THE
AMERICAN
aXis

D0850879

THE
AMERICAN
A X IS

HENRY FORD, CHARLES LINDBERGH, AND THE RISE OF THE THIRD REICH

MAX WALLACE

ST. MARTIN'S GRIFFIN ❦ NEW YORK

Permission to quote from the unpublished papers of Charles Lindbergh granted by the Manuscripts and Archives Department, Yale University Library. Permission to quote from Rabbi Leo Franklin's unpublished manuscript courtesy of Rabbi Leo Franklin Archives, Temple Beth El, Bloomfield Hills, Michigan. Permission to quote from Truman Smith's letters to John O. Beaty, courtesy of University of Oregon Special Collections. Permission to quote from Josephine Gomon's unpublished memoirs courtesy of Bentley Historical Library, University of Michigan. Permission to quote from Thomas Debeuroise's letter to Marcellus Dodge granted by Rockefeller Archive Center. Permission to reproduce photo of Lindbergh German medal (title page) granted by Missouri Historical Society. Permission to reproduce Fight For Freedom photo (page 189) granted by Public Policy Papers Division, Department of Rare Books and Special Collections, Princeton University Library. Photo of Ford-Werke's house newspaper (page 217) courtesy of U.S. National Archives. Photo of Dr. Seuss cartoon (page 237) courtesy Mandeville Special Collections at UCSD. Permission to reproduce photo of Lindbergh, Wheeler, and Norris at AFC rally (page 267) granted by Culver Photos. Photo of Ford's Cologne plant (page 323) is from the report "Research Findings about Ford-Werke under the Nazi Regime," Ford Motor Company archives. Photos on pages 5, 37, and 121 are from the Collections of the Henry Ford Museum, Greenfield Village. Photos on pages 71, 87, 151, 299, and 353 are from the collections of the Manuscripts and Archives Department, Yale University Library.

Title page: Service Cross of the order of the German Eagle, the Third Reich's highest civilian decoration, presented to Charles Lindbergh by Hermann Göring in October 1938. Only three months earlier, the same decoration was bestowed on Lindbergh's friend Henry Ford. Despite a subsequent outcry, both men refused to return their Nazi medals.

Design by Phil Mazzone

www.stmartins.com

Library of Congress Cataloging-in-Publication Data

Wallace, Max.
    The American axis: Henry Ford, Charles Lindbergh, and the rise of the Third Reich / Max Wallace.
        p. cm.
    Includes bibliographical references (page 391).
    ISBN 0-312-29022-5 (hc)
    ISBN 0-312-33531-8 (pbk)
    EAN 978-0312-33531-1
        1. Anti-Semitism—United States—History—20th century. 2. Anti-Semitism—Germany—History—20th century. 3. Lindbergh, Charles A. (Charles Augustus). 4. Ford, Henry, 1863–1947. 5. United States—Ethnic relations. I. Title.
DS146.U6W35 2003
305.892'4073'0904—dc21

                                                          2002045585

First St. Martin's Griffin Edition: December 2004

10 9 8 7 6 5 4 3 2 1

TO THOSE WHO FOUGHT THE GOOD FIGHT

Heroes are created by popular demand, sometimes out of the scariest materials, or none at all.

—GERALD WHITE JOHNSON

CONTENTS

PREFACE		1
CHAPTER 1	Chronicler of the Neglected Truth	5
CHAPTER 2	The Führer's Inspiration	37
CHAPTER 3	Superhero	71
CHAPTER 4	Strange Bedfellows	87
CHAPTER 5	Hate by Proxy	121
CHAPTER 6	History's Stage	151
CHAPTER 7	The Lonely Eagle	189
CHAPTER 8	An Arsenal of Nazism	217
CHAPTER 9	America First	239
CHAPTER 10	Fallen Hero	267
CHAPTER 11	"Will It Run?"	299
CHAPTER 12	Business as Usual	323
CHAPTER 13	Redemption	353
CONCLUSION		385
ACKNOWLEDGMENTS		389
PRIMARY SOURCES		391
NOTES		397
INDEX		453

THE
AMERICAN
AXIS

PREFACE

Twelve years had passed since Germany was compelled to sign the Treaty of Versailles when Annetta Antona arrived at 17 *Brienner Strasse* on the afternoon of December 28, 1931, to interview a rising politician named Adolf Hitler. Thirteen years of stewing in the bile of defeat. Thirteen years of Germany's pondering a suitable scapegoat for its capitulation in World War I and humiliation at the peace conference. Thirteen years of longing to reinvigorate Aryan pride.

A longtime *Detroit News* columnist, Antona was part of a team dispatched by the paper to tell the story of how the defeated nation was rebuilding itself. She was the author of a popular weekly column called "Five Minutes With Men in the Public Eye," wherein she profiled notable figures from the world of politics, literature, and entertainment.

Detroit boasted a significant German immigrant population and the *News* frequently provided its readers with reports from their former homeland. The National Socialist German Workers Party had achieved great strides in the German Reichstag a year earlier, winning 107 out of 556 seats in the national election. That Hitler's message of nationalism and anti-Semitism was appealing to a growing audience was undeniable. Antona believed the man she referred to as the "Bavarian Mussolini" was destined to one day take power. Through a friend who enjoyed influence with the National Socialists, she had secured a five-minute interview with the party leader, although her friend warned that Hitler had a profound dislike for foreign journalists.

At the appointed time, the American columnist arrived at the small

1

brick building—an elegant Munich mansion, nicknamed Brown House, which the Party had recently acquired as its headquarters. Announcing herself to the hard-faced sentry posted at the door, she was ushered into a large office where her subject waited. Flanking a large desk were a pair of red flags bearing the menacing black swastika. But as Hitler welcomed her in, the American's eyes immediately locked on a large portrait hung directly over his desk. It was an incongruous work to encounter in the capital of Bavaria, four thousand miles from home. The imposing oil-painted figure, dressed in a brown suit and gray vest, was immediately familiar to anybody from Detroit—the city's greatest industrialist, automobile pioneer Henry Ford.

Wasting no time, the reporter commenced her brief questioning of the radical nationalist politician she would later describe in print as "the Pan-German Siegfried with a Charlie Chaplin moustache."

Hitler answered each of her questions about the party's political goals, outlining pedantically his vision of a new Reich. Finally, she concluded the interview with a question that the rest of the world would soon be asking: "Why are you anti-Semitic?"

"Somebody has to be blamed for our troubles," came the immediate response. "Judaism means the rule of gold. We Germans are land-minded, not money-minded."

The interview had already extended past the pre-arranged time limit and the journalist rose from her chair, apologizing for taking up so much of Hitler's time. But before she made her exit, she couldn't resist asking for an explanation of the portrait that had loomed over the entire interview.

The reason is simple, explained the future Führer. "I regard Henry Ford as my inspiration."

Nine years later, Hitler ruled the Third Reich and had assembled the most powerful war machine in history. The German *blitzkrieg* was poised to topple France as it continued on its seemingly unstoppable drive toward Britain. It appeared that only American intervention could forestall a Nazi-dominated Europe. But one man was determined that the United States would not thwart Hitler's plans.

The country's most celebrated hero was rallying the isolationist forces to keep America out of the European conflict and prevent military assistance to Britain, despite the desperate determination of President Franklin Roosevelt to supply aid to the beleaguered island nation. On May 19, 1940, Charles Lindbergh took to the airwaves and delivered a national radio address urging America not to interfere with the internal affairs of Europe.

The next day, President Roosevelt was having lunch with U.S. Treasury Secretary Henry Morgenthau at the White House. Midway through the meal, the President put down his fork, turned to his most trusted Cabinet official and declared, "If I should die tomorrow, I want you to know this. I am absolutely convinced that Lindbergh is a Nazi."

CHAPTER 1

CHRONICLER OF THE
NEGLECTED TRUTH

When Henry Ford introduced the revolutionary five-dollar day for his workers in 1914, it transformed American industry forever and made him an overnight hero. Here, thousands of job seekers line up outside the Ford factory the day after Ford's announcement.

The process that brought Henry Ford's portrait to a prominent position behind Hitler's desk began during the summer of 1919, when Ford made the first public sortie in a hate-filled but distinctively American campaign that was to dominate his attention for the next eight years. In July, he announced to the *New York World* that "International financiers are behind all war . . . they are what is called the international Jew: German Jews, French Jews, English Jews, American Jews . . . the Jew is a threat."[1]

From any other figure, the interview might have been dismissed as the ravings of a crackpot. But these words were uttered by the man who was arguably America's most respected and celebrated figure—a man whose achievements had already permanently altered the nation's economic and industrial landscape. This was the first signal that he was about to have a profound impact on America's social character as well.

By 1919, Henry Ford had already secured his place as history's most important automobile pioneer. He had not invented the car or the assembly line, as many believed, but he had revolutionized both, radically changing the country's transportation habits with the introduction of the Model T— the nation's first affordable car. After proclaiming in 1908 that he would "build a motorcar for the great multitude," Ford had by 1913 turned out more than a quarter million units of the car Americans affectionately referred to as the "Tin Lizzie." According to economist Fred Thompson, Ford's car was the chief instrument of one of history's greatest changes in the lives of the common people. Farmers were no longer isolated on remote farms. The horse disappeared so rapidly that the transfer of acreage from hay to other crops caused an agricultural revolution. The automobile became the main prop of the American economy.[2] Within a short period, Henry Ford had joined the likes of Rockefeller, Carnegie, and Mellon as one of the country's industrial giants. Nonetheless, in 1913, five years after he first introduced the Model T, neither *Who's Who* nor the *New York Times* index contained a single reference to Ford or his company.[3] His next innovation, however, was destined forever to put an end to this anonymity.

At the beginning of 1914, the Ford Motor Company found itself in trouble. Two factors in particular were worrying the board of directors. Because of low wages and poor working conditions, it had become increasingly difficult to retain employees. Turnover approached 380 percent, and at one point it was necessary to hire nearly one thousand workers to keep one hundred on the payroll. More worrisome still was a campaign begun the year before by the nation's largest industrial union, the IWW, targeting Ford for unionization and encouraging the workers to stage a slowdown. Union pamphlets featuring such ditties as "The hours are long, the pay is small, so take your time and buck 'em all," had shareholders terrified for their profits.[4]

Ford's assembly line had revolutionized production but it was also being blamed for the increasing dehumanization of workers.[5] A letter to Ford from the wife of one of his assembly-line workers provides a touchingly humble indictment of the conditions in his factory at the time:

> My Dear Mr. Ford—Please pardon the means I am taking of asking you for humanity's sake to investigate and to pardon my seeming rudeness but Mr. Ford I am the wife of one of the final assemblers in your institution and neither one of us want to be agitators and thus do not want to say anything to make anyone else more aggrivated but Mr. Ford you do not know the conditions in your factory we are all sure or you would not allow it. Are you aware that a man cannot "buck nature" when he has to go to the toilet and yet he is not allowed to go at his work. He has to go before he gets there or after work. The chain system you have is a slave driver! My God! Mr. Ford. My husband has come home and thrown himself down and won't eat his supper—so done out. Can't it be remedied?[6]

Her letter reflects nothing more than the norm in American industry at the beginning of the twentieth century. Workers were considered little better than beasts of burden; theirs was a grind of tedious and back-breaking labor from which any consideration for the employee's welfare was absent. The average worker toiled nine hours a day for a salary that barely approached subsistence levels. Profits were based on wages as low as a worker would take and pricing as high as the market would bear. Industrialists were regularly pilloried in the press as robber barons and caricatured in the nation's magazines as inhuman slave drivers. A decade earlier, President Teddy Roosevelt was cheered when he declared war on the industrial trusts he said were ruining the country.

That was about to change. Whether motivated by a genuine concern for the welfare of his workers or a fear of unionization, Ford convened a meeting of his board of directors on Tuesday, January 5, 1914, to announce the revolutionary policy that would alter permanently the worker-employer relationship. Henceforth, he announced to the stunned silence of his colleagues, the minimum wage for Ford workers would be more than doubled from $2.34 a day to $5.00, and the working day would be cut from nine to eight hours.[7] An elaborate system of profit-sharing would be introduced. "Our workers are not sharing in our good fortune," declared Ford. "There are thousands out there in the shop who are not living as they should."[8] The effect was electrifying, signaling nothing less than a new era in American industry. The next morning, every newspaper in the land announced the new policy with blaring headlines. "It is the most generous stroke of policy between a captain of industry and worker that the country has ever seen," wrote the *Michigan Manufacturer and Financial Record*.[9] According to the New York *Globe*, Ford's new wage scheme had "all the advantages and none of the disadvantages of socialism." Overnight, Ford was hailed as a national hero. One newspaper called him "the new Messiah." The only negative note was sounded by his fellow industrialists, who appeared to regard Ford as a traitor to his class, worried that their own workers would expect similar treatment. In an editorial, the *Wall Street Journal*—voice of American Big Business—called the wage blatantly immoral, an "economic crime."[10] Treating workers humanely would set a dangerous precedent that might threaten the entire capitalist system, the paper warned. To his detractors, Ford explained that the new policy was merely sound business practice, not a humanitarian gesture, and would result in increased productivity and higher profits.

But grateful American workers saw humanity in it and sent thousands of letters and telegrams thanking him for his generosity. That week, police had to be summoned to quell a riot when more than 12,000 men lined up at the gates of the Ford plant in hope of a job.

Newspaper reporters descended on the company's Dearborn, Michigan, headquarters to record the new hero's every utterance. Ford was glad to oblige them. His homilies on every conceivable topic blended folksy wisdom with a homespun philosophy on life. On ability: "Whether you think you can or whether you think you can't, you're right!" On self-reliance: "Chop your own wood, and it will warm you twice." On altruism: "A business that makes nothing but money is a poor kind of business." And the quote for which he would be best remembered: "History is more or less bunk." According to one study, Ford's wage hike created more than two million lines of favorable advertising on the front pages of newspapers and thousands and thousands of editorial endorsements.[11]

Ford reveled in his newfound celebrity status. A shameless self-promoter, he used the media to create an entirely new persona, portraying himself as a self-made millionaire who had begun life as the son of a poor farmer in rural Michigan and clawed his way out of poverty to learn a trade and build his first car. He told story after story of the tremendous hardship he had endured as a child. However, according to his sister Margaret, "there was no truth in them." His father was in fact a prosperous landowner who owned a farm along with a number of other enterprises.[12] Moreover, Ford assiduously cultivated the myth that he was a mechanical genius, even though his cars were engineered and designed by others.[13] Instead, he assembled some of the finest mechanics available and used their expertise to build his industry.

"I don't like to read books," he once said. "They muss up my mind." According to one reporter who interviewed him, "Outside of business, where he is a genius, his mind is that of a child."[14] Testifying years later at a libel suit after the *Chicago Tribune* called him an "anarchist," Ford—who never even graduated high school—demonstrated the extent of his historical knowledge under questioning by the paper's lawyer. Asked whether he knew anything about the American Revolution, he responded, "I understand there was one in 1812." *Any other time?* "I don't know of any others." *What about the one in 1776?* "I didn't pay much attention to such things." *Did you ever hear of Benedict Arnold?* "I have heard the name." *Who was he?* "I have forgotten just who he is. He is a writer, I think."[15]

Nothing, however, could diminish Ford's stature with the public or the press. Countless newspapers called on him to run for President. The letters of admiration poured in by the truckload. And as Ford predicted when he instituted the five-dollar day, his company enjoyed an immediate surge in production and skyrocketing profits, making him a billionaire and one of the world's richest men. His name became a verb (to "Fordize" meant to manufacture at a price so low that the common man can afford to buy it) and a noun ("Fordism" referred to mass production resulting in sustained economic growth).[16] Perhaps the best illustration of his new-found status was a nationwide poll in which Ford ranked as the third greatest man in history behind only Napoleon and Jesus Christ.[17]

It is difficult, nearly a century later, to portray accurately the magnitude of Ford's fame and influence brought on by the five-dollar day. In his 1932 classic *Brave New World*, Aldous Huxley attempts to reflect the time in his youth when Ford seemed an omnipresent force. In the novel, set far in the future, Huxley creates a utopian society where universal happiness has been achieved and people are conditioned to love their work. The entire society reveres the "Apostle of Mass Production," Henry Ford, who is worshipped like a God.[18] Time is measured from when Ford first introduced the assembly line. Thus, the story is set in 632 A.F. (After Ford). Adherents cross themselves in the sign of the "T."

Small wonder, then, that when Ford first announced his philosophy toward the Jews to the *New York World* in 1919, it carried no inconsiderable impact. That same year, he quietly purchased a small weekly newspaper called the *Dearborn Independent*, opened an office in an engineering laboratory next to his tractor plant, and assembled a staff in preparation for a crusade that was about to leave a pronounced scar on the face of American society. For the first sixteen months of its operation, under the editorship of former *Detroit News* editor Edwin Pipp, the *Independent* was barely distinguishable from any other weekly newspaper. It supported Prohibition, prison reform and the Versailles Treaty, printed innocuous articles about local issues, and mentioned Jews not at all. But before long, Pipp later recalled, Ford began to bring up Jews "frequently, almost continuously," until his new obsession eventually found its way into the newspaper.[19]

On May 22, 1920, under a banner that announced the *Independent* as "The Ford International Weekly," a huge bold headline fired the opening salvo: THE INTERNATIONAL JEW: THE WORLD'S PROBLEM. For the next ninety-one weeks, each edition of the *Dearborn Independent*—promising its readers to serve as the "Chronicler of the Neglected Truth"—added further embellishments to the picture of a Jewish conspiracy so vast and far-reaching that the tentacles of the Jews supposedly touched every facet of American life. "In America alone," announced the paper, "most of big business, the trusts and the banks, the natural resources and the chief agricultural products, especially tobacco, cotton and sugar, are in control of Jewish financiers and their agents. Jewish journalists are a large and powerful group here . . . Jews are the largest and most numerous landlords . . . They absolutely control the circulations of publications in this country."

Pipp resigned in protest over the paper's new editorial direction and was replaced by former *Detroit News* reporter William J. Cameron, who would serve Ford well over the ensuing two decades.

No American institution, according to the *Independent*, was immune from the grasp of Jewish control. "Whichever way you turn to trace the harmful streams of influence that flow through society, you come upon a group of Jews," it declared. "If fans wish to know the trouble with American baseball, they have it in three words: too much Jew." Jazz music was "Jewish moron music." The Federal Reserve was designed by "Jew bankers" to put the nation's money under the control of a "Jewish cabal."

Each week readers were treated to what Ford's paper called "a lesson" in the insidious tricks Jews used to control the country. These included "the gentle art of changing Jewish names" to disguise their ethnicity. Once disguised as Gentiles, the reasoning went, the Jews' goal was to eradicate Christian virtues.

To Henry Ford, who had famously claimed history is "bunk," the *Independent* was the forum for a history tailored to his own worldview. He dispatched a team of detectives to dig up the evidence that Jews were behind all that was evil in the country. For example, the paper claimed, America was not discovered by Christopher Columbus but by a Jewish interpreter named Luis de Torres—for the purpose of finding and exploiting tobacco, a substance Ford linked to "degeneracy." Benedict Arnold was merely a Jewish pawn who betrayed his country at the behest of Jewish moneylenders.[20] The underlying theme of the series was clear. Jews were attempting to take control of the United States—not by force, but by stealth. In Ford's paranoid conception, the menace was ubiquitous. "If there is one quality that attracts Jews, it is power," the paper announced. "Wherever the seat of power may be, thither they swarm obsequiously."

Anti-Semitism was not unknown to the United States before the *Independent* began its campaign. As early as 1862, one year before Ford was born, President Lincoln was forced to declare anti-Semitism inimical to U.S. government policy after General Ulysses S. Grant issued an order barring Jewish peddlers from selling merchandise to Union soldiers. Lincoln immediately countermanded the order, declaring, "To condemn a class (of people) is to condemn the good with the bad. I do not like to hear an entire class or nationality condemned on account of a few sinners."[21] At the time, such incidents were rare. Yet, a wave of European immigration during the late nineteenth century had brought more than a million Jews to America, resulting in a marked increase in anti-Semitic sentiment, especially among the Protestant upper classes.[22] Caricatures of Jews as crook-nosed moneylenders often appeared in the pages of satirical magazines. Jews were barred from membership in a number of clubs and organizations, and quotas were imposed on levels of Jewish enrollment in many universities as well as on the medical staffs of major hospitals. But Catholics suffered much of the same discrimination (the Ku Klux Klan, for example, originally targeted Roman Catholics as the prime scourge facing the nation along with blacks, while mostly leaving Jews alone in the South, where they had long gained acceptance and respect as the primary merchant class).[23]

The dominant attitude toward Jews among Christian Americans at the time, concludes social historian Leonard Dinnerstein, was an amalgam of "affection, curiosity, suspicion and rejection."[24] Jews may not have been welcomed as fully accepted members of American society and the doors of some institutions may have been barred, but the idea of an organized Jewish conspiracy was still a foreign concept and, on the whole, Jews had assimilated fairly effectively by the end of the nineteenth century.

The influx of European immigrants at the turn of the century, however, brought foreign accents, different cultural mores, and strange fashion styles. And something more insidious—a small body of anti-Semitic literature unfamiliar on America's shores but which had been widely distributed in Europe for some time, especially in countries with large Jewish populations. Among these was an obscure document known as the *Protocols of the Learned Elders of Zion*.[25] Throughout Russia, France, Poland, and England, this document was being circulated as proof that the Jews were plotting to take over the world. The *Protocols* are usually divided into twenty-six separate chapters, each of which comprises a purported Jewish lecture on how to subvert western civilization.[26] "With steadfast purpose," they claim to reveal, "the Jews are creating wars and revolutions . . . to destroy the white Gentile race, that the Jews may seize the power during the resulting chaos and rule with their claimed superior intelligence over the remaining races of the world, as kings over slaves."

Allegedly, the *Protocols* were the confidential minutes of a Jewish conclave convened at the end of the nineteenth century. The document was, in fact, a hoax concocted by a czarist official named Serge Nilus, who edited several editions of the *Protocols*, each with a different account of how he obtained the material. In his 1911 edition, Nilus claimed that his source had stolen the document from (a nonexistent) Zionist headquarters in France. Other editions of the *Protocols* maintained that they were read at the First Zionist Congress held in 1897 in Basel, Switzerland.[27] In reality, the forgery was largely plagiarized from an obscure nineteenth-century satire on Napoleon III called *A Dialogue in Hell Between Montesquieu and Machiavelli*, written by a Frenchman named Maurice Joly, and *Biarritz*, an 1868 novel by the German anti-Semite Hermann Goedsche.[28]

The *Protocols* had already been used in Europe to justify countless incidents of violence toward the Jews. In his 1936 study of the origins of anti-Semitism, Hugo Valentin wrote, "It is no exaggeration to say that they cost the lives of many thousands of innocent persons and that more blood and tears cling to their pages than to those of any other mendacious document in history."[29]

In 1920, shortly after the forgery first made its way to America, a former czarist agent named Boris Brasol arranged for an English translation of the *Protocols* to be sent to the offices of the *Dearborn Independent*. Here was the evidence Ford was looking for to support his suspicion that the Jews were engaged in a sinister conspiracy. Each week a different article attacking the Jews was backed up by one of the twenty-six *Protocols*, skillfully edited to incorporate a contemporary theme. An oft-repeated claim was that the Jews had plotted the recent Russian Revolution and were behind all Bolshevism. The "Soviet," it revealed, was a Jewish institution operating under the Hebrew name "Kahal." The Bolshevik leaders were allegedly all Jews whose sole purpose was to destroy Gentile civilization.[30] In this upheaval, Ford saw tangible evidence of the havoc that Jews could wreak.

Because a figure as prominent as the nation's most respected industrialist had endorsed the *Protocols*, the charges gained instant credibility. The same week in June 1920 that the *Dearborn Independent* revealed their existence, the *Christian Science Monitor* published an editorial entitled "The Jewish Peril," highlighting the *Protocols'* revelations and warning its readers of the dangers represented by international Jews. The next day, in an editorial entitled "World Mischief," the *Chicago Tribune* argued that Bolshevism was merely a "tool" for the establishment of Jewish world control.[31]

Alarm spread throughout the American Jewish community, first because of the *Independent*'s campaign and then because of the rapid pace with which its charges had spread to the mainstream press. In late June, Louis Marshall, director of the American Jewish Committee (AJC), labeled Ford's anti-Semitic campaign "the most serious episode in the history of American Jewry."[32] That week, Marshall convened an emergency session of the AJC's inner circle.[33] Its members unanimously agreed that the *Independent*'s campaign was formidable enough to justify a gathering of all national Jewish organizations. The AJC issued an eighteen-page response to the nation's media, refuting the *Independent*'s claims, rejecting the charge that Jews were behind communism, and exposing the *Protocols* as hate-filled nonsense. The refutation received widespread coverage and earned Ford the epithet "ignoramus" in several newspapers and magazines. *The Nation* deplored the wave of anti-Semitism sweeping the country and declared that "the chief responsibility for the survival of this hoary shame among us in America attaches to Henry Ford."[34]

Ford was undeterred. He explained to a reporter that he was only trying to "awake the Gentile world to an understanding of what is going on. The Jew is a mere huckster . . . ."[35] Not only did he continue to pursue his campaign but in October 1920, Ford published a 200-page pamphlet reprinting the paper's first twenty articles about the "Jewish Question." It was the first edition of *The International Jew*, a series of four pamphlets, each of which exposed a different aspect of sinister Jewish control.[36] The preface to the first edition explained that "the *Dearborn Independent* has not been making a fight but fulfilling a duty to shed light on a matter crying for light."[37] More than a half million copies of *The International Jew* were distributed for free through Ford's vast nationwide network of dealerships; thousands more were sent to some of the country's most influential figures, including college presidents, politicians, bankers, and clergymen. A few months later, Ford compiled the pamphlets and published them in book form.

Jews weren't the only Americans concerned by Ford's relentless crusade. At its annual convention in December 1920, the Federal Council of Churches issued a strong condemnation of the *Independent*'s campaign: "For some time past, there have been in circulation in this country publications tending to create race prejudice and arouse animosity against our Jewish fellow citizens and containing charges so preposterous as to be unworthy of credence."[38]

Louis Marshall appealed to President Woodrow Wilson to intervene and a month later, 119 prominent non-Jewish Americans, including Wilson, former President William Howard Taft, and the new President-elect Warren Harding, signed a manifesto called "The Perils of Racial Prejudice." The document spoke for the "undersigned citizens of Gentile extraction and Christian faith," condemning the introduction into political life of "a new and dangerous spirit." Nowhere did the manifesto mention Ford by name or his newspaper, but its target was clear, as well as its message. "It should not be left to men and women of the Jewish faith to fight this evil, but in a very special sense it is the duty of citizens who are not Jews by ancestry or faith ... to strike at this un-American and un-Christian agitation."[39]

In his book *Henry Ford and the Jews*, chronicling the early history of Ford's anti-Semitism, Neil Baldwin identifies the publication of the "Perils of Prejudice" manifesto as a turning point in Ford's crusade. "After a few weeks," he quotes writer Leon Poliakov, "it was clear that Henry Ford stood alone in the United States."[40] But although it is true that liberals, intellectuals, and a large portion of the mainstream press had turned against him, events were to prove that Ford was far from alone and anything but daunted by the attacks.

Around the same time the "Perils of Prejudice" manifesto was issued in America, the London *Times* published definitive proof that the *Protocols of the Learned Elders of Zion* was a forgery.[41] Extracts from the *Protocols* were printed side-by-side in the influential British newspaper with passages from Maurice Joly's original book, demonstrating that it had been plagiarized almost verbatim. From that point on, the document was almost unanimously dismissed by the media as rubbish. But when a reporter from the New York *World* informed Ford a few weeks later that the *Protocols* could not possibly be genuine, he replied, "The only statement I care to make about the *Protocols* is that they fit in with what is going on. They are sixteen years old, and they have fitted the world situation up to this time. Indeed they do."[42]

Ford was convinced of a truth of his own making and nothing was going to deter him from his determination to expose the international Jewish menace. Moreover, the letters that poured into his office from average Americans convinced him that the people supported his efforts. The Ford Archive has retained thousands of letters that testify to the kind of grassroots support Ford's campaign enjoyed.

Righteous indignation was typical of most of these letters. "The *Independent* is the new Declaration of Independence against the most impudent and rotten domination ever known in this land, and that infernal domination has been the Jew," wrote one reader, echoing the tone of countless others.[43] Several admiring letters came from clergymen, written on the letterhead of their churches. Wrote one priest from Saginaw, Michigan, "I think you will be interested to know that the Jewish Studies are attracting a great deal of attention among the highest authorities in Rome. It seems that the Jews are making themselves particularly obnoxious in the Eternal City. Just recently a request was made from Rome for the volumes containing the stories published in the back numbers of the *Dearborn Independent*."[44] One letter even arrived from a King Kleagle of the Ku Klux Klan offering to procure subscriptions for the paper. Indeed, the *Independent* proved to be a runaway success. When Ford purchased the paper in 1919, its circulation was 72,000. By 1922, it had increased to 300,000, eventually reaching a peak of 700,000 readers two years later.[45] He was tapping into a vein that ran deep in a segment of the American psyche.

The *Dearborn Independent* regularly described the Jews as "an enigma," yet there is probably no more fitting a description of Henry Ford himself. Here was a hitherto shy, gentle man, whose passions included birdwatching, square dancing, country fiddling, and collecting antiques. He showed little intolerance on most other issues and in some respects was quite enlightened, supporting women's suffrage, equal pay for equal work, and anti-lynching laws. In fact, the Ford plant was at one point the largest employer of blacks in the country and many of those who had been in Ford's employ, including the boxer Joe Louis, spoke very highly of him.[46] The source of his fame—the five-dollar day—was perhaps the most progressive labor measure in corporate history. He was so well liked by his friends and employees that, almost without exception, when those closest to him were interviewed in later years about his hate crusade, each attempted to rationalize his odd behavior, convinced that it didn't reflect the Ford he or she knew. Such disbelief merely signaled an inability to explain how or why Ford had come to harbor such hatred.

He consistently ignored attacks against him by the press, which he believed was in the hands of a "Jewish cabal." But, astonishingly, Ford appeared genuinely puzzled as to why his Jewish friends voiced such strong objections to his campaign. To Henry Ford, there were "good Jews" and bad Jews (the latter were the "international element") and he fully expected the good ones to support his efforts and even celebrate them. Company personnel records don't reveal how many Jews worked for Ford, but contemporary accounts indicate the figure was significant. There is no evidence that Henry Ford ever discriminated against Jews in his hiring policies, even at the height of his anti-Semitic campaign. Many of his Jewish workers, including Irving Caesar, who later wrote the hit song "Swanee," had the highest praise for their employer.[47] This is just one of the many puzzling contradictions that has plagued biographers attempting to understand Ford's mind-set.

For years, Ford lived next door to Rabbi Leo Franklin, one of the most respected members of Detroit's Jewish community. Ford regularly entertained Franklin at his home, and as a token of friendship each year, sent the rabbi a Model T right off the line. But in June 1920, a month after the *Independent* first began its attack on the Jews, Franklin sent back the last car with a note explaining, "You claim that you do not intend to attack all Jews but it stands to reason that those who read these articles will naturally infer that it is your purpose to include in your condemnation every person of the Jewish faith."[48]

When he received the note, Ford immediately phoned the rabbi and asked, "What's wrong, Dr. Franklin? Has something come between us?"[49] That he could be so oblivious as to the effects of what he was propagating speaks volumes about Ford's character. His bewilderment was genuine. As the *Independent*'s business manager Fred Black later recalled, "He was very much surprised that the Jews he considered good Jews were opposed to this."[50]

Partially in answer to his critics, who he believed didn't understand "the facts" behind his campaign, Ford published his autobiography, *My Life and Work*, in which he provided the clearest explanation for his anti-Semitic crusade to date. His passage on the "Jewish Question" demonstrates how sincerely he believed that the *Independent*'s exposés reflected no prejudice on his part, but were rather a kind of bitter pill he was administering to the nation for its own good:

> The work which we describe as Studies in the Jewish Question, and which is variously described by antagonists as "the Jew-

ish campaign," "the attack on the Jews," "the anti-Semitic pogrom," and so forth, needs no explanation to those who have followed it. . . . The question is wholly in the Jews' hands. If they are as wise as they claim to be, they will labor to make Jews American, instead of America Jewish. . . . As for prejudice or hatred against persons, that is neither American nor Christian. Our enemies say that we began it for revenge and that we laid it down in fear. Time will show that our critics are merely dealing in evasion because they dare not tackle the main question . . . Time will also show that we are better friends to the Jews' interests than those who praise them to their faces and criticize them behind their backs.[51]

Ford simply wanted to share his important news and proceeded to do it with a kind of befuddled, backwoodsy stubbornness that belied his innovative spirit and prestige. And if the howls of protest didn't halt Ford's "course of education on the Jewish Question," as he called it, they prompted him to explain himself for the first time. Like Rabbi Franklin, most of Ford's friends and associates, both Jew and gentile, were at a loss to explain what had suddenly motivated the great industrialist to embark on the most profound hate campaign in the nation's history.

A clue is to be found in Ford's first high-profile venture into international affairs six years earlier. In April 1915, eight months after the First World War broke out in Europe, Ford had suddenly emerged as a pacifist. In his first public pronouncement on any international issue, he told the *New York Times Magazine* that "Two classes benefit by war—the militarists and the moneylenders . . . the cause of militarism is never patriotism, it is usually commercialism. . . . The warmongers urging military preparedness in America are Wall Street bankers. . . . I am opposed to war in every sense of the word."[52]

Four months later, he announced to the *Detroit Free Press* that he would back his newfound pacifist ideals with his vast fortune, pledging $1 million "to begin a peace and educational campaign in America and the World."[53] Ford was immediately inundated with entreaties for money and support from every pacifist group in the country. Although America would not enter the war for another two years, hundreds of thousands of men had already been killed and gassed in the trenches of France and Belgium.

On November 15, Ford was contacted by a woman named Rosika Schwimmer—a Hungarian Jewish feminist who had recently formed the Woman's Peace Party to advocate the dual goals of women's suffrage and pacifism.[54] Schwimmer had been drawn by Ford's widely publicized pacifist musings—he had recently promised to "have the boys out of the trenches by Christmas"—and she set off to Detroit to seek support for her group. After a two-hour meeting with Ford, she had secured his promise to fund a neutral commission to end the war. A week later, Ford and Schwimmer convened a brain trust of pacifists and intellectuals in New York to discuss ways to "end the carnage." By the conference's end, the group had decided to charter a steamship to sail for Europe and mount an international conference "dedicated to negotiations leading to a just settlement of the war."

On December 15, the *Oskar II*—quickly labeled "Ford's Peace Ship" by the media—set sail from Hoboken, New Jersey, for Norway carrying Ford, Schwimmer, and a delegation of fellow pacifists aboard. The trip was a fiasco. The press mocked its goals, labeling the expedition "Ford's Folly." As respected as he was as a businessman, the mission was seen as a quixotic quest well outside Ford's abilities or understanding. Leave diplomacy to the professionals, the newspapers chided. Midway across the Atlantic, Ford caught cold and spent most of the time in his cabin. What happened in the interval remains a mystery, but when the ship docked two weeks later, Ford immediately separated from his fellow travelers, who were left to flounder with no funds. He returned to the United States, refusing to explain the turn of events, other than to comment, "We learn more from our failures than our successes."[55] The world heard no more of the venture until six years later when Ford granted an interview to the *New York Times*. In it, he attributed his anti-Semitism to something he had learned during the expedition:

> It was the Jews themselves who convinced me of the direct relationship between the international Jew and war. In fact, they went out of their way to convince me.
> On the Peace ship were two very prominent Jews. We had not been at sea 200 miles before they began telling me of the power of the Jewish race, of how they controlled the world through their control of gold, and that the Jew and no one but the Jew could end the war . . .
> They said, and they believed, that the Jews started the war, that they would continue it as long as they wished, and that until the Jew stopped the war it could not be stopped. I was so disgusted I would have liked to turn the ship back.[56]

Most of Ford's biographers have taken him at his word and concluded that his anti-Semitism was born aboard the *Oskar II*, despite the bizarre notion that Jewish pacifists had convinced him the war was a Jewish plot.

However, Schwimmer herself would later dispute the idea that the Peace Expedition was the genesis of his anti-Semitism, noting that Ford was already infected with anti-Jewish sentiments at their first meeting in November 1915, a month before the ship set sail. According to Schwimmer, Ford had announced, "I know who caused the war—the German-Jewish bankers. I have the evidence here. Facts! I can't give them all out now because I haven't got them all yet, but I'll have them soon."[56]

Speculation on the original source of Ford's anti-Semitism has been the subject of countless articles, academic studies, and two books, both entitled *Henry Ford and the Jews*. However, no one has been able to come up with a thoroughly convincing explanation. If Ford's paranoia about the Jews wasn't acquired aboard the Peace Ship, what lay at its root?

When Henry Ford was growing up in rural Michigan shortly after the Civil War, and before the later wave of Jewish European immigration, only 151 Jewish families populated the state.[57] Born of Irish-Scotch heritage, his own religious upbringing consisted of a puritanical Protestantism that preached strict adherence to biblical morality. In his district lived only one Jewish family and it is unlikely that Ford would have had any contact with Jews until much later.[58] During this period, relations between Jews and other ethnic groups were not particularly problematic. Isaac Meyer Wise, one of only 400 Jews living in Detroit at the time, wrote in 1867 that Detroit's Jews "live in the best understanding and harmony with their neighbors and are esteemed as men, citizens and merchants."[59]

That is not to say the young Henry Ford would have been unexposed to anti-Semitism. One of the most popular schoolbooks of his youth was *McGuffey's Eclectic Reader*, the standard text in thirty-seven states, Michigan among them. Schoolchildren were fed daily *McGuffey*'s diet of fundamentalist Christian morality, which was at least mildly anti-Semitic, occasionally denigrating Jewish veneration of the Scriptures. "The Old Testament has been preserved by the Jews in every age, with a scrupulous jealousy, and with a veneration for its words and letters, bordering on superstition," proclaims one edition."[60] Another informs its young readers that "Jews never accepted that the Bible is a Christian book." Ford was undeniably fond of the *McGuffey Reader* and could quote entire passages by heart well into adulthood. However, *McGuffey* hardly bred a nation of Jew-haters.

In his autobiography, Ford's contemporary, Mark Twain—who was also raised on the *McGuffey Readers*—would later describe his own nineteenth-century schoolboy views, admitting that he only thought of Jews in Biblical terms. "They carried me back to Egypt and in imagination I moved among the Pharoahs," he wrote.[61] The great nineteenth-century jurist Oliver Wendell Holmes wrote that he was taught to believe Jews "were a race lying under a curse for their obstinacy in refusing the gospel."[62] However, neither Ford's nor the *Dearborn Independent*'s peculiar form of anti-Semitism ever really attacked the Jews from a religious perspective or applied the epithet "Christ-killers" to them. In fact, Ford seemed to have a respect for the religion itself, as evidenced in his early dealings with Rabbi Leo Franklin, who initially believed Ford to be enlightened about his people.[64] Ford's later anti-Semitism appears, in fact, to reflect a racially based, rather than religious, prejudice.

As more Jews emigrated from Europe to the Detroit area toward the turn of the century, local newspapers recorded a number of anti-Semitic incidents, including an attack on some Jewish peddlers. Yet if Henry Ford ever encountered Jews or anti-Semitism in his early years, there is no record of it and he never spoke of such encounters to friends or associates. In fact, as late as 1916, he was praised by the Detroit *Jewish Chronicle* as an "example to other Christian employers" for allowing his Jewish workers time off to observe the High Holidays.

Among the various theories attempting to trace the source of Ford's anti-Semitism, one of the most persuasive postulates that it was Thomas Alva Edison who first turned Ford against the Jews. The theory, however, rests on a number of questionable foundations.

By the time Ford met Edison in 1898, the scientist/inventor had already profoundly influenced modern society through inventions such as the incandescent lightbulb, the phonograph, and the motion picture camera. The "Wizard of Menlo Park" had been a huge influence on the young Ford, who would later write that Edison "was the chief hero of my boyhood," and "our greatest American." At the time of their first meeting, Ford was the chief engineer at Edison's Detroit electrical substation. At a company banquet, an awestruck Ford received some encouraging words from his idol and, by the time Ford left to start his own automobile company five years later, the two had become close friends. Once Ford became successful, he loaned Edison—a poor businessman who was perpetually in debt—millions of dollars to finance various projects. Eventually he would venerate his mentor by building an institute in his name and moving Edison's entire laboratory from New Jersey to the Ford Museum in Dearborn. To this day, the museum contains a rather odd item proudly displayed by Ford after the inventor's 1931 death—a glass vial purported to contain "Edison's last breath."[65]

In 1914, shortly after the First World War broke out and a year before Ford's Peace Ship expedition, Edison told the *Detroit Journal* that the rise of German commerce fostered the war and that Jews were responsible for Germany's business success. The military government, he added, was a pawn of the Jewish business sector.[66] Years later, in the middle of Ford's *Dearborn Independent* campaign, Edison sent Ford a number of letters indicating his support. In one letter, referring to the Jews, he wrote "they don't like publicity," explaining why Jewish leaders were attempting to stop Ford's campaign.[67] When Ford later sent him a complete leather-bound set of *The International Jew*, Edison mailed a letter of thanks.[68] In turn, Edison regularly sent Ford articles he cut out of the newspaper about Jewish influence. One, headlined "Jews control Soviet Russia," painted a picture of the Jews as the architects of Bolshevism. Edison's accompanying note read, "This is interesting." But at least one company executive later claimed that Edison actually rebuked Ford for his extreme anti-Semitism.[69] Moreover, it is difficult to believe that Edison's own anti-Semitic views could have been responsible for Ford's visceral hatred, so the evidence of Edison's influence on Ford is far from conclusive. It is worth noting, however, that Edison's fortune was later used to fund another of the century's most notorious Jew-baiting organizations after his granddaughter Jean Farrel Edison founded the Institute for Historical Review—a rabidly anti-Semitic organization which has been accused of being at the forefront of the Holocaust denial movement.

Another theory has it that Ford's lifelong animosity was sparked when a Jewish banker turned down his request for a loan. In fact, Ford never had a loan application rejected.[70]

Each of Ford's biographers in turn have trotted out one unsatisfactory theory after another to explain what transformed a once progressive thinker into a narrow-minded racist. There may in fact be no defining incident that can be pinpointed as the indisputable source of his anti-Semitism. However, there is little doubt about who was most responsible for fueling it.

Ernest Gustav Liebold was born in Detroit in 1884 at a time when German immigrants still made up a sizable portion of the city's population. Though he was schooled in the Detroit public school system, Liebold's first language was German and on at least two occasions as a child he traveled to Germany with his parents to visit relatives. By the turn of the century, when Liebold was growing up, Detroit's German community was the primary source of the city's anti-Semitism. In his 1986 study, *Jews of Detroit*, Robert Rockaway writes, "Many of the German residents, themselves recent immigrants, carried to America some of the anti-Jewish sentiments and stereotypes popular in their homeland. . . . Throughout the nineteenth century in Germany, even supposedly enlightened and educated Germans expressed serious reservations about granting citizenship and equal rights to the Jews who they saw as a distinct people who posed a threat to German values and civilization. Thus, German Americans, upon arriving in their new homeland, may have been more likely to view the presence of Jews as a threat than native Americans, who had no such lengthy tradition of anti-Semitism.[71] Jews, in fact, were frequently singled out as a potential source of trouble in the city. During one local election, a Detroit German newspaper warned its readers to "keep an eye on the Jewish population."[72]

In 1911, the story goes, a $70,000 dividend check made out to Henry Ford disappeared, only to be found a few days later in the pocket of a suit Mrs. Ford was preparing to send to the cleaners. As a result, Ford's business partner James Couzens urged him to select a personal secretary to handle his finances and suggested Liebold, who was then a young executive in a local bank that had been set up for the use of the Ford company and the local community.[73] As Ford's "general secretary," Liebold so impressed his employer with his business acumen that Ford came to regard him as "the best financial mind in the country."[74]

Ford's biographers Allan Nevins and Frank Hill describe Liebold as possessing a "cold, ruthless intensity," a quality that served him well as he rose through the ranks.[75] Ford once told an associate that every evening at dinnertime, Liebold liked to march his children around the table military style. When they reached their places, he would bark "*sitzen sie* (sit down)."[76] Before long, he was Ford's most trusted associate. He became the industrialist's gatekeeper, ensuring that Ford saw only the letters that Liebold wanted him to see and met only the people he decided were worthy. "An ambitious martinet, Liebold expanded his authority by exploiting Ford's quirks, such as his dislike for paperwork and refusal to read most correspondence," writes historian Leo Ribuffo.[77] Much like a presidential chief of staff, this gave the secretary enormous power and influence within the company and permitted him undue sway with his employer. Ford trusted him so much that he gave Liebold power-of-attorney to handle all of his personal financial transactions, correspondence, and contracts.

From the time Liebold was hired, many of his colleagues bitterly complained that he had become the most powerful person in the company next to Ford himself. Company business manager Fred Black later described the hold the secretary exerted over his employer: "He was one of the persons Mr. Ford could ask to do things he wouldn't ask other people to do. Mr. Ford knew the others weren't hard enough. For this reason, Liebold had tremendous power . . . After 1921 he was riding high, wide, and handsome."[78]

For all his influence, however, Liebold was at first mostly a background player, content to attend to Ford's business and maintain a low profile within the company itself. That all changed with the acquisition of the *Dearborn Independent*. Several months after Ford bought the small weekly in 1919, he bestowed upon Liebold the position of the newspaper's general manager. At the onset of the *Independent*'s anti-Semitic campaign in May

1920, it was Liebold who signed the press release, marked "authorized by Henry Ford," announcing the paper's new direction. It read: "The Jewish Question, as every businessman knows, has been festering in silence and suspicion here in the United States for a long time, and none has dared discuss it because the Jewish influence was strong enough to crush the man who attempted it."[79]

It was Liebold who coordinated the anti-Semitic campaign and it was he who fended off the criticisms, answering each piece of mail addressed to Ford, including the hundreds of outraged letters from prominent Jews and Gentiles. To most of the criticism, he would politely reply that the reader didn't "understand" the intent of the series. When the Talmud Society wrote demanding that Ford furnish proof supporting his accusations against the Jews, Liebold wrote back, "We will prefer to leave it to you to disprove the statements which are being published."[80]

When Rosika Schwimmer—the Jewish woman who had enlisted Ford in the Peace Ship campaign five years earlier—wrote to ask if, as rumored, she had somehow been responsible for triggering Ford's anti-Semitism, she received a letter back from Liebold stating enigmatically, "All of us affiliated with Mr. Ford have been obliged to and do yet gladly carry a certain measure of responsibility insofar as the articles are concerned. I am just wondering, however, if you have read them because the present campaign is based on facts which we have gathered for some time and is not based on prejudices."[81]

At one point, Liebold boasted in a letter to a friend, "When we get through with the Jews, there won't be one of them who will dare raise his head in public."[82]

Edwin Pipp, the *Independent*'s first editor, had no doubt who "started Mr. Ford against the Jews." In a weekly newspaper he founded to counter Ford's campaign, Pipp wrote, "The door to Ford's mind was always open to anything Liebold wanted to shove in it, and during that time Mr. Ford developed a dislike for the Jews, a dislike which appeared to become stronger and more bitter as time went on . . . In one way and another, the feeling oozed into his system until it became a part of his living self."[83] According to Pipp, Liebold always had an explanation for the problems of the world "with the Jew at the bottom of it." He would share his views on a regular basis with Ford, who resented any attempt to "counteract the poison that was being fed to him."[84]

Most of Ford's biographers have noted Liebold's virulent anti-Semitism and his influence over Ford, but none has been able to pinpoint its motivation or origin. However, a document recently uncovered in the U.S. National Archives casts a new and sinister light on their relationship. On February 8, 1918, the U.S. War Department's Military Intelligence

Division (MID) reported in a file marked "Most Secret" that Ernest Liebold of Dearborn Michigan, private secretary to Henry Ford, is "considered to be a Germany spy."[85] The implications of this document may help explain much of the twentieth-century history of the Ford Motor Company.

In early 1918, as the Great War engulfed Europe, the corporation found itself completely enmeshed in the war effort. After the United States entered the war on April 6, 1917, Henry Ford had suddenly abandoned his antiwar rhetoric and let his patriotism overrule his pacifist ideals, agreeing to put the company's considerable manufacturing resources "at the disposal of the United States government."[86] The result was a number of lucrative defense contracts, including a crucial order to build 5,000 Liberty airplane motors for the army's new fleet of fighter planes.

It appears that the U.S. War Department designation of Liebold as a foreign spy was based on an intercepted letter about this Liberty Motors contract, sent via a Detroit reporter (whose name has been withheld by the government in the declassification process) with close contacts inside the Ford Motor Company. He had sent the letter to a friend, John Rathom, at the *Providence Journal* newspaper, who he knew to be an undercover U.S. intelligence operative. Startled by its revelations, Rathom quickly forwarded the letter to his superiors in Washington.[87]

In this five-page letter, dated December 10, 1917, the reporter/informant—who appears alarmed at a potential threat to the U.S. war effort—is discussing a lunchtime conversation he had overheard at the Ford plant a week earlier, involving two high-ranking company executives, and Ford's legal counsel, whom he identifies as "all avowed and outspoken pacifists."[88] The three men were discussing the recently awarded Liberty Motors contract, he reports, when the conversation shifted suddenly to a discussion of their colleague Ernest Liebold, whom the informant describes as being "closer to Henry Ford than any man alive," noting that he "was the man who brought Rosika Schwimmer into contact with Ford. It was he who promoted and arranged all the details of the Peace Expedition."[89]

In his December 10 letter, the reporter, who was at the time in the process of preparing an article about the Ford Motor Company, provides no further details of the eavesdropped conversation. However, he recalls that, a year before the United States entered the war, an "intimate friend" who worked for the British government had shown him a "coded dispatch from Berlin on its way to Liebold."

There is "no question in my mind," asserts the reporter, "that Liebold is today a German spy." For substantiation of this charge, he points to a visit by A. R. Scharton—a reporter for a New York–based German newspaper, *Staats Zeitung*—who had recently appeared at the Ford plant with a letter of introduction to Liebold. Before meeting Liebold, Scharton walked around the plant attempting "to pump every one he met at the Ford Motor Company about the Liberty Motor." Later that day, the informant reveals, Scharton and Liebold "were surprised in Liebold's office with their heads together, going over the blueprints of the Liberty Motor."

This is a damning accusation. It would have been tantamount to treason if Liebold had disclosed the top-secret Liberty defense plans to any reporter, let alone a correspondent working for a pro-German newspaper. The War Department concluded that the informant was a "credible" source and, according to the recently declassified file, the Military Intelligence Division launched an immediate investigation into Liebold's activities in February 1918—a probe that was eventually discontinued without any action taken when the war ended nine months later.

The pieces begin to fit together. Ford's pacifist campaign of 1915 had been launched just as the fortunes of the German army were beginning to sour in Europe. More important, a strong interventionist campaign had begun to build in the United States for American entry into the war—reasoning correctly that only American military intervention could defeat the powerful German alliance. A negotiated peace, or continued American neutrality, would have benefited the Kaiser and spared Germany the catastrophic defeat it would later suffer. It is entirely conceivable that Liebold engineered and manipulated Ford's pacifist efforts and hatred of the Jews to benefit the German war effort. Rosika Schwimmer, the woman behind the Peace Ship expedition, appeared to hint at this link when she wrote in her unpublished memoirs, "Someone had tried to harness Ford's pacifism into the wagon of anti-Semitism. . . . This is the grossest exhibition of his mental dependence on others in questions where his intuition fails to serve as a flashlight . . . Like managers of a puppet show, they have succeeded in connecting wars and Jews in Ford's mind . . . administering the anti-Semitic poison."[90]

Ford's pacifist campaign ended in vain. America's entry into the war in 1917 ensured a crushing defeat for Germany. But Liebold would have other opportunities to render assistance to the Fatherland.

With Liebold at the helm, the *Independent* continued its relentless drumbeat of anti-Semitic attacks week after week until in February 1922 the campaign came to an abrupt halt. Like much in Henry Ford's history, there are conflicting explanations for the sudden retreat. According to the paper's editor William Cameron, Ford burst into his office one day and told him, "The Jewish articles must stop." Then he told Allan Benson, one of the paper's contributors, "There is too much anti-Semitic feeling. I can feel it around here."[91] This scenario seems improbable, considering that six months later, Ford spoke to the *Detroit Free Press* of the "greed and avarice of Wall Street Kikes."[92] In fact, Cameron's version was related years later when every top official in the company was falling all over himself to distance Ford from the campaign against the Jews. One of the flaws in most Ford biographies is that the authors rely on the select accounts of former company officials, each of whom gives his own self-serving, contradictory and demonstrably false account of events in which he took part.[93]

Publicly, Ford claimed that the "reports" on the "Jewish Question" could cease because Americans now knew enough to "grasp the key."[94] Many observers, however, believed that it was in fact Ford's political ambitions rather than repentance that prompted the sudden termination of the Jewish attacks. Warren Harding's presidency had been scandal-plagued since he took office in 1921, and speculation was rife about who would challenge the embattled president for the White House in the 1924 elections.

Whether it was a grassroots phenomenon or, as seems more likely, a carefully orchestrated effort, "Ford-for-President" clubs suddenly sprung up all over the country in early 1922.[95] The idea of Ford in the White House was not so far-fetched. In 1916, a group of Ford's friends had circulated petitions putting him on Michigan's Republican primary ballot. Without campaigning, he bested the favorite, Senator William Alden Smith, by more than 5,000 votes.[96] Two weeks later, he almost achieved another upset in the Nebraska primary, losing by only 464 votes. In 1916, Ford was a reluctant candidate. But on August 8, 1923, *Collier's* printed an article under his name headlined "If I Were President." Evidently, Ford was beginning to consider the grandeur of high public office. Edwin Pipp, who had resigned as the *Independent*'s editor in 1920, believed that Ford knew he would never win the presidency with the Jewish electorate against him; the *Independent*'s campaign, therefore, had to end.

"Running through New York City, Philadelphia, Cincinnati, Cleveland, and Chicago are strong Jewish influences," Pipp wrote. "They seldom unite or act concertedly on political matters, but with Ford attacking them, they naturally would be solid against him . . . They are human and would not fall for putting their greatest enemy into a high office."[97]

After he retired from the company, former business manager Fred Black laid Ford's political ambitions squarely at the hands of Liebold. "Liebold was the main stimulation of the Ford-for-President boom in 1923," he recalled. "He expected to be the power behind the throne in Washington, as he was then in the company."[98]

Liebold carefully scrutinized the primary laws of every state and planned to flood Ford dealers with free copies of a Ford biography specially prepared for the campaign.[99] In later years, he admitted that he expected to be named vice president if his boss was elected.[100]

According to Ford's biographer Carol Gelderman, "Had Ford wanted the presidency, he probably could have had it. . . . Farmers, pacifists, factory workers, prohibitionists, anti-Semites, labor unionists—all looked on Ford as a hero."[101] Indeed, a June 1923 nationwide *Autocaster* survey tabulated 700,000 ballots and found Ford defeating President Harding by a nearly 2 to 1 margin.[102] A month later, *Collier's* Magazine interviewed 258,000 Americans, with the results showing Ford defeating Harding 88,865 to 51,000.[103]

But when a delegate rose to extol the benefits of a Ford presidency at a convention of the Daughters of the American Revolution in Washington that fall, Ford's wife, Clara, who was in the audience, stormed to the podium and hotly rebuked the speaker: "Mr. Ford has enough and more than enough to do to attend to his business in Detroit. The day he runs for President of the United States, I will be on the next boat to England."[104]

Whether it was because of his wife's opposition or another factor, Ford eventually abandoned his campaign. In the end, he traded his presidential ambitions for an assurance by his leading rival Calvin Coolidge that the latter would support his bid for a watershed on the Tennessee River called Muscle Shoals.[105] Coolidge went on to assume the presidency.[106] Whether Ford was ever serious about running for office is still a mystery but shortly after he abandoned his bid, the *Independent* resumed its anti-Semitic campaign as suddenly as the paper had dropped it two years earlier.

For two years, the *Independent's* pages had been almost completely free of articles dealing with "The Jewish Question"—with only the occasional snipe at "Jewish moneylenders." However, in his weekly column, "Ford's Own Page," Ford continued to attack the "international financiers" and the "international bankers" who had made politicians their pawns.[107] Discerning readers of the *Independent* had little doubt to whom he was referring. But while Ford maintained a disingenuous truce, the ideas that had germinated in the newspaper's columns were beginning to take root across the country and in the highest circles. On March 3, 1923, Senator Robert LaFollette of Wisconsin introduced a motion casting responsibility for World War I on the international bankers and singled out the Jewish Rothschilds in particular.[108] Two books were published by George W. Armstrong, *The Crime of '20* (1922) and *The Story of the Dynasty of the Money Trust in America* (1923), discussing "a Jewish banking conspiracy" to control the money markets of America and eventually world governments.[109] The Ku Klux Klan enjoyed its biggest resurgence since Reconstruction as it added the Jews to its traditional targets, Roman Catholics and blacks.[110] According to the anti-Klan activist Patrick H. O'Donnell, who published

the Chicago-based publication *Tolerance*, Ford "must stand accused of having sedulously nurtured the development of Ku Klux power." According to
O'Donnell, Klan membership was "insignificant in numbers" when Ford
began his campaign but in two years, more than 100 hate publications had
been established.[111] These occurrences, of course, cannot wholly be
blamed on Ford and his campaign. A combination of postwar disillusion-
ment, economic uncertainty, rising Protestant fundamentalism, and fear of
Bolshevism played their part as well. But it was Ford who had most successfully tapped into these feelings of malaise and used his credibility and
platform to exploit them.

He soon resumed the campaign with a vengeance. On April 23, 1924,
the *Independent* carried a huge front-page headline:

JEWISH EXPLOITATION OF FARMERS' ORGANIZATIONS MONOPOLY TRAPS OPERATE UNDER GUISE OF MARKETING ASSOCIATIONS

Setting the tone for a fresh campaign, the article declared, "A band of
Jews—bankers, lawyers, moneylenders, advertising agencies, fruit packers,
produce buyers, professional office managers and bookkeeping experts—is
on the back of the American farmer . . . This organization was born in the
fertile, fortune-seeking brain of a young Jew on the Pacific Coast a little
more than five years ago."[112]

The Jew referred to in the article was a Chicago attorney named Aaron
Sapiro who specialized in farm economics and for some time had been
attempting to draw disaffected midwestern farmers into a new marketing
scheme—a farm co-op—to sell their wheat. The farm co-op movement had
received the support of a number of prominent American Jews—Bernard
Baruch, Julius Rosenwald, and Eugene Mayer. By 1925, Sapiro's plan,
which the *New York Times* described as "one of the greatest agricultural
movements of modern times," had enlisted more than 800,000 farmers.[113]

Henry Ford had never forgotten his roots as a farmer. He maintained a
private farm in Dearborn and subscribed to most of the nation's leading
farm journals. His frequent boasts of his youth on the farm, moreover, had
made him as much a hero among American farmers as his five-dollar day
did among working men. In fact, farmers were some of the Ford Motor
Company's most important customers and had made it the nation's leading
manufacturer of tractors and trucks. Ford was immediately suspicious of
the farm co-op movement. Were the Jews trying to extend their control
into American wheat farming as well?[114] "I don't believe in co-operation,"

Ford said, dismissing the movement. "What can co-operation do for farmers?"[115] During the *Independent*'s first anti-Semitic series four years earlier, Ford had often aired his views on the subject of Jews and agriculture. In an article entitled "How the Jewish Question Touches the Farm," the *Independent* argued that "the Jew is not an agriculturalist"; he only cares about "land that produces gold from the mine and land that produces rents."[116] In one issue, the paper even offered a reward of $1,000 to anybody who could uncover a Jewish farmer.

Now here was a Jew who was successfully organizing Ford's beloved farmers into a powerful force—a phenomenon Ford viewed as suspiciously similar to socialism. For more than a year, under the theme of "Jewish Exploitation of Farmer Organizations," the paper took aim at the Farm Co-op movement. In more than twenty articles, it sought to portray Sapiro as the leader of "a conspiracy of Jewish bankers" forcing farmers into cooperatives. He had "turned millions away from the pockets of the men who till the soil and into the hands of the Jews and their followers." His "strong arm" tactics and squads of Bolshevists had infected farm children with the germs of Communism, making them "modeler's clay" in his hands. His non-Jewish associates were nothing more than "Gentile false fronts . . . human camouflage of the international ring of professional aliens."[117]

Sapiro demanded Ford retract his charges, but to no avail. Then, on April 23, 1925, he launched a million-dollar libel suit, aimed not at the *Independent*, but at Ford himself. Reaction to the suit demonstrates just how successfully Ford had rallied American farmers to his cause. Hundreds of letters poured in from farmers urging Ford to stand up to the "shrewd little Jew" . . . "The Bible says Jews will return to Palestine, but they want to get all the money out of America first." . . . "Sapiro should be kicked out because he is trash." . . . "The sooner the leeches are given a dose of 'Go quick,' the better."[118]

When the case finally came to court two years later, the defense's tack was clear. William Cameron, the *Independent*'s editor and chief witness for the defendant, offered himself as a willing scapegoat. Loyal to his longtime employer, he testified under oath that he was completely responsible for every word the paper had published. Ford, he claimed, had neither read the articles in advance nor talked with him about the "Jewish Question."[119] Whatever credibility this absurd claim may have had was soon undermined when James M. Miller, a former *Dearborn Independent* employee, swore under oath that Ford had told him he intended to expose Sapiro.[120]

The case was about to reach its conclusion when Ford's lawyers alleged that one of the jurors had claimed to have accepted a bribe from Jewish interests to vote against Ford. The judge was forced to declare a mistrial. It later emerged that the allegations were false and had probably been instigated by Ford's defense team in an effort to avoid an unfavorable judgment.

Shortly after the mistrial was declared, U.S. Congressman Nathan Perlman, vice president of the American Jewish Committee, was approached by two of Henry Ford's personal emissaries. They told him that "Ford and his family were anxious to put an end to the controversies and ill feelings" occasioned by the *Dearborn Independent* campaign.[121] When AJC President Louis Marshall heard about the peace feeler, he sent word that only a "complete retraction" would be acceptable, and demanded an assurance that no more attacks would ever be made on the Jewish people.[122]

Two weeks later, the *New York Evening Journal*'s Arthur Brisbane, author of America's most popular syndicated column, "Today," received a document from Ford headquarters. Brisbane had championed Ford in print on a number of occasions, but had recently met with Ford to suggest he discontinue his anti-Semitic attacks, which Brisbane said were hurting his reputation. At that meeting, Ford had dismissed Brisbane's concerns, claiming, "No one can charge that I am an enemy of the Jewish people. I employ thousands of them."[123] Now Brisbane was astonished to receive a three-page letter over Henry Ford's signature, which signaled the official end to what has been called the "most systematic campaign of hatred against a people in American history." Brisbane immediately distributed the letter to four other news agencies for publication and it exploded onto front pages worldwide on July 8, 1927:

For some time past I have given consideration to the series of articles concerning Jews which since 1920 have appeared in the *Dearborn Independent*. Some of them have been reprinted in pamphlet form under the title "The International Jew." Although both publications are my property, it goes without saying that in the multitude of my activities, it has been impossible for me to devote personal attention to their management or to keep informed as to their contents. It has therefore inevitably followed that the conduct and policies of these publications had to be delegated to men whom I placed in charge of them and upon whom I relied implicitly.

To my great regret I have learned that Jews generally, and particularly those of this country, not only resent these publications as promoting anti-Semitism, but regard me as their enemy. Trusted friends with whom I have conferred recently have assured me in all sincerity that in their opinion the character of the charges and insinuations made against the Jews, both individually and collectively, contained in many of the articles which have been circulated periodically in the *Dearborn Independent* and have been reprinted in the pamphlets mentioned, justifies the righteous indignation entertained by Jews everywhere toward me because of the mental anguish occasioned by the unprovoked reflections made upon them.

This has led me to direct my personal attention to the subject, in order to ascertain the exact nature of these articles. As a result of this survey I confess that I am deeply mortified that this journal, which is intended to be constructive and not destructive, has been made the medium for resurrecting exploded fictions, for giving currency to the so-called *Protocols of the Wise Men of Zion*, which have been demonstrated, as I learn, to be gross forgeries, and for contending that the Jews have been engaged in a conspiracy to control the capital and the industries of the world, besides laying at the door many offenses against decency, public order and good morals. Had I appreciated even the general nature, to say nothing of the details, of these utterances, I would have forbidden their circulation without a moment's hesitation, because I am fully aware of the virtues of the Jewish people as a whole, of what they and their ancestors have done for civilization and for mankind toward the development of commerce and industry, of their sobriety and diligence, their benevolence, and their unselfish interest in the public welfare. Of course there are black sheep in every flock, as there are among all races, creeds, and nationalists who are at times evildoers. It is wrong, however, to judge a people by a few individuals, and I therefore join in condemning unreservedly all wholesale denunciations and attacks.

Those who know me can bear witness that it is not in my nature to inflict insult upon and to occasion pain to anybody, and that it has been my effort to free myself from prejudice. Because of that I frankly confess that I have been greatly shocked as a result of my study and examination of the files of the *Dearborn Independent* and of the pamphlet entitled "The International Jew." I deem it to be my duty as an honorable man to make amends for the wrong done to the Jews as fellow-men and brothers, by asking their forgiveness for the harm that I have unintentionally committed, by retracting so far as lies within my power, the offensive charges laid at their door by these publications, and by giving them the unqualified assurance that henceforth they may look to me for friendship and goodwill.

It is needless to add that the pamphlets which have been distributed throughout the country and in foreign lands will be withdrawn from circulation, that in every way possible I will make it known that they have my unqualified disapproval and that henceforth the *Dearborn Independent* will be conducted under such auspices that articles reflecting upon the Jews will never again appear in its columns.

Finally, let me add that this statement is made on my own initiative and wholly in the interest of right and justice and in accordance with what I regard as my solemn duty as a man and as a citizen.

—Signed, Henry Ford, Dearborn, Michigan, June 30, 1927.[124]

Along with the apology, Ford quietly settled out of court with Sapiro for $140,000 and agreed to take measures to stop further distribution of the *International Jew*. On its surface, the claims made in the apology were incredible. Ford had given countless personal interviews since 1920 reiterating the charges against the Jews recounted in the *Dearborn Independent*. As Neil Baldwin has described it, "Jew hatred was now an entrenched, persistent strain on Ford's psyche." The press releases accompanying each issue carried the line: "The *Dearborn Independent* is Henry Ford's own paper and he authorizes every statement incurred therein." And his own autobiography expounds at length about the "Jewish Question." Yet, here was Henry Ford boldly assuring the world that he knew nothing of the attacks against the Jews and that he had always been free of prejudice.

Relieved to be spared from the line of fire, however, the Jewish community was willing to take the apology at face value and even forgive their former adversary. Commenting on Ford's apology, Rabbi Franklin quoted from Leviticus in his diary: "Thou shalt not take vengeance, nor bear any grudge against the children of thy people, but thou shalt love thy neighbor as thyself."[125]

The *Jewish New York Tribune* expressed "profound satisfaction," while *The American Hebrew* quoted Rabbi Isaac Landman as saying, "Henry Ford . . . is the first man in history beguiled by anti-Semitism, who has made a public recantation and apology."[126] Not all Jews, however, were happy to see Ford absolved so easily. The Jewish Telegraphic Agency believed there should be a limit on Jewish forgiveness. Ford's apology, it complained, did not need to be greeted with such an "hysteric outburst."[127]

Most but not all of the mainstream media seemed just as willing to accept the apology as their Jewish counterparts. The *New York Times* wrote, "Mr. Ford has shown superb moral courage in his wholehearted recantation."[128]

The New York *Telegram* editorialized, "If one of the richest men in the world cannot get away with an anti-Semitic movement in this country, nobody else will have the nerve to try it, and of that we can all be thankful, gentiles as well as Jews."[129] But a *Chicago Tribune* editorial noted that there were few things as remorseless as a rich man trying to duck the future consequences of his actions.[130] "Mr. Ford," it wrote, "advances an empty head to explain his cold feet." The *Berliner Tageblatt* pointed out that only recently Ford had given them an interview urging the German nation to "free itself from the slavery of Jewish capital and of the Jewish League of Nations."

The apology was the talk of the country for weeks. Even Tin Pan Alley weighed in when future Broadway impresario Billy Rose released a satirical song entitled "Since Henry Ford Apologized to Me":

> *I was sad and I was blue*
> *But now I'm just as good as you*
> *Since Hen-ry Ford a-pol-ogized to me*
> *I've thrown a-way my lit-tle Che-vro-let*
> *And bought my-self a Ford Cou-pé*
> *I told the Sup-rintendent that*
> *The Dearborn In-de-pen-dent*
> *Does-n't have to hang up where it used to be*
> *I'm glad he changed his point of view*
> *And I even like Edsel too,*
> *Since Hen-ry Ford a-pol-o-gized to me*
> *My mother says she'll feed him if he calls*
> *Ge-fil-te-fish and Mat-zah balls*
> *And if he runs for President*
> *I would-n't charge a sin-gle cent*
> *I'll cast my bal-lot ab-so-lute-ly free*
> *Since Hen-ry Ford a-pol-o-gized to me.*[131]

What motivated the sudden about-face? The *Independent*'s first editor Edwin Pipp claimed business considerations—not remorse—were responsible. The company had begun receiving letters like the one from an Augusta, Georgia, Ford dealer recounting his visit from the city rabbi. No American Jew, the rabbi had told him, would buy a single new Ford until the *Independent* ceased its attacks.[132] In Hartford, Connecticut, organizers of a parade by the local Jewish community declared that there should be "positively no Ford machines permitted in line." And according to Pipp, Gaston Plantiff, Ford's business representative in New York, had recently informed him that sales of his cars were plummeting as the result of an unofficial Jewish boycott. "Whatever his reputation may be," Pipp wrote, "the dollar appeals to Ford as strongly as to any man on earth."[133]

Humorist Will Rogers summed it up best: "Ford used to have it in for the Jewish people until he saw them in Chevrolets, and then he said, 'Boys, I am all wrong.'"[134]

Upton Sinclair, in his 1937 Ford biography, *The Flivver King*, proffered another theory: Ford's detectives had begun to investigate the Jewish film moguls who headed most of Hollywood's major studios. When William Fox, head of Fox pictures, got wind of the investigation, he informed Ford that he would compile footage from "hundreds of cameramen all over the country" of accidents and fatalities involving Ford cars. The resulting newsreel would be projected before every one of his studio's films.[135]

Whatever the reason, Henry Ford never publicly addressed the "Jewish Question" again. But his seven-year campaign would spawn a movement with horrific consequences that would render previous notions of hate obsolete. And if the motivations behind Ford's seven-year campaign remain murky, there can be little doubt about its effects.

CHAPTER 2

THE FÜHRER'S INSPIRATION

Henry Ford, right, with his general secretary and lifelong confidant, Ernest Liebold, center, circa 1919. Liebold has been accused of spearheading Ford's anti-Semitic crusade, and new evidence indicates he was probably a Nazi spy.

In 1935, the city of Nuremberg had played host to the most dramatic rallies ever staged by the ascendant Nazi movement. Ten years later, its destiny reversed, twenty of the most notorious Nazi leaders sat in the dock of a Nuremberg courtroom waiting to hear indictments read against them as the first-ever international war crimes trial got under way.

These men were to be judged for planning and perpetrating the greatest crime in history—what William Shirer calls "a massacre so horrible and on such a scale as to leave an ugly scar on civilization that will surely last as long as man on earth."[1]

Among the first to be indicted—Hermann Göring, Hitler's closest confidante; Hans Frank, the man who oversaw the liquidation of Polish Jewry; Julius Streicher, architect of the Third Reich's anti-Semitic policies—were those considered the leading participants in the implementation of the Final Solution.[2] Only seven months earlier, each had been under the direct command of Adolf Hitler.

At 10:00 A.M. on November 21, 1945, the chief U.S. prosecutor, Robert Jackson, strode to the podium to open the proceedings convened to mete out some semblance of justice for the atrocities carried out in the name of the Third Reich. Pointing forcefully to the defendants, Jackson declared, "In the prisoners' dock sit twenty-odd broken men. What makes this inquest significant is that these prisoners represent sinister influences that will lurk in the world long after their bodies have returned to dust. We will show them to be living symbols of racial

39

hatreds, of terrorism and violence, and of the arrogance and cruelty of power."[3]

As the trial commenced, investigators from the four prosecuting nations presented millions of documents of evidence—the bloody trail of the Nazis' genocidal regime—to support their case against the accused. And one by one, the defendants faced their inquisitors and denied any complicity in the crimes they were accused of.[4]

On the 137th day of the proceedings, it was the turn of Baldur von Schirach, leader of the Hitler Youth, to take the stand. The youngest of the defendants at thirty-nine, the story of the path that brought von Schirach to Nuremberg is a cautionary tale.

Von Schirach had joined the Nazi Party in 1925 shortly after his eighteenth birthday. Slavishly devoted to Hitler, the young adherent rose rapidly through the Party hierarchy as he groomed German youth for the National Socialist cause. In 1932, Schirach was elected to the Reichstag and a year later became the head of the Hitler Youth. He was appointed *Reichleiter* (Reich leader) on June 18, 1933, and quickly assumed a place in Hitler's inner circle.[5] He was so successful in carrying out his new duties that, by 1935, an astonishing 60 percent of German boys had voluntarily enlisted in the Hitler *Jugend*.[6] As he confessed many years later, "I have led millions of German youth to serve a barbaric master."

Von Schirach's efficiency soon caught the attention of Hitler, who in 1940 named him *Gauleiter* (Governor) of Vienna—the city where the Führer claimed to have developed his hatred for the Jewish people two decades earlier. Although most of the later charges against him stemmed from his tenure as Gauleiter, the Nuremberg indictment states that von Schirach had demonstrated a penchant for the baser elements of Nazi ideology long before his promotion. At a 1939 meeting of the National Socialist German Students Bund in Heidelberg, Schirach was invited to deliver the keynote address. After praising the students for devoting so much of their time to the affairs of the Party, he reminded the boys of the service they had rendered during the *Kristallnacht* riots a year earlier when Jewish stores and synagogues were looted and burned. Dramatically, he pointed across the river to the old university town of Heidelberg where several burnt-out synagogues stood as mute witnesses to the students' zeal. "Those skeleton buildings will remain there for centuries," he told them, "as inspiration for future students, as a warning to enemies of the State."[7]

The governorship of Vienna proved the opportunity to put his words into action. On November 7, 1940, von Schirach ordered that the remaining Jews of Vienna be rounded up to implement a massive slave labor operation. "Investigations are being made at present by the Gestapo to find out how many able-bodied Jews are still available in order to make plans for the contemplated mass projects," declared von Schirach's written order, captured by the Allies after the war. "It is assumed that there are not many more Jews available. If some still should be available, however, the Gestapo has no scruples to use the Jews even for the removal of the destroyed synagogues."[8]

According to his Nuremberg accusers, this document indicated that "von Schirach and his immediate subordinates not only knew of the atrocities which had been committed against the Jews by the Nazis in Vienna, but also that they endorsed further forced labor of Jews and worked intimately with the Gestapo and the SS in their measures of persecution."[9]

The enslavement of Jews was merely the first step in the Nazi master plan. Von Schirach was not squeamish about participating in the final phase. In the most serious indictment against him—crimes against humanity—he was accused of sending more than 10,000 Viennese Jews to their deaths. The charge stemmed from a meeting he had with the city council on June 6, 1942, during which he announced that "in the latter part of the summer or in the fall of this year all Jews will be removed from this city, and the removal of the Czechs will then get under way."[10]

In a speech to the European Youth League in Vienna soon after, he stated: "Every Jew who exerts influence in Europe is a danger to European culture. If anyone reproaches me with having driven from this city, which was once the European metropolis of Jewry, tens of thousands upon tens of thousands of Jews into the ghetto of the East, I feel myself compelled to reply: I see in this an action contributing to European culture."[11] The "ghetto of the East" was simply a Nazi euphemism for Auschwitz and other Polish concentration camps.

Now, at war's end, von Schirach stood to answer the charges. On May 23, 1946, the young Nazi leader stepped into the witness box and took the oath required of all defendants: "I swear by God, the Almighty and Omniscient, that I will speak the pure truth and will withhold and add nothing."

When it was his turn, von Schirach's chief counsel, Fritz Sauter, approached the witness box and began his interrogation: Had the Jugend leader's principles been copied from Hitler or had other factors in his youth played a part?

Von Schirach, whom one observer described as "looking like a contrite college boy kicked out of school for some folly,"[12] responded by describing his childhood. The son of a middle-class Heidelberg theater manager, he had always been surrounded by "artistic and intellectual stimulation."

Then, in 1924, a year after the Hitler beer hall *putsch*, at the impression-
able age of seventeen, von Schirach discovered the Nazi Party and gradually became a convert to its ideology.

Had his transformation into a loyal National Socialist come about
through reading the party's literature? Sauter asked. Von Schirach's
response, delivered to a packed courtroom and an international radio audience numbering in the millions, bears disturbing witness to the far reach
and ruinous impact of a long-extinct publishing venture:

> The decisive anti-Semitic book which I read at that time, and
> the book which influenced my comrades, was Henry Ford's book,
> *The International Jew*. I read it and became anti-Semitic. This
> book made in those days a great impression on my friends and
> myself because we saw in Henry Ford the representative of suc-
> cess, also the representative of a progressive social policy. In the
> poverty-stricken and wretched Germany of the time, youth
> looked toward America, and, apart from the great benefactor
> Herbert Hoover, it was Henry Ford who, to us, represented
> America . . . If he said the Jews were to blame, naturally we
> believed him.[13]

One year before he ever heard of Adolf Hitler, Baldur von Schirach
had found inspiration in the hate-laced diatribes of Henry Ford, whose
status as a folk hero extended far beyond the borders of America.

The nineteenth-century German philosopher Hegel wrote eloquently of
Germany's destiny to lead the world in an inspired mission led by
"heroes"—great agents fated by mysterious Providence to carry out "the
will of the world spirit."[14] This veneration of heroes has always figured
prominently in the German psyche.

By 1921, Germans, like Americans, had declared Henry Ford one of
those heroes. In a country where working conditions were even worse
than they were in the United States, news of the American company's
five-dollar-a-day policy had elevated Henry Ford to mythical status.
When his autobiography was published in German, the book became an
instant bestseller in the country and its success was reported in newspapers throughout Europe and America. During the war, while American
newspapers mocked mercilessly Ford's Peace Expedition, the German

press had praised its goals with undisguised reverence for "the great American, Ford." A new word, *Fordismus*, entered the country's vernacular in early 1921 after a Hamburg university professor used it in a lecture on Ford's production methods.

Hegel's concept of "Heroes," first uttered in 1830, would find expression through another German philosopher nearly a century later. Wrote Adolf Hitler in *Mein Kampf*, "World-historical men—the heroes of an epoch—must therefore be recognized as its clear-sighted ones; their words, their deeds are the best of their time."[15] For Hitler, and a generation of Germans, Ford's words as well as his deeds served only to increase his stature in a nation that exalted heroes.

In February 1921, at a time when Hitler was still only a little-known fanatic,[16] the first German-language edition of *The International Jew* was published in Berlin under the title *Der International Jude*.[17] The author's name on the jacket was Henry Ford, though the book, like its American counterpart, was merely a compendium of articles that had appeared in the *Dearborn Independent*.

The book was an immediate success. Germany's humiliating defeat and a postwar recession had sapped the nation's morale. The people were eager to hear Ford's prescription out of the morass. But there was another reason for the book's warm reception. It spoke directly to some of the country's greatest concerns.[18] Much of *Der International Jude* was devoted to exposing a conspiracy to undermine the German nation. Bolshevik Jews, the book claimed, were responsible for the German defeat in the First World War and the humiliating terms of the Versailles Treaty:

> Jewish influence in German affairs came strongly to the front during the 1914–1918 war. It came with all the directness and attack of a flying wedge, as if previously prepared . . . The principal Jewish influences which brought down German order may be named under three heads: (a) the spirit of Bolshevism which masqueraded under the name of German socialism; (b) Jewish ownership and control of the Press; (c) Jewish control of the food supply and the industrial machinery of the country. There was a fourth, "higher up," but these worked upon the German people directly. It will be recalled that the German collapse in that war was directly due to food starvation and material shortages, and to industrial unrest. As early as the second year of the war, German Jews were preaching that German defeat was necessary to the rise of the proletariat.[19]

For a gullible German public desperate to find a scapegoat for its catastrophic defeat, these words pointed the way. We weren't defeated, it told
them, we were betrayed. And, although the *Protocols of the Elders of Zion* had
previously found its way to Germany via White Russian émigrés, it
remained an obscure document there until the German edition of *The
International Jew* gave the forgery legitimacy. In 1921, western leaders were
still debating the establishment of the League of Nations, the international
organization U.S. President Woodrow Wilson envisioned to prevent
another world war. But entry into the League was conditional upon accepting the terms of the Versailles Treaty, and its founding was deeply unpopular in many German circles. Ford's book, meanwhile, was warning of the
consequences of forming such a body, directing its readers to the Fifth
Protocol, which purported to reveal a cabal of Jews vowing, "We will so
wear out and exhaust the Gentiles by all this that they will be compelled to
offer us an international authority, which by its position will enable us to
absorb without disturbance all the governmental forces of the world and
thus form a super-government."[20] Thus, even a proposed instrument of
international peace was suspiciously perceived as a Jewish tool designed to
undermine Germany.

In 1923, American Jewish community activist Samuel Untermeyer
described the impact of *The International Jew* after he returned from a trip
around the world. Translations of the book, he wrote, were to be found in
the most remote corners of the earth:

> Wherever there was a Ford car, there was a Ford agency not
> far away, and wherever there was a Ford agency, these vile
> libelous books in the language of the country were to be found.
> They, coupled with the magic name of Ford, have done more
> than could be undone in a century to sow, spread and ripen the
> poisonous seeds of anti-Semitism and race hatred. These articles
> are so fantastic and so naive in their incredible fantasy that they
> read like the work of a lunatic, and but for the authority of the
> Ford name, they would have never seen the light of day and
> would have been quite harmless if they had. With that name,
> they spread like wildfire and became the Bible of every anti-
> Semite.[21]

And if *The International Jew* was the Bible, observed one historian,
then to the Nazis, "Henry Ford must have seemed like a God."[22] It is still
unclear when Adolf Hitler first read the book but by 1922, a year after he

took control of the National Socialist German Workers Party, he had already clearly lionized the American industrialist.

In December of that year, the *New York Times* ran a small item head-lined "Berlin Hears Ford Is Backing Hitler" long before most Americans or even Germans had ever heard of the obscure nationalist politician:

> A rumor is circulating here that Henry Ford is financing Adolph (sic) Hitler's nationalist and anti-Semitic movement in Munich. Indeed, the *Berlin Tageblatt* has made an appeal to the American Ambassador in Berlin to investigate and interfere.[23]

The reporter offered no specifics other than "a ground for suspicion" that Hitler's lavish spending must be financed from abroad. But a subsequent paragraph offered the first clue that the Ford mystique resonated beyond American shores:

> The wall beside his desk in Hitler's private office is decorated with a large picture of Henry Ford. In the antechamber there is a large table covered with books, nearly all of which are a translation of a book written by Henry Ford. If you ask one of Hitler's underlings for the reason of Ford's popularity in these circles, he will smile knowingly but say nothing.[24]

Three months later, the allegations in the article seemed confirmed by the vice president of the Bavarian *Diet* (parliament), Erhard Auer, when he embarked on a mission to Berlin to meet with German President Friedrich Ebert. Auer had come to the capital to express his concern about Ford's interference in the affairs of a foreign nation.

As he was entering the Reichstag to keep his appointment with President Ebert, Herr Auer was stopped by the foreign correspondent of the *Chicago Tribune*, who inquired about the political situation in Bavaria. The response must have come as a surprise to the American reporter expecting a bland comment about the region's postwar economic improvement. Instead, the politician invoked a familiar name to indict a man previously unknown to any of the *Tribune*'s readers. Henry Ford, he charged, was financing the revolutionary program of a radical Austrian named Adolf Hitler because he was favorably impressed by Hitler's program supporting the "extermination of Jews in Germany."[25] Not only did the quote establish a link between Ford and Hitler, but it appears to be the first reference in the American media, and possibly the first ever published suggestion, that Hitler even contemplated such a plan. According to Auer:

> The Bavarian *Diet* has long had information that the Hitler movement was partly financed by an American anti-Semitic chief, who is Henry Ford. Mr. Ford's interests in the Bavarian anti-Jewish movement began over a year ago when one of Mr. Ford's agents seeking to sell Ford tractors came in contact with Dietrich Eichart (sic), the notorious Pan-German, shortly after Herr Eichart asked Mr. Ford's agent for financial aid. The agent returned to America and immediately Mr. Ford's money began coming to Munich. Herr Hitler openly boasts of Mr. Ford's support and praises Mr. Ford not as a great individualist but as a great anti-Semite.[26]

Neither the *New York Times* story nor the *Chicago Tribune* article quotes Hitler directly, suggesting that neither reporter was able to secure an interview. But two weeks later, on March 8, the *Tribune* ran an expansive interview Hitler had granted to its foreign correspondent Raymond Fendrick. That week, American and German newspapers had been discussing Ford's potential White House candidacy at length, and Hitler seemed overjoyed at the prospect:

> I wish that I could send some of my shock troops to Chicago and other big American cities to help in the elections. We look on Heinrich Ford as the leader of the growing *Fascisti* movement in America. We admire particularly his anti-Jewish policy which is the Bavarian Fascisti platform. We have just had his anti-Jewish articles translated and published. The book is being circulated to millions throughout Germany.[27]

In the interview, Hitler denies Auer's allegation that Ford was providing financial backing for the fascist movement in Germany, but, like a small boy boasting of an autographed baseball card, he adds, "Heinrich's picture occupies the place of honor in [my] sanctum."[28]

The *Tribune* reporter was unconvinced. "If Mr. Ford is not the angel of

Herr Hitler's Fascisti, in spite of the story of the Bavarian government to the contrary, huge sums are coming in from somewhere," Fendrick wrote. Hitler's organization, he noted, includes 5,000 shock troops uniformed in gray and is "spreading by leaps and bounds throughout Germany," sending out Ford's book and other Bavarian Fascisti propaganda by the "car loads."[29]

Shortly after, an American consular official stationed in Berlin named Robert Murphy asked Hitler whether the reports were true. Hitler replied that "unfortunately Mr. Ford's organization has so far made no money contributions to our party" and claimed that most of the Party treasury came from "patriotic Germans living abroad."[30]

The contradictory claims about whether Ford's money financed the early rise of the National Socialists have for more than half a century stymied historians probing one of the enduring mysteries of the Nazi era: Who provided Hitler's early funding?

Certainly, when Hitler assumed control of the Party in the summer of 1921, funding was sparse. According to an early member:

> The Nazi organization itself lived from day to day financially, with no treasury to draw on for lecture hall rentals, printing costs, or the other thousand-and-one expenses which threatened to swamp us. The only funds we could count on were membership dues, which were small, merely a drop in the bucket. Collections at mass meetings were sometimes large, but not to be relied on . . . We never had money enough. Instead of receiving salaries for the work we did, most of us had to give to the Party in order to carry on.[31]

That fall, the National Socialists abruptly canceled a rally that was scheduled to take place at Munich's Krone Circus, citing a "lack of funds."[32] The Party still could not afford to hire a treasurer. Its purchase of a newspaper, the *Volkischer Beobachter*, a year earlier had left it deep in debt. But by the summer of 1923, German newspaper references abound, reporting the National Socialists "flush with cash." The sudden largesse would seem to coincide with the period of the allegation by Vice President Auer—reported in the *New York Times* article—that one of Ford's agents had been successfully solicited for financial aid by Dietrich Eckart.

If Ford gave money to Hitler as early as 1922, then Dietrich Eckart's involvement in the transaction is certainly plausible, although Eckart was no businessman and, under normal circumstances, it seems unlikely he would be consorting with a sales agent. Eckart has often been referred to as the "spiritual godfather of National Socialism." A struggling poet and alcoholic, he had become involved in the German Workers Party, forerunner of the National Socialists, shortly after being released from a mental institution in 1919. A longtime anti-Semite, Eckart could often be found in the beer cellars of Munich advocating the "downfall of the swine"—Jews and Marxists—whom he blamed for his lack of success as a poet.[33]

At a Party meeting in the *Brennessel* wine cellar in 1919, Eckart stood drunkenly on a chair and listed what he considered the ideal credentials in a party leader: "We need a fellow at the head who can stand the sound of a machine gun. The rabble need to get fear into their pants. We can't use an officer, because the people don't respect them any more. The best would be a worker who knows how to talk . . . He doesn't need much brains . . . He must be a bachelor, then we'll get the women."[34]

Shortly after this incident, he met the man who would fit the bill. More than twenty years his junior, Adolf Hitler was still rough around the edges when he joined the party and encountered Eckart, who soon became his mentor, lending him books, coaching the young Austrian hothead in proper German, and refining his oratorical skills considerably. Eckart also introduced Hitler to his wide circle of friends, which included wealthy socialites and talented rabble-rousers—among them, Rudolf Hess and Alfred Rosenberg—who would later figure prominently in the Nazi Party.[35] By 1920, Eckart had succeeded in bringing in the Party's first substantial financial contribution, enabling it to purchase a weekly anti-Semitic newspaper, the *Volkischer Beobachter*, and turning it into the organ of the National Socialists.

Few records exist from those early Party days. What little is known comes from the hearsay accounts of contemporary observers, most of whom identified Eckart as the man responsible for the Party's earliest fund-raising success. As Party fund-raiser, it is conceivable he would have been the logical Nazi official to meet with Ford's financial conduit if one existed. However, the only evidence linking Eckart to Henry Ford, apart from Vice President Auer's accusation, is associated with ideological rather than financial considerations, since many historians believe he is the person who introduced Hitler to *The International Jew*. After Eckart died suddenly in December 1923, the party published a compendium of notes in book form recounting his purported conversations with Hitler. Entitled *Bolshevism from Moses to Lenin: A Dialogue Between Adolf Hitler and Me*, the book was published as Hitler stood trial for his part in the failed 1923 beer hall *putsch* attempt. It soon became a mainstay of anti-Semitic literature and an inspiration for *Mein Kampf*, which Hitler was to dedicate to Eckart a year later. In chapter three of Eckart's posthumous work, the two men are discussing "Jewish Internationalism" when Hitler begins a long monologue on the failure of Jews to give their allegiance to any country:

> "All Israel stands openly in the British camp!" announced the American union leader Samuel Gompers in 1916. And that includes the German Jews too, as the American, Ford, well knew. He has written of the faithlessness of the so-called "German" Jews toward the country where they live, of the fact that they have united themselves with the rest of the world's Jews toward the ruin of Germany. "Why?" jeers the Jew. "Because the German is a vulgar scoundrel, a backward, medieval creature, who hasn't the faintest idea of our worth. And we should help such rabble? No, he has the Jews he deserves!" Such arrogance is indeed staggering to behold.[36]

In their 1964 study of Ford's overseas operation, *American Business Abroad*, Mira Wilkins and Frank Hill insist that no evidence exists in company records proving Ford financed Hitler.[37] What they don't say is that those records are far from complete. According to archivists at the Ford Motor Company, a significant amount of archival material from the company's early days—particularly material pertaining to Ford's anti-Semitism—has been "discarded."[38] This, of course, places severe obstacles in the way of getting at the truth behind these events.

In 1921, a young Bavarian named Kurt Ludecke was introduced to Adolf Hitler for the first time following a Nazi rally in Munich. He was so captivated by the "inescapable power" of Hitler's oratory that he asked for a meeting with the party leader the next day. At the appointed time, Ludecke arrived at Nazi headquarters, a dingy former coffeehouse in a rundown section of the city. By the end of their meeting, Ludecke later recalled, "I had given him my soul."[39] Within months of joining the fledgling movement, Ludecke had so impressed Hitler with his financial acumen that he was appointed the National Socialists' "chief fund-raiser," traveling the globe attempting to secure funding for the Nazi cause. In 1922, while traveling in the United States, during the height of the *Dearborn Independent*'s anti-Semitic campaign, Ludecke had taken a detour to Detroit in order to visit the paper's offices and express his appreciation for the *Independent*'s success in painting Jewry "as a malignant growth on the body of the nation."[40] Two years later, when hyperinflation in Germany had depleted the coffers of the National Socialist Party, the United States held out financial promise and Ludecke was dispatched on a fundraising expedition to America.

On a cold January morning in 1924, he arrived at New York's Waldorf Astoria Hotel on a mission he was convinced would be the salvation of the Nazi movement. His destination was the suite shared by Siegfried Wagner—son of the great operatic composer Richard Wagner—and Wagner's wife Winifred, who had arrived in New York in advance of an American tour where Siegfried was booked to conduct his father's music. Their American agenda, however, had as much to do with politics as it did music. Winifred was one of Hitler's earliest adherents, having joined the Nazi Party in 1921, while Siegfried fully subscribed to his father's written opinion that the Jew "is the plastic demon of decay."[41]

The Wagners, wrote Ludecke, "were on a mission not very different than mine." He claimed his plan was fully embraced by Siegfried, the man "for whose nursing the incomparable *Siegfried Idyll* was prepared," in the bold scheme to save the Nazi Party from collapse. The couple had learned that Ford's wife, Clara, had a "hospitable inclination" toward celebrities. This, Ludecke later recalled, was the "ticket to getting Henry's ear."

Siegfried's concert tour was scheduled to bring him to Detroit in late January 1924. An invitation would be extended to Henry and Clara Ford to attend the concert as a guest of the Wagners. The German couple were counting on a reciprocal invitation so they might discuss how their shared antipathy toward the Jews might find common cause.

"Our plan hinged on whether Mrs. Ford would invite them to be her guests," Ludecke later wrote in his memoir, *I Knew Hitler*. "If this happened, the rest of the plot was obvious—a word in Mr. Ford's presence, a hint, a request."[42]

The gambit worked. The invitation was waiting for the Wagners when they checked into their hotel, the Detroit Statler, on Wednesday, January 30. Late the next morning, Siegfried and Winifred Wagner made the fifteen-minute drive to the Fords' 2,000-acre Fairlane estate, driving through the "winter grimness of Detroit's dreary suburbs." They spent the afternoon at Fairlane with Henry and Clara Ford before driving to the concert with their hosts that evening. The plan was for Frau Wagner, during the concert, to broach the possibility of a meeting between Ludecke and Ford to discuss Nazi funding. As "the heroic themes were springing from Siegfried's baton," the conductor's wife turned on the charm. She later recalled that she was surprised to find that "Ford was very well informed about everything that was going on in Germany. . . . He knew all about the

National Socialist movement."[43] After their spirited discussion, Ford finally agreed to hear Ludecke's appeal the next morning.[44] The German was well aware of the stakes of this meeting. Ford's support, he wrote, was all the Nazis needed to "grasp control of Germany."

The anticipation, Ludecke later recalled, was almost unbearable. "I was to see Henry Ford, the multimillionaire. With one rasp of his pen, he could solve the Nazis' money problem. More than that, if he showed sound vision and goodwill, he could lend us sufficient prestige to push the program ahead like a battering ram. All through the world, wherever there was a road, the name of Ford was known and respected."[45] Ford's influence and prestige, it is clear, was almost as highly coveted as his money.

At the appointed time, Ernest Liebold called at the Statler to fetch Kurt Ludecke and drive him to Dearborn to meet the man Ludecke later described as "a modern myth in his own right." As he sat in Ford's office ready to launch his appeal, a number of thoughts ran through Ludecke's head. "How could I impress this man with the merits of my case enough to divert a fraction of his fortune to Hitler's use? Ford was engaged in a campaign tangent to our own, which was favorable. But no man in the public eye can endow an insurgent revolutionary movement as casually as he would contribute to homeless animals. . . ."[46] Ludecke recognized the magnitude and implications of what he sought from Ford: He was asking an American to aid and abet a radical opposition group based in a foreign nation.

Ford seated himself in his leather armchair, hoisted one foot on the desk, clasped his hand over his knee and looked quizzically at the German visitor, "his gray eyes friendly but keen."[47] For the next fifteen minutes, Ludecke conveyed with the "most emphatic eloquence" at his command the conviction that "the Nazis were offering [Ford] a chance to make history." If his host's anti-Semitic views were sincere, the German argued, it would be worth every penny of his vast fortune. For the Nazis intended, if given a chance, to enshrine into policy anti-Jewish measures the likes of which Ford probably hadn't even imagined. They would represent the practical extremes of ideas he could only write about.

Occasionally, as Ludecke mentioned his great admiration for the work of the *Independent* and the two men's "common campaign," Ford would nod and offer the occasional curt remark: "I know . . . Yes, the Jews, these cunning Jews. . . ."[48] But it soon became apparent, writes Hitler's emissary, that his 4,000-mile journey had resulted in failure. "If I had been trying to sell Mr. Ford a wooden nutmeg, he couldn't have shown less interest in the proposition. With consummate Yankee skill, he lifted the discussion back to the idealistic plane to avoid the financial discussion."[49] Ludecke claims to have returned to Germany with one thought: "What a resounding syllable is a rich man's 'No'!"[50]

This account, published in 1937, has been cited by countless historians and biographers as evidence that Ford did *not* fund Hitler. But not every expert who has investigated the question is convinced. In his landmark 1978 study of Nazi funding sources, *Who Financed Hitler*, historian James Pool writes, "Considering that Ludecke was a Nazi, one would certainly expect him to deny that Ford gave any money to Hitler. . . . If the German people found out that Hitler was financed by Ford, he would be accused of being the puppet of a foreign capitalist. A promise from the Nazis to keep silent about the contribution would probably have been part of the bargain."[51]

However, this is pure conjecture and no tangible evidence exists to prove any such transaction took place. But in 1977, fifty-three years after she arrived in Detroit to help Kurt Ludecke solicit funding for the Nazis, Winifred Wagner revealed for the first time that in the course of her own conversation during the January 31, 1924, concert, "Ford told me that he had helped finance Hitler."[52] Frau Wagner further claimed that when, during the concert, she suggested to Ford that Hitler was now more in need of money than ever, "Ford smiled and made a vague comment about still being willing to support a man like Hitler who was working to free Germany from the Jews. The philosophies and ideas of Ford and Hitler were very similar."[53]

To this day, Winifred Wagner's account remains the only credible suggestion that Adolf Hitler's early financial success was tied to the American industrialist.

But whether or not Ford actually financed Hitler, there can be no doubt about his ideological sway over the Führer-in-waiting.

History records that, unlike Baldur von Schirach, Adolf Hitler was an ardent anti-Semite before he ever read Ford's book *The International Jew*. But there are as many contradictory explanations for the genesis of Hitler's anti-Semitism as there are about the source of his funding.

As a young boy growing up in Linz, Austria, according to Hitler's own account in *Mein Kampf*, he thought very little about the Jewish Question and claimed to abhor any form of discrimination:

It is difficult today, if not impossible, to say when the word, "Jew," first occasioned special thoughts in me. In my father's

house, I cannot recall ever having heard the word, at least while
he lived. . . . Linz possessed very few Jews. In the course of centuries their exteriors had become Europeanized and human-
looking. Indeed, I even took them for Germans. The nonsense
of this conception was not clear to me because I saw just a single
distinctive characteristic, the alien religion. Since they had been
persecuted because of it, as I believed, my aversion toward prej-
udicial remarks about them became almost detestation.[54]

He claimed that after he moved to Vienna as a young bohemian art student in 1908, he still harbored no prejudice. "The Jew was characterized
for me by nothing but his religion, and therefore on grounds of human tolerance, I maintained my rejection of religious attacks. . . ."[55] The turning
point, he writes, came one day when he was strolling the Viennese streets
and "suddenly happened upon an apparition in a long caftan with black
hair locks . . .":

Is this a Jew? was my first thought. They surely didn't look
like that in Linz. I observed the man stealthily and cautiously. But
the longer I stared at this alien face, examining it feature for feature, the more my first question was transformed into a new conception: Is this a German? As always in such cases I began to try
to remove my doubts with books. For a few hellers I purchased
the first anti-semitic brochures of my life. Unfortunately, they all
proceeded from the standpoint that in principle the reader was
conversant with or even understood the Jewish question to a certain degree . . .[56]

If his account can be believed—many historians have questioned it—
Hitler was determined to remedy his "ignorance" of the Jewish Question
and proceeded to bury himself in anti-Semitic literature. It is unclear when
he first discovered *The International Jew*, but his first known anti-Semitic
treatise was written a full year before Ford's book was even published and
almost two years before it was translated into German. Shortly after Hitler
was released from a military hospital in 1919—where he was treated for
wounds he had suffered during the war—he was sent on an army-
sponsored course of systematic political education for demobilizing soldiers that featured Pan-German nationalism, anti-Semitism, and
anti-socialism. On September 12, he was assigned by his army captain, Karl

Mayr, to attend a meeting and infiltrate an upstart political movement called the German Workers Party, which would later evolve into the National Socialists.[57]

Four days later, Captain Mayr referred Hitler to a man named Adolf Gemlich who had written to ask about the Army's position on the Jewish Question. Mayr assigned the response to Hitler.[58] In contrast to the fiery rhetoric that would characterize his later diatribes, Hitler's 1919 letter to Gemlich reveals a sober analysis, emphasizing the need for "scientific anti-Semitism" rather than violence toward the Jews: "The danger posed by Jewry for our people today finds expression in the undeniable aversion of wide sections of our people," he begins. "In his effects and consequences he is like a racial tuberculosis of the nations," the letter continues before rambling on for a full three pages on the same theme.

It is Hitler's prescription for how to treat this "tuberculosis" that is most revealing. "The deduction from all this is the following," he writes: "An anti-Semitism based on purely emotional grounds will find its ultimate expression in the form of the pogrom. An anti-Semitism based on reason, however, must lead to systematic legal combating and elimination of the privileges of the Jews, that which distinguishes the Jews from the other aliens who live among us (an Aliens Law). The ultimate objective [of such legislation] must, however, be the irrevocable removal of the Jews in general."[59] In this context, as most historians agree, Hitler was not referring to a violent removal, but rather a deportation or expulsion.

Historian Albert Lee believes that, while Ford did not necessarily inspire Hitler's hatred of the Jews, he lent him a framework for his burgeoning anti-Semitism. Though Hitler had clearly read Ford's work by the time he served his five-month prison term for treason after the failed 1923 *putsch*, it was not until Hitler was within the comfortable confines of Bavaria's Landsberg am Lech Fortress Prison that his ideas began to crystallize.

While Hitler served his sentence from April to December 1924, he wrote the first volume of *Mein Kampf*, the book whose lessons the world would fail to heed. And in the book that defined his future vision, only one American is mentioned:

> Jews are the regents of the stock exchange power of the American Union. Every year they manage to become increasingly the controlling masters of the labor power of a people of 120,000,000 souls; one great man, Ford, to their exasperation, still holds out independently there even now.[60]

To Hitler, Ford is the lone heroic resister to the Jewish onslaught. There is no further reference to Ford, but his ideas imbue the entire book. Entire passages and numerous ideas are actually lifted verbatim from the pages of *The International Jew*, and when the first English-language edition of *Mein Kampf* was later published in the United States, the editors inserted a footnote after the brief reference to Ford: "These reflections are copied, for the most part, from the *Dearborn Independent*, Mr. Henry Ford's newspaper. Much of the anti-Semitic propaganda once disseminated by this journal is still current in Germany."[61]

The basic theme of Ford's book—and the phrase that inspired its title— is the concept that "International Jews" were responsible for plotting the Russian Revolution and were now planning to extend the tentacles of Jewish Bolshevism to the rest of the world, particularly Germany. Repeatedly, in *Mein Kampf*, Hitler uses this phrase and echoes an identical theme. "The real organizer of the revolution, and the actual wire-puller behind it, the International Jew, had sized up the situation correctly," he writes.[62] Similarly, the *Dearborn Independent* had coined the phrase "gentile front" to describe "their tendency to cover up the evidence of Jewish control." The term "gentile front" appears repeatedly in the pages of Hitler's opus.[63]

Most notably, Hitler, who knew little of agrarian issues, was clearly inspired by Ford's obsession with Jews and farming. The *Independent* declares, "It is necessary for Jewish interests to deplete the land both of laborers and capital." Hitler wrote in the pages of *Mein Kampf*, "The cup is filled to overflowing when [the Jew] draws also the land and the soil into the circle of his mercenary objects." In almost identical phrasing, both Ford and Hitler write, "He himself never cultivated the soil but considered it as an object to be exploited."[64]

The two books share another curious assertion in common: that the Jews perform the remarkable feat of controlling both capitalism and Communism at the same time. Albert Lee has pointed to perhaps the most disturbing of all the hateful passages in *The International Jew* as a precursor to the greatest crime in history:

> Imagine for a moment that there were no Semites in Europe. Would the tragedy be so terrible, now? Hardly! They have stirred up the people in all countries, have incited them to war, revolution, and Communism.[65]

Lee writes, "It takes no imagination to read into this fantasy the precursors of Hitler's Final Solution." But it would probably be more accurate to argue that this passage helped pave the way for many Germans' later acceptance of Hitler's program of *Judenrein* (a Europe free of Jews).

Perhaps the most important influence Ford exerted over Hitler is his "exposé" of the *Protocols of the Elders of Zion* in chapter six of *The International Jew*, "An Introduction to the Jewish Protocols." Although Hitler may have encountered the *Protocols* before, they are never mentioned in the list of the earliest anti-Semitic literature he read before 1920, as cited by his contemporaries. Although it is almost certain that Dietrich Eckart had encountered a Russian edition of the book that was circulating in Munich's anti-Semitic circles, and some later accounts even claim Eckart introduced Hitler to the forged work,[66] there is not a single reference to the *Protocols* in Eckart's posthumously published memoir.[67] Ford, however, is mentioned prominently. Like many of the *Dearborn Independent's* American readers, even Hitler may have needed Henry Ford's endorsement to take the spurious document seriously.[68] According to historian Michael Kellogg, "There was considerable disbelief even in far-rightist circles regarding the "*Protocols'* authenticity."[69]

Wherever he first encountered them, the *Protocols* eventually exerted an enormous influence on Hitler's worldview. Here finally, as he explains in *Mein Kampf*, was the explanation he had sought to make sense of his many unresolved questions about the "Jewish Problem":

> To what extent the whole existence of this people is based on a continuous lie is shown incomparably by the *Protocols of the Wise Men of Zion*, so infinitely hated by the Jews. . . . What many Jews may do unconsciously is here consciously exposed. And that is what matters. It is completely indifferent from what Jewish brain these disclosures originate; the important thing is that with positively terrifying certainty they reveal the nature and activity of the Jewish people and expose their inner contexts as well as their ultimate final aims.[70]

When a Nazi party official brought Hitler proof that *The Protocols of the Elders of Zion* was a forgery in 1930, his curt reply was: "It doesn't matter. The *Protocols* are still true in principle."[71] It is probably no coincidence that his words echoed Ford's own response when confronted with the same facts years before: "The only statement I care to make about the *Protocols* is that they fit in with what is going on." That their lies were predicated on an earlier lie was inconsequential. All the lies dovetailed to a truth of which Ford and Hitler were unwaveringly convinced.

Hitler and many of his fellow Nazis, including propaganda minister Josef Goebbels and the Party's ideologue Alfred Rosenberg, would cite the work repeatedly over the years as the Party's blueprint. Most historians concur that the Russian forgery played a major part in shaping Hitler's genocidal intentions. In her 1968 book, *The Holocaust*, historian Nora Levin argues that "Hitler used the *Protocols* as a manual in his war to exterminate the Jews."[72] In his own 1967 study, Norman Cohn describes them as a "Warrant for Genocide."[73] If Ford's book was indeed the catalyst for Hitler's acceptance of the *Protocols*, the implications are staggering.

A number of historians have scrutinized the early links between Ford and Hitler. Some of them have endeavored to demonstrate conclusively the ideological influence Ford exerted over early Nazi doctrine, comparing passages of Ford's work with Hitler's later writings.

Ron Rosenbaum, author of the acclaimed book *Explaining Hitler*, writes, "One could make the case that without Ford's inspiration and (probably) cash contributions, Hitler and his movement might not have survived to commit mass murder." Hitler, argues Rosenbaum, looked to Ford for his technique, the industrialization of killing perfected in the death camps, the mass production of death by assembly line. Was it an "accident," he asks, that the mechanization of murder in the concentration camps "began with the use of truck motors, with mobile vans turned into gas chambers, using the products of the internal combustion engine to 'motorize' the killing of Jews [and others]? Was it an 'accident' that Auschwitz was run like a hideously efficient automotive assembly line, with its highly efficient division of labor?"[74]

But none of these myriad theories attempting to link the two men explains why Ford singled out Germany as the recipient of his attention and, perhaps, largesse. This, after all, was a man so ignorant of history and world events that he believed the American Revolution took place in 1812 and that Benedict Arnold was a writer. What reason is there to believe that Ford would care anything about the political situation in a country so far away, a country to which he had no discernible connection? The answer, like the genesis of Ford's anti-Semitism itself, likely can be traced to one man, Ford's secretary Ernest Liebold, previously identified as a German spy.

From the earliest days of the *Independent's* campaign against the Jews, Germany is singled out in its pages as the prime example of Jewish influence. In only the second issue of the *Independent*'s anti-Semitic campaign, the paper claimed that the collapse of the German economy, the Armistice and the revolution that prevented Germany from recovery were all the results of a world Jewish conspiracy. The *Independent* had become so German-centered that it falsely declared German Jews "were not German patriots" because they refused to fight for their country during the war.[75] These words had little relevance to the American farmers and laborers to whom they were originally targeted. In fact, many readers must have found it strange to read the frequent articles defending America's former enemy. In the aftermath of the First World War, many Americans had lingering anti-German feelings. But for Ernest Liebold, the sentiments reflected his obsession that the Jews were responsible for the defeat of his beloved Germany.

In his company oral history, Liebold's assistant Harold Cordell later recalled that an inordinate number of visitors to Ford's office during these years were German: "Whenever any German delegation came to the office, the big red carpet was rolled out and royal honors were paid, whereas a United States Senator could just sit in the anteroom for hours and wait for an audience."[76]

On October 25, 1920, an American clergyman named Joseph Schubert wrote Henry Ford revealing that he had "been requested by leading men of the anti-Semitic movement in Germany to submit some very important information to you." According to the recently uncovered correspondence file, Schubert requested a meeting with Ford to discuss this matter.[77] Three days later, Ernest Liebold wrote back informing the minister that he was personally "giving the matter my attention under Mr. Ford's direction and I will be glad to see you at any time you can arrange to come to Detroit."[78] They eventually met a month later, although there is no record about what they discussed.

Again, the destruction of numerous company files makes it difficult to paint a completely accurate picture of what happened next. But there is enough evidence remaining in the U.S. National Archives, the Bundesarchiv in Berlin and other repositories to discern the existence of a shadowy network involving Ernest Liebold, German monarchists, radical right-wing Russian émigrés, disaffected German-Americans, and Adolf Hitler.

The key to unraveling the mystery is the White Russian Boris Brasol, who first brought *The Protocols of the Elders of Zion* to the offices of the *Dearborn Independent* in 1920 and set the stage for the paper's seven-year campaign against the Jews. Brasol, who has been described as a "short man with sharp features and piercing eyes who closely resembled Josef Goebbels,"[79] had arrived in America in 1916 with impressive credentials.

After graduating from law school in St. Petersburg, he rose through the ranks of the Russian ministry of justice where he was peripherally involved in the infamous 1911 "blood libel trial" of a Russian Jew named Mendel Beiliss, who was falsely accused of killing a thirteen-year old boy as part of an alleged Jewish ritual murder that included drinking the blood of a gentile.[80] One of Beiliss' defense attorneys later noted that "the activity of Boris Brasol made him a well-known figure in subsequent Russian political life as a reactionary and anti-Semite."[81] His conduct in that case, and his subsequent bravery on the Polish front during the First World War, so impressed Czar Nicholas II that Brasol was dispatched to the United States in 1916 as chief of the Russian Supply Committee's legal department.[82]

When the Bolsheviks seized power in 1917, Brasol resigned his position rather than serve the new regime. Remaining in the United States, he became active in New York Russian émigré circles, where his fanatical anti-Communism brought him to the attention of U.S. military intelligence. At the time, the War Department was deeply concerned about the Bolshevik threat, and Brasol was offered a position in the Intelligence Branch of the U.S. War Trade Board. Before long, he was appointed senior advisor to Major General Marlborough Churchill, chief of the U.S. Military Intelligence Division (MID), where he succeeded in gaining access to the highest levels of American power.[83]

Brasol was determined to take full advantage of his newfound influence to bring about his cherished dream: to reestablish the Russian monarchy and eliminate the Bolshevik government. The best way to accomplish this task, he calculated, was to discredit Lenin's regime. The vehicle he settled on to carry out this objective was the obscure document *The Protocols of the Elders of Zion*. Its existence had long been rumored but it took Brasol to summon its lies for a campaign that would soon bring devastating results. By this stage, he had already firmly established his anti-Semitic credentials within the War Department. "I know my enemy [the Jew] very well," Brasol wrote to a colleague. "I know his strength, his diabolical cunning, and his systematic treachery and yet I refuse to believe that final victory will be his."[84] Operating under the Code name "B-1," he filed more than thirty reports to his superiors about what he called an "intricate international Jewish web" linking the Federal Reserve Board, New York Jewish bankers, and the American Jewish Committee with Jewish financiers in Russia and Germany. In the face of this danger, B-1 reported, "Christendom remains silent, inactive, dull and inert."[85] The initial response from the upper echelons to these increasingly alarmist reports demonstrated considerable resistance and skepticism about his conclusions.

In 1918, MID launched an investigation into B-1's allegations, con-

ducted by a veteran intelligence officer, Captain Carlton Hayes. His findings, released a month later, dismissed Brasol's "lugging in of the Jewish
question" into every issue, which "can only be viewed as another sign of
the raving tendency of a fanatical if not of a disordered brain."[86] Brasol
knew he would have to furnish real evidence if he was to be taken seriously
in the future.

Its pedigree is still unclear but the first copy of the *Protocols* is thought
to have been brought from St. Petersburg to the United States by a Russian
officer in 1917. It soon ended up in Brasol's hands.[87] On February 1, 1918,
an MID investigator named Nathalie de Bogory—the American-born
daughter of Russian immigrants—learned of the document's existence
from a fellow military intelligence officer, Dr. Harris Houghton, a zealot
obsessed by the idea of a Jewish threat to America's war effort.[88] At
Houghton's urging, de Bogory contacted Lieutenant Brasol in New York
and offered to translate the sensational document into English.

By September 1, 1918, a half dozen typescript copies were being circulated through the War Department under the title "Protocols of the
Meetings of the Zionist Men of Wisdom," where their allegations were met
with considerable alarm. A dossier was opened within MID—file 99-75—
where each War Department memo discussing the "Jewish threat" was
subsequently placed. An astonishing number of these documents reveal
that Brasol had achieved his goal of establishing a deep suspicion of the
Jewish menace. Although some of these memos express skepticism and
question the authenticity of the *Protocols*, many more take its charges seriously. One internal analysis, marked "Most Secret," circulated around
MID comparing extracts from the *Protocols* with contemporary postwar
international currents. One of the excerpts described how the "goy"
working classes must be deceived into undermining industry and producing anarchy. Handwritten next to the excerpt in big letters is the word
SUBSTANTIATION. Then, attached to the original document, is a list of
names of the alleged radical leaders in Russia, South America, Poland, and
the United States. Next to each name and then all the way down the right-
hand margin, someone has typed, more than one hundred times, the
words "JEW, JEW, JEW, JEW, JEW . . ."[89] At one point, MID officer
Captain Robert T. Snow forwarded the document to his colonel, William
W. Hicks, with a handwritten note: "Have you read these documents on
the JEWISH PROTOCOLS? If not, I strongly urge you to read them. I
have read them through very carefully and have underlined several names.
Note the list of Jews on pages 7-8-9. It reads like good dope and recent
world developments would seem to bear out these documents."[90] It is dis-
quieting to contemplate American intelligence officers sitting around

debating the threat posed by Jews based on what they had read in the *Protocols*.

Even before the *Protocols* surfaced, Brasol and other anti-Semitic American intelligence officers had already played no small part in perpetuating a dangerous myth that would become widely believed in the years ahead—the idea that Jews had played a disproportionate role in the Russian Revolution. In fact, while a small number of early Communist figures were Jewish, only 2.6 percent of Russian Jews joined the Communist Party in 1918. Jewish Mensheviks, the arch-enemies of the Communists, outnumbered Jewish Bolsheviks by a substantial margin[91] and, despite the widely touted fact that Karl Marx had Jewish blood, Marx's family had actually converted to Christianity before he was born.

By the time they had circulated through the corridors of Washington for several months, rumors were flying throughout the country about the existence of a document containing "proof" of an organized Jewish conspiracy.

It is unclear when and how Liebold and Brasol first met but, according to the account of Edwin Pipp, the first editor of the *Dearborn Independent*, they had already been in contact at least as early as the spring of 1919. In March that year, Liebold suggested to Pipp that he contact "a Russian who could give us a very interesting article on Russia."[92] The result was "The Bolshevik Menace," written by Brasol and published in the *Dearborn Independent* on April 12, 1919—thirteen months before the paper launched its campaign against the Jews.

It is worth noting that the files of the War Department investigation into allegations Liebold was a German spy end abruptly on October 8, 1918, after they landed on the desk of MID director Brigadier General Marlborough Churchill. At the time, Churchill's chief adviser was none other than Boris Brasol. Could Brasol have derailed the investigation into Liebold's potentially subversive activities?[93]

Churchill himself was clearly among those in the War Department sympathetic to the idea of a world Jewish conspiracy. On a 1921 tour of American embassies in Europe, he sent a cable back to Washington from Bucharest asking to be kept informed on "the isms, Jewry and the like."[94]

While Pipp supervised the day-to-day operations of the *Independent* back in Dearborn, Liebold frequently slipped away to New York for what he referred to as business trips. In reality, he was quietly preparing for the newspaper's transformation into a vehicle to expose the "truth" about the Jewish menace. In this task, he was assisted by Boris Brasol, who was determined to inspire European-style hate crimes in America, under the sponsorship of Henry Ford. "There are going to be the biggest pogroms and massacres here and elsewhere; I will write and precipitate them," Brasol boasted to a fellow émigré. To another friend he wrote, "I have done the Jews more injury than would have been done to them by ten pogroms."[95] In this, he appears to be alluding to his role in shaping the editorial content of the *Independent*. Although his byline appeared only infrequently, his influence is evident in the frequent articles about Jews and Bolshevism.

Brasol soon introduced Liebold to his wide network of contacts within the U.S. intelligence and Russian émigré communities, many of whom were put on the Ford payroll and instructed to gather incriminating information about most of the prominent Jews in America. CC Daniels, brother of the U.S. secretary of the navy, was hired to head the operation, receiving $1,000 per month plus expenses. Harris Houghton, the intelligence officer who had arranged for the original English translation of the *Protocols*, was added to the payroll at the suggestion of Brasol, who resigned from MID around this time. The New York operation was so secretive that each of the special operatives was assigned a code number, a tribute to Brasol's intelligence background. Liebold's was 121 X, Daniels was 120X.[96] Ford himself was referred to as "Mr. Carr" (note the play on words). A number of phrase codes were even employed to shelter communications from prying eyes back in Dearborn. "OBLU" signified acknowledgment of receipt of check; "ACADAM" was the confirmation that "Mr. Ford says OK."[97] According to his FBI file, Brasol himself operated under the code name "Gregory" or "Mr. X," which has caused considerable confusion for biographers and historians seeking to discover evidence in the company archives linking Brasol and Ford.[98] It is intriguing to trace the exodus of this wide array of intelligence officers into the employ of Ernest Liebold, a man their former MID employer had recently classified as a German spy.

The American Jewish Committee had been monitoring the situation carefully for years and fully believed that Brasol was the link to Ford, as evidenced in a letter written by AJC director Louis Marshall to Senator William Borah: "It was through the influence of Brasol that Ford accepted the *Protocols* as genuine . . . It was through him that Ford carried on a campaign of vituperation and defamation against the Jews of this country and sought to inspire hatred and animosity against a large body of loyal American citizens."[99]

Eight months of careful preparation by Brasol and Liebold finally culminated in the May 1920 publication of "The International Jew: The World's Problem" in the *Dearborn Independent*, the article that signaled the start of the paper's soon-to-be infamous campaign. After he resigned from

MID the previous summer, Brasol had persuaded a Boston publisher to issue the *Protocols* in book form. *The Protocols and World Revolution* was published in July 1919 by the Small, Maynard publishing house. But, to Brasol's consternation, the book achieved very little distribution due to what he called a "plot by Jewish bookstores." Undaunted, he turned to Henry Ford's new venture to spread the word and arranged to have the book's printing plates sent to Liebold in June 1920—a month after the paper began its campaign against the Jews.[100] Within a week, the *Protocols* had become the basis for the paper's entire crusade. For Brasol, the *Independent* was the credible vehicle he needed to achieve his obsessive mission of restoring the Imperial Russian monarchy to the throne. Meanwhile, Ernest Liebold was hatching a similar plot to restore the czar's cousin, Kaiser Wilhelm—dethroned by the Versailles Treaty—to his own birthright. Brasol and Liebold had a different goal but a common vehicle, Adolf Hitler, who had assured monarchists from both countries that his movement was their only realistic hope.

The early connections between Ernest Liebold and the Nazis are tenuous but here again Boris Brasol appears to be the link. In his study *Who Financed Hitler*, James Pool identifies Brasol as the most likely conduit between Ford and Hitler. As a U.S. representative of the Russian czar during World War I, Pool argues, Brasol had worked closely with the czar's cousin Grand Duke Cyril Vladimirovich who, after the czar's execution, asked Brasol to collect funds in America for the Russian monarchist cause.

In the early twenties, the White Russian émigré community established strong links with the Nazis and would eventually look to Hitler to rid Russia of the Bolsheviks. Of the two million Russians who fled the motherland after the October Revolution, more than 600,000 ended up in Germany.[101]

In his 1996 book *Hitler's Willing Executioners*, Daniel Joseph Goldhagen claims German anti-Semitism was unique in its viciousness: "What can be said about the Germans cannot be said about any other nationalities or all the other nationalities combined—namely no Germans, no Holocaust."[102] But historian Michael Kellogg disputes this, suggesting that although Nazism developed in a primarily German context, Goldhagen ignores the role Russian émigrés played in laying the ideological groundwork for the Holocaust.[103]

Before Hitler, there was no strong tradition of violent anti-Semitism in Germany. In contrast, between 1881 and 1917, tens of thousands of Russian Jews were killed, raped, and beaten during state-sponsored pogroms organized by the czar's Cossack troops. The worst of these pogroms were engineered by a band of civil servants known as the Black Hundred to which Boris Brasol, then a young lawyer, belonged. His experience there may account for one of the most disturbing passages in *The International Jew*, which eerily presages the arguments of later Holocaust deniers: "This propaganda of pogroms—'thousands upon thousands of Jews killed'—amounts to nothing except as it illustrates the gullibility of the Press. No one believes this propaganda and governments regularly disprove it."[104]

The man who acted as the go-between between the Russian émigrés and the Nazis was Alfred Rosenberg, a fanatical Baltic German who had studied architecture in Moscow before he was forced to flee in 1919 to avoid arrest for his counterrevolutionary activities. Rosenberg came to Munich and became one of Hitler's earliest followers, impressing the party leader with his theories of a Judeo-Bolshevik-Masonic conspiracy. He was later to become the Nazi Party's chief ideologue.[105] Brasol met regularly with Rosenberg and other Nazis when he visited Germany.[106] In 1922, investigative journalist Norman Hapgood, later U.S. ambassador to Denmark, quoted the former head of the Russian constitutional government at Omsk saying, "I have seen the documentary proof that Boris Brasol has received money from Henry Ford."[107]

According to Brasol's FBI file, he traveled from the United States to Europe at least four times between 1923 and 1926, including two trips to Germany.[108] There is evidence that at least one of those trips, and probably all of them, was made on behalf of his friend Ernest Liebold.[109] The FBI reported that in 1923 Brasol sailed to France, on behalf of Liebold and Ford, to gather information proving Jews had been responsible for the murder of Czar Nicholas II.[110]

Here Kurt Ludecke, the Nazis' enthusiastic young fund-raiser, comes back in the picture. Ludecke later claimed that he had made a special visit to Grand Duke Cyril and his wife Victoria at their chateau in Nice, France, in March 1921. By stressing the advantages that would accrue to the White Russians if the Nazis took power, Ludecke hoped to secure some of the rumored Romanoff fortune for the National Socialist movement. But he soon gave up, he claims, when it "became obvious that every rouble they had rescued from the Red Terror was desperately needed to keep up their regal charade."[111] A year after Ludecke's visit, however, Cyril and Victoria suddenly donated the enormous sum of half a million gold-backed *deutschmarks* to General Erich Ludendorff, Hitler's ally and co-conspirator during the 1923 *putsch*. By most accounts, the couple had virtually no funds of their own. "It seems apparent," writes James Pool, "that the half million marks in question were supplied by Henry Ford, with Boris Brasol acting as intermediary."[112]

Pool offers little evidence to back up this claim and it is hard to piece together his logic. But the fact that Brasol traveled to France around this time on behalf of Ford certainly makes the transaction possible. Moreover, the American Jewish Committee Archives contains a letter addressed to Nathan Isaacs, a former War Department colleague of Brasol, from another former U.S. intelligence agent, Casimir Palmer. On Brasol's recommendation, Palmer had been briefly employed as an investigator at Liebold's New York detective agency and would therefore have had inside knowledge about the connections of Ford's secretary. The letter makes no mention of finances but does establish a credible link between Brasol, Ford and the Nazis: "All the Hitlerite intelligence is based on Brasol's, and other, documents gathered through the medium of Mr. Ernest G. Liebold, Henry Ford's General Secretary."[113]

In August 1925, another White Russian named Leonid Druzhelovski stood trial in Moscow, accused of spreading counterrevolutionary and anti-Semitic propaganda. During the course of the trial, Druzhelovski testified that he had met a man named Boris Brasol in Berlin the year before who claimed that he was acting "on behalf of Henry Ford." Brasol, he said, had asked him to fabricate documents that cleared the monarchists of charges they conducted pogroms against Jews.[114] Here again is conclusive evidence linking Brasol's overseas activities to Ford. But it still doesn't prove a financial connection to Hitler.

In 1921, Ernest Liebold—who, as a prewar German spy, owed his allegiance to the Kaiser—reestablished contact with the dethroned German royal family when he dispatched a Ford sales agent named Lars Jacobsen on a mission to Germany to sell tractors. Jacobsen is almost certainly the agent the Bavarian vice president Erhard Auer was referring to when he told the *New York Times* a year later that Ford's interest in the Hitler movement began in 1921 when one of Ford's agents seeking to sell tractors came in contact with Hitler's mentor Dietrich Eckart. Auer told the *Times* that shortly after the agent returned to America, Ford's money began flowing into the coffers of the Nazi Party.[115]

Soon after Jacobsen arrived in Germany, he sent a number of revealing letters to Liebold detailing his clandestine activities. In his first letter, sent March 4, 1921, Jacobsen writes that he has had trouble attempting to do business in Germany: "I knew where the real trouble was, namely the Jews. The method they have used to fight us here is the usual one, what the *Independent* calls the 'whispering drive'. . . . You must remember that there is not a Jew in Europe who does not know about the *Independent* articles and that the articles represent Mr. Ford's views."[116] According to other contemporary accounts, news of Ford's Jew-baiting had indeed spread to every country in Europe by this time. Whether it was having an impact on Ford's overseas business operations is difficult to assess.[117]

In another letter to Liebold three months later, Jacobsen discloses the true nature of his mission to Germany: "After several months of hard trying through different channels, I have finally succeeded in getting in touch with the immediate surroundings of the ex-Kaiser."[118] Clearly, he was not there to sell tractors. He reveals that he had recently met with the Kaiser's son Prince Eitel Friedrich, who told Jacobsen he was a great admirer of Henry Ford. When the Prince inquired why Ford had abandoned his First World War Peace Ship so soon after reaching Europe, Jacobsen responded, "Jewish influence was the cause of this expedition's untimely conclusion and the present campaign of the *Dearborn Independent* constituted nothing more or less than the continuation of the Peace Ship."[119] The Prince then expressed his admiration for the "courage of Mr. Ford in attempting so enormous an undertaking as the exposure of Jewry" and wanted to know if the campaign could be "internationalized." Jacobsen asked the Prince whether the German royal family would be "prepared in their own interest" to assist Ford in exposing the Jewish menace.

"An inevitable phase of the future work of the *Independent* would be an analysis of the real cause of the world war and of placing the blame where it really belonged: the Jews," he informed the Prince.[120]

At the conclusion of his letter to Liebold, Jacobsen reveals that his mission is a dangerous one:

> I have no delusions about what the Jewish revolutionary party in Germany will do to me if they find out that I am communicating with the [Kaiser's family] on behalf of Mr. Ford, in order to secure information that will show the Jews up. If that happens, I am certain that you will not hear from me any more.[121]

Around the same time Liebold's emissary first established contact with the German royal family, the first direct links between the Nazi Party and the deposed German monarchy were established when Crown Prince Wilhelm returned to Germany from exile and met with Hitler, who promised to restore the Imperial crown after the National Socialists took power.[122] With Kaiser Wilhelm's permission, two of his sons, Prince August Wilhelm and Prince Oskar, soon joined the Nazi Party. Liebold maintained close communication with the royal family throughout the 1920s and eventually started communicating with Kaiser Wilhelm directly, even paying a personal visit to the former German monarch at his estate in Doorn, Holland.[123]

In 1929, the Kaiser's grandson, Prince Louis Ferdinand, mysteriously appeared in Detroit, where he was placed on the Ford Motor Company payroll as a "freelance roadman," traveling frequently to Germany on behalf of Ford before and after the Nazis took over. In 1940, Henry Ford was even named godfather of Louis Ferdinand's second son. On one of the Prince's trips to Germany on behalf of Ford in 1934, Louis Ferdinand heard a rumor that the company was contemplating closing its German plant because of business losses. "What a pity it would be if Mr. Ford, who is the father and creator of the motorcar age, would abandon Germany and leave the task to his Jew competitors, the General Motors people," the prince wrote to Ford production chief Charles Sorensen.[124]

Louis Ferdinand was an avowed early admirer of Hitler, writing Liebold in March 1933 that he had voted for the Nazis in the recent elections. "The Nazis have been persecuted for many years by their opponents," he explained.[125] Two months later, when Louis was introduced to Hitler for the first time, he asked the new Führer whether he could "take any message to my American boss in Detroit."[126] According to the Prince, who described the incident in his 1952 memoirs, Hitler responded, "You can tell Herr Ford that I am a great admirer of his. I shall do my best to put his theories into practice in Germany."[127] Some historians have argued that Hitler's veneration of Ford was related merely to his admiration for the industrialist's business methods. But this would appear to be contradicted by an account written by one of the Führer's closest early friends and financial supporters, Putzi Hanfstaengl, in his 1957 memoirs: "The only American figure for whom [Hitler] had time was Henry Ford, and then not so much as an industrial wonder-worker but rather as a reputed anti-Semite and a possible source of funds."[128]

The German royal family still held out hope that Hitler would restore the monarchy and continued to maintain close ties to the Nazi Party for years before eventually turning against Hitler when it became obvious he had no intention of fulfilling his promise.

In his 1937 Ford biography, *The Flivver King*, Pulitzer Prize–winning author Upton Sinclair charges that Henry Ford had transferred $300,000 to Hitler's treasury using Prince Louis Ferdinand as a conduit.[129] Sinclair fails to elaborate and furnishes no evidence to back up the claim; moreover, biographers have been dismissive of the charge because Sinclair's book was partially funded by the United Autoworkers Union during a period when the union was at war with the Ford Motor Company. But this potential connection between Ford and the German royal family appears to stand up to closer scrutiny than many of the other theories.

Liebold later claimed that he kept as much as one million dollars of Ford's personal money in his office safe at any one time—what he called the "kitty."[130] It would have been a relatively simple task for him to designate a portion of this money to the Nazi Party through contacts Liebold had established in the German royal family without any record of the transaction being traced. It could also explain Louis Ferdinand's visits to Germany on behalf of Ford. In his memoirs, the Prince later wrote that Liebold was the Ford official with whom he had "the closest associations."[131] He reveals that once, before he left Dearborn on a trip to Germany, Liebold asked him to deliver a letter to Dr. Otto Meissner, the head of Hitler's Chancellery.[132] At the time, Meissner was very close to the Führer and had personally intervened with President Hindenburg in 1933 to secure Hitler the chancellorship.[133] Later, Liebold would write Detroit German consul Fritz Hailer claiming that Meissner is a "good friend of mine."[134] This letter, and the prince's account, establishes a direct link between Liebold and the highest levels of the Nazi regime at the time but, if they ever existed, any documents conclusively proving Sinclair's assertion that a financial transaction took place have long since been destroyed.

Finally, there is a curious document tucked away in Liebold's own file at the Ford Archives that raises serious questions about his early connections to Hitler. In the early fifties, the Ford Motor Company conducted interviews with hundreds of former relatives, friends, acquaintances, and employees of the late Henry Ford for its company archives, in an effort to reconstruct the history of the company from its earliest days. In one of those interviews, conducted nine years after he left the company, Ernest Liebold speaks at length about his role as Ford's personal secretary and confidant. The transcript of Liebold's interview is filled with exaggerated, self-serving, and sometimes blatantly false accounts of his role in the company, apparently designed to rehabilitate his reputation. But one story which he relates in passing begs attention:

> One day a small shipment of swastika pins came in from Germany. . . . They were passed around to different people. . . . They put about fifty or one hundred of these pins on my desk.[135]

According to Liebold, Ida Steinberg, a Jewish employee of the *Dearborn Independent*, was very upset because she had been forced to wear the pin and "got the devil" from her family for doing so. Liebold reassured her with what he appears to believe were comforting words: "I said, 'Just a minute!' You're Jewish. The people you are working with are not Jewish. You want to bear that fact in mind, but don't let it worry you or bother you.

You are just one of a lot of other Jews who have to go through the same thing."[136] What Liebold doesn't explain about this bizarre exchange is why a boxload of swastika pins were sent to the *Dearborn Independent* during the mid-1920s—a decade before Hitler took power—and why each employee of the newspaper was forced to wear one. Clearly, this episode demonstrates contact between Liebold and the Nazi Party during the earliest period of Hitler's ascendancy and paints him as an enthusiastic supporter of the movement from its nascent days.

It was not the last time Liebold's name would emerge in connection with Adolf Hitler and the Nazi Party.

CHAPTER 3

SUPERHERO

Charles Lindbergh receives a hero's welcome at a New York ticker-tape parade following his historic transatlantic solo flight in 1927.

The crowd had begun to gather the night before. When the first reports flashed over the airwaves that the plane had been spotted through dense fog over St. John's, Newfoundland, and was about to embark on its dangerous journey over the Atlantic, more people arrived, hardly believing the news.

They kept coming all day to Le Bourget airfield, just outside of Paris. Indeed, the whole world awaited anxiously a report on the fate of the small craft bearing its lone passenger. At 8:30 on the evening of May 21, 1927, an hour after the expected arrival time, most assumed the foolhardy pilot and his plane had found the watery grave that most experts had forecast when he set out thirty-one hours earlier. A number of previous solo attempts to cross the Atlantic had ended in tragedy, the pilots never seen again. Still, the crowd waited. By the time the news came that the plane had been spotted over Cork, Ireland, at 9:00 P.M., almost 100,000 people thronged the airfield, many still skeptical. "One chance in a thousand," the radio declared.

Then, at 10:15 P.M., floodlights suddenly drenched the field and the roar of a motor could be heard above the buzz of the crowd. The lights dimmed. A false alarm, announced the gendarmes guarding the airstrip. A minute later, the lights again blazed at the far end of the field, a half mile from where the crowd waited. Descending out of the black night sky was the plane. It lined up to the runway and floated down to earth, consummating the most spectacular achievement in the short history of aviation.

Breaking through the phalanx of six hundred soldiers and policemen,

73

tens of thousands of onlookers raced to the spot where the small plane could be seen taxiing, the words "Spirit of St. Louis" in big bold letters emblazoned on its side. As the craft came to a stop and the door opened, twenty hands reached out and hoisted its pilot in the air, carrying him in a circle around the plane as the crowd cheered deliriously. Even before he touched French soil for the first time ninety seconds later, Charles Lindbergh had joined Henry Ford among the pantheon of America's greatest heroes. The feat, declared the *New York Times*, transformed him "in a frenzied instant from an obscure aviator into an historical figure."[1]

Aviation represented a bold new adventure. Certainly Ford had indelibly marked American industry, but nobody would characterize his achievement as death-defying. Lindbergh, by contrast, had exhibited great daring. He had defied the odds. Americans have always glorified risk-takers.

If Lindbergh's feat was unprecedented, so was the world's reaction. From the moment he landed in France, the public was gripped by mass hysteria—"Lindbergh mania," the reporters called it. For weeks, his every move was front-page news, from what he ate for breakfast the morning after his flight ("perfectly chilled" grapefruit, oatmeal with real cream, bacon, eggs, and crisp buttered toast) to his eclectic assortment of nicknames ("Slim"; "the Lone Eagle"; "Lucky Lindy").

France declared a national holiday. In Paris, a parade in his honor attracted 500,000 people in what the *Times* described as "one of history's greatest mob scenes." Through the initial wave of adulation, one theme emerged again and again—Lindbergh as hero. The refrain echoed from every conceivable forum, including church sermons delivered all over America the following Sunday. "In Lindbergh, we see manifested that indomitable heroism which has made possible the progress of the human race toward the mastery of its world," preached Rev. Russell Bowie of New York's Grace Episcopal Church. "There is a fund of moral heroism as well as a fund of physical heroism among men, which thrills to the challenge of the impossible."[2]

In Congress, one senator declared, "Lindbergh achieved what no person, living or dead, has ever accomplished. . . . He had occupied the front page of every cosmopolitan newspaper in Europe and America . . . he has made himself the hero of every son, the sweetheart of every daughter."[3] In its daily coverage, the *New York Times* began to refer to Lindbergh as "the hero of the Atlantic" while the French parliament passed a resolution proclaiming him "the most audacious hero" of the century. His principal rival in the race to cross the Atlantic, George Byrd, even called him a "Superhero"—a full eleven years before the term was used to describe the comic book character Superman.[4]

The lone dissenting voice came from Gene Tunney, heavyweight boxing champion of the world, who said he failed to see how "mankind is going to benefit from Lindbergh's spectacular stunt." Passing judgment on what he called "this hero business," Tunney gave the upstart flier some advice: "He showed wonderful skill, courage and application—and he had a wonderful motor—but he ought to commercialize his stunt for every cent that's in it, for in a year from now he will be forgotten."[5] Time would prove Tunney wrong.

No one could have been a more engaging hero. In the face of all the attention, Lindbergh charmed the media and the public with his shy, modest demeanor, especially after he said that the reception he received at the Paris airfield was "the most dangerous part of the whole flight."[6] The Vatican newspaper praised him for his "childlike simplicity" after he referred to himself and his plane as "we."[7]

However, the acclaim for Lindbergh's feat was not confined to France and America. The entire world celebrated his achievement. Telegrams poured in from virtually every head of state. "Warmest congratulations for incomparable achievement of your heroic countryman Lindbergh," cabled Albert, King of Belgium, to the American embassy. Italian fascist leader Benito Mussolini wrote, "A superhuman will has taken space by assault and subjugated it. Matter once more has yielded to spirit, and the prodigy is one that will live forever in the memory of men. Glory to Lindbergh and to his people."[8]

But the most fervent reaction outside America came from Germany, where his flight seemed to capture the national imagination. Shortly after he landed, theater performances all over the country were interrupted to announce the flight's successful completion.[9] "Such men as Lindbergh mark the path of humanity," wrote the Berlin newspaper *Vossische Zeitung* the following day.[10] The League of German War Fliers declared, "Lindbergh's flight is more than a big sporting event; for all time, it will remain an act of human enlightenment."[11]

Years later, Lindbergh would describe his initial bemusement at all the attention: "I was astonished at the effect my successful landing in France had on the nations of the world. To me, it was like a match lighting a bonfire."[12] He was catapulted into the rarefied status of international celebrity. He was recognized and revered everywhere. Before he returned to America, he was feted in grand style. The president of France and the kings of Belgium and England showered him with honors. At a Buckingham Palace dinner held in his honor, King George V informed his court that Lindbergh was "quite a feller." He then took the young American aside and asked for a private audience. "Now tell me, Captain Lindbergh," confided the British monarch. "There's one thing I long to know. How did you pee?"[13]

When Lindbergh returned home, he found 500,000 letters, 75,000 telegrams, and two freight car loads of press clippings. New Yorkers staged a giant ticker-tape parade. President Coolidge promoted him to a colonel in the Air Corps Reserves and later awarded him the nation's highest decoration, the Congressional Medal of Honor. *Time* magazine named him its first "Man of the Year." America had never before witnessed adulation of this magnitude. His brief acceptance speech, upon accepting the Distinguished Flying Cross from the President, was compared by some newspapers to Abraham Lincoln's Gettysburg address.[14] The pure adoration everyday Americans felt for the young hero was unending: "Fair-haired Apollo," wrote one woman, "your meteoric traverse of the sea, your transcendent victory over boundless space, shall thunder down the avenues of time."[15]

Fame is often fleeting. However, a number of factors conspired to ensure that Lindbergh's mystique endured. Perhaps the most important was a concerted nationwide effort to hold him up as an example to American youth. James West, chief executive of the American Boy Scout movement, recognized this phenomenon when he paid tribute to Lindbergh in the preface to a widely distributed Scouting pamphlet:

> Every man longs to be the hero to some boy. Overnight, Charles Lindbergh became the hero to millions of American boys. The lone Pathfinder, blazing a trail through the arch of the sky, called to the blood of the pioneer in every American boy. . . . He spoke of his plane as an equal partner in a great enterprise, and found a million echoes in the hearts of boys who know that things of wood and steel can live. He walked with modesty in high places and courtesy in low. . . . And America made him not only its hero, but the symbol of its idealistic Youth.[16]

But the nonstop assault was starting to take its toll, and cracks began to show. As Lindbergh later recalled, "I was unprepared for the world acclaim that followed my landing at Le Bourget."[17] After he showed "angry annoyance" toward a crowd in Amarillo Texas, the Amarillo *News-Globe* accused him of "swellheadedness."[18] Another time, when a crowd gathered on an airfield waiting for hours in the rain to catch a glimpse of him, Lindbergh revved his plane's motor, taxied in circles and deliberately scattered the crowd, not once but twice.[19]

Increasingly disillusioned with the glory that followed him everywhere, he began to dodge reporters and refused every request for autographs. "No more unless he crashes," wired one New York editor to a reporter covering Lindbergh on a Latin American goodwill tour, reflecting the frustration of the press over his unwillingness to cooperate.[20] Whenever a photographer was around, he refused to smile, choosing instead to glower into the lens. One of these photos made it on the front page of the *New York Times* with the caption, "Lindbergh's flying face."

Yet, having created the legend, the media were loathe to pierce it. Rarely was any criticism allowed to make its way onto the pages of the reverential press. More likely, journalists would defend or rationalize his behavior, pointing out that it would be inappropriate to hold the hero up to the same standards as mere mortals. "People forget," wrote W. O. McGeehan in the New York *Herald Tribune*, "that young Lindbergh has been up among the Gods while the world spun beneath him. . . . He saw the world beneath him and measured it for what it was worth."[21]

Commercial offers began to pour in, asking Lindbergh to endorse every conceivable product. $50,000 from a cigarette manufacturer. Half a million dollars plus 10 percent of the gross to star in a movie. He refused each of these requests. "I was advised that if I would enter a political career, there was a good chance I could eventually become President," he later recalled.[22]

According to his biographer Kenneth Davis, a struggle was being waged for the possession of Lindbergh's fame.[23] Along the way, a battle would also be fought for his soul.

By the time Charles Lindbergh died in 1974, many were still at a loss to explain the complexities of the man who had exerted such a profound impact on the twentieth century. His *New York Times* obituary would record, "Lindbergh's life, like his personality, was full of shadows and enigmas."[24] It is a fitting assessment.

Charles Augustus Lindbergh was born in Detroit on February 4, 1902, to C. A. Lindbergh, a successful Minnesota lawyer, and Evangeline Land, a sophisticated schoolteacher, who specialized in chemistry. Orville Wright had not yet made the first sustained airplane flight. His parents lived in the small timber and farming community of Little Falls, Minnesota, on the west bank of the Mississippi River, where his father practiced law and ran a small family farm, but Charles was born in Detroit because his mother's uncle was a physician there. Six weeks after his birth, his parents returned with him to Little Falls, where he would spend a large portion of his childhood.[25] On his father's side, Lindbergh was descended from Swedes who had emigrated to the United States in the middle of the nineteenth century. The media would later frequently invoke his Viking ancestry. His mother's family was of English and Irish stock.

The defining moment of young Charles's youth came when he was four years old and his father was elected to Congress as a Republican. C. A. Lindbergh was something of a maverick, the product of Minnesota's long tradition of populist politics. With the progressive trustbuster Theodore Roosevelt in the White House, C. A. relished the idea of doing battle with the forces of unfettered capitalism—a crusade championed by Roosevelt's Progressive forces at a time when the Republican Party embodied a very different set of values than its modern descendant.

The Progressives were not out to tear down capitalism but to reform it, pushing for anti-trust and regulatory legislation to rein in the excesses of the Morgans and the Rockefellers. C. A.'s pet issue was banking reform and he took up the task with abandon. Declaring war on the "Money Trusts," he demanded to know why bankers "who are no smarter than the rest of us" continually get richer.[26] Time and again, he sided with his farmer constituents against the financial goliaths and soon gained a reputation as an independent-minded politician.

But C. A. paid a personal price for his quixotic political battles. He spent most of his time in Washington planning his crusades and neglecting his young family. His marriage soon fell apart and young Charles found himself in the middle of an ugly domestic situation. The quick-tempered Evangeline was alleged to have once held a gun to her husband's head and may have failed to shoot only because C. A. told her to go ahead and pull the trigger.[27] His mother began to take young Charles on extended visits to her family in Detroit and the boy moved frequently during his childhood, attending at least ten separate schools and performing poorly at all of them.[28]

Meanwhile, C. A. tenaciously continued to take on the powerful financial houses, pursuing an often lonely battle. His colleagues began to distance themselves as his rants about the ubiquitous Money Trust he believed was running America became increasingly paranoid. But his constituents welcomed his battles on their behalf. "Just as long as we treat money as our god and treat useful property as of less value than money . . . most of us will be poor," he barked on the floor of the House, sounding more like a socialist than a Republican.[29]

The younger Lindbergh was anything but removed from his father's preoccupations. He frequently accompanied C. A. to Washington, but appeared singularly unimpressed by his father's profession, writing years later that "his success in politics had no appeal to me. I thought the arguments of lawyers dull and a Congressman's life most tedious."[30] Charles hungered for more exciting pursuits.

He was only six years old when he caught the flying bug for the first time after he heard a buzz in the sky and climbed out of a window onto the roof of his home to witness a biplane sputtering past. "Afterward I remember lying in the grass and looking up at the clouds and thinking how much fun it would be to fly up there among those clouds," he later recalled. "I didn't think of the hazards. I was just interested in getting up there in the clouds."[31]

His father continued his lone crusade. In 1910, C.A. set his sights on the Aldrich Monetary Commission and the central bank it proposed to establish, the National Reserve Association, forerunner of the Federal Reserve Bank. He believed the plan represented the final step in a covert attempt by the Money Trust to take over America's banking and currency system and he attacked it with a vengeance.[32] The Aldrich plan was drafted primarily by Paul Warburg of the investment firm Kuhn, Loeb, and Company. In later years, opponents of a central bank would pointedly refer to the Jewish background of Warburg and his firm, evidence of a supposed Judaic plot to control America's finances. In fact, this would become a favorite theme of Henry Ford's *Dearborn Independent* a few years after C.A. waged battle against the Aldrich plan. Although the elder Lindbergh never explicitly noted Warburg's religion in his public attacks on the scheme, many are convinced that when he talked about the Money Trust[33] he was using a coded language similar to the one Ford employed when he talked about "international financiers" and their sinister control. This is debatable, considering another of C.A.'s favorite targets was the Protestant banker J.P. Morgan.

If there is no public record of prejudice against Jews, however, the same cannot be said for C.A.'s attitude toward the Roman Catholic Church. In 1916, he happened upon a pamphlet distributed by the Kansas-based Free Press Defense League, a small organization that accused the Church of destroying free institutions in the United States. Papists, claimed the League, were out to undermine public schools, the free press, free speech, and freedom of thought.[34] Something had to be done to stop the Church's "pernicious" involvement in American politics and its role "in carrying out the conspiracy to bring the United States of America under the complete domination of the Pope of Rome and the Catholic hierarchy." C.A. had discovered another conspiracy, against which he could stand as defender of the nation. He rose on the floor of the House and enumerated the League's accusations, demanding a congressional investigation into charges that Catholic prelates "in all lands and at all times have been the ally of oppression."[35] This brush with intolerance would later come back to haunt him.

Shortly after the first shots of World War I were fired in 1914, C.A. Lindbergh's crusade against the Money Trust would gain a new focus when he became the nation's most vocal opponent of intervention in the European war. When he took to the floor of the House in September and announced his support for United States neutrality, his views hardly differed from the majority of Americans, who were also strongly opposed to American intervention. "The only way we could get into a war would be to go around with a chip on our shoulder challenging other nations to knock it off," he declared, speaking against a proposed tax increase that would have offset a war-inspired downturn in the economy.[36] He sensed early on, however, that the United States would inevitably be drawn into the conflict. "It is my belief that we are going in as soon as the country can be sufficiently propagandized into war mania," he wrote his daughter Eva in February 1915.[37]

In June 1916, C.A. began a publishing venture designed to mobilize Americans against the threat of involvement overseas. The new journal, called *Real Needs*, attacked his traditional nemesis, the financiers, as well as the "subsidized" press for encouraging American intervention in the European conflict. He charged that Wall Street was helping to finance the Allies and warned, "Nothing but trouble to the United States will come out of the Money Trust speculation with the foreign war nations."[38]

Lindbergh shared with Henry Ford the conviction that somebody must be profiting from the war. C.A.'s more strident opposition coincided with the beginning of Ford's own peace campaign, and their rhetoric sounded remarkably similar. "The warmongers urging military preparedness in America are Wall Street bankers," Ford told the *New York Times* that year.[39]

But after the sinking of the Cunard passenger ship *Lusitania* by the Germans in 1915 with 123 Americans on board, anti-German rhetoric had increased markedly and American opposition to the war began to weaken. Although the majority of the country still opposed U.S. military intervention, support increased sharply for aid to the Allies and containment of German aggression. But the *Lusitania* attack did nothing to sway Lindbergh. He charged that the American public was being "buncoed" on the war issue by "invisible organizers" led by "special privilege" interests.

For the first time, C.A. spoke out against President Wilson, arguing that a citizen had the "right to follow what he believes to be the right course, not only a right but a duty."[40] In 1916, convinced his arguments against the war would reverberate louder in the Senate than in the House, C.A. threw his hat in the ring for the Republican nomination of a vacant Minnesota senate seat. His unpopular stand against the war proved his undoing, however, and he was handed his first political loss on June 19, 1916.

It was during this Senate campaign that fourteen-year-old Charles got his first taste of political action. Having learned to drive at the age of eleven, he chauffeured his father on a number of campaign swings through the state, as C.A. distributed campaign pamphlets and anti-war literature to the farmers who had always provided the backbone of his support.[41]

Undaunted by defeat, Lindbergh Sr. continued his relentless crusade, frequently speaking out on the floor of the House and publishing a book awkwardly titled *Why is Your Country at War? and What Happens to You After the War and Related Subjects.* The book, he explained, was written to counter those responsible for the European conflict, which he identified as an "inner circle" promoting the war for commercial purposes.[42]

In March 1917, as C.A. continued to speak out against American intervention, German submarines sank three American merchant vessels delivering supplies to the Allies. It was the last gasp for American neutrality. President Wilson asked Congress for a declaration of war and got it.

C.A. pledged his immediate support to the U.S. war effort immediately after the formal declaration of war. "If we get into the war, we will have to support it right or wrong," he had written his daughter Eva months earlier.[43] Ever the patriot, C.A. subsumed his personal convictions to the new reality. Now, with the United States committed to war, he believed "it is best not to do anything to discourage, for the thing has been done, and however foolish it has been, we must all be foolish and unwise together, and fight for our country."[44] The commitment made, he would do nothing to undermine it.

In 1918, with the war reaching its end, C.A. decided again to seek higher political office when he ran for Minnesota's Republican gubernatorial nomination on the slate of a farmers' political organization called the Non Partisan League. But his previous anti-war stand had branded him. If it had been unpopular before the United States entered the conflict, it was now considered tantamount to disloyalty, despite his subsequent reversal. As C.A. canvassed the state for support, the campaign against him approached what his biographer Bruce Larson describes as "hysteria":

> Personal abuse and actual physical danger became commonplace for Lindbergh during the campaign. He was run out of town, stoned, pelted with rotten eggs, hanged in effigy at Red Wing and Stanton, and refused permission to speak in a number of places throughout Minnesota.[45]

C.A.'s opponents dredged up every gaffe in his controversial past to discredit him. His book, *Why is Your Country at War?*, and his anti-Catholic speech on the floor of the House two years earlier were potent weapons. The *Duluth Herald* supported efforts to suppress his campaign speeches, declaring, "free speech that prospers a seditious element is a travesty." A *Herald* editorial about his book was headlined "Traitor or Ass?"[46]

One day in the spring of 1918, government agents seized and destroyed the printing plates of C. A.'s book and on June 8, nine days before the election, he was arrested during a campaign meeting on the dubious charges of "unlawful assembly" and conspiracy to violate a federal law prohibiting interference with enlistment. He had anticipated such a tactic, writing his daughter two months earlier, "They may even try to convict me to make a hit. They are desperate."[47] Not surprisingly, Lindbergh ended up losing the primary by a wide margin of almost 50,000 votes.

Throughout the campaign, Charles, now sixteen, often witnessed the abuse and scorn heaped on his father for his anti-war stand and it couldn't have failed to make an impression. Without exception in later years, every biographer of the younger Lindbergh would cite this period as the formative influence on Charles's own controversial stand two decades later. However, at the time, C. A.'s son appeared to have rejected the virtue of his father's stand against the "foolish" war.

"I was not old enough to understand the war's basic issues," Charles later wrote in his autobiography, "yet I felt a pride in the realization that my country was now powerful enough to take a major part in world crises. We would fight for good and right and freedom of the seas. After it was won, peace-loving nations of the world would get together and never fight again. Such an objective justified the sacrifice of life required to destroy the German Hun."[48]

Biographers of Lindbergh Jr. have been notably selective in their attempts to identify which of C. A.'s ideas may have been responsible for Charles's later thinking. Invariably, they ignore or downplay one of the elder Lindbergh's least admirable positions. When he was contemplating his first run for Congress in 1903, the local Little Falls, Minnesota, newspaper asked C. A. to set forth his views on race relations, a hot topic in America at the time following the failure of Reconstruction and President Roosevelt's controversial support for anti-lynching laws. On March 17, he sent the paper a letter entitled "Views on the Race Problem":

> . . . perhaps the three main reasons for limited progress of the Negro are: First, by nature he is inferior to the white race. Second, he is natural to a climate that tends to sluggishness. Third, there is not sufficient inducement for him to become progressive. . . . We may criticize the south for their subordination of the Negro, but we cannot condemn, for we in the northern world would, if we had an equal colored population, render the same treatment. What to do about the Negro is a problem that is practically settled. . . . He will be kept down. There is no question about it. . . . His

future is simply to merge into the white race. . . . It may not elevate the white race but it will eventually lift the black.[49]

On March 21, he sent a follow-up letter to the paper, elaborating on the first:

All coons look alike and, without trying to be original, it is safe to add that all coons act alike. . . . He is the happiest of all the races. The future worries him not in the least. This gay, happy contentment is the strong sustaining influence of the Negro, for it offsets the cloud of race prejudice that holds him down politically and socially. . . . The happy-go-lucky way of the Negro is but an evidence of a lower organization. The above, together with the last letter I sent, gives freely my views of the Negro. It is nothing but what you already know.[50]

Were these racial attitudes merely reflective of their times—a product of the Social Darwinist ideas popular at the turn of the century? According to Harvard University professor Alvin Poussaint, an authority on American race relations, Lindbergh's views were hardly typical in the northern United States. "On any scale of racism and prejudice, he would be in the extreme category," explains Dr. Poussaint.[51]

Given C. A.'s readiness to share his views with the public, it is difficult to imagine that they would have been hidden from his son. However, the only record we have of the younger Lindbergh's early encounter with racial issues arises through an incident he relates ambiguously in his autobiography that involves his mother rather than his father. Recalling a period during his childhood when the family moved to Washington, he describes his first encounter with the "rivalry of the races." When he was five years old, young Charles was walking through a lot adjoining his apartment building when he suddenly came across more than two dozen boys his own age. "They were throwing stones and chunks of brick at one another," he recalls. "Not understanding the seriousness of the situation, I joined in the fight, flinging the first fragment that came to my hand quite ineffectively. In the excitement of the moment, I had not noticed that the boys on my side of the lot were all black, while those on the other side were white. I had no sooner flung my stone than I heard an angry shout from the far side of the lot. 'Look at the white kid fighting with the niggers.'" Charles quickly slipped back into his building, the white children in hot pursuit. "Afterwards," Lindbergh writes, "my mother explained some of the conventions followed in Washington."[52]

Aside from the humiliations of his father's campaign, the war years passed uneventfully for Charles. He tended the family farm in Little Falls where he remained until 1920 when he left to pursue a mechanical engineering degree at the University of Wisconsin. His interest in mechanics was sparked by his aptitude for fixing the equipment that was always breaking down on the farm. But he was a poor student. His low marks found him on academic probation after the first semester and after failing Machine Design, Mathematics, and Physics, Lindbergh was thrown out of the university in February 1922, two days before his twentieth birthday. It proved a wise career move.[53]

Shortly after he left the university, he took a ride in his first airplane. Since the age of six, air travel had captivated his imagination. Now, soaring among the clouds, he knew what he wanted to do. "The life of an aviator seemed to me ideal," he later reflected. "It involved skill. It commanded adventure. It made use of the latest developments of science. I was glad that I had failed my college courses. Mechanical engineers were fettered to factories and drafting boards, while pilots had the freedom of wind in the expanse of sky."[54]

He enrolled in flying school, learning all there was to know about the profession, which, still in its infancy, was a dangerous one. He quickly mastered the spectacular flying feats that had thrilled him as a boy when the barnstormers passed through town, demonstrating their skills at the county fair—wing-walking, parachuting, upside-down flying.

Since he was a teenager, his friends had called him "Slim," a fitting tag to describe his lanky six-foot-one-inch frame. Now his flying feats earned him a new moniker, "Daredevil Lindbergh." C. A. didn't think much of his son's chosen profession. After Charles gave him his first airplane ride in 1921, the elder Lindbergh told his law partner, "I don't like this flying business. See if you can't get the boy to come into our office, study law and join the firm."[55] Charles would have none of it. In 1923, he bought himself a small airplane and earned his first income as a pilot. He charged passengers five dollars a ride and barnstormed through the midwest until on March 24, 1924, he suddenly enlisted in the U.S. armed forces in order to attend the army flying school where he could practice on a better grade of aircraft. Tragedy struck three months later when C. A. died of a brain tumor. Carrying out his father's last wishes, Charles scattered his ashes from a plane over their Little Falls homestead.

In March 1925, he graduated at the top of his flying school class and was commissioned a second lieutenant in the Army Air Service Reserve. But he was still adrift. He continued to barnstorm, demonstrating his new skills as a circus stunt flier before he was hired by the St. Louis–based Robertson Aircraft Company for the first and only real job he would ever have—as the chief pilot on the mail run to Chicago.[56] On these trips, he often found himself contemplating the possibilities of long-distance travel. He constantly wondered about the farthest distance he could fly. It was on one of these flights to Chicago in September 1926 that he suddenly found himself "startled" by a thought that came to him as he soared through the clouds: "I could fly nonstop between New York and Paris."[57] Eight months later, he had transformed this unlikely fantasy into a reality and, in the process, secured a place for himself in the folklore of America.

When Charles Augustus Lindbergh was born in 1902 Detroit, the world had still not heard of Henry Ford, who would sign his first automobile manufacturing contract six months later in an office on the other side of town. The new century had just begun and their paths would not cross for another twenty-five years, but the two men were destined to forge a meeting of the minds and serve as a focal point for an historic crusade.

Their first meeting came in 1927, as Lindbergh flew across America on a goodwill tour shortly after his famous transatlantic flight. One hot day in July, he landed the *Spirit of St. Louis* down at the Ford Airport in Dearborn where Henry Ford had come to meet the only man in America, with the possible exception of the president, who was now more famous than himself. They bonded immediately.

Ford had never before flown in an airplane. His life was too valuable to risk it in one of those "flying deathtraps," argued the officers of his company. But as Ford gazed in awe at the craft that just two months earlier had made the miraculous journey, Lindbergh recognized a kindred spirit. He invited his new friend to take a flight.

Like a child at an amusement park, Ford's eyes glittered. He nodded eagerly. The cockpit had been designed to fit a single person, but Lindbergh made some adjustments and helped his celebrated passenger into the plane. After taxiing down the runway, the two soared skyward. For the next fifteen minutes, bent over, cramped and utterly delighted, Henry Ford experienced his first airplane flight.[58]

The two heroes had much in common. Both had roots in Detroit, both had spent their teenage years working on a farm. Neither had much formal education and each was often called ignorant by their critics, yet both were described as "geniuses" in their chosen field. Both were Freemasons. Both were heralded as the new gods of the machine age. Both were somewhat puritanical: neither smoked nor drank. And, as Americans would soon discover, both men shared a remarkably similar worldview.

CHAPTER 4

STRANGE BEDFELLOWS

Lindbergh is greeted by Major Truman Smith as he arrives at Berlin's Staaken Airport in July 1936 for his first visit to the Third Reich. Smith would prove to exert a major influence over Lindbergh's controversial political ideology.

It was a windy March night. It had been raining on and off since early evening and the late shift had been mostly uneventful for the three state troopers on duty at the Lambertville outpost of the New Jersey State Police. During the previous seven hours, they had only received reports of a runaway from a nearby reform school and a fire at Penns Grove. When the phone rang at 10:25 P.M. Lieutenant Daniel J. Dunn took the call, expecting it to be his wife. Instead, he heard a calm, measured voice on the other end of the line: "This is Charles Lindbergh. My son has just been kidnapped."

Three years earlier, in 1929, Lindbergh, then a twenty-seven-year-old with no discernible interest in women, had married Anne Morrow, a striking twenty-two-year-old East Coast socialite. Among the more than 100,000 telegrams and three million letters of congratulations that had poured in from around the globe after his historic 1927 flight were hundreds of marriage proposals. "I had always taken for granted that someday I would marry and have a family of my own, but I had not thought much about it," he later wrote. "In fact, I had never been enough interested in any girl to ask her to go on a date." He believed that mating involved "the most important choice of one's life. One mates not only with an individual, but also with that individual's environment and ancestry."[1]

But he had been far too busy to pursue women until one day in 1928 after he had landed the *Spirit of St. Louis* in Mexico City following a treacherous 2,100-mile flight. That evening, Dwight Morrow, the U.S. ambassador to Mexico, gave a reception in Lindbergh's honor. In the crowd of well-wishers, only one caught his eye—the ambassador's twenty-one-year-old daughter Anne. He was immediately struck by what he called her "quiet and contemplative nature" and from that point on, they were inseparable. As their courtship progressed, Lindbergh taught Anne how to fly and she became an accomplished aviatrix in her own right, often accompanying him as co-pilot on his frequent globe-trotting flights. As a teenager, Anne had confided to her diary, "I want to marry a hero."[2] On May 27, 1929, she got her wish. The couple were married in a simple ceremony at Dwight Morrow's New Jersey estate. Thirteen months later, on Anne's twenty-fourth birthday, Charles Augustus Lindbergh Jr. was born.[3]

"Perhaps nowhere in the world, at any time in history, had a child been the object of such wide public interest as was the Lindbergh child," wrote the *New York Times* on the birth of the Lindbergh baby.[4] Thousands of gifts poured in from all over the world, countless poems and songs were composed and millions of Americans clamored for any detail about the first-born son of the world's most celebrated couple. But the privacy of baby Charles was carefully guarded by the new parents. For a time, there were rumors that the baby was "deaf or backwards." Why else would the couple refuse to show him off? "Give the Lindbergh baby a chance," *Time* magazine chastised the curious. All over the globe, the new baby was hailed as the "golden child—America's Prince of Wales." The nation of France even "adopted" young Charles in homage to his father, whose feat was still not forgotten in the country where he had ended his groundbreaking solo flight three years earlier.

The impact of fame was crushing, and Lindbergh was not coping well with the adulation. He especially lamented the lack of privacy that came with "belonging to the world." Shortly after his marriage, he began to draw up plans to build a refuge, a 950-acre estate on a wild, lonely stretch of high ground called Sourland Mountain in Hopewell, New Jersey, just outside Princeton.

Construction dragged on for more than two years while the couple lived at the estate of Anne's father in Englewood, New Jersey. By the fall of 1931, the new house—though still not complete—was finally suitable for occupation. Every Friday afternoon the couple and their toddler would drive to Hopewell to spend the weekend, accompanied by a nurse to care for young Charles, a chubby baby with blue eyes and curly hair, often described as a golden-haired replica of his famous father.

On the last weekend of February 1932, however, the Lindberghs broke from their usual routine. The baby was suffering from a cold and they decided to stay over until he was better. And so on the evening of Tuesday, March 1, 1932, Hopewell, New Jersey, was the setting for the event that would become known as the Crime of the Century.

The nurse, Betty Gow, looked into the second-floor nursery to check on the sleeping child. At 7:30, she had tucked little Charlie into his crib and retreated to the servants' quarters for a chat with the butler. The baby's father had returned an hour later from Manhattan, taken a bath, and retired to the library to attend to some correspondence. Anne was in the living room reading.

The still of the March night was suddenly shattered at 10:00 P.M. as Gow walked to the southeast corner of the room to peer into the crib, expecting to see the toddler in his blue sleeping robe. It was empty. At first, the twenty-six-year-old nurse thought one of his parents might have had him, but then she spotted the open window. She sped down the stairs, crying, "Colonel Lindbergh, have you got the baby? Please don't fool me" as the frantic parents raced to the nursery, finding only the empty crib.[5] Charles grabbed a rifle and searched the house. Only on returning to the nursery minutes later did he find the first clues—a set of muddy footprints, an open window screen and, on the lower windowsill, a note, written on a single sheet of folded paper in blue ink:

Dear Sir!
Have 50000$ redy with 2500$ in 20$ bills 1500$ in 10$ bills and 1000$ in 5$ bills. After 2–4 days we will inform you were to deliver the Mony.
We warn you for making anyding public or for notify the polise the child is in gute care.
Indication for all letters are singnature
and 3 holes[6]

Lindbergh ignored the note's warning and immediately summoned the police. Within an hour, a posse of hundreds of state troopers had descended on the estate and the largest manhunt in the nation's history was underway. By 12:40 A.M., the first reporter arrived on the scene and an AP dispatch alerted the nation.

New Jersey State Police detective Colonel H. Norman Schwarzkopf, father of the future Gulf War general, immediately took charge of the investigation. From the start, the search was hampered by the interference of Lindbergh, who insisted on establishing a command headquarters at the Hopewell residence and on overseeing every facet of the search. But Lindbergh's inexperience, as well as infighting between the various local, state, and federal investigative agencies, allowed for a number of serious blunders. Footprints near the house were trampled and pieces of evidence were handled improperly by a variety of people assembled at the compound. Further complicating matters, sightings of the Lindbergh baby were soon reported from all over the country. Each turned out to be a false alarm.

From China to Paris, telegrams of sympathy poured in as the world held its breath, anxiously awaiting news. Albert Einstein declared that the kidnapping reflected a lack of "social sanity" in America. Even the notorious gangster Al Capone, serving an eleven-year federal sentence for tax evasion, was moved to offer a $10,000 award for the baby's safe return. "It's the most outrageous thing I ever heard of," he told the press. "I know how Mrs. Capone and I would feel. . . . If I were out of jail, I could be of real assistance."[7]

Throughout the country, schoolchildren were asked to pray for the baby's safe return. Resolutions of sympathy were adopted by several state legislatures.

For more than two months, the search continued in vain, hampered by dozens of hoaxes that wasted precious time, leading investigators down repeated dead ends. At one point, Lindbergh even paid a $50,000 ransom in a late-night cemetery rendezvous after an intermediary claimed to have been contacted by the kidnappers. The bills were delivered after a series of mysterious graveyard meetings that gave false hope to the couple, who expected to have their baby returned. But it was another cruel deception.

Finally, on May 12, 1932, seventy-two days after the kidnapping, the agonizing wait came to a heartrending end. The decomposed body of a baby was found in the woods a few hundred yards from the Lindbergh home. It was determined that the child had been dead since the night he was taken, most likely dropped accidentally as the kidnapper descended a ladder from the baby's nursery. Two days later, Charles Lindbergh identified the remains of his son and the kidnapping investigation became a murder probe.

The news unleashed a mass outpouring of grief. Not since Abraham Lincoln's assassination had America mourned so deeply. Around the world, there was a cry for justice.

For two years, investigators followed a trail provided by their only concrete set of clues—the serial numbers of the gold certificates that had been carefully recorded before they were delivered to the kidnappers in the graveyard hoax shortly after the baby went missing. After months of little progress and more false leads, the police suddenly announced on September 19, 1934, that they had arrested Bruno Richard Hauptmann, a German-born carpenter living in the Bronx. A search of his garage had uncovered $14,000 of the Lindbergh ransom in a tin can. Hauptmann swore innocence. He was holding the money for a friend who had since died, he insisted, and he swore he knew nothing of the Lindbergh baby. His protestations were ignored and, after a sensational five-week trial, he was convicted of murder and sentenced to die in the electric chair.

Undeniable trauma though it was, whatever lingering scars he suffered from the kidnapping and murder of his first-born son are difficult to gauge because Charles Lindbergh rarely spoke of the incident in later years. When he did, it was in the form of a brief reference to "that New Jersey business." But if the adulation he earned for his transatlantic flight had begun to dissipate by the early thirties, the crime served to rekindle America's reverence for the suddenly tragic hero.

"For the second time in less than five years, the world revolved around Charles Lindbergh," notes his biographer Scott Berg.[8] And, while Lindbergh himself dreaded the assault on his privacy that accompanied the resurgence of his fame, others sensed a unique opportunity.

Before the end of the decade that began with an unimaginable nightmare, Lindbergh would come under the influence of two men who understood how to harness the power of his status as a worshipped hero and who would manipulate it to their own ends.

From the moment the paths of Alexis Carrel and Charles Lindbergh crossed on November 28, 1930, their lives would be inextricably linked. A year earlier, Anne's sister, Elizabeth Morrow, had developed a bout of rheumatic fever that left her with a severely diseased heart valve. The medical prognosis was bleak. The family was told surgery was out of the question. Her heart could not be stopped long enough for surgeons to work on it because the blood could not be circulated without causing a fatal infection.

Lindbergh, whose fame was founded on daring to do the impossible, was unwilling to accept this explanation and challenged her doctors. Why couldn't a device be manufactured, an "artificial heart," to pump the blood while an operation was being performed? Intrigued, a hospital anesthetist referred him to the one man who might be able to facilitate the creation of this invention, a Manhattan scientist performing groundbreaking research into the cultivation of whole organs. Lindbergh made an appointment the next day to discuss his sister-in-law's condition. "For me," he would later recall, "that began an association with an extraordinarily great man."[9]

By the time Lindbergh walked into the Rockefeller Institute for the first time to meet the man who would become his mentor, Alexis Carrel had already established a formidable reputation in the field of medicine. Born in Lyons, France, in 1873, Carrel acquired his medical degree at the age of twenty-seven, at which point he embarked on a course of medical experimentation that has been described as a cross between "medieval alchemy and the weird experiments of Frankenstein."[10] After establishing himself as a brilliant young scientist, he came to North America in 1904 because he felt the research facilities in France were too limiting, but was unable to find a permanent position. After a brief stint as a cattle rancher in Canada, and a year at the Hull Laboratory in Chicago, he was recruited for the staff of Manhattan's newly formed Rockefeller Institute in 1906. There, his pioneering research in suturing small blood vessels during surgery won him the first Nobel Prize ever awarded for medicine and physiology in 1912 after he performed the first modern transfusion by suturing a baby's leg vein to an artery.

A short, stocky man with tiny pince-nez glasses and burning brown eyes, Carrel was an eccentric, famous at the Institute for wearing a black monklike hood and gown while he operated and forcing his subordinates to do the same. His temper was legendary—he would fly into a tantrum at the least provocation—and his officiousness did not make him popular with his colleagues. But from the moment they met, the Nobel Laureate and the aviator developed an extraordinary bond, which evolved into a lifelong friendship. In Dr. Carrel, writes one biographer, the hero found a hero and, in turn, the scientist found a son.[11]

Carrel showed Lindbergh a device he had been testing called a perfusion pump, designed to circulate the blood so that tissue cultures could be kept alive outside the body. The problem, Carrel explained, was that the device had never worked without causing a fatal infection. Lindbergh, whose mechanical abilities had been honed fixing and improving airplane engines, was convinced he could design an effective pump. Carrel offered him full use of his laboratory and together they set out to develop what the media would erroneously call the first "mechanical heart."[12]

By the time Lindbergh entered his life, a quarter century after his groundbreaking research on organs, Alexis Carrel was already seeking broader fields of inquiry. He had lost interest in the purely rational science of medicine and was beginning to experiment with what he called the "metaphysical universe." He had always been a devout Catholic, struggling perpetually to prove there was no inherent contradiction between the objective observations of science and the faith-based dogmas of the Church.[13] At the age of twenty-nine, he had traveled to Lourdes—the French town where miracles were said to occur—and there, he claimed, he witnessed miraculous healing that could have no scientific explanation.

To the dismay of his colleagues, Carrel's research had been veering far off the road of objective science and onto a mystical path of religion, the occult, and supernatural forces. In one paper, he wrote, "Clairvoyance and telepathy are the primary datum of scientific observation." As Lindbergh himself would later describe it, "Carrel's mind flashed with the speed of light in space between the logical world of science and the mystical world of God."[14]

Convinced that he was guided by a spiritual mission to cultivate the body and soul into an ideal being, Carrel soon became obsessed with perfecting all aspects of the physical human condition. Genetics replaced biology as his chosen specialty and eugenics became his new passion. The first public hint that his views had delved from a strictly medical path came in a 1935 interview. "There is no escaping the fact that men were definitely not created equal, as democracy—invented in the eighteenth century, when there was no science to confront it—would have us believe," he told a reporter as they crossed the Atlantic aboard the *Ile de France.* "This fact cannot be suppressed, and it is very sad."[15]

Since around the turn of the century, the eugenics movement had already achieved a certain cachet in the United States, where Social Darwinist ideas had been embraced in some intellectual circles. Darwin's cousin Francis Galton had actually coined the term "eugenics" in 1883, describing it as "the science of improvement of the human race germ plasm through better breeding."[16] The movement's advocates believed that physical and mental problems were caused by inferior genes, or "inheritance." People with good genes, they argued, should be encouraged to reproduce ("positive eugenics") while people with inferior genes should be discouraged from reproducing ("negative eugenics"). Most eugenicists, for example, believed that poverty was caused by "biological inheritance."[17]

The idea of sterilizing the "socially unfit" had first gained acceptance in the United States when a 1927 Supreme Court decision, *Buck v. Bell,* legitimized the procedure, although Indiana had passed the first forced sterilization law (for "mental defectives") as far back as 1907. "It is better for all the world, if instead of waiting to execute degenerate offspring for crime or to let them starve for their imbecility, society can prevent those who are manifestly unfit from continuing their kind. . . . Three generations of imbeciles are enough," wrote Supreme Court Justice Oliver Wendell Holmes in his majority opinion.[18] By 1931, twenty-five states had already passed legislation allowing forced sterilization and by 1944, more than 40,000 Americans classified as "insane" or "feeble-minded" had undergone the procedure.[19]

The movement to preserve America's "racial stock" was accompanied by strident calls to curb immigration. At a time of an unprecedented influx of European immigrants, there were fears the white race would be "polluted" by foreign blood. Among the loudest and most influential voices supporting both the eugenics and anti-immigration movements was Margaret Sanger, the celebrated founder of Planned Parenthood.

Sanger is often described as an inveterate racist,[20] whose pioneering advocacy of birth control, according to her critics, was never meant to liberate women but rather to discourage the poor from reproducing. In recent years, Planned Parenthood has gone to great lengths to whitewash Sanger's early career. And while much of the criticism has come from pro-life groups stretching the truth in an intellectually dishonest effort to discredit the pro-choice advocacy group, Sanger's own words speak for themselves.

"The campaign for birth control is not merely of eugenic value, but is practically identical with the final aims of eugenics," she wrote in 1921. "As an advocate of birth control, I wish . . . to point out that the unbalance between the birth rate of the 'unfit' and the 'fit,' admittedly the greatest present menace to civilization, can never be rectified by the inauguration of a cradle competition between these two classes. In this matter, the example of the inferior classes, the fertility of the feeble-minded, the mentally defective, the poverty-stricken classes, should not be held up for emulation."[21] The following year, she wrote, "Birth control must lead ultimately to a cleaner race."[22] A decade later, in April 1932, she advocated a plan to "give dysgenic groups [people with bad genes] in our population their choice of segregation or sterilization."[23]

Thanks in part to the efforts of eugenicists such as Sanger—who publicly opposed immigration that would pollute "the stamina of the race"[24]— the federal government had effectively barred immigration into the United States with the passage of the 1924 Immigration Act. During the period of 1900 to 1924, immigration levels averaged 435,000 per year but after the act's passage, the rate plummeted 95 percent to 24,430. In fact, it was the restrictions of the Immigration Act that led to the turning away of thousands of Jews fleeing Nazi Germany in the 1930s. After Hitler took power in 1933, there were a number of attempts to waive some of the restrictions so that the eventual Jewish victims of the Holocaust could find asylum. Responding to one of these proposals in 1934, Harry Hamilton Laughlin, director of the Eugenics Division of the Carnegie Institution, submitted a report entitled "Immigration and Conquest" that warned against the "human dross" producing a "breakdown in race purity of the . . . superior stocks."[25]

By 1935, the idea of eugenics had clearly gained acceptance in many quarters. But, as disturbing as the procedure now seems, the preferred eugenic method of forced sterilization hardly compares in its brutality to another eugenic measure that was just beginning to gain support in the movement's more radical circles.

In Germany, the Nazis had long been intrigued by eugenic ideas pioneered in the United States. These seemed to mesh with their own concept of racial purity and in 1934, one of Hitler's staff members wrote to Leon Whitney of the American Eugenics Society and requested, "in the name of the

Führer," a copy of Whitney's recently published book, *The Case for Sterilization*.[26] A few weeks later, Whitney received a personal letter of thanks from Hitler himself. Another Society member, Madison Grant, had written a book called *The Passing Of the Great Race* that analyzed the racial basis of European history. He, too, received a personal note from Hitler, who wrote that the book was his "Bible."[27] Two years after Hitler took power, the Nazis began their own forced sterilization program, operating on more than 360,000 mentally retarded German citizens during the 1930s.[28] Once again, we see the cross-pollination of racist ideas from the United States to Germany.

The German "racial hygiene" movement, as it was called, actually predated Hitler's rise to power by more than a decade. However, it was at first largely confined to a debate within the new medical specialization of psychiatry, whose members were grappling with the problem of how to treat so-called mental defectives.

In 1922, the German psychiatrist Alfred Hoche wrote a paper called "The Release of the Destruction of Life Devoid of Value" that called for the painless elimination of the physically and mentally defective through euthanasia because "the cost of keeping these useless people was excessive." He argued that moral attitudes insisting on the preservation of life would soon disappear and that the destruction of useless lives would become necessary for society's survival.[29]

The reaction was resoundingly negative. Delegates at a psychiatric congress in Dresden that year rejected overwhelmingly a proposal to legalize euthanasia.[30] Henceforth, the radical measure was confined for some time to the movement's fringes and even in the program of the National Socialist Party, it never really gained acceptance.

In 1933, just when Hitler and his party were taking power in Germany, Dr. Alexis Carrel began work on a book that was to express his latest musings on the nature of humankind, ones that embraced eugenics as a tool for social improvement. In a recent paper on sunlight's effects, he had already hinted at his racial outlook: "We must not forget that the most highly civilized races—the Scandinavians, for example—are white, and have lived for many generations in a country where the atmospheric luminosity is weak during a great part of the year. . . . The lower races generally inhabit countries where light is violent and temperature equal and warm." When a reporter asked him in a 1935 interview whether Hitler's Germany might provide a "natural laboratory" for developing "supermen" through a "program of race purification," Carrel replied, "We do not really know the genesis of great men. Perhaps it would be effective if we could kill off the worst of these pure races and keep the best, as we do in the breeding of dogs."[31] This was a preview of the ideas he would expand upon in his new book, published later that year.

First in France, and then in the United States, Carrel's *Man the Unknown* caused an immediate sensation. The new "science," he argued, was the solution to society's ills. "Eugenics is indispensable for the perpetuation of the strong. A great race must propagate its best elements."[32] The passage that ignited the biggest controversy, however, appears in the book's final chapter, "The Remaking of Man":

> There remains the unsolved problem of the immense number of defectives and criminals. They are an enormous burden for the part of the population that has remained normal . . . Why do we preserve these useless and harmful beings? The abnormal prevent the development of the normal. Why should society not dispose of the criminals and the insane in a more economical manner. Criminality and insanity can be prevented only by a better knowledge of man, by eugenics, by changes in education and social conditions. Meanwhile, criminals have to be dealt with effectively. . . . Those who have murdered, robbed while armed, kidnapped children, despoiled the poor of their savings, misled the public in important matters, should be humanely and economically disposed of in small euthanistic institutions supplied with gases. . . . Modern society should not hesitate to organize itself with reference to the normal individual.[33]

In America, the English translation sold 900,000 copies and rose to number one on the *New York Times* nonfiction best-seller list. But, despite the book's success, its repugnant conclusion was largely derided, even among advocates of eugenics. *Time* called the book a "wild rant" and a "colossal joke." Many of the reviews attacked the racism and unscientific methods behind Carrel's arguments.[34]

A year after its American publication, the first translation of Carrel's controversial book appeared in Germany. To accompany this edition, Carrel composed a special introduction in which he appeared to complain that the Nazis' fledgling program of racial hygiene had not yet gone far enough. "In Germany, the government took energetic measures against the increase in the minorities, the lunatics, the criminals," he wrote. "The ideal situation would be that each individual of this kind is eliminated when it was dangerous."

At the time of the book's publication, the Nazis had already introduced forced sterilization, but euthanasia was not yet a part of its eugenic program. In June 1936, German Minister of the Interior Wilhelm Frick introduced the sterilization law, "The law for the prevention of hereditary diseases in posterity." Not until three years later, in 1939, did Hitler order widespread "mercy killing" of the sick and disabled for the first time. The Nazi euthanasia program, code-named *Aktion* T4, was introduced to eliminate "life unworthy of life." Between 1939 and 1945, tens of thousands of "defective" Germans were eliminated by gassing, starvation and injection of lethal drugs at six different psychiatric "kill institutions."[35]

After the war ended, a number of Nazi scientists and physicians were put on trial at Nuremberg for crimes against humanity. During this so-called "Doctors Trial," several German racial hygienists were accused of participating in government-sponsored atrocities. Among those indicted was Hitler's personal physician Karl Brandt, head of the National Socialist program for the killing of the mentally retarded. When it came Brandt's turn to testify in his own defense, he claimed in justification that the Nazi program for sterilization and elimination of "defectives" was actually based on ideas formulated in the United States. To prove his point, he cited the passage advocating euthanasia from Alexis Carrel's book *Man the Unknown*.[36]

If Carrel's radical eugenics bothered Charles Lindbergh, he never said so publicly. On the contrary, he appeared enamored of its possibilities. Indeed, the doctor was exerting a profound influence on the man who once wrote, "I worshipped science. I was awed by its knowledge."[37] Now, under the increasing influence of his mentor, Lindbergh appeared to be embracing the newly discovered pseudo-science that Carrel espoused, and the righteous dogmatism behind it. "It should now be branded on our consciousness that unless science is controlled by a greater moral force, it will become the Antichrist prophesied by early Christians," Lindbergh wrote.[38]

Were the eugenic views embraced by Carrel and Lindbergh merely a product of their times, a reflection of a nation under the sway of social Darwinist ideas? According to historian Carl Degler, "By the 1930s, it was about as difficult to locate an American social scientist who *accepted* a racial explanation for human behavior as it had been easy to find one in 1900."[39] Nevertheless, throughout his life, eugenics would remain one of Lindbergh's enduring passions. He began to shift his focus from an interest in aircraft to "an interest in the bodies which designed and flew them."[40]

Each day, he would drive into Manhattan and spend hours tinkering in Carrel's laboratory. There, he was exposed to the scientist's never-ending barrage of ideas on human nature and the trends of modern civilization. It was a fascinating time for the novice scientist. Once, he looked up from his test tube to find Carrel engaged in a spirited discussion with Albert Einstein about ESP. In the face of the unceasing adulation of the outside world, the laboratory—like the cockpit of a plane—had become a welcome refuge. His sense of awe at working with the doctor increased with every day he spent in Carrel's company. "In Carrel, spiritual and material values were met and blended as in no other man I know," he recalled.[41] Clearly, Carrel had a strong influence on his young protégé, but the two had much in common before they even met. They were both somewhat puritanical. Carrel believed that public dancing, "African" jazz, "immoral films," and overt sexuality were dangerous to the mind and he advocated a ban on cigarettes and alcohol. Lindbergh was largely humorless and he, too, detested cigarettes and alcohol. He shared Carrel's view that Western democracies were in a phase of deterioration, that they were being sapped morally and physically by loose living and a lack of purpose.[42] In the coming years, his words and actions indicated that he agreed with the scientist's philosophy that "we must help the strong: only the elite makes the progress of the masses possible."[43] Carrel regularly argued for a council of superior individuals to guide the future of mankind. Lindbergh appeared to agree, as he would soon make clear after visiting a country where many of Carrel's ideas were already being realized.

For his part, Carrel assiduously cultivated his relationship with Lindbergh, despite widely aired skepticism from his colleagues that the pilot with no scientific credentials was actually contributing anything of genuine value to advance Carrel's research. Indeed, the perfusion pump on which they had been collaborating for years proved something of a failure in achieving its original goal, according to Dr. Sherwyn Warren, former chief of thoracic surgery at Chicago's Lutheran General Hospital, who has researched Carrel's scientific legacy. The closest the pump came to achieving its intended purpose was an impressive 1935 experiment in which it succeeded in keeping the thyroid gland of a cat functioning for eighteen days before cells of the gland were successfully transferred to tissue culture.[44] As much as Carrel hailed the importance of this accomplishment, it was given more attention at the time in mainstream publications than it was in scientific journals, which virtually ignored the experiment. The first successful device for extra-corporeal circulation during surgery would not be developed until 1953 when John Gibbons of the University of Pennsylvania introduced a heart-lung machine, based on an entirely different mechanical principle than the so-called "Lindbergh pump."[45] Many believed Carrel exaggerated its significance, although Carrel's biographer, Dr. Theodore Malinin—who was later Lindbergh's close friend and scientific collaborator—argues that the pump led the way to current research using organ perfusion in surgical transplants.[46] Two of today's top perfusion researchers are Dr. Frank Cerra and Dr. Wei-Shou Hu of the University of Minnesota, who developed a pioneering Bio-Artificial Liver device to revive patients in liver failure. The University of Minnesota Web site claims their device is the "modern day successor of the Lindbergh pump."[47]

But in separate interviews, both Dr. Cerra and Dr. Wei-Shou denied this and claim they are unfamiliar with the Lindbergh pump, saying it is not well known in their field.[48] That is not to say that the research Carrel and Lindbergh performed on the perfusion pump had no scientific value, only that its success, and Lindbergh's role, was perhaps deliberately overstated. According to Dr. Warren, "I think Lindbergh did contribute, maybe not as much as a post-doctoral fellow would have, but certainly at least as much as a lab technician.[49]

Yet, Carrel rarely missed an opportunity to publicize his scientific collaboration with Lindbergh, whom he regularly praised for his "extraordinary" facility and scientific acumen. On July 1, 1935, the cover of *Time* even pictured Carrel and Lindbergh with their "mechanical heart."[50] Many believed that Carrel was using the famous flyer to attract attention and gain credibility for his own controversial ideas. Alexis Carrel had always been a believer in the psychological importance of heroes, writing about their key role in "promoting the optimum growth of the fit."[51] Lindbergh seemed quite content to be used. To him, Carrel's "true greatness lay in the unlimited penetration, curiosity and scope of his mind, in his fearlessness of opinion, his deep concerns about the trends of modern civilization and their effect on his fellow man."[52]

One can only speculate on the appeal for Lindbergh of working with a world-class scientist. Here was a man who had reached the pantheon at the age of twenty-five. How could he ever top the spectacular transatlantic flight in his own field of aviation? What was left to accomplish? Then along came Carrel, who offered him the chance to achieve greatness in a field ordinarily reserved for distinguished scholars. Lindbergh had barely graduated high school and had never demonstrated any academic acumen; now, he was working side by side with a Nobel Laureate who regularly praised him in hyperbolic terms. "He is a great savant," Carrel told *Time* in a 1935 article about the Lindbergh pump, arguing that his protégé's aviation achievements proved his greatness. "Men who achieve such things are capable of accomplishments in all domains." It is easy to imagine how Lindbergh's susceptibility to such flattery could have left him open to swallowing the doctor's more unscientific ideas.

Notwithstanding his unquestionable mechanical ability, it was difficult for many to believe that Lindbergh had made a significant contribution to Carrel's extremely complex medical research. Certainly, few of Carrel's colleagues at the Rockefeller Institute believed that Lindbergh was there as a legitimate collaborator, as a number of them made clear to the nationally syndicated newspaper columnist Dorothy Kilgallen, who publicized their skepticism in her column, "The Voice of Broadway," writing, "The Lindbergh Heart is that in name only. They say Lindbergh merely lent his name to the experiment to popularize it."[53]

Indeed, his scientific contribution—like many of his nonaviation achievements—appears to have been exaggerated by friends and supporters seeking to enhance the Lindbergh legend. There is no question that he worked tirelessly on his experiments, with a passion that he had previously shown only for flying. The considerable mechanical expertise that went into developing the perfusion pump was unquestionably Lindbergh's, despite the skepticism stated by his critics. But many of the Institute's scientists believed he lacked the intellectual rigor and academic background required for scientific success, although he did publish one article in the Rockefeller Institute's respected journal based on his collaboration with Carrel.[54] Was Lindbergh nothing more than a competent mechanic, providing frequent technical adjustments to the pump under Carrel's guidance? Were his scientific contributions illusory? In 1938, the two men collaborated on a book, *The Culture of Organs*,[55] in which they describe their joint research, including repeated references to the Lindbergh pump. They also demonstrated the pump together at a number of scientific forums, impressing the gathered scientists. Years later, Lindbergh said that a number of scientific researchers told him that his experiments on the perfusion pump had been "practical." In the mid-1960s, he was even invited by the U.S. Naval Medical Research Institute to duplicate his experiments. He also reported that Carrel and his staff used the perfusion pump in his Department of Experimental Surgery until World War II and that roughly one thousand perfusion experiments were carried on with these pumps before the department was disbanded.[56] Curiously, however, not a single original document relating to their collaboration, including correspondence between the two men, has been preserved in the Alexis Carrel papers, housed at Georgetown University and the Rockefeller Institute Archives, where they would be available for public and scientific scrutiny. Every scrap of paper, mechanical or scientific jotting, and item of correspondence relating to Lindbergh's role in developing the perfusion pump or Lindbergh's participation in Carrel's research has been inexplicably omitted from the collections. Archivists at both institutions are at a loss to explain their absence. The Lindbergh archives do contain a significant amount of his own scientific research material, but it is still restricted and so cannot be easily examined by scientists to determine its value.

Two days before Christmas, 1935, the world was stunned to wake up and read the news that Charles Lindbergh, his wife, and their three-year-old son had quietly set sail the night before on a freighter bound for England. America's hero had gone into self-imposed exile.

Since the day their first son was kidnapped three and a half years earlier, the Lindberghs had been hounded relentlessly by the press. The public was hungry for any news about America's "royal couple" and rarely a day went by when the front pages were free of Lindbergh news. Throughout the kidnapping investigation and the trial of Bruno Hauptmann, every last detail of the saga was played out in the media, reaching O.J. Simpson–trial proportions in its power to captivate the nation's imagination. Journalist H.L. Mencken called it "the biggest story since the Resurrection." Americans, wrote Lindbergh to a friend in 1937, were a "primitive people" who lacked "discipline" and had "low moral standards . . . it shows in the newspapers, the morbid curiosity over crimes and murder trials."[57]

Six months after Charles Jr. was snatched from his crib, Anne had given birth to another son, Jon. His birth should have helped the couple begin to heal from their tragedy; instead, it brought a new menace. From the moment the media reported his arrival, the new baby was the subject of hundreds of threats. A barrage of letters warned that Jon was "next." Most were dismissed as cranks and the FBI provided round-the-clock protection. But as Anne was driving her son to nursery school one day, their car was sideswiped by another vehicle and almost driven off the road. As she came to a halt, a group of photographers jumped out of the car and began snapping photos of the three-year-old child. This was the final straw, Anne concluded. It was time to leave America.

"And so the man who 8 years ago was hailed as a national hero and a goodwill ambassador between the peoples of the world, is taking his wife and son to establish, if he can, a secure haven in a foreign land," reported the front page of the *New York Times*.[58] News of the family's departure sent shock waves through America. The so-called legitimate press took aim at the tabloids, particularly the Hearst press, whom it blamed for driving the Lindberghs away. The *Christian Science Monitor* wrote that "the newspapers more than kidnappers have exiled the Lindberghs."[59] *Time* added that "long ago the press at large concluded that the Hero Lindbergh's real Herod was yellow journalism."[60]

The Lindberghs chose England because they had been told that "Englishmen respected the rights of privacy and that English newspapers had more respect for law than ours at home."[61] In their newly adopted country, the couple and their baby received a warm reception, free from the harassment that had characterized their time in America. "It was very nice," recalled Anne Morrow Lindbergh years later. "It was very normal. Nobody bothered us. We weren't anybody to them, really. It was a very happy, normal life."[62]

They rented a fourteenth-century farmhouse, Long Barn, from the distinguished British writer Harold Nicolson, who was in the process of completing a biography of Anne's father, Dwight Morrow. "Lindbergh is a surprise," wrote Nicolson in his diary upon their arrival. "There is much more in his face than appears in photographs. He has a fine intellectual forehead, a shy engaging smile, wind-blown hair, a way of tossing his head unhappily, a transparent complexion, thin nervous capable fingers, a loose-jointed shy manner. He looks young with a touch of arrested development. His wife is tiny, shy, timid, retreating, rather interested in books, a tragedy at the corner of her mouth."[63]

At Long Barn, the couple finally achieved the cherished privacy that Hopewell had never provided. "There is a wonderful air of peace and stability in England," Lindbergh wrote a friend.[64] These years were largely uneventful. Anne began work on a book about a flight she and Charles had made to the Far East in 1931.[65] Occasionally, the couple flew to France to visit with Alexis Carrel and his wife, who had a home there. In the spring of 1936, Lindbergh was invited for a tea at the U.S. embassy in London where King Edward VIII happened to arrive with his mistress, Wallis Simpson—the woman who was about to ignite a constitutional crisis. Those first years of Lindbergh's exile were spent in a Europe at peace. But dark clouds loomed.

On March 7, 1936, Hitler stormed the Rhineland, violating the terms of the Versailles Treaty, which had created a permanent demilitarization of the zone. The same day, German Jews were stripped of their right to vote in elections for the *Reichstag*. Throughout the spring, the Nazis continued to build up their military machine as Hitler announced a policy of military conscription, signaling to the world that he might have aggressive intentions.[66]

That spring in Berlin, a brief item in the Paris *Herald* caught the eye of Kay Smith, wife of the U.S. military attaché to Germany, as she sat reading over breakfast. Charles Lindbergh had recently arrived in Paris, where he had been invited by the French government on an inspection tour of its aircraft facilities. She pointed it out to her husband, Truman Smith, and unwittingly set into motion a relationship that would have far-reaching repercussions.[67]

Neither the biographers nor the historians who have written about the events in which Smith and Lindbergh participated have attempted anything more than a superficial examination into the life and character of Truman Smith.[68] However, it is impossible to fully appreciate the historical context of these events without knowing something about the background of the man who would so powerfully influence Lindbergh as he found himself enmeshed in the series of events that would forever define his legacy.

Truman Smith, born in 1893, was the product of old New England stock, his Puritan ancestors arriving in America just after the *Mayflower*.[69] Grandson of a U.S. senator and son of a career army officer, Truman was expected to assume a distinguished career. He entered Yale at the age of nineteen but performed poorly, graduating with mediocre marks and few prospects. When the First World War broke out, Smith, like three generations before him, answered the call. Ten months before the United States entered the war, he was commissioned a second lieutenant in the U.S. army. He had found his career and the kind of environment that suited him well.

The army Smith entered in 1916—a full two years before the Bolshevik Revolution and three years before the *Dearborn Independent* made its first appearance—was already steeped in a long tradition of anti-Semitism. Negative, stereotypical attitudes toward Jews were especially prevalent in the officer corps. "While undoubtedly sharing the ambivalent attitude most Americans had towards Jews, officers as a rule accentuated the negative," writes historian Joseph W. Bendersky in his definitive study of U.S. army anti-Semitism, *The Jewish Threat*. "The concept of the Jew as radical agitator and revolutionary took its place alongside the more traditional Shylock image or its modern equivalent, the exploitive, unprincipled Jewish capitalist."[70]

After the American Jewish Committee wrote a letter to the War Department in 1914 complaining about the treatment of Jews in the army, an internal memo written by an influential colonel attacked AJC director Louis Marshall in brazenly anti-Semitic terms. Jews like Marshall, declared the colonel, had a hereditary instinct for money but knew nothing about the military. "The Jew never was and never will be a soldier," he wrote.[71] At the time Smith underwent his officer training course in 1917, the *Army Manual of Instruction* for Medical Advisory Boards still stated, "The foreign born, and especially Jews, are more apt to malinger than the native born."[72]

Trained and indoctrinated in the army's ethos, it is hardly surprising that Smith's own attitude toward the Jews would reflect the sentiments he had been exposed to constantly among his fellow officers. Years later, describing his World War I infantry company, Smith wrote that the soldiers were a typical cross-section of the American population. He praised the rural Pennsylvanian conscripts as "reliable and intelligent." Fighting besides them were a group of "castoffs," Kansas and Nebraska farm boys who were "stolid, loyal and ever reliable." In contrast, there was another group of "castoffs" attached to the Fourth Infantry—Jews and Italians from New York. These soldiers, Smith writes, were the company's "problem children." In the fighting that year, "these New Yorkers disappeared in droves during every move toward the front, turning up at the company kitchen days, and even weeks later, when 'A' Company had been relieved of front line duty."[73]

Smith shone during his wartime military service, leading his men into several battles on the French front during the closing months of the war. Just after the Armistice, he was promoted to the rank of major, a rapid ascent in less than two years, and was assigned to political liaison duties in postwar Germany as part of the U.S. occupational force.

It is during this period that Smith claims to have gained considerable insight into the German character. He steeped himself in their culture, studying German history, art, architecture, philosophy, and politics, and, by his own account, became "an authority on the postwar German army."[74] His astute insights into Germany's military and political situation soon brought the bright young officer to the attention of the American diplomatic corps, which during the fall of 1922 requested that Smith be "loaned" by the military attaché's office to the political staff of the United States embassy in Berlin.

The American ambassador, Alanson B. Houghton, had for some time been observing the rapid rise of a new political movement in Germany called the National Socialist German Workers Party. Houghton believed Truman Smith, with his thorough knowledge of German affairs, would be the most appropriate person to travel to Munich to interview the party's spellbinding new leader, Adolf Hitler, and evaluate the potential of National Socialism.

During the third week of November 1922, Smith spent eight days in Bavaria, where he succeeded in interviewing more than a dozen political leaders as well as Crown Prince Rupprecht. He had been assigned to familiarize himself with the movement, assess its potential and determine how the National Socialists were viewed by the ruling Bavarian elite. Most of the Germans Smith spoke to described Hitler as a rising star and the movement he led as a rapidly growing political force, a useful if extreme antidote to the burgeoning socialist and Communist parties that were rapidly gaining influence.[75]

On November 18, Smith finally had the opportunity to witness the growing National Socialist phenomenon for himself when he attended a Nazi Street rally at which Hitler was scheduled to review his Brownshirts. "A remarkable sight indeed," Smith wrote in his diary. "Twelve hundred of the toughest roughnecks I have ever seen in my life pass in review before Hitler at the goose-step . . . Hitler, following the review, makes a speech. He promises that next week the National Socialists will clean up the town. He then shouts 'Death to the Jews,' etc. and etc . . . Met Hitler and he promises to talk to me on Monday and explain his aims."[76]

Two days later, Smith arrived at Hitler's residence—"a little bare bedroom on the second floor of a rundown house"—where he listened to the "forceful and logical" arguments of the up-and-coming politician.[77] That afternoon, he became the first-ever American diplomat to interview the future Führer. Smith was clearly taken with his subject. "A marvelous demagogue," he observed in his diary. "Have rarely listened to such a logical and fanatical man."[78] This last passage is particularly telling since, even then, Smith does not appear to view these qualities as mutually exclusive.

Returning to Berlin, Smith recorded his findings in a detailed written report. His ninety-minute interview with Hitler, he revealed, had made a "deep impression." He noted his subject's "fanatical earnestness" and the stridency of his oratory. Each time he asked a question, Smith recalled, "it was as if [I] had pressed a gramophone switch which set off a full length speech."[79] Hitler, he reported, favored withdrawing citizenship from all Jews and excluding them from public office. But subsequent interviews with other leaders of the movement would lead Smith to believe that "anti-Semitism was a propaganda weapon rather than a basic aim of the movement."[80] Later, Smith would lament, he wished "that, on that far off day in 1922, when [I] met the man who was to become the Führer of the Third Reich, [I] could have foreseen the course of history."[81]

Despite initial restrictions on fraternizing with the former enemy, Smith established an impressive number of contacts in the recently vanquished German army corps during his first posting from 1920 to 1924. "During these years," he later recalled, "I became acquainted with a considerable number of German officers, some of whom were to continue as friends until 1964."[82] Among his new friends was Ernst "Putzi" Hanfstaengl, the son of a prosperous Munich art publisher. Smith had attended Yale while Putzi was studying at Harvard, but the two Ivy League graduates didn't meet until after Smith was posted to Germany. Just before he returned to Berlin at the conclusion of his successful Bavarian mission, Smith ran into Hanfstaengl and told him about his recent encounter with Adolf Hitler, advising him "to take a look." On November 21, he advised his friend to attend a Nazi Party rally to witness Hitler firsthand. There are contradictory accounts about whether Smith introduced Putzi to Hitler or whether the young German approached the future Führer on his own. Nonetheless, Putzi was immediately drawn to the charismatic leader and his fledgling nationalist party. Four months later, he loaned the National Socialists the then enormous sum of one thousand dollars to turn its newspaper, the *Volkischer Beobachter*, into a daily.[83] He would later use part of his family fortune to finance the publication of *Mein Kampf*. Putzi remained close friends with Hitler for years and it was widely reported that he actually saved the young agitator's life during the unsuccessful 1923 Munich beer hall *putsch*.[84]

According to Smith, the only other time he met Hitler, more than fourteen years later at a reception for the American ambassador, the Führer asked, "Have I not seen you before?" Taken aback, Smith replied, "Yes, Mr. Chancellor, in Munich in 1922." "Oh yes," came Hitler's response. "You're the one who introduced me to Hanfstaengl."[85]

Smith left Germany in 1924 and would not return in an official capacity for more than a decade. But in December 1932, as the resident "German expert" for the U.S. army, he wrote a strategic survey of the German political situation during a stint at the Army War College in Washington, D.C. In this paper, he wrote that the Nazis were a spent political force, past their peak, and unlikely to take power. He doubted that Hitler had the necessary "political genius" to take over the country.[86] Three weeks later, President Hindenburg appointed Hitler Chancellor and the Third Reich was born.

The gaffe doesn't appear to have hurt Smith's career, as he was appointed U.S. military attaché to Germany two years later. In August 1935, he returned to Berlin in his new capacity, where his prime responsibility was to gather intelligence on the growth of the German military, including new weapons development.[87] Despite the restrictions imposed by the Versailles Treaty, it was clear that Germany was rapidly rearming. According to Smith, Washington did not grasp the magnitude of the "revolution" in military methods currently under way.

Smith's predecessor as military attaché, Colonel Jacob Wuest, was repulsed by what he described as the "terroristic methods" of the Third Reich—the "fanatical attack and hatred against Jews since the new regime took power."[88] In contrast, Smith would describe the "mild anti-Semitism" of the Nazis' early years in a report he wrote to Washington.[89] By this time, he had reversed his conclusion of a decade earlier and now recognized that "Hitler was ardent in his racial and anti-Semitic ideology."[90] But Smith did not believe analysis of the "Jewish question" fell within his area of responsibility and cautiously de-emphasized political reporting "to avoid a possible conflict of views with the Embassy." He was likely referring to what he would later call his "extreme difficulty" with U.S. ambassador William E. Dodd, a liberal New Dealer and an ardent anti-Nazi whom Smith derided as a "pacifist" who paid little attention to military matters.[91] Again, his judgment was less than astute. In fact, Dodd was horrified by the excesses of the Nazi regime, especially its treatment of the Jews, and later ardently supported U.S. military intervention. Hardly the position of a pacifist. It is more likely that Smith's distaste for Dodd stemmed from the fact that the ambassador was not diplomatic enough for the attaché's liking and made no secret of his distaste for the Nazi regime. Smith later questioned Dodd's "fitness for the Ambassadorial post."[92]

By the time he assumed his new post in 1935, Smith's own opinions of the Jews appear to have sharpened since his initial tour of Germany a decade earlier. A sampling of his correspondence, official reports, and internal memos reveals that, while he did not personally approve of the Nazis' brutal treatment of German Jews, he certainly shared some of their thinking on the Jewish Question. Smith clearly believed that "International Jewry" wielded too much power. Its influence, he would note, permeated American society where Jews exercised significant "control."[93]

Nazi racial philosophy was not so outlandish, he concluded. In a detailed 1939 analysis on the subject of National Socialist racial doctrine, he compares the Nazis to "the average white inhabitant of Alabama or Georgia but with a racial feeling towards the Jew rather than towards the Negro."[94]

Like many of his colleagues in the officer corps during this period, Smith "viewed Nazi Germany through the filter of Communism."[95] Any criticism of their excesses, he believed, must take into account practical political considerations. The Nazis were extremists capable of great brutality, the thinking went; their methods were to be avoided. But they were also the best hope of containing the Communist threat and could therefore prove useful. Similarly, Smith seems to have swallowed whole the widespread propaganda circulating among his colleagues linking Jews to international Bolshevism. "It is a fact," he writes in his 1938 analysis "Anti-Semitism in Germany," that "whereas during the World War and in the decade following, the German people became impoverished, the Jewish element in Germany succeeded in markedly increasing their wealth, in gaining influence within the government. . . . Equally important was the role of the Jews in the Russian, German, Bavarian and Hungarian revolutions. . . . Furthermore, the international tendencies of communism appeared to converge exactly with the international tendencies of Jewry."[96] Smith then links the origins of the Nazi Party to a popular reaction in Germany against "this sharp and rapid increase in Jewish influence."[97] As for the steadily growing, systematic persecution of German Jews, Smith felt that might be excused as long as the Soviet Union and not the United States was the target of Nazi fury.

There is no record as to whether Smith ever read the *Protocols of the Elders of Zion*, which was being circulated around the War Department around the time of his 1917 officer's training. But there is evidence that he was a great admirer of a brazen work of anti-Semitism that was nearly as infamous in the canon of hate literature—Houston Stewart Chamberlain's *Foundations of the Nineteenth Century*. Chamberlain was an English Germanophile and the son-in-law of the notoriously anti-Semitic composer Richard Wagner. In 1899 he wrote the *Foundations*, one of the works long credited with helping the Nazis form their racial theories about the Jews. The Germans, Chamberlain wrote, are a "superior race" destined to rule the world; the Jews, by contrast, are a mongrel race and the corrupters of German culture. In 1923, Chamberlain wrote Hitler a letter of near ecstatic admiration. "At one blow you have transformed the state of my soul," he wrote. "That Germany in her hour of need has produced a Hitler testifies to its vitality. Now at last I am able to sleep peacefully and I shall have no need to wake up again. God protect you!"[98]

Years later, Truman Smith would express admiration for Chamberlain's work in a letter to his friend John Beaty, himself an influential anti-Semitic writer who believed that "world Zionist leaders had seized control of Christendom." In his letter, Smith urged Beaty to read the *Foundations of the Nineteenth Century* and singled out the chapter on the Jews as "definitive."[99] In this chapter, entitled "The Entrance of the Jew in History," Chamberlain condemns the Jews as "an Asiatic race," the natural enemy of all Aryans, who are engaged with Jews in a racial and spiritual war for the survival of western civilization.[100]

It is possible that Smith hardened his attitude toward the Jews during the early thirties while he attended the U.S. Army War College, an institution that was designed to develop "the brains of the army," producing more than 50 percent of all future army generals.[101] Since as far back as 1920, officers who attended the college were subject to a steady stream of lectures extolling scientific racism, condemning immigration and painting Jews as an alien culture closely tied to Bolshevism. Geopolitical events were almost always framed in racial terms. According to one War College strategic survey, Russian racial characteristics were "not conducive to military or industrial efficiency" because they were a mixture of the "Orient and the Occident," the white race mixing with the yellow. Their "lack of culture and reasoning logic . . . show the Mongol blood."[102] Lecturers frequently singled out the Jews in particular as inferior because of their "peculiar" racial characteristics.

While he was digesting the *Foundations'* noxious ideas and rationalizing Hitler's anti-Semitic program, Smith's wife, Kay, appears to have formed her own favorable impression of the Reich. In the diary she kept during her German sojourn, she complains that Americans always expected her to "describe horrors" of Nazi Germany whenever she returned to the United States. She attributed this to the media's tendency to stress only the "Jewish troubles" while ignoring the "favorable side" of Germany. After all, she notes, Germany is safe again because "all the drunks, bums, homosexuals, etc. had been put in concentration camps."[103] She seems to share some of her husband's anti-Semitic views as well: "I am beginning to think Hitler is right: a Jew is after all a Jew and a national only when his interests are involved. Certainly the Jews in America, where we have given them everything, now that the test has come, are proving themselves Jews and not Americans."[104] Like both Lindbergh and her husband, she appears to regard the Jews as an alien race, un-American and unpatriotic because they were attempting to draw America into a war with Hitler.

As in his prior posting, Truman Smith wasted no time renewing old acquaintances and making new friends among his counterparts in the German officer corps. To some extent, this was probably a strategic approach. The best intelligence could often be gathered while socializing over drinks or at one of the cocktail parties to which he and Kay were invited every evening. But Smith also had a genuine fondness for Germans and admired their way of doing things. One of his duties as military attaché was to gather information about the growing strength of the *Luftwaffe*, the German air force led by Hermann Göring. Smith believed he had an accurate assessment of the German army's expansion—battle charts, units identified, lists of officers, etc. But he had been much less successful obtaining similar data regarding the German Air Force. What information he had was "fragmentary and unsystematic at best."[105] He was deeply concerned, convinced "that Göring planned a mighty *Luftwaffe*," and that the day was not far off when modern airplanes with powerful new engines would make their appearance in the German skies.[106]

So when he heard the news that Charles Lindbergh had visited a French airplane factory in the spring of 1936, Truman Smith sensed an opportunity. It is important to note that much of the information available about what happened next—and much of what has already been written by historians and biographers—comes from the personal accounts of Charles Lindbergh and Truman Smith, most of it furnished long after the events in question, at a time when both men were anxious to cast their activities in a favorable light.[107] In consideration of this, these events deserve closer scrutiny.

According to Smith's version, he first devised the idea of inviting Lindbergh to Germany as an excuse to gain access to German air factories in order to assess the progress of German aviation. At the time, May 1936, elaborate preparations were under way to showcase the new regime at the Berlin Summer Olympics, scheduled for August of that year. When Germany was awarded the Games in 1931, Hitler was still two years from taking power. But soon after the Nazi ascension in 1933, it became apparent that the 1936 Olympics were to become as much a tool for extolling the virtues of the Third Reich as a sporting event.

A year after the Nazis came to power, American anti-fascists launched a vigorous campaign pressing the United States to boycott the Berlin Games. The debate was heated. American Olympic Committee (AOC) Chairman Avery Brundage, a known anti-Semite and admirer of Hitler,[108] opposed the boycott, arguing "the Olympic Games belong to the athletes and not to the politicians."[109] But the Reich's anti-Semitic policies had already had a significant impact on German sports as Jewish athletes were systematically expelled from athletic clubs and sports associations. Julius Streicher, editor of the Nazis' anti-Semitic newspaper *Der Sturmer*, wrote, "We waste no words here . . . Jews are Jews. And there is no place for them in German sports . . . Germany is the Fatherland of Germans, not Jews."[110]

It was widely expected that Jews would not be allowed to compete for Germany at the Games, prompting Judge Jeremiah Mahoney, president of the American Amateur Athletic Union, to protest that Germany had broken Olympic rules forbidding discrimination based on race and religion. In his view, participation would mean an endorsement of Hitler's Reich.[111]

In 1935, during the heat of the boycott debate, the American consul in Berlin weighed in with his own views, writing to the secretary of state in Washington, "To the Party and to the youth of Germany, the holding of the Olympic Games in Berlin in 1936 has become the symbol of the conquest of the world by National Socialist doctrine. Should the Games not be held in Berlin, it would be one of the most serious blows which National Socialist prestige could suffer."[112] The same year, a Gallup poll found that 43 percent of Americans opposed American participation in the Games.[113] As the boycott campaign gained momentum, Brundage lobbied hard to keep the Games in Germany. In the AOC pamphlet "Fair Play for American Athletes," he argued that U.S. Olympians should not become involved in "the present Jew-Nazi altercation." Later he would allege the existence of a "Jewish Communist conspiracy" to keep the United States out of the Games.[114] In the end, Brundage prevailed. The AOC voted to participate after the Nazis made an unenforceable pledge that Jewish athletes would not be barred from competition.

On May 25, 1936, just over two months before the scheduled Olympic opening ceremony, Truman Smith wrote a letter to Lindbergh, whom he had never met. "In the name of General Göring and the German Air Ministry," Lindbergh was duly invited to inspect the new German "civil and military establishments." From an American point of view, Smith wrote, "I consider that your visit here would be of high patriotic benefit. I am certain that they will go out of their way to show you even more than they will show us."[115]

To this day, it is unclear why Smith would have invited Lindbergh in the name of Göring, Hitler's second-in-command. Ordinarily, a diplomat might pass on or forward an invitation, but this was not the case here. Smith did not go through any official American channels before issuing the invitation and there is no record that his superiors approved it in advance. Not coincidentally, he issued the invitation at a time when his adversary, Ambassador William Dodd, happened to be out of the country, visiting the States. It is highly likely that Dodd would have vetoed the plan if he had been consulted, for he did not tolerate any activities which he believed might strengthen the Hitler regime. Years later, Smith would claim that he decided on his own initiative to approach the German air ministry and suggest a visit by Lindbergh. Upon receiving a positive response, he took it upon himself to invite the flier without consulting Washington. "Only after Lindbergh agreed to come did (I) intend to inform Washington of his plans," he explained.[116]

Lindbergh was clearly excited at the prospect, writing to his mother, "Comparatively little is known about the present status of Aviation in Germany, so I am looking forward with great interest to going there."[117]

The original invitation suggested that Lindbergh arrive in Germany on June 26 and stay for about a week. Lindbergh wrote back on June 5 and accepted the invitation, but said he was unavailable on the dates proposed. He then suggested two alternate dates: any time between July 21 and August 5, or any time after August 25.[118] A week later, Smith requested a meeting with Colonel Hanesse of the German air ministry and proposed a Lindbergh visit beginning July 22. He would return to England on August 1, which just happened to be the opening date of the Olympic Games.

To Smith's "dismay," the German colonel insisted that Lindbergh attend the opening Olympic ceremony as Göring's special guest, Smith recalled in 1956 at a time when he was attempting to justify these events.[119] It is almost impossible to believe that Smith could have issued an invitation for Lindbergh to visit Germany on a date which fell during the Games and not have known the world's most celebrated figure would be expected to attend. Certainly, Lindbergh's suggested dates would have made possible a one-week visit commencing July 22 that would have still seen him depart a full three days before the opening ceremony. Why was his visit extended until August 1, giving the Nazis a chance to exploit his presence at the Games?

In the face of international opposition to what the world was calling "the Nazi Olympics," Hitler's regime desperately craved legitimacy and Smith knew better than anybody that Lindbergh could provide it. In later years, Smith wrote frequently of his initial fear that "the Germans intended to use Lindbergh's visit principally for their own propaganda purposes."[120] Yet it was he who brokered the arrangement to deliver heroism incarnate, and in the process gave the Nazis a vital cog to stage the Games as one of the greatest propaganda coups of the twentieth century. If Smith indeed suspected Lindbergh would be used by the Nazis, he could have easily arranged a shorter visit or switched the dates. Curiously, an account later written by Smith himself completely contradicts his explanation that Lindbergh's appearance at the Olympics was inadvertent, and that the American aviator attended the Games only at the Nazis' insistence. In this account, written during the mid-fifties, Smith appears to admit that he presented the Nazis with the idea of inviting Lindbergh to the Games because it appeared to be an irresistible opportunity to please the *Luftwaffe* generals. "It was (my) impression that the German Air Ministry would like nothing better than to gain favor with Hitler by presenting the world-famous flier as the special guest of the *Luftwaffe* at the Olympic Games," he wrote. Smith notes that it was "clear the Nazis were seeking to attract to the games celebrities from all over the world."[121] With this in mind, he proceeded to contact the German air ministry. Here, he appears to acknowledge that it was originally his idea, rather than the Nazis', for Lindbergh to attend the Olympics. This disturbing contradiction is just one of many unexplained inconsistencies that raise questions about Smith's true motivations.

The news that an American hero was to visit Germany's Olympic propaganda-fest couldn't have come at a worse time. Roger Strauss, co-chairman of the U.S. National Conference of Christians and Jews, immediately cabled Lindbergh to urge him not to go, pointing out that German propaganda would interpret the visit as a gesture of approval for the Nazi regime.[122] But Charles and Anne Lindbergh ignored his entreaty, taking off from England in a rented plane and landing at Berlin's *Staaken* military airport on July 22, 1936, for the start of their eleven-day visit. Awaiting them was a small reception committee comprised of several high-ranking officials of the German air ministry, a number of U.S. military attachés and Göring's personal representative. Also on hand was Truman Smith who, with his wife Kay, had offered to host the Lindberghs at his Berlin apartment for the duration of their visit. A group of German boys approached the plane to welcome the couple as they stepped out on the tarmac. The boys came to a halt, clicked their heels and raised their arms in the Nazi salute. They greeted the distinguished visitors with the first words the Lindberghs would hear on German soil: "*Heil Hitler.*"[123]

The Germans were desperate to avoid alienating international visitors, deliberately downplaying the darker side of their regime. In preparation for the Games, the Nazis had removed all visible signs of their anti-Jewish measures in an effort to put the best face forward for the world. However, Smith's nemesis, Ambassador William Dodd, warned Americans not to be taken in by the facade, reporting to Washington that German Jews awaited "with fear and trembling" the end of the Olympic truce. Three days earlier, German officials had informed Gretel Bergmann, a Jewish athlete who had equaled the German women's record in the high jump and was the gold-medal favorite in the event, that she was denied a place on the Olympic team.[124]

Recognizing the best way to curry favor with Lindbergh, Smith's invitation had promised the publicity-shy celebrity a visit that would allow him "more privacy to your person than can a visit anywhere in the world."[125] Three months earlier, at 8:44 P.M. on April 3, 1936, Bruno Richard Hauptmann was put to death in the electric chair for the kidnapping and the murder of baby Charles, occasioning another onslaught on the couple's privacy from a press corps anxious to record their reaction. Historian Arthur Schlesinger would later say of Lindbergh that the "thing that attracted him about Nazi Germany was the press knew its place and he knew he could go to Nazi Germany without having that kind of incessant and intolerable inquisition and surveillance . . ."[126] But the Nazis had no intention of letting the publicity value of the famous American's visit go to waste. As Anne's biographer Susan Hertog writes, "Adolf Hitler was certain that Charles Lindbergh personified [the future of the Third Reich]. His tall frame, his sandy-haired boyishness, his piercing blue eyes, made him the quintessential Aryan. The Nazis could not have constructed a more eloquent embodiment of their vision."[127]

The promise of privacy was forgotten. For the next ten days, Lindbergh was dogged by reporters and photographers determined to record his every move during a full itinerary of social visits and inspection tours of important aircraft factories. It was the first time any American had been permitted to see the Germans' new state-of-the-art dive bombers—seemingly impressive evidence of Göring's growing air arsenal. Among the journalists reporting on Lindbergh's visit was a German reporter named Bella Fromm, a columnist for Berlin's *Vossiche Zeitung* newspaper. When she returned to her apartment each evening, she recorded the day's events in her diary. In her July 26 entry, Fromm describes a Lindbergh apparently basking in the attentions of his Nazi hosts:

> The Colonel seemed completely spellbound by the honors showered upon him since his arrival in Germany. I overheard several of his conversations. It was obvious he enjoyed the limelight. His words lead to the conclusion that he not only thinks highly of German aviation, but also unmistakably sympathizes with the new Germany . . . They are making wisecracks in the Ministry of Aviation. They say he dislikes publicity but that he enjoyed being snapped with the German and American officers. . . . Alex [von Blomberg, son of the Minister of the Reichswehr] told me that all the officers who had been in touch with Lindbergh reported unanimously that he is very naive and is deeply impressed by the to-do Berlin put on for him. . . . One officer with an especially

sharp tongue said: "If they had a National Socialist party over there and an SA and SS, Lindbergh would certainly run around as group leader."[128]

Noting the unprecedented access Lindbergh had been granted to German aircraft installations, Truman Smith would later portray Lindbergh's first trip to Germany as a "tremendous success" and an "intelligence coup." He appears never to have questioned why the Nazis magnanimously granted this unique access in the first place.

On August 1, a day before his revised departure date, Lindbergh took his seat in Göring's Olympic Stadium box as 100,000 fans roared their excitement at the magnificent spectacle of the Opening Ceremony taking place on the field below. As the parade of nations marched in, the only athlete of Jewish descent representing Germany was the half Jewish fencer Helene Mayer, who was allowed to compete as a gesture to mollify the West. Mayer would eventually claim a silver medal in the women's individual foil competition and, like all other German medalists, gave the Nazi salute on the podium.[129] A few rows away from where Lindbergh watched the pomp on the field, Adolf Hitler sat in his own box. In his letter to Smith, Lindbergh had expressed a desire to meet Hitler, but there's no record that they ever met. Two days earlier, the Führer had confided to his chief architect, Albert Speer, "In 1940 the Olympic Games will take place in Tokyo. But thereafter they will take place in Germany for all time to come, in this stadium."[130]

On August 2, Charles and Anne left Germany, clearly invigorated by their eleven-day visit to the Reich. The next day, German army captain Wolfgang Fuerstner, head of the Olympic Village, killed himself after he was dismissed from active military service because of his Jewish ancestry. Fuerstner's involvement in the Olympic organizing committee had long been hailed by American officials who opposed an Olympic boycott and argued that Jews were not being excluded from the German team. By the time the Games ended two weeks later, Germany had emerged victorious, capturing eighty-nine medals, the most of any country. More important, the Nazis had achieved their goal of putting a human face on the new Germany. "Hitler turned the Olympics into a dazzling propaganda success for his barbarian regime," wrote William Shirer in *The Rise and Fall of the Third Reich*. In his book *Hitler's Games*, the historian Duff Hart-Davis noted that the Nazis were able to project an image of "a perfectly normal place, in which life went on as pleasantly as in any other European country."[131]

But nobody appeared more impressed by what he had witnessed than Lindbergh himself. His defenders would later claim that, at the time,

Lindbergh had little knowledge of the brutality of the Nazi regime. It was only after *Kristallnacht*, the argument goes, that the world understood the true extent of Hitler's brutality. But there is considerable evidence that Lindbergh was in fact well versed in the odious nature of the regime by the time of his July 1936 visit. In March 1934, when Lindbergh was still working with Alexis Carrel in New York, 20,000 Americans—including a wide cross-section of Christian and Jewish leaders—had jammed into Madison Square Garden for a giant mock trial of the Nazi government. Witness after witness testified to the persecution of the Jews carried out since the Nazis took power a year earlier. In the interim, German Jews had been excluded from public office, the civil service, journalism, radio, farming, teaching, filmmaking, and the theater. Collectively, the crowd "indicted" Hitler's government for "crimes against civilization." The trial made front-page news around the country.[132] "We declare," read the indictment, "that the Hitler government is compelling the German people to turn back from civilization to an antiquated and barbarous despotism which menaces the progress of mankind toward peace and freedom, and is a present threat against civilized life throughout the world."[133] In the years since, the American media had frequently written about the savagery of the regime—the book-burnings, the persecution, the racial laws. Few Americans were unfamiliar with Nazi doctrine. Even fewer approved, according to a number of nationwide polls conducted during the mid-1930s.

By the time the Lindberghs arrived for their visit in July 1936, writes Shirer, "the Jews had been excluded either by law or by Nazi terror—the latter often preceded by the former—from public and private employment to such an extent that at least one half of them were without means or livelihood."[134] The Nuremberg laws of September 15, 1935, had deprived all German Jews of German citizenship and designated them as "subjects."[135]

How did the Lindberghs respond to these events, and is it possible that they were unaware of the true nature of Hitler's regime? In a letter to her mother, written three days after she returned to England following the July 1936 visit, Anne Lindbergh reveals that she was indeed well versed in the excesses of her German hosts. "There are great big blurred uncomfortable patches of dislike in my mind about [the Nazis]," she writes. "Their treatment of the Jews, their bruteforce manner, their stupidity, their regimentation. Things which I hate so much that I hardly know whether the efficiency, unity, spirit, that come out of it can be worth it."[136] Charles, for his part, wrote a somewhat defensive letter in September 1936 to his former patron,[137] the Jewish philanthropist Harry Guggenheim, in which he stated, "There is no need for me to tell you that I am not in accord with the Jewish situation in Germany."[138] But publicly he offered no such disclaimer. To the inquiring press, he said little about his impressions of the new regime. However, in a letter to his financial adviser Harry Davison a few months later, Lindbergh wrote of Hitler:

> With all the things we criticize, he is undoubtedly a great man, and I believe he has done much for the German people. He is a fanatic in many ways, and anyone can see there is a certain amount of fanaticism in Germany today. It is less than I expected but it is there. Hitler is undoubtedly a great man who has done much for the German people. On the other hand, Hitler has accomplished results (good in addition to bad) which could hardly have been accomplished without some fanaticism.[139]

Like his wife, Lindbergh's support for Germany was not completely without reservations. In a letter to his friend Henry Breckinridge, he complained of "the instances of incredible stupidity which seems to arise constantly among their actions." But on balance, he found the situation "encouraging . . . rather than depressing," adding that he found Germany to be a "stabilizing factor" at that time. "There seems to be a spirit in Germany which I have not seen in any other country," he wrote.[140]

In a series of correspondence following his 1936 German visit, Lindbergh hints for the first time at his contempt for democracy and his admiration for dictatorship, expressing an attitude that would seem to echo the opinions of his ideological mentor Alexis Carrel, who believed in "rule by elites." "What measures the rights of man or of a nation?" Lindbergh wrote Davison. "Are we deluding ourselves when we attempt to run our governments by counting the number of heads, without a thought of what lies within them?"[141]

Most of his biographers and a number of historians have attempted to discern how Lindbergh could have come away from his first visit to Germany so impressed by Hitler and the accomplishments of the Third Reich. In 1998, after conducting ten extensive interviews with Anne Morrow Lindbergh—the woman who knew him best—Anne's biographer Susan Hertog explained the appeal:

> Clearly, Charles saw the Third Reich as the embodiment of his values: science and technology harnessed for the preservation of a superior race, physically able and morally pure. . . . Social and political equality, together with an ungoverned press, had produced a

quality of moral degeneracy. . . . He did not disdain democracy so much as he did the common man—the uneducated and enfeebled masses. . . . To Charles, Germany under Hitler was a nation of true manhood—virility and purpose. The strong central leadership of a fascist state was the only hope for restoring a moral world order.[142]

In Lindbergh's only public account of his first visit to Germany, published forty years after the fact in his autobiography, he furnished his own explanation: "The organized vitality of Germany was what most impressed me, the unceasing activity of the people, and the convinced dictatorial direction to create the new factories, airfields, and research laboratories . . ."[143]

When he came back to England, Lindbergh immediately threw himself into the task of harnessing his newfound admiration for Germany. He initiated a sustained correspondence with friends and family about his impressions of the Third Reich, its aviation achievements, and Hitler's accomplishments. He was itching to return.

CHAPTER 5

✠

HATE BY PROXY

Henry Ford receives the Third Reich's highest civilian honor, the Grand Cross of the German Eagle, in July 1938.

On the last day of 1927—exactly six months after Henry Ford called a final halt to the *Dearborn Independent*'s anti-Semitic campaign—the paper ceased publication for good. As the staff were packing up the files a few days later, Ernest Liebold asked his boss whether he wished to sell the presses now that they were no longer needed.

According to Liebold's company oral history, Ford replied, "No, don't sell them. I made a deal with those Jews and they haven't lived up to their part of the agreement. I might have to go after those Jews again."[1]

His business sense apparently prevailing, Ford never carried out this threat, at least not publicly. The survival of the company he had successfully built into a corporate behemoth was at stake. Since its introduction in 1908, the Model T had been the Ford Motor Company's mainstay, selling millions of cars worldwide over two decades. But by 1927, the once-fashionable car was obsolete. Chevrolet had introduced its own sleek model to compete with Ford's dinosaur, and sales of the company's flagship car were hurting.

For years, Ford had stubbornly resisted his associates' pleas to introduce a new line or to modernize the Model T. One possibly apocryphal story had Ford telling his associates, "You can paint the Model T any color you want—as long as it's black." Widespread rumors of an unofficial Jewish boycott compounded an already bleak sales outlook. Finally, in 1926, Ford reluctantly authorized the development of the company's first new automobile in two decades—the car that would become known as the "Model A." The company's future depended on the success of this new line. The corporate number crunchers were anxious that no obstacle should hinder Ford's return to preeminence in the automotive world. Ford's son Edsel was especially concerned about the future of his birthright. It was widely believed that it was Edsel who finally convinced his father to call a halt to the seven-year crusade against the Jews.

Years later, Liebold would claim, "I think Edsel was pushing rather hard about the financial loss the paper incurred, and I think the Jewish question brought on the boycotting of the car. A great many of our fleet owners, so called, were told by their financial backers that they ought to buy Chevrolet cars instead of Fords. I think the sales department was complaining quite bitterly about the effect the publishing of the Jewish articles had on business."[2]

Ford was eager to alleviate any lingering resentment in the Jewish community. To this end, the company made the decision to commit $150,000—a staggering 15 percent of its 1927 promotional budget—to advertising the new Model A in American Jewish newspapers, despite the fact that Jews comprised less than 2 percent of the U.S. population at the time.[3] Indeed, from all outward appearances, Ford was honoring his recent pledge to make amends for his anti-Semitic campaign. His efforts yielded results almost immediately.

Many of the *Independent*'s readers were outraged by the apology. Some of the cross-section of letters from the public in the company archives accuse Ford of "turning yellow," selling his "birthright for a mess of porridge," and being "a pitiful quitter." But fully 80 percent of the letters he received in 1927 were written by Jews praising his "courageous and manly statement" and his "breadth of character and broad-mindedness."[4] One New York rabbi wrote, "I am happy that the feelings of my brethren will henceforth cease toward a man who has done so much for a country beloved by all of us."

On January 16, 1928, only two weeks after the *Dearborn Independent* suspended publication, Henry Ford paid a personal visit to Louis Marshall, the longtime director of the American Jewish Committee, who had brokered his apology and retraction six months earlier. At the conclusion of their two-hour meeting, Marshall told reporters that he believed Ford's apology had been completely sincere:

> Mr. Ford told me personally how deeply sorry he was for what had taken place. He said that while the *Dearborn Independent* had been constructing its campaign, he had been unaware of it. Since his published retraction, Mr. Ford told me, he has been doing everything he could to remedy the harm these attacks have

caused. The whole retraction, he told me, had been an immeasurable relief to him and lifted a heavy burden from his mind. He seemed especially pleased that the Jews of America had accepted his retraction so whole-heartedly and happily. He told me he never had anything against Jews as Jews.[5]

According to Marshall, Ford had assured him that the *Dearborn Independent* had ceased to exist, that its editor William Cameron was no longer in Ford's employ, and that Ford himself had destroyed every copy of *The International Jew* he could find.[6] But news of Cameron's dismissal must have come as a surprise to the man himself, because he continued to report for work each day.

As part of his out-of-court settlement with Aaron Sapiro, Ford had in fact promised to fire both Cameron and Liebold. But, as soon became clear, Ford had no intention of cutting loose the two men who had served him so faithfully in carrying out his crusade against the Jewish menace. In order to convey the impression that he was complying with the spirit of the apology, however, Ford had officially dismissed Cameron as editor of the *Independent* soon after the retraction was issued, and quietly reassigned him to other duties. In fact, Ford had not even bothered to inform his loyal deputy before issuing the apology, as a *New York Times* reporter learned when he called for a comment. "It's all news to me," a shocked Cameron stated, "and I cannot believe it is true."[7]

Enter once again Hitler's fund-raiser Kurt Ludecke, whose anti-Semitic affinities with Cameron had sparked something of a friendship since he first dropped by the *Independent*'s offices in 1922 to voice his appreciation for Ford's crusade, two years before his unsuccessful entreaty for funds on behalf of the Nazi party.

In 1927, Ludecke was living in Windsor, Ontario, just across the Canadian border from Detroit, waiting to immigrate to the United States, and he, too, had been stunned when he first heard the news of Ford's retreat. "Though I had abandoned every hope of Ford," Ludecke later recalled, "I never expected one of the richest men in the world to be willing thus to repudiate his editor and to make such a humiliating kowtow to Jewry. Determined to get to the bottom of this, I rushed to Dearborn to catch Cameron before he could make himself invisible."[8]

When he arrived at Cameron's office, Ludecke confronted his "forlorn" friend and demanded to know why Ford had accepted this humiliation. "You must force his hand," the Nazi agent pleaded. "You can turn this whole thing to the advantage of the cause for all of us if you have the guts."

Cameron was hesitant. "I don't know yet what I'm going to do," he replied, "but it is certain that for my part, I will never make any retraction. What I have written will stand. The whole thing is a mystery to me. I know Ford too well not to be absolutely sure that the views set forth (in the articles) are still his views and that he thinks today as he always did."[9]

Ludecke attempted one final appeal. If it was true that Cameron had published the articles in good faith after a careful investigation of the facts, with Ford's explicit consent, then the Jew-baiting editor must make himself heard. The world would listen.

Ludecke's plea must have had an inspirational effect because, in the words of author Neil Baldwin, William J. Cameron—ousted from his bully pulpit—rose "phoenix-like out of the ashes of Henry Ford's doomed newspaper and found a new venue for his philosophy over the next fifteen years."[10] Not long after he was removed from the editorship of the *Dearborn Independent*, Cameron had a new job.[11] He assumed the presidency of a new organization he had recently co-founded called the Anglo-Saxon Federation of America. The Federation was committed to carrying out the philosophy of the British Israelite movement, to which Cameron had long adhered.

The British Israelites subscribed to an odd theology which postulated the belief that Anglo-Saxons, not Jews, were the true sons of Israel, "the real Chosen People," and that Jesus was not a Jew. According to "facts" inscribed on the great pyramids of Egypt, the Anglo-Saxons descended from the ten lost tribes of Israel, while Jews descended from the evil Judeans. Jew-hating was acceptable because it was the manifestation of a long-standing "battle of righteousness" between the Aryan sons of Israel and their Jewish antagonists, a theme that had occasionally surfaced in the *Dearborn Independent* under Cameron's editorship. For example, he had once written that Jewish defensive "propaganda" was infecting the faith of the "uninstructed clergy," leading them "astray." In another issue, British Israelite leader William Pascoe Goard was quoted as proclaiming, "There is not enough room for both Israel and Anglo-Saxondom."[12]

Under Cameron's presidency, the new Federation appears to have taken up where the defunct *Dearborn Independent* left off. From its offices in Detroit's downtown Fox Building, the organization sold and distributed a series of anti-Semitic pamphlets with such titles as: "The Jewish Question," "The Servant Race," and "The Prophetic Forecast of Israel's Destiny." But its bestseller by far was a reissue of the first English translation of *The Protocols of the Elders of Zion*.[13]

Whether Cameron was acting on his own volition in this new endeavor or at the behest of Henry Ford is unclear. Ford Motor Company records reveal that he was never removed from the payroll but that his position had simply been changed to "Director of Public Relations." During the 1930s, in fact, when his anti-Semitic activities at the Federation were at a peak, Cameron was assigned to host a national radio broadcast known as the *Ford Sunday Evening Hour*. Each week, he was given a six-minute sequence to discuss "matters of national interest and concern," sandwiched between "music of familiar theme, with majestic rendition."

In his inaugural broadcast, Cameron promised that the Ford company had "no theories to propagate . . . no political ax to grind . . . no partisan purpose of interest whatever." But, although he remained silent on the subject of Jews, he frequently used what his critics called a "six-minute sermon" to assail the policies of the Roosevelt Administration—venting about one of Henry Ford's pet peeves, the New Deal. Not surprisingly, this was also a favorite theme of the Anglo-Saxon Federation. One of the federation's most popular pamphlets, "The Two Sticks Which Became One," declared, "The present administration has lifted into power more Jews than ever were seen in this government before, and not always the right kind of Jews."[14] One of Cameron's anti-administration diatribes even inspired the pro-Roosevelt United Auto Workers to respond in verse:

> *Do you think, Henry Ford, you exploiter*
> *You can buy with this kind of stuff*
> *The thanks and goodwill of thousands*
> *Who haven't nearly enough?*
> *So you might as well keep your music*
> *And shut old Cameron's yap*
> *For while we enjoy your music*
> *We haven't time for your crap.*[15]

There is no evidence of a direct financial link between the Anglo-Saxon Federation and the Ford Motor Company. But one of Cameron's Ford radio addresses was later reprinted in *Destiny*, the Federation's monthly magazine, suggesting at least an informal link.[16]

As Cameron continued wearing two hats—carrying out his anti-Semitic activities at the Federation during the week while acting as the voice of Ford each Sunday evening over a national radio network[17]—Jewish voices of protest became increasingly louder. In 1934, Samuel Untermeyer, head of the Non-Sectarian Anti-Nazi League, complained in a letter to Ford that some of his company's officials were engaged in "activities considered anti-Jewish." Soon after, Cameron's title of "President" was quietly removed from the official listing of the Anglo-Saxon Federation's officers, and reprinted a month later as "Director of Publications."[18] In this position, he coordinated distribution of the largest body of anti-Semitic literature America had seen since the days of the *Independent*.

Like Cameron, Ernest Liebold had also been publicly offered as what he called a "sacrifice" to the Jewish leaders who had negotiated Ford's 1927 retraction. According to the terms of the settlement, Cameron and Liebold would be fired from the company and Ford's apology would be printed verbatim in the *Dearborn Independent*. None of these things happened. Officially, Liebold was dismissed as general manager of the *Independent*. But since the paper had called a truce with the Jews, he no longer had any interest in working there anyway. His job as Ford's personal secretary, the source of his actual power within the company, remained intact.

Among the other significant concessions Ford had agreed to in his settlement agreement was a commitment to end the worldwide distribution of *The International Jew*. On the surface, Ford appeared to be keeping this promise. Less than a year after the 1927 apology, a letter was sent to each of the book's international publishers asking that Ford's name not be used in connection with its publication and that any copies remaining in print be destroyed. However, it soon became apparent that the letters were having little or no effect. Foreign-language editions of the book continued to proliferate, each bearing Ford's name on the cover.

In 1932, a Brazilian publisher wrote Ford asking to buy the Portuguese translation rights. Liebold promptly wrote back with the helpful information that no permission was necessary because "the book has not been copyrighted in this country."[19] He failed to mention Ford's retraction. The Brazilian publisher proceeded to print 5,000 copies. Eventually, with Liebold's tacit approval, millions of copies of the hate tract were circulating worldwide in more than fourteen languages.

Every time Rabbi Leo Franklin wrote Ford to protest the book's continued distribution, Liebold would send the guilty publishers an official-looking letter of protest, designed to appease the Jewish community critics. However, as Liebold intended, these did little to stem the flow of *The International Jew* into new markets.

Nowhere was the book as well received as it was in Germany. By the time Hitler took power in 1933, *Der International Jude* was already in its twenty-ninth printing. Its Leipzig-based publisher, Theodor Fritsch, was himself a notorious anti-Semitic writer who has been described as "the most influential German anti-Semite before Hitler."[20]

In Germany, advertising for the book exalted Ford, proclaiming, "In America there is today no longer a Jewish question and Henry Ford is the courageous man who has exposed it . . . On this side of the ocean, this problem is moving towards a sure solution, and for the Germans it is of special significance to read the judgments of one of the greatest and most successful Americans."[21] But there was one caveat. In a note inserted in his edition, Fritsch refutes Henry Ford's assertion that there are "good" and "bad" Jews; moreover, he states that he does not share Ford's belief that one day "the eyes of the Jews will be opened to their mistakes." In Fritsch's eyes, all Jews were intrinsically evil and beyond saving.[22]

When a dozen German-language bookstores in New York were found to be selling the German translation openly during the thirties, a furious Rabbi Leo Franklin phoned Liebold to demand that he immediately take steps to halt circulation. The Germans, noted Franklin, were now "using Mr. Ford . . . most effectively" in their resurgent "campaign of anti-Semitism."[23] Liebold assured the rabbi he would pursue the matter. What he failed to tell Franklin was that, upon receiving Ford's request to cease and desist German publication of *The International Jew* in 1928, Fritsch had written back saying that he would only agree to destroy his last 9,000 copies if Ford compensated him for the loss of revenues he would incur—a relatively modest 40,000 *deutschmarks.* "Inestimable mental goods would be lost for mankind," complained the German publisher to Ford. "The publication of this book remains the most important action of your life." How, he asked, could Ford have buckled to the financial power of the Jews? How "could he be made the cat's paw of the most dangerous suppressors of mankind?"[24]

Liebold had expressed similar sentiments himself and was entirely sympathetic to Fritsch's argument. "We understand the matter perfectly and this thoroughly answers our recent inquiry," he wrote back, satisfied that he could now claim he had made the effort.[25] Fritsch, not surprisingly, took this as a green light to continue publication.

Ford's secretary had long ago made it clear where he stood. To one Philadelphia reader who wrote expressing her desire to see *The International Jew* translated into German, Liebold was very helpful. "We wish to advise that Volume One of *The International Jew* has been published in Germany and may be obtained from *Hammerverlag* (Theodor Fritsch) in Leipzig. As we have given our entire attention to the problem in the United States, we are not contemplating the publication of this book in foreign languages, preferring to leave this to the people of the respective countries where such would be of benefit to them."[26]

On May 16, 1933, Rabbi Franklin wrote Ford suggesting he publicly restate his 1927 apology in order to impress upon Fritsch his repudiation of *The International Jew.* In a telephone conversation with Franklin, Ford agreed to do so and asked the rabbi to draft a statement for his signature.

But shortly after he complied with this request, the rabbi was surprised to receive a polite note from Liebold supposedly on Ford's behalf refusing to sign the declaration. Nevertheless, Liebold assured Franklin, Ford had not changed his attitude: anyone attacking the Jews in his name did so without his blessing and with his "definite disapproval."[27]

In many countries, *The International Jew* was proving to be an increasingly influential force. In a 1933 letter to Liebold, the manager of Ford Germany, Edmund Heine, wrote that *The International Jew* had enjoyed government backing since the Nazis took power and was an important factor in educating the nation "to understand the Jewish problem as it should be understood."[28] Many editions, in fact, featured photos of Henry Ford and Adolf Hitler side by side on the cover. Around the same time in South America, which was witnessing a burgeoning Nazi movement, the first Spanish-language translations were beginning to circulate under the title *El Judio Internacional.*

It was time for the American Jewish community's national leadership to enter the fray. On December 5, 1933, B'Nai Brith president Alfred Cohen wrote Liebold to deplore the Argentinean edition of *The International Jew*, which printed not only Ford's name on the cover, but his photo as well. Like most of the foreign-language editions, this version was printed in Germany by Theodor Fritsch and distributed abroad to further the Nazi cause. In his letter to Liebold, Cohen insisted it was "the opportune moment for Mr. Ford to disclaim responsibility for the translation of this book into Spanish, and a denial by him of its authorship." He further demanded that Ford condemn what was being done in his name and put an end to "this latest attempt to worry, harass, and discredit the Jewish people."[29] Again, Liebold dragged his heels, responding that, "the time does not seem opportune for such a public display."[30]

The frustration of the Jewish community mounted. Its leadership wondered openly if Ford was deliberately violating the 1927 agreement. There is no evidence that Liebold ever showed the protest letters to his boss, but it is almost certain Ford knew about the controversy. In December 1933, he saw fit to declare defensively to the *American Hebrew* that "I am not a Jew hater. I have never met Hitler." Incredibly, in the same article Ford goes on to say, "I have never contributed a cent directly, or indirectly, to any anti-Semitic activity anywhere. Jews have their place in the world social structure, and they fill it nobly. I have Jewish friends—many of them—in my business associations."[31]

Even if Liebold was unilaterally pursuing his own clandestine anti-Semitic agenda, it is difficult to believe that Ford did not approve. In his company oral history, Ford's chief chemist J.L. McCloud recalled, "I know, even though [Ford] eventually retracted the *Dearborn Independent*'s statements, he never changed his personal views . . . He said to me one day, with respect to a lawyer whom he knew, that he was a Jew. He said it in the most vindictive fashion I've ever heard Mr. Ford express himself. I realized then that when he said that, it was the worst possible thing he could say of the man."[32] McCloud believed that "Liebold only acted as a red flag in front of a bull."[33]

On March 25, 1933, a revealing exchange of correspondence was initiated between a New York private detective named Casimir Palmer and a Harvard University business professor, Nathan Isaacs. Palmer and Isaacs had worked together as far back as 1918 when they were both agents of the U.S. Military Intelligence Division at the time when Boris Brasol also worked there. After Palmer left MID, he was recruited by Brasol to work for Ernest Liebold's detective agency, digging up incriminating information on prominent Jews to be disseminated in Liebold's *Dearborn Independent*. Now, more than a decade later, Isaacs was a prominent leader of the American Jewish community, chairman of the Zionist Mizrachi movement, and Palmer headed his own New York private detective agency.

In his March 25 letter, Palmer calls Isaacs' attention to the activities of their former colleague Boris Brasol and his association with Ernest Liebold. "It appears that not Ford personally but Liebold was interested in Brasol's activities," he writes. "The information [that he] obtained from Mr. Brasol, Mr. Liebold shared with his old friend Franz von Papen, vice chancellor of Germany. Mr. Liebold by the way is a confirmed anti-Semite and supporter of German monarchists."[34]

The association between Liebold and von Papen cited by Palmer is one more crucial link in establishing Liebold's political ties to the National Socialists. Franz von Papen was a former chancellor in the pre-Nazi Weimar Republic, who was enormously influential in 1932 and 1933 in helping Hitler consolidate his power. Immediately after Hitler was named chancellor, Hitler appointed von Papen vice chancellor in the new Nazi cabinet, making him one of the Führer's most powerful associates. In 1914, before the United States entered the First World War, von Papen had been stationed at the German embassy in Washington as a military attaché. From this post, he supervised a massive German espionage operation designed to keep the United States from entering the war, until he was expelled by American authorities as a spy in 1915. This period happens to coincide with Henry Ford's Peace Ship venture; moreover, von Papen's tenure as the Kaiser's American spymaster comes just before Ernest Liebold himself was identified by the U.S. military intelligence as a German spy. It is conceivable, even probable, that Liebold reported to von

Papen during this period, and that this was the beginning of the relation-ship referred to by Casimir Palmer in his letter.

In this letter, sent only two months after Hitler was appointed chancel-lor, Palmer is clearly alarmed that his former associates, Liebold and Bra-sol, now possessed access to the highest levels of Hitler's government. "Is it not about time that Boris Brasol, Henry Ford, Ernest Liebold . . . and oth-ers' activities who are disseminating anti-Jew propaganda be investigated?" he wrote. "To this day, those fellows have been working overtime to pin something on the Jews and did not succeed."[35] A week later, after Isaacs wrote back expressing his concern about recent attempts by rightist Amer-ican German groups to stop a number of planned anti-Nazi rallies, Palmer wrote him another letter. "I know that most of the German patriots know nothing against the Jews and they could not prove [any] subversive acts against them," he wrote. "It is for this reason that the Hitlerites and other anti-Semites worship Boris Brasol as their benefactor. It was Boris Brasol who contributed much to their 'knowledge.' All the Hitlerite intelligence is based on Brasol's and other documents gathered through the medium of Ernest G. Liebold, Henry Ford's general secretary."[36]

In 1933, five weeks and 4,000 miles apart, two men assumed the leadership of their respective countries. Adolf Hitler, appointed chancellor of Ger-many on January 30; and Franklin Delano Roosevelt, inaugurated presi-dent of the United States on March 4.

The Depression had devastated the economies of both countries and played a decisive role in the elevation of the two leaders. Germans were convinced the Nazis' prescription of fascism and militarism would cure their economic misery; Americans were promised a "New Deal" to lift them out of their own. But while Germans had no opportunity to express their opposition to the new regime—with the Nazis imposing a brutal totalitarian dictatorship soon after taking power—the United States expe-rienced the birth of dozens of organizations opposed to Roosevelt, many of them dedicated to bringing Hitler's brand of fascism to the shores of America. Coincidentally or not, many of them happened to be based in Detroit, Henry Ford's backyard.

The threat of Nazism had hardly permeated the American conscious-ness. But in the heartland of America, a shadow was being cast that would be felt for years to come. As early as 1924, America had witnessed its first sign of native fascism when four German immigrants founded the Free Society of Teutonia in Detroit.[37] The club soon raised a platoon of brownshirts modeled after Hitler's storm troopers.[38] During the next two years, the Soci-ety attracted hundreds of new members, most of them German immigrants, many of them formerly active in Hitler's circle. By 1932, the Teutonians had established branches in five American cities. Less than a year before Hitler took power, Teutonia changed its name to the "Friends of the Hitler Movement" and became increasingly strident in its American political activities, regularly attacking Jews, communism, and the Versailles Treaty.

In May 1933, Hitler's deputy Rudolf Hess—seeking to establish an international base for the newly ascendant Nazi regime—authorized a German immigrant named Heinz Spanknobel, a longtime member of the Teutonia Society, to form a new American Nazi organization, which would come under the direct command of the German leadership. The result was a small, but amply funded, group known as the Friends of New Germany (FONG).[39] When Spanknobel assumed leadership of the new organization, he already had a day job. Like many of his fellow Teutonians, he was on the payroll of the Ford Motor Company. Five months after forming the new organization, Heinz Spanknobel was indicted by U.S. federal authorities for failing to register as a Nazi agent. Before he could stand trial, he fled America to return to Germany, where he would later emerge as an important figure in the Nazi regime.[40]

His successor at FONG, Werner Haag,[41] soon took up where Spanknobel left off, reporting back to his Berlin superiors in September 1933, "It's child's play to make good anti-Semites of the Americans."[42]

They were men on a mission. According to one study conducted by a German American historical society, "Leaders of American Nazi organizations shared Hitler's distorted view of the United States and of the eight million Americans of German stock who lived there. They thought it their duty to 'rescue' their Aryan brothers from the insidious influence of American culture, Jews, and Communists. They expected, ignoring the extent of intermarriage and the variety of American political and racial opinions, that German Americans would heed their cry en masse."[43]

Worried about the rise of pro-Nazi activities in the United States, Congress established a committee in March 1934 to examine the distribution of subversive propaganda.[44] In its February 15, 1935, report, the McCormack-Dickstein committee charged that home-front Nazis were targeting millions of Americans of German descent. Evidence existed, moreover, that Friends of New Germany received funding from the German government.[45]

Nervous that the Nazis' activities were attracting too much negative attention, Hess issued a new directive in December 1935 that effectively disbanded FONG.[46] Three months later, the *Amerikadeutscher Volksbund* (German-American Bund) was born. With considerable fanfare, the Bund held its founding national convention and selected a German immigrant named Fritz Kuhn as its first leader.[47]

Kuhn had arrived in America in the summer of 1927 and immediately settled in Detroit. He later claimed that he had been forced to flee Germany because he had been at Hitler's side during the 1923 Munich *putsch* attempt. This was pure fabrication. In fact, he had been a fugitive from German justice since his indictment for theft in his native Bavaria four years earlier.[48] Upon his arrival in North America, Kuhn worked as a chemist in Mexico City for several years before emigrating to the United States. His scientific credentials landed him a job working in the laboratory of the Henry Ford Hospital, which had been established by Ernest Liebold several years earlier. Under Liebold's administration, in fact, the institution had imposed a policy barring Jews from the medical staff.[49]

After a number of years working in the hospital laboratory, Kuhn was transferred to the chemical division of the Ford Rouge River plant, where he worked until his election as leader of the German-American Bund. Three years before, he had become a naturalized U.S. citizen, an affiliation that would serve him well in a movement dominated by German immigrants, who were subject to deportation. The Bund represented a significant change in approach. The Friends of New Germany had served mainly to establish support for the Nazi regime among German Americans; much of its leadership was comprised of transplanted Nazis who eventually planned to return to Germany. But Kuhn immediately declared the Bund "as American as apple pie" and proceeded to deliver his inaugural speech on a platform emblazoned with both swastikas and the Stars and Stripes.

Shortly after assuming the leadership, Kuhn had led a delegation of Bundists to Germany to attend the Berlin Olympics, where he was received briefly by Adolf Hitler, although Hitler was said to be unimpressed by the ragtag group.[50] Upon his return to America, the organization came to resemble a microcosm of the German Nazi party, with its members sporting swastikas and giving the stiff-armed Nazi salute. But instead of swearing allegiance to Hitler, Bund members were required to recite the following pledge: "I am of Aryan descent, free of Jewish or colored traces. . . . To a free, Gentile-ruled United States and to our fighting movement of awakened Aryan Americans, a threefold, rousing 'Free America. Free America. Free America.' "

In 1937, Kuhn established a training camp in New Jersey, where new recruits could be schooled in techniques for spreading fascism to America. Each morning at Camp Siegfried, aspiring Bundists could be heard singing the Nazi anthem, the "Horst Wessel Song," and other inspirational hymns. One popular camp song contained the chilling refrain:

When Jewish blood drips from the knife
Then will the German people prosper . . .

By this time, the Bund was far from alone in its mission to promote fascism in America. At the time of the *Dearborn Independent*'s disbandment in 1927, there were only five hate organizations active in the entire country, according to the 1941 study, *Organized Anti-Semitism in America*.[51] However, the years 1933 to 1940 witnessed the emergence of an estimated 121 groups preaching fascist, pro-Nazi, and anti-Semitic propaganda, an astonishing increase. Americans, hard-hit by the Depression and anxious to find a scapegoat for their troubles, turned increasingly to these groups. The revived Ku Klux Klan and organizations such as the Silver Shirts, the Defenders of the Faith, and the Black Legion flourished amidst the economic hardship. Although these groups never gained a significant membership, they made a lot of noise and attracted considerable media attention. Historian Francis MacDonnell describes them as a "motley collection of cranks, con men, malcontents and lunatics."[52]

Henry Ford remained uncharacteristically silent on the Jewish Question as these native fascist groups continued to preach the kind of hate propaganda he had pioneered a decade earlier. But, although he never mentioned the Jews by name, his public statements began to take on a codelike quality. In an interview with the *New York Times* in 1934, for example, Ford was asked whether he believed the Depression was an act of God. "No, Depressions aren't 'Acts of God,'" he replied. "Just like wars, they are the work of a small group of men who profit by them. What America needs is to put the national finger on that small group."[53] It took little imagination to figure out who he was referring to. In another interview with the *Times* two years later, he referred to the "underneath government" of financiers who were running the country.[54] References to "international financiers" appear in almost every one of his recorded statements. But publicly, the word "Jew" never passed his lips. His private attitudes, however, can be discerned by the jottings he frequently made in his diary-like notebooks, which were discovered in an attic years after his death. In one of these notebooks he kept during the thirties, he had scrawled a message that provides considerable insight into his mindset at the time: "The Jew is out to enslave you."[55]

As Albert Lee writes, "Ford had started the Jew-hatred snowball rolling and he was now content to stand on the sidelines and watch it grow, with only occasional, and generally covert, encouragement from him along the way."[56]

In 1936, Hitler's favorite filmmaker, Leni Riefenstahl, who specialized in propaganda films extolling the Nazi regime, was vacationing in Chicago when she received an invitation to visit Henry Ford in Detroit. Upon her arrival at the home of the famous American, Riefenstahl later recalled, Ford "quickly made us realize how sympathetic he was towards Germany."

Before she left a few hours later, she claims Ford told her, "When you see the Führer after your return, tell him that I admire him and I am looking forward to meeting him at the coming party rally in Nuremberg."[57] There is no record that Ford ever ended up traveling to Germany to meet Hitler, although his son Edsel did attend the rally.

By the mid-thirties, the enlightened labor policies that had earned Ford his near-mythical reputation were a thing of the past. Both General Motors and Chrysler paid higher wages and treated their workers with considerably more humanity. Ford had incurred the wrath of the Roosevelt administration and had publicly shunned the New Deal by refusing to sign the automobile code of the National Recovery Administration, which stipulated that employees had a right to organize. Conditions in the Ford plant, meanwhile, were abysmal and safety standards were lax. According to the account of one assembly-line worker, any infraction of the plant's "1,001 petty tyrannies" was punishable by instant dismissal: "If you stay too long in the toilet, you're fired. If you eat your lunch on a conveyor, you're fired; if you eat it on the floor, you're fired; if you wait to return stock to the tool crib, you're fired; if you talk to men coming on the next shift, you're fired." Speeded-up quotas, he explained, "combined with the nervous tension present in the plant, results in a high accident rate. No outsider hears of these accidents, for Ford has his own hospital."[58]

The substandard conditions made the company a prime target for unionization and both the CIO and the United Auto Workers (UAW) had long set their sights on organizing Ford's 80,000 employees. To Henry Ford, this meant all-out war. Labor organizations, he declared, "are the worst things that ever struck this earth. . . . We'll never recognize the United Automobile Workers Union or any other union."[59] To lead the battle, Ford needed a general and, as his biographer David L. Lewis notes, "A fiction writer would be hard put to devise a more picaresque or colorful character than the man Ford had designated to handle the union problem."

Harry Bennett claimed to be closer to Henry Ford than any man alive. The former sailor, who had established a reputation as an amateur boxer in the Navy, had been plucked out of the company's art department in 1917 by Ford himself, who asked the burly brawler to be his "eyes and ears" around the plant.[60] Gradually, the assignment was expanded and Bennett was instructed to keep the Ford workers in line. He understood well that this meant keeping them out of the union, which Bennett once described as "irresponsible, un-American and no god-damn good."[61]

To accomplish this task, the ruthless Bennett established an internal paramilitary force, blandly known as the Ford Service Department, and to man it, he embarked on a novel recruiting drive. Explaining to the media that he was deeply committed to "the highest social motive" of giving "unfortunates another chance," Bennett recruited more than 3,000 ex-cons to staff his new service department. Impressed by his apparent social conscience, the *Detroit News* ironically named him one of the industry's "Good Samaritans."[62]

But it soon became apparent that "Bennett's boys" were committed to a policy of intimidation and force to crush the union and keep the workers in their place. Spies were placed everywhere throughout the plant to report any hint of union activity. Workers who showed the least sign of dissent were mercilessly beaten, then fired. In 1932, the American Civil Liberties Union wrote to Henry Ford complaining that "Harry Bennett seems clearly committed to a policy of violence, espionage and lawlessness. It has been charged on reliable authority that your police force is connected with gangsters and racketeers of the underworld."[63] The company's brutal labor policies exploded onto the front pages in May 1937 when a group of UAW organizers distributing union literature outside the gates of Ford's Rouge River plant were badly beaten by Bennett's goons.

In the late 1930s, one of the company's former labor spies recalled his ten years working for what he called Ford's "Gestapo." Bennett's Service Department, charged Ralph Rimar, "covered Dearborn with a thick web of corruption, intimidation and intrigue. The spy net was all embracing. To those who have never lived under dictatorship, it is difficult to convey the sense of fear which is part of the Ford system."[64] Rimar explained that he had joined Bennett's spy ring because he believed he was helping to prevent Communist unions from taking over the plant. But before long, he discovered that fascism, not Communism, was the prime menace. "Pro-fascist ideas flourished in the Ford labor spy ring," he recalled. "Everyone knew that Nazis could be relied upon to fight the CIO; that men with pro-fascist sympathies would hinder, never help, unionism."[65]

Indeed, the Ford plant was a totalitarian state in miniature. Each afternoon, under the watchful eye of Bennett's Service Department, workers coming out of the factory would be greeted by signs in the parking lot reading: "Jews teach Communism; Jews teach Atheism; Jews destroy Christianity; Jews control the Press; Jews produce filthy movies; Jews control money."[66] As one New York newspaper later pointed out, similar signs preceded the Nazi conquest of Poland, Czechoslovakia, and Austria.[67]

Quietly working behind the scenes as Bennett's right-hand man during these years was a Ukrainian immigrant named John Koos. According to Bennett's FBI file, Koos was the most important American leader of a Ukrainian-fascist Fifth Column terrorist group known as the Ukrainian Hetman Organization (UHO), which had its headquarters in Berlin, under the direct control of the Nazi regime. The UHO was closely linked to the White Russian fascist movement, which still dreamed of restoring the czarist monarchy with the help of the Nazis. Among the organization's chief organizers in the United States, in fact, was Boris Brasol, who had brought the *Protocols* to Ernest Liebold years earlier. Brasol continued to promote his virulent anti-Semitic agenda and was working closely with a number of organizations linked to the Nazis. Under Koos's direction, more than two thousand Ukrainians were employed in the Ford Motor Company's labor-espionage operations, and Koos had recruited a substantial proportion of these into the Hetman organization as well. On September 30, 1938, Koos sent a telegram to Adolf Hitler congratulating him on his "settlement of the minority problem." Soon afterward, the Nazis' chief ideologue Alfred Rosenberg dispatched the son of UHO leader General Skeropadsky to Detroit to award Koos a Nazi decoration. Along with the medal, he brought a message from the Führer: When the Third Reich takes over the Ukraine, John Koos will be appointed Minister of Internal Affairs in his native land.[68]

Ralph Rimar later documented the Nazi connections of some fifteen men working at Ford, many holding high-level positions.[69] But by far the highest profile Nazi employed by the company during these years was the chemist Fritz Kuhn, who had recently boasted that he would become the first "American Führer." In a letter to Professor Nathan Isaacs of the American Jewish Committee dated May 11, 1937, detective Casimir Palmer—Isaacs' former colleague in the U.S. Military Intelligence Division—complained that "Henry Ford and his subordinates Ernest G. Liebold, W.J. Cameron, and others have turned the Ford Motor Company Chemical Department into the headquarters of the Nazis here."[70]

At what point Kuhn left his job at Ford is still a mystery. In December 1936, Samuel Untermeyer, president of the non-sectarian Anti-Nazi League, cabled Henry Ford demanding to know why Kuhn was still on the company payroll despite his leadership of the pro-Nazi Bund. Ernest Liebold provided the high-minded reply: "Inasmuch as Mr. Ford has always extended to Ford employees the fullest freedom from any coercion with respect to their views on political, religious or social activities, they cannot be reproved by us for exercising such liberties."[71]

When Untermeyer's telegram was publicized in the *New York Times* and other publications, it was the first time most Americans had learned that the Nazi Kuhn was employed by Ford. Rudolph Heupel, a Ford worker and fellow Bund member, told an inquiring reporter that Kuhn was widely disliked at the Rouge plant because of his Nazi leanings but added, "He was popular with Ford officials because . . . they know that Herr Ford is a militant Jew hater."[72] When the FBI visited the plant to inquire about Kuhn, they were told that he was once caught during work hours "practicing speeches in a darkroom."[73]

Negative publicity about Kuhn's employment appears to have prompted the company suddenly to devise the pretense that the Bund leader's employment had been terminated. A termination date of January 16, 1937, was entered on his company service card. But, when he was confronted with this news by reporters, Kuhn denied he had severed his connection with Ford, explaining that he was merely on a "company-approved leave of absence" to head the Bund. "I was really on vacation when I left the company's employ and I don't know when or whether I will return to my old job," he told a *Detroit Free Press* reporter.[74]

Two years later, *Friday Magazine* obtained a letter William J. Cameron had purportedly sent to Kuhn:

> Dear Fritz: Talked with Bennett just a few minutes ago, he has taken the matter in hand personally and assures me that there will be no evidence whatsoever concerning your status with our chemical department. Several inquiries were made to our personnel department by reporters from New York newspapers asking whether or not you are employed by our organization as a chemist; at each and every instance, we denied knowing you. Some important matters have come up which have to be cleared away before I can leave for New York, but you can look for me by the first of the month, at that time we will outline our next move.[75]

The company claimed the letter was forged and hired a handwriting expert who allegedly verified the claim. Any continued association with Kuhn was denied. But at the end of 1939, Kuhn was convicted of embezzling Bund funds and sentenced to a lengthy prison term for grand larceny. On December 18, he was being escorted by police to Sing Sing prison on a train leaving from New York's Grand Central Station. Just before the train pulled away from the station, none other than Henry Ford appeared on the platform and briefly stuck his head into Kuhn's rail car. He just "chanced to be in the station" at the same time as Kuhn, Ford explained to the *Detroit News* when a reporter asked about the incident.

Ford's war against the unionizers intensified throughout the decade, but it soon became apparent that even Harry Bennett's goons could not permanently stem the labor tide. The Ford Motor Company began studying the more sophisticated union-busting tactics of its arch-rivals Chrysler and General Motors. Both automakers had successfully installed puppet unions to head off the United Auto Workers' efforts. These unions would sprout up overnight and claim to be "for the worker" but opposed to "radical activities." Each was tightly controlled from corporate headquarters to prevent infiltration by legitimate unionists.[76]

Now, Ford realized that he would have to swallow his fierce opposition to labor organizations of any kind and establish his own puppet union if he was to prevent the UAW from taking control. To accomplish this task, he turned to a soon-to-be-notorious Detroit priest named Charles Coughlin.

Born in Hamilton, Ontario, in 1891, Coughlin had started out as a small-town Canadian parochial school teacher before he was granted his own parish in Michigan during the early twenties. In 1926, he was reassigned to the Royal Oak Parish just outside Detroit where his church became known as the Shrine of the Little Flower. When a local Detroit radio station gave him broadcasting time to boost church attendance, it was the start of a hugely successful career in radio. His populist style and Irish brogue were ideal for the new medium; Coughlin soon had so many listeners that he began to purchase radio time in other cities. He called it the Radio League of the Little Flower. Before long, he was a national figure, broadcasting to sixteen stations over the CBS radio network.

Initially, Coughlin's radio shows were aimed at children, combining lessons in religion with some rudimentary politics and economics.[77] But as his fame increased, he began to assail bankers, communists and capitalistic greed. The sermons of the "Radio Priest" took on the tone of a crusade.

Coughlin had firmly supported the President during the first years of the Roosevelt administration and labeled the New Deal "God's Deal." But he soon turned on Roosevelt with a vengeance, apparently convinced that Jews were controlling the White House. By this time, Coughlin's network and influence were reaching more than twenty million listeners across the country—an enormous platform for the priest's increasingly extreme views. He began to express the belief that capitalism was doomed and hardly worth saving. Like many American extremists during the 1930s, he believed that Roosevelt—who he privately referred to as "Rosenfeld"—was secretly a Jew. He began to speak out against the New Deal and proposed a set of fascist controls that he called "Social Justice." To spread his message, he set up a monthly magazine under this name, eventually achieving a circulation of more than a million copies. As the Depression worsened, his followers needed a scapegoat for their economic and social problems. Coughlin provided it for them. Communist Jews, he proclaimed, were behind all America's troubles.

At some point in 1933, Charles Coughlin had become acquainted with Ernest Liebold for the first time. In February of that year, the national media reported that Liebold had suddenly "dropped out of sight" and mysteriously gone missing. When he reemerged two days later, Liebold had no explanation for his whereabouts, only saying that he had just woken up and that he was "totally exhausted." At the time, he had been working on a complicated plan to reorganize Detroit's two largest banks under Ford control.[78] It was speculated that he had suffered a nervous breakdown. From that point on, he ceased to be a power within the company itself, but instead continued to serve as Ford's personal secretary and "confidential aide." In that capacity, he could more fully devote himself to enlightening his employer about their shared passion.

The first time he met Father Coughlin, Liebold later recalled, they discussed "how closely the encyclicals of Pope Leo compared to Henry Ford's ideas." Although the priest was not yet publicly anti-Semitic, Liebold claimed that, "Coughlin came out and talked about Wall Street money interests controlled by Jews. He touched upon the currency issues . . . They were all matters that Mr. Ford was more or less interested in."[79]

According to the Radio Priest's biographer Donald Warren, soon after Coughlin met Liebold, the radical clergyman "was implicated in a series of bizarre and sometimes ludicrous efforts to prevent an independent union from organizing the Ford Motor Company."[80] The first of these came during the summer of 1937 when Coughlin called a press conference to announce the formation of the "Workers Council for Social Justice" at Ford's Rouge, Michigan, plant. The Council would represent Ford workers, or at least those who met Coughlin's membership criteria. Jews need not apply, he declared: "The new Christian Union has no quarrel with the Brahman, the Buddhist or the Jew. But the Workers Council for Social Justice will not compromise nor accept the principles of these philosophies, which are in conflict with Christianity."[81]

The sham union failed to attract any workers and it died a lonely death. Coughlin was undaunted. That summer, the priest invited United Auto Workers president Homer Martin to a secret meeting at his shrine. Ostensibly, the meeting was called to discuss union strategy at the Ford plant. Soon afterward, Martin publicly charged Coughlin with offering him a bribe on Henry Ford's behalf.[82]

There is no direct evidence that Ford rewarded Coughlin financially for these efforts. But Harry Bennett's former labor spy Ralph Rimar described the arrangements between the auto magnate and the priest in an affidavit he signed before the National Labor Relations Board in 1940:

> We knew that Coughlin could be counted upon to combat the CIO. It was an open secret among all of us that the company was collaborating with Father Coughlin in the era of his best violent, anti-democratic oratory. In return for Coughlin's sympathy, the company bought large quantities of *Social Justice* Magazine. Most

of them were never circulated in the plant. I know that thousands
of them were regularly destroyed.[83]

In one of his diary entries, Roosevelt's Secretary of the Interior Harold
Ickes noted that "rich people in the country who are said to include Henry
Ford and other automobile manufacturers . . . are helping to finance
Father Coughlin. . . . He is making a particular drive in New York City and
undoubtedly someone is financing him heavily."[84]

In 1938, Coughlin stepped up his anti-Semitic rhetoric considerably,
both in his weekly sermons and in the pages of *Social Justice*. According to
the study *Organized Anti-Semitism in America*, the most distinct characteristic of his propaganda during this period was "the directness of his quota-
tion from Nazi propaganda material."[85] Indeed, this observation is borne
out by the striking resemblance between Nazi texts and numerous Coughlin diatribes. On September 13, 1935, Nazi Propaganda Minister Josef
Goebbels spoke before the 7th National Socialist Congress at Nuremberg,
bitterly attacking the Jews. The speech was later reprinted in English and
distributed for publication in English-speaking countries. On December 5,
1938, an article entitled "Background For Persecution" ran in *Social Justice*
under Coughlin's byline. The article appears to have been lifted almost
verbatim from the translation of Goebbels's 1935 Nuremberg speech.[86]

By the spring of 1938, Coughlin and Liebold had become regular
lunch companions. At least once a month, the priest dropped by Dearborn
for a chat with Henry Ford, whom he later described as a "sincere man
who knew the truth when he saw it."[87] Praise for Adolf Hitler soon became
a regular feature of Coughlin's sermons. Although the priest occasionally
acknowledged Jewish persecution in Germany, he maintained that the Jews
deserved no pity because they had "shown no sympathy for the persecuted
in their own lands." Soon, Coughlin's efforts were indistinguishable from
those of the young American Brownshirts who idolized the German Nazi
Party. He had become an enormously influential national figure who was
using his platform to disseminate wholesale Nazi propaganda to an audience numbering in the tens of millions.

Who was Coughlin's audience, and why were millions of Americans so
receptive to his hate-laced sermons? According to historian Joshua Krut,
the Depression alone could not explain the appeal of the Radio Priest's
message. Rather, he argues, it was the result of social trends under way for
decades, as the United States was transformed from a largely rural and dif-
fuse society to a highly urban, industrial nation linked by a network of
large institutions. Many Americans, explains Krut, felt threatened by the
intrusion of new, urban values into their lives, and they responded with

increased intolerance of difference, whether it was political, religious, or ethnic.[88]

In a profile of Father Coughlin published in the fall of 1938, *Look* magazine revealed a close friendship between the Radio Priest and Nazi Bund leader Fritz Kuhn. To those familiar with Ford's close relationship to both men, it appeared that the industrialist was quietly abetting the construction of a Nazi Fifth Column in the United States at the same time as he courted the American Jewish community and attempted to convince his critics that he had changed his views.

That same year, another curious item made its appearance in the pages of *Social Justice*. Before 1938, Coughlin had always been careful to include a mix of Jewish and non-Jewish individuals when he provided examples of the "international bankers" he claimed were running America.[89] But at some point that summer, his language and rhetoric became more explicitly anti-Semitic, culminating in the publication of an extensive series of articles introducing the notorious *Protocols of the Elders of Zion*. Invoking the authority of Henry Ford in his introductory article, he wrote, "Yes, the Jews have always claimed the *Protocols* were forgeries but I prefer the words of Henry Ford who said, 'The best test of the truth of the *Protocols* is that up to the present minute they have been carried out.'"[90]

The specter of the *Protocols* once again revived latent fears in the American Jewish community, which believed it had exorcised this demon years earlier with Henry Ford's apology. The audience of *Social Justice* was significantly larger than that of the *Protocols*' first American forum, the *Dearborn Independent*. Moreover, their reappearance could not have come at a worse time. Incensed, the editor of the Detroit *Jewish Chronicle*, Phillip Slomovitz, wrote Coughlin to protest: "You are grossly misled, Father Coughlin, regarding the *Protocols* and many other phases of Jewish life which you have undertaken to criticize at this juncture when dictators are destroying every vestige of human decency and freedom for Jew and Catholic alike."

How did Coughlin come to revive the notorious document and resuscitate a villain most assumed was long buried? His biographer Donald Warren identifies the likely vehicle as none other than Coughlin's new friend, Ernest Liebold.[91] Indeed, Liebold was a constant source of material for the pages of Coughlin's magazine. Each week, he would provide the priest with his personal copy of Hitler's favorite magazine, *Der Sturmer*, the Jew-baiting German weekly, sporting the masthead slogan: "The Jews are our Misfortune." Inevitably, material from *Der Sturmer* would find its way into the pages of *Social Justice* or as a topic for the Radio Priest's weekly sermons. At the Nuremberg trials years later, a 1940 memo written by Joachim Ribbentrop was entered into evidence. Coughlin was a prime example, boasted Hitler's foreign minister, "of the far-reaching influence of Nazi propaganda."[92]

Father Coughlin was not the only Detroit clergyman caught up in Ford's web. In 1937, Ernest Liebold introduced Ford to another charismatic evangelical minister named Gerald L K Smith. Born in Wisconsin in 1898, Smith had earned his preaching credentials in the backwoods of Louisiana before coming to Detroit in the late thirties to combat the "Communist influence" of labor unions.[93] Not surprisingly, Henry Ford became a great admirer of the fiery minister and soon Ford funds were flowing into Smith's coffers. There is evidence that Ford gave Smith at least $2,000 to finance three of Smith's radio broadcasts and later loaned him several "investigators" to help compile a list of alleged union Communists. In return, Smith publicly assailed Ford's critics, whom he labeled "these cantankerous, repulsive, un-American agitators, these Communists, these racketeers, these Reds, who conspire against the spirit of America."[94]

As in the case of Coughlin, the connection between Ford and Smith appears to have been facilitated by Ernest Liebold. According to Smith's own account, he met Ford for the first time when "his personal secretary took me to meet him. He . . . became a great admirer of mine."[95] Smith would later claim that it was Ford who taught him the connection between Jews and Communism. When they first met in 1937, he explained, he was less anti-Semitic than Ford, who he said had gained insight into the Jewish Question because of an attempt by Jews to take over the Ford Motor Company.[96] After Ford told him, "No one can understand the issues of this hour unless he understands the Jewish Question," Smith read *The International Jew* and "embraced the research of Mr. Ford and became courageous enough . . . to use the words 'Communism is Jewish.'" Smith also claims Ford told him that he had never signed the original 1927 statement apologizing for publishing the *Dearborn Independent*.[97] Rather, Harry Bennett forged his name on the document. In his 1951 memoirs, Bennett would later confirm this claim.[98]

Although the two men would later become estranged,[99] Smith resolved to "keep Ford's memory alive" by publishing an abridged version during the forties and fifties of *The International Jew* with his own introduction. In this edition, Smith explains that years before, in the presence of Ernest Liebold, Ford had told him that he intended to republish the work one day. It is, in fact, Smith's version that to this day can be found on hundreds of Internet hate sites devoted to neo-Nazism, anti-Semitism, and Holocaust denial.[100]

While based in Detroit, Smith also established close political and financial ties to his fellow hate-mongers Charles Coughlin and Fritz Kuhn. Together, these men became a sinister force all their own.[101] Noting these close connections, the New York daily newspaper *PM* later wrote, "It may be significant that every time Hitler's efforts bogged down in New York, Chicago or other cities of substantial German-American population, men from Detroit, amply supplied with funds, revived them."[102]

What the newspaper failed to reveal is that each of these men had a common Detroit connection—Ernest Liebold.

On July 30, 1938, not long after the *Protocols* resurfaced in the pages of *Social Justice*, Henry Ford turned seventy-five. For his many admirers, it was a time to celebrate. Congratulatory telegrams poured in from around the globe and several Michigan towns even declared a holiday. In Dearborn, the occasion was festive. As Ford and his wife rode in an ancient 1908 Model T, eight thousand local schoolchildren sang "Happy Birthday" at the County Fair grounds, where the public was invited to share a giant birthday cake and celebrate the milestone. Hardly anybody noticed when Ford briefly slipped away from the festivities without explanation. He had to keep a scheduled appointment at his office with two distinguished foreign guests.

That afternoon, as Ernest Liebold and William Cameron beamed and a company photographer snapped photos, Ford was presented with an award from a longtime admirer. At Dearborn to present Ford with the prestigious decoration was Karl Kapp, German consul-general of Cleveland, and his colleague Fritz Hailer, the German consul of Detroit. On his seventy-fifth birthday, Henry Ford became the first American recipient of the Grand Cross of the Supreme Order of the German Eagle, created by Adolf Hitler a year earlier as the highest honor Germany could give a distinguished foreigner. The medal had previously been bestowed on only four other individuals, including Benito Mussolini.

Hailer opened the red leather box where the award was nestled—a golden Maltese cross surrounded by four small swastikas—while Kapp draped a red satin sash over Ford's white suit and then pinned the medal to his breast pocket.

In Neil Baldwin's account of the proceedings, Kapp then proceeded to read a formal citation from a parchment scroll signed by the Führer, "in recognition of Ford's pioneering auto work in motorization and in making autos available to the masses."[103] In fact, Kapp never actually said these words because the scroll said no such thing. In his otherwise meticulously researched book, Baldwin has been taken in by the clever manipulation of Ernest Liebold. His mistake is understandable. It is the same error made by the *Detroit Free Press* and the *New York Times* in their coverage of the event the following day.[104]

In fact, no newspaper had been there to cover the presentation itself. However, both papers sent a reporter to a gala birthday dinner at Detroit's Masonic Temple that evening, where Ford was feted by more than 1,400 prominent Detroit citizens. There, Liebold issued a press release announcing the German decoration and supplying the fabricated quote.

Buried deep in the Ford archives is the actual citation, a three-page document that contains no reference to Henry Ford "making autos available to the masses." The real citation is somewhat more ironic, perhaps accounting for Liebold's reluctance to publicize the actual words of the Nazi diplomat. The scroll presented by Hailer that afternoon stated that Ford was being presented with the award because of German admiration for his "humanitarian ideals" and his devotion "through many years to the cause of peace, like their Führer and Chancellor has done."[105] This proclamation had been personally signed by Adolf Hitler on July 7. That same week, Hitler had ordered the roundup and arrest of 4,000 Austrian Jews in what is often described as the first significant precursor of the Nazi Final Solution.[106] Many of the Jews arrested that week were sent to a newly opened concentration camp called Mauthausen just outside Hitler's Austrian birthplace, Linz, where most eventually perished.[107]

Three years after Ford received his German decoration, Liebold attempted to cement the deception, in case anybody should uncover his previous lie, by asking Fritz Hailer to write a letter stating that the award had been conferred "in recognition of [Ford's] pioneering in making motor cars available for the masses." On April 25, 1941, Hailer obliged in this charade, supplying Liebold with a letter bearing the fabricated phrase. "Trusting that this will comply with your request," he added.[108]

Even with the innocuous citation, the fallout from Ford's acceptance of the Nazi medal was devastating. The cries of denunciation arose almost immediately. The popular Hollywood entertainer Eddie Cantor fired the first salvo, calling Ford a "damn fool" for accepting the medal. "I question the Americanism of Henry Ford for accepting a citation from the biggest gangster in the world. Doesn't he realize that the German papers, reporting the citation, said all Americans were behind Nazism? Whose side is Mr. Ford on? I question his Americanism and his Christianity . . . The more men like Ford we have, the more we must organize and fight."[109]

Three days later, the Jewish War Veterans of the United States urged Ford to repudiate the award: "This act on your part can only be interpreted as an endorsement by you of the barbarous, indecent, and irreligious Nazi program and philosophy."[110]

Ford was undaunted by the attacks. According to his associate Emil Zoerlein, "All Ford said to me was, 'They sent me this ribbon band. They told me to return it or else I'm not American. I'm going to keep it.' "[111]

Ford stubbornly insisted on keeping the medal, but his acceptance was clearly having an impact on the company's bottom line. Repeating the pattern of the early twenties, sales of Ford and Lincoln cars dropped to a new low. The slump was being particularly felt in the company's eastern sales region, home to the largest Jewish population in the United States. A nationwide Maxon poll found that 80.3 percent of the male American public had heard Ford was an anti-Semite. Another poll reported he had so thoroughly alienated American Jews that they had virtually stopped buying his cars. An internal company investigation concluded that the decline in sales was directly attributable to "an active and effective boycott" of Ford products by Jews and other Americans unsympathetic to the industrialist's views.[112] The report also found that in Hollywood, Jewish executives agreed to ban all Ford units from their studio lots and forbade employees and stars to buy Ford products. According to the *Jackson* (Mississippi) *News*, "Millions of persons regarded Henry Ford as an implacable enemy of the Jewish race."[113] The company's sales division was alarmed by these findings and urged Ford to make a public statement to placate the critics and undo the damage.

The last time Ford's anti-Semitism threatened the financial livelihood of the company, a decade earlier, he was forced to publicly retract his hate-mongering views. It was clear that such a tactic would not work again. Subtler measures were called for this time, reasoned his advisers. The solution was devised by Ford's longtime fixer Harry Bennett, who contacted Ford's old neighbor, Rabbi Leo Franklin. For years, Rabbi Franklin had been writing letters in vain to company headquarters protesting the continued distribution of *The International Jew*. His protests were ignored. Now, Franklin was summoned to Dearborn under the guise that Ford had expressed deep concern over the plight of Jewish refugees from Germany.

On November 13, 1938, Ford convened a meeting in his Dearborn office with Rabbi Franklin, Bennett, and Harry Newman, a Jewish All-American football player who worked for Bennett's Service Department during the off-season. Ford began the meeting by explaining that he wished to hire as many Jewish refugees as possible to help ease the plight of "these displaced people." The rabbi was requested to act as an intermediary and release a letter to the public announcing the decision.[114]

Ford's statement, completed two days later, appeared sincere. It condemned the persecution of Jews in Germany, treatment that "didn't reflect the will of the people but a few Nazi leaders." America, it stated, was the "haven of the oppressed" and Ford pledged to do his utmost to give the displaced Jew "an opportunity to rebuild his life." Neither Rabbi Franklin nor any of the other participants seemed to note the irony of the letter's closing paragraph. "Those who have known me for many years," it read, "realize that anything that breeds hate is repulsive to me."[115]

Rabbi Franklin apparently believed that Ford was at last prepared to atone for his past intolerance. The rabbi personally delivered the letter to two Detroit newspapers, which reported Ford's humanitarian gesture on their front pages the next day.

In 1927, the last time Ford had moved to rehabilitate his image among American Jews with his apology and retraction, his subsequent actions demonstrated that his private views hadn't changed at all. Indeed, he had come to resent the Jews all the more for forcing him to pander to their power as consumers. For Ford, history was repeating itself.

Three days later, a small item on the hiring plan appeared in Father Coughlin's magazine *Social Justice*, warning its readers not to believe what they had heard:

> Social Justice sent its investigators to ascertain the facts of the case. 1) The direct quotation carried in the paper is totally inaccurate and was not written by Mr. Ford but was composed by Rabbi Franklin. 2) Rabbi Franklin came to see Mr. Ford to ask him if his factory would assimilate Jewish refugees, the result of Nazi persecution. Mr. Ford said that there was no persecution of Jews in Nazi Germany.[116]

On his radio show that Sunday, Coughlin launched a vitriolic attack on international Jewish bankers and "devious Jews" such as Rabbi Leo Franklin, repeating the charges that had appeared in *Social Justice*. The letter, he revealed, was not written by Ford, but by Dr. Franklin himself. The priest went on to claim that, according to Harry Bennett, the rabbi had come to the Ford factory to ask if they would assimilate Jewish refugees, the victims of Nazi persecution. "Mr. Ford said that he believed there was little or no persecution in Germany; if any, it was not due to the German government, but to warmongers, the international bankers," Coughlin told his listeners.[117]

An outraged Rabbi Franklin immediately contacted Bennett and urged him to wire the media refuting Coughlin's claim. Bennett refused.[118] Instead, when the press followed up on Coughlin's accusation the next day, Bennett appeared to corroborate the priest's story and also absolved the Nazis of persecution: "Mr. Ford did not attack the German government and did not mention Nazism; and any persecution, if there was any, was not the fault of Hitler or the Nazis."

Had a trap been set for the rabbi? Bennett's denial was a public relations masterpiece, one that neatly pleased the bigot and the bleeding heart alike. According to Ford's biographer Keith Sward:

It cast Ford in a double image. To Jews and anti-Nazis and haters of racial brutishness—and to potential boycotters of the Ford car—the folk hero had been held up once more as the friend of the oppressed, the protector of the little man. But anti-Semites and pro-Nazis and other assorted enemies of democracy had it on the authority of Father Coughlin that the Ford-Franklin interview meant nothing of the sort. It meant only that a wily Jew had put one over on Ford.[119]

When Rabbi Franklin publicly protested that Ford had indeed expressed solidarity with Jewish refugees, he received an official letter from Edward James Smythe, chairman of the Protestant War Veterans of the United States: "You are a liar and you know it. Your tribe has declared war on Christian America. If Henry Ford had said it, he would not have let you give it to the press but would issue it through his publicity bureau."[120]

As Ford continued by stealth to pursue the campaign he had initiated almost two decades earlier, his lieutenant Ernest Liebold remained behind the scenes carefully orchestrating its strategy. And while Ford was being pilloried by the public and the press for his acceptance of the Nazi medal, little attention was given to a quiet ceremony held at Detroit's Harmonie Society Hall on October 12, 1938. On that evening, Detroit's German Consul Fritz Hailer presented Liebold with the Order of the German Eagle, the same medal he had awarded Henry Ford less than three months earlier, but a slightly lesser grade. Like Ford's decoration, the award came with a personal proclamation from Adolf Hitler.[121] In his acceptance speech, Liebold could hardly contain his enthusiasm, declaring his "true friendship" with the German government:

An occasion of this kind becomes one of the outstanding events in our life's history, and leaves an everlasting impression upon our memory . . . This event is all the more important with such recognition coming from a great Commonwealth of 75 million people, who through their Führer and Chancellor, have thus conferred on me the Emblem of the First Order of The German Eagle . . . I ask that you convey to the Führer and Chancellor of the German Reich . . . my humble expressions of sincere gratitude.[122]

CHAPTER 6

HISTORY'S STAGE

Lindbergh's flirtation with Nazism began with his first visit to the Third Reich in 1936. Here, he shakes hands with an unidentified Nazi at a Berlin reception.

By the fall of 1938, as the world stood poised on the brink of war, Charles Lindbergh was about to find himself vaulted onto history's stage in a role once the exclusive preserve of politicians and diplomats. His sole credentials appeared to stem from a thirty-three-hour transatlantic flight. A decade after his celebrated achievement, his remaining claim to fame was fame itself.

In March that year, Adolf Hitler issued a successful ultimatum to Austria's chancellor Kurt von Schuschnigg demanding he resign and allow a Nazi puppet government to take over. Hitler made clear that if this demand wasn't accepted, his troops would march into Austria. Effectively cowed, the annexation of Austria (the *Anschluss*) was soon completed without a shot being fired. Within a month after German anti-Semitic laws were applied in Austria, more than 500 Austrian Jews had committed suicide.

With Austria now integrated into Nazi Germany, its tiny neighbor Czechoslovakia suddenly found itself surrounded on three sides—a prime target for further Nazi expansion.[1] Before long, rumors were rife of German troop concentrations massing near the Czech border.[2]

Slowly rousing from their complacency, European leaders now viewed the possibility of German expansion with alarm. Leaders of Russia, France, and England—who had expressed barely a whimper after the *Anschluss*—warned Hitler to back off.

Emboldened by their callow acquiescence up to this point, the German Chancellor loudly denied that he had any aggressive intentions

153

toward the Czech republic. But on May 28, he summoned his principal military and political advisers to Berlin and declared, "It is my unshakable will that Czechoslovakia shall be wiped off the map. First we will tackle the situation in the East. Then I will give you three to four years' time, and then we will settle the situation in the West."[3] The latter instruction clearly referred to war against England and France. He instructed his generals to draw up a plan for the invasion of Czechoslovakia by the end of September.

The Führer's initial designs centered on the Sudetenland, a small section of Czechoslovakia bordering Germany whose inhabitants were primarily ethnic Germans.

With covert support from Hitler's SS, a faction of pro-Nazi Sudeten Germans began in late summer to foment a rebellion, launching a number of terrorist attacks as well as frequent marches and rallies calling for Sudeten integration with Germany. The Czech militia was dispatched to forcefully repress the unrest.

Exploiting these reprisals as an excuse, the German propaganda machine launched a carefully orchestrated campaign, demanding justice for the "persecuted" Sudeten Germans and incorporation of the Sudetenland into the Greater German Reich.[4] In June, British prime minister Neville Chamberlain, desperately anxious to avoid a confrontation with Hitler, privately admitted that Britain favored ceding the Sudetenland to Germany "in the interests of peace."[5] His country was committed by treaty to defend the Czechs, but only if France committed itself as well. The French cabinet was still wavering. Chamberlain feared the crisis might escalate into another world war and appeared willing to sacrifice land for peace.[6]

Meanwhile, the Czech president Eduard Benes had no intention of giving up the Sudetenland without a fight, reasoning that such a concession would deprive his country of a fortified frontier against the Germans, and he resolutely resisted British pressure to yield to Hitler.

By September, with the situation at an impasse, Benes took to the airwaves appealing for calm and peace. He asked the Czech people to be "firm and have faith in our state, in its health and its strength, in the indestructible spirit and devotion of its people." It was the plea of a desperate politician. The Nazis, frustrated in their plans for another bloodless coup, were furious. Hermann Göring responded to the Czech leader's speech with his own declaration: "This miserable pygmy race without culture, no one knows where it came from, is oppressing a cultured people and behind it is Moscow and the eternal mask of the Jew devil."[7]

The standoff continued.

Hitler himself addressed the situation a week later in a speech to the Nazi Congress in Nuremberg. He railed against the Czechs' intransigence, but appeared to downplay the possibility of military action. However, that week a fresh outbreak of riots in the Sudetenland, and a retaliatory declaration of martial law, prompted the Sudeten German leader Konrad Henlein, acting on Hitler's orders, to issue his own ultimatum.[8] Rescind martial law, recall the reserves to their barracks, and withdraw the state police from the territory, Henlein demanded, or Benes would be responsible for "further developments."[9] There were few doubts in the mind of the Czech, or the British leader for that matter, about the meaning of these words and the consequences of ignoring his ultimatum: War.

The series of events that would embroil Charles Lindbergh in the developing Czech crisis took root soon after he returned from his first visit to Germany in August 1936. His tour of the Reich seems to have ignited a spark. For the first time since the death of his son, Lindbergh appeared animated and optimistic about the future.

"Our visit to Germany was one of the most interesting we have ever made," he wrote Truman Smith on August 6 to thank him for the hospitality the Smiths had extended him and Anne during their stay. "Not alone because of the aviation developments but from many other standpoints as well, I think Germany is in many ways the most interesting nation in the world today, and that she is attempting to find a solution for some of our most fundamental problems."[10]

While he still had some "reservations," Lindbergh wrote, he had come away from his visit with feelings of great admiration for the Germans. The condition of the country left him with the impression that "Hitler must have far more character and vision than I thought existed in the German leader, who has been painted in so many different ways by the accounts in America and England."[11]

The letter, written on a brief stopover in Denmark before the couple even returned to England, initiated a long exchange of correspondence between the two men, who appear to have established a lasting bond during Lindbergh's stay in Berlin.

Smith began to send his new friend reading material updating Lindbergh on the German political situation and, before long, the Lindberghs were inviting the Smiths to visit them in England and writing long breezy letters about their activities. In his letters, Lindbergh repeatedly expresses his wish to visit Germany again.

Meanwhile, he had become an enthusiastic correspondent with a number of Americans involved in the U.S. aircraft industry, describing his positive impressions of German aviation developments.

Smith would later note that Washington "was at last aware of the imposing rearmament program in Germany." Their previous skepticism, he claims, had suddenly "vanished." He implies that this change was brought about by Lindbergh's visit to Germany and his subsequent letters to civilian and military friends.[12] The year 1937 saw the beginning of a virtual pilgrimage of prominent American aviation personalities to Germany, all eager to see for themselves the leap forward in German air technology that Lindbergh had described.

During the summer of 1937, a request from Hermann Göring arrived at Smith's office. Could Lindbergh be "induced" to attend the Lilienthal Aeronautical Society congress in Munich that October?[13] This, according to Smith, was the excuse he had been awaiting, an opportunity to invite Lindbergh for a second visit.

On October 11, Charles and Anne landed their private plane at Prien airfield, thirty miles southeast of Munich. For the duration of the five-day congress, they were hosted by Baron and Baroness Kramer-Klett at their medieval castle, high in the Bavarian Alps. At the Lindberghs' request, Truman and Kay Smith were also to stay at the castle.

Six days before the Lindberghs arrived in Germany, President Roosevelt had delivered a major foreign policy speech in Chicago warning Americans against their continued isolationism. He spoke of the need to "quarantine the aggressors" and urged the community of peace-loving nations to halt the epidemic of world lawlessness.[14]

"War is a contagion, whether it be declared or undeclared," the President stated. "It can engulf states and peoples remote from the original scene of hostilities. Yes, we are determined to keep out of war, yet we cannot insure ourselves against the disastrous effects of war and the dangers of involvement." It was FDR's first public warning to Hitler, who had formally abrogated the Versailles Treaty the previous January. During the interval between Lindbergh's first visit to Germany in July 1936 and his second visit fifteen months later, the Nazis had stripped German Jews of nearly all their remaining rights, including the right to receive a university degree and study medicine.

When the Lilienthal Congress ended on October 16, the Lindberghs accompanied the Smiths back to Berlin where they planned on staying another week as guests of the attaché and his wife. There, Lindbergh embarked on a rather unusual round of sightseeing. Instead of touring museums, cathedrals and monuments, however, he accepted the invitation of Göring's air ministry to inspect the latest additions to the *Luftwaffe's* growing arsenal.

Each day, Lindbergh and Smith were brought to a number of secret aircraft installations where the Germans demonstrated their new bomber, fighter and reconnaissance planes. Lindbergh was even permitted to enter and examine the cockpit of the *Junkers*, the *Messerschmitt*, the *Storch*, and the *Focke-Wulfe* and, at least on one occasion, was invited to take the controls.

Like a kid in a candy store, he delighted in his access to these magnificent aircraft—the first American allowed to view the rapid development of Göring's state-of-the-art fleet. As he toured one hangar after another, he made notes of his impressions: "Design awkward," he jotted after seeing the new Junkers 87. Of the Dornier 17, he proclaims, "Very clean lines." After putting the Storch liaison plane through its paces in a twenty-minute solo flight, he concluded that it was far better than anything of its kind in the United States.[15] Each evening, the Lindberghs were wined, dined and feted by their air ministry hosts.

Shortly before Lindbergh left Berlin at the conclusion of his two-week German stay, Smith made a request of his houseguest. He wondered if Lindbergh might help him prepare a formal intelligence report for Washington, summarizing his conclusions about the progress of German aviation. Lindbergh's expertise, he claimed, could help offset his own "limitations in the air field." Together, they prepared the document that would become known officially as Report #15540, "The General Estimate of Germany's Air Power of Nov. 1, 1937." Smith later emphasized that much of the report was written "in Lindbergh's exact words" but he may have been attempting to distance himself from what had already become a controversial document.

Both men, wrote Smith, were convinced "it was high time that America should awaken to a realization of the German air potential, to the ever-growing, ever improving *Luftwaffe*."[16] The report is written in sensational terms rarely found in an official intelligence document. The burst in aircraft production is described as "miraculous"; German industry is of a "literally amazing" size; Germany's "astounding" growth "must be accounted one of the most important world events of our time."

The report goes on to chastise the British for their policy of "smugness" and declares the German air industry superior to that of both France and England.

Lindbergh's influence is clearly evident in a sentence which credits the technical and scientific skill of the "race" in achieving the "fantastically" large air force. Since his collaboration with Alexis Carrel and his introduction to eugenics several years earlier, he had begun to couch many of his arguments in racial terms.

Near the end of the report, Lindbergh and Smith issue an estimate of the actual size of the German air force, guessing that the *Luftwaffe* possessed an impressive 175 to 225 squadrons and 2,400 first-line planes. The report concludes with an ominous warning that Germany was poised to eclipse American air superiority, especially if the United States made "a single blunder" or allowed political considerations to impede her development.[17]

Lindbergh returned to England on October 25 but his joint report would soon have significant consequences on the other side of the Atlantic, where it achieved wide circulation in the U.S. War Department within days of its dispatch. A bombshell had been dropped and the report's "startling conclusions" were on everyone's lips when the military attaché traveled to Washington on leave a month later. "Finally," Smith wrote, "German air strength was accepted as a fact." Lindbergh's visit had achieved its desired effect. No longer would Smith's warnings of German military superiority be met with skepticism by his superiors.

In later years, Lindbergh's defenders would claim that his visits to Germany were clandestine missions to secure secret military intelligence data on behalf of the United States government. But Lindbergh himself seems to disabuse this notion in a November 1937 letter to Smith discussing his recent visit. "Ever since I have been in Europe," he writes, "I have made a point of not attempting to get military information which was not offered freely. I certainly would not want to go to any country as a guest and impose upon my hosts by prying into information which they considered secret."[18]

Indeed, he specifies that he asked permission of the Germans to share what he had seen because "I did not want to in any way impose on their confidence after I left the country. Their reply was that they had no objection to my discussing the things I had seen with our own people."[19]

Lindbergh's admiration for Germany had not waned. Germany and Italy are the "two most virile countries in Europe today," he wrote in a letter to his financial adviser Harry Davison.[20] The Nazis' fanaticism still disturbed him but this was overshadowed by their "sense of decency and values which in many ways is far ahead of our own." This especially hit home when he walked "among the headlines of murder, rape, and divorce on the billboards of London."

He began spending more time with Alexis Carrel at the doctor's private island, St. Gildas, off the Brittany coast. The two were collaborating on a book called *The Culture of Organs*, which elaborated on their joint scientific research. By this time, Carrel's own fascist leanings were becoming more pronounced. He was a strong supporter of François de la Rocque and his right-wing *Croix de Feu* movement, which had emerged as a powerful force in pre-war French politics. In 1938, Carrel wrote a letter to a friend, stating his refusal to condemn the Austrian *Anschluss*, and criticizing instead "the enormous Bolshevist and Jewish pressure" to start a war.[21]

On May 9, 1938, three weeks before Hitler vowed to wipe Czechoslovakia off the face of the map, Lindbergh sent a letter to Smith thanking him for a report that updated the German situation. This unspecified report apparently made quite an impression, for the tone of his letter differs markedly from their previous correspondence. As Lindbergh later described it, "Nazi Germany was forcing a reorientation of my thought."[22]

In the letter, he has harsh words for Americans and Britons who "blind themselves to all but the worst of German qualities. They are not even willing to recognize that the Germans are our type of people and that, as such, they will be to us either a powerful friend or a dangerous enemy. From either standpoint, they are entitled to a respect which we do not give them."[23]

Midway through the letter, there is a passage that clearly demonstrates the increasing influence of either Carrel or the National Socialists, or both, on Lindbergh's thinking. Describing the recently formed German-Italian Axis, Lindbergh asks Smith if he agrees that "the vulnerable point in this relationship will lie in the difference in *race*."[24] This assertion appears puzzling at first glance. The Italians, after all, are white Europeans like the Germans. But the implication is clear. Race, as Carrel and the Nazis defined it, was not color in the traditional sense. Rather, Italians were racially inferior to Germans because they were not "Aryan," a distinction made by several Nazi racial theorists at the time. In his letter to Smith, Lindbergh appears to echo this bizarre view.

The rambling eighteen-page letter ends with an epiphany of sorts:

> I have become so greatly interested in Germany, and I regard her as being of such great importance in our lives and in our children's lives, that I am willing to make most other things secondary to anything I can do to learn more about Germany, her people and her government. I am extremely anxious to understand more about everything German. In fact, I am seriously considering the possibility of making our home in Germany . . . [25]

Only a week before he wrote this extraordinary letter, Lindbergh had been invited to spend the weekend at the Cliveden estate of Lord and Lady Astor. It was on this visit that Charles Lindbergh became an unofficial member of the "Cliveden Set," a term that journalist Claud Cockburn had coined the year before in the British periodical the *Week*. The "Set" referred to a gathering of powerful politicians, bankers, writers, journalists and aristocrats who regularly assembled at the Astors' Cliveden country estate and at their London mansion in St. James Square. Cockburn frequently portrayed the Astors' circle as a pro-German nest of traitors, a Nazi Fifth Column. Today, they are more likely to be referred to as the "Cliveden Myth" because of Cockburn's pro-Communist bias and frequently exaggerated claims.[26]

An old friend of Anne's mother, Nancy Astor was Britain's first female Member of Parliament and the archenemy of her fellow Conservative politician, Winston Churchill. She also had a long-standing reputation as an anti-Semite. Once, after a 1938 Foreign Affairs Committee meeting, Conservative MP Alan Graham chided Astor for bad behavior. Her retort was, "Only a Jew like you would dare to be rude to me."[27]

The Astors were spectacularly well connected. Nancy's brother-in-law John Jacob Astor was the owner of the powerful *London Times*; their friends included King Edward VIII, British Prime Minister Neville Chamberlain, and the foreign secretary Lord Halifax. And for a time, it appeared that an inordinate number of visitors to Cliveden shared a common belief: that Germany was Europe's best hope to contain the threat of Communist expansion. That is not to say they were necessarily Nazis, as Claud Cockburn charged, so much as to assign them the label that later became synonymous with the Cliveden Set: "Appeasers."

Many believed that Germany had legitimate grievances over the harsh terms of the Versailles Treaty. They didn't think they were doing Britain any harm by saying so publicly. As Nancy Astor wrote in a British newspaper at the end of 1937: "I have desired to restore a sense of security in Europe by treating Germany as an equal. I have worked for the reversal of the policy of goading her people and rulers into restlessness by trying to keep them in a state of inferiority."[28] Integral to this approach was a tendency to downplay the excesses of the Nazi regime.

According to Cliveden regular Thomas Jones, Lady Astor told him that America misunderstood the British attempt to reach a settlement with Germany because of "intensive and widespread anti-German propaganda being conducted by those Jews and Communists. Newspapers are influenced by those firms which advertise so largely in the press and are frequently under Jewish control. One can detect Communist inspiration and promptings, of which most people are quite oblivious."[29]

London Times editor, and Cliveden regular, Geoffrey Dawson was later accused of censoring any information critical of Germany from articles submitted by his reporters. *Times* Berlin correspondent Norman Ebbutt wrote frequently of Hitler's rearmament plans but his dispatches rarely found their way into the newspaper. William Shirer, who was an American correspondent in Germany at the time, noted in his diary: "Ebbutt has complained to me several times in private that the *Times* does not print all he sends, that it does not want to hear too much of the bad side of Nazi Germany and has been captured by pro-Nazis in London."[30]

What Cockburn failed to point out in his frequent attacks on the Cliveden Set was that the Astors' guests also included a number of individuals who could not reasonably be accused of pro-German sympathies, including a number of left-wing politicians. As Cliveden regular Thomas Jones wrote in his diary: "Such was the variety and individuality of the persons gathered that the notion of their forming a Cliveden Set was as grotesque as it would be to expect unity among the passengers of a Cunarder."[31]

Nevertheless, Nancy's preference for visitors who agreed with her political views was undeniable. According to her biographer Christopher Sykes, "These friends were not traitors; they were not Nazis; but until mid-March 1939, they were believers in, and ardent publicists for, Chamberlain's Appeasement policy."[32] Many were also undeniably sympathetic to Adolf Hitler and his policies.

During the weekend in May 1938 that Charles and Anne spent at Cliveden, much of the conversation centered on Germany. At tea that Sunday, Lindbergh sat next to Lady Astor who, he later wrote, wanted "a better understanding of Germany. I was encouraged about the feeling of most of the people there in regard to Germany. They understood the situation better than most Englishmen do these days."[33]

Four days later, he and Anne were invited to lunch at the Astors' London home. Lindbergh's acceptance into the Cliveden circle was confirmed. His luncheon companions that afternoon were the American ambassador to France William Bullitt; Nancy's friend George Bernard Shaw, who had recently expressed publicly a great admiration for Adolf Hitler; Geoffrey Dawson, editor of the London *Times*; and the man who was to become an important political player in the events to come, American ambassador to Britain Joseph Kennedy. The colorful American had been appointed by President Roosevelt to the Court of St. James two months earlier, where he and his young family had already made quite an impression on the British.

Unbeknownst to Roosevelt, who was himself becoming increasingly alarmed at the Nazi threat, Kennedy had already formed strong views on the European situation that were not necessarily in accord with those of the Administration. Only six days earlier, Kennedy had written a private note to the isolationist U.S. senator William Borah expressing his position on Hitler's expansionism: "The more I see of things here," he wrote, "the more convinced I am that we must exert all our intelligence and effort toward keeping clear of any kind of involvement. As long as I hold my present job, I shall never lose sight of this guiding principle."[34]

Kennedy's views on Germany and Jews appeared to mesh closely with those of Lady Astor, who had adopted the ambassador as another member of her Set. Their correspondence during this period offers a revealing insight into their mutual attitudes toward the plight of European Jews. In 1938, Nancy wrote Kennedy that Hitler would have to do more than just "give a rough time" to "the killers of Christ" before she'd be in favor of "launching Armageddon to save them. The wheel of history swings around as the Lord would have it. Who are we to stand in the way of the future?" Kennedy replied that he expected the American "Jew media" to become a problem in the near future and that "Jewish pundits in New York and Los Angeles" were already making noises designed to "set a match to the fuse of the world."[35]

For two hours, Lindbergh listened with fascination to the views of the gathered guests. Naturally, Germany dominated the discussion. When he returned to Long Barn that evening, he recorded the day's events in the journal he had recently begun to compile. The American ambassador appears to have made a particularly strong impression: "Kennedy interested me greatly. He is not the usual type of politician or diplomat. His views on the European situation seem intelligent and interesting. I hope to see more of him."[36]

How much influence Lindbergh's Cliveden discussions had on his political evolution is difficult to assess. But only five days after his visit with the Astors, Lindbergh wrote the letter to Smith announcing that he had made Germany his new priority. His growing obsession is described in the diary of Lindbergh's British landlord, Harold Nicolson:

> Lindbergh is most pessimistic. He says that we cannot possibly fight since we should certainly be beaten. The German Air Force is ten times superior to that of Russia, France and Great Britain put together. Our defenses are simply futile and the barrage-balloons a mere waste of money. He thinks we should just give way and then make an alliance with Germany. To a certain extent his views can be discounted, a) because he naturally believes that aeroplanes will be the determinant factor in war; and b) because he believes in the Nazi theology, all tied up with his hatred of

degeneracy and his hatred of democracy as represented by the free press and the American public. But even when one makes these discounts, the fact remains that he is probably right that we are outmastered in the air.[37]

Soon after, the Lindberghs decided to leave England and purchase a small private island, Illiec, off the coast of Brittany, to be closer to the Carrels, who owned the adjoining island. From this base, they would search for a home in Berlin in which to spend the winter.

By the time he actually left England in June 1938, Lindbergh appears to have become completely disillusioned with the British, an attitude that would play no small part in events to come. With the exception of his new friends, the Astors, and other like-minded Englishmen, he had little good to say about the country where he had spent his three-year self-imposed exile. "I believe the assets in English character lie in confidence rather than ability; tenacity rather than strength; and determination rather than intelligence," he wrote in his journal. "It is necessary to realize that England is a country composed of a great mass of slow, somewhat stupid and indifferent people, and a small group of geniuses." These sentiments may reflect the growing influence of Alexis Carrel, who continued to expound his belief that society must be governed by the elite and that democracy was undesirable because of the inferiority of the masses. Lindbergh singled out the British as an example of this phenomenon. But he had been living in England for three years when these views began to crystallize. It is possible that he would have come to the same conclusion about Americans if he had been living in the United States at the time.

In his newly adopted French island home, Lindbergh spent most of his time with Carrel discussing Germany and "race betterment." Their scientific collaboration took a back seat to concerns arising from the growing threat of a European war. "Why spend time on biological experiments when our very civilization was at stake, when one of history's greatest cataclysms impended?" he despaired.[38]

In late August, at the behest of the American air attaché in London, Lindbergh agreed to embark on a tour of the Soviet Union to survey its progress in aviation. For two weeks, he and Anne toured Kiev, Odessa, Rostov, and Moscow. Their Russian hosts were less inclined to show off their secret air force installations than the Germans had been and Lindbergh was singularly unimpressed by what he had seen. In his journal entries each evening, he had harsh words for almost everything Russian, from the quality of the food, to the art, to their policy of training women in air combat. In stark contrast to his receptive attitude during similar tours of Germany, he dismissed everything the Russians showed him as "Soviet propaganda at its worst." This system, he concluded, "will not work."[39] His harshest judgments were reserved for the state of the Russian air force, which he declared was in a pitiful condition, even though he had not been shown the Soviets' most modern aircraft.

From the Soviet Union, the couple flew to Czechoslovakia in early September, just as the Czech crisis was heating up. It is unclear who arranged the Czech itinerary but, throughout the trip, Lindbergh's journals refer almost exclusively to Czechs who apparently sympathized with German annexation of the Sudetenland. "We were told the Czech army in Sudeten territory had acted more as an army of occupation than protection," he writes on September 4, echoing the Nazi propaganda that filled the German newspapers each day.[40]

On September 8, the Lindberghs returned to Paris, flying directly into the political storm that was about to engulf the continent. That day, talks between the pro-Nazi Sudeten German Party and the Czech government had broken down, leaving the situation on tenterhooks. A day earlier, an editorial in the pro-Appeasement London *Times* advocated cession of the Sudetenland to Germany. But Czech president Eduard Benes was intransigent and war appeared inevitable. On May 30, Hitler had issued a secret directive to his generals, "Operation Green," preparing for a German invasion of Czechoslovakia at the beginning of October.

If Germany did invade, the key question was whether England and France would live up to their treaty obligation and intervene militarily. Both countries were required to come to the rescue of Czechoslovakia, but only by mutual agreement. If either country balked, the Czechs would be left to fend for themselves.

Lindbergh dined the following evening with the French Air Minister Guy La Chambre at the Paris home of U.S. ambassador William C. Bullitt. He was well aware that France's decision was critical, and believed he had to act quickly. He had briefly toured a number of French aircraft factories two years earlier and had come away unimpressed with the state of the French air force. He was convinced that, like England, France was no military match for Germany. Historian Telford Taylor has noted that until that evening, Lindbergh's pronouncements had been those of an influential, but unofficial, American: "Now . . . Lindbergh's opinions appeared to become a part, by no means unimportant, of the official voice of America."[41]

Conversation at dinner centered almost exclusively on a comparison between French and German aviation. Repeatedly, Lindbergh stressed his belief that the French situation was desperate. He warned that it would be impossible to catch up to Germany's air strength for years, if at all. Germany, he claimed, was building 500 to 800 war planes per month while France was producing 45 to 50 and England no more than 70. The only conclusion to be drawn, he told the French minister, is that the German air fleet was stronger than that of all other European countries combined.[42]

La Chambre left the dinner shaken. France had already received a number of similarly sensational reports from its own intelligence sources, but had always been inclined to discount them as unreliable. Now, a seemingly unimpeachable eyewitness source was confirming the worst. The French government was well aware of the shortcomings of its own fleet but had no idea of how it compared to the German air force at the time. How could France and England thwart German designs on Czechoslovakia when the two countries were so clearly outpowered? It would surely be military suicide. The following day, La Chambre reported the alarming prognosis to his cabinet colleagues, who were in the midst of a heated debate about the wisdom of defying Hitler. According to Taylor, whose book *Munich* is considered one of the definitive accounts of the Czech crisis,[43] Lindbergh's warning was the decisive factor in French Foreign Minister Georges Bonnet's sudden turnaround. Bonnet declared that "peace must be preserved at any price as neither France nor Great Britain were ready for war."[44]

The Lindberghs returned to Illiec to spend time with the Carrels and observe the European developments unfold from a distance.

At a Nuremberg rally speech on September 12, delivered before a full stadium of the delirious Nazi faithful, Hitler demanded that the Czechs accept German claims to the Sudetenland, but he stopped short of a war proclamation. Instead, he declared that the Sudeten problem was an internal matter which concerned only the German minority in Bohemia and the Czechoslovak government. But this was all merely part of his carefully constructed "Operation Green" strategy, to sit tight until a "convenient excuse" and "adequate political justification" occurred to spark an attack. This excuse came the following day when, at Berlin's careful instigation, riots broke out in the disputed territory. Predictably, the Czech army responded with brutal ferocity and Benes declared martial law.[45]

A divided French cabinet convened and spent hours debating whether the country should honor its obligations in case of a German attack. Lindbergh's warnings of German air superiority weighed heavily over the proceedings; arguments that the Nazis must be stopped at any price were countered by others adamant that the French and British were no match for Hitler's military.[46]

In England, Chamberlain was emphatic. He was convinced of German military invincibility. Fighting Germany, he told his divided Cabinet, would be like "a man attacking a tiger before he loaded his gun."[47] He favored a compromise that would cede the Sudetenland to Germany in exchange for a guarantee against further expansion, as if Hitler could be relied on to respect the next line drawn in the shifting sand.

Across the Atlantic, President Roosevelt lamented to his own Cabinet that Chamberlain was "for peace at any price," and predicted that England and France, washing the "blood from their Judas Iscariot hands," would leave Czechoslovakia to Hitler's mercy. Sure enough, Chamberlain wired Hitler on September 13 requesting a meeting to discuss German demands. Two days later, the British prime minister flew to Berchtesgaden to meet with the Führer, who immediately demanded England's consent for cession of the Sudetenland. Chamberlain could not commit to the idea without consulting both his Cabinet and the French government. But, to Hitler's delight, he said he recognized "the principle of the detachment of the Sudeten areas." He returned to England intent on pressing his Cabinet toward approving this option. Hitler promised to refrain from any military action until they met again.

On September 18, French prime minister Edouard Daladier and his foreign minister, Georges Bonnet, arrived in London to meet with the British Cabinet and discuss Chamberlain's proposal. After a lengthy debate, both sides at last agreed to Hitler's demands. All territories more than fifty percent inhabited by Sudeten Germans would be turned over to Germany to ensure "the maintenance of the peace and the safety of Czechoslovakia's vital interests." Without a military guarantee from England and France, Czechoslovakia would have no choice but to accept.

On September 22, Chamberlain met Hitler at Godesberg, Germany, to inform him of the joint Anglo-French acquiescence. Public opinion in Britain was deeply opposed to the agreement, which it perceived as a sell-out of the Czechs. Nevertheless, Chamberlain remained convinced it was a small price to pay for peace. He informed the Führer his demands had been met.

But, encouraged by the ease with which the English and French had backed down, Hitler sensed the time was ripe to press on with greater demands. To the Prime Minister's astonishment, his German counterpart informed him that he was "terribly sorry" but the plan was "no longer of any use."[48] Hitler would accept nothing less than a complete German occupation of the Sudetenland.

Chamberlain was shattered. The peace he had assiduously forged almost single-handedly was collapsing "like a house of cards."[49] There were limits to how far even Chamberlain could go to avoid a fight. It appeared England and France now had no choice but to honor their treaty obligation to Czechoslovakia. War seemed imminent.

It was Lindbergh's turn to enter the political stage. On September 19, he received an urgent cable from Joseph Kennedy requesting that he fly to London immediately for consultation. Two days later, he arrived with Anne for a luncheon with the American ambassador. In his journal entry that evening, Lindbergh described the mood:

> Everyone in Embassy is extremely worried. Hitler is apparently ready to invade Czechoslovakia and has his divisions on his border. Hitler told Chamberlain (according to Kennedy) that he would risk a world war if necessary. Kennedy says England is ready to fight, even though not prepared. Chamberlain realizes the disastrous effects of a war with Germany at this time and is making every effort to avoid one. English opinion [says Kennedy] is pushing him toward war.[50]

After lunch, Kennedy told Lindbergh why he had been summoned on such short notice. He needed a report immediately on the state of German aviation.

Documents that have surfaced in recent years reveal that Kennedy's views deviated significantly from U.S. foreign policy. During a visit with German ambassador Herbert von Dirksen three months earlier, Kennedy had assured the ambassador that Roosevelt was unflinchingly opposed to the Nazi regime only because his informants were ill-advised and afraid of the Jews. He promised von Dirksen—who subsequently called Kennedy "Germany's best friend in London"—that he would enlighten the President himself, a task that would be made easier if only the Nazis would conduct their anti-Jewish measures a little less publicly. When German documents were seized by the Allies after the war, the gist of the two diplomats' conversation became clear from a cable von Dirksen had sent to his superiors after meeting Kennedy. On the Jewish Question, von Dirksen reported, Kennedy believed that:

> It was not so much the fact that we wanted to get rid of the Jews that was harmful to us, but rather the loud clamor with which we accompanied this purpose. He himself understood our Jewish policy completely; he was from Boston and there, in one

golf club and in other clubs, no Jews had been admitted for the
past 50 years . . . such pronounced attitudes were quite common,
but people avoided making so much outward fuss about it.[51]

Now, Kennedy believed a stark warning by Lindbergh might tip the
scales against military action by Britain and France. Lindbergh was eager
to comply and spent all night drafting his report, which he delivered to
Kennedy the following day. Fully aware of his potential influence over
world events, his warnings were even more ominous than before, and hit
closer to home:

> I feel certain that German air strength is greater than that of
> all other European countries combined . . . and that she is con-
> stantly increasing her margin of leadership. . . . If she wishes to
> do so, Germany now has the means of destroying London, Paris
> and Prague. There are not enough modern war planes for effec-
> tive defense or counter-attack in England and France combined.
> In the air, France's condition is pitiful. Although better off, the
> British air fleet cannot be compared to their German counter-
> parts . . . I believe that German factories are capable of produc-
> ing 20,000 aircraft per year. Her actual production is difficult to
> estimate. The most reliable reports I have obtained vary from
> 500 to 800 planes per month . . . Judging by the general condi-
> tions in Russia, I would not place great confidence in the Russian
> air fleet . . . Germany, on account of her military strength, is
> now inseparable from the welfare of every civilization, for either
> to preserve or to destroy it is in her power . . . To protect them-
> selves in the air England and France are far too weak. . . . I am
> convinced that it is wiser to permit Germany's eastward expan-
> sion than to throw England and France, unprepared, into a war
> at this time.[52]

In effect, he was saying that it would be military folly for France and
England to stand up to Germany, as they appeared now on the verge of
doing. With little effort, Germany would wipe London and Paris off the
face of the map and then conquer Czechoslovakia and probably the rest of
Europe anyway. Unless the two countries backed off and met Hitler's
demands, it would be suicide.

Lindbergh's report was just the authority needed to fortify the pro-

Appeasement forces. After cabling the document to President Roosevelt and the secretary of state in Washington, Kennedy used his influence to arrange a series of meetings between Lindbergh and some of Britain's most influential policy makers, those likely to have the loudest say in the formation of British policy as the Czech crisis unfolded.

Lindbergh's first meeting was with John Slessor, deputy air staff director of the British Air Ministry. In his notes of that September 22 encounter, Slessor wrote, "He is convinced that our only sound policy is to avoid war now at almost any cost. He spoke with admiration of Mr. Chamberlain and said he felt he had taken the only possible course; he felt that the present situation was largely the fault of the unwise attitude of France, Great Britain, and the United States at Versailles and in the years since the Peace Treaty, and he said the United States was just as much to blame as ourselves and France."[53]

When Lindbergh reemphasized his belief that France and England would lose a war with Germany, doubts began to arise in Slessor's mind as to how much his claims were influenced by German propaganda and carefully staged arrangements designed to impress him. Nevertheless, Slessor later wrote, "it is easy to understand, after talking to him, how he was able to impress the French with the formidable nature of the German threat." Here, Slessor appears, in hindsight, to be blaming the French for the failure to stand up to Hitler rather than acknowledge Britain's role. Although he later claimed to have viewed much of Lindbergh's pessimism with "a grain of salt," he acknowledged that there "was much truth in his story."[54]

Lindbergh met with a bevy of other high-ranking British officials in quick succession, including Air Marshal Wilfrid Freeman, air member for development and production; Sir Ernest Lemon, director general of production; and the entire staff of British air intelligence. Meanwhile, Kennedy met personally with the prime minister and other members of the Chamberlain Cabinet where he frantically relayed Lindbergh's findings. When on September 23 *London Times* editor Geoffrey Dawson called on the ambassador, he found "Kennedy very vocal and excited and full of strange oaths. He had Lindbergh with him, and didn't see how we could go to war effectively."[55] An American correspondent covering the crisis in London later recalled that "Kennedy kept peddling this Lindbergh story. Göring and his crowd had convinced Lindbergh they were so powerful, so he would go scare the Chamberlain people. Joe swallowed all of this and kept repeating it to Chamberlain and every other Englishman."[56]

In the days following Chamberlain's September 22 meeting with Hitler at Godesberg, the political situation had changed dramatically. On

September 26, Kennedy reported to U.S. secretary of state Cordell Hull that sentiment in England and in the cabinet was running against Appeasement and toward war. At Westminster Abbey, religious leaders staged a nonstop prayer vigil for peace. Londoners scurried to obtain gas masks and supplies in expectation of an imminent German attack. In his journal, Lindbergh wrote, "If France and England attack Germany at this time, the result will be chaotic and may easily result in the destruction of democracy. I am afraid it may result in the destruction of European civilization."[57]

Two days later, he attended a meeting of Oswald Mosley's British Union of Fascists at Hammersmith in London, where Mosley was scheduled to speak against going to war over Czechoslovakia. On his way to the fascist gathering, Lindbergh passed a Communist street meeting where protesters held a banner aloft: "Stand by the Czechs."

His assessment of this event—recorded in his journal that evening— has been widely ignored, despite the insight it provides into Lindbergh's political evolution at the time of the Czech crisis. He reports that although he did not find Mosley himself very intelligent, "his meeting, and even his speech, was of a much higher quality than that of the Communists. It always seems that the Fascist group is better than the Communist group. Communism seems to draw the worst of men."[58]

After the meeting, Charles and Anne took the train to Cliveden, where they had been invited to spend the night with Lord and Lady Astor along with a number of other guests. In his journal, Lindbergh describes the mood of the gathering: "Everyone greatly depressed. It was as though war had already begun." At 8:00 that evening, all present gathered around the radio to listen to a speech by Hitler. All expected him to declare war. Two German boys translated Hitler's remarks for the Astors' guests. The Führer spoke for more than an hour, building gradually to a crescendo that William Shirer later described as "the worst state of excitement I've ever seen him in." Benes was determined to exterminate Germany, Hitler bellowed. The Czechs had two days to accept his ultimatum and bow to German occupation of the Sudetenland.

But Hitler did not declare war. Instead, he heaped praise on Neville Chamberlain's peace efforts and assured French and British listeners that he had no further territorial intentions in Europe once this problem was settled.

Fifteen thousand Nazi faithful were packed into the Nazi Party Congress to hear their leader's speech. Now the mob erupted, chanting, "Führer command, we will follow!" Nazi propaganda minister Joseph Goebbels bounded to the microphone and promised that "a November 1918 will never be repeated." Shirer described the memorable scene:

Hitler "looked up to [Goebbels], a wild, eager expression in his eyes . . . leaped to his feet and brought his right hand, after a grand sweep, pounding down on the table and yelled . . . 'Ja!' Then he slumped into his chair exhausted."[59]

The following day, September 27, Lord Astor, who was heartened by Hitler's peace feeler, arranged for Lindbergh to share his German data with a roster of influential Britons. The evening before, Astor had been inclined to press for military intervention in the crisis, prompting Lindbergh to complain that he had been caught up "in the spirit of the Light Brigade." But Lindbergh's bleak assessment of the consequences of such a move for England soon brought Lord Astor back to the Appeasement position maintained by his wife, Nancy, and other members of their circle.

In the afternoon, Lindbergh warned Thomas Jones and a number of other select mandarins that "people are being very badly misled in regard to Great Britain's military situation."[60] From there, he was dispatched in Lord Astor's car to a meeting with former British prime minister David Lloyd George, who still possessed considerable influence. As they drove, they saw signs of war panic everywhere. Two cars passed them with loudspeakers blaring the message that citizens should head for the nearest civil defense station to be fitted for gas masks. Trenches were being dug in every park and open space. The evacuation of schoolchildren had begun.

As Lindbergh toured the corridors of power with Lord Astor, Nancy kept busy with her own lobbying efforts. Opposition leader Hugh Dalton later recalled being approached by Lady Astor, who told him, "You really ought to meet Lindbergh. He said the German air force is the most terrific thing there ever was. No one can stand up to it. He says we ought to make our peace with Hitler as soon as we can."[61]

In Berlin, meanwhile, Hitler appeared resigned to the possibility of impending military conflict. "If France and England strike, let them do so," he told the special British envoy Horace Wilson. "It's a matter of complete indifference to me. Today is Tuesday; by next Monday we shall be at war."[62]

That night, Lindbergh slept fitfully, waking up every hour thinking of England under a bomb attack. The next morning, September 28, he headed directly for an appointment with Ambassador Kennedy at the U.S. embassy, where a huge line of people waited in the desperate hope of obtaining an exit visa before hostilities commenced. Upon his arrival, embassy personnel issued him two gas masks, one for himself and one for Anne. When Kennedy arrived shortly after, he said to Lindbergh, "You may not need them. There's some good news coming in." He rushed out again without elaborating.[63]

The news turned out to be a small break in the dark clouds of the continuing standoff. On the evening of the 27th, Hitler had written a note to the British Prime Minister assuring Chamberlain in a moderate tone that he was ready to negotiate a formal guarantee for the remainder of Czechoslovakia. He appeared to be retreating from his *Sportpalast* ultimatum.[64] Still prepared to trust the German Chancellor's commitments, Chamberlain was eager to grasp at any straw and immediately drafted a conciliatory reply to Hitler's letter. "I am ready to come to Berlin myself at once to discuss arrangements . . . I cannot believe you will take responsibility for starting a world war which may end civilization for the sake of a few days' delay in settling this long-standing problem."[65]

On September 29, Chamberlain, Hitler, Mussolini, and Daladier convened in Munich to resolve the crisis. It was the city in whose beer halls and smoky cafés Hitler had clawed his way to power, never daring to dream that he would one day hold the fate of nations in his hand and have the great European heads of state contorting to his will. Just after noon, the four leaders gathered at the *Führerhaus* to determine whether the immediate future held war or peace. At Hitler's insistence, the Czech prime minister was not invited to participate. Earlier in the day, the Führer had held a private strategy session with Mussolini during which he had explained to his Italian ally his plan to "liquidate Czechoslovakia." If the talks failed, Hitler declared, he would resort to arms. At any rate, he added, "the time will come when we shall have to fight against England and France." *Il Duce* heartily agreed.[66]

The results of Munich were pre-ordained. Neither Chamberlain nor Daladier was in any mood to risk a war and Hitler, recognizing this, bullied his guests throughout the day, winning concessions on one point after another. Shortly after 1:00 A.M., the four leaders affixed their signatures to an accord that gave Hitler virtually everything he had asked for.

On October 1, Chamberlain returned to England triumphant. The country was deeply relieved. Peering out a second story window of his Downing Street residence, he was greeted as a hero by Londoners convinced that he had single-handedly averted war by his last-minute diplomatic coup. After acknowledging the cheers of his countrymen and a rousing rendition of "For He's a Jolly Good Fellow," the Prime Minister waved a copy of the Munich agreement—its ink barely dry—and declared, "Peace for our time." The *Times* echoed the sentiments of the nation when it wrote, "No conqueror returning from a victory on the battlefield has come adorned with nobler laurels."[67]

Only a lone, heretical voice could be heard resisting the consensus. Four days after Chamberlain's return, Winston Churchill—at the time languishing in the political wilderness—rose in the House of Commons and declared:

We have sustained a total and unmitigated defeat, and France has suffered even more than we have. . . . We are in the presence of a disaster of the first magnitude which has befallen Great Britain and France. Do not let us blind ourselves to that. It must now be accepted that all the countries of Central and Eastern Europe upon which France has relied for her safety has been swept away . . . they should know that we have sustained a defeat without a war, the consequences of which will travel far with us along our road; they should know that we have passed an awful milestone in our history . . . and that terrible words have for the time being been pronounced against the Western democracies: "Thou art weighed in the balance and found wanting." And do not suppose that this is the end. This is only the beginning of the reckoning.[68]

To reporters, Churchill announced, "We had to make a decision between the shame and the war. We have chosen the shame and as a reward we will receive a war."

Hitler responded insolently: "Once and for all we request to be spared from being spanked like a pupil by a governess." But Churchill's words were quickly proved prophetic. Within five months, Germany had broken all its promises. Most of Czechoslovakia lay in Nazi hands, demonstrating the hollowness of Appeasement policy. More important, the Munich Pact bought Hitler precious time to strengthen his military machine and prepare for the war that Chamberlain naively believed he had averted.

If Lindbergh's assessment of Germany's overwhelming military superiority had been accurate, then Munich would indeed have represented the diplomatic triumph that Chamberlain heralded on that fall day in 1938 when he announced to the world that he had achieved "peace with honor." Indeed, had Lindbergh been correct, Britain and France would have surely suffered a quick defeat on the battlefield if war had been waged during the fall of 1938.

Within months after the end of the Second World War, however, Lindbergh's 1938 warnings were found to be completely and spectacularly wrong. Göring and his Nazi hosts had so thoroughly deceived their American visitor that he had swallowed and propagated one of history's most damaging lies, a deception destined to have disastrous and tragic consequences in the years ahead.

When German military records were seized by the Allies in 1945, they revealed a grim set of statistics. In his 1938 report prepared for Joseph

Kennedy, Lindbergh had estimated German air strength at 8,000 to 10,000 planes.[69] He believed Germany was producing between 500 and 800 planes per month and was capable of producing 20,000 planes per year. However, German Quartermaster records captured after the war reveal that in fact Germany possessed only a fraction of this number— slightly over 3,307 planes, and many of these were not operational.[70] While Germany still boasted the largest individual air arsenal, the com- bined British and French air forces possessed more than 4,000 planes.[71] Lindbergh had reported it would take England, France, and Czechoslo- vakia many years to catch up to Germany, which he was certain had more planes than all the European countries combined. In reality, they were never behind.[72]

Of course, numbers alone don't tell the whole story. Lindbergh had trumpeted the quality of the *Luftwaffe* as far superior to the obsolete French, British and Czech arsenals. Indeed, officials at the French and British air ministries knew that their fleets were woefully unprepared to wage a war in the fall of 1938. Years of neglect and failure to modernize had reduced their respective air capabilities to disastrous levels. Against the state-of-the-art arsenal described by Lindbergh, they were convinced that it would be impossible to defend against *Luftwaffe* bombers. "Germany now has the means of destroying London, Paris and Prague," Lindbergh wrote Joseph Kennedy in his September memorandum. Again, he turned out to be completely wrong in his assessment. In fact, captured records later revealed, the German air force was as unprepared in 1938 as its French and British counterparts.

In August 1938, the *Luftwaffe* officer responsible for operations against the British Isles told his superiors that Germany's capability to attack Britain would amount to "pin pricks." At the time of the Munich Crisis, General Helmuth Felmy, commander of the German Second Air Force, told the High Command that, given the means at his disposal, "a war of destruction against England seemed to be excluded."[73] Moreover, the state-of-the-art German air force described by Lindbergh after his inspec- tion tours also turned out to be a myth. Like the RAF, much of the *Luft- waffe* fleet was obsolete and was undergoing a major overhaul in 1938. Rearmament was not going smoothly by the time of the Czech crisis. Ger- man testing of the new fighters and bombers heralded by Lindbergh revealed severe weaknesses, including design problems, a shortage of spare parts, inadequate range, poor pilot training and high accident rates. A Ger- man "after-action" report on the Czech crisis acknowledged a severe "lack of readiness in maintenance of flying equipment as well as in technical personnel."[74] As late as May 1939, the *Luftwaffe* chief of staff, Hans Jeschonnek, warned the German High Command, "Do not let us deceive ourselves, gentlemen. Each country wants to outstrip the other in air armament. But we are all roughly at the same stage."[75]

The inflated numbers and exaggerated readiness reports were key elements in a charade masterfully orchestrated by Hermann Göring and his air ministry, using Truman Smith, Lindbergh, and others as pawns. The two Americans had been completely taken in by their amiable Nazi hosts; as intended, they had passed on the false intelligence to Allied military and political leaders who used the bogus data to formulate their response to Hitler's aggression. The German ploy stands as one of the greatest disinformation feats in history. Neither Lindbergh nor Smith had ever sought to verify independently what they were told. They had no data to back up their claims beyond Göring's assurances.

Later on, a handful of Appeasement apologists, including Kennedy and Smith, argued that the Munich pact gave the allies valuable time to rearm and served as a wake-up call to England and the United States. This argument has been almost universally discredited, although it is true that both Lindbergh and Smith had urged the Allies to strengthen their own military forces. What the revisionists fail to point out is that this interval also gave Germany an extra crucial year to build up its own war machine.

According to Winston Churchill, "The year's breathing space said to be 'gained' by Munich left Britain and France in a much worse position compared to Hitler's Germany than they had been in the Munich Crisis."[76] Most military historians agree with this assessment. In fact, the strongest evidence that the western allies had been duped came from the Nazi leaders themselves at the postwar Nuremberg trials. When asked on the stand about the reaction of the German generals to the Munich accord, Field Marshal Wilhelm Keitel, chief of the German Armed Forces High Command, responded, "We were extraordinarily happy that it had not come to a military operation because . . . we had always been of the opinion that our means of attack against the frontier fortifications of Czechoslovakia were insufficient. . . . If war had broken out, neither our western border nor our Polish frontier could really have been effectively defended by us."[77] *Wehrmacht* chief Alfred Jodl confirmed this startling admission: "It was out of the question with five fighting divisions and seven reserve divisions in the western fortifications . . . to hold out against 100 French divisions," he testified. "That was militarily impossible."[78]

The myth of German might in 1938 was a lie of which the military was all too aware. Indeed, General Jodl's diary, captured after the war, reveals that on August 10, 1938, at the beginning of the Czech crisis, Hitler's generals were in a state of near revolt. When one of them cautioned that Germany's western fortifications could only hold for three weeks, the Führer flew into a rage. The German army was in such disarray during this period that a group of generals, led by Franz Halder, had even plotted to arrest and overthrow their Führer if he gave the order to attack Czechoslovakia. They were convinced that such an attack would lead to a disastrous defeat for the German military.[79]

In his epic history *The Rise and Fall of the Third Reich*, William Shirer surmised the likely consequences had England and France called Hitler's bluff at Munich: "Germany was in no position to go to war on October 1, 1938, against Czechoslovakia and France and Britain, not to mention Russia," he writes. "Had she done so, she would have been quickly and easily defeated, and that would have been the end of Hitler and the Third Reich."[80]

This evaluation stands in stark contrast to Lindbergh's September 22, 1938, report confidently claiming that, "If she wishes to do so, Germany now has the means of destroying London, Paris and Prague."[81]

Moreover, it was not Munich that prompted England to accelerate its rearmament efforts, as Kennedy later argued in his own defense; it was Hitler's breach of that pact in March 1939 that many believe finally provoked the British government out of its lethargy.[82]

Sixty-five years later, we know that Lindbergh's 1938 assessment of German air power was completely wrong. The unanswered question, however, is how much influence his false reports had on subsequent events. Certainly, the damage Göring's deception inflicted on Lindbergh's legacy is irreparable. For more than half a century, his reputation has been scarred by charges that he played a major role in the short-sighted Munich debacle. Those seeking to rehabilitate his reputation, however, have gone to great lengths to downplay his influence in these historic events.

Even before Pearl Harbor, charges of grotesque bungling were being leveled regularly at Lindbergh, even though the facts to support the allegations would not surface for years. On January 1, 1939, only three months after Munich, the popular radio commentator and columnist Walter Winchell reported that it was Lindbergh's "now famous report on Germany's power in the air, which was to prove a final factor in Prime Minister Neville Chamberlain's policy at Munich." In May 1941, Louis Fischer, European correspondent for *The Nation*, wrote that the Lindbergh air power reports were "as responsible as anything else" for the Munich deal.

To counter these claims, Lindbergh's authorized biographer Scott Berg attempts to downplay his role in the Munich accord, writing dismissively, "Much of yesterday's hearsay became today's history."[83] To illustrate his assertion that Lindbergh's reputation has been unfairly tarnished by these charges, Berg cites exactly one source, a *New York Times* columnist named Arthur Krock.

On February, 1, 1939, Krock informed his readers that "Criticism of any of [Lindbergh's] activities—in Germany or elsewhere—is as ignorant as it is unfair."[84] In a column entitled "The Invaluable Contribution of Colonel Lindbergh," he stressed that throughout the aviator's missions to Berlin, Lindbergh "has been an official American reporter and adviser on aviation" and that the United States government had been the chief beneficiary of his information and technical appraisal."[85] At the time, of course, Krock had no idea that Lindbergh's information and appraisal were uniformly wrong. Moreover, Krock's assertion that Lindbergh traveled to Germany only to secretly secure air intelligence on behalf of the American government was simply not true, as Lindbergh himself made clear in a letter to his financial adviser Harry Davison, who had sent him a copy of the Krock column. "It seems to be a favorable article," wrote Lindbergh, "but is just as inaccurate as all the others as far as many of the statements are concerned. I suppose that I should be very appreciative of the type of article which Mr. Krock has written. But I prefer to stand upon a foundation of fact rather than of favor."[86]

Furthermore, in citing Krock's defense of Lindbergh, Berg fails to point out that the columnist was a close friend and frequent travel companion of the pro-Appeasement ambassador Joseph Kennedy. Krock was so close to the Kennedy family, in fact, that he "revised and edited" JFK's senior thesis at Harvard, later expanded and published as the best-selling book *Why England Slept*.[87] Many Kennedy experts believe Krock actually wrote most of this work.[88] In the thesis, John Kennedy attempts to downplay his father's controversial role in the Czech crisis by arguing that it was the isolationist character of the British population as a whole, not Britain's political leadership, that had led to Hitler's appeasement.[89]

More than a half century later, a significant body of evidence has emerged from government archives, seized Nazi files, diaries of the participants, and other primary source material that has permitted a substantially more objective assessment. The key to deciphering the importance of Lindbergh's role is to assess how much weight was given to his appraisal of the strength of German air power in the decision-making process over the course of the Czech crisis.

Historian Telford Taylor argues that it was a crucial factor: "Munich was a German military triumph and the prime instrument of that triumph was the German air force: the *Luftwaffe*. It is a remarkable fact that Munich was the only victory of strategic proportions that the *Luftwaffe* ever won."[90] He goes on to explain that the *Luftwaffe* was the "psychological spearhead of German power," arguing that the false estimates spread by Lindbergh and others were a major factor in the diplomatic surrender of England and France.

Historian John E. Wood describes the profound effect of Lindbergh's phantom *Luftwaffe* on Chamberlain's cabinet. "Hitler's *Luftwaffe* possessed neither the operational ability nor the strategic doctrine to attempt the widespread destruction of lives and industry that weighed so heavily on the minds of Britain's leaders," he writes.[91] President Roosevelt, in constant contact with the Chamberlain government during the crisis, later told U.S. ambassador Josephus Daniels that it was a belief in overwhelming Axis air superiority that "made Chamberlain capitulate at Munich."[92]

Lindbergh himself later credited Joseph Kennedy's diplomacy with the steps that led to Munich.[93] But his biographer Leonard Mosley accuses him of excessive modesty: "Without the devastating statistics and predictions with which Lindbergh had provided him, Kennedy never would have been able to convince Chamberlain of the need to appease Adolf Hitler. . . . Moreover, Kennedy's influence had been solely on [Chamberlain], whereas Lindbergh had worked on the French as well."[94] Mosley's first argument is questionable since Chamberlain was inclined toward Appeasement well before Lindbergh or Kennedy came on the scene. But there is no question air power and Lindbergh's reports weighed on the minds of the British and French prime ministers in the interval between the Godesberg meeting on September 22 and Munich a week later, especially after British Cabinet sentiment began leaning toward war.

Lindbergh's powers of persuasion appear to have swayed even the most seasoned of politicians. At the time of the Czech crisis, Thomas Jones, deputy secretary to the Cabinet from 1916 to 1930 and confidante to four successive British leaders, was one of the most influential and universally respected figures in British politics and a well-known supporter of Appeasement. Jones, who had met Lindbergh at Cliveden in September 1938, was so impressed with Lindbergh's warnings about German air superiority that he had introduced the American "expert" to a group of his friends, all influential politicians, at a luncheon on September 28, at the height of the crisis.

In his diary, Jones writes that he initially believed it was necessary for England to fight if Germany moved into Czechoslovakia. But his attitude soon changed. "Since my talk with Lindbergh on Monday," he wrote, "I've sided with those working for peace at any cost in humiliation, because of the picture of our relative unpreparedness in the air and on the ground which Lindbergh painted, and because of his belief that the democracies would be crushed absolutely and finally."[95] Shortly after this meeting, Jones urged his former boss Stanley Baldwin, Chamberlain's predecessor as prime minister, to speak in favor of Appeasement in the House of Lords to "save the country from war."[96]

At the height of the crisis, the BBC political correspondent Sheila Grant Duff cabled Winston Churchill from central Europe, reporting that Lindbergh buttressed the German conviction that England "would be neutral if they attacked Czechoslovakia."[97]

One famous, but apocryphal, story—spread by a British historian, years later—suggested that the Germans had fooled Lindbergh on his air inspection tours by shuttling the same planes from one airfield to another, thus convincing him that their arsenal was much larger than it was. Another account claimed that the Germans placed wooden airplane models on their airfields so that Lindbergh and other observers flying overhead would spot much larger fleets than actually existed. Berg and others point to the falsity of such stories to prove that Lindbergh was unfairly vilified. But *Luftwaffe* lieutenant general Heinz J. Rieckhoff later revealed that the Germans did employ what he described as a "systematic bluff at the top level" to deceive Lindbergh and other foreign observers. He also describes the "willing self-deception of the foreign air observers, who simply refused to believe what their eyes saw and insisted on assuming that there was still more hidden behind it. They had no way of knowing that many of the gigantic hangars they were shown were either completely empty or filled with ancient, dust-covered aircraft."[98]

Many of Lindbergh's defenders have argued that exaggerated accounts of his influence at Munich were later spread by his detractors to discredit him. But in an exclusive interview with Walter Winchell in January 1939, his strong supporter and friend Joseph Kennedy told the influential American radio personality that he had given Lindbergh's air power report to Neville Chamberlain at the height of the Munich crisis and "it was an important factor in the Prime Minister's decision to avoid war."[99]

By no means was Lindbergh the only source officials in England and France had heard from on the subject of German air strength. His inflated estimates merely echoed or confirmed what other British, French, and American intelligence sources had already reported about the strength of the *Luftwaffe*. A number of European air attachés, politicians, and military observers had, in fact, been offered small-scale demonstrations of new German aircraft at select German installations during 1937 and 1938. Each came away impressed and convinced of German air superiority. However, the importance of Lindbergh's information differed from previous such reports for a number of reasons. First, he was the only foreigner who had received allegedly unrestricted access to German air installations and therefore was believed to possess firsthand knowledge that other intelligence sources lacked.[100] Second, as the world's most famous flyer, he was considered something of an expert on aviation matters and his views were more likely to carry weight. Finally, it's true that before Lindbergh arrived in England to share his warnings about German air power, the British government had already obtained similarly pessimistic reports from a number of sources, including its own air attaché in Berlin. However, British government officials had always been inclined to regard these estimates as unreliable.

The quality of their air intelligence at the time was very poor, acknowledged John Slessor, deputy air staff director of the British Air Ministry, in his postwar memoir *The Central Blue*. In the fall of 1938, for example, the British ambassador to Germany, Sir Nevile Henderson, repeatedly urged Lindbergh to do all he could "to make the English realize the quality and size of Germany's aviation program." According to Lindbergh, Henderson said the government didn't believe him when he described it.[101] Hence, the British were predisposed to trust Lindbergh's intelligence estimates because of his presumed credibility on the subject. Indeed, for many, Lindbergh's credibility merely reinforced existing ideas.

Some Lindbergh supporters have argued over the years that his warnings were much more accurate than they have been subsequently portrayed and that Lindbergh was not the "unwitting dupe" described by some historians and biographers. Aviation historian Raymond Fredette supports Lindbergh's contention that at the time of Munich, the British air force was unprepared to take on the superior German fleet, citing contemporary British air ministry accounts to support his case. He also rebuts the common criticism of Lindbergh's 1938 claim that "German factories are capable of producing in the vicinity of 20,000 aircraft each year." Fredette argues that the German aircraft industry had substantial unused capacities that could be tapped in the event of mobilization, as the *Luftwaffe* proved after the war began.[102] In fact, however, much of the Nazis' increased military capacity only resulted from its subsequent invasion of Czechoslovakia months later, when it took control of the giant Skoda Works industrial colossus, a number of air production facilities and, more important, the substantial Czech treasury. Fredette insists that most of Lindbergh's airpower estimates did not come directly from the Germans but rather from the assessment of French intelligence and other sources. Therefore, he argues, charges that Lindbergh swallowed and repeated Nazi propaganda are unfair. This is a dubious point at best, since Lindbergh never revealed the source of his estimates, although some of them did dovetail with French intelligence reports at the time.

While Fredette makes some valid points, he is among a small group of Lindbergh defenders—including Truman Smith, among others—that have posited the idea over the years that Lindbergh's pre-Munich estimates were "substantially correct."[103] Fredette cites the postwar accounts of British air officials to back up this highly questionable assertion. The British, of course, had a vested interest in rationalizing their humiliating Munich capitulation; therefore, such accounts must be taken with a grain of salt, especially now that British and German archives have revealed the actual air power figures. While it is true that Lindbergh's initial air power estimates of November 1937 were not far off the mark, he completely miscalculated German production capacity; thus, he overestimated 1938 German air strength by as much as 300 percent. It was this bungled estimate that proved crucial in the events leading to Munich.

There is no question that some of the criticism of Lindbergh's Munich role has been exaggerated or based on what Scott Berg calls "hearsay." However, the facts speak for themselves and, while Lindbergh was not the only "expert" fooled by German propaganda, he passed on important and damaging intelligence information that has since been proven completely wrong by any objective criteria.

Historian Williamson Murray, senior fellow at the Institute for Defense Analysis, and one of the world's foremost academic experts on German air power and the Munich pact, believes that Lindbergh was merely a pawn used to advance publicly the political agendas of figures such as Truman Smith and the Cliveden regulars who had already made up their minds how they wanted the crisis resolved: "It started with the Germans who played a remarkable shell game with Lindbergh and he played right into their hands. When he got to England with his reports, the false air data was manipulated very skillfully. I don't think Lindbergh changed a lot of minds but, as a famous figure, he was extremely useful in publicly voicing the positions that had already been staked out by Chamberlain, Kennedy and others who never wanted to go to war over Czechoslovakia. He served their purpose quite effectively."[104]

As the German army moved into the Sudetenland two weeks after Munich, the Lindberghs flew to Berlin for their third visit. The ostensible reason for the trip was an invitation to attend the Lilienthal Aeronautical Society's annual congress, but the couple had already decided that Berlin was to be their winter home and Charles was anxious to return to the country of his newfound obsession.

Again, their hosts were to be the Smiths. Truman Smith made what would later prove to be another fatal intelligence blunder on October 5 when he issued a post-Munich intelligence assessment to the U.S. War Department: "Hitler's wish for the immediate future is clear," Smith cabled Washington. "He wants peace . . . Germany wants a period of peace—not a few months, but several years at least, and probably a decade."[105]

For the Lindberghs' visit, the military attaché had arranged another tour of German air installations and a round of diplomatic engagements. Hugh Wilson, the new American ambassador in Berlin, was considerably more receptive to the New Germany than was his predecessor William Dodd. Here was someone with whom Smith could do business, and the two bonded immediately.

Ambassador Wilson was especially anxious to meet Lindbergh and had planned an embassy dinner in honor of the famous American visitor, scheduled for October 18. Meanwhile, a diplomatic contretemps had been ignited by a small item published by Claud Cockburn in *The Week*, the same British newspaper that had coined the term "Cliveden Set" a year earlier. The paper, which Smith referred to as a "scandal sheet," had attributed a series of derogatory remarks to Lindbergh about the state of Soviet aviation following his visit to Russia six weeks earlier. *The Week* claimed he had leveled his criticism at a dinner party hosted by Lady Astor at her London home. He had allegedly claimed that "Russian aviation was in a chaotic condition" and that "the German fleet could whip the Russian, French and English air fleets combined."[106] In fact, this wasn't far off the mark from what Lindbergh had actually said during his London stay. However, the paper also falsely claimed the Russians had invited Lindbergh to be the chief of their Civil Air Fleet. A few days later, a group of prominent Soviet aviators—some of whom had hosted the Lindberghs on their visit to Moscow in August—sent a letter to *Pravda* attacking Lindbergh as pro-Nazi and anti-Soviet.[107]

Alarm spread through the diplomatic community. Under pressure from the Russians, the U.S. military attaché to Moscow begged Lindbergh to issue a statement or, at the very least, to send a private message for the Soviet government denying the remarks attributed to him. But Lindbergh declined, explaining his policy of refusing to comment on press reports, a practice he described as "fatal." It was a policy he appeared to forget a few weeks later when the *New York Times* and other American papers printed a story claiming that he had sent an intelligence report about the *Luftwaffe* to Washington. This time, he phoned the U.S. embassy in Berlin with an urgent request that it contact the German Air Ministry and pass on his apology for the publicity. He was eager, he said, to avoid any "misunderstandings" with the Germans. Truman Smith immediately complied with his request.[108]

Only six days before the Lindberghs arrived in Germany, the Nazis had issued a widely publicized decree ordering German Jews to carry special identification cards, the latest development in the escalating Nazi campaign of persecution. Passports held by Jews were marked with a large red "J" to allow police to easily identify them. All over the country, signs sprung up declaring "Jewry is criminal" and "Jews not wanted." Even an American with no knowledge of German could have identified the mocking caricatures of hook-nosed Jews that accompanied these signs. The Aryanization of the Third Reich was well under way and could not have escaped the notice of a visitor in 1938. But in his defence, historian Richard Ketchum offers an explanation for Lindbergh's seeming indifference to the plight of German Jews: "Lindbergh had the type of mind that absorbed immediately every detail of the airplanes he saw, that took in all the fine points of design and performance . . . but certain political and social implications of what was going on in Germany seem to have escaped him, not because he was indifferent or callous but because such matters were largely beyond the focus of his interests."[109]

On the evening of the 18th, as scheduled, Lindbergh and Smith left for Ambassador Wilson's dinner at the U.S. embassy. Because it was a stag (men only) affair, their wives had not been invited. The guests included Reichsmarschall Hermann Göring, the most powerful man in the Reich after Hitler; General Milch and General Udet from the German air ministry; the Belgian and Italian ambassadors, and a number of American attachés.

Lindbergh had spent some time with Göring during his first visit in 1936 and later described the *Luftwaffe* chief as "charming," although his Nazi host was rumored to have been disappointed when he learned that the Scandinavian-American didn't speak Swedish. Göring's late wife was a Swedish aristocrat and he was said to be enamored of everything Swedish in devotion to her memory.[110] The number two Nazi was himself a distinguished flyer, having served as a commander of the celebrated Richtofen squadron during the First World War where he shot down five enemy planes. He was one of Hitler's earliest followers; the Führer once described Göring as "my paladin," and had reportedly designated him as his chosen successor. Smith would later describe the Reichsmarschall as "magnetic, genial, vain, intelligent, frightening, and grotesque."[111] Lindbergh was looking forward to meeting him again.

Göring was the last to arrive, accompanied by an aide. He wore a blue military uniform with black riding boots and shook hands with the assorted guests. The embassy ballroom was magnificently decorated with flowers, the light from thousands of candles reflected in Mrs. Wilson's finest silver. Minutes after he made his appearance, the portly Nazi air chief caught sight of Lindbergh standing at the back of the room. He strode over, quickly pumped the American's hand and presented him with a red box and a sheaf of papers, announcing "*Im Nahmen des Führer.*" It was the Service Cross of the German Eagle With Star—the highest decoration the Reich could bestow on a foreigner, the same award given to Henry Ford only two months earlier, but a slightly lower grade. "By order of *der Führer*," translated the aide. Inside the box gleamed a shiny cross, to be worn suspended from a ribbon draped around the neck, along with a six-pointed silver star adorned with swastikas, meant to be pinned on the chest.

This event would become one of the defining moments of Lindbergh's career and would be repeatedly summoned by his adversaries in later years to discredit him and his controversial pre-war activities. As a result, there have been many attempts to rewrite the history of the incident to alter its significance. Chief among the later revisionists was Truman Smith, whose association with Lindbergh and the Nazi medal would forever remain a blemish on his own career.

To understand what actually happened on that October evening in 1938, it is important to distinguish between contemporary accounts and those written years after the fact. In 1956, Smith compiled a report for U.S. army intelligence attempting to "set the record straight" about his association with Lindbergh and their controversial air intelligence activities during the 1930s. In this report, for the first time, Smith provides an astonishing revelation about the Göring medal incident. He claims that the Embassy dinner had been arranged by U.S. ambassador Hugh Wilson to obtain Göring's support "for certain measures especially desired by the State Department concerning the easing of the financial plight of the large number of Jews who were being forced to emigrate from Germany in a penniless condition. Mr. Wilson felt that Göring was about the only leader in the Nazi government who might be won over to such a humanitarian measure."[112] This version of the story has since been accepted as fact by a number of chroniclers, including Richard Ketchum in his 1989 history of the period, *The Borrowed Years*,[113] and the 1987 memoir *Uncommon Friends* by Lindbergh's intimate friend James Newton.[114]

Smith's claim is especially surprising because Göring was not generally recognized as sympathetic toward the plight of Jews, and his anti-Semitic views were already well known in U.S. diplomatic circles.[115] On August 11, 1938, only two months earlier, Göring had informed American State Department representative James Riddleberger that "within ten years the United States will become the most anti-semitic country in the world and that the combination of Jews and blacks raise grave questions about America's future."[116] Only a month after he decorated Lindbergh, Göring announced at a meeting with Gestapo leader Reinhard Heydrich that if Germany went to war in the foreseeable future, there would be a "great reckoning with the Jews."[117]

Is Smith's account a fabrication? If, as he claimed, the invitation to Göring had a humanitarian motive, and was Ambassador Wilson's idea, surely Wilson would have recorded it. But the ambassador's personal diary from the month of October contains not a word about the plan to help German Jews,[118] nor did he refer to this in his subsequent report to Washington when he was asked to explain the controversial Lindbergh medal incident.[119] Moreover, it is not mentioned in Lindbergh's journal entries or in his autobiography.[120]

Lindbergh himself always said that the presentation of the medal was a "complete surprise" to him. There is no evidence to dispute this. Similarly, Smith also claimed he had no advance warning about the decoration.[121] However, U.S. embassy records later revealed that the German air ministry had in fact left a message for Smith on the afternoon of Wilson's dinner: "Would the military attaché please note that when Reich Minister Göring arrives at the Embassy that evening, there will be a short ceremony. General Göring intends to present Colonel Lindbergh with a decoration."[122] Smith subsequently claimed in his dubious account that the message had been taken down by a secretary but that she "failed to deliver it."[123]

Smith is also the source of what has become the most repeated story associated with the medal. In this account, the newly decorated Charles returned home that evening and showed the medal to Anne, who prophetically proclaimed it "the Albatross."[124] While it's possible that she said this, Anne's diary entry that evening reveals no such alarm: "C. came back late from his dinner, with a German decoration presented him quite unexpectedly by General Göring. Henry Ford is the only other American to get it. The parchment is signed by Hitler."[125]

In later years, both Ambassador Wilson and Smith claimed that Lindbergh had no choice but to accept the medal. To refuse, Wilson argued, would have been an affront to his German host. "It would have been an act offensive to a guest of the Ambassador of your country, in the House of the Ambassador," he reassured Lindbergh in 1941, when his acceptance of the Nazi medal was under constant attack in the press.[126] The implication was that Lindbergh didn't want to accept the Nazi medal, but he had no choice. Furthermore, the Americans present that evening did not approve of a medal bestowed by such a monstrous regime, but the conventions of diplomatic protocol permitted no alternative. However, Wilson's diary entry on the night of the Göring medal presentation records no such reservations. Describing the incident, he writes: "Dinner at night for Lindbergh and Göring. The latter entered the room with a red box and white envelope. When he came to Lindbergh he handed them over *'Im Nahmen des Führer,'* conferring upon him the Service Cross of the Order of the German Eagle with the Star. Everybody was much cheered and gave Lindbergh a hand."[127] This account is hardly an indication that the medal caused any consternation among the Americans present that night. A letter recently unearthed in the Lindbergh archives is even more revealing. On October 25, a week after the medal presentation, Lindbergh wrote an effusive personal thank you letter to Göring:

> I want to thank you especially for the honor which you conferred on me at the dinner given by Ambassador Wilson. I hope that when the opportunity presents itself, you will convey my thanks to the Reichschancellor [Hitler]. It is difficult for me to express adequately my appreciation for this decoration, and for the way in which you presented it that evening. It is an honor which I shall always prize highly.[128]

Smith later claimed that Lindbergh never wore the decoration. However, in an article printed two days after the ceremony, the *New York Times* reported that Göring had personally pinned the medal on Lindbergh, who "appeared surprised, displayed an embarrassed smile and thanked Marshal Göring but proudly wore the decoration during the evening."[129] *Newsweek* printed a similar account.[130]

In later years, Smith attempted to portray the Göring medal as an innocent recognition of Lindbergh's New York to Paris flight, rather than a gesture of appreciation for his activities heralding Nazi air power. According to Smith's 1956 account, Göring said, upon presenting the medal, that it was being given for Lindbergh's "services to the aviation of the world and particularly for his historic 1927 solo flight across the Atlantic." Smith claimed that Lindbergh confirms this in his journal entry of the incident.[131] At the time Smith wrote this, there was nothing to contradict him. But when Lindbergh published his journal fourteen years later, it revealed that Smith's account was not quite accurate. In his entry of October 18, 1938, Lindbergh had simply written, "I found that he had presented me with the German Eagle, one of the highest German decorations, 'by order of der Führer.'"[132] This is the only reference he provides about Göring's words that evening. Time and again when the facts are scrutinized, Smith's credibility is called into question.

It is worth noting that Lindbergh's Nazi decoration was presented a mere five days after Ernest Liebold received a similar honor from the German consul in Detroit. The citation signed by the Führer accompanying both decorations explained that the medals were given to those "who deserve well of the Reich."[133]

In his monumental biography of Winston Churchill, *The Last Lion*, acclaimed historian William Manchester spent several years researching the Munich crisis and its aftermath. Describing Lindbergh's role in these historic events, Manchester ends his section on Munich with a simple conclusion: "The Lone Eagle had earned his Nazi medal."[134]

CHAPTER 7

THE LONELY EAGLE

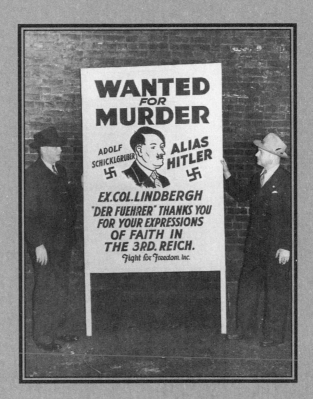

During the Great Debate, both sides flung inflammatory charges at each other as a propaganda tactic. Lindbergh was a favorite target of the interventionist group Fight for Freedom.

In the middle of the night on October 27, 1938, as the Lindberghs were wrapping up their third visit to Berlin, the Gestapo knocked on the door of a Jewish shopkeeper named Zindel Grünspan, rousting him and his family out of their home in the middle of a driving rainstorm. His store and all his possessions were confiscated. Destitute, famished, and soaked to the skin, Grünspan and his family were forced over the Polish border in a boxcar, along with thousands of other Polish Jews living in Germany, many of whom had lived there for generations.[1] As the Polish government had no use for Jews either, the new arrivals were immediately interned in a "relocation camp."

Grünspan's seventeen-year-old son Herschel, who was living with an uncle in Paris when he heard the news of his family's fate, immediately made for the German embassy intending to assassinate the ambassador in revenge. When he learned that his quarry was away, he turned his gun instead on a lesser embassy official, Ernst vom Rath, who died from his wounds two days later.

The Nazis had been waiting for just such an excuse to exorcise German Jews from public life.[2] Propaganda Minister Josef Goebbels immediately declared the assassination a conspiratorial attack by "International Jewry" against the Reich. Gestapo chief Heinrich Müller gave the long anticipated signal to his followers to unleash their fury.[3] On the nights of November 9 and 10, frenzied mobs rampaged through Germany, Austria, and the newly acquired Sudetenland, randomly attacking Jewish targets—homes, synagogues, and businesses. At least ninety-six Jews were killed, thousands more injured as fanatical hordes ran through the streets shouting *"Juden schwein!"* Hundreds of synagogues were burned, thousands of businesses destroyed, cemeteries desecrated, schools vandalized. 35,000 Jews were arrested and sent to concentration camps and a fine of one billion *reichsmarks*[4] was levied against the Jewish community as punishment for the vom Rath assassination.[5] When Goebbels was told the extent of the destruction, he simply responded, "We shed not a tear for them."

The pogrom would become known as *Kristallnacht*, "the Night of Broken Glass,"[6] and it signaled the beginning of a reign of terror that would culminate in the Final Solution. It also marked the beginning of a new attitude in America toward Nazi Germany. For Charles Lindbergh, it would mark the beginning of the end of his days as a universal hero.

American newspapers had paid scant attention to the news of the Göring medal presentation on October 18, twenty-two days before the *Kristallnacht* riots. But as news of the horrific events of November 9 filtered out of the Reich, a wave of revulsion swept America. President Roosevelt held a press conference strongly condemning the anti-Jewish attacks, declaring, "I myself could scarcely believe that such things could occur in twentieth century civilization."[7] Religious leaders from all denominations issued their own harsh denunciations of anti-Semitism as a "wicked folly utterly opposed to the spirit and letter of the teaching of our Lord."[8] An organization representing German Americans issued a statement expressing their "shame and sorrow" for the events in their former homeland.[9] The Nazi regime was no longer considered merely objectionable to Americans for its policies of persecution. It was now recognized as "monstrous" and "barbaric," capable of unspeakable acts of cruelty. And suddenly the media remembered that one American appeared to approve of the regime—a hero, in fact, who only three weeks earlier had been decorated by the Reich and, according to Adolf Hitler, "deserved well" of it.

Only a day after the president assailed the *Kristallnacht* attacks, the *New York Times* published a front-page article revealing that the Lindberghs "plan to move to Berlin." The paper attributed the story to friends of the couple who "said that the recent abandonment of many Jewish homes might make available apartments for rent."[10] The following week, *The New Yorker* magazine wrote, "With confused emotions we say goodbye to Colonel Charles A. Lindbergh, who wants to go and live in Berlin, presumably occupying a house that once belonged to Jews . . . If he wants to experiment further with the artificial heart, his surroundings there should be ideal." A number of editorial cartoons pounded home the theme by depicting Lindbergh wearing a medal in the form of a swastika-shaped heart.[11]

The New Yorker article wasn't far off the mark in its snide attack. The couple had indeed done some serious house-hunting on their recent visit to Berlin with a view toward spending the upcoming winter in Germany. On October 28, they had located what they believed was an ideal home in the Berlin suburb of Wannsee and expressed an interest in leasing it. However, when he asked his friends in the German air ministry for advice on the terms of the lease, Lindbergh was advised not to take it because there "seemed to be something strange about the transaction."[12] It was later revealed that the house had belonged to a Jew; it would not do for a distinguished guest to live there.[13] Instead, he was advised to approach Hitler's chief architect, Albert Speer, who said he would build the couple a house anywhere they wanted.[14] Years later, while Speer was interned at Spandau Prison serving a sentence for war crimes, he recalled Lindbergh's request. "I laugh now when I think about it," he told a reporter. "Imagine an American planning to bring his family to Berlin in 1938–39. He must have been very naive."[15]

In the end, it was Alexis Carrel who gently set the Lindberghs straight. Shortly after the reports of *Kristallnacht* exploded onto the front pages of American newspapers, Carrel wrote the couple from New York with the news that "anti-German feeling" in the United States was running high and "there is a great deal of ill feeling against you." He advised them to cancel their plans. Moving to Germany would not sit well with Americans, appalled by what they had been hearing, Carrel counseled.[16]

On November 14, Eleanor Roosevelt wrote her confidante, Lorena Hickok: "This German Jewish business makes me sick. . . . How could Lindbergh take that Hitler decoration?"[17]

Back in Illiec, Charles read a long account in the London *Times* of what he called Germany's "Jewish troubles." His journal account of November 13 displays his consternation: "I do not understand these riots on the part of the Germans. It seems so contrary to their sense of order and their intelligence in other ways. They have undoubtedly had a difficult Jewish problem, but why is it necessary to handle it so unreasonably? My admiration is constantly being dashed against some rock such as this."[18]

He heeded his friend's advice and canceled his planned move to Germany. To do so at this time, he wrote Carrel, would be "embarrassing to many people and from many standpoints."[19] But his dismay over *Kristallnacht* did not appear to sour him for long on the Nazi regime. He was about to embark on an odd mission, the motivations for which remain murky to this day.

Shortly after he returned to France from Germany in November 1938, Lindbergh was invited by the French government for a series of conferences to discuss how France could improve its air defenses. At one of these discussions, he made a suggestion that raised the eyebrows of each participant in the room, while revealing his apparent oblivion to the state of European affairs: Why not purchase some state-of-the-art Daimler-Benz or *Junkers* engines from the Germans?[20] The suggestion was hurriedly dismissed. Only a month earlier, Germany and France had been at the brink of war. The Munich accord represented a fragile peace at best. Why would Germany willingly help France strengthen its air force? asked the bemused French officials.

Lindbergh persisted, insisting that he had personal contacts in the German air ministry and that there was nothing to lose by sending out a feeler to the Germans. The French finally relented and sanctioned a secret, but unofficial, mission to Berlin.

On December 18, Lindbergh landed at Berlin's Tempelhof Airport on his fourth visit to the Third Reich in two years. The following day, he met his old friend General Ernst Udet of the German air ministry and broached the subject of the engine purchase. Udet immediately expressed interest. On December 20, Lindbergh met with another *Luftwaffe* friend, General Erhard Milch, who also appeared favorably disposed. Milch reassured Lindbergh that neither Göring nor Hitler had anything to do with the recent anti-Jewish demonstrations, leading him to conclude that either Himmler or Goebbels must have been responsible.[21]

It was on this trip, Lindbergh noted in his journal, that he "tried to obtain a better understanding of the German mind in regard to the Jewish problem." He concluded that all Germans seemed to be anti-Jewish, but in varying degrees, and that it appeared to have something to do with the Jews' role in the internal collapse and revolution following the First World War—a time when they owned the most property, "lived in the best houses, drove the best automobiles, and mixed with the prettiest German girls."[22] He did not offer his own opinion of this fiction, a staple of both Nazi propaganda and *The International Jew*.

With a promise from the German air ministry to consider the French offer, Lindbergh returned by train to Paris four days before Christmas, storing his plane in a Berlin hangar so that he would have an "excuse" to make a return trip. Less than a month later, the unlikely arms broker returned to Berlin as scheduled to hear the German answer to his proposal.

On January 16, Lindbergh arrived for an appointment at the air ministry, where General Milch greeted him with the news that the Germans had agreed to the deal. Lindbergh was elated. He flew back to Paris to share the good news with the stunned French government officials, who had believed he was on a fool's errand.

It is obvious, by his journal accounts of these bizarre negotiations, that Lindbergh genuinely believed in the Nazis' good faith, notwithstanding the fact that the deal would have meant the certain strengthening of a future enemy's defenses. Even in the weeks that followed when, with one excuse after another, the German air ministry consistently stalled at finalizing the agreement, he never gave up hope that the engines would be Paris-bound as soon as the paperwork could be completed. Of course, the Germans never had any intention of selling engines to the French; they were merely using Lindbergh once again, this time to convince the French that they had every intention to remain at peace and stand by their Munich promises.

When he left Berlin for the last time in January 1939, Lindbergh turned over the transaction's final details to Paul Stehlin, the French air attaché stationed in Germany. But Stehlin was no more successful than Lindbergh had been in finalizing the agreement. After encountering one stall tactic after another, the French diplomat decided to call upon General Udet at his Berlin apartment for a social visit. He found the *Luftwaffe* general drinking with three of his air ministry colleagues. After a few drinks, the Frenchman casually brought up the subject of the engine purchase, at which the four Germans burst into laughter. Stehlin got the hint. "I realized that the Germans had been bluffing all along," he recalled years later. "They were amazed that Colonel Lindbergh had fallen for the idea, and they were even more surprised that it had been taken seriously by the French."[23]

Shortly after this episode, Stehlin met Lindbergh in Paris and told him of the encounter. "He was quite angry and flared up at me," recalled Stehlin. With some testiness, Lindbergh insisted that General Milch had personally assured him of his goodwill.[24] As if to reassure himself that Stehlin must be mistaken, Lindbergh wrote a defensive note in his journal: "In the contacts I have made to date, no [German] officer has lied to me or attempted to mislead me."[25]

When word of these negotiations leaked years later, it would only serve to fuel accusations that Lindbergh had been acting as a Nazi agent. But undoubtedly a more accurate assessment can be borrowed from Albert Speer: Lindbergh was simply extraordinarily naive.

When he took off from Berlin's Tempelhof Airport at 9:47 P.M. on January 18, 1939, it was the last time Lindbergh would set foot on German soil until six years later when the country he once loved, and the National Socialist vision he once admired, would be reduced to rubble.

Meanwhile, Truman Smith had received some devastating news. The previous September, a routine army physical had revealed the early onset of diabetes. The diagnosis meant an almost certain end to his foreign service career. In early February 1939, Smith was ordered to return to the States and report to Washington's Walter Reed Hospital for further tests. An army medical board would be convened in August to determine whether his military career was also at an end.

The same month, the Lindberghs were invited to England by their old friends Lord and Lady Astor, who were still giddy from the apparent success of the Munich pact four months earlier. Charles had a chance to personally congratulate Neville Chamberlain when the Prime Minister lunched at Cliveden on February 26. That evening, Lindbergh entered into a heated discussion with Britain's Ambassador to Washington, Lord Lothian, about the possibility of war. Lothian worried that a lasting peace could be achieved only so long as the German leadership "does not go mad with the feeling of power and destiny." To this, Lindbergh wrote in his journal, "I think I have a little more confidence in the sanity of German leadership than he has."[26]

Two weeks later, Germany shattered the empty promises of Munich when its army marched into Prague and dismembered Czechoslovakia.[27] In the looting that followed, the Nazis replenished their depleted treasury, took control of the country's sizable air force and seized the giant Czech armaments manufacturer Skoda Works. In the process, the Germans came considerably closer to achieving the military superiority Lindbergh had falsely proclaimed six months earlier. The move was one step nearer to the war Munich had been crafted to prevent.

The invasion prompted the sharpest anti-Nazi rebuke to date from President Roosevelt. His harsh condemnation of Nazi aggression unsettled Washington isolationist circles, raising concerns that the United States would find itself entangled in the European war that was now all but certain.

Smith initiated a new round of correspondence with Lindbergh. In contrast to their previous correspondence that focused mostly on German air power, this series of letters was preoccupied with the imminent European conflict.

The two devised a rudimentary code made up of numbers from 0 to 100, with which Smith would signal his assessment on the odds of war when he corresponded with Lindbergh. Thus, "Yes, 20" meant Smith believed there was only a 20 percent chance that war was imminent.

Lindbergh's week in England appeared to harden his increasing contempt for the British, which became an ever-recurring theme in his journal and correspondence: "The more I see of modern England and the British

people, the less confidence I have in them. . . . I feel sorry for the English . . . No wonder they are desperate." In the English, he saw a lack of
"virility"; they were a people ill-adapted to the modern world, more
attuned to the age of ships than aircraft. The important thing, he concludes, is to avoid letting their shortcomings "overthrow our entire civilization."[28] The balance of power had passed, he decided, and the future
clearly belonged to the New Germany.

When the number in Smith's cable reached "50" at the end of March,
Lindbergh came to a decision. With war clouds on the horizon, his family
was no longer safe in Europe. It was time to return home.[29]

On April 14, the Cunard ocean liner *Aquitania* pulled into New York
Harbor with a prominent passenger aboard. If Lindbergh's four-year European exile had diminished his popularity in any way, it was not evident
from the mob scene of journalists and photographers who jammed the
gangplank hoping for a glimpse of the returning hero. But Lindbergh was
hardly impressed with the reception. "It was a barbaric entry to a civilized
country," he complained in his journal.[30]

He was clearly unhappy at the prospect of returning home: "For twelve
years, I have found little freedom in the country which is supposed to
exemplify freedom," he confided. "The strange thing," he continued, is
that "I found the most personal freedom in Germany."[31]

The next day, before Lindbergh even had a chance to settle in, he was
summoned for a meeting with General Hap Arnold, chief of the United
States air corps. Six months after Munich, the government still had no idea
just how wrong Lindbergh's estimates of German air power had been. As
far as Washington was concerned, he had provided valuable intelligence
data and was a definite asset on the eve of the coming European war.
Arnold invited the reserve colonel back to active duty in the Army air
corps, effective immediately. His advice was needed to help strengthen
American air defenses. Lindbergh did not hesitate to accept, anxious to get
back to his first passion after so many years as a bystander.

Before reporting for duty, he was informed that his new commander-
in-chief President Roosevelt wanted to thank him personally for the service he had provided touring German aviation facilities. Lindbergh had
never met FDR personally, but their paths had crossed five years earlier in
a political battle that neither had ever forgotten.

It had happened in 1934 when Roosevelt issued a surprise presidential
decree announcing the cancellation of all domestic air mail contracts. A
Senate committee had discovered a number of irregularities in the
awarding of the contracts to commercial aviation companies. Henceforth, the President announced, the army air corps would deliver the mail
instead of the allegedly corrupt private firms which had dominated the

industry for years. Three days later, Lindbergh, who had begun his flying career as a mail carrier for one of these private companies, sent a telegram to the White House protesting the cancellation. At the same time, he leaked his communication to the press. The skirmish appeared on the front page of every American newspaper. When it came to aviation issues, even the President of the United States was no match for America's flying hero. Roosevelt was forced to back down in a public and humiliating retreat. Lindbergh, meanwhile, was beginning to understand how his fame could be harnessed to political ends. He and Roosevelt were destined to clash again, only this time in a battle involving higher stakes.

For now, however, both apparently agreed to forget their past differences. Their meeting, lasting less than fifteen minutes, was cordial. They exchanged routine pleasantries, the President bringing up the fact that his daughter had attended school with Anne. Afterward, Lindbergh wrote in his journal, "I liked him and feel that I could get along with him well. . . . But there was something about him I did not trust, something a little too suave, too pleasant, too easy . . . It is better to work together as long as we can; yet somehow I have a feeling that it may not be for long."[32]

He was not the only American wary of Roosevelt in the spring of 1939. As tensions mounted in Europe, political circles in the nation's Capitol were deeply divided among those who favored decisive U.S. intervention to stop the Nazis in their tracks and those who believed America had no business meddling in European affairs. And then there was a smaller clique—anti-Communist, anti-Semitic, and very conservative—made up primarily of military officers, intelligence agents, Republican politicians and former diplomats.[33] This group believed that Hitler could be useful. They were not necessarily pro-Nazi but believed that German aggression could be channeled eastward to rid Europe of the Soviet menace. Many of them were loyal to Roosevelt's predecessor, Republican president Herbert Hoover, and many had served in his administration. Meanwhile, Truman Smith, now back in Washington, was in great demand on the social circuit for his firsthand knowledge about Hitler and the Nazi regime. What are his intentions? Can he be trusted? Will there be war? Ideologically, Smith was immediately drawn to the Hoover group and they to him. He could offer them two very valuable commodities: a vast knowledge of Germany, and his close friendship with America's most popular hero.

The group was rudderless, without any formal organization. Its members shared a common conservative ideology and vision for America but they needed a leader, a man who could publicly crystallize this vision. The natural choice was Herbert Hoover but the former president was still extremely unpopular with the American people, who were convinced he had dragged the country into the morass of the Great Depression.

Smith was officially recuperating from his diabetes, awaiting his appearance at an army retirement board in Washington. But he decided to use his time constructively, preparing for the political battle ahead. In quick order, he introduced Lindbergh to his new Washington contacts: congressmen, senators, intelligence officers, and other conservatives concerned about an imminent European war. And, as Lindbergh made the rounds in Washington during those months in the spring and summer of 1939, he appears to have taken on a new preoccupation.

For years, his private correspondence and journal entries had displayed an obsession with race—its improvement, its degradation, its superior and inferior elements. But as he spent more time with Smith, discussing the shifting political winds, his racial discussions took on an ever narrower focus. For the first time, Lindbergh's attention centered on the Jews and their supposed influence over American foreign policy. On June 30, describing a meeting that afternoon with the powerful isolationist senator Harry Byrd, he writes in his journal, "We are both anxious to avoid having this country pushed into a European war by British and Jewish propaganda, of which there is already too much."[34] On August 23, he strikes a similar note, writing about a meeting with Bill Castle, the assistant chairman of the Republican National Committee:

> We are disturbed about the effect of the Jewish influence in our press, radio and motion pictures. It may become very serious . . . I fear that trouble lies ahead in this regard. Whenever the Jewish percentage of the population becomes too high, a reaction seems to invariably occur. It is too bad because a few Jews of the right type are, I believe, an asset to any country, adding to rather than detracting from its strength. If an anti-Semitic movement starts in the United States, it may go far. It will certainly affect the good Jews along with the others. When such a movement starts, moderation ends.[35]

It is interesting to note the similarities between his notions of "the good Jew" and Henry Ford's use of the same phrase two decades earlier. The paranoia about Jewish propaganda around this time may have had its roots in a movie released by Warner Brothers studio in April 1939, called *Confessions of a Nazi Spy*, which was about a German espionage ring operating in the United States. This film was seen as a turning point in Hollywood, the first motion picture to identify specifically and attack Hitler's regime.[36] Previously, Hollywood studio heads, many of them Jewish, had been reluctant to deal with Nazi themes, for fear that it would call attention to their own religious heritage and spark anti-Semitic attacks on the industry.[37] But after a Warner studio representative named Joe Kaufman was murdered in Berlin in 1936 by a gang of Nazi thugs, Jack Warner decided it was time to warn Americans of the growing Hitler menace.[38] When the studio released *Confessions*, the feared backlash immediately materialized, with the nation's most notorious Jew-baiters seizing on the theme of pervasive Jewish influence. On his popular weekly radio show, the country's highest profile anti-Semite, Father Coughlin, rarely missed a chance to inform his twenty million listeners that the Jews controlled Hollywood and the press.

During a later investigation, the FBI received a report that Truman Smith had approached the notorious American fascist leader James True and asked him to furnish "all available information on the Jewish subject" for Lindbergh.[39] If the report is correct, it may account for Lindbergh's increasingly anti-Semitic attitudes around this time.

It is also possible that, on his travels in the Third Reich, Lindbergh had come across a theme that was popular in Nazi Germany during the mid-1930s. In 1936, Julius Streicher's notorious anti-Semitic daily *Der Sturmer* reported that the abduction of the Lindbergh baby had been a Jewish plot, designed to obtain Charles Jr.'s blood for a religious ritual. The same edition reported a fact that would be repeated in the German press constantly throughout Hitler's reign—that 97 percent of all American newspaper publishers were Jews (the actual figure was less than 1 percent).[40]

There is no evidence that Lindbergh was ever aware of the bizarre anti-Semitic theory surrounding his child's abduction, although many have been puzzled about his strong admiration for Germany, in light of the fact that his son's abductor was German. But he certainly appeared to believe the fiction that Jews controlled his nation's media. For now, however, he kept his opinions behind closed doors.

Commuting between Washington and his new home in Lloyd Neck, Long Island, Lindbergh continued to discuss strategy with a growing circle of isolationists, most of whom had been introduced to him by Smith. The talk was always about Europe, and the growing fear that, in the event of war, the Jews and British would push the United States into a conflict of no concern to Americans. At a July meeting at Washington's Army Navy Club arranged by Truman Smith for Lindbergh and two sympathetic military officers, one of the officers asked his lunch companions how the English "really feel" about Americans. In his journal account, Lindbergh records the other officer's response: "Well, I'll tell you. The English feel about us just the way we feel about a prosperous nigger."[41]

Both Lindbergh and Smith were in regular contact with Hugh Wilson, the former American ambassador to Germany, who had been recalled to Washington by Roosevelt in November 1938 to protest the *Kristallnacht* riots. Wilson was just one of many high-ranking American diplomats who believed Roosevelt's belligerent attitude toward Hitler was the result of a powerful "Jewish lobby."[42] His assessment of Hitler's Germany was remarkably similar to that of Smith, who had become a close friend while the two were stationed in Berlin. Wilson noted in his memoirs that, before the Nazis took power, "The stage, the press, medicine and law, were crowded with Jews . . . the leaders of the Bolshevist movement in Russia, a movement desperately feared in Germany, were Jews. One could sense the spreading resentment and hatred."[43]

Fearful they were being watched by the Roosevelt administration, Lindbergh and Smith worked out a more sophisticated code to complement the rudimentary numbers device they had used until then to discuss the odds of war. They operated like secret agents behind enemy lines. Henceforth, a member of the anti-Roosevelt faction would be referred to as FRIEND. Individual isolationist senators and congressmen were assigned numbers, except for particularly valuable allies who had their own code names. Congressman George Tinkham of Massachusetts, for example, was referred to as BEARD.[44]

As long as Smith remained a G2 intelligence officer, he enjoyed access to valuable intelligence data that could be passed on to members of the anti-Roosevelt faction.[45] However, his privileged access looked likely to be terminated in August when Smith was scheduled to report to an army medical board that would almost certainly recommend his retirement from the military because of his diabetes. But on July 25, shortly before the board was scheduled to determine Smith's fate, Lindbergh intervened on behalf of his friend and requested a private meeting with General George Marshall, the U.S. army chief of staff. Over lunch, he told the powerful general that it would be "inexcusable if the Army failed to make use of Smith's ability and knowledge" by discharging him from a distinguished career simply because of his physical problems.[46] Marshall apparently took heed. A month later, the general personally intervened to overrule the medical board's decision to recommend Smith's retirement. Instead, he ordered Smith back to active duty with G2, the War Department's Military Intelligence Division.[47] Not coincidentally, Marshall was himself an avowed isolationist, believing, like much of the army high command during this period, that true patriotism involved resisting pressures at home or abroad that might involve the United States in a foreign war.[48] However, he only shared these views with trusted confidantes.

Among these pressures was a concerted attempt by the Roosevelt administration to revise the neutrality laws that prevented the United States from sending arms to its allies in case of war, an effort that caused Hitler to accuse the President of engaging in a "holy crusade" against the Reich.[49] Roosevelt was deeply committed to aid the victims of Axis aggression, but was handcuffed by the Neutrality Act of 1935, which forbade the export of arms, ammunition or implements of war to belligerent nations. When his Congressional allies attempted to amend the act, they were immediately met with fierce resistance from a powerful and united Congressional bloc that was to form the core of the isolationist movement in the years ahead. In July, Senator Gerald Nye declared to newsmen that the isolationists were serving "notice to France and Great Britain that we are not going to fight any more of their wars."

Aware that he faced a tough political battle ahead, FDR began to chart a clandestine strategy designed to stop Hitler by stealth before the dictator could swallow Europe whole. He was convinced America could no longer sit comfortably in its isolation. Like Lindbergh, the president believed that nothing short of Western civilization was at stake. Their respective concepts of civilization, however, were very much at odds.

On August 28, Charles and Anne were at home in New Jersey when a coded telegram arrived from Truman Smith. It read, simply, "YES, 80."[50] Four days later, during the early hours of September 1, German *Panzers* poured across the Polish border in a ferocious assault. Without a formal declaration of war, Germany's army, navy, and air force invaded Poland from three directions. The Nazi *blitzkrieg* quickly overpowered any resistance from the outmatched Poles, who rapidly capitulated against the brutal onslaught.

"The German army will fight the battle for the honor and the vital rights of reborn Germany with hard determination," blared Hitler that evening. Forty-eight hours later, England and France honored their treaty obligation to Poland and declared war on Germany.

On the evening of September 3, President Roosevelt promised the American people in a national radio address that the United States would not intervene in the European conflict:

I have said not once but many times that I have seen war and that I hate war. I say that again and again. I hope the United

States will keep out of this war. I believe that it will. And I give you assurance and reassurance that every effort of your Government will be directed toward that end.[51]

In his New Jersey home, Lindbergh listened with Anne to the president's address. His verdict: "It was a better talk than he usually gives. I wish I trusted him more."[52]

Indeed, neither Lindbergh, Truman Smith, nor the other isolationists in their circle trusted the President to keep his pledge of American neutrality. They were convinced he had a plan to get the country into the war "through the back door," a plan they were intent on thwarting. The only way to keep Roosevelt honest, they concluded, was to convince the American public that involvement in the European maelstrom would be a disaster. To achieve this, they needed a voice, a public figure who could counter the President's vast popularity. Roosevelt's enemies had never forgotten that Lindbergh had publicly bested FDR during the air mail dispute five years earlier, handing the President one of his rare political defeats.

On September 10, a week after the declaration of war, Lindbergh received a phone call from his new friend Fulton Lewis Jr., a well-known conservative radio commentator whose broadcasts were carried over the Mutual Broadcasting System, one of America's largest radio networks. Lindbergh had been introduced to Lewis only two weeks earlier at the home of the prominent isolationist Bill Castle, a strongly conservative former undersecretary of state in the Hoover administration, who was currently assistant chairman of the Republican National Committee. It was at this August 23 dinner that the three men had discussed the pervasive Jewish influence in Hollywood and the media.[53] At the same gathering, Lindbergh had wondered aloud whether "it might not be wise," should war erupt, to have a small group ready to become active in opposition to American entry in a European war.[54] Lewis now believed the time had come to activate this group.

Unbeknownst to his many radio listeners, Lewis was on extremely friendly terms with the Nazi embassy in Washington, as a 1939 dispatch captured by the Allies after the war later revealed. In this communiqué, the German press attaché in Washington had cabled the foreign office in Berlin passing along a suggestion from Lewis to Hitler explaining how the Führer could establish a friendly relationship with Roosevelt and ensure continued American neutrality. Lewis even provided the specific wording for the letter he proposed the chancellor send to the American president. In his dispatch to Berlin, the German attaché recommends Lewis as an "admirer of Germany and the Führer and a highly respected American journalist."[55]

With Europe at war, Lewis now set his sights on the Lone Eagle as the isolationists' new hope. He used his network connections to arrange radio air time for Lindbergh to address the American people in a nationwide address with a plea for neutrality. Lindbergh, with his behind-the-scenes shuttle diplomacy during the Czech crisis a year earlier, had maintained a low profile, and had thus gone unnoticed by the public. Few Americans were aware of the influential role he had played in the events leading up to Munich. In fact, since Bruno Hauptmann's execution in 1936, the American media had devoted little coverage to the man who had so frequently occupied the front pages during the previous seven years.

Now he was about take center stage again in a role for which his new friends had been grooming him for months. For five days, Lindbergh carefully drafted and revised the remarks that would mark his first formal radio appearance since August 28, 1931, when he had addressed a group of Japanese dignitaries in Tokyo. The speech would be carried over three national radio networks and reach an audience as large as that of Roosevelt's popular fireside chats.

But on the afternoon of September 15, a rather strange incident threatened to derail the address slated for later that evening. Truman Smith arrived at Lindbergh's Washington hotel room around 4:00 P.M. with an urgent message. Smith explained that the Roosevelt administration was "very much worried" about Lindbergh publicizing his opposition to American entry in a European war. If he would agree to cancel his address, the President was willing to offer Lindbergh a newly created Cabinet position, Secretary for Air, established just for him. As he relayed Roosevelt's offer, Smith could barely contain his glee. "So you see, they're worried," he said, laughing.[56]

According to Smith, the proposition had originated from U.S. Secretary of War Harry Woodring who spoke to General Hap Arnold, who in turn asked Smith to relay personally the offer to his friend. When Smith received the offer from Arnold, he asked the general whether he thought for a minute that Lindbergh would accept. "Of course not," Arnold allegedly replied.

In his journal entry describing the incident, Lindbergh reveals a disdain for the President that already appeared to be pervasive in isolationist circles by the fall of 1939: "The offer on Roosevelt's part does not surprise me after what I have learned about his Administration. It does surprise me, though, that he still thinks I might be influenced by such an offer."[57] In fact, no evidence has ever been found confirming that Roosevelt actually made Lindbergh this offer. We only have Smith's word that it happened.

That evening, millions of Americans gathered around their radios to hear the first shots in an epic battle that would become known as the Great Debate. At 9:45 P.M. a thin, nasal voice announced, "I speak tonight to those people in the United States of America who feel that the destiny of this country does not call for our involvement in European wars."[58]

For half an hour, in a compelling speech that appealed as much to emotion as reason, Lindbergh raised the specter of unprecedented bloodshed: "We are likely to lose a million men, possibly several million—the best of American youth. We will be staggering under the burden of recovery during the rest of our lives." After warning that involvement in a European war "may lead to the end of Western civilization"—the recurring theme of his correspondence for months—he uttered the speech's most memorable line, cautioning his listeners against heeding emotional appeals about the plight of the Europeans: "We must be as impersonal as a surgeon with his knife." It is this cold phrase that was singled out in most of the press coverage the next day. Little attention was given to a cryptic passage buried near the end of the address. In it, he advised his listeners to be wary of the propaganda they were bound to encounter in the months ahead: "We must ask who owns and who influences the newspaper, the news picture, and the radio station. If our people know the truth . . . this country is not likely to enter the war. We must learn to look behind every article we read and every speech we hear."[59]

Lindbergh's reemergence on the national scene was the talk of the nation for days. The Roosevelt administration, sensitive to his popular sway, was initially relieved that he had not explicitly opposed the repeal of the arms embargo that was a cornerstone of the President's new foreign policy, "aid-short-of-war." In their predominantly favorable coverage, many newspapers noted that, in advocating American neutrality, Lindbergh was simply carrying on his father's legacy. This is a theme that would be repeatedly be invoked during the next two years. But there was a very striking difference between Lindbergh's philosophy toward war and the philosophy of his father C.A., who was a self-proclaimed pacifist. In one of his journal entries, Lindbergh would underscore that difference when he wrote, "What luck it is to find myself opposing my country's entrance into a war I *don't* believe in when I would so much rather be fighting for my country in a war I *do* believe in."

Newspaper editorials the week of his radio address were about 90 percent favorable, but they only reflected the general American consensus, which was overwhelmingly against entry into the European conflict.[60] Supportive letters and telegrams poured into Lindbergh's Lloyd Neck estate. One even compared his speech to the Sermon on the Mount.[61]

Lindbergh's radio address was not as well received by two of the world's greatest scientists, who had been contemplating using him as a go-between to send a message to the White House that would forever change the course of history. For several weeks, the exiled European physicists Leo Szilard and Albert Einstein had been discussing how to inform President Roosevelt about a radical new scientific discovery—the realization that a nuclear chain reaction could be generated in a large mass of uranium to produce a bomb capable of unprecedented destruction. With the world on the brink of war, both men were fearful that Hitler's scientists would come to the same conclusion and produce a secret weapon that would win the war for Germany. With deep reservations, they decided that the United States must build an atomic bomb before the Nazis. They desperately sought a way to get the sensitive message directly to the President. They needed an emissary who they believed could place their message directly into Roosevelt's hands. Szilard immediately seized upon Charles Lindbergh as the ideal candidate. Einstein had become acquainted with Lindbergh years before at the laboratory of Alexis Carrel and he agreed to write a letter of introduction, which was dispatched to Lindbergh along with a letter from Szilard on August 16—two weeks before Germany invaded Poland:

> Dear Herr Lindbergh: I would like to ask you to do me the favor of receiving my friend Dr. Szilard and think very carefully about what he will tell you. To one who is outside science, the matter he will bring up may seem fantastic. However, you will certainly become convinced that a possibility is presented here which has to be carefully watched in the public interest, even though the results so far are not immediately impressive. With all respects and friendly wishes, A. Einstein.[62]

By September 13, two days before Lindbergh's radio address, he had still not responded to Szilard, who proceeded to send him a reminder letter. Two weeks later, after Lindbergh's address placed him squarely in the isolationist camp, Szilard wrote a letter to Einstein concluding: "Lindbergh is not our man."[63]

Meanwhile, the isolationists were exceedingly pleased with the success of Lindbergh's radio speech. Herbert Hoover sent his congratulations for "a really great address" and suggested a meeting. On September 21, the two men had lunch at the Waldorf Astoria, where the former President shared his view that the British Empire was in decline and that Germany's expansion was inevitable, whether by force or by diplomacy. They agreed on one more thing: "Roosevelt definitely desires to get us into this conflict."[64]

Their fears weren't entirely unjustified. A week earlier, the President had sent a letter to Winston Churchill that would begin an extraordinary six-year correspondence. With his Munich peace in tatters, Prime Minister Chamberlain had summoned his old nemesis Churchill into the British War Cabinet as first lord of the admiralty, the same position Churchill had held during the First World War. At that time, his American counterpart— assistant secretary of the navy in President Wilson's wartime cabinet—was the young Franklin Roosevelt.

Now president himself, Roosevelt took the opportunity to resume communications with his old ally. On September 11, he wrote an innocuous letter to Churchill inviting him to "keep me in touch personally with anything you want me to know about."[65] What made this letter unusual was the fact that a head of state was communicating with another leader's Cabinet official behind that leader's back.[66]

Churchill would not become prime minister himself for nearly a year but the farsighted, wily politician was already convinced of one thing: If England was to have any chance at all of survival against the powerful Axis, she would need America's help.

The Nazi foreign ministry had come to a remarkably similar conclusion. For the next two years, as Churchill struggled to pull the United States into the war, Germany worked just as hard to keep America neutral. Both battles were fought in secret. The victor of this historical tug-of-war would decide the course of history.

The only wild card was Roosevelt himself. Even today, there is no consensus where he actually stood during this period. Was he, as the isolationists charged, secretly plotting with Churchill to take America into the war? Or was he sincere in his public pledge to remain neutral? One thing is certain. Franklin Delano Roosevelt was the consummate politician and in the fall of 1939, only a year away from re-election, he knew which way the political winds were blowing. The American people had not forgotten the bloody horrors of the Great War two decades earlier. Poll after poll revealed they were in no mood for a repeat.

Only six days after Lindbergh's first radio address—in which he urged Americans not to allow "sentiment and pity" to cloud their judgment— Reinhard Heydrich, head of the Nazi security police, issued an edict clearing the way for the eventual liquidation of Polish Jewry. His infamous *schnellbrief*, entitled "The Jewish Question in the Occupied Territory," ordered the formation of *Judenraete* (Jewish Councils) in Polish towns, the deportation of Jews from areas of northeastern Poland that were earmarked for annexation to the Reich, and the establishment of Jewish ghettoes in large towns situated near railroad junctions.[67]

On the other side of the Atlantic, Lindbergh appears to have cemented his credentials as the leader of isolationism at a remarkably rapid pace, considering his political inexperience. He was clearly no mere figurehead; on October 2, Herbert Hoover himself called and asked his advice about an upcoming speech he planned to deliver about the military prospects for Britain and France in the new European war.[68] But, as Lindbergh was advising ex-presidents, it soon became clear who was shaping his own views. Behind the scenes, Truman Smith was at work steering his political protégé to meetings with potentially useful members of congress and other powerful policy-makers. On September 27, Smith invited Republican congressman George Tinkham of Massachusetts to a meeting with Lindbergh to discuss the isolationists' new policy priority—maintaining the arms embargo against Roosevelt's increasing efforts to repeal it.

The most puzzling aspect of Smith's activities at this juncture is why he was permitted by his superiors to pursue such an obvious political agenda while still on active military duty. Lindbergh himself had been removed from active status[69] in the air corps by General Hap Arnold on September 14, the day before his first radio address, because he planned to take an "active part in politics."[70] Yet, Smith was permitted to continue planning isolationist strategy in a less than discreet fashion. Clearly, many high-ranking members of the U.S. military sympathized with the isolationist cause and were untroubled by Smith's behind-the-scenes plotting, so long as he kept out of the public eye.

After the meeting with Congressman Tinkham, it was decided that Lindbergh would need to go before the nation again, this time with a more focused message. Momentum was building around Roosevelt's campaign to repeal the arms embargo. If the President succeeded, it would be the first step in helping to arm the European allies against the overwhelming strength of the German-Italian Axis. Though still war-shy, a full 60 percent of Americans favored repealing the arms embargo.[71] The isolationists were determined to reverse this trend.

On October 14, Lindbergh returned to the airwaves to deliver his second address, entitled "Neutrality and War." Sounding more confident than in his first radio address a month earlier, he announced, "Tonight, I speak again to the people of this country who are opposed to the United States entering the war which is now going on in Europe." He proceeded to outline a four-point proposal that would continue the arms embargo on "offensive" weapons but offer the European allies all the "defensive" weapons America could spare. As many later noted, this policy was next to useless against a German army well stocked with its own extraordinary offensive arsenal. Without an offensive military capability to strike back at its aggressors, it would only be a matter of time before the Axis smashed through any defense England and France could muster.

Moreover, Lindbergh's proposal would prohibit the United States from extending credit to the cash-starved European nations, making even the purchase of defensive weapons next to impossible. Nevertheless, the most striking chord of this speech, one that would not escape notice, was a passage that appeared to crystallize his increasing obsession with race, nurtured in the laboratory of Alexis Carrel. Since returning to America, Lindbergh had again reunited with Carrel, spending considerable time with his mentor. The two were making plans to establish an "Institute for the Betterment of Man" at the Lindberghs' old Hopewell estate, where their common ideas about eugenics and spiritual development could be advanced, harnessing what Carrel called the "weapons of knowledge and thought which are so abundantly available."[72] Now, Lindbergh was sharing those ideas with the American people for the first time:

> Our bond with Europe is a bond of race and not of political ideology. We had to fight a European army to establish democracy in this country. It is the European race we must preserve; political progress will follow. Racial strength is vital—politics a luxury. If the white race is ever seriously threatened, it may then be time for us to take our part in its protection, to fight side by side with the English, French, and Germans, but not with one against the other for our mutual destruction.[73]

It was as if Lindbergh perceived the European conflict merely as a misguided internecine battle between racial brothers.

In stark contrast to the reaction from his first radio address a month earlier, the attacks commenced almost immediately. On the floor of the Senate the following day, where a debate over amending the Neutrality Act was well under way, one Senator after another lined up to denounce Lindbergh's speech. Senator Key Pittman, the powerful chairman of the foreign relations committee, told his colleagues, "The most unfortunate

part of Colonel Lindbergh's statement is that it encourages the ideology
of the totalitarian governments and is subject to the construction that he
approves of their brutal conquest of democratic countries through
war."[74]

A number of senators pointed out the remarkable similarity in wording between Lindbergh's radio address and a recent talk by Herbert
Hoover. But the harshest words were reserved for his distinction between
defensive and offensive weapons. That morning, Major General John F.
Ryan, commander of the U.S. Army 27th Division, had labeled this distinction as "nonsense." The military aim of the Allies, he declared, was to
smash aggression at its source, not to limit its action to defensive measures.[75]

Attacks began to pour in from the liberal press. The popular and tenacious syndicated columnist Dorothy Thompson—one of the few pundits
to have criticized his first speech—called Lindbergh "a somber cretin," a
man "without human feeling," a "pro-Nazi recipient of a German medal."
Lindbergh, she wrote, dreamt of being "an American Führer."

Even more damaging was an article by the popular First Lady Eleanor
Roosevelt signaling her approval of some of the recent media assaults on
Lindbergh's speech. In her widely read nationally syndicated column, "My
Day," Mrs. Roosevelt wrote, "We were all interested in Mr. Walter Lippmann's column of a few days ago and in Dorothy Thompson's column
yesterday. She sensed in Colonel Lindbergh's speech a sympathy with
Nazi ideals which I thought existed but could not bring myself to believe
was really there."[76] Few doubted that she was reflecting her husband's
views, especially when she atypically used the word "we" to begin the column rather than her tradition of writing in the first person.[77]

Two days later, Lindbergh's old friend and British landlord, Harold
Nicolson, weighed in with an article published in the influential London
magazine *The Spectator.* Part psychological analysis, part biographical portrait, Nicolson's piece is a fascinating, if biased, insight into the man he
once knew well. In the struggle to remain humble after his historic transatlantic flight, Nicolson theorizes, Lindbergh's "simplicity became muscle-
bound; his virility and ideas became not only inflexible but actually rigid;
his self-confidence thickened into arrogance and his convictions hardened
into granite." As a result, he argues, Lindbergh became impervious to anything outside his own legend—"the legend of the lad from Minnesota
whose head could not be turned."

Nicolson believed the tragic death of his child in 1932—and the
accompanying media circus—was the defining point in Lindbergh's transformation, explaining that he emerged from that nightmare with a hatred
for publicity that was "almost pathological":

"He identified the outrage to his private life first with the popular press and then by inevitable associations with freedom of speech and then, almost with freedom. He began to loathe democracy."[78]

Above all, Nicolson's piece attempts to allow the bewildered British people to understand how Lindbergh could repay their three years of hospitality by abandoning them to the mercies of the German military. It reads not so much as a condemnation of his friend, or even an excuse for his behavior, but rather as an explanation:

"The slow, organic will power of Britain eluded his observation; he regarded our indifference to the mechanical as proof that we, as they say in Minnesota, were 'incurable effetes.' "

Nicolson concludes his piece on a warm, almost condescending, note:

"Let us not allow this incident to blind us to the great qualities of Charles Lindbergh; he is and always will be not merely a schoolboy hero but also a schoolboy."[79]

Stung by this broadside from an old friend and the excoriating attacks in the interventionist media, Lindbergh retreated temporarily to the refuge of Lloyd Neck. Anne was not coping well with the cruel return to the public eye. She had long ago become accustomed to the unceasing adulation that came with being Mrs. Charles Lindbergh, wife of an American hero; the cranks and lunatics, the assault on her privacy from press and public. Most of the previous attention, however, had been overwhelming affection. Until her husband went public with his views about the war, she had no idea what it was like to be associated with a controversial public figure. Writing in her diary during this period, she bemoans what she calls the "backwash" from his speeches:

> Bitter criticism. Personal attacks. He has had two threatening letters. He is a "Nazi." He will be punished. Our other two children will be taken. . . . I feel angry and bitter and trapped again. Where can we live, where can we go? C. is criminally misunderstood, misquoted and misused.[80]

Lindbergh's much-criticized remarks on America's racial bond with Europe were merely a preview of an article he had been working on for the conservative magazine *Reader's Digest*, whose isolationist founder DeWitt Wallace had told him recently, "No one in the country is able to exert a deeper influence on public opinion than yourself."[81] The article was published in the November issue under the title "Aviation, Geography and Race," written ostensibly to illustrate the senselessness of a war with

Hitler. The disturbing racial ideas that had been germinating in Carrel's laboratory and nurtured during Lindbergh's growing fascination with the Third Reich appeared to coalesce in this one essay.

In it, Lindbergh posits aviation as a precious tool to be shared exclusively by the western nations as a "barrier between the teeming millions of Asia and the Grecian inheritance of Europe—one of those priceless possessions which permit the White race to live at all in a pressing sea of Yellow, Black and Brown."[82]

To Lindbergh, the war that mattered is a war that "the White race is bound to lose, and the others bound to gain, a war which may easily lead our civilization through more Dark Ages if it survives at all."

Continuing on this undisguised racist theme for three and a half pages, he argues that aviation can be the savior of European culture if only the great white nations come together instead of tearing each other apart: "We, the heirs of European culture, are on the verge of a disastrous war, a war within our own family of nations, a war which will reduce the strength and destroy the treasures of the White race."

But this tragedy is preventable, he argues, if only we can build a "Western Wall of race and arms" to hold back "the infiltration of inferior blood." The answer rests on an "English Fleet, a German Air Force, a French army, an American nation, standing together as guardians of our common heritage." Finally, he concludes with a plea not to "commit racial suicide by internal conflict. We must learn from Athens and Sparta before all Greece is lost."[83]

All white people, then, appeared to have common cause with the Germans in the world that Lindbergh envisioned. This didn't sound like the everyday socialized racism of so many ordinary Americans, but rather the intellectualized racism of the Nazis, as his growing legions of media critics were quick to point out. Nonetheless, most Americans continued to oppose intervention, and Lindbergh was still a hero to millions.

This fact did not escape the attention of the Roosevelt administration, concerned by the well-organized and effective strategy of the isolationist movement and its popular leader. In early December, Roosevelt invited an old friend, Kansas newspaperman William Allen White, to spend a night at the White House. The President wished to elicit White's help in convincing Americans to consider the danger of the Nazi threat "without scaring the people into thinking that they are going to be dragged into this war."[84] At first glance, White was an unlikely leader of the interventionist cause. A lifelong Republican, he had owned the conservative *Emporia Gazette* since 1895. But White was also something of a political maverick, running as an independent for Governor of Kansas in 1924 because of his opposition to the Ku Klux Klan.[85] He cherished freedom and Roosevelt believed he was the ideal candidate to counter the isolationists.

In constant consultation with the Administration, White assembled an influential array of journalists, politicians and strategists to form what would become the country's most formidable interventionist organization, the Committee to Defend America by Aiding the Allies.

Not coincidentally, the public launch of the new committee on May 20, 1940, came only a day after Charles Lindbergh delivered his third nation-wide radio address, entitled "The Air Defense of America."

"We are in danger of war today," Lindbergh announced, "not because European people have attempted to interfere with the internal affairs of America, but because American people have attempted to interfere with the internal affairs of Europe."

In later years, Lindbergh's apologists would defend his isolationist activities on the grounds that, while he preached against aid to the Allies, he consistently argued for a buildup of America's own defenses, indeed contributed significantly to American military strength by warning the nation of the urgent need to re-arm. However, this was nowhere evident in his "Air Defense" speech when he attacked President Roosevelt's plan to build 50,000 new aircraft: "The power of aviation has been greatly under-rated in the past. Now we must be careful not to overestimate this power in the excitement of reaction. Air strength depends more upon the establish-ment of intelligent, consistent policies than upon the construction of huge numbers of planes."

More than one historian has pointed out the inconsistency of this state-ment. For years, Lindbergh had been preaching the gospel of air power, notes Albert Fried. Now that it was being acted upon, he was counseling restraint.[86]

Toward the end of the speech, Lindbergh issued his now standard cryptic warning: "The only reason we are in danger of becoming involved in this war is because there are powerful elements in America who desire to take part. They represent a small minority of the American people, but they control much of the machinery of influence and propaganda."

Increasingly, the media viewed his stance with alarm. The *New York Times* issued a sharp rebuke after his speech, warning that the course advo-cated by Lindbergh would result in a "calamity" for the American people:

> He is an ignorant young man if he trusts his own premise that it makes no difference to us whether we are deprived of the his-toric defense of British sea-power in the Atlantic Ocean. He is a blind young man if he really believes we can live on terms of

equal peace and happiness "regardless of which side wins this war" in Europe. Colonel Lindbergh remains a great flier.[87]

During the seven-month interval between his second and third radio speeches, Lindbergh's dire warnings about German military invincibility appeared prophetic to many as Hitler's army conquered its opponents with ease. But he was wrong about another of his regular assertions. He had always claimed the Germans had no westward expansion plans; their army, he forecast, would march to the East, ultimately directing its powerful arsenal at the Soviet Union. But in August 1939, shortly before the invasion of Poland, Hitler suddenly announced that he had concluded a Non-Aggression Pact with Stalin. Then, after a six-month lull known as the "Phony War," the Nazis had turned the full weight of their *blitzkrieg* toward the west.

In quick succession, the *Wehrmacht* had conquered Denmark, Norway, Belgium, Luxembourg, and the Netherlands in a chilling reminder of how easily a military bully could subdue weaker nations at will. France was next. Within days, the Allies would begin the evacuation of Dunkirk and, a hair's breadth away from military catastrophe, abandon the defense of France. If France fell, England would stand alone.

His Munich peace accord now a humiliating reminder of Appeasement's consequences, Neville Chamberlain was forced to resign as prime minister. To lead them, the British people turned to Winston Churchill, the only politician who had predicted and tried to prevent the current catastrophic state of affairs.

At almost the same moment that Lindbergh was delivering his Air Defense speech on May 19, Churchill spoke to the British people for the first time as prime minister. In a speech broadcast over the BBC, he vowed to save mankind from what he called "the foulest and most soul-destroying tyranny which has ever darkened and stained the pages of history . . . Our task is not only to win the battle—but to win the war," proclaimed the new British leader. "After this battle in France abates its force, there will come the battle for our island—for all that Britain is, and all that Britain means."[88]

If Lindbergh and his fellow isolationists had their way, Britain would face this battle alone. But Franklin Roosevelt had other ideas. How, the president wondered, could anybody wish this fate on the beleaguered island nation, America's historic ally and friend? He could understand Lindbergh's opposition to direct U.S. military intervention. Most Americans wanted to stay out of the war. But this fellow was opposing even indirect assistance, the military aid England desperately needed if it was to stand a chance against the formidable Axis war machine.

On May 20, the day after Lindbergh's air defense speech, the President was having lunch with his treasury secretary, Henry Morgenthau. After a brief discussion of this latest radio address, the President put down his fork, turned to his most trusted Cabinet official and declared, "If I should die tomorrow, I want you to know this. I am absolutely convinced that Lindbergh is a Nazi."[89]

CHAPTER 8

AN ARSENAL OF NAZISM

The cover of *Ford-Werke*'s house organ extols the Führer at a time when the American parent company still controlled its German subsidiary. After the war, a U.S. military investigation would conclude that Ford's German plant, with the full consent of Dearborn, had become an "arsenal of Nazism."

During the final days of summer 1939, Henry Ford was vacationing in Sudbury, Massachusetts, when a local newspaperman caught up to him. What did he think of this bully Hitler, who was again making threatening noises in Europe? "I don't know Hitler personally," came Ford's response, "but at least Germany keeps its people at work." The reporter persisted. What about his increasingly shrill military threats? "They don't dare have a war and they know it," Ford scoffed.[1] The date was August 28. Four days later, Germany invaded Poland, setting off the Second World War.

Back in Detroit a week later, discussion centered on the European war. "There hasn't been a shot fired," Ford told his friend John Dykema. "The whole thing has just been made up by Jew bankers."[2]

A year earlier, former U.S. ambassador to Germany William Dodd, Truman Smith's old nemesis, told a reporter aboard a U.S.-bound ship that "Fascism is on the march today in America. Millionaires are marching to the tune. It will come in this country unless a strong defense is set up by all liberal and progressive forces . . . A clique of U.S. industrialists is hell-bent to bring a fascist state to supplant our democratic government, and is working closely with the fascist regime in Germany and Italy. Aboard ship a prominent executive of one of America's largest financial corporations told me point blank that if the progressive trend of the Roosevelt administration continued, he would be ready to take definite action to bring fascism to America."[3]

Five days after Charles Lindbergh took to the airwaves for his first nationwide address against American involvement in the war, Ford voiced his own views to a Detroit newspaper. He praised the "foolproof" quality of the existing Neutrality Act and warned that if America started shipping arms and war materials to Europe, "We'll be in the war right away." On September 25, he addressed an American Legion convention in Chicago with a similar message, predicting that the conflict would end on its own if only the United States stayed out. "If I were put on the stand," he told the audience of First World War veterans, "I'd say there isn't any war today."[4]

But in November, Roosevelt got his way on the Neutrality Act with a congressional amendment. The path was now clear for the United States to ship war materials to Britain and France.

For months as winter weather forced a lull in hostilities, nothing happened. This was the so-called Phony War. Then, like a thunderbolt, Hitler's army struck, easily crushing its hapless opponents and driving on west toward the English Channel.[5]

On May 16, a worried President Roosevelt asked Congress to shore up America's defenses with a $1 billion appropriation, and proposed an increase in military aircraft production from a few hundred to 50,000 planes per year.

"Let us examine, without self-deception, the dangers which confront us," he declared. "Let us measure our strength and our defense without self-delusion. The clear fact is that the American people must recast their thinking about national protection . . . Our defenses must be invulnerable, our security absolute."[6]

On May 28, Roosevelt appointed the president of General Motors, a former Ford production manager named William S. Knudsen, as U.S. Commissioner for Industrial Production. His task would be to mobilize America's corporate giants for defense work, strengthening a military arsenal that had been weakened by years of neglect. This meant potentially lucrative defense contracts for each of the big three car companies.

The day of the announcement, reporters gathered outside Henry Ford's office to hear his opinion of Knudsen's appointment. His former employee was quite capable, Ford told the newsmen, and his idea of using auto plants to manufacture aircraft was particularly sound: "With the counsel of men like Lindbergh and Rickenbacker [America's most decorated flying ace] . . . and without meddling by government agencies," the Ford company could "swing into production of a thousand airplanes of standard design a day."[7]

Taken aback by this bold assertion, the newsmen pressed him for details. Ford hurriedly stressed that he was referring to defense activity only and repeated his conviction that the United States must not be pushed into the war. Nevertheless, the boast of a thousand planes a day was major news and it was splashed across the nation's newspapers. Such a figure was unheard of. Fifty planes a day would be a significant accomplishment. Still, if Henry Ford said it can be done, who could doubt his word? Miracles of manufacturing were his business.

The sensational claim attracted immediate attention on both sides of the Atlantic. By the spring of 1940, it was widely believed that air power represented England's only chance to defend against the offensive that all sides knew was coming after the humiliating Dunkirk evacuation in May. Miraculously, British forces, pinned to the sea by the German army, had managed to evacuate 300,000 Allied troops to fight another day. The British needed planes, and they needed them in a hurry.

On May 29, 1940, Edsel Ford was summoned to Washington for a meeting with William Knudsen, U.S. Secretary of the Treasury Henry Morgenthau, and other government officials, to discuss the possibility of manufacturing a new fleet of aircraft for the British Royal Air Force. Edsel had been handed the presidency of the Ford Motor Company by his father years earlier, although Henry still retained complete control over the company he had founded.

On May 31, Edsel met with Knudsen and made it clear that it would take months to retool the plant to prepare for aircraft manufacturing. The Ford Motor Company, after all, had not built an airplane since 1933. However, he had an alternative suggestion. The company could be turning out significant numbers of airplane engines in a matter of weeks, Edsel claimed.

By 1940, much of the British air force fleet was obsolete. The RAF possessed a sufficient number of planes, but air ministry officials believed that many of them were slower than the *Luftwaffe*'s newer state-of-the-art fleet, which had been so loudly heralded by Lindbergh. If more powerful engines could be retrofitted into England's older planes, it would go a long way to strengthening England's air defenses. Edsel's offer was timely.

Morgenthau sent word to the British government through its Washington High Commission that Ford was capable of manufacturing aircraft engines on an expedited basis. In London, the news was received with cautious optimism. Sir Henry Self, manager of the British air production division, cabled his air ministry with some reservations about Ford's potential involvement in the contract because of the American industrialist's recent "pacifistic" statements about the war: "Whether he would work directly for the Allies, and if so, whether his past record warrants reliance on him by the Allies are matters for consideration."[8]

At a second meeting with Edsel on June 11, Knudsen proposed that the Ford Motor Company manufacture enough engines to power the entire RAF arsenal, as well as a substantial portion of the U.S. fleet. Edsel agreed in principle, but one obstacle remained. He would have to get approval from his father before he could accept an order from the British government. He promised a quick decision either way.

The next day, Edsel met with his father to discuss the engine order. Six thousand engines would be shipped to England for use of the Royal Air Force, he explained, while an additional three thousand would be sold to the U.S. Air Corps. Each order would require a separate contract. To comply with the remaining provisions of the Neutrality Act, the British government would be required to pay for its own order, even though it was clear the funding was being provided by Washington.[9] The younger Ford was unsure how his father would react to the idea of manufacturing engines for England. But his fears proved unfounded. To his immense relief, he received Henry's go-ahead to accept the contract on June 12.

"I believe the enthusiasm Edsel and I showed for the project influenced his decision," recalled Ford's production chief Charles Sorensen, who also attended the meeting. Edsel was elated. There was nothing more lucrative than government defense work, and it appeared there would be plenty more high-paying Washington contracts for the company in the near future.[10] On the evening of June 12, Edsel phoned Knudsen to confirm his company's acceptance of the order to manufacture 9,000 Rolls-Royce engines. Preparations for tooling and production would begin immediately.

Morgenthau's office promptly relayed the news to Lord Beaverbrook in London. In one of his first acts as prime minister a month earlier, Winston Churchill had appointed the Canadian press baron as minister for aircraft production, responsible for galvanizing the aircraft industry around the British war effort. The task seemed especially urgent, for both Washington and London still wrongly assumed that England's air force was far behind Germany, based on the estimates of Lindbergh and others.

On the 17th, Beaverbrook casually informed British reporters that Ford would be producing six thousand Rolls-Royce Merlin engines for the British government. The news took two days to reverberate across the Atlantic. On June 19th, Henry Ford summoned an Associated Press reporter to his office and flatly denied the Beaverbrook report: "We are not doing business with the British or any other foreign government. If we make six thousand Rolls-Royce Merlin engines, it will be on an order from the United States government."[11]

In Washington, a stunned Knudsen told reporters, "I was assured by Mr. Edsel Ford, President, that this arrangement was satisfactory."[12] American and British government officials scrambled to make sense of the turnaround. Both Edsel and Sorensen confirmed that Henry Ford had been aware of the terms and had approved them.

According to Sorensen's account years later, the elder Ford had summoned him to his Dearborn office the day he learned of the Beaverbrook announcement and vowed, "I won't make any of those Rolls-Royce engines for England."

When Sorensen argued that he had already confirmed the order with Ford's consent, the old man stubbornly restated his position. "We won't build the engines at all. Withdraw the whole order. Take it to someone else. Let them build the engines. We won't."[13] The Ford production chief was at a loss to explain his employer's change of heart.

However, there is a clue that suggests what may have happened to change Ford's mind so abruptly between the day he approved the sale to England and the day he reversed himself publicly a week later. It appears that he had been in contact with his longtime friend Charles Lindbergh, who had been devoting his every waking moment to keeping American war materials out of the hands of the Allies since the beginning of the European war nine months earlier. It may very well have been Lindbergh's influence that turned the tide on the Rolls-Royce engine contract.

Ever since the two men crossed paths in 1927 when Lindbergh gave Ford his first airplane ride, the two had remained friends, keeping in occasional contact. But when Germany invaded Poland in September 1939, their relationship progressed to a new level. During the interval between the start of the European war and the Rolls-Royce engine announcement nine months later, Lindbergh had traveled to Dearborn more than ten times on a series of mysterious missions, each purposely conducted with maximum discretion to keep them from the attention of the press. The only reference to these trips in Lindbergh's journal is a notation on December 28, 1939, when he remarks that he drove to Detroit with Anne because he was "anxious to talk to Ford." He writes only in vague terms about their conversation. Over lunch, they discussed "the war" and "the industrial situation in America." Lindbergh wrote, "He is a combination of genius and impracticability, with genius definitely on top. Ford is a great man and a constructive influence in this country."[14]

To date, the only time their names had been linked in the media was in December 1938, shortly after each received his Nazi medal. Speaking at a banquet, Roosevelt's pugnacious interior secretary Harold Ickes had denounced the two men in no uncertain terms: "How can any American accept a decoration at the hands of a brutal dictator who, with that same hand is robbing and torturing thousands of fellow human beings?" Ickes demanded to know. "Perhaps Henry Ford and Charles A. Lindbergh will be willing to answer."[15]

On June 25, 1939—at the height of the controversy over the Rolls-Royce engine contract—Lindbergh boarded a train to Detroit for yet another visit to Ford.[16] This time, a small Michigan newspaper, the

Petoskey *Evening News*, got wind of the visit and phoned Charles Sorensen for a comment. The Ford production chief confirmed that Lindbergh had been "giving Henry Ford advice on airplane construction" for some time and that they had conferred about the Rolls-Royce contract. "Lindbergh has dropped in on Ford at least a dozen times in the last six months but this is the first time anyone knew about it," Sorensen revealed.[17]

Did Lindbergh say something to influence Ford's sudden reversal on the British order? It's quite conceivable that, when he heard about the RAF engine contract on June 19, he called Ford with an urgent plea not to aid the British war effort. This would have been entirely consistent with his actions over the previous nine months and would also explain his sudden, otherwise unexplained, arrival in Dearborn at the height of the controversy.

Within hours of Lindbergh's arrival for breakfast with Ford on June 26, William Knudsen called a press conference in Washington to announce that negotiations with the company had broken down and that the Rolls-Royce engine deal was dead.[18] In Allied countries, the news was immediately met with outrage. In the Canadian House of Commons the next day, members of Parliament denounced the contract reversal and called for a boycott of all Ford products. MP Michael Coldwell described Ford as a "highly placed saboteur" and called on his government to take over the company's Canadian plants and declare them "enemy property." Declared Coldwell to boisterous applause: "It's no wonder Hitler decorated Mr. Ford."[19]

Meanwhile, Ford reiterated his stand to the press, declaring he would not manufacture materials for any belligerent nation. Most of his biographers and other chroniclers have accepted this explanation. After all, this is the man who had once declared, "I would never let a single automobile get out of the Ford plant anywhere in the world if I thought it was going to be used in warfare."[20]

Even the prominent American historian Doris Kearns Goodwin takes his justification at face value. In her 1994 history of the Roosevelt White House, *No Ordinary Time*, Goodwin writes of Ford, "It was against his isolationist principles to provide war materials to a foreign power."[21]

However, it appears that Henry Ford was willing to make one exception to his rule.

On the afternoon of Saturday, July 24, 1915, a German embassy commercial attaché named Heinrich Albert boarded a New York subway train bound for midtown Manhattan. A few stops along the way, he fell asleep. Two rows behind him sat an American Secret Service agent named Frank Burke, who had been trailing the foreign diplomat for several hours. The moment he saw Albert sink into slumber, Burke grabbed the German's briefcase and exited at the next stop.[22]

The briefcase's incriminating contents were revealed the following Monday morning in the Washington office of U.S. Secretary of the Treasury William McAdoo. They outlined an elaborate sabotage and spy network in which German agents were actively preventing American supplies from reaching England, which was then at war with Germany. The agents had set up dummy American armaments firms to take orders from the English and French military. After promising rapid delivery, the guns and equipment were never sent. Other agents bought up as much gunpowder as they could to keep it out of British hands. One of the most damning documents told of a comprehensive plan to keep the United States from entering the war by influencing American public opinion through the purchase of newspapers, funding of lectureships and other propaganda activities.[23] It was only three months earlier that Henry Ford had embarked on his own pacifist crusade designed to keep America out of the war.

Because America was still neutral, Albert's activities were not officially classified as espionage and he was allowed to remain in the country. However, President Wilson concluded that Albert, whom he called the "kingpin" of German propaganda, was the most "dangerous" agent the Germans had in the United States.[24] When the story of a German spy network was leaked to the New York *Herald Tribune* a few days later, it shocked the nation and helped move America a step closer to entering the war.

As propaganda chief in the United States during the First World War, Heinrich Albert reported directly to the German spy master Franz von Papen, whom the former U.S. intelligence operative Casimir Palmer had identified as a friend of Ernest Liebold.[25] While von Papen oversaw American sabotage operations from the German embassy in Washington, Albert's efforts were conducted in New York, where he opened a small office at 45 Broadway, a few blocks away from the Ford Motor Company's own New York bureau.[26] During this period, Liebold traveled there frequently on company "business" and, when he eventually opened the Ford detective agency to dig up incriminating information on prominent Jews, he chose to establish the office in New York, just down the street from Albert's German spy headquarters.

When America eventually entered the war in 1917, both von Papen and Albert were expelled from the country and returned to Germany. Due to the later destruction of Ford Motor Company documents, it is still unclear whether Albert had any contact with Liebold or the company during his tenure in America. But before long, the fortunes of Heinrich Albert and the Ford Motor Company would be inextricably linked.

• • •

By the time Henry Ford arrived in Germany for his first and only visit in the fall of 1930, the German translation of his book, *The International Jew*, had already sold hundreds of thousands of copies to an adoring German public, who held his industrial achievements and his Jew-baiting in equally high regard. But the purpose of this visit was not a book tour. Five years earlier, the company had established its first German subsidiary in Berlin, a truck and Model T plant called *Ford Motor Company Aktiengesellschaft*, owned 99.9 percent by Dearborn. The success of this operation, and the high demand for the Ford brand, soon necessitated an expansion and in 1929, the company had acquired a fifty-two-acre tract of land in Cologne. On October 2, 1930, Ford arrived with Ernest Liebold to lay the cornerstone for the new plant, which was officially opened in June 1931 on the banks of the Rhine. The goal of the Cologne plant, Ford declared that day, was "to build a bridge from one country to another."[27]

It was not a propitious time to launch a new enterprise. The Depression had hit Germany particularly hard, severely curtailing demand for trucks, tractors and automobiles. Nevertheless, Dearborn was strongly committed to expanding its international operations, and the new German plant was to be a vital part of the company's future.

Dearborn's production chief Charles Sorensen was largely responsible for overseeing the parent company's German interests. When the German corporation was incorporated in 1925, its board of directors was made up entirely of Americans. Henry Ford himself appears to have taken something of a personal interest in the Cologne operation right from the start, sitting on Ford Germany's board for the first two years.[28] When Ford's European operations were reorganized in 1929, American ownership in the company was reduced to 60 percent and, for the first time, Germans were to be represented on the board of directors. Henry Ford issued instructions to find "the best farmer, the best lawyer and the best industrialist" in Germany to serve on the new Board.

The farmer chosen was Alwin Schurig; the industrialist was Carl Bosch; and the lawyer appointed by Dearborn was none other than Heinrich Albert, the notorious First World War German spy.[29] After the war, Albert had been well rewarded for his clandestine activities on behalf of his country, serving for several years as secretary of state in the new German government.[30] After he left the government in the early 1920s, he made good use of the many contacts he had acquired in the United States when he set up a lucrative law practice representing a number of large American firms doing business in Germany.

In 1925, shortly after Ford Germany incorporated its first operation in Berlin, the company hired Albert to handle its relations with the German government. He had represented the company's interests ever since.[31] Joining him on the new Ford Germany board was Sorensen, Edsel Ford, and Albert's fellow German, Carl Bosch, who also happened to be the general manager of a company called IG Farben, the gigantic chemical and pharmaceutical colossus that would soon emerge as the backbone of Hitler's economic base.

As part of the new restructuring, IG Farben was awarded 15 percent ownership in Ford Germany and Bosch was appointed to the board of directors. In exchange, Edsel was appointed to the board of Farben's U.S. subsidiary, American IG Chemical Corporation (later renamed General Aniline & Film), where he sat until 1941.[32] The arrangement officially married the world's largest auto company with the world's largest chemical manufacturer. It was a relationship the Ford Motor Company was anxious to downplay in later years, especially when the full extent of Farben's activities emerged after the Second World War.

Before the National Socialists took power, many Farben executives, including Bosch, had fiercely opposed the Nazi program. But only three weeks after Hitler was appointed Chancellor in 1933, a number of Germany's leading industrialists met with Hermann Göring and SS Chief Heinrich Himmler to discuss how business could find common cause with the new regime. The Nazis promised to eliminate trade unions and any other obstacles that interfered with unfettered corporate profits in the Third Reich. Soon afterwards, IG Farben contributed 400,000 *reichsmarks* to the National Socialist Party's political "slush fund," the largest contribution to the Nazis by any German company.[33] Thereafter, it remained Hitler's single most important corporate ally. According to the report of a wartime U.S. government investigation:

> Without I.G.'s immense productive facilities, its intense research, and vast international affiliations, Germany's prosecution of the war would have been unthinkable and impossible; Farben not only directed its energies toward arming Germany, but concentrated on weakening her intended victims, and this double-barreled attempt to expand the German industrial potential for war and to restrict that of the rest of the world was not conceived and executed "in the normal course of business." The proof is overwhelming that I.G. Farben officials had full prior knowledge of Germany's plan for world conquest and of each specific aggressive act later undertaken.[34]

The financial fortunes of Ford Germany fluctuated considerably during the early thirties, largely because of the continuing worldwide Depression. In 1934 and 1935, for example, the corporation had run a substantial operating deficit. But revenues picked up considerably around the middle of the decade after the company launched an aggressive export program, facilitated by Dearborn. After the war, when Ford Germany was being investigated for complicity with the Nazis, company officials would claim that it had been under constant attack by the Nazi Party throughout the decade because of its status as a "foreign" company. According to political scientist Simon Reich, who was hired by Ford as a consultant on its internal investigation into Ford Germany's activities under the Nazi regime, "[Ford Germany] was persistently treated as an outsider: bullied, manipulated, and denied the material resources allocated to other firms."[35] In fact, this claim appears questionable. It is true that at various times during the 1930s, Ford Germany was criticized by relatively low-level Nazi officials for its American ties and was subject to occasional government interference.[36] But this interference never amounted to anything more than a minor annoyance and it certainly never affected the company's bottom line, as evidenced by the fact that profits continued to mount throughout the decade.[37] Moreover, the company received the ringing endorsement of the only Nazis who really mattered. In 1936, Hitler proclaimed Ford's assembly-line methods to be a model for German industry, at the International Automobile Exhibit in Berlin; a few days later, Hermann Göring bought a Ford Eifel car for his personal use—hardly an indication that Ford was out of favor with the regime.[38]

The German subsidiary benefited tangibly from its American ties. During the three-year period before the war, the U.S. parent company sent Ford Germany crucial shipments of rubber and pig iron, which could only be obtained in the United States. German industry was desperately short of raw materials during this period, a situation that threatened to derail Hitler's rearmament strategy. But in June 1936, Ford Germany—with the full knowledge and approval of Dearborn—entered into an extraordinary barter agreement with the German Ministry of Economics, whereby it agreed to divert a good deal of its American imports to other German companies in return for greater access to foreign exchange funds. This way, according to a subsequent U.S. government investigation, Ford Germany was instrumental in the Reich's war preparations.[39]

Until 1937, virtually all of the German company's manufacturing operations were devoted to civilian passenger vehicles, trucks and tractors. However, one of Heinrich Albert's first priorities upon being appointed chairman of the board in June 1937 was to secure for Ford a portion of the Nazi regime's lucrative rearmament effort.

At Albert's behest, the company dispatched a well-connected employee named Ernst Posekel to Berlin with a mandate to establish favorable relations with "the authorities competent for the placing of official orders."[40] His efforts proved successful. During the spring of 1937, the German War Ministry approached Albert with a proposal to begin manufacturing vehicles for the army.[41] The first government order was to be a special military truck built exclusively for the *Wehrmacht* (German army). However, negotiations bogged down when Ford officials, who had voiced no objections to the idea of manufacturing vehicles for the German military, refused to honor the regime's request that the trucks be built according to German design standards. This was not the way the company did business. Ford vehicles had always been built according to a Ford design. The government also required that the vehicles be manufactured in a designated "safe zone" in the middle of the country, near Berlin. If war broke out, this would help safeguard the plant.

After weeks of negotiation with the government, the issue became moot when the Nazi High Command instead asked the company to manufacture a troop carrier rather than a truck. Ford would be permitted to design the military vehicle to its own standards. In mid-April 1938, Sorensen attended a Ford Germany board of directors meeting in Cologne and cabled Dearborn with the message that the "German plans are turning out very satisfactory."[42] Four days later, with Sorensen in attendance, the board finally approved the scheme to manufacture German military vehicles.[43] The agreement was finalized with the High Command a few weeks later, paving the way for a long-lasting business relationship.

Premises were leased in Berlin and, beginning in 1939, the plant began turning out thousands of military troop carriers. Soon, additional orders from the *Luftwaffe* as well as contracts for other army vehicles and spare parts began to pour in.[44] Eager to keep on the good side of Hitler, the board of directors voted to send the Führer a birthday gift of 35,000 *reichsmarks* in April 1939.[45] There is no record that Dearborn registered any objection to this gift. In fact, although not present at the meeting, Edsel Ford and Charles Sorensen were still members of the board when Ford Germany made the decision.[46]

Meanwhile, the Cologne plant was also in full production. After Ford committed to manufacturing for the military, the company had as many government orders as it could handle. According to an internal company report, Ford Germany's business with the Nazi authorities "developed extraordinarily" during the third quarter of 1938.[47] Dearborn was delighted by the company's success. Business was so good that in September 1938, the American plant shipped one thousand trucks, cabs and platforms to be assembled by Ford in Cologne for the use of the German government and military. In a 1941 letter to the Reich Commissioner for Enemy Property, Albert boasted that these trucks were used in the invasion and occupation of Czechoslovakia.[48]

Thus, by the time Germany invaded Poland in September 1939, Ford had become a vital cog in Hitler's military machine. After the war ended and American authorities scoured the records of Ford Germany, a U.S. army investigator would conclude that "even before the war a portion of German Ford had, *with Dearborn's consent*, become an arsenal of Nazism . . ."[49]

This fact having been established, the question remains to what extent this relationship changed after September 3, 1939, the day England and France declared war on Germany. In 1936, a Nazi Party official had iden-tified the Cologne plant manager Erich Diestel as a Jew and informed a visiting Dearborn executive of the fact. Although there is no evidence that the Nazis demanded Diestel's dismissal,[50] the revelation sparked a series of concerned discussions in Ford corporate offices on both sides of the Atlantic. In the end, it was Heinrich Albert who insisted that Diestel— although he had only one Jewish grandparent—be replaced to keep on good terms with the government.[51] Edsel and Sorensen finally agreed to do so when Albert, on a visit to Dearborn, insisted it was in the German com-pany's best interests.[52]

Albert then recommended that two co-managers, Erhard Vitger and Robert Schmidt, be hired to replace Diestel. Vitger would now be in charge of finances and employment, while Schmidt would be responsible for production and negotiations with the government. In reality, Schmidt had far greater management authority, partly because the Danish-born Vitger was a foreigner. More important, Schmidt had high-level contacts in the Nazi party and could use his connections to the company's advan-tage. In July, the subsidiary received a new Germanized name, *Ford-Werke* (Ford Works).

When the war started in September 1939, Robert Schmidt was in charge of most of the German company's day-to day operations while Heinrich Albert, as chairman of the board, oversaw the company's broader overall activities, particularly its financial situation. And, while they were still accountable to Dearborn, it was clear as the war began that both men now served two different, but not necessarily conflicting, masters. In Octo-ber 1940, Albert sent a letter to Schmidt congratulating him on the fact that the two men were "loyal" to both Henry Ford and the Third Reich.[53]

Shortly after the invasion of Poland, members of the German High Command approached Schmidt and Albert about the possibility of the company diversifying military production beyond the trucks and troop carriers that poured out of the Berlin and Cologne plants in increasing numbers. The *Wehrmacht* was in desperate need of munitions and armaments. Could *Ford-Werke* expand its manufacturing operations to produce these crucial war materials?

As a lawyer specializing in complex corporate maneuvers for German-based American corporations, Heinrich Albert understood the potential public relations risks of manufacturing war materials under the Ford brand name. To get around them, he set up a corporate front, or "cloak" company, in the name of Walter Arendt, a longtime Ford supplier. The principal investor in this new venture, with 76 percent of the stock, was listed as Spolz & Co., a prominent Berlin banking house. In reality, Spolz merely held the shares for the company's real owner, *Ford-Werke* manager Robert Schmidt. The new *Arendt* company was to be operated under the complete responsibility and supervision of German Ford, which was to supply all machinery as well as office and plant workers. Until the end of the war, *Arendt* earned average annual revenues of 1,500,000 *reichsmarks* supplying munitions to the German military—armaments whose deadly force was almost certainly used against American troops after the United States entered the war in December 1941.[54] There is some dispute as to whether Dearborn was ever informed about the cloak operation conducted under its German subsidiary's auspices. Initial conclusions by U.S. army investigator Henry Schneider in 1945 found that the American parent company "apparently was not informed, much less consulted."[55]

But in an affidavit he signed on June 15, 1945, Schmidt provided an ambiguous explanation when he was asked to describe the details of the *Arendt* scheme. He refers to a "decisive" meeting between himself, Albert and "nearly every important member of the Military High Command" to discuss manufacturing munitions for the German army. After explaining that the "entire arrangement was to be kept a strict secret," Schmidt reveals that a memorandum was written up, "a copy of which was received by Ford."[56] Does his reference to "Ford" refer to the German subsidiary or the American headquarters?[57] He never elaborates, and investigators are left to draw their own conclusions. It seems hard to believe that the parent company—which still owned more than 80 percent of *Ford-Werke* at the time—was kept uninformed about its subsidiary's activities, especially since Charles Sorensen made it a point to involve himself so closely in the company's business operations, even flying to Germany to attend regular Board meetings as late as 1938, and micro-managing many management decisions.[58] However, no evidence has been found in the American parent company's corporate archives suggesting that Dearborn knew about the *Arendt* scheme. Nonetheless, German Ford's participation in other integral parts of the Nazi war effort was well known in Dearborn. American executives were fully briefed on *Ford-Werke*'s manufacture of 505 motors for

Luftwaffe boats and landing barges; 20,000 gears for a *Junkers* aircraft plant; and tens of thousands of half ton trucks and troop carriers.[59]

There is no question that American involvement in Ford Germany lessened after September 1939. A number of factors were responsible, not least of which was the company's desire to show the authorities that it was taking steps to "Germanize." No American or British board member, for example, attended a *Ford-Werke* meeting after the start of the war, and communications with the American office were somewhat curtailed, although both Edsel and Sorensen remained on the board until 1941. Nevertheless, the company's most important developments were passed on to Dearborn, and Sorensen received regular reports from both Albert and Schmidt all the way up until Pearl Harbor. In fact, at least 180 letters were exchanged between Dearborn and Ford Germany during the years of 1938 to 1941.[60]

In April 1940, the German board took on a new member following the death of Carl Bosch. Appointed as Bosch's successor was Carl Krauch, who had also succeeded him as chairman of IG Farben. At this stage, Farben still owned 6 percent of *Ford-Werke*, while Edsel Ford remained on the board of Farben's U.S. subsidiary, American IG.

At the time of his elevation to the *Ford-Werke* board, Krauch was preoccupied with plans for a new IG Farben synthetic rubber plant at a small Polish town called Auschwitz, for which both Farben and the Nazi regime had high hopes. Named IG Auschwitz (Buna), the new plant was meant to lessen the Reich's dependence on foreign rubber imports. Soon, the SS would provide Farben with an endless supply of Jewish prisoners, at Krauch's request, to man the Auschwitz operation. Eventually, IG Farben would build its own corporate concentration camp at the site, to eliminate the need to march prisoners several miles to and from the Buna facility every day. This new plant, known as Monowitz, had an infamous sign over the gate which read: ARBEIT MACHT FREI (Work Shall Make You Free).[61]

All the while, Krauch found time to lend his corporate expertise to *Ford-Werke*, acting as Albert's deputy on the company directorate. He attended regular board meetings in Cologne, where it was business as usual as the company began to gradually phase out all passenger-car production and devote its full resources to the increasingly lucrative military contracts which were sending profits soaring to more than twice pre-war levels.[62] The Nazi regime made it clear that it was pleased with Ford's commitment to the war effort, and rewarded the company with one new military contract after another.

Only once prior to Pearl Harbor was this relationship threatened. On June 19, 1940, two days after Lord Beaverbrook prematurely announced in London that Ford had agreed to manufacture Rolls-Royce engines for

Britain, German military officials took immediate notice. To the Nazis, Henry Ford was still considered a friend of Germany and a sworn enemy of the Jews. Now, the military high command demanded an explanation from *Ford-Werke* about how Dearborn could agree to supply the enemy with war materials to be used against the Reich. Heinrich Albert was forced on the defensive.

On June 26, he cabled General Zuckertort an obsequious reply to an angry query received the day before, assuring the general that the reports about "war material from Ford Detroit to Great Britain" were completely false. "Such rumors come up always from time to time," Albert wrote. "We assume that they are circulated by American competition to whom the attitude of Henry Ford is uncomfortable."[63]

But the Nazis were unconvinced, especially when news stories appeared indicating that Ford had initially accepted the contract. They needed more assurance that Ford wasn't playing both ends against the middle. On July 11, Henry Ford received a German Embassy commercial attaché named Gerhart Alois Westrick at his Dearborn office. According to British intelligence, Westrick was a high-ranking Nazi spy. He had been sent to America by German Foreign Minister Joachim Ribbentrop to forge friendly ties between German and American industrialists.[64]

The FBI had been keeping a close eye on the Ford Motor Company's Dearborn headquarters for years, ever since U.S. military intelligence had identified Ernest Liebold as a German spy toward the end of World War I. Consequently, when Westrick paid his visit to Ford in July, the Bureau took immediate notice. That his visit came only two weeks after the company's refusal to manufacture Rolls-Royce engines for Britain appeared especially noteworthy and FBI director J. Edgar Hoover forwarded the information to U.S. Secretary of the Treasury Henry Morgenthau, who had been involved with the Rolls-Royce engine negotiations. On July 31, Hoover personally wrote to Morgenthau about what the Bureau had been able to discern from a "reliable and confidential source":

Information has been received that on or about July 11, 1940 Dr. Gerhart Alois Westrick, Commercial attaché of the German Embassy Washington, D.C., conferred with Mr. Henry Ford of Detroit, Michigan in an endeavor to persuade Mr. Ford to use his influence in keeping the United States and the Government thereof from furnishing any materials of war to Great Britain. Westrick stated that if the source of Britain's war supply were cut off, particularly from the United States, the war would be over in ninety days or by September; adding if the United States fur-

nished Great Britain with war supplies, it would only prolong the
inevitable, the defeat of England.[65]

According to the report, when Henry Ford was asked by the FBI about
Westrick's visit, he claimed he had rebuffed the German diplomat because
he believed that "Westrick was just another crook."[66] The Bureau appears
to have let the matter rest because the United States was not yet at war with
Germany and therefore Westrick had done nothing illegal.

What the FBI did not know, however, was that Westrick also happened
to be the law partner of Heinrich Albert, chairman of the board of Ford
Germany. Their firm handled Ford's German legal interests. Therefore,
Westrick was in fact Ford's attorney at the time of his July 1940 visit. It is
highly conceivable that he informed Ford about the political realities in
Germany. As long as Dearborn refused to sell war materials to Germany's
enemies, the military contracts would continue to pour in at *Ford-Werke*.

France had finally succumbed to the German onslaught in June, thanks
in part to the efficiency of the Ford troop carriers which had performed
magnificently, transporting thousands of soldiers through the spring mud
that could have bogged down the Nazis' westward offensive. In fact, a few
months later, *Ford-Werke* placed a large advertisement in the *Frankfurt
Zeitung* newspaper proudly trumpeting that Ford vehicles had been present
during German army campaigns in Poland, Norway, Holland, Belgium,
and France. "German Ford vehicles were the dependable servants of the
brave soldier," proclaimed the ad.[67]

Immediately following the collapse of France in June, German occupation authorities decided that all Ford plants within its newly conquered
jurisdiction would come under the authority of *Ford-Werke*. The Nazis now
controlled the entire strategic industrial capacity of Western Europe.
Robert Schmidt was appointed commissioner of the new European Ford
plants. However, France was in an unusual position. After its defeat, it had
been immediately divided by the Nazis into two distinct zones. The Germans occupied the northern part of the country while the south retained
"independent" status with a civilian puppet government based in Vichy.

Since September 1939, Ford France had been manufacturing trucks
and engines for the French military at plants located in the towns of
Poissy, Asnieres, Bordeaux and Bourges. In June 1940, Schmidt traveled
to France with his assistant, the son of Heinrich Albert, to assess the state
of operations and to requisition spare parts for Ford's Belgium and Holland plants. Schmidt had developed a plan to reorganize all Ford subsidiaries into a single economic unit under German leadership. But he
hadn't counted on the resourcefulness of the longtime Ford France gen-

eral manager Maurice Dollfuss, whose first loyalty was clearly to his Dearborn employers.

Immediately after the German occupation, Dollfuss had traveled to Paris to meet with the new occupation authorities. According to a July 19 report that he sent to Edsel and Sorensen, Dollfuss managed to persuade the Germans to let him manage the plants independently.[68] In this ten-page report, Dollfuss provides the first clue that Ford had been granted special treatment by the Nazi occupation authorities.

> We are working within a common scheme and I can confirm to you that we shall have the best protection that can be obtained for a purely French concern; and furthermore, we will benefit from the main fact of being a member of the Ford family which entitles us to better treatment from our German colleagues who have shown clearly their wish to protect the Ford interests as much as they can. The damage for us is hence much smaller than in any other company.[69]

He goes on to assure his American employers that the plants are in good condition and that the latest profit figures are "brilliant," adding that the French company has been selling considerable quantities of spare parts, trucks and cars to the German authorities.[70] This letter was written only a month after Henry Ford vetoed the British Rolls-Royce engine contract on the grounds that Ford would never manufacture for a foreign belligerent. On August 19, Sorensen dispatched a reply to Doll-fuss that constitutes Dearborn's first official response to the German occupation:

> We are pleased to learn from your letter of July 18, which we received and read very carefully, that our organization is going along, and the victors are so tolerant in their treatment. It looks as though we still might have a business that we can carry on in spite of all the difficulties.[71]

In other words, business as usual.

On July 28, Robert Schmidt also wrote a letter to Sorensen and Edsel assuring his American employers that he was "safeguarding the interests of the Ford plants in the occupied territory."[72] A month later, Dollfuss again wrote Dearborn but in this letter he revealed more explicitly that the bulk of Ford France manufacturing output was being sold to the German military. He expected the company to soon achieve production of twenty trucks a day, which was considerably better than

> our French competitors are doing. The reason is that our trucks are in very large demand by the German authorities and I believe that as long as the war goes on and at least for some period of time, all that we shall produce will be [bought] by the German authorities.[73]

In the same letter, Dollfuss inadvertently furnishes the first evidence that Henry Ford's refusal to build the British engines two months earlier, and the resulting lost revenues, may have had indirect financial benefits for the company:

> . . . in order to safeguard our interests—and I am here talking in a very broad way—I have been to Berlin and have seen General von Schell himself, who is the highest executive responsible for the motor industry both from the military and civilian points of view.
>
> I will satisfy myself by telling you that my interview with him has been by all means satisfactory, and that the attitude you have taken together with your father of strict neutrality has been an invaluable asset for the protection of your companies in Europe.[74]

Of course, Ford had been anything but "strictly neutral," willingly supplying Germany with military equipment, while refusing to manufacture engines for the British air force.

The news in Dollfuss's subsequent letters just got better. As the German army continued to purchase its entire production from Ford France, profits soared, as Dollfuss trumpeted in a letter to Dearborn on October 11. He makes a particular point of comparing Ford's success to the situation of its French competitors Renault and Citroen, whose sales were only 20 percent of what they had been before the war. Again, he attributes it to the Ford name:

> Naturally the advantages that we have are because we belong
> to the Ford family, but advantages which we cannot overstate
> under the present circumstances.[75]

Two weeks later, Edsel Ford replied, expressing his appreciation: "I think this is a remarkable achievement in view of the difficulties that are present at this time."[76]

In November, Dearborn received a detailed financial statement of the French operation, including statistics on how many vehicles had been sold to the German army in June and July. That same month, Dollfuss's assistant, Georges Lesto, traveled to Dearborn to brief Ford executives on the French situation. When he arrived at company headquarters on November 30, he was carrying two letters addressed to Edsel Ford, containing information that could not be transmitted from France without fear of censorship by German occupation authorities. One was a short personal note written in long-hand, the other a five-page typewritten document. They describe a company that was thriving in its business with the Nazis.

Ford France basked in a freedom other companies did not. Nazi officials, one letter read, were unlikely to interfere with Dearborn's wishes:

> At this stage I would like to outline the importance attached
> by high officials to respect the desires and maintain the good will
> of "Ford"—and by "Ford," I mean your father, yourself and the
> Ford Motor Company, Dearborn.[77]

By the time Dearborn received these letters in early December 1940, the parent company was already well aware of its large financial stake in the German military effort. The Ford board of directors continued to hold monthly meetings in Dearborn to discuss company business, the minutes of which are preserved in company archives. However, from a careful review of this large body of letters, memos, documents and board-level discussions, not a single word of reservation appears to have been expressed at any time about the propriety or moral consideration of doing business with the Nazi regime or fortifying the German military machine. On the contrary, Dearborn sent crucial machinery from the United States to Cologne as late as 1941 to help expand the plant's capacity for war production.[78] This is in stark contrast with the company's official public position that it would not do business with any foreign belligerent. Though to be sure it would have been difficult to resist pressure from Nazi authorities to aid the German war effort, there is no evidence that *Ford-Werke* was ever officially compelled to manufacture for the German military during this period. In fact, Albert and Schmidt, by their own admission, actively courted the military contracts. Schmidt later argued that without their lobbying efforts, "No department of the Government, army, navy or air force would dare to buy Ford cars or trucks."[79]

After the war, Schmidt conveniently claimed that his first loyalty was always to "the American partnership," that he was anti-Nazi, and that his production efforts on behalf of the German military were undertaken strictly for the sake of business expediency.[80] However, this attitude is difficult to discern in a piece he wrote for the *Ford-Werke* employee house organ, published shortly before Pearl Harbor in December 1941, at a time when Dearborn still controlled the German plant and held a majority ownership stake in the company:

At the beginning of this year we vowed to give our best and utmost for final victory, in unshakable faithfulness to our Führer. Today we say with pride that we succeeded.[81]

CHAPTER 9

AMERICA FIRST

Dr. Seuss first gained nationwide prominence with his political cartoons lampooning the isolationist movement, Charles Lindbergh, and the America First Committee.

I have nothing to offer but blood, toil, tears, and sweat. We have before us an ordeal of the most grievous kind. We have before us many, many months of struggle and suffering. I say it is to wage war by land, sea, and air. War with all our might and with all the strength God has given us, and to wage war against a monstrous tyranny never surpassed in the dark and lamentable catalogue of human crime.

—Winston Churchill, May 13, 1940

We are often told that if Germany wins this war, cooperation will be impossible, and treaties no more than scraps of paper. I reply that cooperation is never impossible when there is sufficient gain on both sides.

—Charles Lindbergh, August 4, 1940

On the afternoon of May 21 1940, President Roosevelt retreated to his private White House study to catch up on his correspondence. In recent weeks, he had become increasingly worried about domestic Fifth Column activities. Only three days earlier, Charles Lindbergh had broadcast his "Air Defense of America" speech and the address had injected new life into the isolationist movement.

"When I read Lindbergh's speech, I felt that it could not have been better put if it had been written by Goebbels himself," the President wrote to

Henry Stimson, a Republican politician whom Roosevelt had recently
asked to serve as his new secretary of war. "What a pity that this youngster
has completely abandoned his belief in our form of government and has
accepted Nazi methods because apparently they are efficient."[1]

At the height of the Great Debate, smearing isolationists as traitors and
Nazi sympathizers would become an increasingly common tactic of the interventionist movement and a highly effective propaganda technique. Most of
these attacks were aired in the public sphere where their insinuations would
achieve maximum impact. In contrast, Roosevelt's repeated accusations
against Lindbergh appear in private correspondence and conversations with
trusted advisers, suggesting that he genuinely believed the charges.

As evidence of how seriously he viewed the threat of internal subver-
sion, a few hours after he penned the letter to Stimson, the President issued
a written directive to his attorney general Robert Jackson instructing him
to place wiretaps on the telephones of "persons suspected of subversive
activities against the Government of the United States, including suspected spies."[2] Already, many of the letters and telegrams critical of the
President's defense policies were being forwarded by the White House to
FBI Director J. Edgar Hoover with instructions to "go over" them and
check the names to determine whether any of them had an FBI dossier. To
be sure, FDR was never very tolerant of criticism and had a marked tendency to stifle dissent throughout his four terms in the White House. To
some extent, then, his actions could be put down as occupational paranoia
or political ruthlessness. According to historian Richard W. Steele, "The
President's judgment was strongly conditioned by the hopes of using the
loyalty issue to smear his critics."[3]

Five days later, Roosevelt took to the airwaves to deliver a fireside chat
to the nation. Though he mentioned no names, it was Americans' first taste
of the new interventionist strategy, designed to raise doubts about the
motives of isolationists:

> Today's threat to our national security is not a matter of mili-
> tary weapons alone. We know of new methods of attack. The
> Trojan Horse. The Fifth Column that betrays a nation unpre-
> pared for treachery. Spies, saboteurs and traitors are the actors in
> this new strategy. With all of these, we must and will deal vigor-
> ously.[4]

While Roosevelt's specter of a Fifth Column threat was almost certainly exaggerated, it was not altogether unjustified. Two years earlier, in

February 1938, the FBI had uncovered a well-organized Nazi spy ring centered in New York City that had planted agents within the armed forces and defense industries. The espionage network had been linked to a number of German government officials, and the sensational revelation dominated newspaper headlines for weeks.[5]

The same year, Father Coughlin used his popular radio show to rally his listeners against another threat, urging the creation of a Christian Front to "combat Communism." Within weeks, Christian Front groups, characterized by fierce anti-Semitism, had formed in cities all over the country. In January 1940, the FBI arrested eighteen members of a Christian Front splinter group and charged them with attempting to overthrow the United States government.[6] Their alleged aim was to rally thousands of Irish Catholic members in the police and National Guard to seize the White House and place Major General George Van Horn Moseley in the Oval Office as a military dictator.[7] The group had been planning the coup d'état for years and had secured the support of several high-ranking members of the army and National Guard. At their meetings, they addressed their leader as "Führer" and gave the Nazi salute. Most alarmingly, the plotters had already been given thousands of rounds of ammunition, arms and explosives by an officer of the New York National Guard.

General Moseley was a former commander of the U.S. Third Army who had emerged as a powerful spokesman for the right wing of the isolationist movement. On September 30, 1938, the day he retired from the armed forces, Moseley issued a public attack on the New Deal, which he believed was leading America on a disastrous path toward dictatorship. The Roosevelt administration, he charged, was manipulated by the "alien element in our midst." He warned that Americans must awaken to the sinister motives of "the wrong sorts of immigrants" who wished to replace "our system with their own un-American theories of government." His anti-Semitism became even more explicit when he joined the ranks of the isolationists seeking to prevent American entry in the European war. At a 1939 National Defense meeting in Philadelphia, Moseley declared: "The war now proposed is for the purpose of establishing Jewish hegemony throughout the world." While "your sons and mine" would be conscripted to fight side by side with the Christian-killing Communists, only Jews would profit, he told the audience. The Jews controlled the media and they were about to dominate the federal government, he warned. They were leading America into war to reinstate their power in countries that had banished them.[8] Privately, he described Jews as "crude and unclean, animal-like things. It's like writing about something loathsome such as syphilis."[9]

The ragtag mob that championed his presidency never formally drafted him as their leader. In fact, there is no evidence that Moseley was aware of the Christian Front's coup preparations or their plan to install him in the White House. It is possible that they seized on the general as the ideal leader after he publicly suggested that military resistance to the President may be justified under some circumstances. The army, he stated in a 1939 speech, "is your salvation today. If the administration went too far to the left and asked our military establishment to execute orders which violated all American tradition, that army would demur."[10]

Although Moseley's controversial views gained national publicity and drew widespread criticism, they did not appear to bother his long-time colleague General George Marshall, U.S. army chief of staff, who corresponded with Moseley until the end of World War II, frequently conveying his "respect" and "affection" for the retired general. "I know you will leave behind a host of younger men who have a loyal devotion to you for what you have stood for," wrote Marshall. "I am one of that company, and it makes me very sad to think that I cannot serve with you and under you again."[11] Marshall was the man Truman Smith described as his "mentor" and would later help revive Lindbergh's military career, although there is no evidence that either Smith or Lindbergh had any contact with General Moseley himself.

With the collapse of France in June 1940, Alexis Carrel's attitude toward the Nazis had undergone a fundamental transformation, although he had already begun to express a distaste for Hitler and his policies at least a year earlier. The totalitarian regime whose policies he had once admired had abased his beloved country. Worse still, his wife, who was a nurse, had ignored his entreaties and insisted on staying in France to tend wounded French soldiers. Communications had broken off and he had no idea whether she was still alive.[12] Now, with the swastika flag flying from the Eiffel Tower, Carrel telephoned Lindbergh at his Lloyd Neck home and pleaded with the isolationist spokesman to change camps and back a massive aid package for the Allied nations.[13]

Lindbergh was surprised at his mentor's vehemence. American aid, he argued, would only delay the inevitable and contribute, through indiscriminate bloodshed, to the destruction of European civilization. Exasperated, Carrel shouted back, "It's the Nazis who are destroying western civilization. It's the Nazis!"[14] What on earth did Lindbergh think the Germans would do to France? he asked. His young protégé counseled against believing the anti-Nazi propaganda that permeated the American press. The situation "may not be as bad as people in this country believe," he told the scientist; perhaps Carrel could even work with the new French puppet government.[15]

Many believed Lindbergh's World War isolationist crusade was inspired by his father's own controversial antiwar stand two decades earlier. Charles Lindbergh Sr. became a pariah for opposing American involvement in the First World War. Here, he is hung in effigy from a telephone pole in Stanton, Minnesota, circa 1918. (MINNESOTA HISTORICAL SOCIETY)

Henry Ford, center, aboard the ill-fated Peace Ship in December 1915, as he sails to Europe on an expedition designed to end World War I. (COLLECTIONS OF THE HENRY FORD MUSEUM, GREENFIELD VILLAGE)

French gendarmes hold back the crowds as Lindbergh arrives at Paris's Le Bourget airfield following the completion of his solo flight across the Atlantic on May 21, 1927. (LINDBERGH PICTURE COLLECTION, MANUSCRIPTS AND ARCHIVES, YALE UNIVERSITY LIBRARY)

Charles Lindbergh with his celebrated aircraft shortly after his historic flight in 1927. (U.S. NATIONAL ARCHIVES)

Lindbergh meets Henry Ford for the first time at Ford Airport in 1927. It was the beginning of a lifelong friendship that would culminate in an historic crusade. (COLLECTIONS OF THE HENRY FORD MUSEUM, GREENFIELD VILLAGE)

The Ford International Weekly

THE DEARBORN INDEPENDENT

By the Year **One Dollar**   Dearborn, Michigan, May 22, 1920   Single Copy **Five Cents**

The International Jew:
The World's Problem

"Among the distinguishing mental and moral traits of the Jews may be mentioned: distaste for hard or violent physical labor; a strong family sense and philoprogenitiveness; a marked religious instinct; the courage of the prophet and martyr rather than of the pioneer and soldier; remarkable power to survive in adverse environments, combined with great ability to retain racial solidarity; capacity for exploitation, both individual and social; shrewdness and astuteness in speculation and money matters generally; an Oriental love of display and a full appreciation of the power and pleasure of social position; a very high average of intellectual ability."

—The New International Encyclopedia.

THE Jew is again being singled out for critical attention throughout the world. His emergence in the financial, political and social spheres has been so complete and spectacular since the war, that his place, power and purpose in the world are being given a new scrutiny, much of it unfriendly. Persecution is not a new experience to the Jew, but intensive scrutiny of his nature and super-nationality is. He has suffered for more than 2,000 years from what may be called the instinctive anti-semitism of the other races, but this antagonism has never been intelligent nor has it been able to make itself intelligible. Nowadays, however, the Jew is being placed, as it were, under the microscope of economic observation that the reasons for his power, the reasons for his separateness, the reasons for his suffering may be defined and understood.

In Russia he is charged with being the source of Bolshevism, an accusation which is serious or not according to the circle in which it is made; we in America, hearing the fervid eloquence and perceiving the prophetic ardor of young Jewish apostles of social and industrial reform, can calmly estimate how it may be. In Germany he is charged with being the cause of the Empire's collapse and a very considerable literature has sprung up, bearing with it a mass of circumstantial evidence that gives the thinker pause. In England he is charged with being the real world ruler, who rules as a super-nation over the nations, rules by the power of gold, and who plays nation against nation for his own purposes, remaining himself discreetly in the background. In America it is pointed out to what extent the elder Jews of wealth and the younger Jews of ambition swarmed through the war organizations—principally those departments which dealt with the commercial and industrial business of war, and also the extent to which they have clung to the advantage which their experience as agents of the government gave them.

IN SIMPLE words, the question of the Jews has come to the fore, but like other questions which lend themselves to prejudice, efforts will be made to hush it up as impolitic for open discussion. If, however, experience has taught us anything it is that questions thus suppressed will sooner or later break out in undesirable and unprofitable forms.

The Jew is the world's enigma. Poor in his masses, he yet controls the world's finances. Scattered abroad without country or government, he yet presents a unity of race continuity which no other people has achieved. Living under legal disabilities in almost every land, he has become the power behind many a throne. There are ancient prophecies to the effect that the Jew will return to his own land and from that center rule the world, though not until he has undergone an assault by the united nations of mankind.

The single description which will include a larger percentage of Jews than members of any other race is this: he is in business. It may be only gathering rags and selling them, but he is in business. From the sale of old clothes to the control of international trade and finance, the Jew is supremely gifted for business. More than any other race he exhibits a decided aversion to industrial employment, which he balances by an equally decided adaptability to trade. The Gentile boy works his way up, taking employment in the productive or technical departments; but the Jewish boy prefers to begin as messenger, salesman or clerk—anything—so long as it is connected with the commercial side of the business. An early Prussian census illustrates this characteristic: of a total population of 269,400, the Jews comprised six per cent or 16,164. Of these, 12,000 were traders and 4,164 were workmen. Of the Gentile population, the other 94 per cent, or 153,236 people, there were only 17,000 traders.

A MODERN census would show a large professional and literary class added to the traders, but no diminution of the percentage of traders and not much if any increase in the number of wage toilers. In America alone most of the big business, the trusts and the banks, the natural resources and the chief agricultural products, especially tobacco, cotton and sugar, are in the control of Jewish financiers or their agents. Jewish journalists are a large and powerful group here. "Large numbers of department stores are held by Jewish firms," says the Jewish Encyclopedia, and many if not most of them are run under Gentile names. Jews are the largest and most numerous landlords of residence property in the country. They are supreme in the theatrical world. They absolutely control the circulations of publications throughout the country. Fewer than any race whose presence among us is noticeable, they receive daily an amount of favorable publicity which would be impossible did they not have the facilities for creating and distributing it themselves. Werner Sombart, in his "Jew and Modern Capitalism" says, "If the conditions in America continue to develop along the same lines as in the last generation, if the immigration statistics and the proportion of births among all the nationalities remain the same, our imagination may picture the United States of fifty or a hundred years hence as a land inhabited only by Slavs, Negroes and Jews, wherein the Jews will naturally occupy the position of

The article that signaled the beginning of Henry Ford's seven-year hate campaign against the Jews. (COLLECTIONS OF THE HENRY FORD MUSEUM, GREENFIELD VILLAGE)

Anne Morrow Lindbergh, center, was an accomplished aviator in her own right. Here, she prepares to fly across America with Charles in 1930. (U.S. NATIONAL ARCHIVES)

Charles Lindbergh Jr. celebrates his first birthday. Eight months later, the Lindbergh baby would be snatched from his crib in what would be known as the "crime of the century." (LINDBERGH PICTURE COLLECTION, MANUSCRIPTS AND ARCHIVES, YALE UNIVERSITY LIBRARY.)

June 13, 1938

TIME

The Weekly Newsmagazine

Volume XXXI

LINDBERGH, CARREL & PUMP
They are looking for the fountain of age.
(See MEDICINE)

Number 24

Painted for TIME by S. J. Woolf

Lindbergh's scientific work with Dr. Alexis Carrel helped fuel the Lindbergh legend. In June 1938, a *Time* magazine cover story featured their profusion pump. (TIMEPIX, © 1938 TIME, INC.)

Hitler's second-in-command Hermann Göring receives Charles and Anne Lindbergh in his office during the couple's first German visit in 1936. Two years later, Göring would present Charles with the Third Reich's highest civilian decoration. (BAYERISCHE STAATSBIBLIOTHEK, MUNICH)

1941 Dr. Seuss cartoon in the New York interventionist newspaper *PM*. (MANDEVILLE SPECIAL COLLECTIONS, UCSD)

Dr. Seuss was convinced that Lindbergh's isolationist campaign was a threat to democracy. (MANDEVILLE SPECIAL COLLECTIONS, UCSD)

Charles Lindbergh convinced Henry Ford to finance the America First Committee, which interventionist groups charged with transmitting Nazi propaganda. (DEPART-MENT OF RARE BOOKS AND SPECIAL COLLECTIONS, PRINCETON UNIVERSITY LIBRARY)

1920 stock certificate proving that the Ford Motor Company was the owner and pub-lisher of the *Dearborn Independent* and *The International Jew*, not Henry Ford person-ally, as the company later claimed. (COLLECTIONS OF THE HENRY FORD MUSEUM, GREENFIELD VILLAGE)

Soon afterwards, Carrel visited the office of a longtime friend, New York psychiatrist David Schorr, to express his concerns about "the trend Lindbergh's mind was taking." Carrel told the psychiatrist that Lindbergh "hated the British, and next to them, he hates the United States."[16] In his alarm at the Nazi occupation of his native France, Carrel may have been exaggerating. By most accounts, Lindbergh hated neither Britain nor the United States, but rather what he viewed as the increasing "decadence" of their societies and their governments.

A year earlier, when he reached the mandatory retirement age of sixty-five, Carrel had been forced to retire from the Rockefeller Institute. Suddenly bereft of the Institute's extensive research facilities, the scientist pleaded for an exemption. When the Board of Scientific Directors upheld its policy, he accused the Institute's Jewish members of forcing him out.[17] A subsequent investigation by the Institute's attorney Thomas Debevoise found Carrel's charges "entirely without foundation," since the Board had not a single Jewish member.[18] When news of Carrel's retirement was leaked to the press, the Institute was forced to deny a number of published rumors that his tenure had been derailed by his association with Lindbergh, whose controversial acceptance of the Nazi medal had already made him a pariah in some circles.[19]

By 1940, there were also whispers that Truman Smith's military career was hanging by a thread because of his relationship with Lindbergh. After the fall of France, Smith's name surfaced in a number of newspaper reports linking him to the forces of Appeasement and isolationism. Years later, he would describe this time as "the most unhappy period of my life."

"Almost at once," Smith later recalled, "one columnist after another, among them Drew Pearson and Walter Winchell, launched personal attacks on me for being pro-German and anti-American."[20] By this time, most of official Washington was aware of his close relationship with Lindbergh, who stayed with the Smiths whenever he came to town. Now, this relationship was coming under increasing scrutiny and Smith's role in brokering Lindbergh's isolationist contacts was raising alarm in interventionist circles. The damage was underscored when Walter Winchell published a brief item in his "On Broadway" column on September 17, 1940:

> One of the Washington army officers (whose name has been rumored from time to time as ghosting Lindy's radio speeches) can't deny that when he was in Berlin Mr. Goering gave him a medal inscribed: "To a true friend of Nazi principles."[21]

A week later, FBI director J. Edgar Hoover sent a memo to his assistant Clyde Tolson stating the obvious: "Undoubtedly Walter Winchell had in mind Major Truman Smith."[22] There was never any evidence that anyone other than Lindbergh himself was writing the speeches, and Smith had never received a medal from Göring. But by then, the rumors were widely believed.

The attacks did not let up. In September 1940, Smith was the victim of an anonymous smear, one that threatened to permanently end his army career. Colonel Warner McCabe, his G2 superior, confronted him with reports of a remark he had allegedly made at a cocktail party a year earlier, that "President Roosevelt was paralyzed from the neck up."[23] If he had indeed made the statement, it would have meant an immediate court-martial. But upon further investigation, it was discovered that Smith had been confined to Walter Reed Hospital on the date in question and couldn't have made the remark attributed to him. General Marshall advised him to "avoid the appearance of such a close friendship" with Lindbergh for the time being.[24]

Later, Smith would blame Jews in the Roosevelt administration, whom he referred to as "that crowd," for spreading these stories to discredit him.[25] Like many isolationists, he was convinced that U.S. Treasury Secretary Henry Morgenthau, the only Jew in Roosevelt's cabinet, was manipulating the President toward war. However, a declassified document discovered in the Franklin D. Roosevelt presidential papers points to the more likely source of the rumors. In a memo to FDR's senior aide General Edwin Watson sent on May 27, 1940, a week after Lindbergh's "air defense" speech, the President's secretary Stephen Early discusses Smith's involvement at length:

> Dwight Davis, former Secretary of War, told me Saturday afternoon he had good reasons to believe that Lt. Col. Truman Smith inspired Colonel Lindburgh (sic) to make his radio address last week and collaborated with Lindburgh in preparing his remarks.
>
> Mr. Davis further stated that Colonel Smith had described the President's National Defense Message to the Congress last week as "a hysterical speech."
>
> The former Secretary of War also said that Lindburgh had been the former guest of Colonel Smith who had served many years as Military attaché, and that he was known to be pro-Nazi.[26]

Lindbergh was all too aware that he and his friends had been singled out, as he confided to his journal: "The report is around Washington that the Administration is out to 'get me'. Well, it's not the first time, and it won't be the last."

If his increasingly controversial views were hurting his associates, the fallout was wreaking an even heavier toll at home. Virtually all of Anne's family and closest friends—mainstays of the Eastern liberal establishment—had joined the interventionist side. Her mother, Betty Morrow, was a member of a number of organizations dedicated to aiding what she called "gallant Britain." Her younger sister Constance was married to Aubrey Morgan, assistant chief of the British Information Services in New York, one of the groups Lindbergh claimed was trying to push America into war.[27] They could not understand Anne's decision to stand by her husband, who had become anathema in the Morrows' circle.

Anne's diary and correspondence from the period reflect a deep internal struggle. On the one hand, her natural instinct, like that of her family and friends, was to oppose Nazi tyranny. But on the other, she displayed a stubborn determination to defend Charles's viewpoint: "All the intellectuals are on the other side," she wrote to a friend. "And I can so easily understand that. My heart is there too. I am not on the side of evil. I want evil to be vanquished as much as they—only my mind tells me, perhaps wrongly, that it cannot be done the way they think it can."[28]

For some time, she had been preoccupied with this question of how to reconcile herself to the conflicting forces playing havoc with her loyalties. She appears deeply troubled by her husband's apparent sympathy with Nazi ideals, but at the same time she is struggling to understand his position and find common ground. As far back as April 1940, she had professed to her diary a sense of puzzlement about the true factors behind the war, confiding that she did not believe that the world's problems would be solved simply by eliminating Hitler:

> Nazism seems to me scum which happens to be on the wave
> of the future. I agree with people's condemnation of Nazi methods but I do not think they *are* the wave. They happen to be riding on it.[29]

In September, she decided to expand on this theme and sat down to crystallize her thoughts for public consumption. She had already won great acclaim as a writer for her first two beautifully written books about aviation, *North to the Orient* and *Listen the Wind*. In 1939, *Life* magazine had featured her on its cover, declaring, "The fine sensitive face on the cover belongs to the wife of America's greatest post-war hero. But Anne Morrow Lindbergh is now a celebrity in her own right."[30]

Now, Anne was determined to channel her talents as a writer to make Americans understand what she called her husband's "idealistic" point of view. The result was a forty-one-page treatise published in September 1940, entitled *The Wave of the Future: Confessions of Faith*. The somewhat convoluted essay is her personal attempt to explain the political forces sweeping the world. Democracy, she appeared to argue, was a spent force giving way to an inevitable new political reality. Totalitarianism, she wrote, was merely the manifestation of something deeper:

> What was pushing behind Communism? What behind fascism in Italy? What behind Nazism? Is it nothing but a "return to barbarism," to be crushed at all costs by a "crusade"? Or is some new, and perhaps even ultimate good, conception of humanity trying to come to birth, often through evil and horrible forms and abortive attempts?[31]

Unfortunately, she never actually identifies this force, which may account for much of the confusion that followed. Near the end of the essay, she declares, "There is no fighting the wave of the future, any more than as a child you could fight against the gigantic roller that loomed up ahead of you suddenly."[32]

An uproar greeted Anne's political meanderings in the book that Arthur Schlesinger describes as a "poisonous little best seller" and Scott Berg calls "the book people loved to hate." Surpassed in modern literary history only by *Mein Kampf*, he writes, it became one of the most despised books of its day.[33] Indeed, reviewers reacted with universal scorn, accusing her of attempting to justify fascism and Nazism. These criticisms were somewhat unfair and failed to note one of the essay's most important passages. She had not actually called Nazism the "wave of the future" but rather described it as "the scum on the wave." A careful reading reveals that she had described these totalitarian systems as "barbarisms" and condemned their "tyrannies."

However, even the few fair-minded critics who took note of this distinction were disturbed by another of her arguments. She had appeared to equate the "sins" of the Nazis ("persecution, aggression, war and theft") with the "sins" of the "Democracies" ("blindness, selfishness, smugness, lethargy and resistance to change").[34] This, in her eyes, made both sides equally to blame and there was therefore no justification to fight a war. It was the same argument her husband had been voicing publicly for months and her book confirmed for those around her that she had cast her lot with Charles's "misguided" position. Anne's cousin Richard Scandrett Jr. reflected the view of her family circle in a letter he wrote her shortly after *The Wave of the Future* was released: "Your book seems to me to be the effort of a troubled woman . . . Both you and Charles seem to me to have accepted the totalitarian definition of a democracy as a static or decayed material concept."[35] President Roosevelt's attack dog, Secretary of the Interior Harold Ickes, publicly labeled the book "the Bible of every American Nazi, fascist, Bundist, and Appeaser."[36]

Roosevelt himself had so far remained above the fray, allowing Ickes to voice publicly the sentiments he had himself uttered only in private discussions with his friends and associates. But in his third inaugural speech, a few months later, the President would summon the controversy over Anne's book to take a not-so-subtle shot at her husband's views: "There are men who believe that democracy, as a form of government and a frame of life, is limited or measured by a kind of mystical and artificial fate that, for some unexplained reason, tyranny and slavery have become the surging wave of the future—and that freedom is an ebbing tide," FDR told the nation in January 1941. "But we Americans know this is not true."[37]

On the morning of Monday, September 16, 1940, four men with a mission gathered in Henry Ford's Dearborn office. Ford was joined by his now frequent adviser Charles Lindbergh, along with Douglas Stuart and General Robert E. Wood, to discuss a newly formed national organization known as the America First Committee.[38]

Stuart, the son of a Quaker Oats vice president, was a twenty-four-year-old Yale law student who, with five classmates, had formed a campus-based organization called the Emergency Committee to Defend America First, dedicated to keeping America out of the war.[39] Interviewed in 2003, Stuart, then 86, recalled, "We were very idealistic. We weren't particularly political. We simply believed that this was not America's quarrel." Among the five original members were Sargent Shriver, John F. Kennedy's future brother-in-law, and Kingman Brewster, who would later become president of Yale University. A few months after the campus group was formed, Stuart received a letter from General Robert E. Wood, chairman of the Sears Roebuck Corporation, offering to help the cause by any means at his disposal. Soon after, Wood proposed launching a nationwide movement designed to counter the increasingly effective interventionist propaganda he believed was pushing America toward war. Stuart would be national director of the organization, while Wood would serve as chairman.[40]

The first order of business was to recruit a group of prominent Americans to lend credibility to the fledgling movement. By the time of its official inauguration in Chicago on September 4, its name had been shortened to the America First Committee. Four goals were set:

1. The United States must build an impregnable defense for America.
2. No foreign power, nor group of powers, can successfully attack a prepared America.
3. American democracy can be preserved only by keeping out of the European war.
4. Aid "short of war" weakens national defense at home and threatens to involve America in war abroad.[41]

Twelve days later, Stuart and Wood traveled to Detroit at Lindbergh's invitation to enlist Henry Ford for the National Committee. Stuart had met Lindbergh a month earlier at a Chicago isolationist rally where Lindbergh was the principal speaker. They hit it off immediately, Stuart later describing Lindbergh as a "very sincere and courageous American who has the habit of sticking his neck out."[42] Lindbergh offered to put the new organization in touch with Ford, whom he thought might be willing to lend his name and money to the cause. Lindbergh was by then well aware of his friend's opinions on the subject of the European war. As Ford production chief Charles Sorensen later described his boss's views: "His pet peeve was Franklin Roosevelt, but any mention of the war in Europe or this country's involvement upset him almost to incoherence."[43]

In June, Lindbergh had persuaded Ford to provide financial backing for the American Legion in its campaign against U.S. military intervention.[44] But until now the isolationists lacked an effective national organization dedicated solely to their cause. Although polls consistently found more than 80 percent of Americans opposed to intervention, the movement lacked an organizing force. Ford was at first reluctant to get involved, citing his role in the disastrous Peace Ship expedition a quarter century earlier. But Lindbergh was persuasive, and Ford finally agreed to take an active role on the National Committee and give the AFC his full support.[45]

On September 27, Lindbergh wrote a letter to Ford thanking him for joining the cause: "Your stand against entry into the war has already had great influence, and if we are able to keep out of it, I believe it will be largely due to the courage and support you have given us."[46] Only two weeks earlier, the Pulitzer Prize–winning American playwright Robert Sherwood had delivered a national radio address on the BBC denouncing both Lindbergh and Ford for what he called their "traitorous point of view."[47] Sherwood called the two men Hitler's "bootlickers" and Lindbergh's flirtation with Nazism "a tragic example of a mental aberration."[48]

In the face of all the criticism, the AFC founders forged on. They were determined to make the AFC representative of as wide a cross-section of American society as possible. They vowed to recruit Republicans and Democrats, liberals and conservatives—even socialists. The most important criterion for membership was a belief that America should keep out of the European war. Stuart, however, was anxious to offset any possible controversy that might arise from Ford's membership and invited Lessing Rosenwald, a Jewish director of Sears Roebuck, to join the National Committee. The AFC released the announcement of the two members simultaneously, anxious to avoid accusations of anti-Semitism for including Ford on the committee.[49]

Among the other prominent Americans named to the Executive Committee at the same time were Avery Brundage, the Chicago businessman who, as head of the U.S. Olympic Committee, had blocked efforts to boycott the 1936 Berlin Games; Alice Roosevelt Longworth, daughter of former president Teddy Roosevelt; and World War I flying ace Eddie Rickenbacker.

Lindbergh himself appeared to be the most logical candidate to lead the newly formed movement and was General Wood's first choice. Though he was increasingly under attack by the Roosevelt administration and the liberal press, he remained a widely popular figure, a hero to millions, and had emerged as the leading spokesman for the isolationist cause. But Stuart quickly vetoed the idea. In a memo to his co-founders, he warned that if the Committee were to publicly identify with Lindbergh, it would invite "attacks and smears" on the organization. A moderate, Stuart was particularly concerned with some of the extremist political figures milling around Lindbergh in recent months. Despite later claims by biographers and historians that Lindbergh declined to affiliate with the AFC out of a desire to remain independent of any organization, the truth was that Stuart actively blocked his membership, at least in the beginning.[50] At this point, Lindbergh still had not officially joined any isolationist organization.

It was a gauge of Lindbergh's stigma that he was believed too controversial for the Committee while Ford, a notorious anti-Semite, was welcomed in. Among the extremist figures surrounding Lindbergh throughout this period, in fact, were two men openly aligned with fascism. As early as April

1940, he had been meeting regularly with Merwin K. Hart, head of the right-wing National Economic Council (NEC), whose membership Lindbergh sought for a common isolationist front.[51] Hart's support for fascism began in the mid-1930s when he set up an organization to rally Americans behind the cause of Spanish fascist leader Francisco Franco.

Later, Hart's NEC supported a number of far right American causes and extremist figures, including Henry Ford's friend, the Reverend Gerald L K Smith. Although Hart was fiercely anti-Roosevelt, he reserved most of his scorn for the Jews, whom he described in the Council's newsletter as "alien-minded" outsiders who were responsible for the nation's plight. Through "deceit," "trickery," and "intimidation," he wrote, Jews had become a "mighty force in this land." They threatened the "complete destruction" of America's constitutional government and involved the country in wars.[52] What Douglas Stuart did not know when he expressed concern about Lindbergh's involvement with such characters is that the AFC's own chairman, General Robert Wood, was an avowed admirer and financial backer of Hart's Economic Council. In a private letter to Hart, Wood praised the Council's work, writing, "I admire you for your courage in speaking out on the Jewish Question."[53]

The earliest reference to Lindbergh's political activities in FBI files is in fact related to Merwin Hart, whom the Bureau described as "the alleged promoter of an American Fascist movement." An informant reported that Lindbergh had been approached as early as 1936 by an organization connected with Hart called the "World Movement." The group was said to have "chosen Lindbergh as their world leader because of his youth, his prominence and other characteristics." Lindbergh had "been approached, contact made, and had been converted to the New World viewpoint and since then has been actively working with them."[54] Whether or not the report is accurate, Lindbergh's journal confirms that he met with Hart on at least six occasions between April and November 1940, to discuss "setting up an eastern anti-war organization."[55]

However, it was Lindbergh's association with yet another prominent fascist that caused the greatest hand-wringing amongst his friends. On September 16, 1940, a few hours after he left the meeting with Stuart and Wood at Ford's office, Lindbergh boarded an overnight train for Washington, D.C. Arriving at the station the next morning, he immediately took a taxi to the home of Truman Smith, who had disregarded General Marshall's warning to avoid public contact with his controversial friend. Smith was very anxious for Lindbergh to meet a man whose ideas he believed were very much in keeping with their own, a former American diplomat named Lawrence Dennis.

A product of the eastern liberal intellectual establishment, the Harvard-educated Dennis worked for the U.S. Foreign Service from 1920 to 1927 until he resigned to protest American intervention in Nicaragua. But after Franklin Roosevelt won the White House and introduced his New Deal, Dennis's political ideals, once liberal, shifted rapidly to the right. He set about proposing his own radical solution to the Great Depression: a set of "centralized controls" based on a corporate state. As early as April 1933, he was making references in correspondence to "Good Old Hitler"[56] and writing, "I should like nothing better than to be a leader or a follower of a Hitler who would crush and destroy many now in power."[57] In 1936, he finally named his evolving ideology when he published a book titled *The Coming American Fascism* outlining his vision of a fascist America as a sensible alternative to Communism.[58] The book encountered a lukewarm reception in the United States but was very well received in Germany, where Dennis was invited to attend the 1936 Nazi Party Congress at Nuremberg as a special guest of the regime. There, he met with a number of high ranking Nazis including the party's ideologue Alfred Rosenberg and Putzi Hanfstaengl, the man whom Smith introduced to Hitler in 1922.

By the time Dennis encountered Lindbergh in 1940, the American fascist ideologue had already formed close ties to the Nazi agent Friedrich Auhagen, a Columbia University lecturer who was later indicted by the U.S. government for his clandestine Nazi activities. That summer, Dennis told Auhagen that if he could secure funding from the Nazi government, his efforts on behalf of Germany would be considerably more effective than other American Nazi propaganda.[59] By this time, Dennis was already known as the leading intellectual fascist in America.[60] He published a bulletin called the *Weekly Foreign Letter* in which he argued that wars of conquest were inevitable, and he appeared to welcome the prospect of a Nazi victory.[61]

On the day Smith introduced him to Dennis in September 1940, Lindbergh wrote in his journal, "I must get to know Dennis better. He has a brilliant and original mind—determined to the point of aggressiveness. I like his strength of character, but I am not yet sure how much I agree with him."[62] This is the last reference to Dennis in Lindbergh's published journal, so we never learn whether he eventually formed a stronger opinion. It appears from reading the journal that they had no further contact.

But in 1942, following his indictment by a federal grand jury for sedition, prosecutors seized Dennis's correspondence and other personal documents and discovered numerous references to Lindbergh among them. A week after their first meeting, for example, Dennis sent a special delivery letter to the Nazi agent Friedrich Auhagen: "I saw Lindbergh last week, and will see him often from now on."[63] On December 23, 1940, he wrote to B.B. Kendrick of Greensboro, North Carolina: "I spent hours Saturday with

Lindbergh." In July 1941, he personally gave Lindbergh a copy of a 100-page memorandum he had prepared refuting interventionist charges that "America can't do business with Hitler." In October 1941, he wrote to John Blodgett of Portland, Oregon: "I had a long visit to Colonel Lindbergh here in New York this week."[64]

Later, Dennis was accused of feeding Lindbergh propaganda and even writing his speeches. These charges became especially pointed after Lindbergh declared in a speech that the war in Europe was "not so much a conflict between right and wrong as a conflict between differing concepts of the right." One interventionist group did some research and found that Lawrence Dennis had once written a suspiciously similar passage: "Wars are fought between right and right, not between right and wrong."[65]

Before Dennis died in 1977, he donated his personal and political papers to the Hoover Institution at Stanford University. Many of these papers were annotated with handwritten additions by Dennis, presumably meant for researchers who accessed the papers after his death. One of these notations, possibly facetious, is particularly bizarre. Handwritten underneath a letter he sent to his old friend Truman Smith in 1957, Dennis provides a description of Smith:

> Truman was the US military attaché in Berlin who brought Lindbergh over there. [Roosevelt's friend Bernard] Baruch wanted him fired. But Gen. Marshall stood by him. Truman introduced me to Lindbergh and tried to get Charles to let me brainwash him. I tried but failed. Not enough sessions.[66]

As Lindbergh continued to consort with what his biographer Joyce Milton calls a "collection of second-raters and lunatic fringe types,"[67] the couple were gradually dropped by their old circle: "All the intellectuals are against us," Anne complained in her diary ". . . since I am now the bubonic plague among writers and C. is the anti-Christ!"[68]

Meanwhile, a Nazi invasion of Britain appeared imminent. Before Germany could cross the Channel and complete its seemingly inevitable conquest, however, the *Luftwaffe* would have to soften British resistance. Hermann Göring, who appeared to believe his own propaganda about the weakness of England's air defenses—so convincingly disseminated by Lindbergh two years earlier—was certain that this would be a relatively easy task. He shrugged off the lesson of the battle for France when the *Luftwaffe* had lost a staggering 1,129 out of 5,349 planes, a full 21 percent of its combat aircraft capabilities.[69] Shortly after the Nazis marched into

Paris, Winston Churchill declared, "The Battle of France is over. The Battle of Britain is about to begin. Upon this battle depends the survival of Christian civilization."

In July, with a German invasion fleet waiting in French waters, the *Luftwaffe* launched its campaign to bomb Britain into submission. For three terrible months, the Germans sent thousands of bombers to rain destruction from the skies. Much to the astonishment of both sides, the RAF shot down Göring's planes as fast as he could dispatch them, dealing a ferocious setback to Hitler's invasion plans. So successful was Britain's air defense that by August, England was sending its own planes on nightly missions to bomb German cities. In mid-October, his air force in shambles, the führer finally called off the battle. Roughly 1,700 *Luftwaffe* bombers and fighters had been shot down during the three-month battle, while the RAF had lost just 900 planes. Winston Churchill issued his memorable tribute: "Never . . . was so much owed by so many to so few."[70]

What made the British victory all the more significant was that it was accomplished before most of Roosevelt's promised American military aid arrived. Nevertheless, the Nazis still ruled the continent and most observers believed they would almost certainly make another attempt in the spring.

The British victory goes virtually unmentioned in Lindbergh's journal; his reaction to the battle that put the lie to his predictions of German invincibility is thus unknown. But in August, 40,000 people at a Chicago rally heard him state that cooperation with a victorious Germany might not be such a bad idea: "In the past we have dealt with a Europe dominated by England and France. In the future we might have to deal with a Europe dominated by Germany."[71] He still appeared to believe that a German victory was only a matter of time.

The interventionist media quickly labeled his attitude "defeatist" and resumed its attacks. Nevertheless, the letters pouring into Lloyd Neck were running ten-to-one in favor of his stand, and an overwhelming majority of Americans continued to oppose direct military intervention. Grassroots isolationist organizations were springing up all over the country but Lindbergh still had not publicly committed himself to any of the groups vying for his support.

In May, he had supported the efforts of two conservative isolationists, Douglas Stewart (not the same Douglas *Stuart* who led the AFC) and George Eggleston, to buy the venerable *Scribner's* magazine and convert it into an isolationist mouthpiece called *Scribner's Commentator*, designed to counter the propaganda of the liberal, "Jewish-dominated" interventionist media. In announcing the *Commentator*'s formation, the founders complained that the "great mass of American people who were against the war" had no medium to articulate their opposition. The magazine, and an accompanying isolationist organization, would provide it.[72]

The U.S. Military Intelligence Division (G2) file on Stewart notes that he was a highly educated mathematician who ended up becoming "much exercised over the Communist menace." Out of this grew a violent anti-Semitism, which "took hold of him almost like a disease." He became "pro-Nazi, pro-Fascist and pro-Japanese," condemning Winston Churchill and other leaders as willing tools of the "Jewish International" to destroy capitalism.[73]

In the spring of 1941, Eggleston and Stewart started up a new magazine called the *Herald*, a sister publication of *Scribner's* but considerably more blatant in its pro-Nazi views. The new journal appeared to be flush with cash from the start. When *Scribner's Commentator* and the *Herald* were later investigated by a grand jury for abetting sedition during World War II, Stewart told the FBI that he had received $39,000 from various anonymous sources to fund the two publications.[74] He spun a ludicrous tale about how he had come home one day to find $15,000 in twenty-dollar bills wrapped in a brown manila paper package with no writing on it. On another occasion, he said, somebody tossed a large wad of bills in his living room window. The rest of the money, he claimed, arrived in a similarly mysterious fashion. In a postwar interrogation, Herbert von Strempel, first secretary of the German embassy in Washington, revealed that he had personally delivered $10,000 to $15,000 to Stewart and Eggleston "on instructions from Berlin."[75] Hans Thomsen, chargé d'affaires of the embassy, also acknowledged that the Nazis had "subsidized" *Scribner's Commentator* and the *Herald*. Thus, the magazines were part of the Nazis' sophisticated American propaganda machine, a machine with only one goal: Keep America out of the war. There is no evidence that Lindbergh knew about the magazines' source of funding but, for the next eighteen months, they would be the publications most closely associated with his activities, frequently publishing articles defending his stand. With every paid subscription to *Scribner's*, readers received a complete collection of Lindbergh's radio addresses.[76] In a letter to a friend, Lawrence Dennis called the magazine "Lindbergh's organ."[77] According to a military intelligence report, Stewart told the American fascist leader Harry Jung that "Lindbergh is the leading individual around whom his publishing enterprise is built" and that Lindbergh is "directly or indirectly responsible for the necessary amount of money to carry out the venture."[78]

On August 28, 1940, Lindbergh had dinner with Stewart and Eggleston, who asked him to "form and head some sort of organization—nationalist, anti-war, etc." He allegedly declined, arguing that he was not well suited for such work.[79] Three weeks later, he again dined with the two men and discussed plans for coordinating the activities of all the antiwar groups throughout the country. Their efforts soon culminated in the establishment of a new national isolationist organization known as the No Foreign Wars Campaign, to be headed by an Iowa newspaper editor named Verne Marshall.[80] Lindbergh agreed to launch the new group with a major public address in St. Louis, scheduled for January 1941. But just weeks before the planned speech, the New York *Herald Tribune* revealed that the organization's principal financial backer was a mysterious Texas oilman named William Rhodes Davis, whose fortune was based almost entirely on oil sales to the Third Reich and who was friends with the entire Nazi High Command. When the revelation made headlines, Democratic senator Josh Lee called the formation of the No Foreign Wars Campaign a "diabolically cunning betrayal of the American people." Much of the gasoline that had sent "showers of fiery death" on the defenseless heart of London had been provided by Davis, charged the Senator. The oilman's record demonstrated the "great financial stake he has in a complete Nazi victory in the European war."[81]

That same month, *Scribner's* featured a cover article by none other than Henry Ford predicting a British defeat. Unlike Lindbergh, who had never publicly criticized the Nazi regime, Ford declared that the leaders of Germany and Italy were not necessarily representative of their people. Hitler and Mussolini, he speculated, were merely "puppets" at whose expense greedy financiers had "played a dirty trick."[82] This was simply a continuation of a by now familiar theme that Ford had been trumpeting since 1915: International bankers were behind all war. Before 1927, he happily shared with the public his view on what religion those bankers happened to practice. Now it was up to the readers to figure it out for themselves.

Lindbergh may or may not have been aware of the connection between William Rhodes Davis and the No Foreign War Campaign, but soon after his own role in the Nazi-financed organization was publicized, he backed out of the St. Louis speech and severed all ties with the NFWC.[83] His relationship with Stewart and Eggleston, however, continued unabated; a number of additional meetings with the two men are recorded in his journal. For the interventionist forces, news of Lindbergh's indirect association with a Nazi financier merely provided fresh ammunition for their attacks. Dorothy Thompson, Walter Winchell, and others delighted in using it against him. It was now open season on the isolationist movement's leading spokesman. Still, Lindbergh had his defenders, those who remained untroubled by his alleged fascist connections. The *Christian Century* weighed in against the liberal media onslaught, declaring the venomous attacks had gone far beyond the ordinary canons of debate: "If this man who was once the nation's shining hero had been proved another Benedict

Arnold, he could not have been subjected to more defamation and calumny."[84]

The America First Committee was experiencing its own turmoil during this period. In early December, Lessing Rosenwald—the Jewish director of Sears Roebuck who had been named to the National Committee to prove the AFC wasn't anti-Semitic—submitted his letter of resignation to protest Henry Ford's inclusion on the Committee. In a letter to a friend, AFC director Douglas Stuart confided that Rosenwald was feeling "tremendous pressure from his own people, condemning him for serving on a committee with Mr. Henry Ford." Anxious to minimize the fallout from the resignation before it hit the papers, the AFC board of directors convened on December 3 to expel Ford. America First, the minutes stated carefully, "could not be sure that from time to time Mr. Ford's views were consistent with the official views of the Committee."[85] Publicly, the AFC simply claimed that Ford had been "unable to give any time or attention to the work of the Committee."[86] A number of other prominent Jews were hurriedly invited to sit on the AFC's National Committee but each one declined.[87] In his letter refusing inclusion on the Committee, Bloomingdale's vice president I. A. Hirschmann wrote Stuart, "For me, [Ford's] name represents a black mark on your committee and in American history where minorities are concerned, and unless that can be erased I shall not be able to in any way participate in your work."[88]

By this point, the AFC was rapidly gaining grassroots support around the country, although no one group had yet emerged as the nation's preeminent isolationist organization.

In a radio fireside chat on December 29, President Roosevelt issued his most direct appeal yet for military aid to Britain. He invoked the specter of a Nazi victory in Europe and pleaded that if Britain went down to defeat, the Axis powers would control Europe, Asia, and Africa as well as the High Seas:

> It is no exaggeration to say that all of us, in all the Americas, would be living at the point of a gun—a gun loaded with explosive bullets, economic as well as military. The Nazi masters of Germany have made it clear that they intend not only to dominate all life and thought in their own country, but also to enslave the whole of Europe, and then to use the resources of Europe to dominate the rest of the world.

"No man can tame a tiger into a kitten by stroking it," the President said in reference to the isolationists. "There can be no appeasement with ruthlessness. There can be no reasoning with an incendiary bomb. We know now that a nation can have peace with the Nazis only at the price of total surrender." Issuing his most memorable phrase of the Great Debate, he called on America to become an "Arsenal of Democracy" and urged Congress to supply Britain with the aid she needed to stave off the Nazi military threat.[89]

In a letter to Roosevelt three weeks earlier, Winston Churchill had warned that the time was coming when England's economic situation would be desperate and she would "no longer be able to pay cash,"[90] meaning that, without American military aide, Britain would almost certainly succumb to Nazi conquest. Roosevelt soon came up with a creative solution. On January 6, he submitted to Congress a "lend-lease" bill which would allow the President to sell, transfer, exchange, lend or lease war equipment and other commodities to any country that the President deemed vital for the defense of the United States. Most important, it would authorize the United States to make war materials immediately available to Great Britain to defend against the Axis.

The isolationists were, predictably, furious. Lend-Lease was the most blatant attempt yet to involve America in the war, they charged. The America First Committee declared that Roosevelt "wants a blank check book with the power to write away your man power, our laws and our liberties." Lindbergh appeared more depressed than angry. "The pall of war seems to hang over us today," he wrote in his journal. "More and more people are simply giving in to it."[91]

What the President referred to as a pitched battle for "the soul of the nation" was well and truly under way. In January 1941, Lindbergh was invited by the powerful isolationist congressman Hamilton Fish to testify before the House Foreign Relations Committee hearing on Roosevelt's Lend-Lease bill. A thousand spectators and dozens of photographers thronged the committee room as Lindbergh took his place at the microphone. He sat poised as congressmen questioned him for four-and-a-half hours, reiterating his position eloquently and unequivocally. Finally, it was the turn of the Tennessee Democrat Virt Courtney, who had been looking forward to the opportunity all morning. Congressman Courtney had a simple goal. He was determined to force the witness to commit himself on one question:

> *Whom do you want to win the war?*
> Lindbergh: "I want neither side to win."[92]

While *Scribner's Commentator* was emerging as the mouthpiece of the isolationist movement, the interventionist forces had gained their own media voice when Chicago department store heir Marshall Field III founded a brash New York daily called *PM*. So that it could claim to be "beholden to no one," the newspaper accepted no advertising. Its credibility was assured because, unlike much of the liberal media at the time, *PM* was equally critical of Hitler and Stalin, fascism and communism. Although not exclusively dedicated to combating isolationism, *PM* made no secret of its sympathies with the interventionist cause. On the staff of the new paper was a young editorial cartoonist named Theodor Geisel, who would first achieve national attention in the pages of *PM* with a number of biting cartoons lampooning Lindbergh and his isolationist crusade. Regularly shown cavorting with Hitler, the Lone Eagle was mercilessly portrayed by Geisel as "the Lone Ostrich." Later, the young cartoonist would become better known by his pen name, Dr. Seuss, and by 1941, his trademark style was already evident in a poem accompanying one of his anti-Lindbergh *PM* cartoons:

> *The Lone Eagle had Flown*
> *The Atlantic alone*
> *With fortitude and a ham sandwich*
> *Great courage that took.*
> *But he shivered and shook*
> *At the sound of the gruff German landgwich.*[93]

The rhetoric on both sides was becoming increasingly inflammatory. Interventionist groups, prowar media figures and a number of Jewish organizations had resorted to name-calling against anybody who expressed isolationist views, often unfairly labeling their opponents un-American, anti-Semitic, or pro-Nazi. For their part, isolationists consistently charged that Roosevelt was attempting to impose a dictatorship on the country and that the interventionists were trying to bring America into the war "through the back door." But war was not necessarily what the interventionists were after. William Allen White, chairman of the nation's most powerful interventionist organization, attracted attention in December 1940 when he told a reporter, "The only reason in God's world that I am in this organization is to keep this country *out* of this war."[94] Like many interventionists, White subscribed to Roosevelt's policy of "aid short of war." Millions of Americans who opposed direct intervention still believed it was in America's interest to aid Britain and forestall a Nazi-dominated Europe. When the secret wartime correspondence between Roosevelt and Churchill was revealed to the public decades later, it contained no indication that either leader contemplated American entry into the war before Pearl Harbor, although there is separate evidence that Churchill desired this outcome and that he believed Roosevelt was looking for an excuse to justify open hostilities with Germany. Rather, the President appeared determined to channel America's resources in defense of the British war effort without a commitment of U.S. troops. How much this had to do with the influence of the isolationist movement is open to speculation. Roosevelt was nothing if not politically expedient. In the most comprehensive study ever conducted into America's prewar attitudes toward intervention, *Should America Go to War*, historian James Schneider argues that Roosevelt's failure to intervene before Pearl Harbor was guided by public opinion: "Time and again in private messages to foreign leaders and in conversations with officials, FDR cited public opinion." This apparent political cowardice may also explain Roosevelt's glaring failure to support increased immigration of Jewish refugees fleeing Nazi Germany.

Campaigning for re-election in 1940, the President had promised the American people that he would not involve America in the war abroad. Despite a number of later conspiracy theories and reasoned arguments by academics and historians, no concrete evidence has emerged to prove he intended to break this promise.

Nevertheless, many isolationists, including Lindbergh, remained deeply suspicious. Unquestionably, a number of interventionists veered toward supporting American military involvement. One, New York mayor Fiorello LaGuardia, denounced White's position against direct American intervention, writing him, "You could continue as Chairman of the 'Committee to Defend America by Aiding the Allies with Words' and the rest of us would join a 'Committee to Defend America by Aiding the Allies with Deeds.'"[95] His view was shared by several members of the Roosevelt administration, who believed that Nazi tyranny could only be stopped if the United States entered the war. However, they appeared to be in the minority.

There is no question that many of the media attacks on the isolationist movement as a pro-Hitler Fifth Column were as unfair as they were inaccurate. Most isolationists were simply concerned Americans who wanted to avoid a repeat of the horrifying bloodshed that characterized the First World War. The interventionists, however, appeared to have a stronger case when they charged that Lindbergh himself was acting in league with the Nazis.

When the records of German embassies were seized by the Allies after the war, they revealed a long series of top secret communications between the embassy in Washington—the base of Nazi spy operations in America— and the German High Command in Berlin, describing a vigorous campaign to further the goals of the isolationist lobby in America. A number of these communiqués focused on the activities of Charles Lindbergh, some praising him in almost mystical terms, others suggesting he had at least an indirect relationship with the Embassy.

Throughout 1940, German diplomats in Washington had made it clear that the Embassy's first priority was to win American public opinion over to Hitler and against American aid to Britain.[96] To accomplish this task, they sought to enlist influential Americans sympathetic to the cause who could lobby more effectively than Germans to achieve these ends. Berlin had long since cut all ties to Fritz Kuhn's embarrassing German-American Bund and issued strict orders to its American-based Nazi operatives to refrain from any activities, such as sabotage, that risked jeopardizing American neutrality.[97]

On June 12, 1940, the Embassy's chargé d'affaires Hans Thomsen cabled a coded dispatch to Berlin reporting that a "well-known Republican congressman," working "in close collaboration" with the German embassy, had offered, in exchange for $3,000, to invite fifty isolationist congressmen to the Republican Convention that summer "so that they may work on the delegates in favor of an isolationist foreign policy." The same congressman had asked for $30,000 from Berlin to take out full-page ads in American newspapers to be headed "Keep America Out of War." Another $30,000 would be supplied by his fellow Republicans. The money was quickly authorized by the Foreign Ministry.[98] Sure enough, an ad with this heading appeared in the *New York Times* two weeks later.

On December 25, 1940, Thomsen cabled the Foreign Ministry in Berlin discussing the No Foreign War Committee (a few days after Lindbergh had agreed to speak on its behalf) and the America First Committee. The Nazi diplomat reported, "We have good relationships with both isolationist committees and support them in various ways. In order that this cooperation not be compromised, I request that the work of the committees be passed over in silence in the German press and radio as far as possible."[99]

One of the first known references to Lindbergh in German embassy dispatches can be found in a cable sent jointly by Thomsen and embassy military attaché Friedrich von Bötticher. Marked "Most Urgent Top Secret," it was transmitted to the German Military High Command on July 20, 1940, shortly after Republican presidential candidate Wendell Willkie was nominated to oppose Roosevelt in the 1940 presidential election:

> As the exponent of the Jews who, especially through Freemasonry, control the broad masses of the American people, Roosevelt wants England to continue fighting and the war to be prolonged. . . . The circle about Lindbergh has become aware of

this development and now tries at least to impede the fatal control of American policy by the Jews. Toward Willkie, the candidate of the Republican Party, Lindbergh's attitude is to wait and see whether Willkie will be able to avoid the bondage to Jewry.

Meanwhile, a very trustworthy personage close to Lindbergh has asked me to inform German authorities that the . . . sister of Willkie has pronounced sympathies for Germany and might greatly influence her brother.[100]

On August 6, shortly after Lindbergh spoke at his first public rally, Thomsen and Bötticher again cabled Berlin:

The background of Lindbergh's re-emergence in public and the campaign against him . . .

The forces opposing the Jewish element and the present policy of the United States have been mentioned over and over in my reports taking into account also the importance of the General Staff. The greatly gifted Lindbergh, whose connections reach very far, is much the most important of them all. The Jewish element and Roosevelt fear the spiritual and, particularly, the moral superiority and purity of this man. On Sunday, Lindbergh delivered a blow that will hurt the Jews by declaring that America was not threatened. . . .

The chorus of the Jewish element casting suspicion on Lindbergh in the press, and his denunciation by a Senator as a "Fifth Columnist", that is, a traitor, merely serve to underline the fear of the spiritual power of this man, about whose progress I have reported since the beginning of the war and in whose great importance for future German-American relations I believe.[101]

Lindbergh's speeches had been regularly reprinted and applauded in the pro-Nazi press in America as well as Germany, Italy, and South America. The *New York Times* reported this fact in April 1941, citing an article praising Lindbergh in a Hamburg newspaper. Immediately, Bötticher and Thomsen transmitted another top secret cable to Berlin, earmarked personally for Hitler's foreign minister Joachim von Ribbentrop:

A confidant of Colonel Lindbergh called on General Bötticher and made the urgent request that the German press and

German publications of all sorts refrain from all discussion of
Lindbergh's stand, his fight against the warmongers and his
speeches. Halfield's article in the *Hamburger Fremdenblatt* has
been thoroughly exploited in the American press in order to
prove that Lindbergh is working for Germany.

Lindbergh is of the opinion that he can prevail against Roosevelt's warlike policy if the necessary restraint is observed by the
Germans and also by the Italians. General Bötticher, who is the
only one who can maintain direct contact with these circles
around Lindbergh which are so very important to us, has repeatedly requested the greatest restraint with regard to Lindbergh
and repeatedly pointed to the extraordinary importance of this
man.[101]

A number of other similar Embassy communications refer to this "circle around Lindbergh" and von Bötticher's direct contact with the group.
Yet no names are ever given. Who is the "Lindbergh confidant" who asked
the Nazis to quell media discussion of Lindbergh's stand? It takes little
investigation to conclude that the most likely candidate is Truman Smith.
According to Smith's own account, he first met von Bötticher, then a rising
young German officer, in 1920 when Smith was stationed in Berlin with
the American Occupation authority.[102] The two became friends. While
Smith, to his lasting bitterness, never rose higher than lieutenant colonel in
his own military career, von Bötticher wrote a number of articles and
books on military history that gained him a reputation in Nazi circles as a
deep thinker and impressed his superiors. By the time Hitler took power in
January 1933, he had been promoted to major general and was the chief
military envoy for the whole of North and South America. Three months
later, von Bötticher was dispatched to Washington to serve as military
attaché to the German embassy.[103]

He still held that position when Smith returned to Washington in 1939
from his own posting in Berlin. Before long, the two had resumed their
relationship. There was nothing improper about Smith's acquaintance with
von Bötticher. As the resident German expert in G2, it was his job to keep
track of German military activities and gather whatever intelligence he
could about the Nazi war effort. Indeed, Smith reported these meetings to
his superiors on a number of occasions. However, according to an FBI
report, Smith also "frequently associated socially with the von Böttichers"
away from the embassy.[105]

Historian Ladislas Farago spent several years analyzing captured German Embassy dispatches in preparation for his 1972 book about Nazi intel-

ligence, *Game of the Foxes.* He describes an isolationist American "military clique overly impressed with the precision and might of the German war machine" that viewed "developments with a distinct pro-German bias." Its members met regularly at the Washington home of Truman Smith, whom Farago dubs the "ideologue and *spiritus rector* of the group." He writes that Charles Lindbergh was drawn into this circle and derived considerable inspiration from their firm opposition to war:

> This was no mere study group, not a private debating society of concerned citizens. It had all the characteristics of a cabal. Their meetings were held in circumspect secrecy . . . Classified documents were brought to these gatherings and privileged information was exchanged. Contact was maintained surreptitiously with influential isolationists on Capitol Hill . . .
>
> This was the circle of informants to which General von Bötticher pegged himself, not merely to monitor the mood and morale of the United States Army, but to procure the most reliable factual information he could get.[106]

As disturbing as the implications of these activities may appear today, there was nothing officially improper about Smith's meeting and exchanging information with a high-ranking German operative. Nor was Lindbergh guilty of any treasonous conduct if he conducted his isolationist activities in tacit cooperation with the Nazis during this period. The United States was not yet at war with Germany and, as far as Lindbergh and Smith were concerned, they believed they were simply acting as concerned American patriots.

CHAPTER 10

FALLEN HERO

Charles Lindbergh, flanked by isolationist leaders Burton Wheeler and Kathleen Norris, appeared to many to be giving a Nazi salute in this May 1941 photo, taken at an America First rally at Madison Square Garden. He later claimed they were merely waving to supporters. A closer examination of the photo reveals that a number of other members in the crowd behind them also have their hands raised in a stiff-armed gesture.

In the spring of 1941, an American woman named Alice Crockett, the divorced wife of a U.S. army colonel, appeared in a San Francisco federal court to file a lawsuit that would cast the unwelcome glare of publicity on the alleged Nazi affiliations of both Charles Lindbergh and Henry Ford. In the suit, Crockett alleged that her lover, Germany's San Francisco consul general Fritz Wiedemann, owed her $8,000 in connection with a trip she had taken on his behalf in 1939 to visit Adolf Hitler and other members of the Nazi High Command in Berlin.[1]

Wiedemann was the Nazi who was believed to have enjoyed the longest relationship with Hitler, having served as the future Führer's commanding officer when Lance-Corporal Hitler was still a motorcycle dispatch rider during the First World War. After the National Socialists took power, Wiedemann served as Hitler's personal adjutant from 1935 to 1939, until the two were said to have had a quarrel and he was assigned to the relatively minor San Francisco consular post, where he oversaw Nazi spy operations on the American west coast.[2]

Crockett claimed that Wiedemann had experienced a "serious misunderstanding" with the German regime and had sent her on a private mission to Berlin to gauge the depths of its dissatisfaction. General Wiedemann immediately issued a statement claiming her accusations were "all bunk." The judge eventually concluded that Crockett had aided Wiedemann in "acts of espionage" and the case was dismissed, but not before Crockett recounted a bizarre and elaborate tale of Nazi activities involving both Lindbergh and Ford.

Wiedemann, she charged, was a Nazi spy who directed the German-American Bund and had frequent dealings with IG Farben and its American subsidiary, General Aniline & Film, in the course of his undercover operations. He allegedly told Crockett that he had "used" Lindbergh to "lull America into a false sense of security and into believing that America was safe from Germany and German attack." She said Wiedemann also claimed that he had "worked together" with Ford in "furthering the German and Nazi cause in the United States."[3]

Whether or not her story was true, Crockett, an ordinary San Francisco housewife, certainly appears to have been well connected. While she was in Berlin, she was wined and dined by a number of high-ranking Nazi officials and was even given a special reception by SS chief Heinrich Himmler.[4]

Lindbergh remained silent after Crockett's charges were publicized, but two days after she filed her complaint, Ford's attorney issued a complete denial: "Any statement that Henry Ford is working alone or with anyone else to further any foreign cause whatever is an outrageous lie."[5]

It was the first time the names of Ford and Lindbergh would be linked publicly in connection with the sanctioning of Nazi Germany. Because Crockett's complaint did not allege that either had engaged in illegal activities, the FBI had no grounds to investigate the two men. However, on March 6, a wire story about the lawsuit was brought to the personal attention of FBI director Hoover by his assistant, accompanied by a handwritten notation: "Read this."[6]

The FBI was thought to have had a long-standing interest in both Lindbergh and Ford. In his journal, Lindbergh notes that he had once received an urgent message from Truman Smith claiming that the Bureau had recently begun tapping the telephones of both Lindbergh and the America First Committee. The information, Smith said, had come from "friends" in the Bureau who were "friendly" to Lindbergh.[7]

But an examination of Lindbergh's extensive FBI dossier reveals that no official investigation of him was ever ordered, at least before Pearl Harbor. Some chroniclers have cited the size of Lindbergh's 1,368-page file as evidence that he was unfairly targeted by Hoover. But the contents of his file before Pearl Harbor is not much different than that of any other controversial public figure whom the FBI judged worthy of an informal dossier. The Bureau retained newspaper clippings, anonymous gossip, reports from informants, and correspondence from the public about his isolationist crusade, but the FBI never assigned an agent to monitor his political activities or placed a tap on his telephone. Moreover, there is no evidence in the files of the FBI or in the FDR Presidential Archives at Hyde Park that the White House ever requested any such action be taken, even though Roosevelt had privately authorized the wiretapping of suspected subversives.

Although the President was convinced Lindbergh was a Nazi before Pearl Harbor, neither Roosevelt nor Hoover appeared to believe he was a genuine threat to national security. That is not to say the President and the FBI director remained indifferent to the isolationists as a political force. Both men were clearly wary of the movement and kept a close eye on Lindbergh, mostly by monitoring media coverage of his activities. However, there is no evidence that the President abused his office in an attempt to discredit him. This would seem to contradict claims by Lindbergh and his supporters that the Roosevelt administration "was out to get him" and had engaged in an FBI witch hunt.

The Bureau, however, appeared to be keeping an especially close watch on Ford's secretary, Ernest Liebold. After his nervous breakdown in 1933, Liebold had ceased to wield his previously enormous influence within the company itself, but he still held Ford's personal power-of-attorney and handled all his outside business interests, earning a substantial annual salary of more than $44,000.[8] The two men remained close, and media inquiries to the company about Liebold's status were met with the statement that he was Ford's "confidential aide." A month after the Crockett lawsuit prompted renewed scrutiny of Ford's operations, Hoover personally wrote a letter to Brigadier General Sherman Miles, assistant chief of staff at the War Department's Military Intelligence Division (G2), asking for information about Liebold, noting that Ford's general secretary was one of a number of individuals "considered by the Department of Justice for custodial detention in the event of a national emergency."[9] Three days later, Miles wrote back with a summary of Liebold's dossier, which contained the notation: "Is German and considered German spy . . . is in position to have much secret and valuable information."[10] But this file dated back to the First World War. Liebold's file at the Office of Naval Intelligence—forwarded to the FBI's Detroit bureau shortly after Crockett launched her suit—was considerably more up-to-date, revealing that he was "regarded as pro-Nazi."[11] The Bureau also forwarded a recently received report that Liebold had told a friend, "The entire United States will say within five years that Lindbergh was right."[12]

Meanwhile, reporters for *PM* claimed to have discovered a more substantive link between Ford and Lindbergh. The pro-interventionist newspaper revealed it had uncovered evidence that Ford was compiling a master list of isolationist sympathizers in co-operation with *Scribner's Commentator*, which *PM* called the "Bible of America's super-appeasers."

Secretaries in a locked and guarded room at Ford's New York offices were sorting boxes of Lindbergh's fan mail, lifting the names and addressees, and sending them to *Scribner's* throughout the months of October, November, and December of 1940. This corresponded to the period in which Lindbergh was meeting regularly with *Scribner's* editor and publisher, George Eggleston and Douglas Stewart. According to the report, boxes of Lindbergh's mail were first shipped to the magazine's offices and then on to the Ford operation at 1710 Broadway. As a *Scribner's* employee explained to *PM*, "We thought it best for nothing to go from Lindbergh direct to Ford." Almost every name on the list then received a subscription solicitation to *Scribner's*.[13] The only Lindbergh correspondents who were excluded from the list were those who had names that appeared to be Jewish. According to the report, the secretaries reacted with a "flurry of mirth" whenever they came across one, and the letter was immediately tossed in the trash.

In an editorial, *PM* called on the FBI to launch an investigation into what it called potentially subversive activities. Today, trading or buying mailing lists is a common business practice; indeed, Ford appears to have been guilty of nothing more than shrewd marketing practices on behalf of the movement. In all likelihood, *PM* was simply inflating the issue to take a stab at the isolationists. During a subsequent FBI investigation into the activities of *Scribner's Commentator*, the Bureau concluded that, in addition to mailing lists compiled by Ford and Lindbergh, the magazine also used lists supplied by Father Coughlin's *Social Justice* to aid its subscription drive.[14] After Pearl Harbor, a woman named Esther van Scriver confirmed to the FBI that she had been hired by the Ford Motor Company at $130 per month in the fall of 1940 to do "secret work" that involved compiling a master mailing list for *Scribner's* from Lindbergh's fan mail. According to van Scriver, a large proportion of these letters were from names of "Germanic origin," and many of them referred to Roosevelt as "President Rosenfelt," "that mad man," or "that dirty dog."[15]

In December 1940, Ford's name would be linked even more directly to *Scribner's Commentator* when his byline appeared on an article in the publication that predicted the British would be defeated in the war. In the same article, he declared that Hitler and Mussolini were merely "puppets" at whose expense international bankers and international financiers had "played a dirty trick."[16]

Lindbergh continued his anti-interventionist activities, traveling the country and giving speeches, all the while maintaining an outward appearance of independence from America First, despite entreaties from General Wood and others to become its chairman. With the AFC deeply divided over whether to bring him aboard, Lindbergh claimed publicly that he would not affiliate with any organization, but would instead continue to support the broader anti-intervention movement. However, he remained close to the Committee and met frequently with its leaders. Whenever he received a donation in the mail to support his isolationist activities, he returned the check to the sender along with an AFC circular.

At the same time, a number of other isolationist organizations were competing for his services. Judge William Grace of the Citizens Keep America Out of War Committee wrote Lindbergh a letter urging him to join his group, and complaining that the AFC was uncooperative with other anti-war groups, describing it "as little more or less than an opportunity for some ladies and gentlemen of the social register to bask in the limelight of public attention without mixing up with the *hoi polloi* in the matter of doing the front line soldier rough work which is necessary to win both in war as well as in peacetime activity."[17]

The isolationists, meanwhile, were having little luck in thwarting the President's efforts to aid the British. On March 1, 1941, with London in flames as the result of a renewed German bombing offensive, Congress passed Roosevelt's Lend-Lease bill by a substantial margin. Support for the bill among the American people had risen from 39 percent in February to more than 50 percent in March.[18] The success of the interventionist cause could be largely attributed to Roosevelt's tremendous popularity. Under his leadership, the nation had survived its greatest economic crisis—the devastation of the Depression—and many Americans were grateful. It was clear to the America First Committee that Lindbergh was the only isolationist figure who had the mass appeal to rival the President.

Following the passage of Lend-Lease, the isolationists were despondent. General Wood, who had been acting chairman of the AFC for more than six months, appealed to Lindbergh to take the helm.[19] Wood had convinced Douglas Stuart to shelve his objections and to ignore Lindbergh's continued association with controversial far-right figures. The movement desperately needed his leadership. But the Lone Eagle was used to flying solo. For eighteen months, he had fought passionately for his convictions, giving speeches, writing articles, and carrying on a lonely battle with no one to answer to but himself. Leadership of the organization would entail accountability to an executive committee and a commitment to abide by national policy. Again, he refused Wood's plea but on April 3, Lindbergh relented partially, agreeing for the first time to sit on the National Committee and speak on behalf of the AFC.

The announcement raised immediate alarm in the inner circle of the Roosevelt administration. The president was not especially anxious for a showdown with the tarnished, but still popular, hero. According to historian Wayne Cole, America's foremost academic authority on the history of the isolationist movement:

Franklin D. Roosevelt the political statesman and Charles Lindbergh the aviator were two of the most charismatic Americans of the twentieth century. Each inspired the worshipful adoration of millions; each aroused passionate hatred from others. So long as they performed in separate spheres, there was no contest between them. But when either invaded the domain of the other, the result was a battle of the giants.[20]

Interior Secretary Harold Ickes, fiercely loyal to Roosevelt, had long since taken on the task of discrediting the President's tenacious opponent. Cabinet documents from the period reveal that most members of the Administration resented "the lamentable Lindbergh" but didn't necessarily believe he was a Nazi. Ickes, however, was firmly convinced that Lindbergh was planning to install a totalitarian regime inside America. In one 1941 letter to Roosevelt, he laid out his fears: "An analysis of Lindbergh's speeches—I have a complete indexed collection of them—has convinced me that he is a ruthless and conscious fascist. Motivated by hatred for you personally and for democracy in general, his speeches show an astonishing identity with those of Berlin, and the similarity is not accidental."[21]

On April 13, 1941, four days before Lindbergh's first scheduled America First address, Ickes delivered a speech accusing him of being the "number one Nazi fellow traveler" in the United States and "the first American to hold aloft the standard of pro-Nazism." By this point, Lindbergh simply shrugged off what he called "cheap attacks."

Speaking on behalf of the AFC for the first time on April 17, he grabbed the attention of the capacity crowd of 10,000 at the Chicago arena from the outset of his twenty-five-minute address, declaring, "War is not inevitable for this country. Whether or not America enters this war is within our control." At his every utterance, the crowd broke out in wild applause, interrupting the speech more than twenty-five times. In the eighteen months since he had begun his crusade, the thirty-eight-year-old Lindbergh had become a polished speaker: His once halting delivery was now poised and confident, his shy demeanor replaced by an almost arrogant swagger, and his boyish blue eyes burned with the conviction of the scorned.

In another speech delivered in New York six days later, the loudest cheers were reserved for his call to stop military aid to the British: "I must tell you frankly that I believe this war was lost by England and France even before it was declared, and that it is not within our power in America today to win the war for England."

In his next breath, he appeared to defend Nazi Germany: "In time of war, truth is always replaced by propaganda. I do not believe we should be too quick to criticize the actions of a belligerent nation. There is always the question whether we, ourselves, would do better under similar circumstances."[22]

In the next day's newspapers, this statement brought on some of the most stinging attacks he had yet faced. To his critics, and even to some supporters, he appeared to be welcoming the defeat of Britain. "Almost alone among Americans of distinction," chided *Life* magazine, "he had declined to express even the *hope* that Britain might vanquish her Nazi foe."[23]

Like most of his fellow isolationists, Lindbergh argued that the United States should stay out of European affairs because they were none of America's business, reasoning that, even if the Nazis invaded Britain and ruled the continent, they would pose no military threat to the United States. During this period, Arthur Schlesinger, who would later emerge as one of America's most prominent historians, was a Harvard postgraduate fellow and deeply concerned about the isolationist trend on campus. Schlesinger sympathized with the argument that America should not be the world's policeman unless its vital interests were at stake, but he strongly believed that a Europe ruled by Hitler posed a genuine threat to the United States. In 1940, he spelled out his fears in a letter to the Harvard student newspaper, asking what would happen to democracy when the Americans who thought the United States could do business with Hitler came to power. He envisioned the day when "every frustrated, unsatisfied hoodlum in America will start buying colored shirts and parading with his local fascist party, when it will be impossible to criticize fascism, lest it disturb relations with our good neighbors and customers beyond the seas. Hitler won't have to invade America until it is so torn by inner conflict that the German army could cross the ocean in canoes."[24] Meanwhile, a young Kurt Vonnegut wrote an editorial in his own campus newspaper, the Cornell *Sun*, describing Lindbergh as "one helluva swell egg" and mocking interventionist attacks on the man he believed to be "a sincere and loyal patriot."[25]

Although Lindbergh had publicly declared in the New York speech that it would be a "tragedy to the world—even to Germany—if the British Empire collapsed," his actions seemed to belie these words. Indeed, privately he appeared almost annoyed at the continuing British resistance and Roosevelt's role as a willing accomplice. In a letter to a friend around this time, he wrote that America's encouragement of England merely "complicated the readjustment that had to take place in Europe."[26] It was as if he wished Britain would just bow to the inevitable and accept defeat.

Yet not everybody was convinced that Lindbergh was hostile to Britain. Sir John Wheeler-Bennett, a British Foreign Office official who was close friends with Lindbergh's uncle Aubrey Morgan, later offered an alternate view in his own account of the period: "He was not anti-British. He had lived in Britain and had appreciated the way in which his desired anonymity had been respected. He had simply written Britain off as a bad bet. He disapproved of Roosevelt's policy of 'all aid short of war' on grounds that there was no point in throwing good money after bad . . ."[27]

Lindbergh's defenders have pointed out that his isolationist activities merely reflected the mindset of mainstream American society at the time. The overwhelming majority of U.S. citizens, after all, opposed intervention in the European war. Lindbergh was just one of many with a similar viewpoint. In later years, this would become the chief argument in the effort to rehabilitate Lindbergh's reputation and repair his legacy. Poll after poll would be cited to prove Lindbergh's views were in lockstep with the majority of his fellow Americans during this period. However, these polls don't quite tell the whole story. It is undeniably true that the vast majority of Americans opposed direct military intervention in the European war. A Gallup poll conducted April 26, 1941, one week after Lindbergh's Chicago speech, found that only 19 percent of Americans supported U.S. entry into the war against Germany and Italy. However, the very same poll revealed that more than 70 percent of the American people *favored* military aid to Britain if it meant England might otherwise lose—a stand fiercely opposed by Lindbergh.[28]

This was in fact the core of the Great Debate. Before Pearl Harbor, neither Roosevelt nor the majority of his fellow interventionists ever actually advocated direct American military involvement in the European war. Only a small group, known today as "extreme interventionists," publicly voiced this option. The majority simply wanted to provide the means for England to defend itself against Nazi aggression. This was the thrust of Roosevelt's "aid-short-of-war" policy. Yet, in speech after speech, Lindbergh opposed aid to Britain, leaving him open to charges that he was siding with the Nazis. Even many of his fellow isolationists agreed that his was an extreme position, and supported British military aid so long as America kept out of the war. In a 1941 speech to the American Legion, for example, General Wood declared, "We sympathize with Britain. We hope she will not be defeated; we favor sending her aid."[29] Many even rejected the label "isolationist," preferring the term "anti-interventionist" as a more accurate description of their political philosophy.

Lindbergh's emergence as a spokesman for America First and his continuing attacks on American assistance to Britain now appeared to be the last straw for the President, who had thus far refrained from publicly attacking him. At a White House press conference on April 25, a reporter asked Roosevelt why Colonel Lindbergh had not been asked to rejoin the

United States army. In his still memorable response, the President proceeded to compare Lindbergh to the infamous Ohio congressman Clement L. Vallandingham who, during the Civil War, had led the "Copperheads," a movement of Yankees who supported the Confederacy.

"Well, Vallandingham, as you know, was an appeaser," Roosevelt responded. "He wanted to make peace from 1863 on because the North 'couldn't win.' And there were an awful lot of appeasers at Valley Forge that pleaded with Washington to quit, because he 'couldn't win.' "

A reporter asked if the President was still talking about Lindbergh, to which FDR simply responded, "Yes."[30] It was tantamount to calling Lindbergh a traitor. The battle lines had been drawn.

Two days later, Lindbergh made what many considered a disastrous tactical error. He sent a letter to Roosevelt tendering his resignation as a colonel in the U.S. army air corps, to protest the President's slur on his patriotism—and in the process, called that very patriotism into question. Leonard Mosley believes FDR's seemingly off-the-cuff remark was calculated to elicit just such a response: "It was a fatal move to have taken and one which President Roosevelt had obviously deliberately set out to provoke, having sized up his opponent. A more astute antagonist would have refused to fall into the trap which had been set out for him."[31]

Truman Smith recognized the folly of Lindbergh's resignation and argued passionately against it, but to Lindbergh "a point of honor was involved."[32] The next day, the *New York Times* took him to task in an editorial: "Mr. Lindbergh shocked those who believed him to be a loyal American—though a sadly mistaken one—by his petulant action."[33] The influential newspaper, however, also pointed out that no evidence existed to justify the President's comparing him to the traitorous Vallandingham.

"The pressure for war is high and mounting," Lindbergh lamented in his journal on May 1. "Most of the Jewish interests in the country are behind war, and they control a huge part of our press and radio, and most of our motion pictures."[34] He was determined to turn the tide, but he believed it would take considerable sums of money to combat these powerful forces aligned against the isolationist cause. In a May 9 Gallup poll, 63 percent of Americans said they *disagreed* with Lindbergh's foreign policy stand. Only 24 percent agreed with him.[35] This contrasts sharply with later intellectually dishonest claims by the biographers and historians who wrote that Lindbergh's stand was supported by the majority of his fellow Americans. Lindbergh's views, in fact, were anything but mainstream.

On May 12, he flew to Detroit to meet the one man with the resources and conviction that Lindbergh believed might help reverse these discouraging statistics. At lunch with Henry and Clara Ford that day, he made his case: "I told him America First was badly in need of money for an advertising campaign and that I hoped he might be able to assist in this respect," Lindbergh noted in his journal.[36]

Ford came through with an offer to underwrite a $250,000 national advertising campaign on behalf of the Committee, using the services of the Ford Motor Company's favored advertising firm, Maxon. To Lindbergh's astonishment, Harry Bennett informed him the next day that this was just the beginning of the company's generosity. Henry Ford had authorized this amount just for the first month's campaign. After that, Bennett implied, there would be no limit to the backing Ford was prepared to provide.[37] In his 1951 memoirs, Bennett claimed that Ford had instructed him to immediately take $10,000 in cash out of the safe to send to General Wood in Chicago. But, because of Bennett's "uneasiness" about the business risk of publicly associating the company with America First, he convinced Ford to reverse the decision and to cancel the advertising campaign.

It was a discouraging setback. In his journal, a disappointed Lindbergh speculated that "government pressure in the form of defense contracts" may have been responsible for the reversal.[38] The Ford Motor Company had recently been awarded a series of substantial defense contracts by the U.S. War Department, so it's entirely conceivable that this was indeed a factor. However, Lindbergh also suspected that Ford may have been paranoid about "General Wood's connection with the partially Jewish-owned firm of Sears Roebuck."[39]

Without Ford's largesse, the committee was forced to seek funds elsewhere. Three months earlier, on February 21, President Roosevelt had sent a memo to his secretary Stephen Early attached to an America First Committee bulletin. The memo read, simply: "Will you find out from someone—perhaps FBI—who is paying for this?"[40] Early forwarded the request to J. Edgar Hoover, who commenced an immediate investigation into the source of the Committee's funding. The probe would turn up no direct Nazi funding of the AFC, although German Embassy dispatches captured after the war later revealed that significant Nazi funds had been funneled to more extremist elements of the isolationist movement as well as to a number of Republican congressmen, and that the Nazis claimed to have supported the AFC in "various ways."

Until that point, General Wood had refused to answer repeated media queries about where the Committee was getting its funding. He had also declined to issue detailed financial statements, simply stating that the AFC relied on grassroots donations from its membership. Later, he bent slightly to mounting pressure and released a "partial list of funders," explaining that "numerous contributors had preferred not to have their names mentioned."[41]

By this time, Lindbergh had already delivered a number of hugely popular speeches for America First, and the organization's ranks were swelling. Since he had accepted the role of spokesman, thousands of new members were signing up each week. But as the movement grew, the criticism reached new heights. On April 23, he was scheduled to address 10,000 AFC faithful at New York's Manhattan Center. Outside the arena, hundreds of protesters picketed the proceedings while a new interventionist group, Fight for Freedom, distributed cardboard replicas of Lindbergh's Nazi decoration bearing the inscription, "Lindy quit the U.S. Army but kept the Nazi medal."

Leon Birkhead, a Unitarian minister who headed the interventionist group Friends of Democracy, had predicted before the rally that it would be "the largest gathering of pro-Nazis and pro-Fascists" since the German American Bund had packed Madison Square Garden years before.[42] His prediction appeared prophetic. In its coverage the next day, *PM* wrote that the rally included "a liberal sprinkling of Nazis, fascists, anti-Semites, crackpots and just people. The just people seemed out of place." According to a number of press accounts, loud boos accompanied every reference to Roosevelt. Several people in the crowd were seen giving the Nazi salute.

America First's founders had been determined to keep the organization free of the extremist elements that characterized the membership of other isolationist groups. In its manifesto, the AFC declared it would "bring together all Americans, regardless of possible difference on other matters, who see eye to eye on our principles. This does not include Nazis, Fascists, Communists, or members of other groups that place the interests of any other nation above those of our own country."[43] But as the organization gained in strength and effectiveness, becoming America's preeminent anti-war group, it was stamped with a sinister seal of approval by far-right groups throughout the land.

As far back as January 1941, a Nazi shortwave radio broadcast emanating from the Propaganda Ministry in Berlin appeared to endorse the AFC by declaring, "The America First Committee is true Americanism and true patriotism."[44] On May 1, the German-American Bund's newspaper *The Free American* encouraged its members to join the committee.[45] Soon afterward, members of the American fascist leader William Dudley Pelley's Silver Shirts, the Ku Klux Klan, Father Coughlin's Christian Front, and scores of other fascist groups also entered the AFC ranks. Nazi agent Werner C. Clemm offered his services as a fund-raiser; another Nazi agent, George Viereck, developed propaganda for the Committee. Garland Alderman, former secretary of the pro-Nazi National Workers League, joined the AFC and later revealed, "I wanted to keep America out of the war, and I thought I could do it better by spreading anti-Semitism."[46]

When a newspaper reported that the April 23 Manhattan Center rally was riddled with extremists, Edwin Webster, secretary of the AFC's New York chapter, downplayed the charge: "Although certain of the people mentioned were probably at our rally, they were in the very small minority. No press tickets or tickets of any sort are given to the people in question."[47] But a week later, when an undercover FBI agent purchased a copy of the Nazi Bund newspaper, he was handed two complimentary tickets to Lindbergh's next AFC speech, scheduled for May 23 at Madison Square Garden.[48]

There is no evidence that anybody on the National Committee, including Lindbergh, encouraged these far-right forces to join the AFC. But it soon became apparent that extremist elements had successfully hijacked the movement, if not the leadership of the Committee itself. And, as these elements swelled the ranks of the America First Committee, there was clearly a new force drawing them in: Lindbergh himself, who had become the darling of the American extreme right.

In a letter to General George Van Horn Moseley dated April 23, 1941—less than a week after Lindbergh gave his first AFC address—fascist leader William Dudley Pelley, the former Hollywood screenwriter who dubbed his followers the "Silver Shirts," named the four men he needed to bring about a Nazi revolution in America: Senator Burton Wheeler, who would lend his prestige on Capitol Hill; Moseley, who would convince the Army personnel; Charles Lindbergh, who would provide "glamour to assure the interest of the public"; and Henry Ford, with his "wealth to finance remedial action."[49]

Invoking Roosevelt's widely publicized attack on Lindbergh, a new organization was formed by Bund member Ellis Jones calling itself the "National Copperhead Association," declaring Lindbergh to be "our man on horseback."[50] The Nazi Bund immediately instructed its members to join the Copperheads. Coughlin's Jew-baiting *Social Justice* magazine regularly featured Lindbergh on its cover. As Scott Berg writes, "The more Lindbergh attracted such bigots, the more people judged him by his followers."[51] But if his vilification was simply a matter of guilt by association, Lindbergh repeatedly declined to publicly disassociate himself from the growing array of extremists who cloaked themselves in his aura.

What had started out as a patriotic organization composed of mostly sincere American pacifists had by the summer of 1941 degenerated into something very different from what its founders had intended. In July, *Time* magazine called the AFC a "garden" in which "the weeds had gotten out of hand," a group full of "Jew-haters, Roosevelt haters, England haters, Coughlinites." Henry Hobson, the Episcopal Bishop of Southern Ohio, called America First "the first fascist party in this nation's history."[52]

A year earlier, an Armenian-American named Arthur Derounian had infiltrated American fascist organizations as an undercover informant for the FBI.[53] Writing under the pseudonym John Ray Carlson, Derounian described the early days of America First as a gathering of "reliable and sincere elements, as American as Plymouth Rock,"[54] but proceeded to document the group's gradual evolution into "a cesspool of hate and deceit." In his sensational 1943 bestseller *Under Cover: My Life in the Nazi Underworld,* Carlson reports his repeated encounters with anti-Semitism, fascism and pro-Nazi sentiment in the America First Committee. In one passage, he relates that members of America First had participated in a giant Ku Klux Klan rally in Rockford, Illinois, attended by 50,000 Klansmen after the Klan had urged its members to enroll in the AFC: "The resurgence of the Klan was symbolic of the riffraff which now began to flow unchecked into the America First fold."

Nowhere in his investigation did Derounian encounter evidence that Lindbergh himself was a Nazi—characterizing him rather as "the most naive of men politically," willing to be "led by the nose"—but he describes the Committee's most popular speaker as "a hero to countless American fascist groups looking for a Führer."[55]

Derounian's book, like many pro-interventionist tracts, is far from objective and has to be discounted to some extent, but his description of the reaction to one Lindbergh America First speech at Madison Square Garden in May 1941 mirrors a number of similar press accounts: "The wildest demonstration I ever heard met Lindbergh. It was unlike anything else I had known. A deep-throated, unearthly, savage roar, chilling, frightening, sinister and awesome. And what of the blond god who for six full minutes smiled like an adolescent as the mob stood to its feet, waved flags, threw kisses and frenziedly rendered the Nazi salute."[56] In fact, a number of newspapers the morning after this rally had carried photos of Lindbergh standing next to the extreme right-wing senator Burton Wheeler and the novelist Kathleen Norris, a popular AFC speaker. Each had their right arms raised in the air in what appeared to many as a Nazi salute, although they later claimed they were simply waving to their supporters and the photo was taken out of context.

In the same book, Carlson also describes Henry Ford as a hero to the far right, reporting that his *Dearborn Independent* articles were still used as a reference source by each American Nazi leader.[57] On one visit to the New York office of the American Nazi Party in 1941, Carlson claims he saw a stack of petitions with the heading, "Ford For President To Restore Americanism."[58]

Despite the increasing presence of extremist elements among the grassroots membership of the movement, neither anti-Semitic nor explicitly pro-fascist views were ever expressed from the podium at national AFC rallies or in the Committee's literature, at least not in the first year of the organization's existence. But the files of the AFC between January and November 1941 reveal considerable alarm among some of its founders at the direction the organization had taken.

At one rally, Joe McWilliams, leader of the pro-fascist American Destiny Party, was spotted sitting in the front row. In response, AFC National Committee member John Flynn, who was considered the leader of the Committee's so-called liberal wing, took to the podium and publicly rejected the support of "Communists, Fascists, Bundists and especially Joe McWilliams." During the second half of 1941, one of the AFC's most popular speakers was another famed pilot, Laura Ingalls, who had gained notoriety in September 1939 when she dropped antiwar leaflets over the White House. Occasionally sharing an AFC platform with her fellow aviator Lindbergh, Ingalls was often described as the "heroine" of the isolationist movement. In 1942, she was convicted and jailed by the United States government for failing to register as a foreign agent. An investigation revealed that she had been on the Nazi payroll for years, working for U.S. Gestapo chief Baron von Gienanth, who told her, "The best thing you can do for our cause is to promote the America First Committee."[59] There is no record that her AFC association caused any particular concern within the Committee's leadership or that the Executive knew of her Nazi ties, despite her frequently expressed pro-German views.

Although many interventionist groups freely labeled all isolationists as Fifth Columnists or Nazi sympathizers, some were more circumspect. As the AFC attracted ever more extremist elements, Leon Birkhead, the National Director of Friends of Democracy, wrote Lindbergh expressing alarm at the direction the country's most influential isolationist organization was taking. Assuring Lindbergh that his group, despite its strong support for interventionism, had a "high regard for sincere isolationists," Birkhead was anxious to bring Lindbergh's attention to the increasing exploitation of the AFC by "pro-Nazi forces throughout the country." Does it make sense, he asked, that a Committee calling itself "America First" is being used by those "who give aid and comfort to the enemy?" Birkhead ends his letter by urging the AFC to "either clean house or disband."[60] Lindbergh ignored the letter.

During the summer of 1941, a rift occurred between the liberal and conservative wings of the AFC over the ever-increasing number of Father Coughlin's followers joining the movement. Flynn wanted to expel the Coughlinites because of their loud anti-Semitic and pro-fascist views. After the media reported in July that Coughlin's followers would be expelled from America First, prompting an angry editorial in the pages of *Social Justice*, General Wood hastily wrote a letter to the magazine denying the report: "I have not rejected the Christian Social Justice movement. I welcome their support in our common objective—preventing this country from getting into the war."[61] By now, of course, the two organizations were indelibly linked with Lindbergh in the public eye, and the popular columnists Dorothy Thompson and Walter Winchell seized on the opportunity to take their increasingly vitriolic attacks a step further. Lindbergh, they wrote, was "the leader of the American Nazi movement."

By this point, he was used to this kind of inflammatory rhetoric and the attacks hardly seemed to bother him. In his journal entry of May 1, Lindbergh blames the "British agents who are allowed free rein" in a list of forces, including the Jews, that he believed were responsible for such propaganda. Isolationists had regularly leveled this accusation, convinced that England had planted agents in cooperation with Roosevelt to incite the nation to war. Their charges had always been dismissed by interventionists as "paranoia." But years later, information surfaced to suggest that some of Lindbergh's suspicions may have been justified.

Operating out of an office in New York's Rockefeller Center throughout the years 1940 and 1941 was a highly secretive unit known as British Security Coordination (BSC). Its operations were overseen by the legendary British spymaster William S. Stephenson, who was code-named "Intrepid." Its mission was straightforward: to discredit the isolationist movement and influence American public opinion in favor of aid to Britain, although not necessarily toward direct American involvement in the war. British agents regularly provided resources to interventionist groups, manipulated public opinion polls and leaked damaging information to a number of prominent reporters and columnists, among them Lindbergh's harshest critics, Walter Winchell and Dorothy Thompson. BSC, in fact, was not above resorting to dirty tricks to achieve its ends. On one occasion, the unit printed up and distributed a set of duplicate tickets to an America First rally featuring Lindbergh at Madison Square Garden, hoping to spark fights and turmoil in the arena over seating. But the plan backfired when the original crowd proved smaller than expected and the phony tickets only succeeded in inflating attendance.[62]

Both sides, then, were being manipulated by outside forces bent on using the well-meaning grassroots membership as pawns in a heated battle for supremacy over U.S. public opinion. Through it all, the American people, oblivious to these machinations, remained deeply and bitterly divided as the Great Debate raged on.

Before the spring of 1941, many inside the Roosevelt administration still believed that Ickes and others were simply guilty of hyperbole in their repeated accusations that Lindbergh was a Fifth Columnist. That changed on May 23 when the AFC spokesman addressed a Madison Square Garden rally. Speaking to 20,000 fervent supporters, he decried the results of the November presidential election—which Roosevelt had won convincingly—and called for "a change of leadership in this country."[63] An outcry ensued. What did he mean by a change of leadership? Did he want to oust the President? The next day, Lindbergh denied he was referring to Roosevelt. He explained that he merely wanted "a change in the interventionists" who were surrounding and influencing the President. "Neither I nor anyone else in the America First Committee advocate proceeding by anything but constitutional methods," he told the Associated Press.[64]

The *New York Telegram* was only one of many newspapers who questioned his explanation: "Is he thinking of having President Roosevelt impeached? In that case, look who he is going to get as a new president: Henry Wallace [the left-leaning vice president]. Or is he thinking of imposing it by other means, in which case we'll get a Nazi?" Lindbergh continued to deny either option. But in his journal entry of May 31, a week later, he reveals that ousting Roosevelt was indeed very much on his mind. Describing a meeting he attended that afternoon with former president Herbert Hoover—another influential isolationist leader—Lindbergh writes, "At one time during our conversation, we discussed the possibility of Roosevelt being impeached before his term expires."[65]

Since the "Copperhead" accusation in the spring of 1941, President Roosevelt had chosen to publicly ignore the America First Committee and its popular spokesman. However, the group's growing strength made this impossible. From the time Lindbergh joined the AFC in April, its membership had swelled from 300,000 to nearly 800,000 members.[66] Something would have to be done to put the brakes on. Again, it was left up to Ickes to lead the attack. Speaking at a Bastille Day rally in support of the Free French forces at New York's Manhattan Center on July 14, the interior secretary fired the most direct hit at Lindbergh to date, calling him a mouthpiece of the Nazi Party line in the United States:

> No one has ever heard Lindbergh utter a word of horror at, or even aversion to, the bloody career that the Nazis are following, nor a word of pity for the innocent men, women and children who have been deliberately murdered by the Nazis in practically every country in Europe . . . I have never heard this Knight of the German Eagle denounce Hitler or Nazism, or Mussolini or fascism.[67]

Here, Ickes had finally seized upon an effective strategy. Instead of the cheap and increasingly stale propaganda tactic of labeling isolationists as

Nazi sympathizers and Fifth Columnists, he seized on what he believed was concrete proof—the Nazi medal Lindbergh had accepted three years earlier—and began to refer to its recipient as the "Knight of the German Eagle." Why not return it, Ickes demanded, to demonstrate his opposition to the Nazi regime? This was one of the interior secretary's favorite topics. At a White House Cabinet meeting a year earlier, Ickes had steered discussion to Lindbergh's Nazi medal. When Roosevelt's secretary of the navy Charles Edison mentioned that, upon receiving the decoration from Göring in 1938, Lindbergh didn't know what to do with it, the President barked, "I would have known what to do with it all right."[68]

It was a theme that had growing resonance, even among Lindbergh's supporters. Why wouldn't he publicly come out and condemn Hitler? His failure to do so was only fanning the flames and providing ammunition to those who accused him of harboring Nazi sympathies. The chairman of the German-American Congress for Democracy, Dr. Frank Bohn, accused him of being the "leader of the fascist youth of the United States."[69] Even General Wood urged him to come out with a public statement against all the "isms," including Communism, fascism and Nazism, in order to silence the "whisper campaigns that he is pro-Nazi."[70]

But Lindbergh refused. He believed that America already had "far too many of the type of articles and addresses that bend with the changing winds of popular opinion."[71] However, he was not altogether unmindful of the need to safeguard appearances to maintain his credibility. In March, he had written Truman Smith that he thought it "inadvisable" to meet with a friend of Smith's who was visiting from Germany, lest he provide fresh ammunition to his critics: "I have had no communication with Germany, or with German citizens, since I left Europe in April 1939, and I think it is important for me to say this whenever the question arises. It is a stupid situation, and I do not intend to govern my actions by such considerations indefinitely."[72] Of course, Smith himself was bound by no such restrictions. According to an FBI report, "Since his return to the United States from Germany, Colonel Smith has been in continual contact with the German Embassy."[73]

Lindbergh had never before publicly responded to Ickes or his other detractors. But now he sensed an opportunity to turn the tables. In his journal, he wrote, "Nothing is to be gained by my entering a controversy with a man of Ickes's type. But if I can pin Ickes's actions on Roosevelt, it will have the utmost effect."[74]

On July 16, Lindbergh wrote a letter to the President demanding an apology for the interior secretary's comments and reminding Roosevelt that he had received the Göring medal "in the American Embassy, in the presence of your Ambassador." He insisted that he had no connection with any

foreign government and offered to open his files for inspection.[75] The letter
was ignored. The Administration noted that the letter's credibility was
undermined by the fact that Lindbergh had leaked it to the press before it
even reached the White House. Ickes seemed positively gleeful that Lindbergh had reached for his bait, writing in his diary: "Up to that time, I had
always admired Lindbergh in one respect. No matter how vigorously he had
been attacked personally, he had never attempted to answer . . . I had begun
to think that no one could get under his skin enough to make him squeal.
But at last I had succeeded. I suspect that it was my reference to him as a
'Knight of the German Eagle' that got him."[76]

Ickes wasted no time exploiting his new tactic, telling reporters, "If Mr.
Lindbergh feels like cringing when he is correctly referred to as a Knight
of the German Eagle, why doesn't he send back the disgraceful decoration
and be done with it? Americans remember that he had no hesitation about
sending back to the President his commission in the United States Army."

The well-known Broadway impresario Billy Rose sent Lindbergh a
telegram detailing a list of documented Nazi atrocities and offered to rent
Madison Square Garden at his own expense if he would melt down his
Nazi medal at the rally.[77] Lindbergh ignored the bait.

Ickes sensed that he had his opponent on the ropes: "He has now made
it clear to the whole country that he still clings to the German decoration,"
he wrote in his diary. "For the first time, he has allowed himself to be put
on the defensive and that is always a weak position for anyone."[78]

To friends and supporters, Lindbergh claimed that condemning Nazi
atrocities or returning his medal would jeopardize his policy of strict "neutrality." But this policy of refraining from criticism of a foreign belligerent
appeared only to apply to Nazi Germany. At an America First rally on July
1, 1941, he issued a brutal condemnation of the "barbarism and godlessness" of the Soviet Union, which had been invaded by the Nazis only a
week earlier when Hitler abandoned his Non-Aggression pact with Stalin
and turned his *blitzkrieg* toward Russia.

In the two years since the pact was signed in 1939, making Russia a
nominal Nazi ally, Lindbergh had never once publicly criticized the Soviet
Union. The same restraint toward its former nemesis was evident in the
Nazi press, which, since the signing of the Non-Aggression pact, had also
conspicuously refrained from its once common blistering attacks on the
Soviets. But only ten days after Hitler declared the Soviet Union an enemy
of the Reich, Lindbergh told a San Francisco rally, "I would a hundred
times rather see my country ally itself with England, or even Germany with
all her faults, than with the cruelty, the godlessness and the barbarism that
exist in Soviet Russia . . . An alliance between the U.S. and Russia should be
opposed by every Christian, and every humanitarian, in this country."[79]

The timing of his sudden turnaround was not lost on his critics, who renewed their attacks with a vengeance, convinced he was simply parroting the Nazis. The criticism was having a devastating effect on his reputation. More than two hundred American libraries pulled Lindbergh's books from their shelves. His hometown of Little Falls, Minnesota, repainted its water tower, which for years had proudly proclaimed the town's Lindbergh connection. The airline TWA no longer ran advertisements featuring its famous slogan, "The Lindbergh Line." Even his closest friends and associates began to turn against him. Writing in the *American Magazine*, Harry Bruno, who had served as his public relations adviser before and after the 1927 flight, wrote that Lindbergh was attracted to the Nazi philosophy because of its dehumanizing nature: "He never learned that people do not act like machines. His admiration for a new order that tries to make men act like machines is therefore not so strange."[80]

In July, a coalition of twenty-one youth groups issued a public statement declaring:

> We're the youth who named our dogs Lindy. . . . We're the youth who built models of *The Spirit of St. Louis* . . . we're the youth who used to crowd the airports and streets of the towns you visited to catch a glimpse of you. But now you've disappointed us, Mr. Lindbergh. Now you ask us to follow you—a wearer of the Nazi German Cross—an embittered isolationist, a man who would have us make peace with a mad dictator. . . . We're the American youth—do you hear us? We don't have to be goose-stepped into defending our freedom. But instead of leading us in our fight against Hitler, as we truly felt you would, Mr. Lindbergh, you plead with us to accept slavery willingly. Heroes fight for freedom. You are no longer a hero, ex-Colonel Lindbergh.[81]

Yet in the face of the relentless attacks, continuous scorn, and accusations of treason, it was clear that for a segment of the American population, Lindbergh did remain a hero. Thousand of letters of support poured in from the heartland. America First membership rolls continued to grow and local AFC chapters throughout the country desperately vied for a speaking engagement, knowing that a Lindbergh speech was guaranteed to fill an arena. His support appeared to be strongest in the midwest—the same rural constituency that had supported his father and Henry Ford in their own crusades decades earlier.

What accounts for Lindbergh's enduring popularity in the face of accusations of treason, sedition and association with an odious regime?

His biographer Walter Ross attempts an explanation: "Ever since his first public appearance at the American embassy in France, in 1927, he had a kind of hypnotic effect on people. His utterances, therefore, had more force than those of others." Contemporary media accounts confirm that wherever Lindbergh appeared, the crowds appeared mesmerized just being in his presence.

Unlike many other larger-than-life characters, he wasn't a particularly charismatic figure on the surface. In person, he was rather shy and he was never entirely comfortable in front of large crowds. On the radio, where most Americans encountered his isolationist appeals, his delivery was often halting and, while he eventually became an accomplished speaker, nothing in his style appears to account for the "frenzy" that media reports often described as the reaction to his speeches.

But it seems that the Lindbergh legend had taken on a life of its own over the years, fed by the media he hated, which had built him up into an almost superhuman figure. In 1929, Marquis Childs captured the public mood best when he wrote in the New York *Herald Tribune*, "Five centuries have been required to make a saint of Joan of Arc, but in two years Colonel Lindbergh has become a demigod."[82] Most of his enormous nationwide following, in fact, had placed Lindbergh on a pedestal of hero worship long before they ever heard him on the radio or saw him speak.

Thus, it appears to be the mystique of Lindbergh rather than his personality, ideas or physical presence that commanded the loyalty and adoration of millions. For a significant portion of the American population steeped in the legend, nothing could bring him down from his pedestal. People wanted to believe him, and believe *in* him.

On the afternoon of September 2, Lindbergh drove to Dearborn to attend what he called an important "conference" with Henry and Clara Ford. For an hour, they discussed the "war situation and the America First Committee." It is difficult to ascertain exactly what the two men discussed at their frequent meetings. In his journal entry that day, Lindbergh simply notes, "Every time I see Ford I am impressed both by his eccentricity and his genius . . . I always come away refreshed and encouraged after a meeting with Ford. I only wish the country had more men like him."[83] His journal contains many such generalities after every meeting with Ford but fails to provide any details about what they discussed. But Ford's FBI file offers a clearer, and somewhat more disturbing, glimpse of their conversations.

Around the time of Pearl Harbor, J. Edgar Hoover became suspicious that Lindbergh may have leaked classified information to the Germans.[84] Hoover knew that Lindbergh was an adviser to Ford, whose company had recently been awarded a number of U.S. military defense contracts, and may therefore have been privy to classified material. He assigned Detroit's FBI chief John S. Bugas to interview Ford and determine how much Lindbergh knew about Ford's military contracts. But Ford quickly reassured him. "When Charles comes out here, we only talk about the Jews," he told the agent.[85] The old man's anti-Semitism was as virulent as ever. What it lacked, since the *Independent*'s demise, was a credible mouthpiece.

When Lindbergh took the podium at an America First rally on September 11 in Des Moines, Iowa, a week after the meeting with Ford, his speech began on a familiar note: "It is now two years since this latest European war began. From that day in September 1939, until the present moment, there has been an ever-increasing effort to force the United States into the conflict."

Since the start of his public involvement with the interventionist cause twenty-four months earlier, Lindbergh had regularly hinted that there were invisible forces pushing the country toward war, but he had never identified those forces by name. Now, he indicated that was about to change:

> The subterfuge and propaganda that exists in our country is obvious on every side. Tonight, I shall try to pierce through a portion of it, to the naked facts which lie beneath. National polls showed that when England and France declared war on Germany, in 1939, less than 10 percent of our population favored a similar course for America. But there were various groups of people, here and abroad, whose interests and beliefs necessitated the involvement of the United States in the war. I shall point out some of these groups tonight, and outline their methods of procedure. In doing this, I must speak with the utmost frankness, for in order to counteract their efforts, we must know exactly who they are.

As the crowd of 8,000 midwesterners waited in hushed expectation, he proceeded to carry through on this promise:

> The three most important groups who have been pressing this country toward war are the British, the Jewish and the Roosevelt administration.

A massive roar from the crowd greeted these words as thousands rose to their feet to cheer. When they quieted, he continued, proceeding to outline the case against Britain, the first group he named, which he said was in a "desperate" position and therefore had to draw America into the war. He then came to the second group:

> It is not difficult to understand why Jewish people desire the overthrow of Nazi Germany. The persecution they suffered in Germany would be sufficient to make bitter enemies of any race.
>
> No person with a sense of the dignity of mankind can condone the persecution of the Jewish race in Germany. But no person of honesty and vision can look on their pro-war policy here today without seeing the dangers involved in such a policy both for us and for them. Instead of agitating for war, the Jewish groups in this country should be opposing it in every possible way for they will be among the first to feel its consequences.
>
> Tolerance is a virtue that depends upon peace and strength. History shows that it cannot survive war and devastations. A few far-sighted Jewish people realize this and stand opposed to intervention. But the majority still do not.
>
> Their greatest danger to this country lies in their large ownership and influence in our motion pictures, our press, our radio and our government.
>
> I am not attacking either the Jewish or the British people. Both races I admire. But I am saying that the leaders of both the British and the Jewish races, for reasons which are as understandable from their viewpoint as they are inadvisable from ours, for reasons which are not American, wish to involve us in the war . . . [86]

In September 1941, Arnold Forster was a young lawyer in his second year as the chief attorney of the Anti-Defamation League, America's leading organization against anti-Semitism and racial prejudice. Sixty-two years later, he continues to serve as general counsel for the ADL. Interviewed in 2001, Forster, then ninety-two, remembered Lindbergh's Des Moines speech as if it were yesterday:

> When I heard him utter those words, I—along with every Jew in America—felt as if we had been kicked in the gut. We had come so far, yet with this one statement he did a tremendous

amount of damage. Here was this so-called hero saying these things and it was like an invitation for anti-Semites to blame us. For the average American at the time who wouldn't know a Jew from Adam, it said the Jews want to get your son killed. Of course, Lindbergh was never known for his brains. Somebody was obviously feeding him these things.

When asked about the common argument that Lindbergh merely reflected the attitudes of the times—that a lot of Americans were anti-Semitic in 1941, and he was only echoing mainstream opinion—Forster was dismissive:

> That's horse's ass logic. Sure, most Americans didn't want their daughter to marry a Jew and the rich didn't want us in their country clubs, but there is a very great difference between that kind of anti-Semitism and the kind of poison he preached that day. And if anybody thinks he was only saying what most Americans believed, they only have to look at the reaction to the speech to realize that is ludicrous.[87]

Indeed, the firestorm ignited by the speech was so far ranging—from Jews and Gentiles, from interventionists and isolationists, from Republicans and Democrats—that almost overnight the America First Committee came close to collapse. Resignations poured in from all over the country. Even the organization's most adamant media supporters were outraged. "The assertion that Jews are pressing this country into war is unwise, unpatriotic and un-American," charged the fiercely isolationist Hearst chain. "The voice is Lindbergh's but the words are the words of Hitler," declared the San Francisco *Chronicle*. "The speech was so intemperate, so unfair, so dangerous in its implications," thundered the Des Moines *Register*, "that it disqualifies Lindbergh from any pretensions of leadership."

The invective flew from all sides. One columnist wrote that Lindbergh had plummeted from "Public Hero number one to Public Enemy number one." The Republican standard bearer Wendell Willkie—for whom Lindbergh had voted the year before—called the speech "the most un-American talk made in my time by any person of national reputation."[88] *Liberty* magazine called Lindbergh "the most dangerous man in America." Christian leaders joined Jewish groups demanding that he retract his remarks.[89]

Roosevelt's presidential secretary Stephen Early noted that there was "a striking similarity" between the Des Moines speech and "the outpourings of Berlin in the last few days."[90] The Texas House of Representatives adopted a resolution telling Lindbergh to stay out of Texas. But the most widely publicized attack of all came from Lindbergh's own cousin Augustus, who told the media that "Charles is one of Hitler's most valuable helpers."[91] Walter Winchell captured the remarkable transformation of the one-time hero's image when he declared, "Lindbergh's halo has become his noose."

Lindbergh may have believed his Des Moines speech was sympathetic to Jews, as he later claimed, but he was one of the few who believed it. Besides the ominous tone of his remarks, critics immediately questioned their accuracy, particularly Lindbergh's implication that a Jewish media conspiracy was behind the interventionist movement. Arthur Robb, editor of the media trade journal *Editor and Publisher*, noted that out of 1,700 owner-publishers in America at the time, only fifteen—or less than 1 percent—were Jewish.[92]

Ninety prominent Americans, including Eleanor Roosevelt, along with many isolationists and Republicans, signed a public statement urging a debate on national policy without any attempt to "pit religion against religion."[93]

From the tone of the criticism, Lindbergh's greatest sin was not that he identified the Jews as one of the groups pushing for war. What alarmed most Americans was the implied threat carried in the speech—the warning that Jews would be "the first to feel the consequences" of a war. It sounded a little too close to Hitler's own Reichstag speech in January 1939, when he warned that if Jewish bankers plunged the world into war, it would result in "the annihilation of the Jewish race in Europe."[94] Equally controversial was Lindbergh's assertion that interventionist Jews were un-American.

In his journal entry the evening following delivery of the speech, Lindbergh seemed oblivious to the uproar: "When I mentioned the three major groups agitating for war, the entire audience seemed to stand and cheer. At that moment, whatever opposition existed was completely drowned out by our support."[95] Four days later, he seemed bemused by the subsequent reaction: "My Des Moines address has caused so much controversy that General Wood has decided to hold a meeting of the America First National Committee in Chicago. I must, of course, attend. I felt I had worded my Des Moines address carefully and moderately. It seems that almost anything can be discussed in America except the Jewish problem. The very mention of the word 'Jew' is cause for a storm."[96]

Lindbergh's later defenders, including a number of historians seeking to downplay his anti-Semitism, have argued that the Des Moines speech does not actually attack Jews, merely their influence, which is a distinction that has long been popular with anti-Semites. Jews, the argument goes, are not vilified for what they are, but what they do. Even his authorized biographer A. Scott Berg, who does acknowledge Lindbergh's "genteel" anti-Semitism on a number of other occasions, maintained that in the speech, "Lindbergh had bent over backwards to be kind about the Jews" and that the Des Moines speech contained the only public reference to Jews that Lindbergh ever made during the Great Debate, although Berg does devote considerable space to the firestorm of criticism ignited by the speech. The files of the America First Committee—now housed at Stanford University's Hoover Institution—reveal that some of the AFC's own leaders were shocked at Lindbergh's words. As the founders met to debate how to salvage their badly damaged movement, National Committee member John Flynn wrote a memo to Stuart and Wood expressing his disbelief. "It was incredible that Lindbergh, acting alone, literally committed the America First Movement to open attack on Jews," he wrote. In a separate letter to Lindbergh, who believed he had done nothing wrong, Flynn explained why the speech was harmful. "We know that New York's Jewish community is practically unanimous for war, and they had tried to brand all war opponents as anti-Semitic or pro-Nazi, a responsibility that should be brought home to them," he wrote on September 15. "But this is a far different matter from going out on the public platform and denouncing 'the Jews' as the warmongers. No man can do that without incurring the guilt of religious and racial intolerance and that character is poison in a community like ours."[97]

Anne was deeply distressed, writing in her diary that the speech had thrown her into a "black gloom." She writes that she had attempted to persuade her husband not to mention the Jews in his Des Moines speech, pleading that it would be taken as "Jew-baiting" and merely serve to rally the anti-Semitic forces around him. She had hoped he would say, "I call you people before me tonight to witness that I am not anti-Semitic nor have I attacked the Jews." When he refused her pleas, she attempted to rework the paragraph dealing with the Jews, rewriting it to "avoid all trace of rancor and bitterness" and inserting the brief section expressing sympathy with their plight.[98] But as she sat listening to the speech on September 11, the frenzied applause of the crowd frightened her. "Can he keep in control what he has in his hands?" she asked her diary.[99] Anne continued to grapple with the repercussions of the speech. In her diary three days later, she attempts to come to terms with her feelings of "revulsion" at Charles's comments. Though she believed he spoke the truth about the three groups pushing for war, she instinctively knew there was something wrong about stating it publicly. To her own question: "Why is naming the Jews 'un-American'?" she provides a clear-eyed answer: "Because it is segregating them as a group, setting the ground for anti-Semitism . . . it is a match lit near a pile of excelsior."[100]

Needless to say, the American far right was overjoyed with the Des Moines speech, particularly its warning of the consequences for Jews if they continued to support intervention. In Germany, the press upheld Goebbels' strict orders to refrain from praising Lindbergh for fear of "jeopardizing" his efforts in America.[101] But in New York, the official newspaper of the pro-Nazi Bund, the *Free American*, called the Des Moines speech "truthful," and echoed its implication that the Jews' "elimination in this country" might be "less gentle."[102] Father Coughlin's *Social Justice* and *Scribner's Commentator* also had high praise for the speech. In light of the Des Moines address, America's most prominent fascist leader, Joe McWilliams, believed he was having a positive influence on Lindbergh's thinking. According to the undercover FBI informant Arthur Derounian, McWilliams claimed his disciples were responsible for indoctrinating the America First spokesman: "I'll tell you how Lindbergh is getting his education. He is getting it from the men I have been talking to for months . . . Lawrence Dennis is one. I can't tell you who the others are. For months, I've been talking to intellectuals on the Jewish question, coaching them and giving them our literature. Lindbergh talked to these men after I educated them. Indirectly, Lindbergh got his education from me." Asked whether he believed America would ever be governed by National Socialism, McWilliams replied, "Hell yes. Can't you see the way the AFC is gradually coming our way? Just wait six months."[103]

Meanwhile, a Gallup poll revealed that an overwhelming majority of Americans disagreed with Lindbergh's assertion that Jews were responsible for inciting war. The poll, released October 24, asked Americans what groups are most active "in trying to get us into a war." The "Roosevelt Administration" was the overwhelming response, followed by "Big Business." Only one in sixteen respondents—less than 7 percent—listed the Jews.[104]

How typical was anti-Semitism in late-Depression America? Many historians and biographers have cited a January 1939 Gallup poll reporting that 83 percent of Americans opposed the admission of a larger number of Jewish refugees. However, they usually fail to point out that most Americans were opposed to increased immigration of any kind during this period,[105] as much because of economic conditions and high unemployment as anything else. As early as 1937, a majority of Americans told pollsters they would be willing to elect a Jewish president.[106] In a 1940 poll, Americans by an overwhelming 3 to 1 margin said they would be less likely to elect a member of Congress if he was "against the Jews."[107] The same year, only 12 percent of those polled responded favorably to the idea of a "campaign against the Jews."[108] Clearly, however, a large portion of the population was anti-Semitic, egged on by the propaganda of Father Coughlin and other extremists who consistently blamed the Jews for the country's economic problems. Another poll found that one-third of the American people believed Jews were more radical than other Americans and possessed a number of unpleasant qualities, including greed, dishonesty and selfishness.[109] A disproportionate percentage of anti-Semitic attitudes could be found in the midwest rural constituencies where support for Coughlin, Lindbergh and the America First Committee was highest and where the *Dearborn Independent* had enjoyed its strongest popularity fifteen years earlier.[110] However, it is difficult to gauge how much of a role anti-Semitism played in the isolationist movement as a whole.

As the criticism mounted, Lindbergh's public crusade appeared undaunted. Two weeks after the Des Moines speech, he addressed an AFC rally in Fort Wayne, Indiana, warning the crowd of 1,500 supporters that Roosevelt might suspend the 1942 congressional elections and impose a dictatorship on the United States. Lindbergh knew that most Americans valued democracy above all and that this argument would strike a chord. The Administration wasted no time responding to the accusation, matching its foe in the escalating war of rhetoric. Speaking at the Harvard Club, Assistant Secretary of State Adolf A. Berle Jr. charged that Lindbergh was "following the exact line which has been laid down in Berlin for the use of Nazi propagandists in the U.S." Berle revealed that the FBI had intercepted orders from Berlin to its American supporters instructing them on how to undermine the interventionists. He said these orders included instructions that "a howl was to be raised that Roosevelt would impose on America the kind of dictatorship that Hitler has imposed on Germany."[111]

It was not the first time Lindbergh had been publicly accused in a credible forum of following the Nazi line. In August, *Life* quoted Lindbergh telling a Philadelphia America First rally, "If we say our frontier lies on the Rhine, they (the Germans) can say it lies on the Mississippi." A few days earlier, the magazine had secured an interview with Adolf Hitler, which had not yet been published. In this interview, Hitler had said that he had not yet seen "anybody in Germany say the Mississippi River was a German frontier." The magazine was quick to seize on the similarity between the two quotes. "This coincidence, like many that have occurred in Lindbergh's speeches, appears to have been a result of parallel thinking," writes *Life* correspondent Roger Butterfield, noting that no actual evidence existed suggesting Lindbergh deliberately followed the party line or had any contact with German agents.[112]

On September 11, the FBI interrogated Friedrich Auhagen, leader of the American Fellowship Forum, who was later imprisoned for failing to register as a Nazi agent. Under questioning, he told the agents that the America First Committee was "the leading propaganda organization" in the United States. The chief problem of the German government, claimed Auhagen, was "to keep the Committee advised of all available propaganda."[113] For two years, Auhagen published a magazine called *Today's Challenge*. Among the contributors was Lindbergh, as well as a number of pro-Nazi agents who were later charged with sedition after Pearl Harbor, including Lawrence Dennis.[114]

With the AFC in disarray, the Executive Committee convened on September 18 to decide whether to repudiate Lindbergh's comments. The isolationist movement as a whole was clearly hurting. A number of prominent anti-interventionists, including Republican congressman Everett Dirksen of Illinois, publicly switched sides and supported the Roosevelt administration's stand for the first time. On October 5, one of organized labor's most prominent isolationists, Carpenter Union chief William Hutcheson, abandoned his anti-intervention position and resigned from America First.[115] John Flynn pleaded that, unless the AFC acted quickly, the movement was in danger of collapse. But many members of the National Committee insisted that Lindbergh had merely spoken the truth and refused to admonish him. Lindbergh reported that telegrams to the Committee were running overwhelmingly in his favor. Flynn's was the lone dissenting voice when the committee voted 10 to 1 to stand by its most valuable asset and resist the pressure. Instead, a statement was issued by the America First leadership on September 24 declaring that the attacks on Lindbergh were merely an attempt by the interventionists to hide the real issues by flinging false charges:

> Colonel Lindbergh and his fellow members of the America First Committee are not anti-Semitic. We deplore the injection of the race issue into the discussion of war or peace. It is the interventionists who have done this. . . . There is but one real issue—the issue of war. From this issue we will not be diverted.[116]

Many isolationists defected to other organizations such as the Keep America Out of War Committee, whose director had written that Lindbergh's speech did "more to fan the flames of anti-Semitism and push 'on the fence' Jews into the war camp than Mr. Lindbergh could possibly imagine."[117]

On November 12, the AFC in shambles, Lindbergh approached the one man whom he believed could save the movement. Over breakfast at his Dearborn home, Henry Ford told his young friend that he wanted to do something more to help oppose American intervention and promised to donate a monthly sum to keep the America First Committee afloat.[118]

The next day, Hans Thomsen, chargé d'affaires of the German embassy in Washington, dispatched a cable marked "secret" to the foreign ministry in Berlin. The AFC's plight had sounded alarm in American Nazi spy circles. Attention from the FBI—which had recently begun investigating *Scribner's Commentator* and the *Herald* as the two principal publicity vehicles of the America First Committee—was particularly worrisome. Thomsen's cable indicates that he still believed the Nazis could manipulate the AFC to do its bidding:

> The danger exists that many leading members of the Committee will be so intimidated by these methods that they will resign. In order that this useful organization not disintegrate, the press officer, through his confidential agents, is endeavoring to ensure that should General Wood, who is the present chairman, resign, Lindbergh would take over the leadership. . . . The negotiations are conducted in such a way that the Embassy's part in them can not be discerned.[119]

So high was Nazi esteem for Lindbergh that its agents failed to comprehend that he was no longer an asset to their cause in America, but had instead become a liability. In the words of Anne's sister Constance, reflecting on America's new attitude toward Lindbergh, "In just fifteen years, he had gone from Jesus to Judas."[120] Nevertheless, thousands of letters from everyday Americans continued to pour in supporting his stand, and he could still fill an arena. On October 30, 1941, 20,000 New Yorkers packed Madison Square Garden to hear Lindbergh call for "the right to demand integrity in the leadership of this nation."

Throughout most of the Great Debate, the focus on both sides had been the war in Europe. Little attention was paid to developments in Asia, despite faint rumblings over Japanese aggression in China and the announcement that Japan had signed a tripartite pact with Germany and Italy. But when the Roosevelt administration blocked all Japanese assets in America in July 1941 and moved to cut off its oil supplies in Asia, isolationists paid attention to Asian developments for the first time.

In the late fall of 1941, the *America First Bulletin* carried a blaring

front-page headline: BLAME FOR RIFT WITH JAPAN RESTS ON ADMINISTRA-
TION, charging that the Japanese had only peaceful intentions and were
being unfairly vilified by Roosevelt.[121] The same day, the New York chapter of the AFC fired off an angry letter to the President: "What's all this
sabre-rattling in connection with Japan?"[122]

Less than twenty-four hours later, the Japanese bombed Pearl Harbor.

CHAPTER 11

"WILL IT RUN?"

Shunned for his prewar isolationist views after Pearl Harbor, Lindbergh was anxious to prove his patriotism. Barred from reenlisting by the Roosevelt administration, he ended up flying more than twenty-five missions in the South Pacific as a "civilian observer," shooting down at least one Japanese Zero. Here, he is pictured in the cockpit of a Corsair fighter in New Guinea.

The date was December 17, 1941, only ten days after the Japanese attack on Pearl Harbor plunged the United States into the Second World War. Shortly after 7:00 P.M., guests began arriving at the Greenwich Village townhouse of Edwin Webster Jr., secretary for the New York chapter of the America First Committee. The occasion was a farewell dinner to honor selected America First organizers, in recognition of their tireless efforts on behalf of the isolationist cause.[1] About forty guests, including Charles Lindbergh, were invited to attend.

The AFC, like the rest of America, was reeling from the sneak attack. As news bulletins of the Japanese bombing were still pouring in on December 7, the Committee's national headquarters had issued a statement urging its followers to support America's war effort against Japan. America First suspended all non-interventionist activity, postponed rallies already scheduled and immediately halted the distribution of all isolationist literature until further notice. But the statement had deliberately left open the possibility of resuming opposition to involvement in the European war.

"Well, he got us in through the back door," General Wood told Lindbergh the morning after the attack, reflecting the cynical attitude of many America First members about Roosevelt's motives.[2] Three days later, on December 11, a group of prominent AFC officials convened in Chicago to discuss whether to disband. Lindbergh did not attend but sent a telegram opposing dissolution. He suggested simply "adjourning" the Committee, a course that would involve "burning no bridges."[3] In a straw poll taken at the meeting, seventy-seven members backed Lindbergh's position, while forty-four voted to dissolve the Committee. Despite the majority vote, the national leadership opted to cease AFC operations because of "disunity" within the ranks.[4]

Humbled irrevocably by the historical circumstances, members of the Committee were gathering in Webster's living room for one final self-affirmation before their voices were drowned out by war. But not every member had accepted the abandonment of their historic crusade as inevitable. After supper, a Brooklyn America First organizer named Horace Haase rose to address the assembled guests:

> It's obviously necessary for leaders of America First like Wood and Webster to keep quiet. But the organization should not be destroyed. . . . We must be ready for the next attack which must be made upon this Communistic administration . . . If and when the moment comes, I feel sure that our leaders, and especially the Colonel [Lindbergh], will take the leadership and take us to victory.[5]

At the invocation of Lindbergh's name, the other members present urged him to address the gathering. He was at first reluctant, arguing that he was simply there to honor the "street workers." But his colleagues insisted, and the movement's most popular leader, two months shy of his fortieth birthday, rose to make one final speech. Among those present that evening were informants for both the FBI and the U.S. Military Intelligence Division, who relayed summaries of Lindbergh's remarks to their respective agencies.

Lindbergh, they noted, was discouraged by the United States government because it "had no plan" and did not appear "to know for what it is fighting." He deplored the fact that America had for years been talking of the "yellow peril," but now found itself "fighting on the side of the Russians and the Chinese." He said he accepted the fact that America must fight the Germans, but he appeared distinctly distressed at the prospect:

> There is only one danger in the world—that is the yellow danger. China and Japan are really bound together against the white race. There could have only been one efficient weapon against this alliance. Underneath the surface, Germany itself could have been this weapon. The ideal set-up would have been to have had Germany take over Poland and Russia, in collaboration with the

British, as a bloc against the yellow people and Bolshevism. But instead the British and the fools in Washington had to interfere. The British envied the Germans and wanted to rule the world forever. Britain is the real cause of all the trouble in the world today.[6]

The Committee would live again when German military superiority was made manifest, Lindbergh confided to the gathering. He still appeared convinced that a German military victory was inevitable:

Of course, America First cannot be active right now. But it should keep on the alert and when the large missing lists and losses are published, the American people will realize how much they have been betrayed by the British and the Administration. Then America First can be a political force again. We must be quiet a while and await the time for active functioning. There may be a time soon when we can advocate a negotiated peace.[7]

Like his father, who a quarter century earlier had set aside his initial passionate opposition to the First World War to support the U.S. war effort, Lindbergh presented a patriotic face to the public. The day after Pearl Harbor, he released a statement through the AFC: "We have been stepping closer to war for many months. Now it has come and we must meet it as united Americans regardless of our attitude in the past toward the policy our government has followed. Whether or not that policy has been wise, we have been attacked by force of arms, and by force of arms we must retaliate."[8]

With his country at war, Lindbergh was anxious to be of some service and demonstrate his patriotism. He was keenly aware, however, that not everyone would welcome his participation. "What part am I to take in the war in view of the obvious antagonism of the Administration?" he mused to his journal.[9] On December 20, he wrote a personal letter to General Hap Arnold, chief of the U.S. air corps, offering his military services while conceding the "complications" created by his previous political stand.[10] Ten days later, when the offer was leaked to the media, it set off an immediate uproar. Letters poured in to Arnold's office urging him to reject the offer. "I consider him to be the most dangerous man in America today," wrote one veteran of the First World War. "Why doesn't he return that medal to Hitler, at least, so he can come into the service of the country

with clean hands?"[11] Another letter demanded that Lindbergh be given no
position except "that of an orderly in a concentration camp, where he
should have been a long time ago."[12]

In the Washington office of Harold Ickes, Lindbergh's attempt to re-
enlist was met with crushing scorn. On December 30, the interior secretary
wrote a memo to President Roosevelt charging that Lindbergh's actions
were "coldly calculated with a view to attaining ultimate power for himself"
and that it would be a "tragic disservice to American democracy to give one
of its bitterest and most ruthless enemies a chance to gain a military
record." Describing Lindbergh as a "ruthless and conscious fascist, motivated by hatred for you personally and a contempt for democracy in general," Ickes urged the President to reject the offer and instead bury
Lindbergh in "merciful oblivion."[13] Roosevelt promptly responded: "What
you say about Lindbergh and the potential danger of the man, I agree with
wholeheartedly."[14]

Officially, the administration only told Lindbergh his offer was "under
consideration." Most of the media shared Ickes's cynicism, but the *New
York Times* noted that Lindbergh had done nothing illegal and believed his
offer "should and would" be accepted—ironically belying his paranoia
about the agenda of the Jewish-owned press.

On January 12, Lindbergh decided to broach the subject with Secretary of War Henry Stimson, imploring the former Republican turned
Roosevelt loyalist to give him a chance. Stimson was blunt. He was
"extremely hesitant" to put the former isolationist spokesman in any position of command. Anybody who held such views, he confided, should not
be involved in the armed forces because he doubted "such a person could
carry on the war with sufficient aggressiveness." Moreover, Stimson could
not be entirely convinced about Lindbergh's "loyalty" or the sincerity of
his change of heart. Lindbergh confirmed that he had not changed his
views at all, that he believed it had been a mistake for the United States to
get into the war, but that at this point, "my stand was behind the country,
as I always said it would be." He offered to help in whatever way he could
be most effective.[15]

The next day, Lindbergh met with General Arnold, chief of the air
corps, and Robert Lovett, assistant secretary of war for air. Lovett pointed
out that Lindbergh had attacked Roosevelt very strongly. Could he serve
the President loyally? Lindbergh acknowledged that he had "very little
confidence" in the Roosevelt administration and intended to vote against it
at the first opportunity, but "would follow the President of the United
States as Commander in Chief of the Army." In view of the positions he
had taken in the past, Arnold asked, did Lindbergh really believe that his
associates in the air corps would have any confidence in him?

Ultimately, their suspicions convinced Lindbergh to abandon his plans. After a half-hour discussion, he told the officers it would be a mistake for him to return to military service, given the ill feelings he had generated. Perhaps, he suggested, he could be more useful to the war effort working in the civilian aviation industry. Did they think the administration would have any objection? Lovett said he believed the War Department would support such a move.[16]

Lindbergh proceeded to put out feelers, contacting Pan American Airways, United Aircraft, and Curtiss Wright Aviation offering his services. But it soon became apparent that Lovett had overestimated the administration's capacity for forgiveness. On January 26, Lindbergh received a phone call from his old friend, Pan Am chairman Juan Trippe. "Obstacles had been put in the way" of hiring Lindbergh as a consultant. The White House had made it clear that such a move would not be viewed favorably.[17] Similar calls came from Curtiss Wright and United Aircraft. The situation, explained Curtiss Wright president Guy Vaughan, was "loaded with dynamite."[18] As the rejections poured in, Lindbergh's frustration increased. Suddenly desperate to participate in a conflict that he had long opposed, he complained in his journal, "I am beginning to wonder whether I will be blocked in every attempt I make to take part in this war."[19]

Scott Berg and other biographers have attributed these obstacles to vindictiveness on the part of the Roosevelt administration. Berg cites a meeting at which the president allegedly told a group of senators, "I'll clip that young man's wings."[20] But military intelligence files reveal that there may be more to the administration's initial veto than petty revenge in the months immediately following the outbreak of war. Only weeks earlier, the White House had been informed by the FBI that Lindbergh was under investigation as the potential source of a serious military leak.

A number of historians have suggested that Roosevelt regularly used the Bureau to stifle political dissent, abusing the power of the presidency against his political enemies. However, a series of Freedom of Information Act requests reveal that the Administration had never once asked the FBI to formally investigate Lindbergh, nor did J. Edgar Hoover do so on his own initiative, although he was fond of leaking incriminating information about the President's political opponents, including Lindbergh, to the White House and the press. As distasteful as Lindbergh's activities may have been to the president, there was nothing illegal or treasonous about professing pro-Nazi sympathies before Pearl Harbor. The closest Roosevelt appears to have come to abusing the Bureau's investigative powers against the isolationist movement is when he asked his secretary in February 1941 to inquire about the source of AFC funding.[21] During most of his political crusade, Lindbergh had never been a law enforcement target.

That situation changed dramatically eleven days before Pearl Harbor when the FBI received a disturbing advisory from the War Department's Military Intelligence Division. On November 26, Colonel J. T. Bissell of MID informed Hoover that when Lindbergh returned to the United States in 1939, a civilian inventor, Marvin Rutherford, had sent him a complete set of plans for a "self-sealing gas tank." Lindbergh had received the plans via registered mail as chairman of the air corps' New Devices Committee. Not long afterwards, Colonel Bissell reported, the *Luftwaffe* happened to develop its own self-sealing gas tank for airplanes, which was discovered on a German plane shot down in England. Rutherford suspected that Lindbergh had transmitted the plans to the German government. A subsequent search by MID determined the plans Lindbergh had received were missing from the War Department files. Suspecting that Lindbergh may have leaked the plans to Germany, Bissell reported that he had written to Lindbergh requesting the plans or an explanation of what became of them.[22]

Before Pearl Harbor, Bissell's report appears to have sparked little concern at FBI headquarters. In fact, Hoover had received a similar report from the Bureau's Dallas office in July 1941 but, because the United States was not yet at war with Germany, he concluded that, even if true, no federal violation would have occurred.[23] However, on the day of the Japanese attack, an informant's account of a recent conversation with Ford Motor Company executive Harry Bennett reignited the FBI's interest and cast new suspicion on Lindbergh's loyalty.

During this conversation, Bennett allegedly claimed that Lindbergh had boasted that much of the factual information he used in his isolationist speeches came from officials in the U.S. War Department.[24] Three days before Pearl Harbor, the fiercely isolationist *Chicago Tribune* had leaked the War Department's contingency plans, code-named the Victory Program, as evidence that Roosevelt planned on secretly bringing the United States into the war. The President was livid and ordered Hoover to find out who leaked the information. The FBI investigation concluded that an anti-Roosevelt army officer had leaked the plans. Now, with the informant's report, Hoover was convinced that Lindbergh was the conduit for the leak.

Hoover promptly dispatched the FBI's Detroit bureau chief John Bugas to the Ford plant to interview Bennett about Lindbergh's claim. What Bennett told the FBI agent did little to reassure the Bureau. He said he had been present at a conversation between Ford and Lindbergh three weeks earlier in which the two men discussed the war in Europe, at which point Lindbergh revealed that he was getting much of his confidential information directly from U.S. army officials.[25] He claimed that he had a regular contact in the Washington officer corps, who had similar political views, but Lindbergh no longer went to see this officer because he felt they were "being watched or followed." Bennett could not recall the officer's name.[26]

Three weeks later, Bennett called Bugas and said he had learned that Lindbergh's army contact was probably a general in Hap Arnold's office named Ralph Cousins. But from Bennett's description, Lindbergh was almost certainly referring to Truman Smith, not Cousins, as his War Department source. During a subsequent investigation, FBI agents learned that Lindbergh barely knew Ralph Cousins.[27] Hoover immediately circulated a memo to his chief deputies advising them of his preferred course of action. If Lindbergh refused to reveal his War Department contact, he wrote, "We can then give consideration as to whether he should be called before a Grand Jury . . . He either should be made to put up or shut up."[28]

Lindbergh's name had also recently come to the Bureau's attention in connection with a shadowy right-wing movement that the FBI suspected of succeeding the America First Committee. The Bureau had been receiving a number of reports that some former AFC members had been meeting and discussing the formation of a new movement or political party with Lindbergh at the helm. Agents were dispatched around the country to investigate these reports.

On January 26, 1942, the bureau was alerted by Vice-President Henry Wallace about the potentially subversive activities of the prominent Brigham family of New York, many of whom were former members of America First. A subsequent FBI investigation revealed that the family matriarch Ethel Brigham was reported to have said, upon the declaration of war with Japan, "Lindbergh was right and we will not win this war. We are getting no more than we deserve." Her daughter Constance Brigham allegedly said, "I would like to kill Roosevelt." Another daughter, Barbara Brigham, said she knew of a secret organization in the United States financed by a millionaire with a membership of over 500,000, all of whom were armed and ready to take up arms against the President. She implied the group was associated with the AFC.[29] Barbara Brigham happened to be one of the forty AFC members present at the exclusive Greenwich Village gathering on December 17 when Lindbergh warned against the "yellow danger."[30]

The Bureau could find no evidence that Lindbergh was acting in league with the Brighams in planning anything subversive. Nor did a subsequent investigation implicate him in any seditious activity after Pearl Harbor. But in a letter to the President's secretary Edwin M. Watson on February 13, 1942, Hoover reveals that the White House had good reason to be concerned about Lindbergh's potential involvement in the war effort. To this point, Hoover's reports about Lindbergh had always been surprisingly objective, paying little attention to the raw data, rumors, and innuendo that characterize the FBI files of many public figures. Though Hoover had received hundreds of letters from citizens urging that he investigate Lindbergh for Fifth Column activities, the Bureau had always ignored these accusations, never so much as placing a wiretap on the Lindberghs' telephone. So the first paragraph of Hoover's letter to Watson couldn't have failed to attract the attention of the White House:

> I have been confidentially informed that members of the America First Committee entertain the hope that the Committee may again become a political force; that they are biding their time in contemplation of this eventuality. While the organization ostensibly went out of existence following the entrance of the United States into the present war, I am informed that the Committee has in reality gone underground, under the leadership of Charles A. Lindbergh.[31]

Nothing in the letter, however, explicitly stated that Lindbergh was guilty of any crime or that the America First Committee was engaged in treasonous activity. It appears that the FBI had found no evidence proving Lindbergh had leaked sensitive military information to the Germans. The Bureau was determined to remain vigilant but no action was recommended. Meanwhile, Lindbergh remained a pariah, unable to secure a single civilian job in the American aviation industry.

Scrutinized, mistrusted, scorned outright, and blocked from serving his country at every turn, he still had one powerful friend who would not shun him—a friend who, in the words of Leonard Mosley, "could not be pressured. He loathed Roosevelt even more than Charles Lindbergh did. He also despised democracy, was anti-Semitic, and employed a ruthless thug to break the affiliations, the spirit, or the heads of those who got in the way. But not even the United States Government was strong enough to challenge him, or prevent him from saying or doing pretty well what he wished."[32]

On March 21, 1942, Lindbergh received word that Henry Ford wanted to see him. Three days later, he arrived in Detroit to meet with Ford, Harry Bennett and a group of high-ranking company officials. After lunch, they drove to a massive clearing west of Dearborn where the Ford Motor Company had recently constructed a mammoth manufacturing plant known as Willow Run. The plant had been built to accommodate the major contract Ford had secured a year earlier to build B-24 bombers for the U.S. War Department. For the sake of the national defense effort, the

Roosevelt administration had put aside its historical antagonism against Henry Ford and his company, believing its legendary manufacturing expertise could be channeled toward strengthening a long-neglected military arsenal.

Nicknamed "the Liberator," the B-24 was to be the cornerstone of American supremacy over the skies. Ford had persuaded the government to contribute a staggering $200 million to the plant's construction after promising to build one B-24 every hour. Adapting a 24-hour/7-day work week, the company threw itself into the project accompanied by a massive publicity campaign painting the Ford Motor Company as a vital cog in the U.S. war machine. The company even attempted to rewrite history, downplaying its controversial 1940 refusal of the British Rolls-Royce Merlin Engine contract. A company spokesman told the media that the Ford Motor Company had only refused the Merlin contract because Henry Ford "didn't like the design," not for any political motive.[33] This explanation, of course, was pure fiction.

As they toured the Willow Run site, Ford suddenly asked his young friend whether he would be willing to move to Detroit to help the company with its B-24 program. Lindbergh jumped at the offer. Here, finally, was a chance to make a contribution to the war effort, after being rebuffed for months by other companies fearful of the Administration's retributive reach. But before he would get his hopes up, Lindbergh suggested that Ford seek clearance from the Roosevelt administration to ensure that his employment wouldn't jeopardize any military contracts. Initially incensed at the idea of having to ask permission to do anything in his own company, Ford finally relented and instructed his subordinates to contact the War Department for approval. Lindbergh was equally chagrined. "It annoys me to have to ask the government's permission to make a connection with a commercial company; it's too damn much like Russia," he complained in his journal.[34]

The FBI had still not found any credible evidence to suggest Lindbergh posed a security risk, and Secretary of War Henry Stimson gave the go-ahead a week later. Lindbergh enthusiastically moved his family to Detroit and reported for work—his first real job in almost twenty years. But news that the two Nazi medal recipients were working together on behalf of the U.S. war effort raised hackles across the country. Hundreds of angry letters poured into the White House complaining about a "Detroit Fifth Column." Nor were Ford's own employees thrilled to be working with a man who had smugly implied a German victory was nigh only a few months earlier. On April 10, the Foundry Workers Union passed a resolution, approved by 10,000 Ford workers, charging that "laboring men had been given a slap in the face" by the hiring of the former isolationist leader. A Ford spokesman dismissed the resolution as "communist-inspired."[35]

But the doubts persisted. In July, *Liberty* magazine ran an open letter to Lindbergh headlined, "Have You Changed Your Mind?" challenging him to publicly affirm to the nation that he was "wholeheartedly behind our government and the President in the struggle to win the war." Lindbergh immediately crafted a handwritten reply, refusing to retract any of his prewar views and restating his conviction that the alternative to a negotiated peace in Europe was "either a Hitler victory or a prostrate Europe and possibly a prostrate America as well." The Roosevelt administration, he charged, had so far pursued a course that "had led to a series of failures and disasters almost unparalleled in history." Perhaps sensing the firestorm that would ensue if these views were made public while America was at war, he decided against mailing the letter.[36]

Still, the Lindbergh name kept popping up in a number of unsavory contexts. Since Pearl Harbor, the U.S. government had been investigating the allegedly fascist and pro-Nazi activities of a number of individuals and organizations. Before the war, these activities were protected by the constitutional right to free speech. Now they were potentially seditious. One of the most notorious American fascists was William Dudley Pelley, leader of the Silver Shirt storm troopers. Patterned after the Nazi Brown Shirts, the organization's announced purpose was "a wholesale and drastic ousting of every radical-minded Jew from the United States."[37]

Shortly after Pearl Harbor, Pelley was indicted by a grand jury on eleven counts of criminal sedition for conspiring to overthrow the government. In early August, as Pelley's trial convened in Indianapolis, the defense suddenly called Charles Lindbergh as a surprise witness. Two years earlier, Pelley had written a letter to the extreme right-wing isolationist leader George Van Horn Moseley confiding that he would like to enlist Lindbergh, along with Ford, in an American Nazi revolution. This letter could have suggested a potentially damning connection between the two men. But it was the defense, not the prosecution, who called Lindbergh to testify, and the move appeared to be little more than a publicity stunt since there was no evidence the two men had ever even met. Indeed, when Lindbergh appeared in court on August 4, he was called on to answer only three inconsequential questions. Asked about American public opinion regarding war before Pearl Harbor, he testified, "It was my impression that a majority of the people opposed entering the war before we were attacked."[38] He was off the stand in less than fifteen minutes but the mere association in the public eye with a notorious figure such as Pelley only served to reinforce American suspicions that Lindbergh could not be trusted.

On September 18, 1942, President Roosevelt paid a visit to Willow Run to inspect the B-24 bomber program for which the Allies had such high hopes. Lindbergh's animosity toward the president had not changed and he decided to take the afternoon off rather than chance being at the plant when Roosevelt arrived.[39] Each morning, Ford liked to pay a visit to his favorite employee where they discussed world events, the war and other shared interests. "Charles in much of his thinking is much like me," he told *Fortune* magazine in February 1943.[40] A week before Roosevelt's visit, Ford had visited Lindbergh's office to express disgust with the president's policies. "People like that always get what's coming to them," Ford hissed.[41] He went on to blame the DuPonts, owners of arch-rival General Motors, for most of the country's troubles, an increasingly common theme of his private rhetoric. The DuPont family was originally Huguenot (French Protestant)[42] but Ford was convinced they were Jewish and acting in league with Roosevelt to destroy the country.

Lindbergh humored the old man and continued to report for work at Willow Run each day. However, privately, he was becoming increasingly frustrated with the B-24 project, which was not going as smoothly as the company pretended. Ford officials regularly boasted to the media that publicizing Willow Run's production plans would "scare Hitler to death" and the company painted itself as an important element in President Roosevelt's "arsenal of democracy." The March 1942 cover of *Time* magazine featured an image of Henry Ford standing before a huge factory from which streams of tanks and bombers flowed. The caption stated, "Out of enormous rooms, armies will roll and fleets will fly."[43] Even today, the Ford Motor Company boasts of its work on the B-24 as a significant contribution to the Allied victory in World War II. And, although the company eventually did produce significant numbers of B-24s and other war material, the facts in 1942 suggested a very different story—that of a fiasco in the making.

The mismanagement, incompetence, and plain bungling at Willow Run were plainly evident and Lindbergh appeared embarrassed to be associated with the project. His journal told the story. After a meeting with Air Corps Chief General Arnold on August 11, Lindbergh relates that Arnold told him combat squadrons greatly preferred the B-17 bomber to the B-24 because "when we send the 17's out on a mission, most of them return. But when we send the 24's out, most of them don't."[44] A month later, Lindbergh visited the Dearborn engineering laboratory with Ford production chief Charles Sorensen, who told the company's new consultant that he thought the workmanship on the B-24 was as good as other companies' and that the plant was well ahead of their production schedule. That evening, Lindbergh confided to his journal, "I had to say bluntly that we were *not* making schedule and that the workmanship on the first bombers that went through Willow Run was the worst I had ever seen."[45]

It appears to be Lindbergh's devotion to Ford, who had long since replaced Alexis Carrel as his father figure, that prevented him from resigning from the disaster-plagued program. On Ford's seventy-ninth birthday, Lindbergh sent his boss a congratulatory note that reflected his continued admiration:

> My friendship with you is one of the things I value most highly in life. You combine the characteristics I admire most in men—success with humility, firmness with tolerance, science with religion.[46]

As young American B-24 test pilots continued to be killed in the flying deathtraps, which the company had promised would help vanquish Hitler, the government began to ask questions. As early as February 1943, rumors had begun to surface about shoddy B-24 production standards at Willow Run when *Fortune* reported that aircraft manufacturers believed the plant should have been named "Will it run?"[47] Two months later, a national defense congressional committee headed by Senator Harry Truman sent investigators to look into problems with the B-24. Their report to Congress three months later was devastating. Investigators severely criticized the Ford Motor Company for setting up the B-24 production line like an automobile assembly line, "despite the warnings of many experienced aircraftmen." The report contrasted the work at Willow Run with another military contractor, San Diego–based Consolidated Aircraft, which was turning out B-24s at a much faster rate. It criticized Ford for failing to send production engineers to San Diego to determine why the Consolidated program was so much more successful, and lamented the project's "waste and confusion."

Underlying the committee's findings were the lofty promises made by the Ford Motor Company in its bid to convince the government to hand over $200 million to build Willow Run a year earlier. The company promised that Ford's legendary production resources would turn out a B-24 every hour as well as thousands of spare parts to be used by other aircraft manufacturers who were engaged in producing B-24s across the country. However, by July 1943, Ford had failed to supply any of the parts for which it had contracted, forcing the army to switch its parts manufacturing to a plant in Tulsa and setting the Consolidated B-24 plant at Fort Worth, Texas, far behind schedule.

By far the most damning finding, however, was the revelation that, until shortly before the report was released, "the Ford Motor Company had not produced at Willow Run a plane which was capable of use at the front."[48] Senator Monrad Wallgren, chairman of the Truman subcommittee, publicly described the employees of Willow Run as "aircraft workers who have never produced a plane."[49]

Around this time, U.S. military intelligence reported that a delegation from the Ford UAW local planned to ask the United Auto Workers Convention "what Lindbergh is doing as a consultant at the Ford Motor Company" and demand an investigation of the company's war production effort, which "they charge is being shamefully retarded."[50] The delegation appears to have abandoned this plan before the convention.

The problems with the B-24 program were said to be taking a tremendous toll on company President Edsel Ford, whose health had been rapidly failing for months under the strain. Twice, he was hospitalized suffering from gastric ulcers, although the company repeatedly downplayed his medical problems. Then, on May, 25, 1943, the forty-nine-year-old Edsel suddenly lapsed into a coma while home in bed. The next day, the Ford empire was shaken by the news that Henry's only child had died during the night. The elder Ford, just shy of his eightieth birthday, was a broken man. "Maybe I pushed the boy too hard," he lamented to friends.[51]

As it faced its most serious crisis in years, the company appeared rudderless. However, Edsel's death appeared to have been welcomed by at least one company official, who moved quickly to take advantage of the void. Edsel had always despised Ford's ruthless security chief Harry Bennett and the feeling was entirely mutual. Each regularly complained to Henry Ford about the other. Only Henry's intervention had prevented Edsel from firing Bennett years before. But by the time the mourning period was over, Bennett had consolidated his power in the company with remarkable agility, joining the Ford board of directors alongside Henry and Clara, and Edsel's two sons, Benson and Henry Ford II. His company title was switched in the summer of 1943 from head of the Ford service department to director of administrative affairs—a position that gave him enormous additional powers. Now, he reported only to Henry, who had reassumed the President's mantle, but was reported to be in failing health himself. In what Ford biographer Keith Sward describes as a "palace revolution," Bennett plotted to purge a number of longtime enemies, many loyal to Edsel, from the company's executive ranks. But there was one Ford employee whom Bennett wanted out above all others.

As far back as 1933, he had set his sights on Ernest Liebold's removal from the company payroll. Liebold had long since ceased to be a major power within the company itself, but had remained personally close to

Henry and Clara Ford, handling their personal investments, retaining their power of attorney, and continuing to exert a good deal of influence over his boss of thirty years. Simple jealousy may have been a factor in the conflict, as Bennett competed for Ford's undivided attention and would tolerate no rival. In his autobiography, Bennett would presumptuously claim to have been closer to Ford "even than his only son."[52] For years, Bennett had attempted to persuade Ford to fire Liebold, accusing the longtime secretary of embezzling company funds and a number of other improprieties. Ford had resolutely refused these entreaties. Bennett later said he believed Ford was "afraid" of Liebold and that is why he refused to dismiss him.

In his 1951 memoir, Bennett insisted that Ford had first become disenchanted with Liebold following Edsel's death: "After that he wasn't anti-Semitic or anything else. He was just a tired old man who wanted to live in peace. He reached a point where he didn't want to see either Liebold or (William) Cameron."[53] Like many of the stories in his self-serving memoir, there is very little evidence to back up this account. It was Bennett who didn't want Liebold around and he set about his task in earnest.

His long-awaited opportunity was inadvertently set in motion in late 1943 by none other than Charles Lindbergh, who had returned from a trip to Washington with some disturbing news. The Willow Run disaster was the talk of the Capitol, he reported. High-ranking military officials had intimated "that the government might take the plant over." Lindbergh suggested remedial action before it was too late. "You'd better be prepared and see if you can't do something about it," he told Ford officials.[54] This wasn't the first time this threat had flashed on the company's radar screen. As early as January 1941, Eleanor Roosevelt had told an audience of Yale University students that her husband could "declare a state of national emergency at any time and can even take over Mr. Ford himself tomorrow."[55] More recently, Washington columnist Drew Pearson revealed that the U.S. War Production Board had let it be known that if Willow Run continued to flounder, the government was prepared to commandeer Ford's plant and run it for him.[56]

Here, Ford's old friend, the Jew-baiting minister Gerald L K Smith, reenters the picture. Smith had refused to accept the decision of the mainstream isolationist movement to disband after Pearl Harbor, maintaining the widely held conviction that President Roosevelt had secretly engineered the attack as an excuse to push the United States into the war. According to Smith's biographer Glenn Jeansonne, "His hatred for Roosevelt was deep and emotional, far beyond simply opposing his policies. Smith loathed the President and accused him of evil intentions, corrupt acts and endless ambition. He was obsessed with removing President Roosevelt from office."[57] To this end, Smith formed his own political party to challenge Roosevelt in the

1944 presidential election, calling it the America First Party, although there was no discernible connection between Smith's party and the former AFC. For Smith, only one man had the public profile to successfully dethrone the popular president. He met with Charles Lindbergh at the Dearborn Inn on July 10, 1942, to persuade him to carry the new party's banner.[58] But Lindbergh allegedly declined, explaining he had no political ambitions.

Next, Smith offered the party's presidential nomination to the popular General Douglas MacArthur, whose extremist political views had long made him a darling of the American far right. When he was rebuffed once again, Smith finally decided to run for president himself. To have any chance of success, however, he knew he would require two things: significant funding and the endorsement of prominent Americans. To this end, he spent the next two years attempting to contact both Lindbergh and Ford, but by this time, it was clear that Smith was treading dangerously close to crossing the line between free speech and sedition. Both Ford and Lindbergh had been warned by colleagues to distance themselves from the increasingly unstable clergyman, who was under almost constant surveillance by various law enforcement agencies. According to FBI reports, Smith left repeated unreturned messages for both Lindbergh and Ford.

This is not to say Lindbergh or other former AFC officials had abandoned the idea of unseating Roosevelt, still the cherished dream of the American right. According to his journal, Lindbergh lunched with Wood and other former members of the AFC National Committee at the end of 1943 to discuss the possible presidential candidacy of General MacArthur. These discussions coincided with Smith's own attempt to enlist MacArthur as a presidential candidate, but it's difficult to determine whether the efforts were related. In August 1942, a month after he met with Lindbergh at the Dearborn Inn, Smith nominated Lindbergh for the post of assistant secretary of war for aviation, although there is no evidence Lindbergh ever consented to this.[59]

Nobody was more aware of Smith's activities than Harry Bennett, who had provided substantial financial support to the Reverend over the years, most likely on behalf of Henry Ford.[60] Bennett had long been close to the FBI's Detroit bureau chief John Bugas, who, in an FBI field report, once described Bennett as "a friend of the Bureau."[61] In early 1944, Bennett made Bugas an offer he couldn't refuse, luring him away from the FBI as his assistant at a salary more than three times what the veteran agent had been earning at the Bureau. As his first task, Bugas was asked to write a memorandum detailing his inside knowledge of Ernest Liebold's activities. To this day, the three-page memo, entitled "re: Ernest Liebold," sits in a file at the Ford Motor Company's archives. When the company donated its corporate papers to an independent museum repository in

1964—supposedly in the interest of opening up its history to the public—
it chose to keep the Liebold memo where it lay, far from the prying eyes
of historians.[62]

Bugas's memo tells an astonishing story. It reveals that on the day after
Pearl Harbor, December 8, 1941, a federal warrant had been issued for
Liebold's arrest "along with several hundred other dangerous individuals."
But while the subsequent FBI sweep had taken countless Nazi agents and
other potential national security threats into custody, the Liebold arrest
warrant was never served. It was eventually countermanded, the memo
reveals, "due principally to Liebold's affiliation with Ford."[63] Bugas implies
that Ford himself intervened to save his trusted secretary from arrest but
provides no further details.

Though Liebold escaped detention, the FBI continued to keep close
tabs on his activities. By 1944, reveals Bugas, Liebold had "for four years
been very suspiciously regarded by federal law enforcement agencies."[64]
The memo goes on to describe how, at a time when the Ford Motor Com-
pany was working on a number of highly classified military contracts,
Liebold met frequently with a man named Edmund G. Heine whom he
had befriended in the early 1930s when Heine was manager at the *Ford-
Werke* plant in Cologne. In 1941, years after Heine stopped working for
Ford, he was living in the United States when he was apprehended by the
FBI for sending information about the American aviation industry to Nazi
Germany. He was convicted on two counts of espionage and sentenced to
eighteen years imprisonment.[65]

Details of the Heine-Liebold relationship are troubling. In the months
leading up to his arrest, according to the Bugas memo, Heine's movements
were being monitored twenty-four hours a day at a time when "he was
intensively engaged in espionage activities, which the FBI was observing
unknown to him." During this period, "he visited the office of Liebold frequently and was in constant communication with him." After Heine's
arrest, Liebold attempted to procure the services of a Ford attorney to represent the accused spy. According to a separate FBI report, Liebold had
mysteriously advised Heine in September 1940 that he had gone to Washington "to get the data."[66] Around the same time, Heine approached
Liebold asking for his help to secure a U.S. passport to return to Germany.
Liebold informed his friend that the Ford Motor Company could probably
"send him on a mission" as a pretext for securing the passport. Later,
Liebold asked Heine to help him obtain a first edition of *Mein Kampf*.[67]

After Pearl Harbor, the Bugas memo continues, Liebold had "continuous contact" with several Nazi organizations such as the "German American Bund, the German Relief Fund and a number of agencies that have
since the war been outlawed." In addition, Liebold "was a recipient of con-

siderable and various expert and effective German propaganda, and actually disseminated same."[68]

In the memo, Bugas also establishes a direct connection between Liebold and the Reverend Gerald Smith. "He was a fairly frequent visitor with Gerald L K Smith who had, over a period of years, until fairly recently, almost open access to Liebold's office."[69] It is this finding that Bennett hoped would persuade Henry Ford to fire Liebold because of the fear that the Smith association could trigger punitive action by the Roosevelt administration.

As Bennett almost surely intended when he asked Bugas to write the memo, the former FBI chief concluded with an unequivocal recommendation: "The purpose of this is to tell you, in so far as I know, the type of man Liebold is, which in itself thoroughly justifies, in my opinion, severance of this man's employment with the company and with Mr. Ford."[70]

The details of what happened next are still sketchy. In his memoirs, Harry Bennett makes no reference to the Bugas memo but appears to allude to it when he writes, "In the spring of 1944, I learned some things I hadn't known about Liebold." Armed with this information, Bennett "finally got a chance to fire Liebold—the only executive I ever did fire."[71]

Bennett claims that when he took up the matter of Liebold's unsavory activities with Ford, the old man responded, "Oh, it isn't that bad." Bennett then attempted a different tactic. Because Liebold held Ford's personal power-of-attorney, he explained, the secretary could give away all Ford's money if he so desired. Ford appears to have never before grasped this legal concept. A few phone calls to his lawyers confirmed it. Bennett describes what happened next: "He then spoke the words I had been waiting to hear for so long: 'Well, you just get him out of here.' "[72]

Bennett immediately asked Ford's executive secretary Frank Campsall to revoke the power-of-attorney. Liebold, explains Bennett, had always been paid directly by Henry Ford, rather than the company, meaning that Bennett had no official power to dismiss him. To get around this complication, he claims he took the necessary steps to place Liebold, who was in Mexico on vacation, on the company payroll: "Once that was accomplished, it put him under my jurisdiction, and I fired him."[73]

Bennett's account, repeated by a number of biographers, implies Liebold's disturbing activities over the years were those of a private individual working for Henry Ford. They were thus completely removed from the Ford Motor Company itself. But, according to personnel records found in the company's industrial archives, this claim was simply not true. The records reveal that, although Liebold worked privately for Ford from 1911 to 1915, he was added to the company payroll on October 1, 1915, and his substantial salary was paid by the Ford Motor Company for nearly thirty years.[74] This proves that Bennett's account is likely a fabrication. Like many Ford loyalists, he appears to be deliberately seeking to distance Liebold's actions from the corporation, thus protecting the reputation of both Henry Ford and the company.

Nevertheless, Bennett's version of the story contained some truth. Liebold returned from his Mexican vacation in May 1944, only to be informed by Campsall that his power-of-attorney over the finances of Henry and Clara Ford had been revoked. Stunned at losing this last vestige of influence over the company founder, he tried in vain to change Ford's mind. The decision was final, but Henry never told him the reason for the abrupt revocation. Years later, in his oral history, Liebold was still apparently bewildered by his fall from grace. While he was away in Mexico, he recalled, "I found that Gerald L K Smith had been at my office. I always believed it was Gerald Smith's visit to my office which apparently aroused Mr. Ford."[75] Until his death twelve years later, Liebold would frequently claim that Harry Bennett had deliberately turned Ford against him and that Bennett, not himself, was disloyal to the United States.

The *Detroit Free Press* and the *New York Times* carried prominent stories marking "the end of an era" at Ford. Both papers quoted Liebold as saying he had been dismissed, an assertion that has been generally accepted over the years. However, according to company personnel records, Ford never actually fired his longtime confidante—even after learning that he was probably a Nazi spy. This lenience is hardly surprising, considering that Ford had apparently intervened to prevent the government from arresting his secretary as a threat to national security after Pearl Harbor three years earlier.

Instead, Liebold was offered another position at the company's Rouge River facility.[76] But the prospect of losing precious access to Ford's inner sanctum, only to take a meaningless office job, was more than Liebold could bear and he left in a huff, not even bothering to clean out his office.

The personal effects he left behind offer a revealing insight into the man who had at one time occupied a position of unrivaled power within the company. Among the boxes of documents and files found in Liebold's office were copies of a speech by Adolf Hitler, a number of publications issued by the Nazi propaganda agency *Deutsche Fickte Bund* and a letter from the German consul general thanking Liebold for a donation he had made to the German Winter Relief Fund, a well-known Nazi financial front.[77]

For almost three years after the United States entered the war, at a time when the Allies were relying on the Ford Motor Company to manufacture some of its most important weapons delivery systems, Liebold had all but unrestricted access to every phase of company operations, including sensitive military systems.[78] During this same period, a Senate committee accused Ford of seriously mismanaging the most important of these systems, the B-24 bomber—dealing a staggering setback to the Allied war effort. However, there is no conclusive evidence proving that Liebold sabotaged the bomber program. Although Ford's B-24 production increased significantly after Liebold left the company, the bomber had already become a reliable mainstay of the U.S. air corps, its once frequent glitches a thing of the past.

Meanwhile, Lindbergh's frustration over the B-24 fiasco apparently convinced him to abandon most of his duties at Ford shortly before Liebold left the company. Although he never officially resigned his position as a consultant on the B-24 and he continued to offer occasional advice, Lindbergh quietly took another position as a consultant with the United Aircraft Corporation, where he was charged with improving the company's well-respected Navy marine Corsair fighter. Ever since he had been rebuffed in his bid to rejoin the U.S. military, Lindbergh had been itching to see some action. Although he was still uncomfortable at the prospect of fighting Germans, he had no such qualms about going to war against the Japanese, whom he had referred to as "the yellow danger" at the beginning of the war.

In January 1944, Lindbergh traveled to Washington to seek permission to go to the South Pacific combat zone to survey Corsair operating bases. The war against Japan was entering its most crucial phase and Lindbergh was anxious to be a part of it. He was not optimistic about his chances, fearful that the Roosevelt administration would veto the trip. But a day after a meeting with Brigadier General Louis Wood, he received the go-ahead to fly to the Pacific war zone. Here again, the White House could have placed obstacles in the way and chose not to do so, despite the claims by Lindbergh's friends and supporters that they were out to get him. In fact, there is not a single piece of convincing evidence—only rumors related by Lindbergh himself in his journal—that the Administration ever interfered with his requests to help the war effort as a civilian.

In April 1944, the Allies established a beachhead in Hollandia, New Guinea, after a surprise invasion caught the Japanese off guard. This was to be Lindbergh's first Pacific war zone destination.[79] He arrived in May eager to join the front lines after more than two years working at a desk. His presence at first was not well received by American troops, many of whom still regarded him as traitor for his defeatist speeches, and there was considerable grumbling in the ranks wherever he appeared.[80] But many high-ranking officers, including Pacific commander Douglas MacArthur, had been sympathetic to the isolationist movement before Pearl Harbor and still regarded Lindbergh as a hero.

As a civilian, Lindbergh was forbidden from acting in anything more than an observer role, but his officer friends knew there were many ways to skirt the regulations. If he was flying along as a passenger and his plane was shot at by an enemy fighter, surely nobody would object if he acted in self-defense. That's just what happened as he flew along as an "observer" on daily missions, regularly drawing enemy fire and firing back on a number of occasions. Stories—many of them exaggerated—began to spread throughout the South Pacific of a civilian pilot dive-bombing enemy positions, sinking barges and evading Japanese zeros. On May 29, Lindbergh was flying a Corsair fighter-bomber over Kavieng when he dropped a 500-pound high explosive bomb on a section of the city which he described as an area "where we know there is Jap military activity." His bomb missed its intended target, landing on a strip of buildings instead and almost certainly killing innocent civilians. In his journal that night, he wrote:

> I don't like this bombing and machine-gunning of unknown targets. You press a button and death flies down. One second the bomb is hanging harmlessly in your racks, completely under your control. The next it is hurtling down through the air, and nothing in your power can revoke what you have done. The cards are dealt. If there is life where that bomb will hit, you have taken it.[81]

Flying along as an observer on almost fifty missions, Lindbergh was reported to have shot down at least one Japanese Zero in "self-defense." He also taught American pilots how to conserve fuel so their own bombing missions would be more efficient. A number of officers, impressed with Lindbergh's exploits, suggested he make another attempt to regain his military commission, but he demurred. In his journal, he explained his reluctance: "There are political complications, and I am hesitant to accept a commission under Roosevelt even if I could obtain one." But these complications became moot in April 1945 when, a few weeks short of V-E Day, the President died suddenly at his Georgia retreat. Lindbergh had temporarily suspended his journal so there is no record how he felt about the death of his greatest nemesis. However, in her own unpublished memoirs, Truman Smith's wife Kay provides a revealing insight into the mindset of the circle of Roosevelt's longtime enemies who surrounded Lindbergh. She recalled that on the day they heard of the President's death:

> In blew Connie Brown (Constantine Brown of the *Washington Star*). His eyes popping out of his head, sparkling, his face one large beaming smile. He said not a word but hugged me violently.

Rushed to Truman, embraced him. Threw his arms high in the air in exultation. Whirled around and flew out the door leaving me speechless. Truman and I burst into roars of laughter. We had not yet heard the news but we knew only one thing could have given him such fierce delight! The evil man was dead!

Writing this in the year of 1974, I know how right we were to hate him so bitterly. Our decline, our degeneracy stems from that man and his socialist, blinded greedy wife.[82]

CHAPTER 12

BUSINESS AS USUAL

Ford's Cologne plant, on the banks of the Rhine, was instrumental in the Nazi war effort, employing thousands of forced laborers supplied by the regime, including inmates from a nearby concentration camp.

In the beginning of October 1942, a convoy of German occupation troops suddenly swept through the Russian city of Rostov without warning, abducting children as young as fourteen and placing them into cattle wagons bound for Germany. The city's Jewish population had already been massacred by Nazi death squads three months earlier. Armed soldiers traveled from house to house, forcing the remaining residents to register at a German labor depot and wait until their number was called. Among the group of detainees was a sixteen-year-old schoolgirl named Elsa Iwanowa. On October 8, Elsa and two thousand other young Russians were herded like livestock, driven by blows from the butts of German rifles, onto a transport heading west. After a grueling three-week journey, she arrived in the city of Wuppertal, Germany, where she and thirty-eight other Russian teenagers were put in line and displayed before a group of waiting businessmen shopping for human cargo.[1]

Seven months earlier, the Nazis had appointed Fritz Sauckel as the Plenipotentiary General for the allocation of labor, responsible for supervising a massive slave labor operation designed to alleviate the Reich's severe manpower shortages. The Nuremberg war crimes trial would later reveal that, following Sauckel's appointment, "manhunts took place in streets, at motion picture houses, even at churches and at night in private houses." More than seven and a half million people were forcibly deported from Nazi-occupied territories to Germany to support the war effort.[2] A significant number of these civilian forced laborers were the nearly three million young adults and minors, most of them female, who were captured by the Nazis in the Soviet Union beginning in March 1942.[3]

Pursuant to Sauckel's directive, German industries were encouraged, but not required, to bid for forced laborers in order to meet production quotas.[4] When Elsa arrived in Wuppertal, she was purchased like a common beast of burden by a representative of *Ford-Werke*.[5]

Sixty years later, Iwanowa—seventy-six years old and living in Antwerp, Belgium—describes what happened next:

> They took us by truck to the Ford plant in Cologne. We were just children, we were frightened, calling out for our mothers, crying all the time. At first, they told us it would only be for a few months and then we would go home, but they lied to us, they never let us go. At Ford, we were treated like dogs, thrown into a barracks without any heat, running water or sewage. It was freezing in the winter, terrible, just terrible. The bunks had no mattresses, just wooden planks with a little straw and they only fed us a bowl of cabbage and water broth twice a day with a slice of bread. We were always hungry. I sat all day dreaming about food. If you asked for seconds, they would beat you.
>
> I was forced to work from seven in the morning until seven at night drilling holes in engine blocks while the foremen, who were like animals, supervised us. We had no names, only numbers. Whenever a worker got sick, they took them away. We later heard they were shot. If we didn't meet our quota, we were beaten.[6]

Elsa Iwanowa was just one of thousands of forced laborers who toiled under brutal conditions at *Ford-Werke* during the Second World War. According to a postwar U.S. military investigation, as much as 40 percent of the total workforce during 1943 and 1944 were "foreigners." Approximately one-third of those were Russian POWs, while another third consisted of Russian civilians such as Iwanowa.[7] The balance of the foreign workers came from other countries the Nazis had conquered. French, Dutch, Belgian, Polish, and Yugoslav prisoners were separated by nationality in different compounds. A prisoner's ethnic origin appeared to be the determining factor in how he or she was treated. According to former *Ford-Werke* toolmaker Fritz Theilen, who was German, "The French weren't treated so badly, but Poles, and Russians and Yugoslavs, those were the so-called sub-humans."[8] In the "New Order" he described in *Mein Kampf*,

Hitler had long ago envisioned the Slavic peoples as a service caste, eter- nally subordinate to their Aryan masters.[9]

For more than half a century, the series of events that brought Elsa Iwanowa and thousands of other forced laborers to *Ford-Werke* had never been brought to light. While most other German-based American companies had been seized by the Nazis as "enemy property" after Pearl Harbor, the *Ford-Werke* plant continued operating for months as if nothing had changed. This wasn't mere happenstance, but the result of concerted efforts on the part of its se- nior executives to protect Dearborn's financial interests.

Two weeks before the Japanese sneak attack, board chairman Heinrich Albert had recognized the signals and was already taking preemptive action to safeguard the company's independence in the event that the United States entered the war. In a memo written November 25, 1941, Albert argued that Ford should be spared from Nazi control even if the Americans declare war on Germany. He makes a convincing case for continued association with the American parent company, reasoning that, with Dearborn's assistance, *Ford-Werke* had been a strong supporter of the Nazi war effort from the begin- ning, and there was no reason this relationship could not continue. Moreover, he argued, a continuing link to Dearborn meant a number of eco- nomic advantages for *Ford-Werke* and for the Nazis:

> Among the reasons speaking against a complete Germaniza- tion of the capital, the first one is the excellent sales organization which, thanks to its connection with the American company, is at the disposal of the German *Ford Werke* . . . As long as *Ford Werke* A.G. have an American majority, it will be possible to bring the remaining European Ford companies under German influ- ence. . . . As soon as the American majority is eliminated, each Ford company in every country will fight for its individual exis- tence. . . . A majority, even if it is only a small one, of the Ameri- cans is essential for the actually free transmittal of the newest American models as well as for the insight into American produc- tion and sales methods.[10]

Albert's arguments were persuasive. By December 1941, 250 American firms operating in Germany owned more than $450 million in German assets. Ranked sixteenth by investment holdings, Ford held 1.9 percent of the total American investment.[11] In the months following Pearl Harbor, the Nazis declared most of those companies "enemy property" and incorporated many into the *Hermann Göring Werke*, a giant industrial combine set up by Göring when he was placed in charge of the Nazis' four-year plan. But while the assets of one American company after another were seized by the Nazis, *Ford-Werke* was somehow spared, its shares remaining in the hands of Dearborn.

After the war, *Ford-Werke*'s deputy board chairman Carl Krauch was tried at Nuremberg for war crimes in connection with his directorship of IG Farben, the company that at one time controlled 15 percent of *Ford-Werke* stock.[12] During his 1946 interrogation by Allied investigators, Krauch provided a telling explanation for German Ford's inexplicable continuing independence after almost every other American company was taken over by the Nazis:

> I myself knew Henry Ford and admired him. I went to see Göring personally about that. I told Göring that I myself knew his son Edsel, too, and I told Göring that if we took Ford independence away from them in Germany, it would aggrieve friendly relations with American industry in the future. I counted on a lot of success for the adaptation of American methods in Germany's industries, but that could be done only in friendly cooperation. Göring listened to me and then he said, "I agree. I shall see to it that the German Ford Company will not be incorporated in the Hermann Göring Company." So I participated regularly in the supervisory board meetings to inform myself about the business processes of Henry Ford and, if possible, to take a stand for the Henry Ford Works after the war had begun. Thus, we succeeded in keeping the Ford Works working and operating independently of our government's seizure.[13]

For several months, the plant operated independently, producing military vehicles at a remarkable rate with virtually no government interference. Its allegiances, however, were clear. In March 1942, company manager Robert Schmidt penned a motivational plea to his employees in the company's internal organ: "It depends upon our work whether the front can be supplied with its necessities . . . therefore, we too are soldiers of the Führer."

The industrial sector was, by now, inseparable from Germany's war machine. Finally, in May 1942, the plant's autonomy was curtailed slightly when the Cologne Superior Court declared *Ford-Werke* to be an "enter-

prise under authoritative enemy influence" and demanded the appointment of a trustee.[14] However, unlike most foreign companies so designated, which saw the selection of a Nazi-appointed custodian to safeguard
the *Reich's* interests, the authorities saw no need to impose an outsider. In a
February 1942 letter to the Nazi Party leadership, the Party's regional economic adviser in Cologne recommended appointing Schmidt himself as
custodian because of the "German character" of *Ford-Werke* and his "confidence" in Schmidt, who had always been a willing and obedient servant of
the führer. Nor did the trusteeship entail any change in Dearborn's majority ownership. All profits and dividends would simply be placed in an
escrow account for distribution to the American parent company after the
war.

The new arrangement couldn't have been more satisfactory for the
company, considering how little actually changed. Schmidt was merely
required to report to the Reich commissioner every three months and seek
approval before determining profit margins. Government regulations also
required that *Ford-Werke* management obtain permission from the Reich
commissioner before purchasing or disposing of property and assets.

Under Schmidt's continued management, Ford Germany amassed
huge profits without interruption, operating its production lines in full service to the Nazi military effort. Of the 350,000 trucks which the motorized
German army possessed in 1942, at least 120,000 were built by Ford.[15]

With a significant portion of the German male work force called into
armed service, the plant was in desperate need of labor in order to keep up
its extraordinary output and maintain rapidly rising profits. As the war progressed, the company lost a significant portion of its workers to the military
draft and, with the government demanding a rise in production quotas, the
labor shortage was becoming more acute.[16] The minutes of *Ford-Werke's*
custodial advisory council in January 1943 illustrate the company's growing
concern: "The labor question has gotten extraordinarily difficult. Military
recruitment is no longer sparing our key people."[17]

The Nazis were all too willing to provide a solution.

In August 1944, Nazi armaments minister Albert Speer ruled that the
automotive industry was essential to the German war effort and decided to
make 12,000 concentration camp inmates available to ensure that the
industry produced up to its maximal capacity. Following a meeting
between Robert Schmidt and the head of the German Automotive Industry Economic Group in August, the nearby Buchenwald concentration
camp drew up a list of prisoners to be sent to work at *Ford-Werke*.[18]
Buchenwald was one of the most notorious of the Nazi prison camps and
had become one of the largest labor-exploitation centers in Europe, supplying slave laborers to a number of German industries, including IG Far-

ben, which maintained a factory there. After Schmidt paid the SS an undis-closed sum to purchase the inmates, fifty were delivered to the Ford plant, although it is impossible to determine how many of these inmates were Jews.[19] Right through to the end of the war, Buchenwald prisoners would continue to be dispatched to the Cologne plant.

Contrary to common myth, the company was not compelled to employ slave laborers or concentration camp inmates, nor were they automatically assigned these workers by the regime. Rather, Ford had to "purchase" the workers or fill out an application with Nazi authorities, detailing the com-pany's needs. Like the German industrialist Oskar Schindler—the real-life subject of Steven Spielberg's epic film—*Ford-Werke* had the choice to treat its laborers humanely. Instead, it chose to exploit them as slaves. According to German historian Mark Spoerer, an authority on wartime forced labor, "Normally, a company had quite a lot of discretion." He explains that "a firm which treated its workers decently could always find an excuse" because this was simply conducive to efficient armaments production on behalf of the Nazi regime.[20]

In a postwar interrogation, Robert Schmidt claimed that the forced laborers from the East were paid a monthly wage based on about 1.28 *reichsmarks* per hour. Documents retained by the plant suggest that a pay-roll record was indeed maintained for many of the forced laborers but that a substantial percentage was deducted from the workers' "wages" for taxes as well as for food, clothing, and lodging supposedly provided by *Ford-Werke*. Some foreign prisoners later reported that they were in fact given "a few Marks."[21] But, according to Elsa Iwanowa, "I never received any money in the three years I worked for Ford. Nothing. Never."[22] Other forced laborers working at the Cologne plant told a similar story in oral histories collected after the war.

In early March 1945, as the Allies pushed relentlessly across Germany, American troops exchanged fire with German soldiers on the opposite bank of the Rhine, damaging a portion of the *Ford-Werke* plant in the pro-cess. After a short battle, the Allies took Cologne on March 6, two months before the Nazi High Command surrendered, ending the war in Europe. When American troops entered *Ford-Werke*, they found more than five hundred foreign workers still confined behind barbed wire; hundreds more had already escaped days earlier during the battle for Cologne. Elsa Iwanowa was still at the plant on March 7 when an American army unit told her she was free to go. "It was the happiest day of my life," she recalls. "The nightmare was over. I truly believed I would die at Ford before I would be set free."[23] A report by U.S. Occupation authorities three days later revealed that conditions at the plant were "foul in the extreme and most of the Russian women were reported to be suffering from VD," suggesting they had been raped by their captors.[24] Most of the foreign workers, including Elsa, were sent to displaced-persons camps operated by the United States army.[25]

Allied intelligence had long known that *Ford-Werke* was a vital part of the German war machine but had decided recriminations would have to wait until the war was won. Rather than close down the plant, its resources would be channeled by the Allies to helping defeat Germany. Less than three weeks after the plant's liberation, a U.S. army officer met with Schmidt to discuss using it for servicing American army vehicles. On April 27, eleven days before V-E Day, occupation authorities authorized the plant to begin assembling trucks for the U.S. army. On May 8, the day after the Nazis officially surrendered, an American documentary camera crew recorded the first post-war truck coming off the *Ford-Werke* assembly line.[26]

As early as March 10, a combined British and American intelligence team had begun investigating the plant's complicity in the Nazi war effort. The team questioned a number of forced laborers and German *Ford-Werke* employees and interviewed Robert Schmidt on several occasions. On June 9, Schmidt was arrested and taken into custody by American military authorities, though not in connection with his tenure as wartime plant manger of *Ford-Werke*. Rather, the arrest order stated that he was to be "held for questioning in connection with the IG Farben investigation."[27]

The full extent of Farben's crimes was just beginning to emerge as the world learned the horrifying truth about the Nazi Final Solution. Soon, the name Auschwitz was indelibly linked with history's most monstrous crime and it was clear to Allied investigators that IG Farben was, more than any other company, complicit in the events that would soon be referred to as the Holocaust.

The chairman of IG Farben was Carl Krauch, who was also deputy chairman of the *Ford-Werke* board. Krauch was appointed to his position at *Ford-Werke* not by the Nazis but by Ford, with the full knowledge and consent of Dearborn. It seemed clear that Ford's connection to Farben ran deep. The chemical giant owned as much as 15 percent of *Ford-Werke* stock and until 1941, Edsel Ford had sat on the board of Farben's American subsidiary, General Aniline & Film, which was later exposed as a Nazi front.

Farben's culpability for the Holocaust extended far beyond the fact that its rubber factory made up an integral part of the Auschwitz concentration camp complex. Investigators soon discovered that, with Krauch's knowledge, an IG Farben subsidiary, *Degesch*, manufactured a poisonous gas known as *Zyklon B*, which was used by the Nazis in Auschwitz and other death camps to exterminate hundreds of thousands of Jews and other prisoners. At Nuremberg, Krauch was charged with crimes against humanity and with enslaving and murdering civilian populations. During his subsequent trial, little was said about his high-level connection to Ford.[28]

Schmidt was interrogated by Allied investigators for more than three months. He was compelled to write a series of affidavits detailing his knowledge of Farben's activities as well as *Ford-Werke*'s wartime operations, before authorities finally released him in September.

On September 5, 1945, a civilian investigator for the U.S. army named Henry Schneider issued a devastating report outlining Dearborn's role in its German subsidiary's complicity with the Nazi war machine. The report charged that *Ford-Werke*'s American ties had made it "a valuable asset to the Reich" and that "without continuing American technological assistance, German Ford might have lost most or all of its value."[29] Even before the war, Schneider concluded, *Ford-Werke* "had, *with Dearborn's consent*, become an arsenal of Nazism."[30]

Schneider reveals that the company had sought to win military contracts for the Reich as early as 1936. Once war came, "German Ford stepped into the position of a major supplier of vehicles" for the army. "Ford trucks prominently present in the supply lines of the Wehrmacht were understandably an unpleasant sight to men in our Army," he writes. In addition, "as much as 7 or 8 percent of total output during the war years consisted of more specialized war material."

Schneider's report touches only briefly on the use of forced labor: "As was common in other German enterprises, Ford increasingly resorted to use of prisoners of war and other slave labor . . . The foreigners employed rose to over 40 percent of its labor supply in 1944. The usual Nazi discriminations in wages and working conditions were practiced."[31]

When the investigators' findings were made public, they received little attention from the German-based American media corps, whose attention had been captivated by a more sensational wartime story—the emergence of almost daily revelations of Nazi monstrosities and the inconceivably horrific plan described as the Final Solution. One story that did register with the American press was the discovery of Heinrich Albert's November 1941 memo asking whether a Nazi takeover of *Ford-Werke* would be "necessary or advisable" should the United States enter the war. The influential syndicated columnist Drew Pearson exposed the Albert memo in a July 1945 column headlined, "How Ford Helped Nazis." But it failed to gain broader notice because it appeared on July 17, the same day President Truman met Stalin and Churchill at Potsdam to discuss how to deal with the defeated Germany.[32] For more than half a century, Ford largely escaped the consequences of its business dealings with the Nazis. The world soon forgot about Ford and other American corporations that conducted business as usual while Hitler was building up his powerful war machine. But one woman wouldn't forget.

On March 4, 1998, fifty-three years after she was liberated from the German Ford plant, Elsa Iwanowa demanded justice, filing a class-action lawsuit in U.S. District Court against the Ford Motor Company and its German subsidiary. She demanded compensation on behalf of herself and the thousands of other forced laborers who were compelled to work at *Ford-Werke* during the Second World War under "utterly barbarous conditions." Four months earlier, German courts had lifted the statute of limitations on such lawsuits, permitting slave laborers to seek compensation for the first time.

In a court submission responding to her suit, the Ford Motor Company acknowledged that Iwanowa and others were "forced to endure a sad and terrible experience" at its German plant but maintained that redressing such "tragedies" should be "a nation-to-nation, government-to-government concern."[33] Dearborn maintained that it bore no responsibility for their plight.

At first, Ford claimed that it did not profit in any way from forced labor at its Cologne plant. Ford spokesman John Spellich publicly defended the company's decision to maintain business ties with Nazi Germany on the grounds that the U.S. government continued to have diplomatic relations with Berlin up until the Japanese attack on Pearl Harbor in December 1941.[34] But a few months after the suit was filed, the company did a sudden about-face. Spellich told the *Washington Post* that company historians found documents showing that after the war, Dearborn had indeed received dividend payments for profits accrued at *Ford-Werke* between 1940 and 1943. Meanwhile, the BBC had broadcast a documentary about the use of slave labor at *Ford-Werke*. To a company that had always bragged about its contribution to the Allied war effort, the headlines were devastating. The company's strenuous attempts to restore friendly relations with the Jewish community, which included contributions in the millions to Jewish causes, had made Henry Ford's hate campaigns seem the misguided obsessions of a cranky old eccentric. Now, with revelations that its entire board of directors had approved dealings with the Nazi regime, fresh horrors were awakened. Something had to be done.

A damage control team was assembled in 1998 to discuss how best to address the serious issues raised by the Iwanowa lawsuit and stem the public relations nightmare it had created. Calls went out from corporate watchdog groups for an independent investigation into the company's wartime role, but the company rejected them. It chose instead to conduct an internal investigation, carefully controlled from within, and appointed a team of forty-five researchers, historians, and archivists, promising an "exhaustive and uncompromising assessment regarding accusations of profiteering, collaboration and the use of forced and slave labor." To avoid accusations of a whitewash, the company hired an outside consultant, University of Pittsburgh political science professor Simon Reich, to "assist in locating materials, to read and comment on the research team's findings, and to ensure that the report was an accurate reflection of the materials collected." Another academic consultant, Lawrence Dowler, was hired as an expert on research methodology.

In truth, the company had little choice but to conduct this investigation. As much as being an inescapable public relations exercise, it needed to determine the facts to avoid any unpleasant surprises when the Iwanowa case went to court. At stake were billions of dollars in potential damages and untold lost profits. But in September 1999, a U.S. federal judge dismissed the class-action suit—not on its merits, but because he ruled the resolution of such matters should be left to international treaties between countries.[35] Iwanowa's lawyers appealed the judgment, confident it would be overturned. But on the eve of the appeal in late 1999, a number of German and American companies agreed to a five-billion-dollar international settlement of slave labor and Holocaust-related claims. As part of the settlement, all outstanding class action suits were dropped and Iwanowa's appeal was moot. To its credit, Ford continued with its internal investigation and promised to release the team's findings, whatever they revealed.

The company made good on its promise two years later but it chose a strange time to go public with its findings. On December 6, 2001—at the height of the U.S. war in Afghanistan when the media and most Americans were paying attention to other matters—the Ford Motor Company held a press conference to release its 198-page report, entitled "Research Findings About *Ford-Werke* under the Nazi Regime."[36] Did the company rush its report to take advantage of the media's distraction with the War on Terror? Company spokesperson Tom Hoyt steadfastly refused to answer any questions concerning the chronology of the report's release, nor would he disclose when the company came to the decision to release its report on the date in question, although it's certainly possible the timing is coincidental.[37]

Contrary to expectations, the report itself came to no conclusions, explaining in its preface that it "consciously tries to avoid interpretation" and allows readers to draw their own conclusions. But at the press conference called to unveil the final report, Ford sent the company's chief of staff John Rintamaki to "spin" the findings for journalists who had no time to read the full report and its 98,000 accompanying pages in order to come to their own conclusions. "The use of forced and slave labor in Germany, including at *Ford-Werke*, was wrong and cannot be justified," Rintamaki told the assembled media. "In looking back, it must be remembered that all companies operating in Germany at that time had to use labor provided by the German government, and that the Nazi regime chose to provide forced and slave laborers to industry. By being open and honest about the past, even when we find the subject reprehensible, we hope to contribute toward a better understanding of this period of history."[38]

The journalists had no reason to doubt Rintamaki's claim; the next day, they dutifully reported the company's assertion that *Ford-Werke* had no other choice but to use slave labor. But a careful reading of the report and its accompanying source material reveals Rintamaki's assertion—that the company had to use forced labor provided by the government—does not stand up under scrutiny. The slave laborers were in fact there at the behest of *Ford-Werke*, not the Nazis.

One of the most disturbing revelations in the report was never addressed in the press conference, nor in the media release that accompanied the report. Repeatedly, the company has emphasized that it lost control over *Ford-Werke* after Pearl Harbor and therefore can't be held responsible for what happened. When he was asked by a reporter about the company's responsibility for the use of forced labor, Rintamaki responded that what happened at Ford Germany was "a process we could not influence or control."[39] But, according to the documentation accompanying the report, the first forced laborers arrived at the plant *before* the United States entered the war, as early as September 1940, when between 100 and 200 French prisoners of war were requisitioned by the company to help fill a government contract to build army barge motors, in violation of Article 31 of the Geneva Convention governing prisoners of war. The 1929 convention, agreed to by Germany, stated, "Work done by prisoners of war shall have no direct connection with the operations of the war."[40] These prisoners were among the more than one million French citizens detained for forced labor by the Nazis after the fall of France in June and made available to companies that requested their services. At this time, Dearborn still controlled the German company.

Rintamaki's assertion that *Ford-Werke*'s hands were tied on the matter of slave labor also does not hold up under scrutiny. German historian Karola Fings ascribes such arguments to the collective denial of guilt by scores of firms that used morally unacceptable means to profit from the war. In *Working for the Enemy*, her book about forced labor in the auto industry during World War II, Fings writes, "The corporations that made use of forced labor during the war met any and all accusations in later decades with a defense borrowed from the Nuremberg Trial defendants. They argued that the Nazi state forced companies to accept slaves, that businesses were left with no choice and no influence in the matter. A long series of studies have exploded this myth."[41]

In the most detailed study ever conducted on the use of wartime forced labor in German industry, historian Mark Spoerer discovered that the companies almost always lobbied the government to supply forced laborers, rather than the other way around. In only one of the twenty-four cases Spoerer studied did the German state actually coerce a private company to use forced labor. Even more significantly, he discovered five separate cases where the Nazi regime proposed the use of slave labor but was unable to force the German companies to comply. Thus, it was possible for a company to refuse the use of forced labor without repercussions.[42]

For, in fact, the country had no genuine labor shortage. Companies manufacturing for the German war effort always had another choice. They could have chosen to employ the large available supply of German women to work in their plants—a business strategy implemented with great success by the Allied countries in their own defense industries. A substantial amount of forced laborers in Germany, after all, were foreign women and girls. But these companies would have had to pay German women a living wage, thereby cutting into corporate profits. The use of forced labor, therefore, appears to have been motivated by greed rather than necessity.

Indeed, neither Rintamaki nor the Ford Motor Company has been able to provide any evidence that Ford was forced by the Nazi regime to use slave labor.[43] The report's accompanying documentation, in fact, makes it clear that it was *Ford-Werke* that requested additional forced laborers from the government. Even if the company felt pressured to use forced labor in order to meet increased government production quotas, no one was able to point me to a single piece of evidence that proves it was the Nazis who were responsible for most of the brutal treatment of the slave laborers within the plant. The Eastern workers were beaten, raped, forced to live through the winter with no heat and given the most meager of food rations by *Ford-Werke*—at a time when the company was reaping unprecedented profits from their labor.

Possibly in an attempt to absolve himself of responsibility for war crimes, Robert Schmidt would claim after his 1945 arrest that the Gestapo had taken over "the housing and feeding of all workers, foreign and German.[44] However, Elsa Iwanowa and other forced laborers dispute this and the research team failed to produce any independent evidence to verify Schmidt's claims.[45] Moreover, the company first began to employ forced labor in 1940, two years before the Gestapo had any jurisdiction there.

It is true that, after Pearl Harbor, Nazi guidelines officially required the supervisor of the eastern forced laborers to be jointly appointed by the Gestapo and the German Labor Front. But like many such Nazi rules, an exception appears to have been made for Ford. In a July 13, 1942, letter to the Gestapo, a *Ford-Werke* employee named Werner Buch informed the secret state police force that if the Gestapo approved, the company had chosen its own candidate, Josef Wierscheim, to oversee the Eastern workers. Permission for Wierscheim's appointment was duly received.[46] This left a Ford employee, rather than a Nazi official, in charge of Elsa and other Russian forced laborers. This conforms to a pattern repeated throughout the war. *Ford-Werke* consistently received permission from German government authorities to run its own affairs, with minimal interference from the Nazi regime. Although some slave laborers reported the occasional presence of Gestapo officials and other Nazis at the Cologne plant, most of the Nazis appear to have performed a security role rather than in a day-to-day supervisory capacity.[47] When a prisoner attempted to escape, the Gestapo was called in to interrogate and punish the offender. When a worker showed any anti-Nazi tendencies, the Gestapo moved in. Iwanowa says most of the guards were in fact fellow prisoners or German "gendarmes" who did not wear the Nazi badge.[48] The Ford Motor Company and the investigative team have failed to provide any evidence demonstrating that the Nazis were directly responsible for the inhuman treatment of the Eastern prisoners.[49]

A substantial portion of the *Ford-Werke* slave labor report relies on the postwar affidavits of Robert Schmidt and Heinrich Albert, who were both interrogated by Allied investigators after the war. Both men, of course, had a clear interest in downplaying their own involvement in the crimes of the Reich. When I asked the Ford Motor Company whether it made any independent attempt to verify their claims, a company spokesperson pointed out that the investigation team, led by the company's chief archivist, employed a typical archival approach to gathering evidence. I was referred to an accompanying report.

"For the archivist, the aim is to copy any relevant document, rather than read and evaluate each piece of evidence," wrote Lawrence Dowler, who was hired by Ford to supervise the team's research methods.[50] In other words, the report was not so much an investigation looking for specific answers as an attempt to locate all relevant material and let readers draw their own conclusions. This makes Rintamaki's subsequent attempts at spin all the more troubling since he effectively made claims to the media that are not necessarily backed up in the actual research findings.

One thing appears clear from the report. After Pearl Harbor, as Ford claims, Dearborn did lose effective day-to-day control over the *Ford-Werke* plant. According to Simon Reich, the consultant hired to oversee the project, the plant's relationship with Dearborn became increasingly "attenuated" during the 1930s and nonexistent after Pearl Harbor.[51] Reich makes the point that, "short of divestment by the American parent, Ford's German managers had little choice but to try to address Nazi demands."[52] This may or may not be true. A significant body of evidence shows that it was Ford Germany, with the full consent of Dearborn, that solicited the Nazis to begin awarding the company military contracts in the first place. The Nazis never in fact forced the company to manufacture on behalf of its military machine. But, for the sake of argument, it can be assumed that the government may have eventually compelled the company to assist the German war effort. If that had happened, as Reich argues, Dearborn would have been left with only two choices. The parent company would either be forced to comply with government demands or divest its German holdings, sacrificing potentially large profits.

In 1940, of course, Henry Ford and his company chose "principles" over profits, opting to give up the British Rolls-Royce engine contract because of his alleged reluctance to "manufacture for a foreign belligerent," thereby sacrificing millions of dollars in lost revenues. Before Pearl Harbor, when it still controlled its German subsidiary, Dearborn could have done the same thing, refusing to participate in the German war effort. Instead, as Reich acknowledges, "Ford did absolutely everything they could to ingratiate themselves to the Nazi state."[53]

Reich maintains that after 1939, the German subsidiary acted with growing autonomy from the American parent company, which was "often ill-informed" about activities in Germany.[54] This assertion is certainly not borne out by a letter *Ford-Werke* chairman Heinrich Albert sent Edsel Ford in July 1940, seeking permission to hire Albert's own son to work at the Cologne plant.[55] This evidence of Dearborn micromanagement almost a year after the war began hardly demonstrates the German subsidiary's growing autonomy.

It is almost impossible to ascertain exactly how much Dearborn knew about the German plant's activities before and after Pearl Harbor. The Ford research team had access to more than one hundred letters exchanged between *Ford-Werke* and Dearborn before Pearl Harbor, and Reich insists there is no evidence in the letters to indicate that the parent company knew about the use of forced labor.[56] But this paper trail doesn't reveal the whole story. In September 1940, V. Y. Tallberg, a former chief inspector at the Cologne plant, sailed from Germany to the United States with instructions from *Ford-Werke* management to "tell the people in Dearborn how conditions were and what we were doing in the plant."[57] No record exists about what he reported but it is likely that Dearborn was much better informed about the activities of its German plant than the surviving documentation would suggest.

In fact, the possibility of missing documents was the only real constraint faced by Reich and the Ford research team. "We could only work with what was there," says Reich.[58] However, it is impossible to determine how much wartime documentation is actually missing from the company's archives. The recollections of former Chrysler chairman Lee Iacocca—who began his automotive career at the Ford Motor Company in the 1950s working under Edsel's son, Henry Ford II—suggests there may be a great deal. In his 1984 autobiography, Iacocca recalls his employer's attitude about preserving company documentation: "Henry actually used to boast that he never kept any files. Every now and then he would burn all his papers. He told me, 'That stuff can only hurt you. Some day you could be crucified for keeping all that stuff.'"[59]

Although it acknowledges that it had a controlling financial stake in the plant throughout the war, the Ford Motor Company has always claimed that it lost all communication with *Ford-Werke* after Pearl Harbor and therefore had no knowledge of, or responsibility for, its activities after December 7, 1941. But in 1944, a former *Ford-Werke* employee named Oscar Bornheim told U.S. military authorities that former plant co-manager Erhard Vitger had "been in communication via radio-telephone with the Detroit offices of the Ford Motor Company" subsequent to 1942.[60] If true, this would have represented a serious violation of U.S. Trading With the Enemy laws, presenting grounds for prosecution of the parent company. However, there was no way of proving the allegation and authorities were forced to drop the investigation. Nevertheless, it underscores a point that the company has been anxious to downplay since the charges of wartime Nazi complicity first surfaced. Unlike most other American corporations operating in Germany after America entered the war, *Ford-Werke* was not actually run by Nazis; it was still being operated by longtime Ford employees, most of them hired by Dearborn more than a decade earlier and fiercely loyal to the parent company's interests. In an affidavit supporting Elsa Iwanowa's slave labor lawsuit, *Ford-Werke*'s wartime head of production Hans Grande denied that the Nazis were calling the shots:

> We on the floor, we didn't have the impression we were working for the Government but that we were still owned by the [American] shareholders and that we were working for Ford, for the Ford Motor Company.[61]

Grande, who went on to become Ford's vice president of European operations after the war, acknowledged that "Our first priority was to look after the company's interests, even after Pearl Harbor."[62]

In an effort to absolve Dearborn from any responsibility, Ford has painted itself as an unwitting victim of the Nazi regime. According to Simon Reich, "The evidence provided by the data suggests that there was no complicity on the part of Ford's Dearborn management in assisting the Nazi government's wartime effort."[63] This is a carefully worded, and potentially misleading, statement that lends a subjective interpretation to a report from which readers are supposed to "draw their own conclusions." Reich may be correct that no evidence exists proving Dearborn directly aided the Nazi war effort, but this is true only after the United States joined the war. There is substantial evidence that, before December 1941, Dearborn was highly complicit in strengthening the German war machine, becoming, in the words of a postwar U.S. military report, "an arsenal of Nazism."

"I think there is a big difference in my own mind between if you were actively involved in the manufacture of chemicals for gas chambers or if you were actively involved in the manufacture of trucks," declares Reich, overlooking Ford's close political and financial relationship with its part-owner, IG Farben, the company that manufactured the chemicals for the gas chambers.[64] Moreover, *Ford-Werke* was manufacturing more than just trucks. According to a U.S. military investigation, as much as 8 percent of the company's total wartime output was devoted to more specialized war munitions materiel, including the turbine for the V-2 rockets that killed thousands of civilians in London during the Blitz.[65]

Certainly no one has called into question Reich's integrity. Indeed, the investigation itself appears to have been very thorough and there is no indication that the company is trying to cover up its wartime past. However, it is the interpretation of the report's findings that is most crucial to an objective assessment of Ford's wartime role. The Ford Motor Company has repeatedly bragged about its "transparency" during this investigation, arguing correctly that it has been more open than any other U.S. company operating in Germany during the war. But critics have pointed out that hiring a paid consultant such as Simon Reich to provide an interpretation of the team's research data undermines the objectivity of the report itself, much like doctors who make a career of testifying for the plaintiff in medical malpractice cases. Reich's six-page commentary—which describes his involvement and offers his opinion about the research team's findings—was released by Ford in December 2001 to accompany the team's 144-page report of their findings. Ford refuses to disclose how much it paid Reich to participate in the investigation and "comment on the research team's findings." At the same time it released its findings, the Ford Motor Company also announced that it has hired Reich to assist in setting up a new center for the study of human rights issues with a two-million-dollar endowment from Ford.[66] Thus, the independent consultant hired by Ford to evaluate its slave labor practices remains on the company payroll.[67]

In December 2001, New York University law professor Burt Neuborne told the *Los Angeles Times* that no conclusions can be drawn about Ford's wartime conduct until a fully independent review of the documents could be made.[68]

As the first independent researcher to access the documentation accompanying the report, I spent weeks examining a significant portion of the 98,000 pages of source material deposited by the research team at the Ford Museum archives, following the completion of its investigation. An exhaustive review of these documents raised as many questions as they answered, and I requested an interview with John Rintamaki to clarify some of the claims he made at the December 2001 press conference. But, although the company made Rintamaki available to reporters on December 6—before any of them had a chance to examine the documentation— my request was refused. "Mr. Rintamaki has nothing to add to what has already been released or stated at the briefing with news media on Dec. 6, 2001 when the report was released," responded Ford spokesperson Tom Hoyt.[69] Instead, I was asked to submit any questions I had in writing. When I did so, I still received no direct answers or elaboration, only an email referring me to relevant sections of the report that still did not answer my questions.

One of the most contentious issues raised by the report is the company's claim that it did not profit from forced labor. At the press conference, Rintamaki stated, "The statements that we profited, that Ford U.S. profited, from Ford Germany are just not true." However, a close examination of the documentation accompanying the report appears to suggest otherwise. As part of the investigation, Ford hired the accounting firm PricewaterhouseCoopers to conduct an independent analysis of the company's financial activities during the war. The results are revealing.

According to its findings, *Ford-Werke* reaped a substantial net profit of 9,605,519 *reichsmarks* ($3,626,207 U.S.)[70] between 1939 and 1943. In 1944, the last full year of the war, the company suffered a net loss of 2,731,689 *reichsmarks* ($1,092,675 U.S.). This means that the company realized an overall net operating profit of $2,533,532 U.S. during the entire wartime period up until the end of 1944. In 1945, *Ford-Werke* suffered another large operating loss due to the military defeat of its biggest client. However, the company only operated under the Nazis during the first two months of the year so it would be misleading to count its 1945 loss in the wartime calculations.[71] Even if the full 1945 loss is counted, the company still enjoyed a substantial net operating profit of well over one million U.S. dollars during the war years.

The foundation underlying Ford's argument that it did not profit from *Ford-Werke* stems from losses it allegedly incurred in the heavy Allied bombing of the Cologne plant during the closing months of the war. But in fact, according to the post-war account of Robert Schmidt, the plant suffered relatively minor damage and its production facilities remained largely unaffected.[72] Two decades after the war ended, the U.S. government implemented a war-damages claim commission that allowed Dearborn to submit claims for bombing losses and other lost revenues it sustained at its German and Austrian plants. In 1965, the Ford Motor Company submitted a claim to the commission in the amount of $7,050,052. Two years later, the government awarded the company $785,321 for its share of allowable losses under the program.[73] Ford appears to base part of its claim that it did not profit from *Ford-Werke* on the fact that it only received 10 percent of its damage claims in compensation. However, this statistic is very misleading.

Some of the company's damage claims stem from Allied bombing of its slave labor barracks. Presumably, these barracks were no longer required after the war ended so these claims are moot.

The question of whether or not Ford profited from its German wartime operations rests on extremely complex accounting principles. When I asked Ford for permission to interview the PricewaterhouseCoopers accountant who supervised the financial review, in order to clarify its findings and to confirm Ford's claim that it never profited from *Ford-Werke*, I was refused. Certainly, nowhere in the PricewaterhouseCoopers report does it explicitly state that Ford did not profit during the war.

In March 1998, John Rintamaki told the BBC that Dearborn had looked at the records and "As far as we can tell, Ford did not receive any profits or dividends from its operations in Cologne."[74] But, according to the findings of the research team, the company did indeed collect dividends after the war based on its German subsidiary's wartime profits. When war came, states the report, the German government blocked payment of dividends to *Ford-Werke*. Instead, the money was safeguarded in an escrow account to be paid to the American parent company after the war. Between 1939 and 1943, *Ford-Werke* declared a total of $600,000 U.S. in dividends. Dearborn's share of these were not paid out until 1951. By this time, the German government had established a new currency, the *deutschmark*, devaluing the old *reichsmark* by 90 percent. This left Dearborn's share of *Ford-Werke* dividends at $60,000 U.S., which the company used to purchase its outstanding shares back from IG Farben after the chemical conglomerate was liquidated by the courts because of the company's complicity in Nazi war crimes. These additional shares are today worth tens of millions of dollars to Dearborn.[75]

Today, the Ford Motor Company points to this dividend payment as the only direct wartime profit it realized from *Ford-Werke*. However, the dividend only tells a small part of the story. In the same Pricewaterhouse-Coopers report, financial investigators revealed that the total value of *Ford-Werke* had increased an impressive 14 percent during the war.[76] It is this statistic that Elsa Iwanowa's attorney Mel Weiss says is most significant. During the war years, *Ford-Werke* reinvested most of its profits to increase production capacity, which directly benefited Dearborn after the war when it regained control of its German subsidiary. The increased value, he argues, is an indirect profit—much of it derived from the use of forced labor: "If the case had gone to court, it would have been extremely easy to prove that Ford profited, despite all their accounting mumbo jumbo that claims otherwise."[77] Weiss says that Ford was eager to demand compensation from the U.S. government after the war for "losses" due to bomb damage to its German plants and therefore should also be responsible for any benefits derived from forced labor:[78] "They were out to profit, pure and simple, and they didn't care how it was earned or who was abused in the process."[79] Immediately after the war, he notes, "*Ford-Werke* continued to produce trucks at substantial profit at a time when much of Europe was devastated, benefiting from economic reserves and production capacity that had, in large part, been derived from the work of unpaid, forced laborers."[80] Weiss notes that today, *Ford-Werke* is the headquarters for the Ford Motor Company's entire European operations, which produce billions of dollars in annual revenues.

Even if, as the company claims, Dearborn didn't profit from *Ford-Werke*'s wartime activities, it fails to acknowledge the profits it realized from other Ford subsidiaries such as Ford France that did significant business with the Nazis during the war. According to business historians Mira Wilkins and Frank Hill in their 1964 study *American Business Abroad*, "The [Ford] European companies operated at a handsome profit in all years except 1945." They estimated that the Ford family's net paper profit from these operations during the war years came to just under $11 million U.S.[81] However, the *Ford-Werke* research team was not asked to determine the extent of profits realized by the company at other Ford companies operating in Nazi-occupied Europe. As a result, the company appears to have deliberately ignored the big picture by simply claiming that it did not profit from its wartime Nazi business dealings *in Germany*.

The press conference called by company officials to herald the report's release focused on the activities of *Ford-Werke* and slave labor. Many news accounts the following day simply reiterated Ford's claim that it did not profit from its German plant and that it had lost control of *Ford-Werke* after Pearl Harbor. The casual reader could have easily come to the conclusion that the company had been vindicated by the report and that Ford's involvement with the Nazis ended after the United States entered the war. But when Rintamaki told reporters that the report proved Ford was committed to being "open and honest about the past," it appears that he, like Simon Reich, neglected to mention its most damaging finding.

Several months before Ford released its *Ford-Werke* report in December 2001, I was conducting my own research into the Ford Motor Company's wartime activities when I discovered an astonishing series of government documents, most of which had never before publicly surfaced. These documents, found at the U.S. National Archives, focus on a criminal investigation into Ford's Nazi complicity that centered on an ill-timed wartime business letter from Edsel Ford.

In July 1942, after Ford of France transferred the head office of its African subsidiary company, Ford-Afrique, from Paris to Algeria—at the time a French colony, governed from neutral Vichy—the American Consul General at Algiers became suspicious. He was puzzled as to why the move to a neutral country had been initiated by a company operating out of Nazi-occupied France.[82] He wondered whether the Germans, with "the connivance of the Ford Motor Company," had engineered the move in order to receive shipments of Ford products to a neutral country that would eventually make their way into Germany.[83] The consul, Felix Cole, immediately notified Washington, triggering a Treasury Department investigation that would soon have far-reaching implications in Dearborn.

On December 7, 1942, a Treasury investigator named John Lawler made a surprise appearance at Ford Motor Company headquarters with a document ordering the company to immediately open its complete books and files, under the authority of the 1917 Trading With the Enemy Act. The Act, which was intended to prevent any economic activity that could benefit enemy powers, prohibited U.S. firms from having any contact with enterprises in occupied Europe. Lawler instructed the company to locate all records relating to its French subsidiary's operations since the fall of France in June 1940.[84] For weeks, investigators combed the company's files, copying thousands of documents relating to Ford France. For an additional three months, Treasury Department attorneys in Washington carefully scrutinized the mountain of paperwork, looking for any sign that the company had violated federal statutes. Finally, on May 25, 1943, the investigation complete, a Treasury attorney named Randolph Paul dispatched a copy of the Lawler report to U.S. Treasury secretary Henry Morgenthau with a memo summarizing its most significant findings:

> 1) the business of the Ford subsidiaries in France substantially increased; 2) their production was solely for the benefit of Germany and the countries under its occupation; 3) the Germans have "shown clearly their wish to protect the Ford interests" because of the attitude of strict neutrality maintained by Henry and Edsel Ford; and 4) the increased activity of the French subsidiaries on behalf of the Germans received the recommendation of the Ford family in America.[85]

The accompanying report is damning. It reprints the extensive correspondence between Dearborn and Ford France managing director Maurice Dollfuss, including numerous letters to and from Edsel proving that Dearborn knew and approved of the French company's substantial manufacturing efforts on behalf of the German military (see chapter 8). For two years, Dearborn had applauded Dollfuss's efforts, praising as a "remarkable achievement" the huge profits he realized manufacturing on behalf of the Nazi war machine.[86] Because the overwhelming majority of this correspondence was exchanged before Pearl Harbor, it broke no U.S. federal laws.

However, Treasury investigators immediately seized on a series of eleven letters exchanged between Dollfuss and Dearborn between January and October 1942—after the United States had entered the war. The base of Ford's French operations was located in Poissy in the Nazi-occupied zone. The Poissy plant was therefore classified by the American government as enemy property. Any communications between Poissy and Dearborn would have violated the Trading With the Enemy Act. But Dollfuss had figured out a loophole around these restrictions. Because Ford France also had a plant located in neutral Vichy, Dollfuss was able to dispatch his assistant Georges Lesto, acting as a courier, to Vichy in order to send and receive correspondence between Ford France and American corporate headquarters in Dearborn.[87]

From previous correspondence with Dollfuss, Dearborn was well aware that its French plants were generating enormous profits manufacturing vehicles for the German military. Edsel frequently commended Dollfuss for his efforts. Before Pearl Harbor, there was nothing officially improper about these Nazi military contracts. But on January 28, 1942, Dollfuss's letters took on a more circumspect tone. He writes Edsel admitting that, "since the existence of a state of war between the United States and Germany, correspondence is difficult." He reveals that Ford continued to profit from Nazi military contracts, despite U.S. entry into the war, noting that "production is continuing at the same rate despite difficulties." Dollfuss goes on to boast that the company's military production is distributed between the collaborationist Vichy government and the Nazi military authorities in Occupied France, adding that "this production rate is the best of all the French manufacturers." He confides that he is still relying on Vichy to "preserve the interests of the American shareholders."[88]

On February 11, Dollfuss sent another letter to Dearborn, reporting the company's 1941 net profit at 58,000,000 francs. A month later, Dollfuss cabled Edsel informing him that the Poissy plant had been severely bombed and that one man was wounded.[89] On May 11, 1942, Edsel finally responded to Dollfuss's letters, writing, "It is interesting to note that you have started your African company and are laying plans for a more peaceful future." At this point, he refers to the recent bombing of the Poissy plant, revealing that photographs of the plant on fire were published in American newspapers but "fortunately no reference was made to the Ford Motor Company."[90] Treasury investigators paid particular attention to this phrase, noting Edsel's eagerness to avoid alerting the public to the fact that a Ford plant was manufacturing for the Nazis.

On June 6, Dollfuss wrote Edsel again, informing him that the Poissy plant had now been bombed four times but that the government had agreed to compensate the company for any damages incurred. He hoped Edsel would show the letter to his father and Ford Production Chief Charles Sorensen. On July 17, Edsel responded, stating that he was pleased that the company was in good health and that Dollfuss was "carrying on the best way possible under the circumstances":

> I have shown your letter to my father and Mr. Sorensen and they both join me in sending best wishes for you and your staff, and the hope that you will continue to carry on the good work you are doing.[91]

The team of Treasury investigators were stunned by this letter. The previous correspondence clearly demonstrated that a Ford company was complicit in helping to send thousands of Allied soldiers to their deaths on the bloody battlefields of Europe. The Nazis frequently commended the efficiency of Ford-produced military vehicles in the success of their combat operations. Now, here was apparent evidence that Edsel Ford approved of these efforts and wanted them to continue. On May 25, 1943, Morgenthau forwarded a copy of the Lawler report to President Roosevelt, directing the President's attention to what he calls the "amazing and shocking correspondence" between Edsel Ford and Dollfuss. Although the Lawler report was never made public, Eleanor Roosevelt was almost certainly referring to it in her "My Day" column in September 1945 when she wrote:

> I recall hearing after France fell and after we went into the war, that the heads of a big industry in this country cabled congratulations to their managers in France because the latter were keeping the plant going—although they were keeping it going by making what the Germans asked them to make . . . Business complications do strange things to our patriotism and ethics.[92]

On May 26, 1943, only one day after the Treasury Department completed its investigation, Edsel Ford died suddenly at the age of forty-nine. His premature death had always been blamed on stress over the company's bungled B-24 program, but Edsel was well aware that government investigators were investigating his involvement in potentially treasonous activities. It is entirely conceivable that his worry over a potential federal indictment in fact contributed significantly to the rapid decline of his health and even his death.[93]

On the same day Edsel died, copies of the Lawler report were forwarded to the U.S. Military Intelligence Division, the Office of Naval Intelligence, and the FBI.[94] After a three-month Justice Department investigation, the United States assistant attorney general dropped a bombshell. An examination of the correspondence between Edsel and Dollfuss concluded that there was the "basis for a case" against Edsel Ford under the Trading With the Enemy Act.[95]

From the pattern of his correspondence with Maurice Dollfuss, it was clear that Edsel had sanctioned continued business dealings between his company and the Nazi regime with whom his country was at war. But, taken individually, each letter was ambiguous enough to provide cover. Justice Department attorneys worried that Ford's July 17 letter urging Dollfuss to keep up the "good work" could be argued in court as nothing more than a "polite expression of appreciation" from an employer to his subordinate. Moreover, investigators could not obtain enough evidence for an indictment against the company itself. Although Edsel had indicated that he had informed his colleagues, there was no written documentation of this, making a prosecution case against the Ford Motor Company untenable.

In his correspondence after Pearl Harbor, Edsel had dispatched his letters to Dollfuss through neutral Vichy. If the letters had remained in unoccupied France, they would have broken no laws. But, as the Justice Department studied the correspondence, it concluded that he deliberately intended his letters to be sent on to Dollfuss in Nazi-occupied territory. This was a clear violation of section 3(c) of the Trading With the Enemy Act. Justice Department attorney David Bookstaver concluded there was "a basis for a case."[96] The Ford Motor Company's president was almost certainly guilty of violating one of the nation's most serious federal wartime statutes and could have gone to prison. Only treason would have carried a stiffer penalty. Indeed, a number of historians have referred to violation of the Trading With the Enemy Act as "corporate treason."[97] However, by the time the investigation was concluded, Edsel had been dead for three months and the Justice Department was forced to abandon its investigation because his death "made any discussion of criminal liability purely academic."[98]

When the *Ford-Werke* investigative team came across the same documents I had discovered about the existence of the Lawler investigation along with the Justice Department's startling conclusions, they briefly noted their findings in the December 2001 report. However, this section appears to have been completely ignored in Simon Reich's accompanying commentary as well as at the December 6 Ford Motor Company press conference. Consequently, the damaging findings were not mentioned in any of the subsequent media accounts. The company has refused to comment directly on the revelation that its former President may have been guilty of Trading With the Enemy. Officially, the Ford Motor Company will only say that "the report speaks for itself."[99]

If Edsel Ford violated federal laws by continuing to do business with the Nazis after Pearl Harbor, he was not alone. In a small box housed among the U.S. National Archives Trading With the Enemy files sits an explosive series of documents implicating another prominent American family in this serious crime. On October 20, 1942, ten months after the United States entered the Second World War, the U.S. Alien Property Custodian, Leo T. Crowley, issued Vesting Order 248 under the Trading With the Enemy Act, seizing all assets of the Union Banking Corporation of New York, which was being operated as a front for "enemy nationals."[100] According to a federal government investigation, Union Banking was not a bank at all, but a cloak operation, laundering money for Germany's power-ful Thyssen family. The Thyssens were instrumental in financing Hitler's rise to power and had supplied the Nazi regime with much of the steel it needed to prosecute the war.[101]

One of the partners of the Union Banking Corporation, the man who oversaw all investments on behalf of the Nazi-affiliated owners, happened to be Prescott Bush, grandfather of the American president George W. Bush. Through the connections of his father-in-law, Bert Walker (George W.'s maternal great-grandfather), who has been described by a U.S. Justice Department investigator as "one of Hitler's most powerful financial support-ers in the United States,"[102] Prescott Bush specialized in managing the invest-ments for a number of German companies, many with extensive Nazi ties. These included the North American operations of another Nazi front, the Hamburg-Amerika Line, which was directly linked to a network set up by IG Farben to smuggle agents, money and propaganda for Germany.[103] Accord-ing to a 1934 Congressional investigation, the Hamburg-Amerika line "subsi-dized a wide range of pro-Nazi propaganda efforts both in Germany and the United States."[104] Both Walker and Bush were directors of a holding com-pany, the Harriman Fifteen Corporation, that directly financed the line.

Shortly before the government seized the assets of the Union Banking Corporation, in fact, it had also seized American-held assets of the Ham-burg-Amerika Line under the Trading With the Enemy Act. A few weeks after the government seized Bush's shares in Union Banking, it seized the assets of three other Nazi front companies whose investments were han-dled by Bush—the Holland-American Trading Corporation, the Seamless Steel Equipment Corporation, and the Silesian-American Corporation. The paper trail indicated that the bulk of Prescott Bush's financial empire was being operated on behalf of Nazi Germany.[105]

According to former United States Justice Department Nazi war crimes investigator John Loftus, who has investigated the Bush family's considerable ties to the Third Reich, Prescott Bush's investment prowess helped make millions of dollars for various Nazi-front holding companies, and he was well paid for his efforts. "The Bush family fortune that helped put two members of the family in the White House can be traced directly to the Third Reich," says Loftus, who is currently president of the Florida Holocaust museum.[106]

In his own investigation, Loftus discovered a disturbing trail connect-ing the Bush family's money laundering efforts to the Thyssens and their role in building up the Nazi war machine. He believes these connections deserve more scrutiny: "There are six million skeletons in the Thyssen family closet, and a myriad of criminal and historical questions to be answered about the Bush family's complicity."[107]

Fortunately for Bush, who was later elected a United States senator, his name never surfaced in the news when his Union Banking shares were seized by the U.S. government. The only media reference related to the seizure was a brief 1944 item in the *New York Times* announcing that "The Union Banking Corporation, 39 Broadway, New York, has received authority to change its principal place of business to 120 Broadway."[108] The article neglected to point out that the company's assets had been seized under the Trading With the Enemy act or that 120 Broadway was the address of the U.S. Alien Property Custodian. If the news had been publicized, it might well have derailed Bush's political career as well as the future presidential aspirations of both his son and grandson. According to Loftus, however, the potential scandal did affect the short-term career plans of Prescott's eldest son, George Herbert Walker Bush.

As the government investigation into Prescott's Nazi dealings heated up, Loftus reveals, the eighteen-year-old Bush abandoned his plans to enter Yale and enlisted instead in the U.S. Army in an attempt to "save the family's honor."[109] Meanwhile, Prescott Bush, in an effort to avoid potential government prosecution, volunteered to spy for the OSS, precursor of the U.S. Central Intelligence Agency. These efforts at cleansing his Nazi ties appear to have been successful. He was never indicted. In 1951, Union Banking assets valued at $1.5 million were released back to the Bush family.

While the Ford Motor Company and the Union Banking Corporation were being investigated for trading with the enemy, hundreds of other American companies continued to carry on business in Nazi Germany and other Axis-controlled territories after Pearl Harbor. However, most of these companies came under immediate seizure by the Nazi Enemy Property Commission. In his commentary accompanying the *Ford-Werke* report, Simon Reich goes out of his way to stress that Ford was not the only American car company operating in the Third Reich. General Motors, he argues, played a much larger role in Germany, "dwarfing Ford's production there."[110] Indeed, GM's Opel subsidiary was involved in Nazi war preparations as far back as 1935, manufacturing heavy trucks for the *Wehrmacht*.

In succeeding years, Opel became an integral part of the German military machine, eventually building engines for the *Luftwaffe* air fleet as well as military vehicles for the German army. Like Ford, GM's shares in Opel were never seized after Pearl Harbor, although an enemy property custodian was appointed to oversee the plant in November 1942. Opel, likewise, employed thousands of forced laborers in its own wartime operations. However, General Motors did not appear to enjoy the same cozy relationship with the Reich as did Ford after the United States entered the war. Beginning in August 1942, Opel was forced to fight numerous attempts by the Reich War Ministry to expropriate and even "liquidate" its German operations.[111] Up to the present day, GM, like Ford, appears to have escaped the moral consequences of its own extensive business dealings with Nazi Germany. According to company spokesperson Dee Allen, "We lost complete control of the company after Pearl Harbor so we can't be held responsible for anything that happened at Opel during the war."[112]

Perhaps the most notorious example of U.S. corporate collaboration with the Reich was exposed by historian Edwin Black in his explosive 2001 book, *IBM and the Holocaust*. Black reveals for the first time how IBM's German subsidiary developed the information technology that helped Hitler efficiently implement the Final Solution by identifying Jews so they could be rapidly rounded up, deported, imprisoned and ultimately exterminated. With the American parent company's full knowledge and guidance, the automation of persecution was enthusiastically perfected and sold to the Nazis for massive profits.

It may be significant to note that *Ford-Werke*'s attorney and Board Chairman Heinrich Albert also served as the German attorney for IBM. It was in fact Albert who advised the company before Pearl Harbor on how to maintain its independence and protect its profits should America enter the war. IBM has remained largely silent on its wartime role since Black's book made headlines in 2001.[113]

Objectionable though the Nazi business dealings of Prescott Bush, General Motors and IBM may be, however, they differed from Ford in one significant respect. As Edwin Black writes about IBM's Nazi collaboration, "It was never about the anti-Semitism, never about the Nazism. It was always about the money. As far as IBM was concerned, 'business' was its middle name."[114]

In fact, it is an incident involving IBM president Thomas Watson that provides the starkest possible contrast between the philosophies of the two company's founders. At a Berlin Economic Congress in June 1937, the German government bestowed on Watson the Merit Cross of the German Eagle, a slightly lower-grade Nazi decoration than the Grand Cross Henry Ford would receive a year later.[115] Ford consistently refused public calls to return his own medal, even after the United States entered World War II. He believed the Jews were behind efforts to take it away from him, telling an associate, "They told me to return it or else I'm not American. I'm going to keep it."[116]

Watson's Nazi decoration never received the kind of publicity accorded to Ford's own Cross of the German Eagle; hence, there was no similar public clamor for the IBM president to return his medal. But in May 1940, as the Nazi *blitzkrieg* swept westward toward France, Watson wrote a letter to Hitler, returning the medal the Führer had bestowed on him three years earlier, writing, "The present policies of your government are contrary to the causes for which I have been working and for which I received the decoration."[117] Like Ford, however, he never returned Hitler's money.

After the Iwanowa slave labor lawsuit against Ford was dismissed in 1999, a number of German companies, including GM's subsidiary Opel, agreed to pay into a $5.1 billion "humanitarian aid fund" to compensate the victims of wartime slave labor.[118] At the time, Ford's director of global operations, Jim Vella, told reporters that Ford had no intention of contributing to the fund: "Because Ford did not do business in Germany during the war—our Cologne plant was confiscated by the Nazi government—it would be inappropriate for Ford to participate in such a fund."[119] But in March 2000, after considerable negative publicity, Ford did a sudden about-face, announcing that its German subsidiary would contribute to the fund after all. According to the company's press release announcing this change of heart, "*Ford-Werke* wants to make a humanitarian contribution to help former forced laborers who are still alive and others who suffered particular hardship during the National Socialist regime." The company announced that it expected to contribute approximately $13 million to the fund, although the exact amount had "not been finalized."[120]

In 1995, a group of historians invited Elsa Iwanowa and a number of other former Ford slave laborers to Cologne to tour the same *Ford-Werke* plant where they had been forced to toil at gunpoint during the war. During their tour, a company official presented each member of the group with a small lapel pin bearing the Ford company logo. "Just a pin for three years of labor and starvation," Iwanowa recalled. "We were humiliated by this ridiculous present."[121]

As of May 2002, the pin remains the only compensation the seventy-six-year-old Iwanowa has received for her years as a teenage slave laborer. She has not received a dime from Ford or from the "humanitarian aid" fund to which the company contributed in 2000. As time passes, she grows increasingly bitter: "I think they are waiting for all of us to die so they won't have to pay us," she says from her home in Antwerp. "Ford is still pretending that they bear no responsibility for my nightmare, but somebody owes me for my three years in hell. It's sixty years later, and I'm still crying."[122]

CHAPTER 13

REDEMPTION

During the last years of his life, Lindbergh's white supremacist racial views were
transformed as he traveled the world, visiting what he called "primitive" tribes on cultural conservation missions.

As the plane circled over Mannheim on its final approach, the signs of destruction were poignantly evident below. Once a thriving industrial metropolis, the German city had been reduced to rubble, its factories and homes obliterated, its streets deserted. Lindbergh landed his C-47 on the damaged airfield shortly after noon on May 17, 1945, ten days after the Nazis surrendered, ending the war in Europe.

The last time he had set foot in the country six years earlier, he mused to his journal, his beloved Germany was still "proud and virile." Now, as he surveyed the damage, it reminded him of a Dali painting, its "hellish feel" symbolizing "death without dignity, creation without God."[1] The first accounts of Nazi atrocities were already filtering out of the newly liberated Germany; horrors beyond imagining had only begun to pervade the public consciousness. Lindbergh was determined to see for himself whether the reports were just another example of the anti-German propaganda he had once dismissed as the exaggerations of a Jewish-dominated media.

His first destination was Hitler's former headquarters at Berchtesgaden in the Bavarian Alps. As he stood in the bombed-out ruins of the mountain retreat, he could not help but ruminate on the initial promise of Hitler's vision, one that could have brought "much human good" but instead had turned to "such resulting evil." In Lindbergh's journal entry, inscribed as he stood in the ruins, the Führer took on the traits of a tragic figure: "A few weeks ago, he was here standing, looking through that window, realizing the collapse of his dreams, still struggling against overwhelming odds."[2]

Lindbergh had long argued that a Nazi defeat would only replace one totalitarian regime with something worse—a Communist-ruled Europe. Now, as he imagined what Hitler must have been feeling during those final days, he believed events had vindicated him:

> . . . Germany overrun by the forces he feared most, the forces of Bolshevism, the armies of Soviet Russia; much of his country, like his own room and quarters, rubble—flame-blacked ruins. I think of the strength of pre-war Germany."[3]

Officially, Lindbergh's trip had been undertaken to survey German developments in high-speed aircraft. As on his mission in the South Pacific a year earlier, he was traveling as a civilian representative of United Aircraft. Permission to travel in U.S.-occupied Germany required clearance from the State Department, but this presented no serious obstacle. Lindbergh believed that, since Roosevelt's death, official attitudes toward him had softened considerably. "The vindictiveness in Washington [has] practically disappeared as far as I was concerned," he wrote General Wood.[4]

For weeks, he toured the country, becoming increasingly angry with the misery he witnessed among the newly conquered German people. And, while conceding that the Nazis were ultimately responsible for the situation, he placed most of the blame for their continuing misery on the "well-fed" Americans who "stuffed their faces" while the German people suffered. In his journal, he asked, "What right have we to damn the Nazi and the Jap while we carry on with such callousness and hatred in our hearts?"[5]

On June 11, Lindbergh and his party arrived at Camp Dora, a secret underground German rocket factory and death camp in the Harz Mountains. Twenty-seven thousand slave laborers had been exterminated there by the Nazis after they had outlived their usefulness. As he stared into a huge pit overflowing with the residue of the furnaces—small chips of human bone—the true horrors of the Nazi regime were brought home for the first time:

> Here was a place where men and life and death had reached the lowest form of degradation. How could any reward in national progress even faintly justify the establishment and operation of such a place. When the value of life and the dignity of death are removed, what is left for man?[6]

But as he looked down at the evidence of one of history's greatest crimes, he could not bring himself to fully condemn the Germans responsible. Staring at the human debris, "a strange sort of disturbance" entered his mind. He was suddenly reminded of his mission to the South Pacific a few months earlier when, on a visit to the caves on the island of Biak, he saw a bomb crater filled with stacks of rotting Japanese bodies. Victorious U.S. troops had dumped a load of garbage over their bodies, to Lindbergh's disgust. It had left a lasting impression.

A few moments later, he met a Polish prisoner recently liberated from Camp Dora, who looked "like a walking skeleton; starved, hardly any flesh covering the bones." Where, Lindbergh asked himself, had he witnessed starvation like that before? Also on Biak Island, where he had seen Japanese prisoners "thinner even than this Pole." Again, he cast responsibility on the Americans, who "had let them starve themselves in the jungle by simply not accepting their surrender." Lindbergh proceeds to recall several more stories he had heard about the inhuman treatment of Japanese prisoners by American troops, and in his journal, he makes a telling comparison:

> I look down at the pit of ashes (twenty-five thousand in a year and a half). This, I realize, is not a thing confined to any nation or to any people. What the German has done to the Jew in Europe, we are doing to the Jap in the Pacific.[7]

Invoking a Biblical passage, he writes: "Judge not that ye not be judged. . . . It is not the Germans alone, or the Japs, but the men of all nations to whom this war has brought shame and degradation." His sudden concern for the plight of the Japanese people, whom he had only recently dismissed as the "yellow danger," appears to be motivated as much by his antipathy toward American "hypocrisy" as a genuine concern for their welfare. When his *Wartime Journals* were published in 1970, the *New York Times* described Lindbergh's comparison between the Holocaust and isolated American excesses against Japanese prisoners as "grotesque."[8]

With billions of dollars in potential military contracts at stake after Pearl Harbor, the Ford Motor Company had been anxious to obtain its fair share of government largesse once the United States entered the war. To that end, company officials were determined to remain on good terms with the Administration. Like many Americans on the far right, Henry Ford and his colleagues were convinced that the Roosevelt White House was dominated by Jews. Worried that Henry's anti-Semitic reputation still haunted the company, Ford Motor Company public relations officials had convinced him to meet with Richard Gutstadt, national director of the Anti-Defamation League, to clear the air.

On January 7, 1942, soon after this meeting took place, a letter bearing Ford's signature was sent to hundreds of American newspapers, once again disassociating himself and his company from anti-Semitism. "In our present national and international emergency," Ford wrote, "I consider it of importance that I clarify some general misconceptions concerning my attitude towards my fellow citizens of Jewish faith. . . . It is my sincere hope that now in this country and throughout the world, when this war is finished and peace once again established, hatred of the Jew, commonly known as anti-Semitism, and hatred against any other racial or religious group, shall cease for all time."[9] This time, American Jewish groups were not as willing to accept his words at face value. The Philadelphia *Jewish Exponent* was the first to sound a skeptical note:

> The revocation now is hardly sufficient to palliate the great injury that he has done to the Jewish people in the many years when he lent his name and his wealth to the spread of the libelous charges against them which have poisoned the minds of so many and the fruits of which are still a source of peril and misery to thousands of our people.[10]

In his memoirs, Harry Bennett also insisted that Ford had irrevocably abandoned his anti-Semitic views. But a number of contemporary accounts indicate that Ford's visceral hatred for Jews continued unabated throughout the war years. Like his previous public renunciations of anti-Semitism, the letter appeared to be merely another insincere attempt at window-dressing. Shortly after the war ended, a reporter asked him whether he had any plans to take his company public. Ford's reply is revealing: "I'll take down my factory brick by brick before I'll let any of the Jew speculators take stock in my company."[11]

Each person had their own unique reaction to the stories coming out of Germany immediately after the war ended but none perhaps as ironic—some would say fitting—as Henry Ford's. In the spring of 1946, the American government released a public information film called "Death Stations" documenting the liberation of Nazi concentration camps by U.S. troops a year earlier. In May, Henry Ford and a number of his colleagues attended a private showing of the film at the auditorium of the Ford Rouge River plant, a few days before the documentary was to be released to the American public.

Most of the assembled Ford executives sat rapt as the first gruesome images of the Majdanek concentration camp flickered on the screen. They reeled in horror at the graphic footage, which included stark images of a crematorium, Gestapo torture chambers and a warehouse filled with the victims' belongings. When the lights went on an hour later, the company executives rose, shaken, only to find Henry Ford slumped over in his seat, barely conscious. Sitting there witnessing the full scale of Nazi atrocities for the first time, the old man had suffered a massive stroke, from which he would never fully recover. The story sounds apocryphal and is never mentioned in any company history or Ford biography, but the account comes from a credible eyewitness source. It is described in the unpublished memoirs of one of the Ford Motor Company's highest-ranking executives— Josephine Gomon, director of female personnel at the Willow Run bomber plant—who was present at the screening. Ford's lesson, she wrote, seemed appropriate:

> The man who had pumped millions of dollars of anti-Semitic propaganda into Europe during the twenties saw the ravages of a plague he had helped to spread. The virus had come full circle.[12]

Just before midnight on April 7, 1947, Henry Ford suffered a cerebral hemorrhage, and died in sleep at the age of eighty-three. As his body lay in state at Ford's Greenfield Village Museum, 100,000 people filed past for a last glimpse of the man who had made such a lasting impact on American society. On the day of his funeral, every industrial worker in the state of Michigan was asked to observe a moment of silence.[13] Laudatory editorials filled the nation's newspapers, few mentioning his anti-Semitic past.

His eldest grandson, Henry II, had been appointed president of the company more than a year earlier and was so far proving himself up to the task. Rather than preserving his grandfather's legacy, however, Edsel's son appeared to be going out of his way to demolish it. In quick order, he fired Harry Bennett and purged the remaining elements of the paramilitary force that continued to spy on Ford employees. He established peace with the labor unions, concluding a decades-long battle between the company and its workers and ended what *Fortune* magazine called "a feudal dynasty." And once and for all, Henry II moved to disavow any remaining vestiges of anti-Semitism on behalf of the company, publicly stating that copies of *The*

International Jew published by Gerald L K Smith were without the author-ization of his grandfather, the Ford Motor Company or himself.

"It is the policy of the Ford Motor Company and members of the Ford family," he wrote, "to urge all American citizens to combat any movement the purpose of which is to foster hatred and prejudice against any group."[14] By war's end, when Americans began to purchase cars again, the Jewish community was in no mood to forgive a company that had been so publicly associated with anti-Semitism and Nazism over the years. But under the leadership of Henry II, the corporation spent millions of dollars advertis-ing in Jewish publications, donating generously to Jewish causes, and ensuring that these initiatives received wide publicity in the Jewish media. On the surface, it appeared that the company was genuinely committed to repudiating its tarnished past and restoring the family name. At the same time, however, on the other side of the Atlantic, and far from the scrutiny of the American press, a series of events were calling the depth of this commitment into question.

As part of the denazification of Germany then under way, the U.S. mil-itary occupation government barred many of the country's industrial lead-ers from working at their former companies until they could prove that they had never been a member of the Nazi Party. In July 1946, the Dena-zification Committee placed *Ford-Werke's* wartime manager Robert Schmidt in Category 3 (minor wrongdoer or mid-level Party member) and denied him the right to return to his old position.[15] But in October 1947, after one unsuccessful appeal, Schmidt tried again and this time was offi-cially cleared. Investigators could find no evidence that he had ever joined the Party. Days later, Schmidt wrote a letter to Henry Ford II asking to be reinstated at *Ford-Werke*. A number of Schmidt's former employees protested, reporting that he had held strong pro-Nazi views, and for two years Dearborn stalled on a decision.[16] But in January 1950, with the full consent of the American parent company, Robert Schmidt finally was allowed to return to *Ford-Werke* as a technical adviser and member of the management board. Ford International executive A.J. Wieland praised Schmidt's return as "an expedient solution to some of *Ford-Werke's* most pressing problems."[17] The company was struggling to regain its preeminence with German consumers, and company executives believed Schmidt's experience was sorely needed. His tarnished past did not appear to factor in the decision. Eight years later, he retired from the company with a lucra-tive compensation package, including a pension, expense allowance, annu-ity payments and a two-year consulting agreement.[18] He was immediately elected to the *Ford-Werke* board of directors, again with Dearborn's con-sent, and served four years until his death in 1962.

Notwithstanding all his carefully publicized efforts to erase the stain of his company's past, no evidence has emerged that either Henry Ford II or any other top-level Ford Motor Company executive ever raised any moral objections to rehiring the man who had presided over one of the company's darkest chapters. Before Pearl Harbor, when Dearborn still controlled *Ford-Werke* but professed to know little of its goings on, Schmidt had entered into an illegal arrangement to manufacture munitions for the Nazis, using Ford's resources to supply the regime with the means to kill thousands of British civilians during the Blitz. Also before Pearl Harbor, Robert Schmidt wrote in a company publication, vowing "to give our best and utmost for final victory, in unshakable faithfulness to our Führer."[19] Before Pearl Harbor, he imported hundreds of POWs as forced laborers, in defiance of the Geneva Convention, to fill yet another German military contract. After Pearl Harbor, he literally purchased thousands of slave laborers and oversaw their brutal treatment at the hands of his own employees, while the company enjoyed unprecedented profits. There is no evidence that he had any qualms about these acts or that they were performed under coercion from the Nazi regime. Robert Schmidt was acting on his own initiative as a loyal servant of the Ford Motor Company; after the war, he was well rewarded for his efforts by Ford, a company that today claims it could not "influence or control" the wartime events over which Schmidt had presided and therefore had no responsibility for his actions.

If his newly acquired firsthand knowledge of Nazi atrocities convinced Lindbergh that his pre-war position had been mistaken, it was nowhere evident as he returned to America and plunged head-long into another political controversy. A new international body, the United Nations, was being proposed to forge a lasting peace. Lindbergh was not necessarily opposed to this idea, but he firmly rejected one of the new body's guiding principles—human equality. In a speech before Washington's Aero Club on December 17, 1945, he proposed his own alternative to the UN, envisioning a world organization that would possess overwhelming military might and be guided by "Christian ethical principles."[20] Human beings were obviously *not* equal in ability, he argued. An equal governing power must not be given to the Russians, the Chinese, and the Indians, who constituted the majority of the world's population. Instead, the organization must be governed by peoples of "ability"—Westerners who had developed modern science, aviation and the atomic bomb.[21] He pointed to the Nazi excesses as an example of what happens when power is not tempered with Christian morality and argued that only "Christian virtues" could save Western civilization. He also condemned the recently commenced war crimes trials at Nuremberg for their spirit of "vengeance" against the

Nazis who had perpetrated the Final Solution. The media took up where they left off before Pearl Harbor, excoriating Lindbergh for these views. Wrote the *New Republic*:

> He is saddened by the lack of Christian qualities in the post-war world as shown by our "complacency" at the hanging of Mussolini, at the "court trials of our conquered enemies," and in "our attitude toward the famine-stricken peoples we have defeated." There is no similar concern for the victims of Nazism.[22]

In a statement to the *Chicago Tribune*, Lindbergh implied that the destruction of Nazi Germany had been a disastrous error and that the "seeds of a Third World War were already being sown."[23] He later wrote, "A civilization had collapsed, one which was basically our own, stemming from the same Christian beliefs, rooted in similar history and culture."[24]

Meanwhile, Lindbergh's old friend Truman Smith was growing increasingly bitter about his own treatment at the hands of the U.S. military. He had been finally forced to retire in 1941 without attaining the position of general that he had so coveted, even though most of his friends had long since been promoted to the army's highest rank. In his letters to far-right figures after the war, Smith repeatedly claimed that he had been the victim of Jewish members of the Roosevelt Administration, who had targeted him because of his association with Lindbergh. To understand how "that crowd" operated, he urged friends to read the fanatically anti-Semitic writings of the British ideologue Houston Stewart Chamberlain.[25] Recalls Smith's daughter Katchen Coley, "There is no question that his friendship with Lindbergh destroyed my father's career. He did not deserve the terrible things they did to him. He was completely apolitical, he never even voted because he said it would compromise his objectivity. But Lindbergh had a lot of enemies and they took it out on my father."[26]

Smith was determined to redeem his reputation, but this would not be possible while Lindbergh remained a pariah. After the hostile reaction to his 1945 Aero Club speech, Lindbergh was determined to keep a low profile. But, as Leonard Mosley notes, Smith had other ideas. All of Lindbergh's prewar prophecies were beginning to come true, the former military attaché wrote his friend. The British Empire was collapsing; a good part of Europe had come under the totalitarian control of the Soviets. In Asia, the Red hordes of China were sweeping their enemies into the sea. Why, then, should Lindbergh not now be recognized as the prophet who had been maligned unjustly, and vilified only because he had insisted upon telling his fellow countrymen the truth?[27] Smith urged Lindbergh to redeem himself with the American people by publicly reminding them of this reality. The result was a slim volume, in essay form, that Lindbergh published in 1948 under the title *Of Flight and Life*.

Not for the last time, Lindbergh contended that, although they had enjoyed a military victory, the Allied nations had not really won the Second World War:

> Most of the issues for which we fought have not been settled. Our underlying objectives have not been attained. Our victory has not brought peace to the world. It has established neither democratic ideals nor the security of nations . . . As England won a war and lost an empire, we have stamped out the menace of Nazi Germany only to find that we have created the still greater menace of Soviet Russia, behind whose "Iron Curtain" lies a record of bloodshed and oppression never equaled.[28]

A few years earlier, these words would have been dismissed as another attempt to justify his long-held pro-German views. Now, at the dawn of the Cold War, they resonated with a military and political establishment that saw the Soviet Union as the new enemy. Figures of the far right began arguing that their defense of the Nazis before the war had been merely a bulwark against the greater, Communist threat. Hitler, they pleaded, was simply the lesser of two evils. And, while many conservatives had indeed argued this point, Lindbergh's friends preferred to forget that his support for the Nazi regime had been based on more than simply anti-Communism.

In the years ahead, as Lindbergh was hailed by Smith and other supporters as a "prophet," it became nearly impossible to find any reference to his very frequent prewar sermons about racial purity or his publicly and privately voiced anti-Semitic statements. Rarely was there an admission that many of Lindbergh's closest friends and associates before Pearl Harbor openly advocated fascism and received direct financing from the Nazi government. Smith himself never acknowledged that Lindbergh, even while disagreeing with their excesses, had frequently expressed admiration for Hitler and the Nazi regime, and had at one time planned to move his family to Nazi Germany because it was there that he felt most at home.

Lindbergh was being recast from a Nazi sympathizer to an outspoken Cold Warrior. By the time the Republicans took control of the White House in 1953 after twenty long years in the political wilderness, Nazi ties were no longer necessarily a political liability. Expunging their records of war crimes, the U.S. government had allowed thousands of former Nazi scientists and their family members into the United States after the war to assist in developing an American missile and rocket program.[29] Without this program, dubbed "Operation Paperclip," the United States would never have beaten the Soviet Union to the moon or developed some of the sophisticated missile technology that gave it a military edge during the Cold War. The most notorious of these German scientists was Dr. Wernher von Braun, who would have almost certainly been convicted of Nazi war crimes for his part in developing the V-2 missile if he had not been recruited by the Americans. Although much of the information surrounding the operation is still classified, it is likely that one of these former Nazi scientists requested to work with Lindbergh, whose well-known interest in rocketry derived from his efforts in the early 1930s to persuade the Guggenheim Foundation to finance the experiments of America's foremost rocket pioneer, Robert Goddard. The German scientists were fully aware that Lindbergh would be an asset to any rocket program. In fact, it was later revealed that his postwar German visit in May 1945—which included the visit to the Nazi V-2 rocket factory and extermination camp at Camp Dora—had actually been undertaken to help locate and recruit former German rocket scientists on behalf of the United States government.[30]

In April 1954, the Eisenhower administration suddenly and inexplicably announced that Lindbergh's military commission had been restored and that he had been promoted to the rank of brigadier general in the Air Force reserves. Many of his former isolationist friends had gone to work for the new Republican president, Dwight D. Eisenhower, and immediately rose to the defense of Lindbergh's prewar activities. Although the rank was largely ceremonial, it meant that he could be granted a top secret security clearance to work on von Braun's rocket program as a member of the Air Force Scientific Advisory Board, which may have been the genuine reason for the restoration of his military commission.[31] The newly promoted general continued his secret work on the rocket program for more than a decade and even made a small contribution to NASA's manned space program.

But Lindbergh's interests during this period were not merely confined to aviation and rocketry. Scott Berg and other biographers have written at length about the passion for conservation that would consume Lindbergh until the end of his days. Indeed, he threw himself into the cause of protecting birds, whales and other wildlife, working closely with the World Wildlife Fund and other groups dedicated to saving endangered species. "I realized if I had to choose," he once stated, "I would rather have birds than airplanes."

Even as a conservationist, however, Lindbergh could not escape his controversial past. When he explained that he wanted to preserve nature because "I don't want history to record my generation as being responsible for the extermination of any form of life," the syndicated columnist Max Lerner opined, "Where the hell was he when Hitler was trying to exterminate an entire race of human beings?"[32]

Perhaps Lindbergh's most notable postwar venture was his well-publicized 1972 foray into the jungles of the Philippines to study a long-lost primitive stone-age tribe called the Tasaday. The tribe had been allegedly discovered by the Philippine cultural minister Manuel Elizalde, who claimed they had lived an isolated existence for hundreds of years in a Philippine rainforest, without any contact with outsiders. Years earlier, Lindbergh had struck up a friendship with the country's brutal dictator Ferdinand Marcos, who became a patron of his conservationist causes. Instead of allowing trained anthropologists to study the recently discovered Tasaday tribe, Marcos invited Lindbergh to lead the first expedition to the colony of this cave-dwelling people, whose discovery was soon hailed as one of the great anthropological finds of the century.

After living among the Tasaday for a week, Lindbergh told reporters he had never seen a "happier people." Soon after, the Philippine government strictly prohibited all contact between outsiders and the Tasaday, leaving Lindbergh's description one of the only accounts available to academic researchers. Again, Lindbergh was hailed for his nonaviation achievements, adding to the carefully cultivated legend. More than just a great aviator, he was now regularly portrayed as a world-class scientist for his work with Carrel and a renowned conservationist and anthropologist for his work with the Tasaday. "For one of the few times," writes Scott Berg, "the media reports about Lindbergh did not exaggerate." But Berg's assessment may have been misplaced.

Soon after Marcos was ousted from power in 1986, a Swiss journalist and an anthropologist entered the Tasaday area—the first outsiders to do so in more than a decade—and came out declaring the Tasaday were a hoax. They told reporters the primitive tribesmen were in fact Filipino farmers who had been paid by Marcos to move into the forest and pretend to be Stone Age cave dwellers to fool anthropologists and journalists.[33] According to one of the so-called Tasaday:

> We didn't live in caves, only near them, until we met Elizalde . . . Elizalde forced us to live in the caves so that we'd be better cavemen. Before he came, we lived in huts on the other side of the mountain and we farmed. We took off our clothes

because Elizalde told us to do so and promised if we looked poor
that we would get assistance. He gave us money to pose as Tasaday and promised us security from counter-insurgency and tribal
fighting.[34]

Elizalde had allegedly perpetrated the hoax in an effort to increase
tourism to the Philippines, although he had come to realize that his ruse
would easily be discovered by trained anthropologists, forcing him to
shield the Tasaday from outsiders. The Swiss newspaper *Neue Zurcher
Zeitung* exposed the sensational claims in a story headlined, "The Stone
Age Swindle." It was being called the greatest hoax since Piltdown man.
Some academics claimed that the journalists themselves were the hoaxers[35]
but soon after, at a Philippines University conference, an anthropologist
presented genealogical evidence proving that each of the Tasaday came
from one of the two neighboring language groups, the Blit Manobo or
Taboli. Since then, the majority of anthropologists who have studied the
controversy agree that the story of the Tasaday as a cave-dwelling people
who had lived for hundreds of years without any outside human contact
was a hoax.[36] However good his intentions, it appeared that once again
Lindbergh had allowed himself to be used to further the agenda of a dictator. This incident, like many others in Lindbergh's past, speaks more to his
naiveté than to any sinister motive on his part.

It would probably be a gross exaggeration to call Lindbergh "one of the
twentieth century's greatest conservationists"—a description used by more
than one writer after his death. But there is no doubt that he was sincere in
his conservation efforts and made some important contributions to envi-
ronmental consciousness during the sixties and early seventies. However,
his biographers have paid little attention to another of Lindbergh's greatest
passions during the same period.

With the shocking postwar revelations of the Final Solution, the American eugenics movement that had so inspired the Nazis fell into almost
universal discredit. No longer was race betterment considered an acceptable field of scientific inquiry. However, the disclosure of Nazi euthanasia
methods did not appear to sour Lindbergh on a movement he had
embraced ever since his mentor Alexis Carrel introduced him to its principles during the early 1930s. Long after the war ended, Lindbergh
remained committed to the cause of race betterment, contributing money,
advice and time to the American Eugenics Society (AES), which had
retained only a fraction of its prewar membership. From 1955 to 1959,
Lindbergh even served as a Director of the Society, concentrating his
interests mainly on the concept of so-called "positive eugenics," including

selective breeding.[37] "I believe the simplest knowledge of eugenics, if taught in schools, would have a tremendous long-term effect," he wrote AES secretary Frederick Osborn in 1967.[38] However, Lindbergh's youngest daughter Reeve, who was born shortly after the war ended, says she can't remember ever hearing her father talking about concepts of racial purity:

> We grew up in suburban Connecticut where I heard racist and
> anti-Semitic comments on the block almost constantly. But in our
> house, my father never talked like that. He didn't seem to hate
> anyone. I never heard him talk directly about eugenics, though he
> used to speak in almost mystical terms about Alexis Carrel. Later
> on, I read Carrel's writings and they were truly scary. I never
> understood what my father saw in him.[39]

In November 1944, Carrel had died in Paris, his reputation in tatters. After the fall of France in 1940, Lindbergh had suggested that the doctor might be able to return to France to work with the new Nazi-backed Vichy regime.[40] Following his protégé's advice, Carrel traveled to Paris in 1941. There, he obtained financial support from the collaborationist Vichy leader Marshal Pétain to establish a Foundation for the Study of Human Problems[41] to promote many of the eugenic concepts Carrel had advocated in his 1935 book, *Man the Unknown*. With almost $8 million in Vichy funds, Carrel established his Institute in Paris and pursued his research for more than three years.[42] Following the liberation of France in 1944, however, members of the Resistance immediately fingered the doctor as a Nazi collaborator, an accusation Carrel vigorously denied, as did almost all collaborators after the war. Along with 4,000 other accused civilian collaborators, he was rounded up and detained at the Palais des Sports in Paris.[43] A "purging" committee was set up to determine the extent of their collaboration with the Nazis.[44] But three months later, before he could face a tribunal to answer the charges against him, Carrel died of a heart attack at the age of 71.

With reports of his death, news about Carrel's alleged Nazi collaboration soon reached his former friends and colleagues in America. Many refused to believe the charges, since he had occasionally expressed anti-Nazi sympathies before the war and had even chided Lindbergh for his pro-German views following the Fall of France.

Shortly after V-E Day, on his way to Germany, Lindbergh decided to take a brief detour to France in order to determine personally the circumstances of Carrel's wartime activities. Upon arriving in Paris, he spoke to a French duchess who was with the scientist frequently during his final days and who claimed Carrel's collaboration with the Germans had been greatly exaggerated and the charges against him unfair. He had merely gone to the German Embassy, she explained, to argue against the closing of his Institute, but his meeting with the Nazis had been misinterpreted by the Resistance.[45] However, the duchess herself was pro-Vichy so her claims probably carried little credibility. The French Minister of Health Valery Radot publicly announced that he had "important new evidence" proving Carrel had collaborated with the Germans.[46] Many other witnesses also attested to Carrel's collaboration. Indeed, it is difficult to believe he could have secured millions of dollars in funding for his Institute without some collaboration, although this doesn't mean that Carrel had changed his mind about the Nazis. Lindbergh himself appears to have eventually accepted the veracity of the claims. But as a prewar Nazi sympathizer himself, who had counseled Carrel to return to France and work with the Nazi puppet regime, he was hardly disposed to condemn his longtime friend. Indeed, Lindbergh defended Carrel's activities in his journal shortly after hearing of the accusations:

> What could Carrel do but cooperate with the government of occupation? Carrel was never a pro-Nazi but he thought the Communists were worse . . . I have heard him say many times that if he had to choose between Fascism and Communism, he would take Fascism without hesitation.[47]

Lindbergh spent a good part of his remaining years attempting to redeem his mentor's reputation and in 1970 provided financial support to establish a foundation at Georgetown University to "promote the study and dissemination of the ideas expounded during his lifetime by the late Alexis Carrel."

After the war, the Lindberghs moved to Darien, Connecticut—a suburban WASP enclave that legally barred Jews and blacks from owning homes by employing restrictive real estate covenants. The town was so notoriously anti-Jewish that it was used as the setting for the Oscar-winning 1947 Gregory Peck film, *Gentleman's Agreement*, about anti-Semitism in America.

Life in the Lindbergh household during those postwar was anything but idyllic for his growing family. His children remember a father who was loving but severe. Reeve recalled that one moment Charles could be playful, running imaginary animals across her back, while the next he could be a stern and exacting father who, when he returned from his frequent absences, called each of his five children into his office to peruse a handwritten list of their achievements and failures.[48] In 1998, Reeve published a memoir, *Under a Wing*, in which she confronts her father's prewar history. When as an adult she read his Des Moines speech, delivered years before she was born, she read a "chilling distinction in his mind between Jews and other Americans" but says it didn't reflect the Charles Lindbergh she remembered growing up. Nor could she entirely sympathize with his prewar isolationist stand. "Knowing him as I did, it didn't compute, somehow, until I understood that my father represented his country and his time inescapably, in ways that even he didn't understand. All the same, he was a very principled and a very compassionate man."[49] Overall, she believes that "the Lindbergh legacy is very profoundly the legacy of this country, and that his contradictions are our own."[50]

Another daughter, Anne, remembered, "There were only two ways of doing things—Father's way and the wrong way." He barred television and comic books from the house and when his wife suggested she needed a new stove, he asked her to postpone the decision until they could talk over the purchase together "from personal, economic and military standpoints."[51] Once, when she replaced some old mattresses in the guest room, purchasing a set of new mattresses on sale at Bloomingdale's, he accused her of contributing to the fall of civilization.[52] Lindbergh's stern manner appeared to take its severest toll on his wife, who suffered from severe bouts of depression and spent most of her days in her room crying, before learning to cope after years of psychiatric treatment. Eventually, husband and wife spent most of the year apart as Charles traveled the globe on various projects and Anne compared herself to a "widow." When she underwent painful knee surgery in the spring of 1960, she was devastated when Charles failed to show up at the hospital. "Where are you?" she wrote him bitterly two weeks after the operation when he had still failed to visit.[53] During their increasingly rare periods together, she complained, he expected Anne's attention to focus exclusively on him, his self-absorption reaching what Scott Berg calls "comical proportions."[54] Occasionally, when he thought Anne was spending too much time on the telephone talking to friends, he would get his gun from the closet and threaten to shoot the phone. He frequently responded to her complaints with explosive rages, accusing her of "making mountains out of molehills." Anne would later write about the "banked" bitterness she felt toward her husband and admitted that, to relieve the loneliness, she had an extramarital affair with a surgeon who had removed her gallstones.[55]

Lindbergh had all but disappeared from the spotlight during those postwar years. The man who had once dominated the front pages of American newspapers now rarely registered in the public eye. In some years, in fact, there is not a single reference to him in the *New York Times* index. The notable exception was 1957 when Hollywood presented a screen adaptation of his Pulitzer Prize–winning memoir, *The Spirit of St. Louis*, starring James Stewart. Released with mammoth publicity on the thirtieth anniversary of Lindbergh's historic flight, the film was a giant box-office flop. Producer Jack Warner allegedly called it the "most disastrous failure" in the history of his studio.[56] Critically acclaimed and packed with excitement, nobody could account for the film's lack of success. Perhaps many Americans were still hostile to Lindbergh for his prewar isolationist stance and his flirtation with Nazism. Warner Brothers, in fact, experienced considerable difficulty in even booking the film into theaters because of Lindbergh's enduring reputation as an anti-Semite.[57]

During the 1960s, Lindbergh demonstrated that his antiwar views were decidedly selective when he strongly supported U.S. military intervention in the Vietnam War. When his youngest son Scott threatened to renounce his U.S. citizenship and move to Europe in 1967 to avoid the draft, Lindbergh called him an "ass" and the two remained estranged for many years.[58]

He frequently claimed to friends that the controversy over his pre-war isolationist activities had never in the years since caused him a moment of concern. But in 1970, he appeared to go out of his way to sanitize his own past when he published his *Wartime Journals*, covering the years 1938 to 1945. In his introduction to the thousand-page volume, publisher William Jovanovich insisted that the book omits only the insignificant "details of day-to-day living," some material of "intimately personal content" and a number of "repetitive" passages.[59] But when Scott Berg was allowed to access the original journals, he found that a number of distinctly anti-Semitic passages had been deliberately excised from the published version, including an entry in which Lindbergh complains about too much Jewish immigration into the United States.[60]

Berg explains his subject's attempts at censorship: "Without realizing that some of his comments were anti-Semitic, he intuitively deleted them. His admiration for Germany's accomplishments got soft-pedaled."[61]

In his own introduction to the published journals, the 68-year-old Lindbergh made it clear that he had still not changed his mind about his prewar stand. Looking back from the vantage point of a quarter century, he writes, America may have won World War II in a military sense, but in a broader sense "it seems to me we lost it." In order to defeat Germany and Japan, he argues, the Allies supported the greater menaces of Russia and China:

> It is alarmingly possible that World War II marks the beginning of our Western civilization's breakdown, as it already marks

the breakdown of the greatest empire ever built by man [the British Empire]. . . . Much of our Western culture was destroyed. We lost the genetic heredity formed through eons of many million lives.[62]

In a testy editorial response to Lindbergh's argument, the *New York Times* took issue with his contention: "If any war can said to be worth fighting and winning, it was World War II. Even vanquished nations gained, since Japan and Germany are far richer and freer today than they were in 1939. There is no doubt who won the war. Mankind won it."[63]

On August 26, 1974, Charles Augustus Lindbergh succumbed to cancer at his Maui home, never having acknowledged that his prewar stand may have been mistaken. Long newspaper obituaries commemorated his passing—the first time in years that the American public or press had paid much attention to the onetime hero. His historic flight had not been forgotten but the controversy surrounding his isolationist activities was only briefly noted, much of the American prewar generation having taken any lasting bitterness toward Lindbergh to their graves.

In 1976, a British journalist named Leonard Mosley published the first major Lindbergh biography—a somewhat unflattering account that resurrected many of the stories about his Nazi sympathies. As a foreign correspondent, Mosley had covered Lindbergh's trips to Germany during the thirties and later interviewed many former members of the Nazi High Command, including Hitler's Armaments Minister Albert Speer, about Lindbergh's activities. Lindbergh's friends and supporters immediately moved to discredit the book, pointing out, among other things, that Mosley's book wrongly said Truman Smith was still alive in 1975, when in fact Smith had died in October 1970.[64]

Historian Wayne Cole, who had written a number of books sympathetic to the isolationist movement, published his own account of Lindbergh's prewar anti-intervention activities shortly before Lindbergh's death. This book is often cited today as the definitive account, but Cole counted himself as a friend of Lindbergh and so could hardly be objective.[65] Nevertheless, he raises some important points, asking the reader to consider "beyond mere passion and prejudice" the issues raised by the prewar isolationist movement. Cole personally believes that Americans have been too quick to judge Lindbergh for his political stand:

America's opinion-forming elite has concluded that he was wrong. Any judgment in depth, however, must wrestle with difficult

questions about the consequences of alternative courses of action—
those proposed either by Lindbergh or others. . . . Would the alternative courses of action urged by Colonel Charles A. Lindbergh
from 1937 through 1941 have provided a more or less secure, free
and stable world for Americans and others than they find today? To
what extent did the "Great Debate" and the tactics by both the isolationists and the interventionists enhance or undermine democracy, freedom, peace and security for the United States?[66]

A decade after these books appeared, a New York freelance journalist
named Susan Hertog was sitting at the departure gate of a Minnesota airport when Anne Morrow Lindbergh suddenly sat down beside her. Hertog
introduced herself, thrilled to be in the presence of a woman she had long
admired. At that moment, Hertog resolved to write Anne's life story. Two
years later, in 1987, she was invited to Anne's mountain chalet near
Geneva, Switzerland, where Anne told her that, despite her lifelong aversion to publicity, she wanted "to set the record straight" about her life with
Charles. Over the next two years, Hertog met with her subject ten times,
during which Anne talked candidly about her life with Lindbergh.

No published journalist or biographer had ever been given complete
access to the Lindbergh papers and correspondence, spread throughout
archival repositories around the country. Anne Morrow Lindbergh's will
specified that they could only be accessed with written permission from
the family.[67] After negotiations with Anne during the late 1980s, Hertog
believed she was at one point close to gaining full access to the papers,
but negotiations broke down after the family intervened, concerned
about the direction her book appeared to be taking.[68] When Hertog's
work was published in 1999, two years before Anne's death, the Lindbergh family moved quickly to discredit the work, accusing her of misleading Anne by claiming she was writing a "feminist study" rather than
a biography.[69] Nevertheless, the book is a valuable contribution to the
Lindbergh canon. The hours of detailed interviews Anne granted Hertog represent perhaps the most complete and candid account of Lindbergh's life by the person who knew him best, as well as a fascinating
portrait of a remarkable woman.[70]

In the early 1990s, another writer named A. Scott Berg began corre-
sponding with Anne about the possibility of writing a biography of her
husband. Berg, whose best-known previous book was a respected biography of film mogul Samuel Goldwyn, had long been fascinated with Lindbergh, and it was evident from his persistent letters to Anne that Berg's

portrayal of her husband's life would be a sympathetic one. After a year of correspondence and a series of meetings, she finally agreed to allow Berg unfettered access to the Lindbergh family papers.[71] Although Berg clearly admired his subject,[72] he made it clear to the family that he would only agree to write the biography if he was allowed unrestricted freedom to write what he chose.[73] Anne consented, shortly before she suffered a stroke that would leave her incapacitated for the rest of her life. Although her marriage to Charles was often stormy and unhappy, it was also frequently rich, fascinating and rewarding. "My life began when I met Charles Lindbergh," she told Susan Hertog. Anne was clearly committed toward the end of her life to preserving her husband's legacy and safeguarding his reputation, despite his deathbed admonition to his wife and children not to "spend your life defending mine."[74]

After years of research, the family-authorized biography finally appeared in 1998, attracting immediate attention and acclaim. Because Berg acknowledged Lindbergh's anti-Semitism—even discovering previously unreported examples—the book appeared to be a warts-and-all biography. It portrays Lindbergh as a great, but flawed, historical figure— unfairly excoriated for his isolationist views. The book received a number of glowing reviews, became a *New York Times* bestseller, and went on to win the 1999 Pulitzer Prize for Biography. Indeed, the book is an important work, meticulously researched, and thorough in many respects. But a number of prominent reviewers more familiar with Lindbergh's prewar activities noticed that, while Berg addressed Lindbergh's anti-Semitism and prewar Nazi sympathies, he appeared to deliberately play them down. In one passage, for example, Berg quotes Lindbergh expressing his belief that admitting excessive numbers of Jewish refugees into the United States would cause "chaos" and that "there are too many in places like New York already." Inexplicably, Berg then claims that "Lindbergh was not singling Jews out for persecution; indeed, he could have just as easily written the same about any other minority."[75] In another unaccountable defense of his subject's actions, Berg writes that in his reviled Des Moines address, "Lindbergh had bent over backwards to be kind about the Jews."[76] This assertion is especially puzzling since even Lindbergh's daughter Reeve acknowledges that the speech was anti-Semitic.[77] In fact, Anne's diary reveals that her husband only inserted the brief positive passage about the Jews at her insistence. Berg also writes that most of Lindbergh's references to Jews "express Lindbergh's affinity and admiration for them."[78] In his section about the events leading up to Munich, Berg downplays Lindbergh's role in Britain's appeasement of Hitler, attributing subsequent accounts about his influence as "hearsay."[79] On his book tour promoting the biography, Berg regularly described Lindbergh's views as a "genteel brand of anti-Semitism that was prevalent in this country up until the 1960's."[80]

These attempts to rationalize Lindbergh's behavior were too much for a number of prominent critics, including *New York Times* columnist Frank Rich, who accused Berg of "sanitizing the all-American hero's anti-Semitism by tossing in bizarrely off-key 'everyone-did-it' disclaimers."[81] Similarly, *Business Week* magazine criticized Berg's "failure to confront Lindbergh's anti-Semitism head-on, or to explain why it was that he buried his head in the sand when confronted with the crimes of inhumanity that repelled so many others."[82]

Although most reviewers wrote that Berg was the first biographer ever granted unrestricted access to the Lindbergh archives, that distinction actually belongs to the prominent aviation historian, and former U.S. intelligence officer, Colonel Raymond Fredette, who got to know Lindbergh before his death and had received permission from Lindbergh himself to write a book about his military activities. Two years later, Anne Morrow Lindbergh authorized Fredette to "write the definitive biography of my husband." Although Fredette has yet to complete his book, he has had unrestricted access to the Lindbergh archives for more than twenty-five years and was harshly critical of Berg's biography when it was published. In a review of the book for the journal *Air Power History*, Fredette wrote, "Berg approaches Lindbergh and his accomplishments with awe, and a hero worship that harkens back to the time the flight to Paris was made."[83] Fredette's book, scheduled to be released in 2004, is expected to reveal some controversial personal details that he believes will shed new light on Lindbergh's character and reputation.

Shortly before the publication of Berg's biography in 1998, director Steven Spielberg acquired the film rights to the book sight unseen and announced plans to produce a major Hollywood biopic of his "boyhood hero" Lindbergh. However, shortly after the book's release, Spielberg's involvement was severely criticized by many American Jews, who were afraid that the film, like the book, would downplay Lindbergh's anti-Semitism and Nazi sympathies. One of a number of scathing letters to New York's prominent Jewish newspaper, the *Forward*, lambasted the planned Spielberg film project: "Any person who has read even a single book on the life of Charles Lindbergh already knows what the author of this family-authorized biography tried so hard not to reveal—that the Lone Eagle was a disgrace."[84]

Having a filmmaker of Spielberg's stature affirm Lindbergh's heroism would significantly influence his enduring legacy. But shortly after the criticism hit its peak, Spielberg told Britain's *Guardian* newspaper that he had put plans to direct the Lindbergh film on hold, claiming he had not been fully aware of Lindbergh's anti-Semitism until he read the book. He explained that making *Schindler's List* and developing the Shoah Foundation, documenting the testimonies of survivors, had reshaped his thinking about the Holocaust era:

> They've given me more of a moral responsibility to make sure I'm not putting someone else's agenda in front of the most important agenda, which is trying to create tolerance. We'll probably make *Lindbergh*, but one of the reasons I've considered not being the director is that I didn't know very much about him until I read Scott Berg's book and I read it only after I purchased it. I think it's one of the greatest biographies I've ever read but his "America First" and his anti-Semitism bothers me to my core, and I don't want to celebrate an anti-Semite unless I can create an understanding of why he felt that way. Because sometimes the best way to prevent discrimination is to understand the discriminator.[85]

An angry Berg publicly disputed Spielberg's claim that he was unaware of Lindbergh's anti-Semitism until he read the book, telling *New York* magazine that he had fully discussed it with the director when he sold him the rights. "When he and I first met, topic A was anti-Semitism," said Berg. "And I would say topic Z was anti-Semitism, too."[86] As of December 2002, Spielberg's film has been shelved indefinitely.

More than anything, the publication of Berg's biography, as Anne undoubtedly intended, marked the first step in the carefully crafted rehabilitation of a tarnished hero.

Although Spielberg has thus far declined to participate in Lindbergh's redemption, the director inadvertently played a role in helping to rehabilitate the reputation of Henry Ford and the company he founded. On February 23, 1997, when NBC broadcast the television premiere of Spielberg's epic drama *Schindler's List*, its presentation was unique. Accompanying the massive publicity blitz that heralded the broadcast was the following announcement: "By foregoing commercials during the screening, the Ford Division of the Ford Motor Company will make TV history as the sole sponsor of the program."[87]

Hardly a peep was heard from the Jewish community about the irony of Ford's sponsorship of a Holocaust epic. Only a few media voices pointed out the incongruity. When the *New York Times* contacted the Ford Motor Company to ask whether the sins of the founder had influenced its decision, company spokesperson Gerry Donnelly denied the connection: "Many of our people were involved in this project and no one ever mentioned Henry Ford. I think quite a few are not even aware of this background."[88]

Indeed, so successfully has the company repaired its image over the years that few Americans are aware of its founder's sordid past or its own complicity in the events portrayed in *Schindler's List*. As Ron Rosenbaum writes in his acclaimed book *Explaining Hitler*, "It's remarkable how easily—or conveniently—Ford's contribution to Hitler's success has been lost to memory in America."[89]

When details about Ford's controversial past surface, as they occasionally do, the corporation has been remarkably successful at distancing itself from any moral responsibility for his actions, just as it distanced itself from the wartime activities of *Ford-Werke*. When I began researching this book, I found that a number of files relating to the *Dearborn Independent* and Ford's early anti-Semitism had been "discarded" from the company archives decades ago. In a March 2002 interview with Ford Motor Company archivist Elizabeth Adkins, I asked whether she thought the *Independent* files might have been destroyed because they represented "the darkest period in the history of the Ford Motor Company."[90] Her e-mailed response took me by surprise: "In fact, Ford Motor Company did not own the *Dearborn Independent*. The publication was owned by Henry Ford, but was separate from the company."[91]

I was intrigued. Implicit in the letter was the notion that Henry Ford's hate campaign was just another of his many eccentricities and had nothing to do with the company, an argument I had encountered on a number of occasions since starting this book. I resolved to determine the facts, despite the gaping holes in the archives.

The company refused me access to its own industrial archives but, after hours scouring the archives of the independent Ford museum, I finally located the information I was seeking: the original stock certificates of the Dearborn Publishing Company, publisher of both the *Dearborn Independent* and *The International Jew*. They reveal that one thousand shares of stock capital were issued on April 22, 1920—less than a month before the *Independent* began its anti-Semitic campaign. Of these original shares, 997 were in fact owned by the Ford Motor Company; one share was held by Henry Ford, one share was held by Ernest Liebold, and one share was held by another company executive.[92] In a gesture of remarkable confidence, the Ford Motor Company had even authorized Ernest Liebold to hold its voting proxy.[93] Moreover, receipts and letters attest to significant cash advances paid by the Ford Motor Company to the Dearborn Publishing Company "to finance operations of this company."[94] In addition, Ford dealers were regularly compelled by the company to sell the *Dearborn Independent* and *The International Jew* at their dealerships. As late as February 1926, a memo to all branch company managers instructed Ford dealers and salesmen to put greater effort into selling the *Independent*.[95]

When I brought these facts to the attention of Ford spokesperson Tom Hoyt, and asked why Elizabeth Adkins—the keeper of the company's corporate history—had falsely informed me that Henry Ford personally owned the *Independent*, Hoyt simply replied, "Elizabeth was mistaken."[96] When I asked him whether, given these new facts, the Ford Motor Company might bear some responsibility for the consequences of its seven-year hate campaign, Hoyt's only response was, "The company's position against anti-Semitism is well-documented."[97]

The records of the Dearborn Publishing Company also dispel a myth repeated by many biographers: the belief that Edsel Ford never approved of his father's anti-Semitism.[98] In fact, both Edsel and Henry's wife Clara sat on the Dearborn Publishing Company board of directors during the entire first phase of the paper's anti-Semitic campaign and, according to records, neither ever protested its Jew-baiting content. Edsel even served as the publishing company's first secretary and treasurer. Only in 1923, one year *after* the *Independent* called a halt to its first hate campaign, did Edsel and Clara resign from the Board.[99] When the paper's attacks against the Jews resumed a year later, Edsel's objections to continuing publication of the *Independent* appeared to be related to the fact that it was costing the company business more than to any moral consideration about the paper's content.[100] This becomes particularly significant in light of Edsel's subsequent wartime business dealings with the Nazi regime.

With the death of Anne Morrow Lindbergh in 2001, an opportunity presented itself that would have been out of the question while she lived. I wrote Reeve Lindbergh requesting unrestricted access to her father's political papers at Yale University, which remain sealed under the terms of her parents' will.[101] I informed the Lindberghs' youngest daughter that my account would not necessarily be a favorable one but argued that only by granting access to an unauthorized biographer could the family lay to rest the lingering suspicion that it has something to hide. Scott Berg, Lindbergh's authorized biographer, had previously been allowed access to this material, but it remained restricted. After months of negotiations and correspondence, during which she consulted extensively with her siblings, I was finally granted unrestricted access during the summer of 2002 to the papers I had requested.

After reading through thousands of pages of his incoming and outgoing correspondence, uncensored journal entries and unpublished writings, I discovered no smoking gun proving that Lindbergh was motivated by anything but sincere—albeit misguided—motives for his prewar isolationist activities or that he was disloyal to America. I did not expect to.

What I did discover was further evidence that Charles Lindbergh was anything but the one-dimensional figure often portrayed by his critics and supporters. I also found additional material that sheds considerable light on his prewar views and the evolution of his social and political thought.

Many of his critics, including a number of historians, have described Lindbergh as a "Nazi," at least before the onset of the Second World War. However, it is clear from reviewing his correspondence and unpublished writings that this description is largely inaccurate. Throughout this book, I have referred to his "prewar Nazi sympathies." Although this description is perhaps closer to the truth, even it does not tell the whole story.

Clearly, during the years following his first visit to Germany in 1936, Lindbergh sympathized with many of the Nazi ideals and accomplishments that he had witnessed on his repeated tours of the Third Reich. Compared to the decadence and freedoms he deplored in the western democracies, he admired the "dictatorial direction" and "virility" of the New Germany and believed Hitler was "undoubtedly a great man who has done much for the German people."[102] Despite Lindbergh's own anti-Semitism, however, he appeared to be genuinely disturbed by the Nazis' overt persecution of the Jews, along with many of their extreme methods. Nevertheless, he appeared to be willing to overlook or rationalize this extremism, writing a friend, "Hitler has accomplished results (good in addition to bad) which could hardly have been accomplished without some fanaticism."[103]

During his initial postwar rehabilitation, many of Lindbergh's friends and supporters argued in his defense that his trips to Germany were in fact clandestine missions designed to gather secret military intelligence on behalf of the United States government—that he was in effect acting as a double agent. Moreover, they claimed, he never admired Nazi Germany but viewed the Nazis as a useful antidote to Communism. He was actually something of a prophet, they argued—a Cold Warrior before his time. In his private correspondence, however, Lindbergh makes it clear that this was not the case. He refused to pass on any German air intelligence information to the U.S. government unless he had first received approval from his Nazi hosts.[104] And he makes no mention of Communism at all in his initial 1936 references to his admiration for Hitler, Nazi Germany, and National Socialist ideals. In fact, it would be an additional two years before he began to regularly criticize the Communists, during which time he was frequently exposed to the Nazis' frequent denunciations of the Soviet Union.

Was Lindbergh, then, a fascist with a contempt for democracy? This is more difficult to answer. Following his first visit to Nazi Germany, he appears to be captivated by the concept of "rule by elites" advocated by his ideological mentor Alexis Carrel, rejecting the democratic ideal of one person, one vote. "What measures the rights of man or of a nation?" he wrote a friend in 1937 after a visit to the Third Reich. ". . . Are we deluding ourselves when we attempt to run our governments by counting the number of heads, without a thought of what lies within them?" Later, he appeared captivated by a British fascist rally in 1938, comparing it favorably to a Communist meeting he had recently witnessed: "It always seems that the Fascist group is better than the Communist group. Communism seems to draw the worst of men."[105] He never fully resigned himself to the contradictions inherent in his virulent anti-Communist sermons, frequently condemning the Soviets' "godlessness," "brutality" and "totalitarian" nature, while refusing to acknowledge that each of these traits was also a fundamental element of Nazi ideology. Like his wife, he appeared to believe democracy was a spent force, destined to be replaced by an unspecified "wave of the future." But, while Anne believed instinctively that Nazism was merely the "scum on the wave," he never appears to have rejected its tenets outright, only its excesses.

Yet, throughout the course of his prewar isolationist activities, Lindbergh seemed uncomfortable with some of the extremist and pro-Nazi elements surrounding him and moved to distance himself from direct Nazi contacts. Whether this was out of political expediency or genuine discomfort with Nazi extremism is still unclear. Publicly, he refused to criticize the Nazis or return the medal presented to him by Hermann Göring in 1938, given to those who "deserve well of the Reich."

Did he desire a Nazi victory in Europe, at least before Pearl Harbor? It appears so, reviewing his private correspondence. Time and again, he makes it clear that he is annoyed by continued British resistance to Nazi domination of Europe. The bulk of his isolationist activities were not devoted to keeping America out of the European war, as many believe. They were devoted to preventing American military aid to Britain as the beleaguered island nation attempted to stave off a German military invasion. Yet his supporters, including a number of respected historians, argue that Lindbergh merely wanted to prevent "good money being thrown after bad." He did not necessarily welcome a German victory, they insist, but believed it inevitable. He merely wanted the British to accept defeat so Hitler could get on with a much-needed "readjustment" of Europe, which included the destruction of Bolshevism. Then, a democratic America could live in peaceful coexistence with Nazi Europe.

In his correspondence, Lindbergh argues that he favored a negotiated peace with the Nazis to avoid "the destruction of Western civilization."[106] Evidently, however, he would have still advocated such a readjustment even if he knew it would lead to the Nazi extermination of millions of Jews and other Europeans. Even after the full horrors of the Holocaust were revealed following the war, he continued to believe he was right, arguing that America had, in fact, lost the war because the Communists were allowed to swallow Eastern Europe. He appears to believe that a negotiated peace, or a Nazi victory resulting in the destruction of the Soviet Union, would have been preferable to the greater Soviet menace and its "record of bloodshed and oppression never equaled."[107]

Was Lindbergh a "witless dupe"—the description applied to him by the *New York Times* in a 1975 review of Leonard Mosley's biography? This simplistic view discounts the complexities of Lindbergh's character and personality. Certainly, the Nazis had sized up his naiveté early on and used him as a pawn in their sophisticated propaganda charade. But it is important to remember that he was far from the only person fooled and that the Nazis had also successfully deceived foreign intelligence agencies that were anything but witless. Time and again, his friends describe Lindbergh as "honest"—perhaps too honest for his own good. A woman who once worked for him said, "He cannot tell a lie, even if he knows the truth is going to hurt. . . . He just has to tell the truth, and he expects other people to tell the truth to him."[108] As objectionable as some of his "honestly" expressed views were, his private correspondence reveals that this assessment may not have been far off the mark. When the pro-Appeasement *New York Times* columnist Arthur Krock defended him in a 1939 column, falsely arguing that Lindbergh was acting almost as an American double agent during his prewar trips to Nazi Germany, Lindbergh was furious, despite the column's tone of exoneration. In an extraordinarily revealing letter to a friend, he wrote, "I suppose that I should be very appreciative of the type of article which Mr. Krock has written. But I prefer to stand upon a foundation of fact rather than of favor."[109] Lindbergh clearly believed that the Nazis—who had extended such hospitality to him and his wife— were also committed to the same honesty, and he could not begin to imagine that they would attempt to deceive him. Truman Smith and Alexis Carrel appear to have understood this aspect of Lindbergh's malleability early on. Once he trusted somebody, they knew, he was open to manipulation, and both men used this knowledge to instill their own unsavory ideas into his receptive mind.

The subject of Lindbergh's honesty, however, is still open to question. We know that he deliberately excised damaging information about his attitude toward Jews from his journals before they were published, presenting the public with a less-than-honest portrait of his true views. At the time I visited the Lindbergh archives, there was no way of knowing whether the archival materials accessed by Scott Berg and myself represented a complete set of Lindbergh's papers or whether he removed incriminating documents at some point that might have harmed his reputation. But in 2003, an extraordinary story emerged out of Germany when it was revealed that Lindbergh had secretly fathered a second family with a Munich hatmaker named Brigitte Hesshaimer, producing three children between 1958–1967, while traveling to Germany under the pseudonym Careu Kent during the couple's seventeen-year affair. At first, the story was met with skepticism, especially by Berg, who told the media it would have been "out of character" for Lindbergh to have carried on such an affair. But in late 2003, DNA tests confirmed that Lindbergh had indeed fathered the three German siblings. The story took another bizarre twist when the German magazine, *Focus*, revealed that Lindbergh had also fathered a second German family, producing two additional children with Brigitte Hesshaimer's sister, Marietta. It remains to be seen what other damaging secrets Lindbergh might have excised from the official record.

Berg himself noted a curious discovery while researching Lindbergh's papers: "He left messages to me, his future biographer. He would write on a letter, 'Do not believe this man. What he says isn't true.' At times, I thought he was trying to control me from the grave." Clearly, then, Lindbergh was conscious of influencing his own historical legacy.

As is the case with Henry Ford, the genesis and evolution of Lindbergh's racial views are difficult to pinpoint. A comprehensive analysis of his early correspondence reveals that racial or anti-Semitic animus is entirely absent from his thinking in the years before he encountered Carrel and Smith. Only after he began to spend time with Carrel, who was preoccupied with the study of eugenics and wrote about the "salvation of the white races," did Lindbergh's own racial views begin to form. Soon, he would be arguing that white people must not resist Hitler but should instead unite with the Nazis in a "western wall of race and arms" to hold back "the infiltration of inferior blood."[111] Similarly, there is not a single known example of anti-Semitism—either in his private writings or in anecdotal accounts by those who knew him—in the years before he encountered Smith. In fact, one of Lindbergh's closest early friends was the Jewish philanthropist Harry Guggenheim, whose foundation sponsored his nationwide goodwill tour in 1927. Lindbergh was so fond of Guggenheim that he felt compelled to assure his friend somewhat defensively that he did not approve of Hitler's anti-Semitic policies[112] after his first visit to Germany in 1936, although he refused to express similar sentiments publicly. As his friendship with Smith intensified, however, Lindbergh's journal entries became increasingly obsessed with the Jewish Question, especially the idea of pervasive Jewish influence over the press and the interventionist movement. In his biography, Scott Berg cites a number examples of Lindbergh's anti-Semitism previously censored from his journal, most of them relatively mild.

However, Berg appears to have ignored an entry that, perhaps more than any other, speaks volumes about Lindbergh's attitude toward the Jews. On November 19, 1938, only a week after *Kristallnacht* shocked the world, Lindbergh was standing on a Paris train platform when he spotted a group of Jewish refugees leaving to catch an American-bound ship. That evening, he recorded his impressions in his journal:

> The station platform is filled with Jews leaving for America. They were a poor looking lot on the whole . . . I have never been anti-Jewish and have great respect and admiration for Jews I know. Some of them are among my best friends. But this group on the station platform gave me a strange feeling of pity and disgust. These people are bound to cause trouble if many of them go to America.[113]

It is especially revealing to learn how closely Lindbergh's anti-Semitism parallels that of his friend Henry Ford, who also believed there were "good" and "bad" Jews. Smith, then, appears to have instilled in Lindbergh the idea that Jews were a dangerous political force, while Ford influenced his racial thinking.

Another revealing passage, which Lindbergh also censored from his published journals, sheds light on his reaction to the Des Moines controversy. Describing a recent rebuke of his speech by AFC Executive Committee member John Flynn a week after Des Moines, Lindbergh appears unrepentant:

> Apparently he would rather see us get into the war than mention in public what the Jews are doing, no matter how tolerantly or moderately it is done. On the other hand, I feel: (1) that the people of this country should know what Jewish influence is doing; and (2) that the Jews should be warned of the result they will bring onto their shoulders if they continue their present course.[114]

Berg argues that in later years, after traveling extensively throughout the world and living among people of all skin colors, Lindbergh had discarded his odious racist views, writing a friend, "The idea of racial inferiority or superiority is foreign to me."[115] Yet throughout his life, Lindbergh remained a passionate advocate of eugenics and as late as 1967, his correspondence reveals that he was anything but color blind. In a letter to his father's biographer Bruce Larson, written at the height of the civil rights movement, Lindbergh wrote, "I don't feel anti any race; and I don't see how anyone can intelligently speak of racial superiority without referring that superiority to some framework such as civilization . . . but I believe race is important, and that differences in race are desirable. If you know a man's race, you already know a lot about him."[116]

His daughter Reeve Lindbergh has been struggling for years to make sense of some of her father's views that she describes as "painful" for the family. In July 2002, she wrote me a letter attempting to explain what she calls his "blind" spot: "I know he didn't hate others individually, or in groups, but it was acceptable to see them in groups—'others'—and I think this was (and especially now, is) unacknowledged but pervasive."[117]

It is easy to understand, after reviewing Lindbergh's private papers, how many of his friends and critics appear to agree on only one word to describe him. Like Henry Ford, Charles Lindbergh was very much an enigma. But if an accurate assessment of what motivated the two men is still elusive, the consequences of their actions are all too evident.

CONCLUSION

The year 2002 marked both the centenary of Henry Ford's first automobile contract and Charles Lindbergh's birth, as well as the seventy-fifth anniversary of Lindbergh's transatlantic flight. As the media reported on these milestones, the focus was mostly on the achievements of the two men rather than their controversial pasts. The fanfare marking the anniversary of Lindbergh's flight indicates that he stands to serve as a role model for a new generation of young Americans. Schools and libraries mounted Lindbergh expositions extolling his historic feat and pioneering spirit.

Society tends to have a short memory. In a 1999 end-of-the-century Gallup Poll, an overwhelming 85 percent of Americans said they admired Henry Ford. Soon after, the Ford Motor Company advertising department commissioned a series of national TV ads featuring company CEO Bill Ford reflecting nostalgically on the legacy of his great-grandfather. Meanwhile, *The International Jew* continues to circulate on hundreds of Internet hate sites worldwide, and at least one edition is still in print, its influence perhaps increasing in proportion to the rehabilitation of Ford's own reputation.

The revived, rose-colored view of these deeply flawed men requires us to confront some important issues about American society. In his book *The Hero in America*, historian Dixon Wecter argues that hero worship in the United States fills an urgent need: The country elevates exceptional men to heroes in order to validate America's sense of destiny as a great nation.

Perhaps, then, the popular crusades of Ford and Lindbergh are an

385

indictment of our society's tendency toward idolatry. After all, in both cases, the public adulation that placed these two men on a pedestal offered them the undeserved credibility outside of their recognized areas of expertise to spearhead their campaigns. Moreover, both men were clearly manipulated by others, who understood the nature of hero worship and chose to channel it toward their own destructive ends. Yet naiveté alone cannot explain or excuse the actions of Ford and Lindbergh.

At the start of a new millennium, the men who were once revered as two of America's greatest heroes, then reviled as traitors, are once again widely admired. In the recent celebrations of their lives, there appears to be a deliberate effort to define their importance by their historic achievements rather than the detrimental sociopolitical consequences of their actions, which have been largely downplayed, rationalized, or ignored. Many argue that it is unfair to judge historical figures by today's standards—that they must be judged in the context of their times. An oversimplification at best, this argument must never be used as an excuse to blind ourselves to certain troubling facts.

Modern defenders argue that Ford and Lindbergh were vilified by their enemies for propaganda purposes, that they were unfairly cast as traitors, despite a proven record of patriotism. Many insist that while their isolationist activities were misguided, they stemmed from sincere conviction rather than from sinister motives. Today, the two men are often portrayed as undeniably great, albeit flawed, figures whose racial views simply reflected the society they lived in. The Ford Motor Company insists that it bears no moral responsibility for the actions of its founder or for its own use of slave labor during World War II. They argue that their contributions to Jewish causes demonstrate their commitment to combating anti-Semitism.

Conspicuously absent from these arguments, however, is the notion of accountability. In any honest assessment of these men's lives, we are obliged to evaluate the whole of their legacies in an effort to understand the enduring impact of two deeply contradictory figures.

At a time when the western world stood on the brink of catastrophe, both men allowed their prejudices to blind them to egregious horror. With Hitler's armies on the march, Ford and Lindbergh actively chose to impair the Allied war effort, jeopardizing the survival of democratic Europe. During a period when Jews were struggling to establish equality for themselves in American society, both men fanned the flames of anti-Semitism. Ford's company put profit over principles when it became an arsenal of Nazism. After the war, it chose to rehire the men who had perpetrated unspeakable human rights abuses.

In recent years, there appears to be a conscious attempt to portray these actions as mere character flaws. At worst, we are told, each man's conduct was a blemish on his otherwise exemplary career. Yet, their prewar crusades had a devastating impact that cannot be ignored.

Unless biographers and historians factor in the moral responsibility Ford and Lindbergh bear for the consequences of their actions, they do a disservice to the past, and to the future.

The specters of racial genocide in Kosovo and Rwanda, and a renewed wave of anti-Semitism in Europe, have once again cast a pall over world affairs. On the eve of the 2003 Iraqi war, U.S. Congressman James Moran told his constituents that "American Jews are responsible for pushing the country to war with Iraq," in a speech eerily reminiscent of Lindbergh's Des Moines address sixty-two years earlier. Unless we honestly examine the phenomena that fueled the destructive social forces championed by Ford and Lindbergh, we ignore—at our peril—a cautionary tale of intolerance, abuse of power, and reckless hero worship just as applicable to our own times.

ACKNOWLEDGMENTS

This book could never have come to fruition without the valuable assistance of many people, who I must gratefully acknowledge. First, my agent Noah Lukeman, for believing in this book; and my editor at St. Martin's Press, Alicia Brooks, whose unlimited patience, perspective, and sage advice made the editing process a painless one. Thanks also to Edwin Black, who offered invaluable advice on navigating the minefield of Holocaust-era research.

I would also like to thank my tireless international team of research assistants, who patiently scoured dusty archival repositories all over the world looking for just one more clue: Barry Stahlmann (Canada); Greg Murphy (Washington, D.C.); Carolyn Gammon (Berlin); Dina Leytes (Stanford); Devhra Bennett Jones (Cleveland); Tiyani Behanzin (London). Thanks also to my foreign language translators Carolyn Gammon (German) and Sasha Grinspun (Russian). I am especially grateful to Jacquie Charlton, Tod Hoffman, and Margaret van Nooten for reading and proofing the manuscript in progress, editing, and offering advice as the book progressed.

I am indebted to both Albert Lee and Neil Baldwin, whose own pioneering research into Ford's early anti-Semitism has made an invaluable contribution to the field, as well as Joseph W. Bendersky for his groundbreaking research into the history of anti-Semitism in the United States Army. I am also grateful to the unsung archivists and librarians all over the world who took time out of their busy schedules to offer assistance above and beyond the call of duty. Thanks especially to Cathy Latendresse at the

Henry Ford Museum, Greenfield Village; Brad Bauer at the Herbert Hoover Presidential Library; John Taylor, U.S. National Archives; Roland Bulatoff, Hoover Institution Archives; Holly Teasdle, Leo Franklin Archives; and Judith Schiff at the Yale University Manuscript and Archives Division.

Thanks also to the following for their much appreciated support and assistance: Phyllis Bailey; Mel Wallace; Elsa Iwanowa; Arnold Forster; Reeve Lindbergh; Dr. Sherwyn Warren; Heather Grewar; Prof. Jane Vieth; Lee Barton; Mel Weiss; Carol Leadenham; Morag York; Father Joseph Durkin; Prof. Barbara Farnham; Michael Kellogg; Greg Bradsher, Bill Walsh, Ed Barnes, and Milt Gustafson, U.S. National Archives; Liane Keightley; Joseph Bendersky; Francesca LoDico; David Kahn; R. Douglas Stuart Jr.; Prof. Williamson Murray; Prof. Bob Pearce; Prof. Alvin Poussaint; Astrid Link; Prof. Glen Jeansonne; David Nanasi; Heather Robb; Todd Shapiro; Gustavo Lever; Lee R. Hiltzik; Prof. Andrew Thorpe; Prof. Wayne Cole; Phil Fine; Prof. T J Davis; Andrew Schornick; Randy Sowell, Truman Presidential Library; Louise King, Churchill Archives Center; Beate Schreiber; Robert Fleming; Robert Parks; Lynda Claasen; Diane E. Kaplan; Richard Minear; Jeremy Wallace; Michele Anish; Duffy Knaus; Jennifer Parker; Little Falls Public Library; Sharon Smith and Ellen Thomasson, Missouri Historical Society; Esmond Choueke; Oliver Lechat; Mark Falzini; Nick Regush; Nonny McLaughlin; Marjean Kremer; Ian Halperin; Tessa Stirling; Irwin Miller; and Robert Dunnett.

PRIMARY SOURCES

Manuscripts

AJC—American Jewish Congress Archives, New York, NY

AJCA—American Jewish Committee Archives, Cleveland, Ohio
Louis Marshall papers
Nathan Isaacs papers
American Jewish Committee papers
"Anti-Semitism" papers

APS—American Philosophical Society Archives, Philadelphia, Pennsylvania
American Eugenics Society papers

BA—Bundesarchiv, Berlin, Germany
Reichsministerium für Volksaufklärung und Propaganda papers
Sicherheitsdienst (SD) of the Reichssicherheitshauptamt (RSHA) papers

BHC—Burton Historical Collection (Detroit Public Library), Detroit, Michigan

BHL—Bentley Historical Library, University of Michigan, Ann Arbor, Michigan
Josephine Gomon papers
Gerald LK Smith papers

CDAA—Committee to Defend America by Aiding the Allies Papers, Seeley G. Mudd Manuscript Library, Princeton University

FA—Rabbi Leo Franklin Archives, Temple Beth El, Detroit, Michigan

FDRL—Franklin Delano Roosevelt Presidential Library, Hyde Park, New York
  Franklin Roosevelt Presidential papers
  Franklin Roosevelt Personal papers
  Henry Morgenthau papers
  Stephen Early papers
  Eleanor Roosevelt papers

FFF—Fight For Freedom Papers, Seeley G. Mudd Manuscript Library, Princeton University

FMC—Ford Motor Company Industrial Archives, Dearborn, Michigan

GU—Georgetown University Library, Washington, D.C.
  Alexis Carrel papers

HFM—Henry Ford Museum, Greenfield Village Archives, Dearborn, Michigan

HHPL—Herbert Hoover Presidential Library, West Branch, Iowa
  Truman Smith papers
  Katherine Hollings Smith papers
  Hugh Wilson papers

HIA—Hoover Institution on War, Revolution and Peace, Stanford, University, Stanford, California
  America First Committee papers
  Lawrence Dennis papers
  Robert E. Wood papers
  Truman Smith papers

HLRO—House of Lords Record Office, London, UK
  Lord Beaverbrook papers

KSHS—Kansas State Historical Society

LC—Library of Congress, Washington, D.C.
  Harold Ickes papers
  Henry "Hap" Arnold papers
  William E. Dodd papers
  Boris Brasol papers
  William Allen White papers
  Amos R. E. Pinchot papers

LFPL—Little Falls Public Library Archives

MHS—Missouri Historical Society

MNHS—Minnesota Historical Society

NARA—National Archives and Research Administration, Washington, D.C. &
College Park, Maryland

NJSPA—New Jersey State Police Museum Archives

NUR—Proceedings of the Trial of German Major War Criminals,
Nuremberg, Germany

NYPL—New York Public Library Manuscripts and Archives Division
Rosika Schwimmer/Lola Maverick Lloyd collection

PRO—British Public Records Office, Kew, London, UK
AVIA—Records of the Air Ministry
FO—Records of the Foreign Office
PREM—Records of the Prime Minister's Office

PUL—Princeton University Library
Charles & Anne Lindbergh papers

RIA—Rockefeller Institute Archives, Sleepy Hollow, New York
Alexis Carrel papers

STAAT—Bavarian State Library, Munich

UCSDA—Mandeville Library, University of California, San Diego
Leo Szilard papers

UOL—University of Oregon Library
John Beaty papers

YU—Yale University Library
Charles Lindbergh papers

FBI Files (Freedom of Information Requests)

Charles Lindbergh
Henry Ford
Harry Bennett
Ford Motor Company
America First Committee
Boris Brasol
Truman Smith
Prescott Bush

Scribner's Commentator
Americans For Peace
No Foreign Wars Committee
Lawrence Dennis
Anglo-Saxon Federation
American Fellowship Forum
Edmund G. Heine (NARA)
Ernest Liebold

U.S. Military Intelligence Division (G2) Files

Truman Smith
Charles Augustus Lindbergh
Charles Lindbergh Sr.
Henry Ford II
Ernest Liebold
Harry Bennett
America First Committee
Ford Motor Company
Lawrence Dennis
Douglas Stewart

U.S. Office of Naval Intelligence Files

Charles Lindbergh
Ernest Liebold

Personal Interviews

Reeve Lindbergh
Katchen Smith Coley
Elsa Iwanowa
Tom Hoyt, Ford Motor Company
Elizabeth Adkins, Ford Motor Company
Arnold Forster
Cathy Latendresse, Henry Ford Museum, Greenfield Village Archives
Susan Hertog
Rainer Rohrbach

Edwin Black
Mel Weiss
Adolph Koch
David Kahn
Lee R. Hiltzik
Lee Barton, Royal Air Force
Dr. Sherwyn Warren
Father Joseph Durkin, Georgetown University
Darwin H. Stapleton, Rockefeller University Archives
Prof. Simon Reich, University of Pittsburgh
Dr. Williamson Murray, Institute for Defense Analysis
Prof. Barbara Farnham, Columbia University
Prof. Jane Vieth, University of Michigan
Prof. Bob Pearce, University of Edinburgh
Prof. Andrew Thorpe, University of Exeter
Prof. Emeritus Wayne S. Cole, University of Maryland
Prof. TJ Davis, Arizona State University
Prof. Alvin Poussaint, Harvard University
Prof. Glen Jeansonne, University of Wisconsin
R. Douglas Stuart Jr.
John Loftus
Mark Spoerer

Legislative & Government Documents

Elimination of German Resources for War, Senate Military Affairs
Subcommittee on War Mobilization, 79th Congress, 1945

Special Committee Investigating National Defense Program. Aircraft report.
(Truman Committee) July 10, 1943. Report 10, part 10, 78th Congress, 1st session

Public hearings before the special committee on un-American activities, House
of Representatives, 73rd Congress, second session, June 5, 6, 7, 1934, investigation of un-American Propaganda Activities in the United States

DGFP—*Documents on German Foreign Policy* (Captured German diplomatic dispatches)

FRUS—*Foreign Relations of the United States* (U.S. Dept. of State dispatches)

NOTES

Chapter 1. Chronicler of the Neglected Truth.

1. HFM, Acc. 7, Clipbook, 1919.
2. Fred Thompson, "Fordism, Post-Fordism and the Flexible System of Production," Willamette University School of Management.
3. Carol Gelderman, *Henry Ford: The Wayward Capitalist* (New York: Dial Press, 1981), p. 59.
4. Stephen Meyer III, *The Five Dollar Day* (Albany: State University of New York Press, 1981).
5. In Charlie Chaplin's 1936 film classic *Modern Times*, there is a famous scene of an endless factory assembly line with a figure closely resembling Henry Ford hovering over the workers. Satirizing the dehumanization of the industrial age, Chaplin's Tramp character is literally fed by a machine and then becomes the "food" in the cogs and gears of another machine.
6. HFM, Museum exhibit, "Henry's Stories," Jan. 23, 1914.
7. HFM, Museum exhibit, "Henry's Stories," Minutes, Ford Motor Company Board of Directors Mtg., January 15, 1914.
8. Gelderman, p. 52.
9. Ibid., p. 52.
10. HFM, Acc. 7, Clipbook, 1914.
11. Albert Lee, *Henry Ford and the Jews* (New York: Stein and Day, 1980), p. 8.
12. Ford Bryan, *Fords of Dearborn* (Detroit: Harlo, 1989), pp. 93–112.
13. In 1896, as an engineer at the Detroit Edison and Illuminating Company, he built a self-propelling "quadricycle" vehicle, but it was based on technology invented by others.

14. Norman Hapgood, "The Inside Story of Henry Ford's Jew Mania," *Hearst's International*, June 1922.

15. HFM, Acc. 572, Box 5, Folder: 9.4, *Chicago Tribune* Suit.

16. Fred Thompson, "Fordism, Post-Fordism and the Flexible System of Production," Willamette University School of Management.

17. Jonathan R. Logsdon, "Power, Ignorance, & Anti-Semitism," *Hanover Historical Review*, Volume 7, Spring 1999.

18. http://www.huxley.net (accessed April 14, 2003).

19. EG Pipp, *Henry Ford: Both Sides of Him* (Detroit: Pipp's Magazine, 1926), p. 68.

20. Lee, p. 31.

21. David Herbert Donald, *Lincoln* (New York: Simon & Schuster, 1995), p. 338.

22. Leonard Dinnerstein, *Antisemitism in America* (New York: Oxford University Press, 1994), p. 58. From 1890 to 1914, more than 16 million immigrants arrived in the United States. About 10 percent were Jewish.

23. Author interview with Marjean Kramer, Memphis Jewish Historical Society, conducted, August 18, 2000.

24. Leo Ribuffo, "Henry Ford and The International Jew," *American Jewish History*, vol. 69 (1980), p. 440. Ribuffo classifies three types of American anti-Semitism during this period: First, "polite" anti-Semitism, which restricted admissions into clubs, resorts, universities and the professions; second, the "Anglo-Saxon" cult; third, the association by many politicians and commentators of Jews with radicalism and Bolshevism.

25. Sometimes referred to as the *Protocols of the Wise Men of Zion*.

26. Holocaust History Project, Short Essays, "What are the Protocols of the Elders of Zion?"

27. Anti-Defamation League, Special Reports, *"Protocols of the Elders of Zion."*

28. Nizkor Project. Printed in Brussels in 1864 by an anonymous author, the book had actually been written in 1858 by Maurice Joly, an anti-Semitic French lawyer and monarchist from an old Catholic family. There are over 175 passages in the *Protocols* that are taken directly from Joly's novel. For example:

Joly, Brussels Edition 1864:
"Like God Vishnu, my press will have one hundred
arms, each hand of which will feel all shades of
public opinion." (p. 141)

From Nilus' "Protocols of the Learned Elders of Zion":
Like the Hindu God Vishnu, they will have one
hundred hands, each one of which will feel the
pulsation of some intellectual tendency." (p. 43)

29. Lee, p. 26.

30. *Dearborn Independent*, miscellaneous issues, 1920–22; Jonathan Norton Leonard, *Tragedy of Henry Ford* (New York: G. P. Putnam's Sons, 1932), p. 202.

31. *Chicago Tribune*, June 21, 1920, p. 8; Dinnerstein, p. 315. The *Monitor*'s edito-

rial appears to refer to the recent publication in England of a book about the *Protocols* entitled *The Jewish Peril*. But it seems that only after Ford gave them respectability, did the newspaper see fit to highlight its "warnings."

32. Previously, Marshall had been reluctant to respond to the *Dearborn Independent*'s campaign for fear of dignifying it, but now he decided he had to address the "puerile and venomous drivel."

33. Ibid.

34. Dinnerstein, p. 83.

35. Ibid., p. 81.

36. *The World's Foremost Problem, Vol. 1, 1920; Jewish Activities in the United States, Vol. 2, 1921; Jewish Influence in American Life, Vol. 3, 1921; Aspects of Jewish Power in the United States, Vol. 4, 1922.* The four pamphlets together were published in book form as *The International Jew*.

37. *International Jew: The World's Foremost Problem* (Dearborn: Dearborn Publishing Company, 1920).

38. Dinnerstein, p. 83. The FCC's condemnation made no actual reference to Ford or the *Independent*. It was left to the public to figure out who they were condemning.

39. Neil Baldwin, *Henry Ford and the Jews: The Mass Production of Hate* (New York: Public Affairs, 2001), p. 150.

40. Ibid. p. 151.

41. On August 16, 17, and 18, 1921, the *New York Times* ran articles by Phillip Graves, a *London Times* correspondent. Much of the *Times* account was drawn from the 1921 article *History of a Lie* by the American writer Herman Bernstein, editor of the *Jewish Tribune*. His article, later expanded into a book, first appeared in the *American Hebrew*, Volume 108, Number 17, p. 484–491. In fact, many other newspapers, as well as the book *The Jewish Bogey and the Forged Protocols of the Learned Elders of Zion* (London: *Committee of the Jewish Board of Deputies*, 1920) had already exposed the *Protocols* as a lie before this date but the side-by-side comparison offered the first conclusive proof, or at least received the first worldwide attention.

42. *NY World*, February 17, 1921. The *Independent* responded to the claims by writing, "The document itself is comparatively unimportant; the conditions to which it calls attention are of a very high degree of importance."

43. HFM, Acc. #1, Box 121, *DI*-Mail, 1921.

44. Ibid.

45. Dinnerstein, p. 81.

46. On the whole, African-Americans who worked for Ford were given the worst jobs and were excluded from managerial positions. Still, Ford almost singlehandedly created a large Black middle class in Detroit at a time when Blacks were suffering great economic hardship in the rest of the country.

47. HFM, Irving Caesar oral history.

48. HFM, Franklin to Ford, June 14, 1920, Acc. 572, Box 2, Rabbi Franklin.

49. Baldwin, p. 133.

50. HFM, oral history, Fred Black, p. 37.

51. Henry Ford, *My Life and Work* (Garden City, N.Y.: Doubleday, 1922), pp. 250–252.

52. "Commercialism Made This War," *New York Times Magazine*, April, 1, 1915, p. 14.

53. HFM, Acc. 7, Clipbook, 1915.

54. Jane Addams, *Peace and Bread in Time of War* (New York: Macmillan, 1922), p. 5.

55. "Henry Ford is Dead at 83 in Dearborn," *New York Times*, April 8, 1947.

56. *New York Times*, December 25, 1921. Eventually Ford identified the editor of the *Jewish Tribune* Herman Bernstein—the same writer who exposed the *Protocols* as a forgery in his article *The History of a Lie*—as the man who told him Jews were responsible. Bernstein successfully sued Ford for libel.

57. NYPL, "The Beginning of Henry Ford's Anti-Semitism" (ca. 1921–1922), Rosika Schwimmer-Lola Maverick Lloyd Collection.

58. Robert A. Rockaway, *Jews of Detroit* (Detroit: Wayne State University Press, 1986), p. 26.

59. Lee, p. 147. By 1920, when the *Independent* started its campaign, only five Jews lived in Dearborn, according to Neil Baldwin (p. 30).

60. Rockaway, p. 26.

61. Skipp Porteous, "Anti-Semitism: Its prevalence within the Christian right," *Freedom Writer*, May 1994.

62. David Gerber, *Anti-Semitism in American History* (Chicago: University of Illinois Press, 1986). In 1899, Twain would write an essay entitled "Concerning Jews" in which he attempted to address anti-Semitism.

63. Ibid., p. 68.

64. FA, Franklin Archives, "Leo Franklin, Unpublished Memoirs."

65. Ford somehow convinced Edison's son to sit by the dying inventor's bedside, clamp a test tube over his mouth, then plug it with a cork.

66. Lee, p. 154. He would later write a letter to the Jewish writer Herman Bernstein claiming he had been misquoted and that he had actually said, "If one went down to the bottom of things in the great and most successful industries, one would dig up a Jew who furnished the ability to make them a success." He never, however, publicly protested the quote or denied its authenticity.

67. Ibid., p. 154.

68. Albert Lee discusses the theory of Edison's influence in his book *Henry Ford and the Jews* without completely subscribing to the theory but Neil Baldwin, in his later book of the same title, disagrees that Edison's anti-Semitism was a factor. Baldwin claims this was one of the reasons he wrote his own book about Ford's anti-Semitism.

69. Ibid., p. 155. The official was Harry Bennett, head of Ford's Service Department, who said Ford denied being anti-Semitic in response to Edison's rebukes "on more than one occasion."

70. In Harry Bennett's memoir *We Never Called Him Henry*, he writes, ". . . some of those close to him began to poison his mind. I believe they convinced him that some difficulties he had with a bank loan he'd made was part of a Jewish plot" (p. 46). According to Edwin Pipp, Ford never had a bank loan rejected.

71. Rockaway, p. 26.

72. Ibid., p. 24. The paper was referring to the candidacy of a Jew named Liebman Adler, who later attacked the newspaper for its "stupid and dangerous incitement."

73. Neil Baldwin gives the date of Liebold's hiring as 1910 (p. 24), Nevins & Hill give the date as sometime after 1912 (p. 23). But in his Oral History, Liebold himself gives the date as 1911 and there is no reason to believe this is incorrect.

74. "Twenty Years With Ford," *New York Times*, March 1, 1933, p. 4.

75. Allan Nevins & Frank Hill, *Ford* (New York: Scribner, 1954), p. 13.

76. Bennett, p. 48.

77. Ribuffo, p. 444.

78. HFM, Fred Black oral history, Acc. 65, Box 6, pp. 130–131.

79. James Pool, *Who Financed Hitler?* (New York: Dial Press, 1979), pp. 82–83.

80. HFM, Liebold to Talmud Society, August 5, 1921, Acc. 572, Box 2.

81. Ibid., p. 223.

82. *"The International Jew,"* Anti-Defamation League, Special report.

83. BHL, "What started Mr. Ford against the Jews," *Pipp's Weekly*, March 5, 1921, pp. 2–3.

84. Ibid., p. 2.

85. NARA, RG 165, Entry 65, Box 1854, File #2801-445-123.

86. Mira Wilkins, *American Business Abroad* (Detroit: Wayne State University Press, 1964), p. 79.

87. NARA, RG 165, Entry 65, Box 2524, File 10104-379. The name of the writer is excised from the intercepted letter, which is addressed to John R. Rathom of the *Providence Journal*, who appears to be an underground military intelligence operative or informer. He writes, "I am confident the material and information will be of tremendous value to you and the government" so he seems to be reporting these facts under the impression that they will make their way to Washington. This report in itself is not enough to indict Liebold as a German spy but, in a subsequent follow-up by military intelligence, the source is called "reliable." When military intelligence receives raw data from a source, they will label it "Reliable," "Unreliable," or "Unknown," depending on the source. Usually, according to the department, a source will be labeled "Reliable" if he or she has previously furnished information on a number of occasions which has been proven to be accurate.

88. He identifies the three men as "Smith, in charge of the Ford chemical research work; Alfred Lucking, legal counsel for Henry Ford, and Knudsen, Ford manager of production."

89. Ibid.

90. NYPL, "The Beginning of Henry Ford's anti-Semitism" (ca. 1921–1922), Rosika Schwimmer–Lola Maverick Lloyd Collection.

91. Baldwin, p. 164.

92. Ibid., p. 165.

93. Harry Bennett, for example, blames EG Liebold for much of the negative goings on within the company in his memoir *We Never Called Him Henry* (New York: Gold Medal Books, 1951). William Cameron accuses Liebold, while Liebold, in his company oral history, blames both William Cameron and Harry Bennett.

94. Ribuffo, p. 461.

95. Gelderman, p. 245.

96. Reynold M. Wik, *Henry Ford & Grassroots America* (Ann Arbor: University of Michigan Press, 1972), p. 163. Ford received 83,058 votes to 77,872 for Smith.

97. BHL, "The Real Henry Ford," *Pipp's Weekly*, April, 8, 1922, p. 8.

98. HFM, Fred Black oral history.

99. Gelderman, p. 245.

100. HFM, Liebold oral history, p. 520.

101. Gelderman, p. 264.

102. Wik, p. 174.

103. Ibid., p. 174.

104. Gelderman, p. 246.

105. Ford had offered to lease the dam for 100 years at an annual rental of 4 percent of the $68 million construction costs, which would be provided by the government. The power produced by the dam would be available to Ford who also offered to pay an annual maintenance fee and a percentage of a complicated financial pool arrangement. The offer was considered by many government analysts much too beneficial to Ford and considerable pressure was put to bear to reject his bid.

106. When Harding died suddenly in 1923, Coolidge, his vice president, took office and went on to win the 1924 presidential election.

107. *Dearborn Independent*, October 28, 1922; Nevins & Hill, p. 653, note 22.

108. Michael Dobkowski, *Ideological Anti-Semitism in America* (Ph.D. thesis, New York University, 1976), p. 458.

109. Ibid.

110. To be sure, some elements of the Klan had occasionally shown anti-Semitic tendencies before this time, particularly when it tried to establish a foothold in Northern cities like New York or Chicago, but Jew-baiting didn't become a regular feature of its propaganda and activities until the 1920s.

111. Jonathan R. Logsdon, "Power, Ignorance, & Anti-Semitism," *Hanover Historical Review*, Volume 7, Spring 1999, p. 12.

112. *Dearborn Independent*, April 23, 1924, p. 1.

113. *New York Times*, March 12, 1927, p. 17.

114. David Lewis, *Public Image of Henry Ford* (Detroit: Wayne State University Press, 1976), p. 143.

115. Baldwin, p. 207.

116. Ibid., p. 207.

117. Logsdon, "Power, Ignorance, & Anti-Semitism."

118. Ibid., p. 99. Many of the farmers' letters give specifics of their complaints: "The price of tobacco is 30 cents a pound, I got 15 cents from the pool" (Gelderman, p. 229). But most studies of the farm co-op movement contend that its members fared considerably better than those farmers who were not part of the co-op. Sapiro himself had often been accused of dishonesty—including a well-publicized charge of corruption by his Colorado marketing director—and shady business practices in his management of the co-op. Indeed, he became very wealthy during his tenure. But the *Independent* was not attacking Sapiro for his business practices, it was attacking his Jewishness, and that is what he said prompted the lawsuit (although the judge later ruled that this was irrelevant to the case).

119. Gelderman, p. 232. Cameron claimed that the first conversation he had with Ford about the Sapiro series was only after he received the demand for a retraction. Ford, he claimed, asked what they were being asked to retract. "The Sapiro arti-

cles," Cameron replied in his dubious account. "What are they?" his employer asked, then told him, "If you're wrong, take it back, if you're right, stand by it."

120. "The International Jew," ADL Special Report.

121. Baldwin, p. 236. The emissaries were Earl J. Davis, former assistant U.S. Attorney General, and Joseph Palma of the New York field office of the Secret Service.

122. Ibid., p. 236.

123. Ibid., p. 235. Baldwin writes that it was at that same meeting that Ford had first suggested he was going to discontinue his attacks on the Jews and cease publishing the *Independent*, at which point Brisbane allegedly offered to buy the paper for $1 million.

124. HFM, Acc. #1, Box 122, *DI*-Shapiro, 1927–1928; Neil Baldwin (p. 237) and others have claimed that the letter was actually written by Louis Marshall of the AJC and then approved by Ford without him having read it, at which point his signature was forged by the head of his security department, Harry Bennett. This story is taken in part from Bennett's memoir *We Never Called Him Henry*. Bennett, who claims it was he who had urged the Sapiro settlement and apology, wrote that after he had received the text of the apology, he phoned Ford and told him, "It's pretty bad." Ford allegedly replied, "I don't care how bad it is, you just settle up. The worse they make it the better" (p. 56). It is hard to believe that the text, worded the way it is, could have been written by Louis Marshall. Why would Marshall have inserted phrases blaming others on the paper for its sentiments and completely clearing Ford of responsibility for its contents? In his unpublished memoirs, Rabbi Leo Franklin denies that Marshall wrote the apology.

125. FA, "Leo Franklin, Unpublished Memoirs," p. 139.

126. Gelderman, p. 234.

127. Logsdon, *Hanover Historical Review*.

128. Howard Sachar, *History of Jews in America* (New York: Knopf, 1992), p. 319.

129. Edwin Black, *The Transfer Agreement* (New York: Macmillan, 1984).

130. This line was taken from Logsdon, *Hanover Historical Review*, and may be a paraphrase from the original *Tribune* story.

131. Logsdon, *Hanover Historical Review*.

132. HFM, George Lombard to Ford, December 6, Acc. 1, Box 121, *DI*-Mail 1921.

133. Ibid.

134. Lee, p. 85.

135. Upton Sinclair, *The Flivver King* (Paris: Stock, 1938), pp. 126–127.

Chapter 2. The Führer's Inspiration.

1. William Shirer, *Rise and Fall of the Third Reich* (New York: Fawcett, 1950), p. 1480. There were actually 22 defendants indicted but Gestapo Chief Ernst Kaltenbrunner was temporarily ill and did not attend the opening session. Hitler's secretary and confidante Martin Bormann was missing but tried in absentia.

2. Robert Ley, former head of the German Labor Front, had committed suicide

before the trial began; industrialist Gustav Krupp was considered too frail to stand trial. Perhaps it is an overstatement to call the original defendants the most important. Each of the four prosecuting nations—the United States, England, France, and Russia—were allowed to designate names to the tribunal for indictment. Some defendants, chosen by the USSR, were indicted first at the insistence of the Soviets, although their crimes were significantly less severe than other members of the original 22.

3. NUR, Opening Statement of the Prosecution, 21 November 1945.

4. The exceptions were Nazi Armaments Minister Albert Speer, who assumed some "collective guilt" for the atrocities of the Third Reich and Hans Frank, who acknowledged some responsibility.

5. *The Encyclopedia Britannica* (London: 1994), Volume 5, p. 951.

6. Louis L. Snyder, *Encyclopedia of the Third Reich* (New York: McGraw-Hill, Inc., 1976), p. 256.

7. NUR, Proceedings of the Nuremberg International Military Tribunal, p. 890. This was presented in accompanying prosecutorial documentation outlining von Schirach's participation in a "conspiracy to persecute the Jews."

8. Ibid., p. 890.

9. Ibid., p. 891.

10. Ibid., p. 891.

11. Ibid., p. 892.

12. Shirer, p. 1482.

13. NUR, Proceedings of the Trial of German Major War Criminals (British transcript), 14th May to 24th May, 1946, One Hundred and Thirty-Seventh Day: Thursday, 23rd May, 1946 (London: His Majesty's Stationery Office, 1946). On October 1, 1946, the judgment was read: 12 of the defendants were sentenced to death, 3 sentenced to life imprisonment, 4 given prison sentences ranging from 10 to 20 years, and 3 were acquitted. Von Schirach was found guilty of count 4, Crimes Against Humanity, and sentenced to 20 years. After serving the full sentence, he was released from Berlin's Spandau prison in 1966.

14. Shirer, p. 144.

15. Ibid., p. 161.

16. Hitler had not yet taken over the leadership of the National Socialists, which he would assume in the summer of 1921.

17. Conflicting accounts give the date of the first German publication as 1920 and 1921. The latter date seems more likely, given that the book was only published in America in 1921.

18. Lee, p. 48.

19. *The International Jew: The World's Foremost Problem* (Dearborn: Dearborn Publishing Company, 1921), Chapter 24, "The High and Low of Jewish Money Power."

20. Ibid., chapter 6, "An Introduction to the Jewish Protocols."

21. ADL, *International Jew*, Special Report.

22. Pool, p. 71.

23. "Berlin Hears Ford is Backing Hitler," *New York Times*, December 20, 1922, p. 2.

24. Ibid.

25. "Says Ford Aids Royalists," *New York Times*, February 8, 1923, p. 3.

26. Ibid.

27. "Heinrich Ford Idol of Bavaria Fascisti Chief," *Chicago Tribune*, March 8, 1923, p. 2. The references to "Fascisti" stem from the name of Mussolini's original fascist movement in Italy—Hitler's inspiration.

28. Ibid.

29. Ibid.

30. Robert Murphy, *Diplomat Among Warriors* (Garden City, N.Y.: Doubleday, 1964), p. 23.

31. Pool, p. 27.

32. Joachim Fest, *Hitler* (New York: Harcourt Brace Jovanovich, 1974), p. 166.

33. Shirer, p. 65.

34. Ibid., p. 65.

35. Ibid., p. 65.

36. Dietrich Eckart, *Bolshevism From Moses to Lenin* (New York: Historical Review Press, 1998), chapter 3. Neil Baldwin writes that in recent years, some scholars, notably Albrecht Tyrrell, have questioned the authenticity of this work.

37. Shirer, p. 235.

38. Interview with Ford archivist Elizabeth Adkins, conducted via e-mail, March 27, 2002. Adkins says that when the company moved its archives into a central location in 1962, many files were "discarded," including a number pertaining to the Dearborn *Independent*.

39. Kurt Ludecke, *I Knew Hitler* (New York: C. Scribner's Sons, 1937), p. 16.

40. Ibid., p. 193.

41. Ibid., p. 194.

42. Ibid., p. 194.

43. Pool, p. 93.

44. Ibid.

45. Ibid.

46. Ibid., p. 195.

47. Ibid.

48. Ibid., p. 197.

49. Ibid.

50. Ibid., p. 201.

51. Pool, p. 95.

52. Pool, p. 93. Frau Wagner revealed Ford's admission during an October 1997 interview with James Pool while he was conducting his research into Hitler's early funding sources.

53. Ibid., p. 93.

54. Adolf Hitler, *Mein Kampf* (14th ed., Munich, 1932), Translated by Richard S. Levy, pp. 54–70. Many historians have disputed Hitler's claim that he did not grow up anti-Semitic and a number of later accounts from his contemporary acquaintances have contradicted much of his *Mein Kampf* description about the origins of his antipathy toward the Jews.

55. Hitler, p. 47.

56. Ibid. Most historians believe that Hitler's account was exaggerated or concocted to show that he was conversant with the "Jewish question" early on.

57. "Adolf Hitler's First Anti-Semitic Writing," G-Text Primary Source Archives, H-German Discussion Network.

58. Ibid.

59. Ibid.

60. Adolf Hitler, *Mein Kampf* (New York: Reynal & Hitchcock, 7th edition, 1939), p. 929. In later American editions, the reference to Ford is inexplicably excised and replaced by the passage "Only a few great men, to their exasperation . . ."

61. Ibid., p. 30, footnote. The note seems to be referring to the previous passage about the United States rather than the entire book, although numerous historians have stated the book was "plagiarized" or "copied verbatim" from the *International Jew*. See Lee, p. 59.

62. Lee, p. 62.

63. Ibid., p. 64.

64. Ibid., p. 60.

65. Ibid., p. 51. The passage is actually an alleged quote from a letter written by a Russian anti-Semite.

66. Although the *Protocols* were not published in German until later, they had surfaced in Germany in 1919 as part of an obscure book distributed in German aristocratic circles, written by Captain Müller von Hausen (editor of the newspaper *Auf Vorposten*) writing under the pseudonym of Gottfried zur Beck, who added numerous notes and commentaries to the appendix of Nilus's original forgery, and included them in pages 68 to 143 of his book entitled *Die Geheimnisse der Weisen von Sion*. There is no evidence that Hitler read von Hausen's book, although it was discussed at length in the April 1920 edition of the *Munchener Beobachter*—the newspaper that was later renamed the *Volkischer Beobachter*. However, the newspaper did not become the official organ of the Nazi Party until December 17th of that year so there is no reason to assume Hitler read this article since it is not mentioned in the earliest accounts of Hitler or his associates. The future party ideologist Alfred Rosenberg, who also met Hitler during this period and may have discussed the *Protocols* with him, was greatly influenced by them, writing five pamphlets about the documents between 1919–23. But these were written in Russian for the émigré community of Munich in which he traveled. The first Nazi Party edition of the *Protocols* wasn't published until 1933.

67. Eckart did mention the *Protocols* on at least two other occasions, however, including a 1920 reference in the anti-Semitic weekly *Auf Gut Deutsch* in which he writes that they show the "dastardly nature of Jewry."

68. According to UCLA historian Michael Kellogg, Ford's endorsement of the *Protocols* probably helped Hitler and others to believe in their validity.

69. Author interview with Kellogg via e-mail, February, 2002.

70. Hitler, *Mein Kampf*, pp. 307–308.

71. "Not all Conspiracy Theories are Created Equal," *Sierra Times*, August 28, 2001, p. 3.

72. Nora Levin, *The Holocaust: The Destruction of European Jewry, 1933–1945* (New York: T.Y. Crowell Co., 1968), p. 19.

73. Norman Cohn, *Warrant For Genocide* (New York, Harper & Row, 1967).

74. "Ford to Hitler: Have You Bought a Gas Chamber Lately?," *Challenge*, January 13, 1999, Volume 35, No. 20. I have been unable to locate the source of the origi-

nal quote and Rosenbaum failed to return several emails and phone messages inquiring about whether or not he wrote this passage.

75. Lee, p. 48.

76. HFM, oral history, Harold M. Cordell.

77. HFM, Schubert to Ford, October 25, 1920, Acc. 572, Box 2.

78. HFM, Liebold to Schubert, October 28, 1920, Acc. 572, Box 2.

79. Pool, p. 87.

80. "Protocols of the Elders of Zion," *American Jewish History*, vol. 71, 1981, p. 55.

81. Ibid., p. 55.

82. Ibid., p. 56; Brasol FBI file, FOIA. Before coming to America, Brasol briefly served with the Russian legation in London.

83. Bendersky, p. 56.

84. Baldwin, p. 140.

85. Bendersky, p. 58.

86. Ibid., p. 58.

87. NARA, RG 165, Entry 65, Box 138, File 99–75, Letter to MID Director, Brigadier General Marlborough Churchill, from Captain John B. Trevor, April 3, 1919.

88. Bendersky, p. 63.

89. Joseph Bendersky, *The Jewish Threat* (New York: Basic Books, 2000), p. 138. This book is a superbly researched, eye-opening account of the history of anti-Semitism in the United States Army and U.S. Army intelligence.

90. Ibid., p. 138.

91. Lee, p. 50.

92. BHL, *Pipp's Weekly*, "The Russian Lieutenant and Ford's Attack on the Jews," March 26, 1921, p. 1.

93. NARA, RG 165, Entry 65, Box 2524, File 10104-379. The file reached Churchill's desk after an inquiry by the U.S. Bureau of Citizenship about a planned trip to Mexico by Liebold on company business. Churchill forwarded the allegations that Liebold was a spy and then the file mysteriously ends. It is possible the end of the war one month later made the investigation moot but there is no document confirming the investigation is closed, as would be customary.

94. NARA, RG 165, MID 2610-37, Churchill to Colonel Sherman Miles, March 30, 1921.

95. Boris Brasol FBI file, FOIA.

96. "The Inside Story of Henry Ford's Jew Mania," *Hearst's International*, June, 1922.

97. HFM, "Departmental Communication," August 24, 1927, Acc. 572, Box 2.

98. Boris Brasol FBI file, FOIA.

99. "Protocols of the Elders of Zion," *American Jewish History*, vol. 71, 1981, p. 72.

100. There has been significant confusion about Brasol's role due to an incident involving a Russian woman named Pacquita Shishmareff (alias Leslie Fry). Fry approached Liebold in 1920 offering to sell him the "original" version of the "Protocols" for $25,000. Liebold turned her down because, according to his later account, he couldn't verify their authenticity. But it is not Fry who originally gave the paper the forgery, it was Boris Brasol, operating under the code name "Gregory." According to the Ford files, the original copy came via WG Eynon,

district supervisor of Ford operations in Delaware. On June 10, Eynon sent the text to Liebold, who immediately arranged to incorporate it into the paper's campaign. The Eynon/Delaware connection is still unclear.

101. Michael Kellogg, "Hitler's Russian Connection, White Émigré Influence on the Genesis of Nazi Ideology, 1917–23," Doctoral Dissertation Prospectus, UCLA, 2001.

102. Kellogg, p. 2.

103. Ibid., p. 3.

104. ADL, "The International Jew."

105. Israel Gutman, *Encyclopedia of the Holocaust* (New York: Macmillan, 1990), "Alfred Rosenberg."

106. Michael Kellogg, "Hitler's Russian Connection, White Émigré Influence on the Genesis of Nazi Ideology, 1917–23", Doctoral Dissertation, UCLA, 2001.

107. Hapgood, "The Inside Story . . .," June 1922.

108. Brasol FBI file, NY file 97-318, form 1, p. 2.

109. HFM, Brasol to Liebold, November 30, 1923; Brasol to Liebold, October 22, 1923; Brasol to Liebold, February 14, 1924, Acc. 572, Box 2.

110. Brasol FBI file. In a 1942 interview with an FBI Special Agent, Brasol claimed that he was traveling on behalf of Ford's attorneys to gather information that would help defend Ford in the libel suit filed against him by Herman Bernstein in 1923 after Ford claimed Bernstein told him that Jews were responsible for the First World War. He denied having any personal contact with Ford himself but, since he was not asked about Ernest Liebold, he makes no mention of him.

111. Pool, p. 88.

112. Ibid., p. 89.

113. AJCA, Palmer to Isaacs, March 29, 1933, Nathan Isaacs Collection.

114. *Forward*, August 10, 1926, p. 7.

115. *New York Times*, December 20, 1922, p. 2.

116. HFM, Lars Jacobsen to Liebold, March 14, 1921, Acc. 572, Box 2.

117. ADL, "*The International Jew*," Special Report.

118. HFM, Jacobsen to Liebold, June 11, 1921, Acc. 572, Box 2.

119. Ibid.

120. Ibid.

121. Ibid.

122. William J. Gilwee, "The End of An Era: The Passing of the Hohenzollerns," *Relevance*, Volume Five, Issue Four, Fall 1996. Hitler did not live up to his promise about restoring the monarchy. In 1933, Hermann Göring told the Kaiser that he could no longer draw income from his German estates but that he and his sons would be paid an allowance from the German government. The Kaiser was warned that if any of them spoke out against the Nazis, the allowance would end.

123. HFM, Liebold oral history, p. 260.

124. HFM, Louis Ferdinand to Sorensen, June 26, 1934, Acc. 572, Box 26, Folder: "Germany 1930s." Later, after Hitler broke his promise to restore the Imperial monarchy, Louis Ferdinand—like the rest of the German royal family—turned against the Nazis.

125. HFM, Ferdinand to Liebold, March 21, 1933, RG 23, Box 6.

126. Louis Ferdinand, *The Rebel Prince* (Chicago: Henry Regnery Company, 1952), pp. 240–241.

127. Ibid., 241.

128. Ernst Hanfstaengl, *Hitler: The Missing Years* (London: Eyre & Spottingswood, 1957), p. 41.

129. Sinclair, p. 118. He also claims Hitler funded the distribution of *The International Jew* in Germany.

130. HFM, Liebold oral history.

131. Louis Ferdinand, p. 154.

132. Ibid., p. 154.

133. *Who's Who of Nazi Germany* (London: Wiederfield & Nicolson, 1982), "Otto Meissner."

134. HFM, Liebold to Hailer, September 27, 1934, Acc. 285, Box 1610, Folder: 448 A—Mr. Fritz Hailer.

135. HFM, Liebold oral history, p. 461. The swastika was adapted by the Nazis as their official emblem in 1920. Liebold doesn't give a date for this incident but it had to be sometime between 1919 and 1927, the publication life of the *Dearborn Independent*.

136. Ibid., p. 462.

Chapter 3. Superhero.

1. "Daring Lindbergh Attained the Unattainable With Historic Flight Across Atlantic," *New York Times*, August 27, 1974.

2. "Lindbergh's Daring Raised in Pulpits," *New York Times*, May 23, 1927, p. 3.

3. Susan Hertog, *Anne Morrow Lindbergh: Her Life* (New York: Nan Talese, 1999), p. 66

4. "'Superhero,' Says Byrd," *New York Times*, May 22, p. 3.

5. Kenneth Davis, *The Hero: Charles A. Lindbergh and the American Dream* (Garden City, N.Y.: Doubleday, 1959), p. 220.

6. "Called Lucky but Says Luck isn't All," *New York Times*, May 23, 1927, p. 1.

7. "Capt. Lindbergh's 'We' charms Vatican Paper," *New York Times*, May 27, 1927, p. 2.

8. Davis, p. 214.

9. "Lindbergh's flight is hailed in Germany," *New York Times*, May 23, 1927, p. 4.

10. *New York Times*, May 24, 1927, p. 3.

11. "Lindbergh's flight is hailed in Germany," *New York Times*, May 23, 1927, p. 4.

12. Charles Lindbergh (hereinafter CAL), *Autobiography of Values* (New York: Harcourt Brace Jovanovich, 1978), hereinafter *AOV*, p. 310.

13. Barry Schiff, "The Spirit Flies On," *AOPA Pilot*, May 2002.

14. Dixon Wecter, *The Hero in America* (Ann Arbor: University of Michigan Press, 1966, c. 1941), p. 426.

15. CAL, *AOV*, p. 430.

16. Wecter, p. 432.

17. Ibid., p. 12.

18. Davis, p. 270.

19. Decter, p. 437.

20. Isabel Leighton, *Aspirin Age* (New York: Simon and Schuster, 1949), "The Lindbergh Legends," p. 201.

21. Ibid., p. 246.

22. CAL, *AOV,* p. 14.

23. Davis, p. 217.

24. "Daring Lindbergh Attained the Unattainable With Historic Flight Across Atlantic," *New York Times*, August 27, 1974.

25. Ibid.

26. Joyce Milton, *Loss of Eden* (New York: Harper Collins, 1993), p. 12.

27. "Fallen Eagle," *New York Times*, Sept. 27, 1998.

28. Ibid.

29. Bruce Larson, *Lindbergh of Minnesota* (New York: Harcourt Brace Jovanovich, 1971), p. 110.

30. CAL, *AOV,* p. 309.

31. "Daring Lindbergh Attained the Unattainable With Historic Flight Across Atlantic," *New York Times*, August 27, 1974.

32. CAL, *AOV,* p. 107.

33. In 1912 Woodrow Wilson won the Democratic party's nomination for president, and seemed to take up Lindbergh's themes when, in his acceptance speech, he warned against the "money trusts," and advised that "a concentration of the control of credit . . . may at any time become infinitely dangerous to free enterprise."

34. CAL, *AOV,* p. 207.

35. Ibid., pp. 207; 227.

36. Larson, p. 180.

37. Ibid., p. 182.

38. Ibid., p. 183.

39. "Commercialism Made This War," *New York Times Magazine*, April 1, 1915, p. 14.

40. Larson, p. 189.

41. Ibid., p. 196.

42. Ibid., p. 211.

43. Ibid., p. 204.

44. Ibid., p. 205.

45. Ibid., p. 235.

46. Ibid., p. 235.

47. Ibid., p. 236.

48. CAL, *AOV,* p. 61.

49. Little Falls *Daily Transcript*, March 17, 1903, p. 3.

50. Ibid., March 21, 1903, p. 3. His daughter Eva later claimed that C. A. eventually repudiated his racist views and came to a more enlightened view of the "Negro Question," but there is no public record that he ever did so, even on the floor of Congress, where anti-lynching laws were frequently debated.

51. Author's interview with Dr. Alvin Poussaint, conducted via e-mail, March 12, 2002.

52. CAL, *AOV*, p. 54–55.
53. Berg, p. 60.
54. CAL, *AOV*, p. 63.
55. Lardner, "Lindbergh Legends," p. 196.
56. "Daring Lindbergh Attained the Unattainable With Historic Flight Across Atlantic," *New York Times*, August 27, 1974.
57. Ibid.
58. CAL, *AOV*, p. 98.

Chapter 4. Strange Bedfellows.

1. "Lindbergh," *American Experience*, PBS, 1990.
2. Hertog, back cover.
3. Because of a technicality, he was referred to as Charles Jr. instead of Charles III even though his father and his grandfather were both named Charles.
4. "World Hails Birth of Lindbergh Child," *New York Times*, March 2, 1932.
5. Betty Gow police statement, March 10, 1932; FBI report.
6. New Jersey State Police Museum, Trenton, N.J.
7. Lindbergh FBI file, FOIA, press clippings.
8. A. Scott Berg, *Lindbergh* (New York: Berkley, 1999), p. 245.
9. "Daring Lindbergh Attained the Unattainable With Historic Flight Across Atlantic," *New York Times*, August 27, 1974.
10. Davis, p. 340.
11. Berg, p. 223.
12. According to their friend and fellow scientist Richard Bing, "When Lindbergh approached him with his idea of operating on the bloodless heart to rescue his sister-in-law from certain death, Carrel was not overly enthusiastic, knowing that these techniques were still in the future." Dr. Bing claims that Carrel and Lindbergh never really pursued this technique in their research. Instead, he says, Dr. Carrel "suggested that Lindbergh participate with him in a study that was more to Carrel's taste, the culture of whole organs, a system to maintain an organ outside the body by circulating nutrient fluid through its artery."
13. Davis, p. 340.
14. "Daring Lindbergh Attained the Unattainable With Historic Flight Across Atlantic," *New York Times*, August 27, 1974.
15. Davis, p. 348.
16. Francis Galton, *Memories of My Life* (London: Methuen, 1908).
17. Garland E. Allen, "Flaws in Eugenics Research," Washington University, Image Archive on the American Eugenics Movement.
18. Ibid. Recent scholarship, reveals Garland Allen, has shown that Carrie Buck's sterilization was based on a false "diagnosis" and her defense lawyer conspired with the opposing lawyer to guarantee that the sterilization law would be upheld in court.
19. Andre Sofair, M.D., and Lauris Kaldjian, M.D., Yale University School Of Medicine Study, February 2000.

20. Planned Parenthood claims that "Sanger uniformly repudiated the racist exploitation of eugenics principles." This is not quite true. The group's defense of their founder is less distorted and out of context than the numerous attacks on Sanger by pro-life groups. Nevertheless, much of it is not borne out by the facts. Much of what Sanger believed is unconscionable today and was abhorrent to progressive thinkers in her own day.
21. Margaret Sanger, "The Eugenic Value of Birth Control Propaganda," *Birth Control Review*, October 1921, p. 5.
22. Margaret Sanger, *Woman, Morality, and Birth Control* (New York: New York Publishing Company, 1922), p. 12.
23. Margaret Sanger, *Birth Control Review*, April 1932.
24. Margaret Sanger, "Plan For Peace," *The Birth Control Review*, April 1932, p. 106. She wrote, "The main objects of the Population Congress would be to keep the doors of immigration closed to the entrance of certain aliens whose condition is known to be detrimental to the stamina of the race, such as feebleminded, idiots, morons, insane, syphilitic, epileptic, criminal, professional prostitutes, and others in this class barred by the immigration laws of 1924."
25. Mike Richmond, *Life Advocate*, January/February 1998, Volume XII, Number 10.
26. Jonah Goldberg, "Westminster Eugenics Show," *National Review Online*, February 13, 2002. http://www.nationalreview.com/goldberg/goldberg021302.shtml (accessed April 10, 2003).
27. Jonathan Marks, "Eugenics—Breeding a Better Citizenry Through Science," Department of Sociology and Anthropology, Berkeley University.
28. David Morgan, "Study Says US Eugenics Paralleled Nazi Germany," *Reuters*, February 15, 2000.
29. Bernhard Schreiber, *The Men Behind Hitler*, translated by H. R. Martindale, available online at http://www.toolan.com/hitler (accessed January 28, 2003).
30. Ibid.
31. Davis, p. 348.
32. Alexis Carrel, *Man the Unknown* (London: Harper & Bros., 1935), p. 220.
33. Ibid., pp. 318–319.
34. Hertog, p. 276.
35. NUR, USA vs. Karl Brandt et al., Trials of War Criminals before the Nuremberg Military Tribunals under Control Council Law No. 10. Nuremberg, October 1946—April 1949. Washington, D.C.: U.S. G.P.O., 1949–1953. There is no accurate record of how many people were killed in the Nazi euthanasia programs. Estimates range from 20,000 to 400,000. On his deathbed, Franz Ziereis, the former commandant of Mauthausen Concentration Camp, estimated the total at 400,000.
36. Ibid., Trial of Karl Brandt, Defense exhibit 78, presented June 26, 1947.
37. Joyce Milton, *Loss of Eden* (New York: Harper Collins, 1993), p. 33.
38. Charles Lindbergh, *Of Flight and Life* (New York: Charles Scribner's Sons, New York, 1948), p. 42.
39. Bendersky, p. 262.
40. Berg, p. 225.
41. CAL, *AOV*, p. 17.
42. Mosley, p. 220.

43. Ibid., p. 220.

44. "Carrel of Discontent," speech delivered to The Chicago Literary Club by Sherwyn Warren, MD, former Chief of Thoracic Surgery, Lutheran General Hospital, November 8, 1999.

45. Ibid.

46. "Malinin to Discuss Lindbergh Perfusion Pump," *News and Notes*, newsletter of Rockefeller University March 12, 1999, p. 2.

47. The site's address is http://mbbnet.umn.edu/multimedia/gal3.html (accessed January 28, 2003).

48. Author interview with Dr. Wei-Shou Hu and Dr. Frank Cerra, September 11, 2002.

49. Interview with Dr. Sherwyn Warren via e-mail, September 17, 2002.

50. *Time*, July 1, 1935, cover.

51. "Daring Lindbergh Attained the Unattainable With Historic Flight Across Atlantic," *New York Times*, August 27, 1974.

52. Ibid.

53. RIA, "Voice of Broadway," Alexis Carrel papers, RG2, Rockefeller Boards, Pensions, Dr. Carrel's Retirement 1938–1940, Box 51, Folder 525. The item appeared in April 1939 several months *before* Lindbergh took his unpopular war stand so, unlike much of the later newspaper coverage of his activities, it was not designed to discredit him. Kilgallen used the word "intimates" rather than colleagues.

54. On September 1, 1935, the *Journal of Experimental Medicine* published "An apparatus for the culture of whole organs" by C.A. Lindbergh about his research but there is no way of knowing how much if any of this paper was written by Carrel.

55. Alexis Carrel and Charles Lindbergh, *The Culture of Organs* (New York: Paul Hoeber, Inc., 1938)

56. YU, Lindbergh to Father Joseph Durkin, May 20, 1966, Lindbergh papers, Series I.

57. Cole, *CAL*, p. 38.

58. *New York Times*, December 23, 1935, p. 1.

59. Hertog, p. 281.

60. Ibid., p. 281.

61. CAL, *AOV*, p. 145.

62. Interview with Anne Morrow Lindbergh, "Lindbergh," *American Experience*, PBS, 1990.

63. Harold Nicolson, *Diaries and Letters* (London: Collins, 1966).

64. Berg, p. 355.

65. The result would be *North to the Orient*, published in 1935.

66. Holocaust Timebase, 1938, Humanitas International.

67. HHPL, *Unpublished Manuscript of Katherine Holling Allister Smith*, p. 91.

68. The exception is a rather incomplete 1984 volume called *Berlin Alert* (edited by Robert Hessen, Hoover Institution Press, 1984, Stanford) compiled by the Hoover Institution which houses Smith's papers. This volume purports to be a cross-section of Smith's reports and attempts to shed light on his role in the controversial events involving Lindbergh. The volume completely ignores Smith's own anti-Semitism and appears to be attempting to whitewash Smith's role in these events, painting his activities in the most favorable light possible.

69. Robert Hessen, *Berlin Alert: The Memoirs and Reports of Truman Smith* (Stanford: Hoover Institution Press, 1984), p. 3.

70. Bendersky, p. 37.

71. Ibid., p. 38.

72. Ibid., p. 38.

73. Hessen, p. 11.

74. Ibid., p. 16.

75. Shirer, p. 75.

76. HIA, "Hitler and the National Socialists." Notebook and report of Captain Truman Smith, Infantry, U.S. Army, Assistant Military Attaché, Berlin, Germany, describing a visit to Munich from November 15 to November 22, 1922. Report, 1924, Truman Smith papers, Box 2, Speeches and writings, 1924–1956.

77. Ibid.

78. Ibid.

79. HIA, "Hitler and the National Socialists," November 15–22, 1922, p. 7, October 12, 1960, Truman Smith Papers, Box 2.

80. Ibid.

81. HIA, "Hitler and the National Socialists," November 15–22, 1922, p. 7, October 12, 1960, Truman Smith papers, Box 2.

82. Hessen, p. 62.

83. Shirer, p. 76.

84. William E. Dodd, *Ambassador Dodd's Diary, 1933–1938* (New York: Harcourt, Brace & Co., 1941), p. 360.

85. HIA, "Hitler and the National Socialists," November 15–22, 1922, Truman Smith papers, Box 2, p. 9.

86. Bendersky, p. 231; HIA, Truman Smith papers, "War College Monographs," 1932–1933, Individual Staff memoranda, Army War College Course, 1932–1933.

87. Hessen, p. xv.

88. Bendersky, p. 229.

89. NARA, MID, Truman Smith, "Anti-Semitism in Germany," File #2657-B-801.

90. Bendersky, p. 237.

91. Hessen, p. 79.

92. Ibid., p. 79.

93. Bendersky, p. 237.

94. NARA, "Anti-Semitism in Germany," January 12, 1939, RG 165, Box 1640, File #2657-B-801, p. 2.

95. Bendersky, p. 230.

96. NARA, "Anti-Semitism in Germany," RG 165, Box 1640, File #2657-B-801, p. 2. To some extent, this sentiment seems to be Smith interpreting Hitler's sentiment. However, in other parts, he makes it clear when he disagrees with the Nazis' viewpoint. In this context, he appears to be agreeing that the rise of Communism coincided with the rise of international Jewry. At any rate, he definitely expressed similar sentiments throughout his career.

97. Ibid. In some ways, Smith's analysis of the skill with which the Nazis exploited German anti-Semitism was quite brilliant. It would be unfair to say he agreed with most of the Nazis' attitudes toward Jews or their prescriptions for how to address

the "Jewish problem." But clearly his reports did not contain sufficient alarm or adequately emphasize the danger represented by Nazi anti-Semitism, especially since he was present at a rally in 1922 where he heard Hitler call for "Death to Jews." Like Lindbergh, he appeared to believe Nazi extremism could be channeled for the greater good of eliminating Soviet Bolshevism.

98. Holocaust Timebase, 1923, Humanitas International.

99. UOL, John Beaty papers, letter from Col. Truman Smith to John O. Beaty, March 24, 1955, incoming correspondence file.

100. Bendersky, p. 238.

101. Ibid., p. 171.

102. Ibid., p. 263.

103. HHPL, *Unpublished Memoir of Katherine Hollings Smith*, 1939–45, p. 3.

104. Ibid., "Diary."

105. Hessen, p. xvi.

106. Ibid., p. 85.

107. Smith frequently claimed that the records documenting these events had been "destroyed" during the war or seized by the Russians and therefore he had to rely on his and Lindbergh's recollections (see Hessen, 109). He claims that he didn't keep a diary during 1937, the year of the most significant developments in their collaboration.

108. "Marty Glickman's Stolen Medal," *Chapters in American Jewish History*, American Jewish Historical Society, chapter 81.

109. U.S. Holocaust Memorial Museum exhibit, "1936 Berlin Olympics."

110. "Berlin, 1936: At the Olympics, Achievements of the Brave in a Year of Cowardice," *Washington Post*, July 6, 1996, p. D1.

111. Ibid.

112. "China: A Dangerous Decision," editorial, *National Review Online*, August 6, 2001. http://www.nationalreview.com/6aug01/editorial080601a.shtml (accessed April 10, 2003).

113. "Give Me the Keys Please," *Journal of Sport History*, Vol. 18, No. 2, Summer 1991.

114. U.S. Holocaust Memorial Museum exhibit, "1936 Berlin Olympics."

115. HIA, Smith to Lindbergh, May 25, 1936, Truman Smith Collection, Lindbergh Correspondence.

116. HIA, Truman Smith, "Air Intelligence Activities (With special reference to the services of Colonel Charles A. Lindbergh, Air Corps)." Truman Smith Collection, Box 1, Air Intelligence Activities, p. 21.

117. Berg, p. 356.

118. HIA, Truman Smith, "Air Intelligence Activities (With special reference to the services of Colonel Charles A. Lindbergh, Air Corps)." Truman Smith Collection, Box 1, Air Intelligence Activities, p. 91.

119. Ibid., p. 27.

120. Ibid., p. 19.

121. Ibid.

122. Wayne S. Cole, *Charles A. Lindbergh and the Battle Against American Intervention in World War II* (New York: Harcourt Brace Jovanovich, 1974), p. 34.

123. "Lindberghs Arrive For German Tour," *New York Times*, July 23, 1936, p. 1;

Anne Morrow Lindbergh, *The Flower & the Nettle* (New York: Harcourt Brace Jovanovich, 1976), p. 82.

124. U.S. Holocaust Museum Exhibit, "1936 Berlin Olympics."

125. HIA, Truman Smith Papers, Lindbergh Correspondence, Smith to Lindbergh, May 25, 1936.

126. Interview with Arthur Schlesinger, "Lindbergh," *American Experience*, PBS, 1990.

127. Hertog, p. 293.

128. "Nazis banked on Lindbergh," *PM*, October 12, 1941, p. 10.

129. U.S. Holocaust Museum Exhibit, "1936 Berlin Olympics."

130. Ibid.

131. "China: A Dangerous Decision," editorial, *National Review Online*, August 6, 2001. http://www.nationalreview.com/6aug01/editorial080601a.shtml (accessed April 10, 2003).

132. Shirer, p. 323.

133. "Nazis 'Convicted' of World Crime by 20,000 in Rally," *New York Times*, March 8, 1934, p. 1.

134. Shirer, p. 323.

135. Ibid., p. 323.

136. AML, *The Flower & The Nettle*, letter from Anne to her mother, dated March 5, 1936, p. 101. After returning from Germany, Anne appeared to gain a brief respect for the Führer when she wrote her mother, "Hitler, I am beginning to feel, is a very great man. . . . a visionary who really wants the best for his country and on the whole has rather a broad view." She censored this letter from her published papers.

137. Guggenheim's foundation had sponsored his nationwide tour in the Spirit of St. Louis following the 1927 flight.

138. LC, Harry Guggenheim papers, Correspondence, Lindbergh to Guggenheim, September 15, 1936; YU, Lindbergh to Guggenheim, September 15, 1936, Lindbergh papers, Series 1.

139. YU, Lindbergh to Harry Davison, January 23, 1937, Lindbergh papers, Series I.

140. YU, Lindbergh to Col. Henry Breckinridge, September 23, 1936, Lindbergh papers, Series I.

141. Ibid.

142. Hertog, p. 324.

143. CAL, *AOV*, p. 147.

Chapter 5. Hate by Proxy.

1. HFM, Liebold oral history. It is hard to take anything in Liebold's oral history at face value but, given the subsequent events and other contemporary accounts, it is not at all unlikely that these words were uttered by Ford.

2. HFM, Liebold oral history, p. 504.

3. Lewis, p. 146. The company advertised in no other ethnic newspapers.

4. Ibid., p. 146.

5. "Marshall Says Ford is Sincerely Sorry," *New York Times*, January 17, 1928.

6. Marshall may have publicly declared his belief in Ford's sincerity but forgiveness only went so far. When Ford offered him a gift of a new Model A at the end of the meeting, Marshall refused the offer. "I respectfully declined, informing him of my devotion to pedestrian locomotion," Marshall wrote his son.

7. *New York Times*, June 1, 1927.

8. Ludecke, p. 313.

9. Ibid., p. 314.

10. Baldwin, p. 267.

11. Albert Lee claims that it was a few weeks later, Neil Baldwin claims it was three years later.

12. Lindbergh FBI file, FOIA, "Memo re: Anglo-Saxon Federation," J. Edgar Hoover to Wendell Berge; *PM*, August 14, 1940, p. 8; Lee, pp. 88–90; Baldwin, pp. 264–267.

13. HFM, Acc. 1, Box 122, Judaism 1930–1942, 'Anglo-Saxon Federation', by Boake Carter; Lee, p. 89.

14. HFM, Richard Gustadt to Harry Bennett, December 31, 1941, Acc. #1, Box 122, Judaism, 1930–1942.

15. Lewis, p. 328.

16. *PM*, September 20, 1940, p. 14.

17. Before the war, the *Ford Sunday Evening Hour* was carried on the CBS Radio network as well as the Canadian Broadcasting Corporation until the CBC decided the show was too politically motivated and decided to drop it.

18. *PM*, September 20, 1940, p. 14.

19. Lewis, p. 148.

20. His most popular and influential book *Handbuch der Judenfrage* (Handbook of the Jewish Question) became officially sanctioned reading in the schools of Germany after Hitler took power.

21. Baldwin, p. 273.

22. Ibid., p. 272.

23. Ibid., p. 272.

24. HFM, Acc. 285, Box 572; Gelderman, p. 235.

25. HFM, Liebold to Heine, November 27, 1933, Acc. 285, Box 1769, Folder: Frankl-Frar.

26. HFM, Acc. 285, Box 572.

27. Ibid.

28. HFM, EC Heine to Ernest Liebold, November 7, 1933, Acc. 285, Box 572.

29. HFM, Cohen to Liebold, December 5, 1933, Acc. 1, Box 122, Judaism, 1930–1942.

30. HFM, Liebold to Cohen, November 29, 1933, Acc. 1, Box 122, Judaism, 1930–1942.

31. *American Hebrew*, December, 1933.

32. HFM, J. L. McCloud oral history, p. 405 and p. 348.

33. Ibid.

34. AJCA, Nathan Isaacs Collection, Casimir Palmer to Nathan Isaacs, March 25, 1933.

35. Ibid.

36. AJCA, Nathan Isaacs Collection, letter from Casimir Palmer to Nathan Isaacs, March 29, 1933.

37. Some accounts give Chicago as the birthplace of the Teutonia Society but there is no question that Detroit and its large German population became its central organizing center at some point in 1924.

38. Carlson, p. 111.

39. For a time, the organization was known simply as the "Friends of Germany."

40. Francis MacDonnell, *Insidious Foes* (New York: Oxford University Press, 1995), pp. 42–43.

41. Haag was actually the organization's vice-president who briefly held the presidency until a successor for Spanknobel could be selected.

42. Michael Sayers, *Sabotage* (New York: Harper & Brothers, 1942), p. 141.

43. http://www.geocities.com/Heartland/Plains/2407/german.htm (accessed April 10, 2003). In reality, Americans of German descent seemed no more influenced by Nazi propaganda than anyone else. In the 1930s, one pollster found that 70 percent of the German Americans he interviewed were "totally indifferent" to international Nazism.

44. The committee also investigated subversive communist activities as part of its mandate but much of its focus was on native fascist groups.

45. MacDonnell, p. 43.

46. Hess actually issued an edict forbidding German citizens living in the United States to be members, which amounted to the same thing.

47. Kuhn had in fact been appointed provisional leader of Friends of New Germany in December, 1935 after the edict was issued barring German nationals from membership. Since he was a naturalized American, the edict didn't apply to him, unlike most of FONG's previous leadership.

48. There are a number of conflicting versions about the circumstances of his emigration. Some accounts claim he served a four-month jail term and then left Germany because, as a convict, he couldn't get a job.

49. Keith Sward, *The Legend of Henry Ford* (New York: Rinehart, 1948), p. 137.

50. There is no evidence that the Nazi regime gave any financial support to the Bund, despite Kuhn's later suggestions to the contrary. The German leadership appeared worried that the Bund's fanatical activities would hurt its credibility in the United States.

51. Donald Strong, *Organized Anti-Semitism in America* (Westport, Conn.: Greenwood Press, 1941), pp. 15–16.

52. MacDonnell, p. 47.

53. "Ford puts trust in Pioneer Spirit to bring recovery," *New York Times*, July 22, 1934.

54. "Ford Calls Crop Curtailment 'Thievery' Promoted by Financiers for Own Profit," *New York Times*, March 25, 1936, p. 1.

55. "Ford's Papers to be Dedicated Today," *New York Times*, March 7, 1953, p. 7.

56. Lee, p. 91.

57. Leni Riefenstahl, *The Sieve of Time* (London: Quartet, 1992), p. 238.

58. "The Great Ford Myth," *New Republic*, March 16, 1932, p. 118.

59. Sward, p. 370.

60. Harry Bennett, *We Never Called Him Henry* (New York: Gold Medal, 1951), pp. 10–11.

61. Sward, p. 370.

62. Ibid., p. 328.

63. Lee, p. 98.

64. *In Fact*, July 21, 1941; *PM*, May 1–4, 1941.

65. *PM*, May 1, 1941.

66. Ibid., August 14, 1940, p. 8.

67. Ibid.

68. Harry Bennett FBI file, FOIA, "Nazi-Ukrainian Sabotage and Espionage Ring and Fifth Column Activities," file # 61-10497-45.

69. *PM*, August 14, 1940, p. 8.

70. AJCA, Palmer to Isaacs, May 11, 1937.

71. "Ford Disclaims Book," *New York Times*, January 7, 1937, p. 44. Liebold may have been referring to Kuhn in this reply or he may have been referring to the continued association of William Cameron with the Anglo-Saxon Federation. It is ambiguous.

72. Lee, p. 97. Heupel later denied making this statement.

73. Harry Bennett FBI file, FOIA.

74. *Detroit Free Press*, March 12, 1937, p. 3. In his self-serving memoir, *We Never Called Him Henry*, Harry Bennett claims that he fired Kuhn in 1937 after the Bund leader made "unwelcome advances" to a nurse at the Henry Ford Hospital (p. 131). There appears to be no evidence to support this claim.

75. *PM*, September 20, 1940, p. 15.

76. Sward, p. 379.

77. Strong, pp. 57–58.

78. "Ford Secretary, Missing, is Found," *New York Times*, March 1, 1933, p. 4.

79. HFM, Liebold oral history, p. 1397.

80. Warren, p. 146.

81. Lee, p. 104.

82. Warren, p. 148.

83. "Pro-Fascists Dominate Ford Spy Ring," *PM*, May 1, 1941.

84. Warren, p. 148.

85. Strong, p. 61.

86. Ibid., p. 61.

87. Baldwin, p. 297.

88. "Safe but Not Secure," *Michigan Jewish History*, vol. 6, 1995–96, p. 12.

89. Warren, p. 149.

90. Ibid., p. 150.

91. Ibid., p. 150.

92. Ibid., p. 282.

93. Gerald L K Smith, FBI file.

94. Glen Jeansonne, *Gerald L K Smith: Minister of Hate* (New Haven: Yale University Press, 1988), p. 74.

95. Ibid.

96. Ibid.

97. "Introduction by Gerald L K Smith," *The International Jew*, originally published by Smith in abridged form during the late 1950s and now available on many Internet hate sites.

98. Bennett, p. 56.

99. Gerald L K Smith, FBI file.

100. Anti-Defamation League Special Report, *"The International Jew,"* 1998.

101. Ibid.

102. *PM*, August 14, 1940, p. 8.

103. Baldwin, p. 284.

104. "Ford, at 75, Looks to 'Going Ahead'; Huge Parties Given Him in Detroit," *New York Times*, July 31, 1938, p. 1; *Detroit Free Press*, July 31, 1938, p. 1.

105. HFM, Acc. #285, Box 2149, Fritz Hailer—Grand Cross of the German Eagle. The closest the citation comes to mentioning his automobile work is a brief reference to the admiration of the German people for what Ford has done "in your special field—the automobile industry."

106. Holocaust Timebase, 1938, Humanitas International.

107. The Holocaust Project Timebase, 1938, Humanitas International. Mauthausen was officially opened in early August—one week after Ford received his medal—to house the newly arrested Jews.

108. HFM, Hailer to Liebold, April 25, 1941, Acc. 285, Box 2149, Fritz Hailer-Grand Cross of the German Eagle.

109. "Nazi honor to Ford stirs Cantor's Ire," *New York Times*, August 4, 1938, p. 13.

110. "Urge Ford to reject German decoration," *New York Times*, August 7, 1938.

111. HFM, Emil Zoerlein oral history.

112. Lewis, p. 153.

113. Ibid.

114. FA, Unpublished memoirs of Rabbi Leo Franklin, pp. 148–152.

115. FA, Ford/Coughlin Anti-Semitism Collection, Box 2.

116. *Social Justice* Magazine, December, 1938.

117. FA, Folder: "News From All Over The World, Coughlin/Ford/Franklin," 1938.

118. FA, Unpublished memoirs of Rabbi Leo Franklin, p. 155.

119. Sward, p. 456.

120. FA, Smythe to Franklin, December 1, 1938, Folder: Correspondence: anti-Semitism, 1933–1938.

121. The medal given to Liebold was of a slightly lesser grade than Ford's medal in the Nazi hierarchy of citations.

122. HFM, Transcript of Liebold Acceptance Speech, Acc. #64, E.G. Liebold papers, 1938.

Chapter 6. History's Stage.

1. Old Time Radio, "The Munich Crisis."

2. Crisis over Czechoslovakia: March–September 1938, "The May Crisis," Department of Modern History, University of St Andrews.

3. Nizkor Project, Nazi Conspiracy & Aggression, "The Execution of the Plan to Invade Czechoslovakia," Volume I, Chapter IX.

4. Ibid.

5. Ibid.

6. "British Reaction to the Munich Crisis," *Student Historical Journal*, Loyola University, vol. 25, 1993–94.

7. Nizkor Project, Nazi Conspiracy & Aggression, "The Execution of the Plan to Invade Czechoslovakia," Volume I, Chapter IX.

8. Crisis over Czechoslovakia: March–September 1938, "Hitler's instructions to Heinlein," Department of Modern History, University of St Andrews.

9. Ibid.

10. HIA, Lindbergh to Smith, August 6, 1936, Truman Smith papers, Box 1, Lindbergh folder.

11. Ibid.

12. Hessen, p. 105.

13. Smith claimed that he received a telephone call in early September from Colonel Hanesse of the Air Ministry relaying the request by Göring. (See Hessen, p. 108.) But on August 23, Lindbergh had already written Smith informing him that he planned on attending the Lilienthal Congress and asking him to forward his letter of acceptance to the Air Ministry. (HIA, Lindbergh to Smith, August 23, 1937, Truman Smith papers, Box 1.)

14. Holocaust Timebase, 1937, Humanitas International.

15. Hessen, p. 111.

16. HIA, Truman Smith papers, "General Estimate as of November 1, 1937," Box 1, General Estimate folder.

17. Ibid., pp. 113–118.

18. YU, Lindbergh to Smith, November 4, 1937, Lindbergh papers, Series I.

19. Ibid.

20. YU, Lindbergh to Davison, October 28, 1937. Lindbergh papers, Series I.

21. Leon Sokoloff, "Alexis Carrel and the Jews at the Rockefeller Institute"; *Korot*, Vol. 11, 1995, p. 68.

22. CAL, *AOV*, p. 147.

23. YU, Lindbergh to Smith, May 9, 1938, Lindbergh papers, Series I.

24. Ibid., author's italics.

25. Ibid., p. 15.

26. Many historians believe that Cliveden regular King Edward VIII and his mistress, Wallis Simpson, worked in league with the Nazis to keep England from standing up to Hitler. But when Cabinet documents about the abdication crisis were made public in 2003, they contained no evidence of this.

27. "A Reevaluation of Cockburn's Cliveden Set," John Taylor, *Ex Post Facto*, vol. VIII, 1999.

28. Ibid.

29. Ibid.

30. William L. Shirer, *Berlin Diary* (New York: A.A. Knopf, 1941), p. 42. Dawson's support for Appeasement didn't mean he was a fan of Hitler. At one point during the Sudeten crisis, he protested in the *Times* that Germany was "applying the physical strength of the bully!"

31. Thomas Jones, *A Diary with Letters*: 1931–1950 (London: Oxford University Press, 1954).

32. "A Reevaluation of Cockburn's Cliveden Set," *Ex Poso Facto*, vol. VIII, 1999.

33. YU, 05/01/38, Lindbergh papers, Series V.

34. David Koskoff, *Joseph P. Kennedy* (Englewood Cliffs, N.J.: Prentice-Hall, 1974), p. 136.

35. Edward Renehan Jr., *The Kennedys at War* (New York: Doubleday, 2002), p. 45.

36. YU, 5/05/38, Lindbergh Papers, Series V. For his part, Lindbergh seems to have had a significant influence on Kennedy's attitude towards Germany, as the German Ambassador to England Herbert von Dirksen reported back to the Nazi foreign ministry on June 13, 1938, after meeting with Kennedy earlier that day:

> Although he [Kennedy] did not know Germany, he had learned from the most varied sources that the present government had done great things for Germany and that the Germans were satisfied and enjoyed good living conditions. The report by the well-known flier Colonel Lindbergh, who had spoken very favorably of Germany, made a strong impression on Ambassador Kennedy . . . (DGFP, von Dirksen to Foreign Ministry June 13, 1938)

37. Nicolson, *Diaries and Letters*. Lindbergh later claimed that he never said Germany was 10 times superior, merely that it was stronger than all the other countries combined.

38. Berg, p. 373.

39. YU, 08/17/38–08/31/38, Lindbergh papers, Series V.

40. YU, 09/04/38, Lindbergh papers, Series V.

41. Telford Taylor, *Munich: The Price of Peace* (New York: Doubleday, 1979), p. 764.

42. Taylor, p. 765. The French had received previously pessimistic intelligence estimates about German air strength but La Chambre appears to have discounted them as unreliable or else he was using Lindbergh's confirmation as an excuse to drive home the point to his Cabinet colleagues.

43. Taylor was the chief prosecutor at the post-war Nuremberg War Crimes trials and later wrote nine acclaimed historical books, most of them dealing with World War II.

44. Taylor, p. 765.

45. Shirer, p. 520.

46. Ibid., p. 520.

47. Michael Beschloss, *Kennedy and Roosevelt* (New York: Norton, 1980), p. 176.

48. Shirer, p. 531.

49. Ibid., p. 532.

50. YU, 09/21/38, Lindbergh papers, Series V.

51. Taylor, p. 768.

52. LC, Cordell Hull papers, Correspondence, 1938, Kennedy to Hull, September 22, 1938, containing the Lindbergh air power memo.

53. John Slessor, *The Central Blue* (London: Cassell, 1956), p. 219.
54. Ibid., p. 220. It is difficult to give much weight to this, or any other, postwar account. By that time, Appeasement had been thoroughly discredited and each player attempted to downplay their role in the embarrassing episode. The result is a number of self-serving revisionist accounts of the September 1938 events. The only credible source materials are the contemporary accounts from that month (e.g. memos, diary entries, official reports, etc.).
55. Koskoff, p. 152.
56. Ibid., p. 152.
57. YU, 09/23/38, Lindbergh papers, Series V.
58. Ibid., 24/09/38.
59. Steve Lehrer, *A City-by-City Guidebook* (New York: McFarland & Co., 2001), "Sportspalast."
60. YU, 09/27/38, Lindbergh papers, Series V.
61. Hugh Dalton, *The Fateful Years: Memoirs, 1931–45* (London: F. Muller, 1953–1962), p. 192.
62. NUR; Testimony of Hjalmar Schacht, April 30, 1946.
63. YU, 09/28/38, Lindbergh papers, Series V.
64. Shirer, p. 544.
65. Ibid., p. 545.
66. Ibid., p. 559.
67. Ibid., p. 567.
68. Winston Churchill, *Blood, Sweat and Tears* (New York: G. P. Putnam's Sons, 1941), pp. 75–80.
69. French intelligence had also come to a similar conclusion, although officials in the French government were skeptical of this estimate. Only when Lindbergh met with the French Air Minister Guy La Chambre in early September 1938 did the French appear to take this estimate seriously. In November 1937, Lindbergh estimated that Germany possessed 2400 first line planes. To arrive at his assessment of German air strength in September 1938, he or Truman Smith appears to have estimated how many planes were likely produced during the interval.
70. Williamson Murray, *The Change in the European Balance of Power, 1938–1939* (Princeton: Princeton University Press, 1984), pp. 247–249.
71. On October 1, British first-line strength was 1,606 planes with 412 aircraft in reserve. France possessed approximately 1,454 aircraft with 730 in reserve, according to British reports. Germany had virtually no aircraft in reserve.
72. German Military History Research Bureau, Specialty Group 6: Air Force and Aerial Warfare History; Davis, p. 225.
73. Williamson Murray, *Luftwaffe: Strategy For Defeat* (Baltimore: Nautical and Aviation Publishing Company of America, 1985), p. 18.
74. Williamson Murray, *The Change in the European Balance of Power*, p. 246.
75. Cajus Bekker, *Luftwaffe Air Diaries* (London: Macdonald, 1967), p. 24.
76. Shirer, p. 574.
77. Ibid., p. 572.
78. Ibid., p. 572.
79. Ibid., pp. 508–509.
80. Ibid., p. 575.

81. LC, Kennedy to Hull, September 22, 1938, Cordell Hull papers, Correspondence, 1938.

82. Williamson Murray and Allan Millett, *A War to be Won* (Cambridge: Belknap, 2000).

83. Berg, p. 384.

84. "In the Nation," *New York Times*, February 1, 1939, p. 19.

85. Ibid.

86. YU, Lindbergh to Harry Davison, March 31, 1939, Lindbergh papers, Series I.

87. Andrew Ferguson, "The Myth Machine," *Time*, November 1, 2001. http://www.time.com/time/covers/1101010813/myth.html (accessed May 7, 2003).

88. A. J. Langguth, *Our Vietnam The War, 1954–1975* (New York: Simon & Schuster, 2000).

89. PBS *American Experience* Web site: *The Presidents*, "Kennedy," available on-line at http://www.pbs.org/wgbh/amex/presidents/frames/featured/ken/kenee.html (accessed January 28, 2003).

90. Barbara Farnham, *Roosevelt and the Munich Crisis* (Princeton: Princeton University Press, 1997), n. 109.

91. John E. Wood, "The *Luftwaffe* as a Factor in British War Policy, 1935–1939" (Ph.D. thesis, Tulane University, 1965), p. 345.

92. Farnham, pp. 149–150.

93. YU, 09/29/38, Lindbergh papers, Series V.

94. Mosely, p. 231.

95. Taylor, p. 851.

96. Baldwin never did so.

97. William Manchester, *The Last Lion* (Boston: Little, Brown, 1983), p. 317. Duff had been working as a publicist for the Czech government.

98. Richard Suchenwirth, *Development of the German Air Force, 1919–1939* (New York: Arno Press, 1968), p. 190.

99. Taylor, p. 850.

100. The French air force chief, General Joseph Vuillemin, had visited Berlin and was taken on a tour of select German air installations in August 1938, exclaiming "I'm amazed" after a demonstration of the He-100 fighter. Although he was given nowhere near the same access as Lindbergh, he too returned to Paris with frightening stories of the Luftwaffe's might.

101. YU, 10/16/38, Lindbergh papers, Series V.

102. YU, "Lindbergh & Munich," Col. Raymond Fredette critique of Leonard Mosley's biography, *Lindbergh*, Lindbergh papers, Series X.

103. YU, Col. Raymond Fredette to Anne Morrow Lindbergh, April 3, 1976, Lindbergh papers, Series I.

104. Interview with Dr. Williamson Murray, conducted via telephone, December 26, 2001. Murray believes that Chamberlain and the Appeasers "did not necessarily surrender Czechoslovakia because of fear that Britain might lose a war" but rather because "of a desperate fear of war." In a controversial theory—disputed by many other historians—Murray argues that British government officials always knew they could easily beat Germany in 1938.

105. FRUS, Smith to War Department, October 5, 1938, 1938, Vol. 1, pp. 716–719.

106. PRO, Chilston to Lord Halifax, October 14, 1938, FO 371/22301.

107. Lindbergh FBI file; YU, 10/10/38, Lindbergh papers, Series V; Hessen, p. 129.

108. YU, 01/7/39, Lindbergh papers, Series V.

109. Richard M. Ketchum, *The Borrowed Years* (New York: Random House, 1989), p. 106.

110. HIA, Truman Smith, "Air Intelligence Activities (With special reference to the services of Colonel Charles A. Lindbergh, Air Corps"), Truman Smith Collection, Box 1, Air Intelligence Activities, p. 43.

111. Ibid., p. 42.

112. HIA, Truman Smith, "Air Intelligence Activities (With special reference to the services of Colonel Charles A. Lindbergh, Air Corps"), Truman Smith Collection, Box 1, Air Intelligence Activities, p. 92.

113. Ketchum, pp. 104–105.

114. In his 1987 book *Uncommon Friends* (New York: Harcourt Inc., 1987), Lindbergh's friend James Newton repeats this version, which he said Lindbergh told him as they sat together on an island beach in 1941. But Newton, who was also close friends with Alexis Carrel and Henry Ford, continuously uses his book to paint a favorable portrait of his friends, and his version can probably be considered unreliable and drawn from the Truman Smith account. Lindbergh himself never repeated this story in public or in his posthumously published autobiography. Presumably, he would have been anxious to do so in order to cast the medal incident in a more favorable light. Newton was a devotee of Frank Buchman and the fundamentalist Christian "Moral Re-armament" movement. Buchman himself was a one-time sympathizer of Hitler. He said in 1936, "I thank Heaven for a man like Adolf Hitler, who built a front line of defense against the anti-Christ of Communism." He also called SS chief Heinrich Himmler "a good lad," although it's probably overstating it to say that he approved of Hitler's Jewish policies. Asked about this, Buchman once replied, "Of course I don't condone everything the Nazis do. Anti-Semitism? Bad, naturally. I suppose Hitler sees a Karl Marx in every Jew." Nevertheless, these early Buchman views have always tainted the Moral Re-armament movement, much to the frustration of its followers.

115. Göring is sometimes referred to as a "moderate" on the Jewish question when compared to his more fanatical colleagues Himmler and Bormann. He once overlooked the fact that the wife of his trusted General Milch was of Jewish blood but many high-ranking Nazis also were known to ignore such issues for practical reasons. He was the Nazi who orchestrated Jewish slave labor operations during the height of the war. There is no question of Göring's intense hatred for the Jews.

116. Richard Breltman, *The Architect of Genocide: Himmler and the Final Solution* (New York: Alfred A. Knopf, 1991), p. 56.

117. Ibid., p. 56.

118. HHPL, diary of Hugh Wilson, October 7–October 31, 1938, pp. 57–62.

119. NARA, Cable from Wilson to Secretary of State re: "Presentation of medal to Colonel Lindbergh by General Field Marshal Göring," October 31, 1938, RG 65, State Department decimal file #093.622/45.

120. In the 1976 introduction to her published diaries and letters for the years

1936–1939, *The Flower & the Nettle*, Anne Morrow Lindbergh quotes the account in Truman Smith's 1956 intelligence report, suggesting that she and Charles had never heard the dubious story until Smith told it for the first time eighteen years after the event took place.

121. Hessen, p. 133.

122. Mosley, pp. 233–234.

123. HIA, Truman Smith, *Air Intelligence Activities (With Special Reference to the Services of Colonel Charles A. Lindbergh)*, 1956, Truman Smith papers, Folder: Air Intelligence Activities, Box 1, p. 9.

124. Ibid., p. 134. According to the Jesuit priest Joseph Durkin, a friend of Lindbergh and Alexis Carrel, Anne told him a different version. "Mrs. Lindbergh told me that when it happened she said, 'there's the weight of the world around your neck.'"

125. AML, *F&N*, 10/18/38, p. 437.

126. HIA, Truman Smith, *Air Intelligence Activities (With Special Reference to the Services of Colonel Charles A. Lindbergh)*, 1956, Truman Smith papers, Folder: Air Intelligence Activities, Box 1, p. 101.

127. HHPL, diary of Hugh Wilson, October 18, 1938, p. 59.

128. YU, Lindbergh to Göring, October 25, 1938, Lindbergh papers, Series V.

129. "Hitler Grants Lindbergh High Decoration," *New York Times*, October 20, 1938, p. 1.

130. "Lindy's Nazi Eagle," *Newsweek*, October 31, 1938, p. 19; Lindbergh's friend Prof. Ernst Heinkel, who was present when the medal was awarded, later wrote that, upon the presentation, Lindbergh "looked strangely at Göring, shook his head, and shoved the decoration into his trousers pocket like a handkerchief, without casting a glance around" (Richard Suchenwirth, *Development of the German Air Force, 1919–1939*, p. 191). Again, this account differs sharply from the contemporary account of Ambassador Wilson, who recorded a very different reaction in his diary that evening and whose account can probably be trusted as more reliable since it was not meant for public consumption and therefore could have no ulterior motive.

131. HIA, Truman Smith, *Air Intelligence Activities (With Special Reference to the Services of Colonel Charles A. Lindbergh)*, 1956, Truman Smith papers, Folder: Air Intelligence Activities, Box 1, p. 101.

132. YU, 10/18/38, Lindbergh papers, Series V.

133. Manchester, p. 317.

134. Ibid., p. 317.

Chapter 7. The Lonely Eagle.

1. Holocaust cybrary, "*Kristallnacht* Perspective."

2. Ibid. According to this historical analysis of the events, the Führer had "decided that such demonstrations are not to be prepared or organized by the party, but so far as they originate spontaneously, they are not to be discouraged either." The

Gauleiters (district chiefs), Kreisleiters (county chiefs), and the SA and SS leaders were accustomed to reading between the lines of such declarations. If they had any doubts, they were resolved by a teletype message sent out a few minutes before midnight by Heinrich Müller, the head of the Gestapo, to all central police stations.

a) Actions against the Jews and in particular against their synagogues will occur in a short time in all of Germany. However, it is to be made certain that plundering and similar lawbreaking will be held to a minimum.

b) Insofar as important archive material is present in the synagogues, it is to be secured by immediate measures.

c) The seizure of some twenty to thirty Jews in the Reich is to be prepared. Wealthy Jews above all are to be chosen. More detailed directives will appear in the course of this night.

3. Muller's title was actually "Chief of Operations."
4. A *reichsmark* equaled about forty American cents at the time.
5. Jewish Virtual Library, *"Kristallnacht,"* American-Israeli Cooperative Enterprise.
6. Contrary to popular belief, the pogrom actually stretched over two consecutive nights.
7. "Roosevelt Condemns Nazi Outbreak," *New York Times*, November 16, 1938, p. 1.
8. "Anglicans Strike at Anti-Semitism," *New York Times*, December 19, 1938, p. 4.
9. "Nazi Persecution Scored," *New York Times*, December 19, 1938, p. 4.
10. "Lindbergh Said to Plan to Move to Berlin," *New York Times*, November 16, 1938, p. 1.
11. Milton, p. 368.
12. YU, 10/29/38, Lindbergh papers, Series V.
13. Mosley, p. 237.
14. YU, 10/29/38, Lindbergh papers, Series V.
15. Mosley, p. 416.
16. YU, Carrel to Lindbergh, November 18, 1938, Lindbergh papers, Series I. Additional correspondence in Lindbergh's Yale University papers indicate that he may have changed his mind about moving to Germany even before receiving Carrel's letter.
17. FDRL, Eleanor Roosevelt papers, E. Roosevelt to L. Hickok, Nov. 14, 1938.
18. YU, 11/13/38, Lindbergh papers, Series V.
19. YU, Lindbergh to Carrel, November 28, 1938, Lindbergh papers, Series I.
20. HIA, Truman Smith, "Air Intelligence Activities (With special reference to the services of Colonel Charles A. Lindbergh, Air Corps"), Truman Smith Collection, Box 1, Air Intelligence Activities, p. 113.
21. YU, 12/20/38, Lindbergh papers, Series V.

22. YU, 12/22/38, Lindbergh papers, Series V.

23. Mosley, p. 240.

24. Ibid., p. 240.

25. CAL, *WJ*, 12/20/38, p. 130.

26. YU, 26/02/39, Lindbergh papers, Series V.

27. The invasion was staged jointly by the German, Romanian and Hungarian armies at Hitler's behest. In October 1938 Slovakia and Subcarpathian-Ruthenia respectively gained autonomy. On March 14, 1939, both had declared their independence. The next day Germany annexed the remainder as the "Reichsprotektorat" Bohemia & Moravia, while Hungary annexed Subcarpathian-Ruthenia and some more parts of Slovakia. (See Mark Sensen, "Carpatho-Ukraine, 1939.")

28. YU, 03/31/39 & 03/07/39, Lindbergh papers, Series V.

29. A number of writers, including the Lindberghs' biographer Joyce Milton, incorrectly state that Lindbergh returned to the United States at the request of the Roosevelt Administration or the U.S. military. But, according to Lindbergh's own account, he decided on his own to return because of his fear of an imminent European war. He was only invited back to active duty the day after he returned to America.

30. YU, 04/14/39, Lindbergh papers, Series V.

31. YU, 03/20/39, Lindbergh papers, Series V.

32. YU, 04/20/39, Lindbergh papers, Series V.

33. There were also a number of conservative southern Democrats in this isolationist group.

34. YU, 06/30/39, Lindbergh papers, Series V.

35. YU, 08/23/39, Lindbergh papers, Series V; Berg, p. 393. This passage was heavily censored in the original published edition of his *Wartime Journals*. The additional anti-Semitic comments were discovered and printed by A. Scott Berg when he was granted access to the Lindbergh papers.

36. MacDonnell, p. 62.

37. *Hollywoodism: Jews, Movies, and the American Dream*, 1998. Director: Simcha Jacobovici.

38. MacDonnell, p. 218.

39. Lindbergh FBI file, FOIA, Mumford to Ladd, Aug. 21, 1942 ("re: Charles Augustus Lindbergh").

40. Hertog, p. 355.

41. YU, 07/13/39, Lindbergh papers, Series V.

42. Mosley, p. 252.

43. Hugh Wilson, *Diplomat Between Wars* (New York: Longmans, Green Press, 1941).

44. Mosley, p. 253.

45. That is not to say that Smith leaked top secret data illegally. Intelligence officers have discretion whether to share intelligence information with members of Congress, diplomats and military officers with the proper security clearance. There is no evidence that he shared such intelligence with inappropriate civilians.

46. YU, 07/25/39, Lindbergh papers, Series V.

47. On August 29, the medical board recommended Smith be ordered before an army retiring board, "with a view to being retired from active service."

48. Bendersky, p. 275.

49. "Roosevelt Calls for Peace in Europe," *New York Times*, April 15, 1939; p. 1.

50. YU, 08/28/39, Lindbergh papers, Series V.

51. FDRL, "Presidential speeches," Sept. 3, 1939.

52. YU, 09/03/39, Lindbergh papers, Series V.

53. YU, 08/23/39, Lindbergh papers, Series V.

54. Wayne Cole, *CAL*, p. 71.

55. *Documents on German Foreign Policy (DGFP)* (Washington: Government Printing Office, 1949), vol. X, 1939, p. 298.

56. YU, 09/15/39, Lindbergh papers, Series V.

57. Ibid.

58. "Lindbergh's Appeal For Isolation," Text of Lindbergh speech, *New York Times*, Sept. 16, 1939, p. 9.

59. Ibid.

60. YU, 09/20/39, Lindbergh papers, Series V.

61. Berg, p. 397.

62. UCSDA, Szilard to Lindbergh, containing Einstein's letter of introduction in German, Aug. 16, 1939; Translation into English from Ronald W. Clark, *Einstein: The Life and Times* (New York: Avon Books, 1972), p. 674. Lindbergh later claimed he had never seen Szilard's letters.

63. Clark, p. 676.

64. YU, 09/21/39, Lindbergh papers, Series V.

65. Joseph P. Lash, *Roosevelt and Churchill 1939–1941* (New York: Norton, 1976); p. 23.

66. Churchill later claimed that Chamberlain had given him permission to communicate with Roosevelt. However, it is highly unlikely that the Prime Minister knew the nature of their communications or he surely would not have permitted it.

67. Yad Vashem, "Chronology of the Holocaust," 1939–1941.

68. YU, 10/02/39, Lindbergh papers, Series V.

69. His new designation was "inactive-active."

70. YU, 09/14/39, Lindbergh papers, Series V.

71. Gallup poll, October 14, 1939.

72. Georgetown University Archives, Alexis Carrel papers, "Memorandum as to a Proposed Center of Integrated Scientific Research," 1939.

73. "Neutrality and War: Text of Colonel Lindbergh's speech," *New York Times*, October 15, 1939; p. 9.

74. "Lindbergh Speech Assailed in the Senate," *New York Times*, October 15, 1939; p. 1.

75. "Lindbergh Thesis Disputed by O'Ryan," *New York Times*, October 15, 1939; p. 2.

76. FDRL, Eleanor Roosevelt papers, "My Day," October 19, 1939.

77. "Mrs. Roosevelt Attacks Colonel Lindbergh," *Christian Century*, November 1, 1939, pp. 1323–1324.

78. "British Host Gives Lindbergh Excuse," *New York Times*, October 22, 1939; p. 4.

79. Ibid.

80. Anne Morrow Lindbergh, *War Within and Without: Diaries and Letters of Anne*

Morrow Lindbergh, 1939–44 (Harccourt Brace Jovanovich: New York, 1980), 10/28/39, p. 64.

81. Berg, p. 395.

82. Charles Lindbergh, "Aviation, Race and Geography," *Reader's Digest*, November, 1939; pp. 64–67.

83. Ibid.

84. Cole, *CAL*, p. 128.

85. Kansas State Historical Society, "William Allen White."

86. Albert Fried, *FDR and His Enemies* (New York: St. Martin's Press, 1999), p. 194.

87. *New York Times* editorial, May 22, 1940, p. 6.

88. Complete Speeches of Winston Churchill, The Churchill Center, Washington, D.C., "Be Ye Men of Valour," BBC, May 19, 1940.

89. FDRL, Henry Morgenthau Jr., Presidential diaries, May 20, 1940, p. 563.

Chapter 8. An Arsenal of Nazism.

1. HFM, Acc. 7, Clipbook, 1939.

2. Warren, p. 148.

3. *Federated Press*, January 7, 1938.

4. Nevins & Hill, p. 172.

5. Warren, p. 173.

6. FDRL, "Collected Presidential Speeches," May 16, 1940.

7. HFM, Acc. 7, Clipbook, 1940.

8. PRO, Sir Henry Self to Rowland, June 8, 1940, AVIA 381724.

9. Knudsen told a United Press reporter on June 26 that the United States and England had a "gentleman's understanding." Ostensibly, the Americans were paying England for the "rights" to the British Rolls-Royce patent, which was a convenient way for the Americans to pay for the entire order without Congressional approval.

10. *Detroit Times*, June 26, 1940.

11. HFM, Acc. 7, Clipbook, "English Contract is Denied by Ford," 1940.

12. Ibid.

13. HFM, Charles Sorensen, *My Forty Years with Ford*, pp. 273–274.

14. CAL, *WJ*, 12/28/39, p. 300.

15. "Ickes Hits Takers of Hitler Medals," *New York Times*, December 19, 1938.

16. CAL, *WJ*, 06/25/39, p. 362.

17. "Lindbergh advises Ford on Airplanes," Petoskey *Evening News*, June 29, 1940.

18. HFM, Acc. 7, "Ford Plane Deal Dropped," Clipbook, 1940.

19. Ibid., "Canadian Denounces Ford as a Saboteur," AP, June 28, 1940.

20. HFM, Acc. 7, Clipbook, 1915.

21. Doris Kearns Goodwin, *No Ordinary Time* (New York: Simon & Schuster, 1994), p. 229.

22. NARA, T.H. Ball to O.A. Schmidt re: Heinrich Albert, RG 131, entry 247, Box 170, Germany General File Vol. II.

23. MacDonnell, p. 17.

24. NARA, Woodrow Wilson to Robert Lansing, December 5, 1915; RG 59: State Department decimal file #701.6211/327.5.

25. AJCA, Casimir Palmer to Nathan Isaacs, Mar. 25, 1933.

26. Frank J. Rafalko, "American Revolution to World War 2," *Counterintelligence Reader*, Vol. 1.

27. FMC-AR-98-213541, European Corporate, Box 131, Folder: 25 Years of Company History—Cologne.

28. Ibid., Appendix B, p. 123.

29. Ibid., p. 6. It is unclear whether these men were chosen by Dearborn directly or by Lord Perry, Chairman of Ford's British subsidiary, which oversaw the operations of Ford Germany for a time.

30. FMC, AR 98-213541, Box 131, Briefing Binder–Part N.

31. NARA, RG 407, Entry 368 B, Box 1032, 270/69/23/5, "Report on *Ford-Werke Aktiengesellschaft*" (hereinafter referred to as Schneider Report), exh. 2, "Dr. H.P. Albert," affidavit signed by R.H. Schmidt, June 22, 1945.

32. Ibid., p. 6. Edsel did not attend American IG Board meetings but was kept fully apprised of its activities.

33. NARA, RG 407, Entry 368 B, Box 1032, Schneider Report, exh. 65.

34. *Elimination of German Resources for War*, U.S. Congressional Committee Hearing, 79th–82nd Congresses, hearings before subcommittee on Military Affairs (1945–52), p. 943.

35. Simon Reich, "Ford's Research efforts in assessing the activities of its subsidiaries in Nazi Germany," November 2001, p. 6.

36. FMC, *Research Findings about Ford-Werke under the Nazi Regime*, prepared by Ford Motor Company archives, December, 2001, pp. 19–21.

37. FMC, AR-75-63-430, Box 90, File: *Ford-Werke* Finance 1938–1948, Business Report for 1938-Balance Sheet, December 31, 1938.

38. FMC, *Research Findings*, p. 21.

39. NARA, RG 407, Entry 368 B, Box 1032, Schneider Report, p. 3.

40. Ibid., p. 5.

41. Ibid., p. 5; FMC, *Research Findings*, p. 25.

42. FMC, *Research Findings*, p. 27.

43. Ibid., p. 6.

44. NARA, RG 407, Entry 368 B, Box 1032, Schneider Report, p. 6.

45. NARA, RG 407, Entry 368 B, Box 1032, Schneider Report.

46. Neither Ford nor Sorensen were present at this Board meeting but both were kept fully informed of the German company's decisions.

47. FMC, *Research Findings*, p. 28.

48. BA-L, R 87/6205, Schmidt and Albert to Reich Commissioner, June 18, 1941 (English translation, BAL 12930).

49. NARA, RG 407, Entry 368 B, Box 1032, Schneider Report, p. 6 (author's italics).

50. Albert claimed that he had been subject to "continuous bombardment" by Party officials. There are conflicting stories about whether Diestel was eventually replaced because of his Jewish blood or whether his "dictatorial" management style was no longer acceptable to the Board.

51. At first, Albert appears to have resisted the idea of replacing Diestel, arguing in

a letter to Sorensen that it is "ridiculous" for Diestel to be labeled a Jew with only one Jewish grandparent. But he appears to have changed his mind in an October 1935 letter to Sorensen when he admits that the "Jewish Question" could materialize into real sales resistance.

52. FMC, *Research Findings*, p. 12. Initially, Edsel and Sorensen had resisted Albert's efforts to fire the German manager.

53. NARA, RG 407, Entry 368 B, Box 1032, 270/69/23/5, Albert to Schmidt, October 31, 1940, exhibit 11, "Report on *Ford Werke Aktlengesellschaft*," p. 14.

54. Ibid., p. 7.

55. Ibid., p. 6.

56. NARA, RG 407, Entry 368 B, Box 1032, Schneider Report, exhibit 163, Affidavit of Robert H. Schmidt, June 15, 1945.

57. In many of his postwar affidavits, Schmidt uses Ford to refer to *Ford Werke* but he also uses the term to refer to Dearborn so it is inconclusive. My personal opinion is that he is referring to German Ford, not the American company. Therefore, there is no conclusive evidence Dearborn knew about the *Arendt* scheme.

58. Neither Sorensen nor Edsel Ford attended any *Ford Werke* Board meetings after April 1938 when Sorensen approved the contract with the German military.

59. NARA, Schneider Report, p. 7.

60. FMC, *Research Findings*, pp. 85–86.

61. Holocaust Cybrary, "IG Farben's Auschwitz Diet."

62. FMC, *Research Findings*, p. 114.

63. NARA, Schneider Report, exhibit 171, Heinrich Albert to General Zuckertort, June 26, 1940 (translated Aug. 22, 1945).

64. O. John Rogge, *The Official German Report* (New York: A. S. Barnes and Co., 1961), p. 292

65. Henry Ford FBI file, FOIA, Cross-References, J. Edgar Hoover to Henry Morgenthau, July 31, 1940.

66. Ibid.

67. *Frankfurt Zeitung*, January 1, 1941.

68. NARA, RG 60, Entry 114, Classification 146–39, Box 4, File: 146-39-24, Foreign Funds Control memo, May 25, 1943, pp. 21–22.

69. Ibid., p. 23.

70. Ibid., p. 23.

71. Ibid., p. 24.

72. Ibid., p. 25.

73. Ibid., p. 26.

74. Ibid.

75. Ibid., p. 31.

76. Ibid., p. 30.

77. Ibid., p. 34.

78. Reinhold Billstein, Karola Fings, Anita Kugler & Nicholas Levis, *Working For the Enemy* (New York: Berghahn Books, 2000), p. 112.

79. NARA, Schneider Report, exhibit 163, June 15, 1945, Schmidt affidavit.

80. See NARA, Schneider Report, exhibits 161, 163, 171; FMC, *Research Findings*, p. 103.

81. NARA, Robert H. Schmidt, Ford House Organ, *Ford Werkzeitung*, Dec. 1941, RG 407, entry 368 B, box 1032, Schneider Report, p. 10, footnote 4.

Chapter 9. America First.

1. YU, Roosevelt to Henry L. Stimson, May 21, 1940, Henry Lewis Stimson Papers, Manuscripts and Archives, Microfilm Reel 101, HM 52.

2. Although the FBI maintained an extensive FBI file on Lindbergh's political activities, there is no evidence that a wiretap was ever placed on his telephone.

3. Richard W. Steele, *Propaganda in An Open Society: the Roosevelt Administration and the Media, 1933–1941* (Westport, Conn.: Greenwood Press, 1985).

4. Mid-Hudson Regional Information Center, "Radio Address of the President," May 26, 1940.

5. MacDonnell, p. 49.

6. Ibid., p. 38. The charges were dropped after the jury failed to reach a unanimous verdict. It was later revealed that one member of the hung jury was a cousin of Father Coughlin's top aide, Father Edward Brophy.

7. "Prout Gave Bishop US Ammunition," *New York Times*, May 14, 1940, p. 17.

8. Bendersky, p. 255.

9. Ibid., p. 256.

10. Ibid., p. 257.

11. Ibid., p. 309.

12. YU, 06/22/40, Lindbergh papers, Series V.

13. Milton, p. 389.

14. Ibid., p. 389; YU, 05/28/40, Lindbergh papers, Series V.

15. YU, 06/22/40, Lindbergh papers, Series V.

16. Lindbergh FBI file, FOIA. Foxworth to Hoover, February 10, 1942. Dr. Schorr's nurse overheard the conversation and relayed the information to her friend, an FBI informant.

17. RIA, Handwritten note to Marcellus Dodge; RG2, Box 51, Folder 525.

18. Ibid., Thomas Debevoise to Marcellus Dodge, May 12, 1938, RG 2, Box 51, Folder 525.

19. Leon Sokoloff, "Alexis Carrel and the Jews at the Rockefeller Institute," *Korot*, vol. 11, 1995; p. 70.

20. Hessen, p. 33.

21. Walter Winchell, "On Broadway," *New York Daily Mirror*, September 17, 1940.

22. Truman Smith FBI file, FOIA, Clipping enclosed with a memo from Hoover to Clyde Tolson, September 26, 1940.

23. HHPL, Katherine A. H. Smith, *My Life: The War Years, 1939–46*, unpublished memoir, p. 32.

24. YU, 05/29/1940, Lindbergh papers, Series V.

25. University of Oregon Library, Smith to John O. Beaty, Beaty papers, incoming correspondence.

26. FDRL, Early to Watson, May 27, 1940, VF, Col. Lindbergh.

27. Mosley, p. 263.

28. Anne Morrow Lindbergh, *War Within and Without*, letter to Mina Curtiss, September 21, 1940, pp. 146–147.

29. Ibid., 04/29/40.

30. *Life*, May 15, 1939.

31. Anne Morrow Lindbergh, *Wave of the Future* (Rahway, N.J.: Quinn & Boden, 1940), pp. 15–16.

32. Ibid., p. 34.

33. Berg, p. 406.

34. Mosley, p. 275.

35. Ibid., pp. 275–276.

36. Lindbergh FBI file, FOIA.

37. "Third Inaugural Address of Franklin D. Roosevelt, January 20, 1941," Avalon Project, Yale Law School.

38. YU, Lindbergh papers, Series V, 09/16/40.

39. CDAAA, "America First" Subject File/America First, October 1940, Box 7, Seeley Mudd Library, Princeton University.

40. The first announcement on September 4, 1940, did not list Wood as chairman but he appears to have taken on the position soon afterwards.

41. America First Committee FBI file, FOIA.

42. Cole, *CAL*, p. 118.

43. HFM, Sorensen, pp. 273–274.

44. YU, 06/27/40, Lindbergh papers, Series V.

45. YU, 09/16/40, Lindbergh papers, Series V.

46. YU, Lindbergh to Ford, Sept. 27, 1940, Lindbergh papers, Series I.

47. "Sherwood Assails Ford, Lindbergh," *New York Times*, August 26, 1940, p. 9.

48. "Lindbergh-Ford Point of View Called Traitorous by Sherwood," *PM*, August 26, 1940, p. 8.

49. Wayne Cole, *America First: The Battle Against Intervention, 1940–41* (Madison: University of Wisconsin Press, 1953), p. 132.

50. Cole, *America First*, p. 118.

51. Lindbergh FBI file, FOIA.

52. Bendersky, p. 412.

53. Ibid., 413.

54. Lindbergh FBI file, FOIA, "Memorandum re: Colonel Charles A. Lindbergh," August 21, 1942, Special Memoranda Unit, FBI, file # 65-11449-152.

55. YU, Lindbergh papers, Series I, 07/10/40; Lindbergh FBI file, FOIA.

56. O. John Rogge, *The Official German Report* (New York: A. S. Barnes & Co., 1961), p. 174.

57. Ibid., p. 174.

58. Justus D. Doenecke, "The Isolationist as Collectivist: Lawrence Dennis and the Coming of World War 2," *Journal of Libertarian Studies*, April 28, 2000, p. 191.

59. Rogge, p. 182. Rogge, the assistant U.S. Attorney General, was the federal prosecutor in the 1944 sedition case against Dennis. *The German Report* was a published version of the report Rogge submitted to the U.S. Justice Department

summarizing his findings about Nazi penetration into the United States. When Dennis was indicted in 1942, the government seized all his correspondence and other documents in his possession. These seized documents form the basis of Rogge's report about Dennis' activities. Today, Lawrence Dennis is a darling of the far right, who contend he was persecuted for his "patriotic" ideas. They accurately point out that Rogge was for a time pro-Communist and even defended one of the Rosenberg defendants after he left the Justice Department. Whether or not Dennis was guilty of sedition (the case was dismissed and charges against Dennis and other defendants were dropped after the judge died midway through the trial), these letters are authentic and they reveal a number of Nazi ties, at least up until Pearl Harbor.

60. Justus D. Doenecke, "The Isolationist as Collectivist: Lawrence Dennis and the Coming of World War 2," *Journal of Libertarian Studies*, April 28, 2000, p. 191.
61. Ibid.
62. YU, 09/17/40, Lindbergh papers, Series V.
63. Rogge, p. 282.
64. Ibid., p. 282.
65. "Lindbergh," *PM*, October 3, 1941, p. 8.
66. HIA, Lawrence Dennis papers, Dennis to Truman Smith, June 14, 1957.
67. Milton, p. 392.
68. Anne Morrow Lindbergh, *War Within & Without*, diary entry of January 1941, p. 161.
69. Dr. Richard P. Hallion, "The Battle of Britain in American Context and Perspective," an address given at the Air Force History and Museums Program, Bollings Air Force Base, September 5, 1998.
70. BBC News Web site, "The Battle of Britain," available on-line at http://news.bbc.co.uk/hi/english/static/in_depth/uk/2000/battle_of_britain/default.stm (accessed January 28, 2003).
71. "Lindbergh Urges We 'Cooperate' With Germany if Reich Wins War," *New York Times*, August 5, 1940, p. 1.
72. *PM*, "Marshall's No-War Group Hailed by Nazis," December 23, 1940, p. 10.
73. Lindbergh FBI file, FOIA, Military Intelligence Division file on William Rhodes Davis, #10261-372, Report from Basil Walker to General Sherman Miles, December 30, 1940.
74. FBI file, *Scribner's Commentator*, FOIA, file #100-2685, p. 23.
75. Rogge, p. 301.
76. FBI file, *Scribner's Commentator*, FOIA, Eggleston subscription letter, March, 1941.
77. Rogge, p. 302.
78. NARA, Lindbergh IRR file, "Loyalty and Character Report, Charles Lindbergh," Open File 2667.
79. YU, 08/28/40, Lindbergh papers, Series V.
80. This would soon be renamed the No Foreign Wars Committee.
81. Lindbergh FBI file, FOIA.
82. Sward, p. 460.
83. YU, 14/01/41, Lindbergh papers, Series V. Lindbergh claimed that Marshall had prematurely publicized his planned St. Louis speech, disregarding Lindbergh's

specific request not to do so. This, among other things, he said, soured him on the organization.

84. Berg, p. 409.

85. HIA, AFC papers, Minutes of AFC Board of Directors Meeting, December 3, 1940.

86. This was another reason cited for Ford's expulsion in the Board resolution asking him to resign, although it is clearly a face-saving measure designed to cloud the real reasons, which are also stated in the resolution.

87. Cole, *America First*, p. 133.

88. HIA, AFC papers, I.A. Hirschmann to Stuart, November 1, 1940.

89. *PM*, "Text of President's Fireside Chat on the Crisis," December 30, 1940, p. 2.

90. Cole, *CAL*, p. 92.

91. YU, 01/06/41, Lindbergh papers, Series V.

92. *Life*, February 3, 1941.

93. Neil & Judith Morgan, *Dr. Seuss & Mr. Geisel: a Biography* (New York: Da Capo Press, 1996), p. 102.

94. Cole, *CAL*, p. 137.

95. Ibid., p. 138.

96. Shirer, p. 984.

97. Postwar Allied interrogations of most German Embassy officials based in Washington before Pearl Harbor as well as captured dispatches to and from the Nazi High Command confirm that Berlin took this directive very seriously, despite widespread fears encouraged by the American media that Nazi Fifth Columnists were plotting to sabotage American industrial and military production.

98. *DGFP*, Thomsen to Foreign Ministry, June 12, 1940, Series D (1937–1945), Vol. IX, pp. 550–551.

99. *DGFP*, Thomsen to Foreign Ministry, December 25, 1940, Series D, Vol. XI, "The War Years, September 1, 1940–January 31, 1941" (London: Her Majesty's Stationery Office, 1961), p. 949.

100. *DGFP*, Thomsen and Bötticher to High Command, July 20, 1940, Series D (1937–1945), Vol. IX.

101. *DGFP*, Thomsen and Bötticher to High Command, August 6, 1940, Series D (1937–1945), Vol. IX.

102. *DGFP*, Hans Thomsen and Friedrich Bötticher to Ribbentrop, April 27, 1941, Series D, Vol. XII, "The War Years, February 1, 1940—June 22, 1941" (Washington: Government Printing Office, 1962), p. 651.

103. Hessen, p. 24.

104. NARA, Interrogation of Friedrich von Bötticher, Nuremberg, Germany, October 12, 1945, RG 238, Entry 7A—Interrogations, Summaries & Related Records, M1270, Roll #1, Frames 1171–1187.

105. Lindbergh FBI file, FOIA, 65-28688-409.

106. Ladislas Farago, *Game of the Foxes* (New York: D. Mackay Co., 1972). In her unpublished memoirs, p. 37, Truman Smith's wife, Kay, claims that Farago's description of a "cabal" that met at her house was false, claiming that she never met any of the men whom Farago claims gathered for regular meetings at her house.

Chapter 10. Fallen Hero.

1. Alice Crockett vs. Fritz Wiedemann, U.S. District Court, Northern District of California Southern Division, June 9, 1941.

2. Louis Snyder, *Encyclopedia of the Third Reich* (New York: Paragon House, 1989), pp. 1046–1047.

3. Ford FBI file, FOIA, "Nazi Consul is Charged as Spy," *Associated Press*, March 5, 1941.

4. Higham, p. 196.

5. Ford FBI file, FOIA, "Story Ford Aided Bund is Termed 'Outrageous Lie,'" *Associated Press*, March 5, 1941.

6. Ibid.

7. YU, Lindbergh papers, Series V, 07/07/41. He claims he told Smith to tell the FBI to "go on tapping my phones." He had nothing to hide.

8. FMC, AR-73-17965, Box E:60, Folder: Executive Personnel records. He was earning a monthly salary of $3,733.00.

9. NARA, Hoover to Miles, April 22, 1941, RG 165, Entry 65, Box 1854, File # 2801-445-123. Liebold's name was included on a list of other names about whom Hoover requested information.

10. NARA, Miles to Hoover, April 25, 1941, RG 165, Entry 65, Box 1854, File # 2801-445-123.

11. ONI, Ernest Liebold dossier, June 9, 1941, file #97-331-4X.

12. NARA, Lindbergh IRR file, Letter from FBI, Grand Rapids, Michigan.

13. FBI file, Henry Ford, FOIA, "Ford Secretly Compiles Who's Who of Appeasers," *PM*, February 9, 1941, pp. 16–17.

14. FBI file, *Scribner's Commentator*, FOIA, file #100-2685, February 7, 1942.

15. FBI file, *Scribner's Commentator*, FOIA, file #100-2685, July 15, 1942.

16. Sward, p. 460.

17. Cole, *CAL*, p. 122.

18. Cole, *America First*, pp. 49–50.

19. YU, 01/01/41, Lindbergh papers, Series V.

20. Cole, *CAL*, p. 125.

21. FDRL, Ickes to Roosevelt, December 30, 1941 VF, Charles Lindbergh.

22. *New York Times*, April 24, 1941, p. 12.

23. "Colonel Lindbergh Tells House Committee He Hopes Neither Side Will Win," *Life*, February 3, 1941, p. 18.

24. Arthur M. Schlesinger Jr., *A Life in the Twentieth Century* (Boston: Houghton Mifflin, 2000), pp. 243–244.

25. "We chase a Lone Eagle and end up on the wrong side of the Fence," Cornell *Sun*, circa 1941.

26. Cole, *CAL*, p. 84.

27. Sir John W. Wheeler-Bennett, *Special Relationships: America in Peace and War* (London: Macmillan, 1975), pp. 131–132.

28. YU, 04/25/41, Lindbergh papers, Series V.

29. Manfred Jonas, *Isolationism in America, 1935–1941* (Ithaca, N.Y.: Cornell University Press, 1966), p. 240.

30. FDRL, "Presidential Press Conferences of Franklin D. Roosevelt," April 25, 1941.

31. Mosley, p. 284.

32. YU, 04/26/41, Lindbergh papers, Series V.

33. *New York Times*, April 28, 1941.

34. YU, 05/01/41, Lindbergh papers, Series V.

35. Gallup Organization, "Do you agree or disagree with what Charles Lindbergh says concerning American foreign policy?" Poll conducted between April 27 and May 1, 1941, surveying 1500 Americans. 13% registered no opinion. The poll was conducted only among Americans "familiar with his views."

36. CAL, *WJ*, May 12, 1941, p. 488.

37. YU, 05/13/41, Lindbergh papers, Series V.

38. YU, 05/20/41, Lindbergh papers, Series V.

39. Ibid.

40. FDRL, Early to Hoover, February 21, 1941; VF, America First Committee.

41. FDRL, Hoover to Watson, January 26, 1942; VF, America First Committee.

42. Cole, *CAL*, p. 148.

43. America First FBI file, FOIA.

44. CDAAA, "America First Committee, the Nazi Transmission Belt" (Friends of Democracy, Inc.), Publications/Pamphlets (1941), Princeton University Library, box 36.

45. "Join the America First Committee and continue to bombard your representatives in Congress," *Free American*, May 1, 1941, p. 1.

46. John Roy Carlson, *Under Cover* (New York: E. P. Dutton & Co., 1943), p. 330.

47. Cole, *CAL*, p. 149.

48. Lindbergh FBI file, FOIA.

49. Rogge, p. 357.

50. Charles Lindbergh FBI file, FOIA.

51. Berg, p. 402.

52. Cole, *America First*, p. 108.

53. Derounian was not an actual agent. He may have originally been working for the interventionist group Friends of Democracy but at some point in 1941, he appears to have been added to the FBI's payroll as an informant.

54. Carlson, p. 242.

55. Ibid., p. 250.

56. Ibid., p. 250.

57. Ibid., p. 206.

58. Ibid., p. 33.

59. Cole, *America First*, p. 121.

60. YU, Birkhead to Lindbergh, March 11, 1941, Lindbergh papers, Series I.

61. "Coughlinites, America First Part Company," *PM*, July 4, 1941; Carlson, p. 253.

62. Thomas E. Mahl, *Desperate Deception* (Dules, Virginia: Brassey's, 1999), p. 35.

63. Lindbergh FBI file, FOIA.

64. "Lindbergh Denies He Hinted At Overthrow of Government," *Washington Post*, June 10, 1941.

65. YU, 05/31/41, Lindbergh papers, Series V.

66. Many accounts gave false estimates of the AFC membership. In dispatches to Berlin, the German Embassy claimed the AFC had 15 million members while many interventionist organizations claimed the figure was closer to 85,000. AFC records now housed at Stanford's Hoover Institution reveal the organization's membership actually peaked at between 800,000 and 850,000 members in 1941.

67. "Lindbergh called Nazi Tool by Ickes," *New York Times*, July 15, 1941, p. 13.

68. LC, Harold Ickes papers, "Secret Diary of Harold Ickes."

69. "Lindbergh Leads Fascist Youth, Dr. Bohn Charges," *Washington Post*, June 30, 1941.

70. Cole, *CAL*, p. 146. Wood asked AFC member George Peek to approach Lindbergh about the idea.

71. Ibid., p. 145.

72. YU, Lindbergh to Smith, March 6, 1941, Lindbergh papers, Series I.

73. Lindbergh FBI file, FOIA, 65-39945-19.

74. YU, 07/16/41, Lindbergh papers, Series V.

75. FDRL, Lindbergh to Roosevelt, July 16, 1941, PPF, Box 1080.

76. LC, Ickes papers, "Secret Diary of Harold Ickes," pp. 581–582.

77. Lindbergh FBI file, FOIA.

78. LC, Ickes papers, "Secret Diary of Harold Ickes."

79. "Lindbergh Prefers Nazis to Soviets," *PM*, July 2, 1941.

80. *International News Service*, "Man is Machine to Lindbergh, Friend Writes," July 2, 1941.

81. FFF, "You're Not Our Hero, Ex.-Col. Lindbergh," Box 32, subject file: Lindbergh.

82. Decter, p. 432.

83. YU, 09/02/41, Lindbergh papers, Series V.

84. Lindbergh FBI file, FOIA, Memo from G. C. Burton to Ladd, November 26, 1941, 65-11449-104.

85. Harry Bennett FBI file, FOIA.

86. Historychannel.com, "Charles A. Lindbergh, Jr., American isolationist, Urges U.S. neutrality in World War II."

87. Author's interview with Arnold Forster, December 10, 2001.

88. Schlesinger, p. 257.

89. Berg, p. 428.

90. Cole, *CAL*, p. 175.

91. Charles Lindbergh FBI file, FOIA, "Cousin Assails Lindbergh as Hitler Helper."

92. Ibid., "Lindy Misrepresented Facts in Anti-Semitic Talk," *Chicago Daily News*, September 24, 1941.

93. Ibid.

94. Ketchum, p. 109.

95. YU, 09/11/41, Lindbergh papers, Series V.

96. YU, 09/15/41, Lindbergh papers, Series V.

97. YU, Flynn to Lindbergh, September 15, 1941, Lindbergh papers, Series I.

98. Anne Morrow Lindbergh, *War Within and Without: Diaries and Letters of Anne Morrow Lindbergh, 1939–1944* (New York: Harcourt Brace Jovanovich, 1980), 11/09/41, pp. 220–221.

99. Ibid., pp. 221–222.

100. Ibid., 14/09/41, p. 223.

101. BA, Press conferences, German Propaganda Ministry, Berlin, September 16, 1939; February 7, 1940, instruction A1042, A272, Brammer collection, Coblenz. Goebbels himself discusses this on a number of occasions in his diary, captured by the Allies after the war.

102. "New York Paper Praises Lindbergh," *PM*, September 26, 1941.

103. Carlson, p. 255.

104. "Jews Listed 5th in Pro-War Groups," *New York Times*, October 25, 1941, p. 7.

105. Robert Herzstein, *Roosevelt and Hitler* (New York: Paragon House, 1989), p. 265.

106. Ibid., p. 400. Forty-seven percent said yes; 46 percent said no.

107. Ibid., p. 371. The poll asked voters questions about a hypothetical congressional candidate. Respondents said his being "against the Jews" would negatively influence their judgment of said candidate.

108. Ibid., p. 371.

109. Ibid., p. 372.

110. Donald Stuart Strong, *Organized Anti-Semitism in America: The rise of group prejudice during the decade 1930–40* (Westport, Conn.: Greenwood Press, 1979, c.1941).

111. Charles Lindbergh FBI file, FOIA, "Lindy Follows Nazi Line"—Berle, October 6, 1941.

112. "Lindbergh: A stubborn young man of strange ideas becomes a leader of wartime opposition," *Life*, August 11, 1941, p. 70.

113. America First Committee FBI file, FOIA, J. Edgar Hoover to Edwin Watson, January 26, 1942.

114. Charles Lindbergh FBI file, FOIA, Memo re: Registration Act, SAC Sackett to Hoover, March 17, 1941.

115. "Isolationist Movement in US Labor Collapses," *PM*, October 7, 1941, p. 13.

116. Cole, *America First*, p. 152.

117. Ibid., p. 178.

118. YU, 11/12/41, Lindbergh papers, Series V.

119. *DGFP*, Thomsen to Foreign Ministry, November 13, 1941, pp. 772–773.

120. Berg, p. 433.

121. *America First Bulletin*, December 6, 1941.

122. FDRL, Leonard Conrad to Roosevelt, December 6, 1941, VF, America First Committee, file 4330.

Chapter 11. "Will It Run?"

1. According to Lindbergh, the gathering was also a celebration of Webster's recent marriage engagement.

2. Cole, *CAL*, p. 209.

3. Ibid., p. 210.

4. America First Committee FBI file, FOIA, "re: Laura Ingalls," Flinn to Ladd, December 22, 1941.

5. Michael Sayers and Albert Kahn, *Sabotage* (New York: Harper & Brothers, 1942), pp. 241–242.

6. Lindbergh FBI file, FOIA, Memo Re: Charles Augustus Lindbergh, Mumford to Ladd, August 21, 1942, file 65-114.449.1.54. When some of this speech was leaked to the press, Lindbergh later denied that he had talked about the "yellow danger" or about England and Germany getting together. Instead, he said that he had told the gathering that since the United States was attacked, it must fight, that the America First Committee was correct in dissolving and that all Americans should concentrate on conducting the war successfully. In his journal, he puts the date of the gathering at December 16, not the 17th. He does not reveal what he said at the gathering beyond defending the decision to dissolve the Committee. He does concede that "some of the more radical groups were represented at the dinner, and some of them were not at all in sympathy with the decision to dissolve the AFC." He doesn't mention that he was originally one of those people.

7. Ibid.

8. YU, Lindbergh to RD Stuart, December 8, 1942, Lindbergh papers, Series I.

9. YU, 12/26/41, Lindbergh papers, Series V.

10. LC, Henry Arnold papers, Lindbergh to Arnold, Lindbergh folder, December 20, 1941.

11. Ibid., James Herz to Hap Arnold, undated.

12. Ibid., G.H. Branaman to Arnold, December 30, 1941.

13. FDRL, Ickes to Roosevelt, December 30, 1941, VF, Charles Lindbergh.

14. FDRL, Roosevelt to Ickes, December 30, 1941, VF, Charles Lindbergh.

15. YU, 01/12/42, Lindbergh papers, Series V.

16. YU, 01/13/42, Lindbergh papers, Series V.

17. YU, 01/26/42, Lindbergh papers, Series V.

18. YU, 01/25/42, Lindbergh papers, Series V.

19. Ibid.

20. Berg, p. 437.

21. FDRL, Early to Hoover, February 21, 1941, VF, America First Committee.

22. Lindbergh FBI file, FOIA, Memo from G.C. Burton to Ladd, November 26, 1941, 65-11449-104.

23. Lindbergh FBI file, SAC Kitchin to Hoover, June 27, 1941; Hoover to McGuire, July 18, 1941; McGuire to Hoover, July 29, 1941.

24. Ibid., Bugas to Tamm, "re: Charles Lindbergh," December 13, 1941.

25. Ironically, Bennett also made the dubious claim that, during the same conversation, Ford had scolded his young friend for his recent anti-Semitic Des Moines comments.

26. Lindbergh FBI file, FOIA, Bugas to Hoover, December 13, 1941, 65-11449-105.

27. Ibid., interview between Edward Tamm and Lieutenant Lowell Bradford, file 62-4443, January 16, 1942.

28. Ibid., memo from Hoover to Tolson, Ladd & Tamm, December 12, 1941, file 65-11449-105.

29. FDRL, Hoover to Watson, re: Ethel F. Brigham, Barbara Brigham, January 26, 1942, VF, America First Committee.
30. Lindbergh FBI file, FOIA, D.A. Flinn to Ladd, re: Laura Ingalls, December 22, 1941, 100-34712-119.
31. FDRL, Hoover to Watson, February 13, 1942, VF, America First Committee.
32. Mosley, p. 312.
33. HFM, Acc. 7, Clipbook, 1941.
34. YU, 03/24/42, Lindbergh papers, Series V.
35. Ford Motor Company War Department MID file, FOIA, April 4, 1942, MID 004.4 Ford Motor Company.
36. YU, Unsent letter to *Liberty* magazine, circa July 1942, Lindbergh papers, Series 1.
37. "Nazi Sympathizer Pelley Dies at 65," Associated Press, February 7, 1965.
38. Lindbergh FBI file, FOIA, 65-14449-A.
39. YU, 18/09/42, Lindbergh papers, Series V.
40. Sward, p. 462.
41. YU, 09/11/42, Lindbergh papers, Series V.
42. One of the family matriarchs, Mary Belin DuPont, had some Jewish blood but it would be ludicrous to call the family Jewish. Many American anti-Semites at the time were also convinced that Roosevelt was Jewish and attempted to prove that his bloodline had Jewish blood in order to prove their point. According to a number of oral histories by Henry Ford's associates, he always invoked the "Jewish DuPonts" during his diatribes against Roosevelt, so he may have believed this fiction.
43. FMC, *Research Findings*, p. 16.
44. YU, 08/11/42, Lindbergh papers, Series V.
45. Ibid., 09/04/42.
46. YU, Lindbergh to Ford, July 30, 1942, Lindbergh papers, Series I.
47. Sward, p. 447.
48. Special Committee Investigating the National Defense Program, Aircraft," 77th Congress, July 10, 1943, pp. 6–7.
49. Sward, p. 448.
50. NARA, Lindbergh IRR file, "Loyalty and Character Report, Charles Lindbergh," open file # S1-4960.
51. Baldwin, p. 316.
52. Bennett, p. 5.
53. Ibid., p. 168.
54. Ibid., p. 160.
55. "Mrs. Roosevelt Says Ford Could Be Taken Over," *New York Herald Tribune*, January 28, 1941.
56. Sward, p. 449.
57. Jeansonne, p. 152.
58. Lindbergh FBI file, FOIA, "Internal security Sedition report, Gerald L K Smith," file 62-1126.
59. NARA, Lindbergh IRR file, Lindbergh MID file, "Additional references on above subject."
60. Harry Bennett FBI file, FOIA.
61. Ibid.

62. I discovered the memo while poring through the tens of thousands of pages of documentation accompanying the *Ford-Werke* report, which were deposited at the independent Henry Ford Museum at the completion of the investigation. (See chapter 12)

63. FMC, "re: Ernest Liebold"; Folder: International executive Files; JS Bugas, VP Industrial Relations, Industrial Consultant, AR 68-5, Box 8.

64. Ibid.

65. One of the espionage accounts was reversed on appeal in 1945.

66. NARA, RG-60, Heine FBI file, Box 24, file # 146-43-278.

67. Ibid.

68. FMC, "re: Ernest Liebold"; Folder: International executive Files; JS Bugas, VP Industrial Relations, Industrial Consultant, AR 68-5, Box 8.

69. Ibid.

70. FMC, "re: Ernest Liebold"; Folder: International executive Files; JS Bugas, VP Industrial Relations, Industrial Consultant, AR 68-5, Box 8.

71. Bennett, pp. 172–173.

72. Ibid., p. 173.

73. Ibid., p. 173.

74. FMC, AR-73-17965, Box E-60, Folder: Executive Personnel records.

75. HFM, Liebold Oral History, p. 1271.

76. In his oral history, Liebold claims that he had never been offered another position but a letter in his personnel record claims that he had "refused" the position.

77. FMC, AR-68-5, "Liebold, Ernest G." May 17, 1944, Box 8, Folder: International—Executive Files; J.S. Bugas, VP International.

78. In 1941, Bennett told the FBI that Liebold was in "the bad graces" of Henry Ford and had been removed as his personal secretary. Because of Liebold's strong pro-German sympathies, Bennett claimed, he didn't have any access to company military contracts. However, like much of Bennett's account, this is simply not credible.

79. Berg, p. 449.

80. Ibid., p. 449.

81. YU, 05/29/44, Lindbergh papers, Series V.

82. HHPL, *Unpublished Memoir Of Katherine Hollister Smith*, p. 126.

Chapter 12. Business as Usual.

1. Author interview in Russian with Elsa Iwanowa, April 14, 2002, via telephone (translation by Sasha Grinspun).

2. *Elsa Iwanowa vs. Ford Motor Company and Ford Werke A.G.*, United States District Court, District of New Jersey, March 4, 1998.

3. Nicholas Lewis, "Introduction," *Working For the Enemy*, p. 6.

4. Ibid.

5. Ibid. Thirty-eight other young Russian girls were also purchased by *Ford-Werke* that day.

6. Author interview with Elsa Iwanowa, April 14, 2002.

7. FMC, *Research Findings*, p. 53.

8. Fings, p. 180.

9. Nicholas Lewis, p. 6.

10. NARA, RG 407, Entry 368 B, Box 1032, 270/69/23/5, Albert memo, November 25, 1941, "Report on *Ford Werke Aktiengesellschaft*," exh. 1.

11. FMC, *Research Findings*, p. i.

12. IG Farben's ownership stake in *Ford-Werke* was constantly revolving, reaching a low of 6 percent and a high of 15 percent.

13. Charles Higham, *Trading With the Enemy* (New York: Delacorte Press, 1983), p. 156.

14. FMC, *Research Findings*, p. 33.

15. NARA, RG 407, Entry 368 B, Box 1032, 270/69/23/5, "Report on *Ford Werke Aktiengesellschaft*," p. 7.

16. Fings, p. 142.

17. Ibid., p. 142.

18. FMC, *Research Findings*, p. 68.

19. "Forced Labour," BBC documentary, March 1998.

20. Interview with author, via e-mail, May 13, 2002.

21. Fings, p. 188.

22. Author interview with Elsa Iwanowa, April 14, 2002.

23. Ibid.

24. Elsa Iwanowa says she was not raped.

25. FMC, *Research Findings*, p. 71.

26. Fings, p. 118.

27. Ibid., p. 99.

28. Museum of Tolerance Multimedia Learning Center, "Carl Krauch's Links to the Nazis." Krauch was convicted and sentenced to six years imprisonment.

29. NARA, RG 407, Entry 368 B, Box 1032, 270/69/23/5, "Report on *Ford-Werke Aktiengesellschaft*," p. 4.

30. Ibid., p. 6 (author's italics).

31. Ibid.

32. Billstein, p. 109.

33. "Ford and GM Scrutinized for Alleged Nazi Collaboration Firms Deny Researchers' Claims On Aiding German War Effort," *Washington Post*, November 30, 1998, p. A1.

34. Ibid.

35. "Ford Says WW2 Study Clears Firm," *Los Angeles Times*, December 7, 2001, Section 3, p. 1.

36. When I contacted the company to determine when it decided on a December 2001 release date, Ford spokesperson Tom Hoyt replied, "We chose to release the report at that time because that was when the report was finished." The timing certainly appears suspicious and Hoyt's reluctance to answer simple chronological questions makes the company's "transparency" claims all the more puzzling. From my own experience, the company has not been at all transparent or truly open in this process.

37. E-mail from author to Tom Hoyt, May 10, 2002; e-mailed response from Hoyt to author, May 10, 2002. Instead of answering the question, Hoyt simply

responded, "As we said in the report, it was a 3-½ year research project. The report was released on December 6, 2001."

38. John Rintamaki at Ford Motor Company press conference, December 6, 2001.

39. "Ford study can't end Forced-Labor Link to Nazis," *Detroit Free Press*, December 7, 2001.

40. Convention relative to the Treatment of Prisoners of War. Geneva, 27 July 1929.

41. Fings, p. 136.

42. Interview with author, via e-mail, May 13, 2002; Nicholas Lewis, p. 12.

43. Author email to Tom Hoyt, April 26, 2002.

44. FMC, *Research Findings*, p. 58.

45. I e-mailed the Ford Motor Company on April 29, 2002, asking for any such evidence.

46. FMC, *Research Findings*, p. 60.

47. In a postwar oral history, a *Ford-Werke* slave laborer named Inna Kulgina claimed that the "administration" wore black and she thought they may have been Gestapo but she was unsure.

48. Iwanowa claimed that one of the foremen, whom she described as an "animal," wore a swastika.

49. Email from author to Tom Hoyt, April 29, 2002, asking whether the company can provide any evidence demonstrating that it was the Gestapo rather than *Ford Werke* that was responsible for the food and lodging of the prisoners.

50. FMC, *Research Findings*, Lawrence Dowler, *An Independent Assessment of the Ford Motor Company Research Project of* Ford-Werke *Under the Nazi Regime*, November 2001, p. 19.

51. Ibid., p. 6.

52. Ibid., p. 7.

53. "Ford and GM Scrutinized for Alleged Nazi Collaboration Firms Deny Researchers' Claims On Aiding German War Effort," *Washington Post*, November 30, 1998, p. A1.

54. Simon Reich, *Ford's Research Efforts in Assessing the Activities of its Subsidiary in Nazi Germany*, p. 7.

55. HFM, Albert to Edsel Ford, July 11, 1940, Acc. 6, Edsel Ford Office Papers, Box #321, Briefing Binder, Section R.

56. Ibid., p. 7.

57. HFM, V.Y. Tallberg, "Oral History," p. 98.

58. Simon Reich interview with author, conducted via telephone, March 22, 2002.

59. Lee Iacocca, *Iacocca: An Autobiography* (Toronto: Bantam, 1984), pp. 99–100.

60. NARA, Hoover to Assistant Attorney General Tom Clark, December 16, 1944, RG 60, Entry 114 BV-Classified Sub. Files, Box # 4, File # 146-39-24.

61. *Elsa Iwanowa vs. Ford Motor Company and Ford Werke A.G.*, United States District Court, District of New Jersey, March 4, 1998.

62. "Forced Labour," BBC documentary, March, 1998.

63. Ibid., p. 7.

64. "Ford study can't end forced-labor link to Nazis," *Detroit Free Press*, December 7, 2001.

65. NARA, RG 407, Entry 368 B, Box 1032, Schneider Report, p. 6.

66. Ford Motor Company press release, December 6, 2001.

67. In response to my question about the terms of Reich's agreement with Ford, company spokesperson Tom Hoyt responded in an email sent August 2, 2002, "There's no formal contract. He's consulting. It's open-ended."

68. "Auto maker's report says it did not profit from a plant in Germany where Nazis used force," *Los Angeles Times*, December 7, 2001.

69. E-mail from Tom Hoyt, May 6, 2002.

70. The report says "net income." PricewaterhouseCoopers calculated the exchange rate as 1 *reichsmark* = 40 U.S. cents.

71. Most of *Ford-Werke*'s 1945 loss that year resulted from the military defeat of its largest customer. If the loss is pro-rated for those two months, it would take another $230,000 US off the company's net profits for the period, leaving a net wartime gain of more than $2 million. However, when the Ford Motor Company calculates the loss in its own attempt at spin, they prefer to calculate the loss for the whole year. Technically, 1939 only saw four months of war but the company's revenues that year were almost exclusively derived from the Nazi military effort.

72. NARA, RG 407, Entry 368 B, Box 1032, 270/69/23/5, "Report on *Ford-Werke Aktiengesellschaft*."

73. FMC, *Research Findings*, p. 109. Dearborn owned 58.5 percent of *Ford-Werke* at war's end so it only claimed this percentage of total losses.

74. "Forced Labour," BBC, March, 1998.

75. The company declined to place an exact value on these shares.

76. HFM, Acc. *Ford-Werke Under the Nazi Regime*, Box 1, "Financial Overview, *Ford-Werke* 1933–1953," PricewaterhouseCoopers Report, August 24, 2001, p. 4.

77. Author interview with Mel Weiss, January 28, 2002.

78. "Ford and GM Scrutinized for Alleged Nazi Collaboration Firms Deny Researchers' Claims On Aiding German War Effort," *Washington Post*, November 30, 1998, p. AI.

79. "Forced Labour," BBC documentary, March 1998.

80. *Elsa Iwanowa vs. Ford Motor Company and Ford Werke A.G.*, United States District Court, District of New Jersey, March 4, 1998.

81. Fings, p. 121.

82. NARA, RG 131, Entry 47, Box 131, "Lawler report."

83. NARA, RG 60, Entry 114 BV, Box 4, Bookstaver to McInerney, August 5, 1943, file # 146-39-24.

84. NARA, RG 131, Entry 47, Box 131, "Lawler report," J.W. Pehle to Ford Motor Company, December 7, 1942.

85. Ibid., Paul to Morgenthau, May 25, 1943.

86. NARA, RG 60, Entry 114, Classification 146–39, Box 4, File: 146-39-24, Foreign Funds Control memo, May 25, 1943.

87. Lesto used the U.S. Embassy in Vichy as a conduit for these letters.

88. NARA, RG 60, Entry 114, Classification 146–39, Box 4, File: 146-39-24, Foreign Funds Control memo, May 25, 1943, p. 54.

89. Ibid., p. 55.

90. Ibid., p. 56. The emphasis is provided in the Lawler report.

91. Ibid., Morgenthau to Roosevelt, May 25, 1943.

92. FDRL, "My Day," September 19, 1945.

93. Conflicting reports claimed that Edsel either died of a perforated ulcer or stomach cancer. For months before his death, the company referred to his illness as "ulcer problems."

94. NARA, RG 131, Entry 47, Box 131, "Lawler report," Paul to Morgenthau, May 25, 1943.

95. NARA, Bookstaver to McInerney, August 5, 1943, RG 60, Entry 114BV, Classified Sub. Files, Box 4, File #146-39-24, Ford Motor Company Report; Treasury Department report on Possible Violation of Trading With the Enemy act of 1917. Bookstaver concluded that while Ford's letters to Dollfuss had not appeared to violate section 3(a) of the Act, they did apparently violate section 3(c).

96. Ibid.

97. Charles Higham's 1983 book, *Trading With the Enemy*, is a shocking indictment of U.S. corporate complicity with the Nazis, although the book's lack of footnotes and occasionally exaggerated claims call some of Higham's findings into question.

98. NARA, RG 60, Entry 114, Box 4 Folder: DOJ Division records, 146-39-24, Bookstaver memo, August 5, 1943.

99. Telephone interview with Tom Hoyt, May, 2002.

100. NARA, Vesting Order 248, October 20, 1942, RG 131, B190//80/8/2, Box 341.

101. NARA, Vesting Order 248, Memo from Homer Jones to Executive Committee of the Office of Alien Property Custodian, October 9, 1942, RG 131, B190//80/8/2, Box 341. The investigation found that the shares of Bush and other stockholders were being held for the benefit of Bank voor Handel en Scheepvaart, N.V. Rotterdam, which was controlled by the powerful Thyssen family.

102. John Loftus and Mark Aarons, *The Secret War Against the Jews* (New York: St. Martin's Press, 1994), p. 358.

103. Ibid., p. 359.

104. Ibid., p. 359.

105. Ibid., 361.

106. Interview with author via telephone, April 29, 2002.

107. Toby Rogers, "Heir to the Holocaust," available on-line at http://www.john loftus.com/Thyssen.asp (accessed January 28, 2003).

108. *New York Times*, December, 16, 1944.

109. Loftus and Aarons, p. 360.

110. Simon Reich, *Ford's Research Efforts in Assessing the Activities of its Subsidiary in Nazi Germany*, p. 6.

111. Anita Kugler, "Airplanes For the Fuhrer," *Working For the Enemy*, pp. 73–74.

112. Interview with author, conducted via telephone, April 29, 2002.

113. In a statement shortly after the release of Black's book, the company said it "regrets" its past.

114. Edwin Black, "IBM's solutions for the Holocaust in Poland," *Jerusalem Post*, April 7, 2002.

115. Edwin Black, *IBM and the Holocaust* (London: Little Brown and Company, 2001), p. 133.

116. HFM, Emil Zoerlein oral history.

117. Black, *IBM and the Holocaust*, p. 217.

118. General Motors confirms that Opel paid into the fund but refuses to disclose the amount.
119. Ken Silverstein, "Ford and the Fuhrer," *The Nation*, January 24, 2000.
120. *Ford-Werke* press release, "Ford Joins German Foundation," March 28, 2000.
121. "Forced Labour," BBC documentary, March, 1998.
122. Author interview, April 14, 2002.

Chapter 13. Redemption.

1. YU, 17/05/45, Lindbergh papers, Series V.
2. YU, 18/05/45, Lindbergh papers, Series V.
3. Ibid.
4. Berg, p. 463.
5. YU, 05/23/45, Lindbergh papers, Series V.
6. YU, 06/11/45, Lindbergh papers, Series V.
7. Ibid.
8. *New York Times*, September 6, 1970.
9. AJC, Ford to Sigmund Livingstone, January 7, 1942, *Jewish Ledger*, January 16, 1942, Anti-Semitism files, Henry Ford.
10. "Henry Ford's Letter," *Jewish Ledger*, January 30, 1942.
11. Lacey, p. 473.
12. BHL, "Poor Mr. Ford," Josephine Gomon papers, Box 10, Folder: Ford Motor Company, University of Michigan, p. 1.
13. Sward, p. 479.
14. LFA, Henry Ford II to B'Nai B'rith, March 25, 1947.
15. FMC, *Research Findings*, p. 103.
16. The managers of Ford's wartime plants in Holland and Belgium both spoke on his behalf, denying he was pro-Nazi.
17. FMC, *Research Findings*, p. 104.
18. Ibid., p. 104.
19. NARA, Robert H. Schmidt, Ford House Organ, *Ford Werkzeitung*, December 1941, RG 407, entry 368 B, box 1032, Schneider Report, p. 10, footnote 4.
20. Davis, p. 425.
21. Ibid., p. 426.
22. Ibid., p. 426.
23. Cole, *CAL*, p. 234.
24. Davis, p. 424.
25. UOL, John Beaty papers, Col. Truman Smith to John O. Beaty, March 24, 1955, incoming correspondence file.
26. Author interview with Katchen Smith Coley, via telephone, May 1, 2002.
27. Mosley, pp. 340–341.
28. Charles Lindbergh, *Of Flight and Life* (New York: Charles Scribner's Sons, 1948), pp. 25–26.
29. "What's Good For General Motors," *New York Times*, December 2, 1998.

30. Mosley, p. 352.

31. According to Scott Berg's account, Air Force chief of Information Services Robert Lee Scott Jr. convinced Air Force Secretary Harold Talbott to restore Lindbergh's commission because Talbott was looking for ways to secure his own place in history.

32. Berg, p. 526.

33. "History of the Tasaday." http://www.tasaday.com

34. Anthropological Webcourse, University of Iowa, "The Tasaday Hoax?: Lost Tribes, Sunken Continents and Ancient Astronauts: Cult Archaeology and Creationism." http://www.uiowa.edu/~anthro/webcourse/lost/Tasaday/Tasaday.htm

35. Lawrence A. Reid, "Another Look at the Language of the Tasaday," Social Science Research Institute, University of Hawaii.

36. Ibid., p. 2. Linguist Lawrence Reid still believes that the Tasaday are authentic and he explains the similarity between their language and the neighboring languages using complicated linguistic principles. Most anthropologists, however, now appear to concede that the story is a hoax. In 1988, the American Anthropological Association asked Thomas Headland to organize a special session on the "Tasaday Controversy" for its 88th Annual Meeting. Eighteen speakers presented papers on both sides of the controversy, although the majority believed the Tasaday were a hoax. In 1993, Headland told the PBS Television program NOVA, "The widely-hailed story that these people were Stone-Age cavemen living in cultural and linguistic isolation for hundreds of years is patently false."

37. APS, Frederick Osborn to Lindbergh, January 21, 1955.

38. Ibid., Lindbergh to Osborn, May 10, 1967.

39. Interview with the author, via telephone, April 26, 2002.

40. CAL, *WJ*, 06/22/40, p. 361.

41. Also known as the Institute of Man.

42. In addition to eugenic research, the Institute conducted studies in areas such as child development, work-related illnesses, fatigue and work psychology.

43. Hertog, p. 415.

44. "Carrel of Discontent" by Sherwyn Warren, M.D., delivered to The Chicago Literary Club, November 8, 1999.

45. CAL, *WJ*, 05/16/45, p. 940.

46. Hertog, p. 415. Carrel had denounced Radot when the latter was head of the Pasteur Institute. Radot suspended Carrel from the Foundation and set up a "purging" committee to determine the extent of his collaboration.

47. Ibid., p. 941.

48. "Fallen Eagle," *New York Times*, September 27, 1998.

49. E-mail from Reeve Lindbergh to author, May 13, 2002.

50. E-mail from Reeve Lindbergh to author, August 6, 2002.

51. "Fallen Eagle," *New York Times*, September 27, 1998.

52. Berg, p. 548.

53. Ibid., p. 512.

54. Ibid., p. 548.

55. Ibid., pp. 497, 507.

56. Ibid., p. 502.

57. YU, Lindbergh to Bruce Larson, April 7, 1967, Lindbergh papers, Series I.

58. Berg, pp. 530–531.
59. CAL, *WJ*, p. xviii.
60. Berg, p. 386.
61. Ibid., p. 545.
62. CAL, *WJ*, p. xv.
63. *New York Times*, September 6, 1970.
64. In fact, Mosley had attempted to interview Smith in spring 1970—a few months before Smith died—and was told the former attaché was too ill to see anyone. After Mosley submitted the book to his publisher, an editor inserted a footnote erroneously claiming "Smith is still alive in 1975," basing the error on Mosley's introduction, which discusses his attempt to interview Smith.
65. In a 1974 letter to Lindbergh discovered in the Lindbergh papers at Yale University, Cole writes, "I hold you in highest regard always and treasure your friendship." Cole was given limited access to the Lindbergh papers years earlier under the supervision of Lindbergh himself.
66. Cole, *CAL*, pp. 238–240.
67. E-mail from Reeve Lindbergh to author, March 24, 2002.
68. Author interview with Susan Hertog, via e-mail, May 6, 2002.
69. Hertog claims to have documented evidence proving that she informed the family she was writing a "biography."
70. Anne Morrow Lindbergh suffered a stroke shortly after A. Scott Berg began research on his own biography so it's unclear if he had the same access to Anne that Hertog enjoyed, although he did have complete access to Anne's papers, which Hertog did not.
71. The Lindbergh papers at Yale reveal that Anne had previously chosen Colonel Raymond Fredette to write an authorized biography more than a decade earlier, and Fredette was also given unrestricted access to the papers.
72. Berg told the *Yale Alumni Magazine* that he found Lindbergh "more admirable than likable." Publicly, Berg claims he set out to write the book because, as he told ABC News, "Charles Lindbergh's was the greatest untold American story of the century . . . the story of one of the great heroes of the century, one of the great victims of the century, and one of the great villains of the century."
73. Berg, p. 565.
74. E-mail from Reeve Lindbergh to author, July 2002.
75. Berg, p. 386. Berg does note that "it is difficult to imagine him making the same comment about White Anglo-Saxon Protestants."
76. Ibid., p. 427.
77. Reeve Lindbergh, National Public Radio interview, "Fresh Air," September 21, 1998.
78. Berg, p. 385.
79. Ibid., p. 384.
80. Interview with A. Scott Berg, NPR "Morning Edition," October 21, 1998.
81. "What's Good For General Motors," *New York Times*, December 2, 1998.
82. "The Hero Who Fell to Earth," *Business Week*, November 9, 1998.
83. "In Pursuit of Charles Lindbergh," *Air Power History*, Summer, 1999.
84. Letter to the editor by Ronelle Delmont, *Forward*, December 18, 1998.
85. "Inside the Dream Factory," *Guardian*, March 21, 1999.

86. *New York*, November 15, 1999, p. 12.

87. Baldwin, p. 323.

88. Ibid., p. 323.

89. Ron Rosenbaum, *Explaining Hitler* (New York: Random House, 1998), p. xxxix.

90. Author's interview with Elizabeth Adkins conducted via email, March 25, 2002.

91. E-mail response from Elizabeth Adkins received March 27, 2002.

92. HFM, "Transfer of Assets," Acc. 305, Box 1.

93. HFM, "Minute Book," Acc. 305, Box 1.

94. HFM, Charles Zahnow to AC Benter, August 31, 1922, Acc. 305, Box 1.

95. HFM, Acc. 2, box 572, "Memo to all branches," February 11, 1926.

96. Author interview with Tom Hoyt, via telephone, April 26, 2002.

97. Ibid.

98. In the *Legend of Henry Ford*, Keith Sward writes, "He disapproved of his father's anti-Semitism in the 20's" (p. 464). Many Ford biographies repeat this claim without furnishing any examples to back up the assertion.

99. HFM, Minutes of meeting of shareholders of Dearborn Publishing Company, April 1923, Acc. 305, Box 1. They don't give a reason for their resignation but the newspaper had long since discontinued its anti-Semitic campaign so this could not have been a factor. The *Independent* resumed its attacks against the Jews a year after Edsel and Clara Ford resigned.

100. HFM, Liebold oral history, p. 504.

101. E-mail from author to Reeve Lindbergh, January 20, 2002. I did not ask for access to Lindbergh's family correspondence or his strictly personal papers, only material relevant to the period I was researching.

102. YU, Lindbergh to Harry Davison, January 23, 1937, Lindbergh papers, Series I.

103. Ibid.

104. YU, Lindbergh to Smith, November 4, 1937, Lindbergh papers, Series I.

105. YU, 23/09/38, Lindbergh papers, Series V.

106. YU, 23/09/38, Lindbergh papers, Series V.

107. Charles Lindbergh, *Of Flight and Life* (New York: Charles Scribner's Sons, 1948), pp. 25–26.

108. Ketchum, p. 642.

109. YU, Lindbergh to Harry Davison, March 31, 1939, Lindbergh papers, Series I.

110. "In Search of Lindbergh," *Vanity Fair*, September 1998, p. 238.

111. Charles Lindbergh, "Aviation, Race and Geography," *Reader's Digest*, November 1939; pp. 64–67.

112. YU, Lindbergh to Guggenheim, September 15, 1936, Lindbergh papers, Series I.

113. YU, 11/19/38, Lindbergh papers, Series V.

114. YU, 09/18/41, Lindbergh papers, Series V.

115. Berg, p. 529.

116. YU, Lindbergh to Bruce Larson, April 7, 1967, Lindbergh papers, Series I.

117. Reeve Lindbergh to author, July 4, 2002.

INDEX

Adkins, Elizabeth, 377
Afghanistan war, 334
African Americans
  Ford Motor Company, 16
  Lindbergh, C. A., 82–83
agriculture
  farm co-op movement, 29–31
  Hitler, 55
  Lindbergh, C. A., 78, 81
Aktion T4 (euthanasia) program, 99
Albert, Heinrich, 224–225, 226, 227,
  228–229, 230, 231, 232, 233, 234, 238,
  327, 332, 337, 338, 351
Albert (king of Belgium), 75
Alderman, Garland, 279
Aldrich Monetary Commission, 79
Allen, Dee, 351
Amarillo *News-Globe* (newspaper), 76
America First Committee (AFC), 239. *See
  also* isolationist movement
criticism of, 291–295
defections from, 296–297
dissolution of, 301–302
fascism, 279–283
FBI investigation of, 307–308
Ford, Henry, 278
founding of, 249–251

funding of, 278
Japan and, 297–298
Lend-Lease program, 259
Lindbergh, Charles, 239, 249, 250–251,
  272–275, 276, 279, 281, 289–296
public support for, 258, 297
Roosevelt, Franklin Delano, 283–284, 305,
  315
America First Party, 315
American Civil Liberties Union (ACLU),
  137
American Destiny Party, 282
American Eugenics Society (AES), 366–367
The American Hebrew (newspaper),
  33
American Jewish Committee (AJC), 14, 31,
  62, 65, 105, 124, 138
American Legion, 250, 276
American Magazine, 287
American Olympic Committee (AOC),
  111–112
Anglo-Saxon Federation of America,
  126–128
Anschluss, 153, 159
Anti-Defamation League (ADL), 290,
  358
Anti-Nazi League, 127, 138

anti-Semitism
  America First Committee, 251, 258, 281
  Anglo-Saxon Federation of America,
    126–127
  Austria, 153
  Brasol, Boris, 59–60
  British Israelite movement, 126
  Carrel, Alexis, 245
  Communism and, 14, 144, 198–199, 243,
    256
  England, 160, 162
  Ford, Henry, 7, 11–12, 14–18, 19–25, 27,
    29, 31–35, 42, 46, 49, 51, 57, 63, 65, 123,
    124, 127, 130, 135, 138, 147–149, 199,
    289, 311, 333, 351, 357–359, 376, 382
  Ford Motor Company, 137, 359–360,
    375–377
  Germany, 43, 63, 104, 108, 117, 128–129,
    146, 156, 182–183, 184, 207–208,
    262–263
  Hart, Merwin K., 252
  Hitler, Adolf, 1, 2, 40, 52, 54, 56–57, 106,
    107
  Kristallnacht riots, 40, 117, 191–193, 201,
    381
  Liebold, Ernest, 131–132
  Lindbergh, Charles, 199–200, 277, 283,
    290–294, 363, 370, 373, 374–375,
    381–382
  Nazi party, 40–42
  Olympic Games of 1936, 111–112, 114,
    116
  Russia, 63–64
  Smith, Truman, 105, 108–110, 200, 201,
    246, 362
  United States, 12–15, 16, 22–23, 60–61,
    133–135, 138, 140, 142–145, 167–168,
    198–199, 291, 294–295, 368
  U.S. War Department, 105, 110
  World War I, 28, 43–44, 194
Antona, Annetta, 1–2
Arendt company, 231
arms embargo, United States, 202, 207,
  208–209
Armstrong, George W., 28
Arnold, Benedict, 10, 12, 57, 257–258
Arnold, Hap, 197, 204, 208, 303, 304, 307,
  311
Astor, John Jacob, 160, 170, 171, 196
Astor, Nancy, 160, 161, 162, 170, 171, 196
atomic bomb, 206
Auer, Erhard, 45, 46, 47, 48, 65
August Wilhelm, Prince (Kaiser Wilhelm's
  son), 66
Auhgaen, Friedrich, 253, 295–296
Auschwitz concentration camp, 232, 331
Austria
  annexation of, 153, 159
  anti-Semitism, 191

Baldwin, Neil, 15, 33, 126, 145
Baldwin, Stanley, 178–179

Baruch, Bernard, 29, 254
Battle of Britain, 255
Beaty, John, 110
Beaverbrook, Lord, 222, 232
Beiliss, Mendel, 59
Benes, Eduard, 154, 155, 164, 165, 170
Bennett, Harry
  America First Committee, 278
  anti-Semitism, 144, 147, 148–149, 358
  FBI, 306–307, 315
  firing of, 359
  labor policy, 136–137, 139, 141
  Liebold, Ernest, 313–314, 317–318
Benson, Allan, 26–27
Berg, A. Scott, 93, 176–177, 181, 248, 280,
  293, 305, 364, 365, 369, 370, 372–374,
  377, 381, 382
Bergmann, Gretel, 114
Berle, August, Jr., 295
Berlin Olympic Games of 1936, 111–116,
  134, 251
Berliner Tageblatt (newspaper), 34, 45
Birkhead, Leon, 279, 282
birth control, eugenics movement, 96
Bissell, J. T., 306
Black, Edwin, 351
Black, Fred, 17, 23, 27
Black Legion, 135
blacks
  Ford Motor Company, 16
  Lindbergh, C. A., 82–83
Blodgett, John, 254
Blomberg, Alex von, 115
"blood libel trial," 59
B'Nai Brith, 130
Bohn, Frank, 285
Bonnet, Georges, 165, 166
Bookstaver, David, 348
Borah, William, 62, 162
Bornheim, Oscar, 339
Bosch, Carl, 226, 227, 232
Bötticher, Friedrich von, 262, 263, 264
Bowie, Russell, 74
Brandt, Karl, 99
Brasol, Boris, 14, 58–65, 131, 132, 138
Braun, Werner von, 364
Breckinridge, Henry, 118
Brewster, Kingman, 249
Brigham, Barbara, 307
Brigham, Constance, 307
Brigham, Ethel, 307
Brisbane, Arthur, 31
Britain. *See* England
British Israelite movement, 126
Brown, Constantine, 320–321
Brundage, Avery, 111, 112, 251
Bruno, Harry, 287
B24 bomber program, 308, 309, 311–313,
  319, 347
Buch, Werner, 337
Buchenwald concentration camp, 329–330
Buck v. Bell, sterilization, 95

Bugas, John S., 289, 306, 307, 315–317
Bullitt, William C., 161, 164
Burke, Frank, 224–225
Bush, George Herbert Walker, 350
Bush, George W., 349
Bush, Prescott, 349–350, 351
Business Week (magazine), 374
Byrd, George, 74
Byrd, Harry, 199

Caesar, Irving, 17
Cameron, William J., 11, 26, 27, 30,
    125–128, 138, 139, 145, 314
Camp Dora, 356, 357, 364
Campsall, Frank, 317, 318
Cantor, Eddie, 146
Capone, Al, 92
Carlson, John Ray, 281
Carrel, Alexis
  career of, 93–95
  death of, 367
  eugenics movement, 97–98, 157–158
  Lindbergh, Charles, 99–102, 104, 117, 118,
    158–159, 163, 165, 193, 209, 212,
    244–245, 312, 365, 366, 379
  Nazi party, 244
  retirement of, 245
  Vichy government, 367–368
Castle, Bill, 199, 203
Central Intelligence Agency (CIA), 350
Cerra, Frank, 100–101
Chamberlain, Houston Stewart, 109–110,
    362
Chamberlain, Neville, 154, 160, 161,
    166–167, 169, 170, 172, 173, 176, 178,
    179, 196, 207, 214
Chevrolet, 123, 124
Chicago Tribune (newspaper), 9, 14, 34, 45,
    46, 306, 362
Childs, Marquis, 288
China, Japan and, 297
Christian Century (journal), 257–258
Christian Front, 243–244, 279
Christian Science Monitor (newspaper), 14, 103
Chrysler Corporation, 136, 139
Churchill, Marlborough, 59, 61
Churchill, Winston, 160, 187, 241, 256,
    332
  Munich Pact, 172–173, 175, 179
  prime minister, 214
  Roosevelt, Franklin Delano, 207, 259,
    260–261
  World War II, 222, 255
Citizens Keep America Out of War
    Committee, 273
Clemm, Werner C., 279
Cliveden Set, 160, 161, 162, 181, 182
Cockburn, Claud, 160, 161, 182
Cohen, Alfred, 130
Cohn, Norman, 57
Cold War, 363, 364
Coldwell, Michael, 224

Cole, Felix, 344
Cole, Wayne, 273–274, 371–372
Coley, Katchen, 362
Collier's Magazine, 27, 28
Committee to Defend America by Aiding the
    Allies, 213
Communism
  anti-Semitism and, 14, 144, 198–199, 243,
    256
  Lindbergh, Charles and, 286, 356, 378–380
  Nazism, 160, 170, 363
Communist Party (Russia), Jews in, 61
Confessions of a Nazi Spy (film), 199–200
conservationist movement, Lindbergh,
    Charles, 364–365, 366
Consolidated Aircraft, 312
Coolidge, Calvin, 28, 76
Cordell, Harold, 58
Coughlin, Charles, 140–145, 148–149, 200,
    243, 272, 279, 280, 282–283, 294, 295
Courtney, Virt, 259
Cousins, Ralph, 307
Couzens, James, 23
Crockett, Alice, 269–270, 271
Cross of the German Eagle. *See* Grand Cross
    of the German Eagle; Merit Cross of the
    German Eagle; Service Cross of the
    German Eagle
Crowley, Leo T., 348
cultural observation missions, Lindbergh,
    Charles, 353, 365–366
Curtiss Wright Aviation, 305
Czechoslovakia
  England and, 166, 169–173
  France and, 164, 165, 166
  German aggression against, 154–155,
    164–167, 180, 181
  Munich Pact, 172–173, 176

Dalton, Hugh, 171
Daniels, CC, 62
Darwin, Charles, 95
Davidson, Harry, 118
Davis, Dwight, 246
Davis, Kenneth, 77
Davis, William Rhodes, 257
Davison, Harry, 158, 177
Dawson, Geoffrey, 161, 169
Dearborn Independent (newspaper), 11, 12, 14,
    15, 16, 17, 21, 23, 24, 26–27, 28, 29, 30,
    32, 33, 34, 43, 49, 51, 55, 57–58, 61, 62,
    63, 65, 66, 68–69, 79, 123, 124, 125, 126,
    130, 131, 143, 281, 289, 295, 376–377
Dearborn Publishing Company, 377
Debevoise, Thomas, 245
de Bogory, Nathalie, 60
Defenders of the Faith, 135
Degler, Carl, 99
Deladier, Edouard, 166, 172
Dennis, Lawrence, 252–254, 256, 296
Derounian, Arthur, 280–281, 294
Der Sturmer, 112, 200

Des Moines, Iowa speech (Lindbergh), 289–295, 373, 382, 387

Des Moines *Register* (newspaper), 291

Detroit Free Press (newspaper), 18, 27, 139, 145, 318

Detroit Journal (newspaper), 21

Detroit News (newspaper), 1, 11, 137, 139

Diestel, Erich, 230

Dinnerstein, Leonard, 13

Dirksen, Everett, 296

Dirksen, Herbert von, 167

Dr. Seuss. *See* Geisel, Theodor (Dr. Seuss)

Dodd, William E., 108, 112–113, 114, 182, 219

Dollfuss, Maurice, 235–237, 345–346, 347, 348

Donnelly, Gerry, 376

Dowler, Lawrence, 334, 337

Druzhelovski, Leonid, 65

Duff, Sheila Grant, 179

Duluth Herald, 81

Dunkirk evacuation, 221

Dunn, Daniel J., 89

DuPont family, 311

Dykema, John, 219

Early, Stephen, 246, 278, 292

Ebbutt, Norman, 161

Ebert, Friedrich, 45

Eckart, Dietrich, 45, 47–49, 56, 65

Edison, Jean Farrel, 22

Edison, Thomas Alva, 21–22

Editor and Publisher (journal), 292

Edward VIII (king of England), 104, 160

Eggleston, George, 255, 256–257, 272

Einstein, Albert, 92, 99, 206

Eisenhower, Dwight D., 364

Elizalda, Manuel, 365–366

England
  Battle of Britain, 255
  Czechoslovakia, 154, 164, 166–167, 169–173
  Dunkirk evacuation, 221
  Germany and, 160–161
  Lindbergh, Charles and, 102–104, 161, 163, 196–197, 275–276, 283, 290, 303
  spies in United States, 283
  World War II declared by, 202

eugenics movement. *See also* race purity
  Germany, 96–97, 98–99
  Lindbergh, Charles, 99, 157–158, 366–367, 382
  United States, 95–96

euthanasia, 97, 98–99, 366

Farago, Ladislas, 263–264

Farm co-op movement, 29–31

fascism. *See also* Germany; Nazi Party
  America First Committee, 279–282
  Carrel, Alexis, 159
  England, 160

Ford Motor Company, 137–140
  Lindbergh, Charles, 252–254, 363, 379
  United States, 132–135, 200, 219, 252, 253, 294, 310

Federal Bureau of Investigation (FBI), 347
  America First Committee investigation, 278, 280, 295–296, 297
  Bennett, Harry investigation, 137
  Brasol, Boris investigation, 64
  Christian Front investigation, 243
  fascism investigations, 138, 200, 252, 256, 264, 272, 281, 285
  Ford Motor Company investigation, 233–234
  kidnapping threat, 103
  Liebold, Ernest investigation, 315–317
  Lindbergh, Charles investigation, 270–271, 288–289, 294, 302, 305, 306–308

Federal Council of Churches, 15

Felmy, Helmuth, 174

Fendrick, Raymond, 46–47

Ferdinand, Louis, 66–67, 68

Field, Marshall, III, 260

Fight for Freedom, 279

Final Solution. *See* anti-Semitism; Holocaust

Fings, Karola, 335–336

Fischer, Louis, 176

Fish, Hamilton, 259

The Flivver King (Sinclair), 35, 67

Flynn, John, 282, 293, 382

forced labor
  compensation fund for, 352
  executions of, 356
  Ford-Werke, 323, 329–330, 332, 333–337, 341, 343–344, 361
  Germany, 325–327
  Opel subsidiary, 350

Ford, Benson (son), 313

Ford, Bill (great-grandson), 385

Ford, Clara (wife), 28, 50, 277, 313, 318, 377

Ford, Edsel (son)
  anti-Semitism, 124
  Dearborn Independent (newspaper), 377
  death of, 313, 314, 347
  Ford France, 344, 345–348
  Ford Motor Company, 221
  Ford-Werke, 227, 229, 230, 235, 237, 328, 338
  Germany, 136
  IG Farben, 232, 331
  Rolls-Royce engines, 222

Ford, Henry, 37, 313
  America First Committee, 249, 250–251, 258, 278, 281, 297
  anti-Semitism, 7, 11–12, 14–18, 19–25, 27, 29, 31–35, 42, 44, 46, 49, 51, 57, 63, 65, 123, 124, 127, 130, 135, 138, 147–149, 199, 289, 333, 351, 357–359, 376, 382
  apology by, 31–35, 124–125, 128, 143
  Brasol, Boris, 62
  career of, 7–8
  childhood of, 20

Ford, Henry (*continued*)
   Dearborn Independent (newspaper), 376, 377
   death of, 359
   farm co-op movement, 29–31
   fascism, 280
   FBI, 270
   Germany, 42–45, 50–52, 57–58, 64–65,
     66–67, 219, 226
   Grand Cross of the German Eagle award,
     121, 145–147, 149, 184, 185, 223, 351
   Great Depression, 135
   Hitler, Adolf, 2, 45–48, 49, 54, 55, 56, 57,
     67, 135–136, 376
   Holocaust, 358–359
   isolationism, 219–220, 224
   Kuhn, Fritz, 139
   labor policy of, 5, 8–9, 136–137, 141
   legacy of, 385–387
   Liebold, Ernst, 313–314, 316, 317, 318
   Lindbergh, Charles, 85, 223–224, 249,
     271–272, 277–278, 288, 297, 308, 312
   Nazi party, 143, 233–234, 257, 269, 328
   pacifism, 18–19, 80, 131, 225
   personality of, 16–17
   popularity of, 9–11
   presidential ambitions of, 27–28, 46
   Roosevelt, Franklin Delano, 127, 136, 250,
     311
   Smith, Gerald L K and, 144, 315
   World War I, 25, 80, 131
   World War II, 221–224, 235, 278
Ford, Henry II (grandson), 313, 339,
   359–360, 361
Ford Motor Company, 306. *See also Ford-
   Werke* (German subsidiary); IG Farben
   America First Committee, 278
   anti-Semitism, 137, 359–360, 375–377
   Ford, Henry, II, 359–360
   French subsidiary of, 234–237, 343, 344–348
   German subsidiary of, 217, 226–238, 316
   hiring policies, 16, 17
   IG Farben, 331–332
   innovation at, 123–124
   labor policy at, 8–9, 136–137, 139–140, 141
   Lindbergh, Charles, 309–312
   Nazi party, 137–140
   payroll of, 62, 66–67, 133, 134, 317–318
   Roosevelt, Franklin D., 311
   sales at, 147
   wages at, 5, 8–9
   World War I, 24–26, 225
   World War II, 220–223, 232–233, 235,
     236, 278, 289, 308–309, 311–313, 314,
     318–319, 357–358
Ford-Werke (German subsidiary)
   compensation fund for forced labor, 352
   denazification, 360
   forced labor in, 323, 326, 329–330, 332,
     333–337, 341, 343–344, 361
   Nazi party and, 327–329, 332–333,
     336–337, 338, 339–340
   profits of, 329, 333, 338, 341–343

Reich report, 340–341
   U.S. military liberates, 330–331
   U.S. ties of, 331, 332, 335, 337–339, 361
Forster, Arnold, 290–291
Fortune magazine, 311, 312, 359
Forward (newspaper), 374
Foundry Workers Union, 309–310
Fox, William, 35
France
   Czechoslovakia and, 154, 164, 165,
     166–167, 169, 173
   fall of, 234, 244, 254–255
   fascism, 159
   Ford Motor Company, 234–237
   Lindbergh, Charles, 164–165, 194–195
   World War II declared by, 202
Franco, Francisco, 252
Frank, Hans, 39
Frankfurt Zeitung, 234
Franklin, Leo, 17, 18, 21, 33, 128, 129–130,
   147–149
Fredette, Raymond, 180–181, 374
The Free American (newspaper), 279, 294
Freeman, Wilfrid, 169
Free Press Defense League, 79
Free Society of Teutonia, 132–133
Frick, Wilhelm, 98–99
Friday Magazine, 139
Fried, Albert, 213
Friedrich, Eitel, 66
Friends of Democracy, 279, 282
Friends of Hitler Movement, 133
Friends of New Germany (FONG), 133, 134
Fritsch, Theodor, 128, 129, 130
Fromm, Bella, 115
Fuerstner, Wolfgang, 116

Galton, Francis, 95
Geisel, Theodor (Dr. Seuss), 239, 260
Gelderman, Carol, 28
Gemlich, Adolf, 54
General Aniline & Film, 227, 270, 331. *See
   also* IG Farben
General Motors, 67, 136, 139, 220, 311,
   350–351, 352
Geneva Convention, 335, 361
George V (king of England), 75
German-American Bund, 133–135, 138–139,
   143, 262, 270, 279, 280, 294
German Eagle award. *See* Grand Cross of the
   German Eagle; Merit Cross of the
   German Eagle; Service Cross of the
   German Eagle
German Workers Party, 54
Germany. *See also* Nazi Party
   aggression of, 153–155, 164–165
   anti-Semitism, 43, 63, 96, 108, 117,
     128–129, 146, 156, 182–183, 187,
     191–193, 207–208
   denazification, 360
   England, 160–161, 166
   eugenics movement, 96–97, 98–99

Germany (*continued*)
  euthanasia, 99
  forced labor, 325–327
  Ford, Henry, 42–45, 50–52, 57–58, 121,
    128–129, 145–147, 149, 219, 226
  Ford Motor Company subsidiary in, 217,
    226–238
  Great Depression, 132
  Holocaust, 331
  Jewish extermination, 325
  Lindbergh, Charles, 75, 114–119, 155–158,
    159–160, 162–163, 168, 173–187,
    194–195, 212, 285, 303, 355–357, 378
  military strength of, 174–176
  monarchists, 63, 66, 67
  Olympic Games of 1936, 111–116, 134
  Poland invaded by, 202, 230
  Smith, Truman, 106–108, 111, 181–182
  Soviet Union, 214, 286
  spies in United States, 224–225, 241–244,
    253, 256, 261–262, 269–270, 282,
    295–296, 297, 316, 349
  United States, 161–162
  World War II, 104, 214
Gestapo, *Ford-Werke*, 336–337
Gibbons, John, 100
Gienanth, Baron von (U.S. Gestapo chief),
  282
Goard, William Pascoe, 126
Goddard, Robert, 364
Goebbels, Josef, 57, 58, 170–171, 191, 194,
  241, 294
Goedsche, Hermann, 13
Goering. *See* Göring, Hermann
Goldhagen, Daniel Joseph, 63
Goldwyn, Samuel, 372
Gomon, Josephine, 359
Gompers, Samuel, 49
Goodwin, Doris Kearns, 224
Göring, Hermann, 39, 111, 112, 113, 115, 116,
  154, 156, 157, 169, 173, 175, 176, 183–186,
  192, 194, 227, 228, 246, 254, 255, 286, 328
Gow, Betty, 91
Grace, William, 273
Graham, Alan, 160
Grand Cross of the German Eagle, Ford,
  Henry awarded, 121, 145–147, 149, 184,
  185, 223, 351
Grande, Hans, 339–340
Grant, Madison, 97
Grant, Ulysses S., 12
Great Depression, 132, 253
  Ford, Henry, 135
  Germany, 226, 228
Grünspan, Herschel, 191
Grünspan, Zindel, 191
Guardian (newspaper), 374
Guggenheim, Harry, 117
Gutstadt, Richard, 358

Haag, Werner, 133
Haase, Horace, 302

Hailer, Fritz, 68, 145, 146, 149
Halder, Franz, 176
Halifax, Lord, 160
Hamburg-Amerika Line, 349
Hanesse, Colonel (German air ministry), 113
Hanfstaengl, Ernst "Putzi," 67, 107, 108, 253
Hapgood, Norman, 64
Harding, Warren, 15, 27, 28
Harriman Fifteen Corporation, 349
Hart, Merwin K., 252
Hart-Davis, Duff, 116
Hauptmann, Bruno Richard, 92–93, 115, 204
Hayes, Carlton, 60
Hegel, G. W. F., 42, 43
Heine, Edmund G., 316
Henderson, Nevile, 180
Henlein, Konrad, 155
Henry Ford and the Jews (Baldwin), 15
Herald (journal), 256, 297
Hermann Göring Werke, 328
heroism
  Lindbergh, Charles, 74–77
  social aspects of, 385–387
Hertog, Susan, 115, 118–119, 372, 373
Hess, Rudolf, 48, 133
Heupel, Rudolph, 138
Heydrich, Reinhard, 184, 207–208
Hicks, William W., 60
Hill, Frank, 23, 49
Himmler, Heinrich, 194, 227, 270
Hindenburg, Paul von, 68, 108
Hirschmann, I. A., 258
Hitler, Adolf, 39, 40, 272, 295, 318, 363
  aggression of, 153–155, 164
  anti-Semitism, 40, 52, 54, 55–57, 96
  appointed chancellor, 132, 264
  childhood of, 52–53
  Coughlin, Charles, 142
  Czechoslovakia, 166, 167, 169, 170–172,
    175–176
  Dennis, Lawrence, 253
  England, 161
  eugenics movement, 97, 99
  forced labor, 326–327
  Ford, Henry, 2, 43, 44–48, 49, 57, 67, 130,
    135–136, 145, 146, 149, 219, 376
  Ford Motor Company, 228, 229
  German-American Bund, 134
  Göring, Hermann, 183
  Lewis, Fulton, Jr., 203–204
  Lindbergh, Anne Morrow, 247
  Lindbergh, Charles, 115, 118, 183–184,
    185–186, 192, 355–356
  monarchists, 63, 66, 67
  Olympic Games of 1936, 116
  Poland invaded by, 202
  rise of, 1, 42, 48–49, 349
  Roosevelt, Franklin Delano, 156
  Smith, Truman, 106–108, 181–182
  Soviet Union, 286
  Wiedemann, Fritz, 269
  World War I, 53

Hitler Youth, 40
Hobson, Henry, 280
Hoche, Alfred, 97
Holland-American Trading Corporation, 349
Holmes, Oliver Wendell, 20, 95
Holocaust
    denial movement, 22, 64
    eugenics movement, 366
    Ford, Henry and, 358–359
    IBM and, 351
    IG Farben and, 331–332
    Lindbergh, Charles and, 357, 362,
        380
    media, 332
    Spielberg, Steven, 374–375
    World War II, 331
Hoover, Herbert, 42, 198, 199, 203,
    206–207, 208, 210, 284
Hoover, J. Edgar, 233–234, 242, 246, 270,
    271, 278, 289, 305, 306, 307–308
Hoover Institution (Stanford University),
    254, 293
Houghton, Alanson B., 106
Houghton, Harris, 60, 62
hours of labor, Ford Motor Company, 9
Hoyt, Tom, 334, 341, 377
Hu, Wei-Shou, 100–101
Hull, Cordell, 170
Hutcheson, William, 296
Huxley, Aldous, 11

Iacocca, Lee, 339
IBM, Holocaust and, 351
Ickes, Harold, 142, 223, 249, 274, 283–286,
    304
IG Farben, 227, 232, 270, 328, 329–330,
    331, 340, 342–343, 349. See also General
    Aniline & Film
immigration
    anti-Semitism, 12, 13, 20, 21, 22–23
    eugenics movement, 95–96
Immigration Act of 1924, 96
Industrial Workers of the World (IWW), 8
Ingalls, Laura, 282
Institute for Historical Review, 22
The International Jew (Ford pamphlet series),
    14–15, 22, 31, 32, 33, 42, 43–44, 48, 52,
    53, 55, 56, 62, 64, 125, 128, 129, 144,
    147, 194, 226, 359–360, 376, 377, 385
interventionist movement
    Lindbergh attacked by, 189, 257–258, 279
    PM (newspaper), 260
    public opinion, 251, 255, 276
    Roosevelt, Franklin Delano, 212–213,
        258–259, 261, 273
    tactics of, 242, 260–261, 271–272, 282
Isaacs, Nathan, 65, 131, 132, 138
isolationist movement. See also America First
    Committee (AFC)
    Ford, Henry, 219–220, 224, 225
    Hoover, Herbert, 284
    Lend-Lease program, 259, 273

Lindbergh, Charles, 203, 204, 205–207,
    208–209, 241–242, 251, 255–257, 267,
    272–275, 370–372
    Moseley, George Van Horn, 243–244
    Nazi party and, 262
    public opinion, 251, 255, 276
    Smith, Truman, 200–201, 245–246
    tactics of, 260–261, 271–272
    United States, 198–199, 212
Iwanowa, Elsa, 325, 326, 327, 330, 333–334,
    336, 337, 339, 343, 352. See also forced
    labor
IWW. See Industrial Workers of the World
    (IWW)

Jackson, Robert, 39–40, 242
Jackson (Mississippi) News (newspaper), 147
Jacobsen, Lars, 65–66
Japan
    America First Committee and, 297–298
    Lindbergh, Charles, 357
    World War II, 319–321
Jeansonne, Glenn, 314
Jeschonnek, Hans, 174–175
Jewish Chronicle (newspaper), 143
Jewish Exponent (newspaper), 358
Jewish New York Tribune (newspaper), 33
Jewish refugees, 96, 261
Jewish Telegraphic Agency, 33
Jewish War Veterans of the United States,
    146
Jodl, Alfred, 175
Joly, Maurice, 13, 15
Jones, Ellis, 280
Jones, Thomas, 160, 161, 171, 178–179
Jovanovich, William, 370
Jung, Harry, 256

Kapp, Karl, 145
Kaufman, Joe, 200
Keep America Out of War Committee, 296
Keitel, Wilhelm, 175
Kellogg, Michael, 63
Kendrick, B. B., 253–254
Kennedy, John F., 177, 249
Kennedy, Joseph, 161–162, 167–170, 171,
    173–174, 175, 177, 178, 179, 181
Ketchum, Richard, 183, 184
Kilgallen, Dorothy, 101–102
Knudsen, William S., 220, 221, 224
Koos, John, 137–138
Kosovo genocide, 387
Kramer-Klett, Baron (Lindbergh host), 156
Krauch, Carl, 232, 328, 331–332
Kristallnacht riots, 40, 117, 191–193, 201,
    381. See also anti-Semitism; Holocaust
Krock, Walter, 177, 380
Krut, Joshua, 142–143
Kuhn, Fritz, 133–135, 138–139, 143, 144,
    262
Ku Klux Klan, 12, 16, 28–29, 135, 213, 279,
    281

labor conditions, Ford Motor Company, 8–9
La Chambre, Guy, 164, 165
LaFollette, Robert, 28
LaGuardia, Fiorello, 261
Landman, Isaac, 33
Larson, Bruce, 81, 382
Laughlin, Harry Hamilton, 96
Lawler, John, 344, 345, 347, 348
League of Nations, 44
Lee, Albert, 54, 55, 135
Lee, Josh, 257
Lemon, Ernest, 169
Lend-Lease program, 259, 273
Lenin, V. I., 59
Leo (pope of Rome; Coughlin influence), 141
Lerner, Max, 365
Lesto, Georges, 345
Levin, Nora, 57
Lewis, David L., 136
Lewis, Fulton, Jr., 203–204
Liberty magazine, 291, 310
Liberty Motor, 25–26
Liebold, Ernest Gustav, 37, 51, 123, 128,
    145, 226
    anti-Semitism, 23–25, 57–58, 61–62, 64,
        68–69, 124, 125, 129, 130, 134, 138
    Bennett, Harry, 313–314, 317–318
    biography, 22
    Coughlin, Charles, 140–141, 143
    Dearborn Independent (newspaper),
        376–377
    dismissal of, 317–318
    FBI, 271, 315–317
    Ford Motor Company, 23
    Ford presidential ambition, 27–28
    German medal award, 186–187
    German monarchists, 65, 66, 67–68
    German spies, 25–26, 131–132, 225, 233
    Nazi Party, 63, 131, 146, 149
    Smith, Gerald L K, 144
Life magazine, 248, 275, 295
Lilienthal Aeronautical Society, 156
Lincoln, Abraham, 12, 76, 92
Lindbergh, Anne (daughter), 369
Lindbergh, Anne Morrow (wife), 104, 156,
    161, 163, 198, 372, 374, 375
    anti-Semitism and, 369
    death of, 377
    German medal, 185
    isolationism, 211, 247–249, 293–294
    kidnapping, 90, 91, 103
    marital relationship, 369
    marriage of, 89
    Nazi Party, 117, 118
Lindbergh, Augustus (cousin), 292
Lindbergh, C. A. (father), 77–85, 205, 303
Lindbergh, Charles, 71, 220
    America First Committee, 239, 249,
        250–251, 272–275, 276, 279, 280, 281,
        289–296, 301–303
    anti-Semitism, 199–200, 277, 290–294,
        363, 370, 373, 374–375, 381–382

attacks on, 189, 209–211, 213–214, 257–258,
    260, 275, 279, 283, 284–285, 287
Carrel, Alexis, 93, 94–95, 99–102,
    158–159, 163, 244–245, 367, 368
childhood of, 77–84
Cold War, 363
conservationist movement, 364–365, 366
cultural observation missions, 353, 365–366
Czechoslovakia, 164, 168–171
death of, 371
Dennis, Lawrence, 252–254
Des Moines, Iowa speech, 289–295
education of, 84–85
England, 102–104, 161, 163, 245, 275–276,
    283, 290, 303
eugenics movement, 99, 157–158,
    366–367, 382
family life of, 368–369
fascism, 252–254, 363, 379
FBI, 270–271, 306–308
Ford, Henry, 85, 223–224, 249, 271–272,
    277–278, 288, 297, 308, 312
Ford Motor Company, 309–312, 314, 319
France, 164–165, 194–195
Germany, 75, 114–119, 151, 155–158,
    159–160, 162–163, 168, 173–187, 212,
    285, 303, 355–357, 378
Hart, Merwin K., 252
heroism, 74–77
Hitler, Adolf, 115, 118
Holocaust, 357
honesty, 380–381
isolationist movement, 203, 204, 205–207,
    208–209, 213, 255–257, 259, 262, 267,
    272–273, 370–372
Japan, 357
kidnapping case, 89, 90–93, 210
Kristallnacht riots, 192–193
legacy of, 371–375, 378–383, 385–387
marriage of, 89–90
Marshall, George, 244
Munich Pact, 176–181
Nazi Party, 3, 75, 114–119, 151, 158, 159,
    215–244–245, 247, 261–265, 269–270,
    271, 274–275, 287, 295, 297, 356, 378–380
personality of, 100
popularity of, 287–288, 297
race purity, 209, 211–213, 302–303, 353,
    361–362, 367
rocket program, 364
Roosevelt, Franklin D., 2–3, 197–198,
    204–205, 214–215, 241–242, 249, 271,
    273–274, 276–277, 283–284, 285–286,
    295, 304, 305, 310, 311, 320
Service Cross of the German Eagle award,
    183–187, 223, 285–286, 303
Smith, Gerald L K, 315
Smith, Truman, 87, 104, 111, 112–115,
    155–156, 196–197, 202, 245–246, 285,
    362–363
Soviet Union, 163–164, 182, 286
trans-Atlantic flight of, 73–74, 385

Lindbergh, Charles (*continued*)
  Vietnam War, 370
  World War II service of, 299, 303–305,
    319–321
Lindbergh, Charles, Jr. (son)
  birth of, 90
  kidnapping of, 90–93, 103, 115, 210
Lindbergh, Evangeline Land (mother), 77, 78
Lindbergh, Eva (sister), 80, 81, 82
Lindbergh, Jon (son), birth of, 103
Lindbergh, Reeve (daughter), 367, 368–369,
    373, 377, 382–383
Lindbergh, Scott (son), 370
Lippmann, Walter, 210
Lloyd George, David, 171
Loftus, John, 349, 350
London *Times* (newspaper). *See Times* of
    London (newspaper)
Longworth, Alice Roosevelt, 251
Look magazine, 143
Los Angeles Times (newspaper), 341
Lothian, Lord (British foreign minister), 196
Lovett, Robert, 304, 305
Ludecke, Kurt, 49–50, 51–52, 64, 125–126
Ludendorff, Erich, 64
Luftwaffe, 157–158, 174, 177–178, 179, 180,
    182, 183, 194, 195, 221, 229, 232,
    254–255, 306, 350
Lusitania sinking, 80

MacArthur, Douglas, 315, 319
MacDonnell, Francis, 135
Mahoney, Jeremiah, 112
Malinin, Theodore, 100
Manchester, William, 187
Marcos, Ferdinand, 365
Marshall, George, 201, 244, 246, 254
Marshall, Louis, 14, 15, 31, 62, 105, 124–125
Marshall, Verne, 257
Martin, Homer, 141
Marx, Karl, 61
Mauthausen concentration camp, 146
Mayer, Eugene, 29
Mayer, Helene, 116
Mayr, Karl, 53–54
McAdoo, William, 225
McCabe, Warner, 246
McCloud, J. L., 130–131
McCormack-Dickstein committee, 133
McGeehan, W. O., 77
McGuffey's Eclectic Reader, 20
McWilliams, Joe, 282, 294
Mein Kampf (Hitler), 43, 48–49, 52, 54, 55,
    56, 107, 248, 316, 326–327
Meissner, Otto, 68
Merit Cross of the German Eagle, Watson,
    Thomas awarded, 351–352
Michigan Manufacturer and Financial Record
    (newspaper), 9
Milch, Erhard, 183, 194, 195
Miles, Sherman, 271
Miller, James W., 30

Milton, Joyce, 254
Model A Ford, 123–124
Model T Ford, 7, 8, 123, 145
monarchists, German, 63, 66, 67, 68
Morgan, Aubrey, 276
Morgan, Constance Morrow (sister-in-law),
    247
Morgan, J. P., 79
Morgenthau, Henry, 3, 215, 221, 222,
    233–234, 246, 345, 347
Morrow, Betty (mother-in-law), 247
Morrow, Dwight (father-in-law), 89–90,
    104
Morrow, Elizabeth (sister-in-law), 93
Moseley, George Van Horn, 243, 280, 310
Mosley, Leonard, 178, 277, 308, 362, 371,
    380
Mosley, Oswald, 170
Müller, Heinrich, 191
Munich Pact
  assessment of, 175
  Czechoslovakia, 172–173
  Lindbergh, Charles, 176–181, 196
Murphy, Robert, 47
Murray, Williamson, 181
Mussolini, Benito, 75, 145, 172, 257, 272,
    362
My Life and Work (Ford), 17

Napoleon III (Louis-Napoleon, emperor of
    France), 13
National Aeronautics and Space
    Administration (NASA), 364
National Economic Council (NEC), 252
National Labor Relations Board (NLRB),
    141–142
National Recovery Administration (NRA),
    136
The Nation (magazine), 14, 176
Nazi Enemy Property Commission, 350
Nazi Party. *See also* Germany
  America First Committee, 278, 279
  anti-Semitism, 41–42, 108
  Carrel, Alexis, 367–368
  Cold War, 364
  Communism, 160, 170, 363
  denazification, 360
  eugenics movement, 96–97, 98–99
  euthanasia, 99
  financing of, 47–48, 49–50, 51–52, 64–65,
    68, 107
  forced labor, 325–327
  Ford, Henry, 143, 233–234, 257, 269–270,
    328
  Ford France, 346–347
  Ford Motor Company, 137–140, 227–228,
    230, 232–234, 237–238
  Ford-Werke, 327–329, 332–333, 336–337,
    338, 339–340
  General Aniline & Film, 331
  General Motors, 350–351
  Holocaust, 331

Nazi Party (*continued*)
  isolationist movement, 262
  Liebold, Ernest, 69, 131, 318
  Lindbergh, Anne Morrow, on, 247–249
  Lindbergh, Charles, 3, 75, 114–119, 151,
    158, 159, 215, 247, 261–265, 269–270,
    271, 274–275, 287, 295, 297, 356,
    378–380
  monarchists, 66
  Nuremberg trials, 39–40
  Olympic Games of 1936, 111–114
  rise of, 1, 48
  Smith, Truman, 106–107, 263–264
  Union Banking Corporation of New York,
    349
  United States, 132–135, 142, 243
  White Russian émigrés, 63, 64, 137–138
  World War II, 104
Neuborne, Burt, 341
Neue Zurcher Zeitung (newspaper), 366
neutrality, Roosevelt, Franklin Delano,
  202–203, 207
Neutrality Act of 1935, 202, 209, 220,
  222
Nevins, Allen, 23
New Deal, 253
  Coughlin, Charles, 140
  Ford, Henry, 127, 136
  Great Depression, 132
Newman, Harry, 147
New Republic (magazine), 362
Newsweek (magazine), 186
Newton, James, 184
The New Yorker (magazine), 192–193
New York Evening Journal (newspaper), 31
New York *Herald Tribune* (newspaper), 77,
  225, 257, 288
New York magazine, 375
New York Telegram (newspaper), 34, 284
New York Times Magazine, 18
New York Times (newspaper), 8, 19, 29, 33,
  45, 46, 47, 65, 74, 77, 80, 90, 98, 103,
  135, 138, 145, 177, 182, 186, 192,
  213–214, 262, 263, 277, 304, 318, 350,
  357, 370, 371, 373, 374, 376, 380
New York World (newspaper), 7, 11, 16
Nicaragua, 253
Nicholas II (czar of Russia), 59, 64
Nicolson, Harold, 103–104, 162–163,
  210–211
Nilus, Serge, 13
No Foreign Wars Campaign, 257, 262
Non-Aggression Pact (Germany-USSR),
  214, 286
Non Partisan League, 81
Norris, Kathleen, 267, 281
Nuremberg laws (1935), 117
Nuremberg trials, 39–40, 41–42, 99, 175,
  325, 328, 332, 336, 361–362

O'Donnell, Patrick H., 28–29
Office of Strategic Services (OSS), 350

Olympic Games of 1936, 111–116, 134, 251
Opel subsidiary, 350–351, 352
Operation Paperclip, 364
Osborn, Frederick, 367
Oskar, Prince (Kaiser Wilhelm's son), 66

pacifism, Ford, Henry, 18–19, 25, 26. *See also*
  isolationist movement
Palmer, Casimir, 65, 131, 132, 138, 225
Pan American Airways, 305
Papen, Franz von, 131, 225
Paul, Randolph, 344–345
Peace Ship expedition, 19–20, 24, 25, 26,
  42–43, 66, 81, 131, 250
Pearl Harbor attack, 232, 261, 270, 272, 276,
  289, 296, 298, 301, 333, 336–337, 338,
  339
Pearson, Drew, 245, 314, 332
Peck, Gregory, 368
Pelley, William Dudley, 279, 280, 310
perfusion pump, 93, 94, 100–102
"Perils of Racial Prejudice" (manifesto), 15
Perlman, Nathan, 31
Pétain, Philippe, 367
Philippines, Lindbergh, Charles, 365–366
Pipp, Edwin, 11, 24, 27, 34–35, 61
Pittman, Key, 209–210
Planned Parenthood, 96
Plantiff, Gaston, 35
PM (newspaper), 145, 260, 271–272, 279
Poland, Germany invades, 202, 230
Poliakov, Leon, 15
Pool, James, 52, 63, 64
Posekel, Ernst, 229
Potsdam Conference, 332
Poussaint, Alvin, 83
Pravda (newspaper), 182
presidential ambitions, Ford, Henry, 27–28,
  46
Pricewaterhouse-Coopers report, 341, 342,
  343
prisoners of war, 335
profit-sharing, Ford Motor Company, 9
Progressive Party, 78
Protestant War Veterans of the United
  States, 149
Protocols of the Learned Elder of Zion (Nilus,
  anti-Semitic tract), 13–14, 15–16, 32, 44,
  56, 58, 59, 60–61, 62–63, 109, 126, 138,
  143, 145

race purity, Lindbergh, Charles, 209,
  211–213, 302–303, 319, 353, 361–362,
  363, 367, 382. *See also* African Americans;
  anti-Semitism; eugenics movement
racism, U.S. War Department, 110
Radot, Valery, 368
Rath, Ernst von, 191
Rathom, John, 25
Reader's Digest (magazine), 211
Reich, Simon, 228, 334, 337–338, 339,
  340–341, 344, 348, 350

Ribbentrop, Joachim von, 143, 233, 263–264
Ribuffo, Leo, 23
Rich, Frank, 374
Rickenbacker, Eddie, 220, 251
Riddleberger, James, 184
Rieckhoff, Heinz J., 179
Riefenstahl, Leni, 135–136
Rimar, Ralph, 137, 138, 141–142
Rintamaki, John, 334–335, 336, 337, 341,
    342, 344
Robb, Arthur, 292
Rocque, François de la, 159
Roenberg, Alfred, 48
Rogers, Will, 35
Roman Catholic Church
    Carrel, Alexis, 94
    discrimination against, 12
    Lindbergh, C. A., 79
Roosevelt, Eleanor, 193, 210, 292, 314, 321,
    347
Roosevelt, Franklin Delano, 161, 253, 255,
    272, 347
    America First Committee and, 283–284,
        315
    Churchill, Winston, 207, 259, 260–261
    Coughlin, Charles, 140
    Czechoslovakia, 166
    death of, 320–321, 356
    Ford, Henry, 127, 136, 250, 311
    inauguration of, 132
    interventionism, 212–213, 242, 258–259,
        261, 273, 276
    Japan, 297–298
    Kennedy, Joseph, 167, 169
    Kristallnacht riots, 192, 201
    Lindbergh, Charles, 2–3, 197–198,
        204–205, 214–215, 241–242, 249, 271,
        273–274, 276–277, 283–284, 285–286,
        295, 299, 304, 305, 310, 311, 320
    mobilization, 220
    neutrality, 202–203, 207
    Smith, Gerald L K, 314–315
    Smith, Truman, 246, 362
    World War II, 156
Roosevelt, Theodore, 78, 82, 251
Rose, Billy, 34, 286
Rosenbaum, Ron, 57, 376
Rosenberg, Alfred, 57, 64, 138, 253
Rosenwald, Julius, 29
Rosenwald, Lessing, 251, 258
Ross, Walter, 288
Rupprecht, Crown Prince (Bavaria), 106
Russian Revolution. See also Soviet Union
    anti-Semitism, 14, 43, 44, 55, 61, 64
    Brasol, 59
Rutherford, Marvin, 306
Rwanda genocide, 387
Ryan, John F., 210

San Francisco Chronicle (newspaper), 291
Sanger, Margaret, 95–96
Sapiro, Aaron, 29, 30, 33, 125

Sauckel, Fritz, 325
Sauter, Fritz, 41, 42
Scandrett, Richard, Jr., 249
Scharton, A. R., 25–26
Schindler, Oskar, 330
Schindler's List (film), 375, 376
Schirach, Baldur von, 40–42, 52
Schlesinger, Arthur, 115, 248, 275
Schmidt, Robert, 230, 231, 232, 234, 235, 238,
    328, 329, 331, 332, 336, 337, 342, 360, 361
Schneider, Henry, 231, 332
Schneider, James, 261
Schorr, David, 245
Schubert, Joseph, 58
Schurig, Alwin, 226
Schuschnigg, Kurt von, 153
Schwarzkopf, H. Norman, 91
Schwimmer, Rosika, 18–20, 24, 25, 26
Scribner's Commentator (journal), 255–256,
    257, 259, 271–272, 294, 297
Seamless Steel Equipment Corporation, 349
Self, Henry, 221
Service Cross of the German Eagle,
    Lindbergh, Charles awarded, 183–187,
    223, 285–286, 303
Seuss, Dr. See Geisel, Theodor (Dr. Seuss)
Shaw, George Bernard, 161
Sherwood, Robert, 251
Shirer, William, 39, 116, 117, 161, 170, 176
Shriver, Sargent, 249
Silesian-American Corporation, 349
Silver Shirts, 135, 279, 280
Simpson, Wallis, 104
Sinclair, Upton, 35, 67, 68
Skeropadsky, General (Ukrainian Hetman
    Organization leader), 138
slave labor. See forced labor
Slessor, John, 169, 180
Slomovitz, Phillip, 143
Smith, Gerald L K, 144–145, 252, 314–315,
    317, 360
Smith, Kay, 104, 110–111, 114, 156,
    320–321
Smith, Truman, 219, 320–321
    anti-Semitism, 105, 108–110, 200, 246,
        362
    attacks on, 245–246
    biography of, 104–106
    death of, 371
    Dennis, Lawrence, 254
    Germany, 106–108, 111, 175, 181–182
    health of, 196, 198, 201
    isolationism, 200–201, 203, 208
    Lindbergh, Charles, 87, 104, 111,
        112–115, 155–158, 180, 183, 184–186,
        196–197, 198–199, 202, 204, 245–246,
        252, 270, 277, 285, 307, 362–363, 382
    Marshall, George, 244
    Nazi Party, 263–264
Smith, William Alden, 27
Smythe, Edward James, 149
Snow, Robert T., 60

Social Darwinism, 83, 95
Social Justice (magazine), 143, 145, 148, 272, 280, 282, 294
Sorensen, Charles, 67, 222, 223, 224, 226, 227, 229, 230, 231, 232, 235, 250, 311, 346
Soviet Union. *See also* Russian Revolution
  anti-Semitism, 63–64
  German occupation of, 325
  Germany and, 214
  Lindbergh, Charles and, 163–164, 182, 286, 363
  Operation Paperclip, 364
Spanknobel, Heinz, 133
The Spectator (magazine), 210
Speer, Albert, 116, 193, 195, 329, 371
Spellich, John, 333
Spielberg, Steven, 330, 374–375
The Spirit of St. Louis (film), 370
Spoerer, Mark, 330, 336
Stalin, Josef, 214, 286, 332
Steele, Richard W., 242
Stehlin, Paul, 195
Steinberg, Ida, 68
Stephenson, William S., 283
sterilization
  eugenics movement, 95, 96
  Germany, 96–97, 98–99
Stewart, Douglas, 255–257, 272
Stewart, James, 370
Stimson, Henry, 242, 304, 309
Strauss, Roger, 114
Streicher, Julius, 39, 112, 200
Strempel, Herbert von, 256
Stuart, Douglas, 249–250, 251, 252, 258, 273, 293
Sudetenland, 154–155, 164, 165, 166, 191
Supreme Court (U.S.), sterilization, 95
Sward, Keith, 148–149, 313
Sykes, Christopher, 161
Szilard, Leo, 206

Taft, William Howard, 15
Tallberg, V. Y., 338
Talmud Society, 24
Tasaday people, 365–366
Taylor, Telford, 164, 165, 177–178
Teutonia Society, 132–133
Theilen, Fritz, 326
Thompson, Dorothy, 210, 257, 283
Thompson, Fred, 7
Thomsen, Hans, 256, 262, 263, 297
Thyssen family, 349
Time (magazine), 76, 90, 98, 101, 103, 280, 311
Times of London (newspaper), 15–16, 160, 161, 169, 172, 193
Tinkham, George, 208
Today's Challenge (magazine), 296
Tolson, Clyde, 246
Trading With the Enemy Act of 1917, 344, 345, 347, 348, 349, 350
transatlantic flight, Lindbergh, Charles, 73–74, 385

Treaty of Versailles, 1, 43, 44, 63, 104, 108, 133, 154, 160, 169
Trippe, Juan, 305
True, James, 200
Truman, Harry, 312, 313, 332
Tunney, Gene, 74–75
TWA, 287
Twain, Mark, 20

Udet, Ernst, 183, 194, 195
Ukranian Hetman Organization (UHO), 137–138
Union Banking Corporation of New York, 348–350
unionization, Ford Motor Company, 8, 9, 136
United Aircraft Corporation, 305, 319, 356
United Auto Workers Union, 67, 127, 136, 137, 139–140, 141, 313
United Kingdom. *See* England
United Nations, Lindbergh, Charles, 361
United States
  anti-Semitism, 12–15, 16, 20–21, 22–23, 28, 60–61, 105, 110, 133–135, 138, 140, 142–145, 167–168, 291, 294–295
  arms embargo, 202, 207, 208
  British spies in, 283
  fascism, 132–135, 200, 219, 252, 253, 294, 310
  German spies in, 224–225, 241–244, 253, 256, 261–262, 269–270, 282, 295–296, 297, 316, 349
  Germany, 161–162, 327
  immigration policy, 96
  isolationism, 198–199, 205–206, 212, 276
  Nazism in, 132–135, 137–138, 142, 203–204
  Olympic Games of 1936, 111–112
  World War II, 330–331
United States Military Intelligence Division (MID, G2), 59–60, 61, 62, 63, 131, 138, 201, 256, 271, 302, 306, 347
United States National Conference of Christians and Jews, 114
United States War Department, 24–25, 59, 61, 105, 110
Untermeyer, Samuel, 44, 127, 138

Valentin, Hugo, 13
Vallandingham, Clement L., 277
van Scrivner, Esther, 272
Vaughan, Guy, 305
Vella, Jim, 352
Versailles Treaty, 1, 43, 44, 63, 104, 108, 133, 154, 160, 169
Vichy government
  Carrel, Alexis, 367–368
  Ford France, 345–346
Viereck, George, 279
Vietnam War, Lindbergh, Charles, 370
Vitger, Erhard, 230, 339
Vladimirovich, Cyril, 63, 64

Volkischer Beobachter (newspaper), 47, 48, 107
Vonnegut, Kurt, 275
Vossische Zeitung (newspaper), 75, 115
V-2 missile, 340, 364

wages
  automobile industry, 136
  Ford, Henry, 5, 8–9, 16
Wagner, Richard, 50, 109
Wagner, Siegfried, 50
Wagner, Winifred, 50, 52
Walker, Bert, 349
Wallace, DeWitt, 211
Wallace, Henry, 284, 307
Wallgren, Monrad, 313
Wall Street Journal (newspaper), 9
Warburg, Paul, 79
Warner, Jack, 200, 370
Warner Brothers studio, 199–200
Warren, Donald, 141, 143
Warren, Sherwyn, 100, 101
Washington Post (newspaper), 333
Washington Star (newspaper), 320
Watson, Edwin, 246, 307, 308
Watson, Thomas, 351–352
Webster, Edwin, Jr., 280, 301–302
Wecter, Dixon, 385
Weekly Foreign Letter (fascist bulletin), 253
The Week (newspaper), 182
Weiss, Mel, 343
West, James, 76
Westrick, Gerhart Alois, 233–234
Wheeler, Burton, 267, 280, 281
Wheeler-Bennett, John, 275–276
White, William Allen, 212–213, 260, 261
White Russian émigrés, Nazi party and, 63,
    64, 137–138
Whitney, Leon, 96–97
Wiedemann, Fritz, 269
Wieland, A. J., 360
Wierscheim, Josef, 337
Wilhelm (kaiser of Germany), 63, 66
Wilkins, Mira, 49

Willkie, Wendell, 262, 263, 291
Willow Run plant (Ford Motor Company),
    308–309, 311–313, 314
Wilson, Hugh, 182, 183, 184, 185, 186, 201
Wilson, Woodrow, 15, 44, 80, 207, 225
Winchell, Walter, 176, 179, 245–246, 257,
    283, 292
Wise, Isaac Meyer, 20
Women's Peace Party, 18
Wood, John E., 178
Wood, Robert E., 249–250, 251, 252, 273,
    276, 278, 282, 285, 292, 301, 302, 315,
    356
World War I, 105
  anti-German sentiment, 58
  anti-Semitism, 28, 43–44, 194
  Ford, Henry, 18–19, 131
  Ford Motor Company, 24–26
  German spies, 224–225
  Hitler, Adolf, 53, 269
  Liebold, Ernest, 131–132
  Lindbergh, C. A., 79–82
  Versailles Treaty, 1, 43, 44, 63, 104, 108,
    133, 154, 160
World War II
  Battle of Britain, 255
  Ford Motor Company, 220–223, 232–233,
    235, 236, 278, 289, 308–309, 311–313,
    314, 318–319, 357–358
  Germany, 214
  Holocaust, 331
  Lindbergh, Charles, 299, 303–305,
    319–321
  outbreak of, 104, 202–203, 219
  Soviet Union invaded by Germany,
    286
World Wildlife Fund, 364
Wright, Orville, 77
Wuest, Jacob, 108

Zoerlein, Emil, 146
Zuckertort, General (German army), 233
Zyklon B (poisonous gas), 331–332, 340

ABOUT THE AUTHOR

MAX WALLACE is a veteran investigative journalist and Holocaust researcher. For three years, he worked as an interviewer and researcher for Steven Spielberg's "Shoah Project," documenting the testimonies of Holocaust survivors. He is also a former executive director of the Anne & Max Bailey Center for Holocaust Studies. Winner of the *Rolling Stone* Magazine Award for Investigative Journalism, he is also an award-winning documentary filmmaker. In 2001, he was nominated for a Gemini Award (Canada's equivalent of an Emmy) for his first documentary, *Too Colorful for the League*, about racism in hockey. Wallace has been a guest columnist for the Sunday *New York Times* and contributed to the BBC. His previous books include the international bestseller *Who Killed Kurt Cobain?* and *Muhammad Ali's Greatest Fight: Cassius Clay vs. the United States of America*, about Ali's controversial stand against the Vietnam War. A native of New York City, Max Wallace lives in Montreal, Canada.